RIOR DESIGNERS · ART DEALERS · AUCTIO
GAR BARS AND CLUBS · LLEGES · SMET
NT AGENCIES · EVENTS · TION · FITNES
HOTELS · JEWELRY AND ES · LAND
EMS · PARTY ORGANIZERS CATERERS
OGRAPHERS · PRIVATE CLUBS · REAL ESTAT
Y ONSULTANTS · SPAS AND CLINICS · SP
MANAGEMENT · WINE MERCHANTS · WIN
RCHITECTS AND INTERIOR DESIGNERS · AR
FFEUR SERVICES · CIGAR BARS AND CLUBS
HOOLS · EMPLOYMENT AGENCIES · EVENT
HAIR AND BEAUTY · HOTELS · JEWELRY AN
MS · MEDIA · MUSEUMS · PARTY ORGANIZER
ERS AND PHOTOGRAPHERS · PRIVATE CLUB
OOLS · SECURITY CONSULTANTS · SPAS AN
ANTS · WEALTH MANAGEMENT · WINE MER
T · ANTIQUES · ARCHITECTS AND INTERIO
ASINOS · CHAUFFEUR SERVICES · CIGA
NS · CULINARY SCHOOLS · EMPLOYMEN
RISTS · GOLF CLUBS · HAIR AND BEAUTY
ARCHITECTS · LAW FIRMS · MEDIA · MUS
CLUBS · PORTRAIT PAINTERS AND PH
TS · RESTAURANTS · SCHOOLS · SECURIT
Y SHOPS · TRAVEL CONSULTANTS · WEALT
KERS · YACHTING · AIRCRAFT · ANTIQUES
EALERS · AUCTION HOUSES · CASINOS
OLLEGES · COSMETIC SURGEONS · CUL
NTS · FASHION · FITNESS · FLORISTS · GOI
AND WATCHES · LANDSCAPE ARCHITECTS
NIZERS AND CATERERS · POLO CLUBS · PO
ATE CLUBS · REAL ESTATE AGENT · RESTA
PAS AND LINICS · SPE ALTY SHOPS · TRA
NE MERCHANTS · WINEMAKERS · YACHTI

America's Elite 1000

The Ultimate List
Millennium Issue

Inspired by Gabrielle Rose O'Mahony-Kelly. A truly stylish woman.

Publisher &
Editor in Chief
Kevin Kelly

Deputy Editor
Michael Slimmer

Managing Editor
Lynda Weatherhead

Associate Publishers
Mark D. Kelly
Francine S. Stessel

Art Director
Kevin Sullivan

Picture Editor
Oksana Pidhoreckyj

Color origination by D&B Reproductions, New York City
Printed and bound by Mondadori Printing, Verona, Italy

First Published in November 1999 by Cadogan Publications Ltd.
27 West 24th Street, New York, NY 10010, USA
Telephone: +1-212-633-6488

UK Address:
50 Hans Crescent, London SW1X ONA, UK
Telephone: +44-171-581 1805

America's Elite 1000–The Ultimate List
Copyright © Cadogan Publications Ltd. 1999

British Library Cataloging in Publication Data
A catalog record for this book is available from The British Library.

ISBN 0-9671694-0-2

AMERICA'S ELITE 1000
THE ULTIMATE LIST
MILLENNIUM ISSUE

EDITED BY
TREVOR WHITE

CP

CADOGAN PUBLICATIONS

A Gallery in the New York townhouse of Juan Pablo Molyneux.

FOREWORD

Sophisticated Europeans are visiting the United States in greater numbers than ever before. They come to buy businesses and to shop on Madison Avenue or Rodeo Drive. They ski in Aspen, take a house in the Hamptons, play golf at Augusta and visit the wineries of the Napa Valley.

Based on the acclaimed *Europe's Elite 1000,* this is the first of an annual series in which the United States of America is explored from a European perspective. We hope that the book will be of considerable interest not only to visitors but also to Americans who, because of the vast size of their country, have little opportunity to be familiar with everything that this great land has to offer.

Designed to sit on the coffee tables of the finest houses in the world, the book provides a lavish record of the best of the best in America today, from the top florists to the most celebrated restaurants, and the finest galleries to the smartest country clubs. We have also incorporated a range of stories which we believe discerning readers will enjoy. For instance, our keynote feature, *Those Amazing Americans,* provides portraits of 100 people whose style, energy and creativity have inspired the admiration of Europeans and Americans alike.

Putting the book together has been a labor of love, involving a mammoth effort on the part of a dedicated team of writers, advisors and contacts across the country. Hopefully you will be as enthralled as we are by the talent and opportunity celebrated in *America's Elite 1000.*

KEVIN KELLY
PUBLISHER &
EDITOR IN CHIEF

AMERICA'S ELITE 1000

THE LISTINGS

The 1000 names on our list are the editors' choices of the finest shops, services and luxury goods that America has to offer. Every company or individual proposed for inclusion has been checked and cross-checked by our network of contributors, advisors and contacts, to ensure that inclusion is merited. The names have been selected on the basis of the current excellence of their products and services, rather than simply a high profile or impressive past reputation. Equally, all names have been judged against a pan-American standard of excellence, rather than being selected on a state-by-state basis. All of the entries will be reviewed and updated annually.

While the *Elite 1000* naturally includes the acknowledged greats, it also contains many less predictable names. Readers may be surprised to find certain famous names missing from the list. If they did not qualify, it is because they appear to have succumbed either to the temptation of resting on their laurels, rather than constantly reviewing and upgrading their standards, or to the temptation of becoming too commercial and populist.

Entries described as *Best Kept Secrets* are specialty shops and services. Many of the names are already well-established but deserve to be more widely known. Some of them are hardly known outside the inner circle of America's cognoscenti. All of them offer outstanding quality and an indefinable 'something special.'

We have also highlighted *Rising Stars,* those firms which, in our opinion, will soon make it to the very top in their particular field. Some of these firms may not have yet fulfilled their potential or proved that they have real staying power but their commitment to excellence is unquestioned.

HOW TO USE THIS BOOK

The *Elite 1000* is published in alphabetical order, across all product categories. The names are cross-referenced in three indexes, to enable you to use this book in a variety of ways. For example, if you are traveling to a particular city, you would use the city index to discover the best of everything in, say, Washington, D.C. On the other hand, if you are seeking the best in a certain field—say jewelers or antique dealers—you would use the product category index, which will list all names under the relevant category heading. In addition, there is a straight alphabetical index of all names which have been included in the Listings section of the book.

CONTENTS

9

McAlpine's America

Lord McAlpine reflects on his travels in the United States

17

A Life of Style

Debra Scott meets Juan Pablo Molyneux in his New York home

33

The Dream 18

Tom Doak selects the best golf holes in America

45

The Irish in America

Tom O'Gorman tells a tale of patriots, poets and dreamers

57

The Elite 1000

The best luxury goods, shops and services in the United States of America

201

Banking for Billionaires

How do the super-rich manage their money? Robinson Clark investigates

207

Those Amazing Americans

100 people whose achievements epitomize what Europeans admire in Americans

273

The Modern Acropolis

Trevor White describes the genesis of the Getty Center in Los Angeles

287

The Private Playground

An Insider's guide to the Hamptons

299

Index I

Alphabetical

305

Index II

By State

313

Index III

By Category

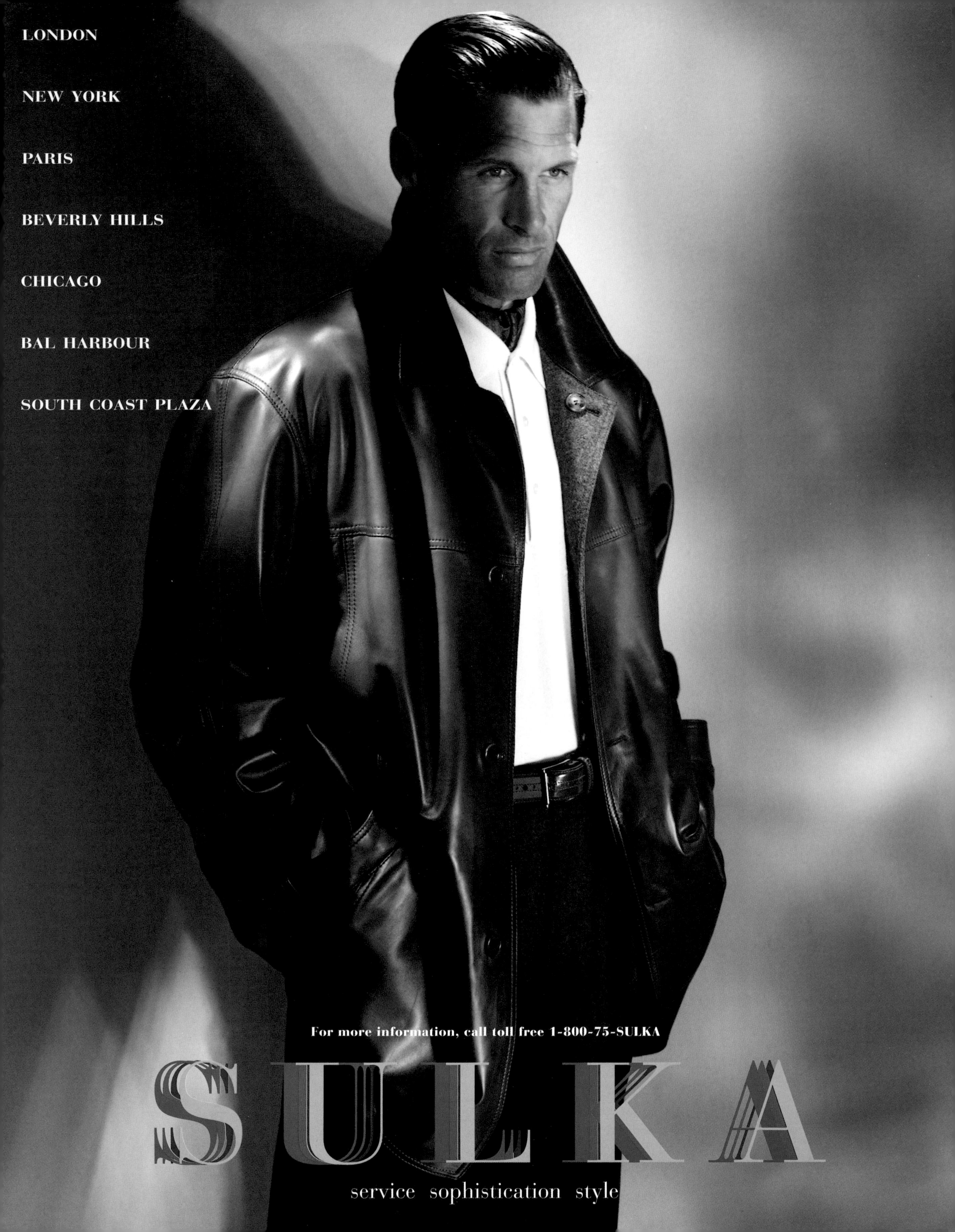
LONDON
NEW YORK
PARIS
BEVERLY HILLS
CHICAGO
BAL HARBOUR
SOUTH COAST PLAZA
For more information, call toll free 1-800-75-SULKA
SULKA
service sophistication style

McAlpine's
America

Lord Alistair McAlpine is one of England's great treasures—
journalist, author, art historian, politician, philosopher and collector of beautiful things.
For many years he has journeyed through America, sampling its cultural
(and culinary) delights. Here are some of his favorite moments from those travels.

To arrive by boat is the most romantic way to set eyes upon a coastal city, and of all the world's coastal cities, New York is by far the greatest. In 1957, aboard the old *Queen Elizabeth,* I first saw the Manhattan skyline. In those days Europe had cities where the tallest buildings seldom exceeded the height of a fireman's ladder. To a young boy of fifteen, the sea trip on that giant liner was an adventure; the first sight of New York a miracle.

The *Queen Elizabeth* was a truly luxurious vessel. Each night my father put on his dinner jacket and my mother, what would now pass for, a ball gown. In the Veranda Grill we ate caviar, chateaubriand and crepes suzettes, which were flamed at the table. Whenever my family ate crepes suzettes my father trotted out the same story about a chef whose beard had caught fire at the table. As children we laughed and laughed. Forty two years later I still smile when I recall the crepes suzettes on that liner.

The captain of the *Queen Elizabeth* had expected to be met by tugs as he sailed up the East River. The tug crew were on strike, so the ship would have to wait until the strike was over. The *Queen Elizabeth,* however, waited for no-one. The captain berthed that giant liner without help from anyone. It was the first time that this had ever been achieved. Only when the ship was alongside the berth and we looked down on the stevedores (small ants moving hither and thither on the dock) did we realize what a considerable achievement this had all been. One wrong move and the great ship would have destroyed the wharf.

We were met by our hosts as we passed through customs and we piled into limousines as long as buses. We were whisked away to the countryside of Westchester County, a place that seemed urban to me. We traveled as a clan; parents, grandmother, brother and other relatives. We stayed in the large home of the Shicks (kind but jealous hosts), sailing on their motor launch, visiting the local shops and visiting their Shaver Factory. It was like many other factories, although the Amish communities that we saw nearby were fascinating.

There was a niece of the Shicks who lived not far away in New Canaan; an attractive and intelligent girl, she was determined to take my older brother to New York to listen to jazz at Birdland. But the elder Shicks seemed equally determined to keep us from New York. The attractive niece was never seen by us again and I have often wondered what happened to her.

However, on one occasion we all broke free of the Shicks' stranglehold and set out for New York, where we were to have lunch at the 21 Club. Finding a taxi, my father instructed the driver to take us there. "I hope that you have plenty of money" he said. "It's the most expensive place in town." This information was not a bit welcome for the British currency controls restricted the amount of money that you could take overseas to a derisory sum. "Are you from England?" the driver continued, "I hate people from England. There's only one Englishman that I like; he's Winston Churchill. What a fine man he is." I began to understand why the Shick parents had tried to keep us out of New York.

At the 21 Club we ate and drank well and the whole meal was on the house. My father was deputy chairman of the Dorchester Hotel in London. "I love your hotel more than anywhere in the world," said Max Crindler, the owner. I was taken down to the kitchens where a chef poked a skewer into a small hole in the wall, which swung open to reveal a cellar filled to the ceiling with fine wine.

In 1966 I returned to New York on the successor to the *Queen Elizabeth,* the QEII. The city still fascinated me: search for a rare Staffordshire pottery figure and in New York you find a shop with ten of them. By now I was buying the paintings of the abstract expressionists and New York colorists like Mark Rothko and Morris Louis.

A giant of a city, New York has the best of most things and amongst them is Cipriani's, where Arrigo Cipriani is always attending to his guests. Whenever I am in Venice I find him doing the same thing in Harry's Bar; he has the most extraordinary ability to be in two places at once, bringing quality to the lives of his customers. Among the other places where I like to eat are the Oyster Bar in Grand Central Station (now beautifully restored), Elaine's, The Colonial (which serves the best Vietnamese food in town) and the Carlyle Hotel, where on Sunday I like to take my lunch.

I still haunt the galleries and antique shops. These days I buy old textiles and Venetian beads from Himalayan Imports on Broadway. For unusual textiles I visit the Craft Caravan in Soho. When I am wandering the streets of this fascinating area I take lunch at Barolo, a fine Italian restaurant.

Page 9:

Top Left: The Statue of Liberty; a gift from the French to the American people, it was designed by Fréderic-Auguste Bartholdi and unveiled in New York's East River in 1886.

Top Right: Plaque from the facade of the Beverly Hills Hotel, California, former home to celluloid stars like Marlene Dietrich and Rudolph Valentino.

Bottom Left: Mount Rushmore National Memorial, South Dakota. Carved into the granite cliff are the faces of (L-R) Presidents George Washington, Thomas Jefferson, Theodore Roosevelt and Abraham Lincoln.

Bottom Right: The iconic Cable Cars of San Francisco are now more of a tourist attraction than simply a mode of transportation.

Left: The Lower Manhattan Skyline spanning City Hall Park to the World Trade Center.

Below: New York City's Grand Central Station, a gateway to the city and a fine example of the Beaux Arts movement, opened in 1913 .

After the great museums of New York like the Metropolitan and the Frick, most people would consider the Newark Museum small beer. For me it was a delight, its object wonderful, its size perfect, about as much as I could usefully take in on a Sunday morning. I was also particularly taken by the Firehouse Museum, a tribute to firemen and fire fighting.

Los Angeles, on the other side of the continent, is the very antithesis of New York. When New York is cold, Los Angeles is warm. While New Yorkers are smart and thirsty, Los Angelenos are laid back and merely clever. They are creative people who wear open neck shirts and seem to lazily pass their way through life with unimaginable success. This is the home of imagination and new cultures. A city that wanders for miles, a city where a friend can live twenty miles away and still be called a neighbor. The Ivy is my favorite restaurant (plates carry enough food for two) while the Beverly Hills Hotel is one of the most luxurious in the world. Luxury, that is, in the old sense, not the luxury of towering foyers of glass and brass: the luxury of soft beds and deep carpets, of armchairs that are reluctant to give you back to the real world. A fantasy hotel, with a garden freshness about the place .

I dine alone at the Beverly Hills Hotel's Polo bar. In fact I sit at the bar and drink 25 year old MacCallans while I nibble on buffalo wings. People come and go; Americans are friendly and seldom pass without wishing me well or commenting on my ties (I have ten thousand of them).

For those who like to shop and want to break away from the upmarket multiple names of the world, Los Angeles is paradise. Here, the obscure is commonplace. Visit the Watts Towers in Watts County, an incredible monument built on some derelict land, largely out of broken pottery, by a lonely old man known as Sam who, after working 33 years on this bizarre project, just moved on, abandoning his life's work. After that visit, I went to the Gene Autry Museum to see everything to do with cowboys, the memorabilia of the film set and the wild frontiers.

Inland from Los Angeles, a few hours drive along a straight road through the desert, is Las Vegas. The Luxor Hotel, where I stayed, boasts a thousand rooms or so, built as a pyramid. The lifts are called inclinators because they move sideways as well as upwards. From my hotel room I could see that the desert started a few hundred yards from its walls and went to distant hills. I suppose for a gambler this place is paradise, while for me it is one of the wonders of the modern world. Try as they may no one anywhere has been able to reproduce or better Las Vegas. For kitsch, for vulgarity, for sheer unashamed exhibitionism, this place takes the biscuit. White tigers sitting on white rocks in a white cage, performing twice a day with a trainer in a white suit: I ask you! If it is America that you wish to see do not miss Las Vegas.

Up the coast from Los Angeles, I drove to San Francisco, first traveling through wine country, then along the coast where giant waves roll against the rocks that are torn from nature. About half way on my journey I came upon San Simeon, Randolph Hearst's surreal monument to the great wealth of America. As you travel to San Francisco, do not miss Carmel–not Carmel on the Sea, rather Carmel Valley. A place of peace and plenty, it has the look of Japan about it. Here you will find Ruth and John Picard, the proprietors of one of the world's few bead museums, which traces the history of the Venetian Trade Bead, once used in trade from Alaska to Africa. The Picard Trade Bead Museum is a fascinating place to spend an hour or two.

It was in 1960 that I first visited San Francisco and I returned several times in the following few years. In those days hippies lived on Haight and Ashbury streets. Candles burned in the windows of the houses–sometimes these candles set fire to the buildings (like my father's crepe suzettes) but for the most part the hippies lived in their own psychedelic world offering strangers a flower and wishing the peace. In the 1980s I returned to San Francisco: the hippies were gone, and restaurants seemed to have taken over. I dined at the Zuni Restaurant, drinking the best of California wine and eating their famous Tuscan chicken. When I returned to San Francisco this year the Zuni was as good as I had remembered it, perhaps even better. I enjoyed fresh oysters and prawns, the Tuscan chicken and a bottle of old Telegram. The antique shops on Jackson Square are better organized, their stock less haphazard.

The whales still pass by San Francisco and the Sea Lions still sit on the rocks, defying the rolling surf and roaring at the fog as it begins to cloak the city in wondrous mystery.

For a change of climate head to Monument Valley, where traders still sell the silver and pottery made by native Americans–not the usual tourist rubbish. For most small boys brought up on Western movies Monument Valley is no great novelty. I have seen "indians" appear from behind those great monoliths with almost monotonous regularity. Despite their familiarity, I was hopelessly unaware of their scale. As I approached the valley I pulled my car to the side of the road and just sat, inspired by the giant majesty of these rocks that rise a thousand feet from the flat floor of the desert. The drive from Monument Valley to Santa Fe is long but fascinating. I have seen most of this country from the comfort of an airplane: along the Grand Canyon, over Salt Lake City, across mountain ranges and dry deserts, but nothing is the same as driving across that virgin countryside. On a lonely road you marvel at the resolve of the settlers. What an intrusion they must have been on the population who already lived there!

Slowly the land rose as I drove up to the high plateau, into New Mexico and then Santa Fe, where the buildings fit so perfectly into the landscape that they are only visible when your eyes adjust to look for buildings rather than boulders. Here I read a plaque on the wall of a bookshop: "In this building Billy the Kid was held prisoner." Then he escaped.

I like Santa Fe. The food is hot and the weather crisp. On one occasion I saw a terrific performance of *Don Giovanni*. The next day I returned and was shown behind the scenes as the singers rehearsed, standing in an open space amongst the buildings that had become their homes for a summer season.

Between Santa Fe and Taos there are many small chapels, in their way quite as beautiful as the grand churches of Europe. On a detour I crossed one of the highest suspension bridges in the world, spanning the canyon through which the Rio Grande runs. In this canyon, a small cut in the plain (really quite narrow, perhaps 30 yards wide), the river can be seen a long, long way below: a remarkable sight. But Taos itself is really a skiing resort and I arrived in the summer.

On the drive to Denver one occasionally passes through a small village with a church of character, more often just a house or two and a general store, selling items as exotic to me as the goods in any bazaar: mouse lures, chewing tobacco, jerky and something called moose urine, much used in hunting or so I was told by a proprietor who was shocked that I did not know. Saddened that I did not see a grizzly bear or a mouse as I drove over high hills and along large valleys (their sides clad with pines), I asked at the next store where these curiosities could be found. "Not in my store," he said, "but I can give you a good strong political argument if you would like one."

As a small boy I was obsessed with cowboys, their boots, their clothes, their cattle, their guns, so I took a trip to Fort Worth to see the stock yards. That evening I ate in the gardens of a Mexican restaurant. During our meal a helicopter flew over, with a search light that illuminated the ground underneath it. "What is that helicopter doing?" I asked. "Searching for criminals," was the reply. It was all a bit different from the Texas I had seen at the cinema where Wyatt Earp used to catch the criminals at the local saloon.

The mayor of New Orleans was once asked why the average age of death in his town was so low. He replied, "We pack ninety years into our lives, so it makes no difference." I love the wonderfully decadent atmosphere of this town, where a good breakfast is no excuse for missing lunch. I can recall no city in America where the people have so much fun. Once I spent New Years Eve there, taking a car to visit the antebellum mansions around the city. I loved the mansions and ate so well at lunch time that I had to retire to bed without dinner, missing the arrival of the New Year and many hours of merry making.

On, then, to Maryland, where my memories are again culinary, like eating crabs with my fingers and the help of a wooden mallet. Not just one crab but rather a pile of fresh crabs tipped onto a brown paper covered table; or devouring corn on the cob, an equally messy business (but a certain amount of mess seems to add a special enjoyment to the act of eating). The satisfaction of cleaning yourself up, replete after a good meal of hands-on food, cannot be equaled by the greatest wines and finest linen of a Parisian bistro.

Not far away is Washington D.C., the capital of the greatest nation on earth. Journalists and politicians lurk in the bar of the Willard Hotel, passing the gossip that makes the wheels of government turn. But fascinating as politicians are it is not them and their history that is the delight of Washington; rather it is the city's great museums. If you were to visit the Smithsonian every day for several years you would still find plenty of wonders to see. Over in Georgetown there are shops and restaurants to keep the gourmet satisfied for a decade, during which time of course a whole swag of new restaurants will have opened. Washington is an exciting and immensely interesting city to visit.

When traveling in America it is easy to forget Hawaii, which is almost further from America's capital than London. My first visit to Honolulu was on a great ship called the Oriana. As we came down the gang plank, beautiful Hawaiian women placed leis of Frangipani blossoms around our necks. What a place this was! Hawaiian guitars, hula dancing and the first shopping center I had ever seen–in the late 1950's such things did not exist in Britain. My mother bought muu muus, I think more taken with the garments name than with its shape. Being English and quite reserved (almost the same thing!) I refused to buy Hawaiian shirts. Little did I know as I rejected these beautiful garments that a particularly fine specimen could one day fetch a fortune.

We stayed but a day or two more in Honolulu and then set sail for Vancouver. As our ship sailed the Honolulu police band stood by the dock; tall, fine looking men played their instruments and sang the songs of these proud islands. It was an emotional occasion. Girls clad in floral prints called to us "Come back, come back!" and we threw the floral leis that we had been given over the stern of our ship. Behind us was the fading music and a trail of floating flowers that seemed to beckon us back to these wonderful islands. I will return. Ⓐ

Pages 12-13:
Sailing on the Bay is one of the finest ways to marvel at the beauty of San Francisco's Golden Gate Bridge.

Above:
The Grand Canyon, 277 miles long and more than one mile deep at its lowest point.

CHRISTIE'S

**HELPING COLL
SINCE 1766**

Jasper Johns
Two Flags. 1973
Sold in New York for $7,152,500

20 Rockefeller Plaza
New York, New York 10020
212 636 2000

219 East 67th Street
New York, New York 10021
212 606 0400

360 North Camden Drive
Beverly Hills, California 90210
310 385 2600

A LIFE OF STYLE

*America boasts many handsome residences, where architects and
interior designers have created enduring emblems of good taste.
Here, Debra Scott looks at the life and work of Juan Pablo Molyneux,
whose designs grace some of the country's finest homes.*

Once you have had the privilege of viewing a Molyneux interior, with its particular blend of palatial airiness, historical significance and contemporary nuances, you will always be able to identify the designer's inimitable homescapes. His moniker is stamped on his residential works from the moment you cross the threshold of his grand entry halls till you enter his gardens where arboreal delights politely harmonize with both internal and external structural elements.

Though other interior designers and architects can be said to have an eclectic approach, Molyneux's style is no random whimsy. With an academic's knowledge and an aesthete's sensibility, the architect takes an intellectual approach to his projects. To put it simply, he knows his stuff.

Page 17: Mr. and Mrs. Juan Pablo Molyneux in the library of their Manhattan townhouse. Coffee table by Mallet. On the table sits a 17th century horse by Susini. Photo: Brian Dobin.

Left: A guest room in the Molyneux's Manhattan townhouse. 18th century French day bed. Directoire Bergere by Jacob. Engravings of the Colonna Trajana and the Colonna Antonina by Piranesi. Painting by DeJuan. Photo: Billy Cunningham.

Below: La femme qui marche. Alberto Giacometti, 1934. Photo: Brian Dobin.

Below: Second floor landing—The walls are covered in red cotton velvet. The marble console is a Molyneux design. The engraving is French 18th century by LeBrun. The busts on columns are Italian 19th century. The urns are alabaster. Photo: Billy Cunningham.

Page 21:

Top left: A carved, gilded Neapolitan 18th century mirror. A German 18th century chair. An Italian, 18th century marble console table. Four Lapis Lazuli obelisks mounted on rock crystal animals. Photo: Jaime Ardiles Arce.

Top right: Entrance Hall-Empire Italian Console Table with dogs supporting marble top. Directoire Chandelier and Russian chairs. Photo: Billy Cunningham.

Bottom right: Japanese and Chinese table setting. Juan Pablo Molyneux designed the chair in the background. It was built by David Linley. P.C. Billy Cunningham.

Bottom left: Silk pillows, hand painted by Anne Harris. Photo: Billy Cunningham.

Although he is now an American citizen, Molyneux was born in Chile to an affluent family of partly English heritage. He was trained, as he puts it, "in rigid modernism before rebelling against that minimalist doctrine" by enrolling at the École des Beaux-Arts, where he formed his lifelong passion for the neoclassical. Yet, despite his latterday affection for the Greco-Roman tradition, the Versailles aficionado still retains a place in his oeuvre for modern touches. Let's call it Palladio meets Le Corbusier—by way of South America.

Molyneux has "done" the homes of some of the most discerning clients in the world today, but the best way to know the essence of his work is to visit one of his own homes, which he shares with his wife of twenty-five years, Pilar. They own a ski chalet in Vail, an eighteenth century farmhouse in the Berkshires and a family home in Chile. But the couple's main residence—and the hub of the designer's work—is a seven-story late-nineteenth century French townhouse on New York's East 69th Street.

The handsome designer (think Hugh Grant with a Spanish accent) with his slight, but toned build, begins every morning with a predawn swim in the jet stream of his continuous-lap pool on the limestone house's exquisitely planted roof. Depending on the season, he breakfasts on fruit beneath a vine-wrapped pergola or on the terry cloth covered arm chair in the adjoining gym. After working out on state of the art machines next to a wall-sized photographic mural of himself riding one of his beloved Harley-Davidsons (wearing only boots, sunglasses and hat), he heads downstairs to join his staff of 18 designers and architects who are headquartered in the rear of the house's first two floors. Allowing his clients to sit at the drafting tables, review plans and fool around with sketches themselves, he takes measure of their understanding of a project. "It is also something people love to do," he says.

Page 22:
Top left: Entrance hall with 18th century
George III gilded console table.
At the back there is a Venus de Milo,
by Jim Dine. Above the console table
there is a Larry Rivers painting.
Photo: Billy Cunningham.

Top right and bottom left:
Dark green marble with white inlay lines this
gentlemen's bathroom. Mahogany woodwork.
Photo: Billy Cunningham.

Bottom right: Contemporary marble floor in
a neo-classical hallway, with an 18th century
Chinese paneled wall.
Photo: Billy Cunningham.

Page 23:
This showroom was created for the Kips Bay
Boys and Girls Decorator's Show House.
Three pictures, a Rauschenberg adjacent to
a Veronese, above a Veneto portrait, illustrate
the breadth of Molyneux's influences.
Photo: Jaime Ardiles Arce.

Right:
Inspired by Tiepolo, this dining room ceiling
was painted to depict the four continents.

Page 26:

Top left: 18th century Swedish chairs.
Karelian birch gueridon.
The tea set is porcelain de Paris.
Photo: Peter Vitale.

Top right: 18th century Roman sconce;
Late 18th century Central European
black commode. Painted canvas in
the grotesque manner. Photo: Peter Vitale.

Bottom left: Four Lapis Lazuli obelisks
mounted on rock crystal animals,
beneath a pumpkin leaf carved 18th century
Italian mirror. Through the mirror you can
see the reflection of a Veronese portrait.
Photo: Jaime Ardiles Arce.

Bottom right: 18th century Russian chairs.
Russian late 18th century chandelier.
George III Dining table.
Gilded Regency console table.
Photo: Billy Cunningham.

Across the hall from the piano nobile is the vast refuge that doubles as Molyneux's office and a reception room for guests. The room is a museum-like repository for a bold profusion of color, pattern, furniture, architectural details and objects that could only spring from the mind of Molyneux: red and white striped walls, floor to ceiling red silk curtains, larger than life bookshelves that nearly brush the ceiling; a 19th century Russian arm chair; a Chinese coffee table; an English Regency mirror; an early 18th century Flemish tapestry; a French mantelpiece; a contemporary sculpture by Fontana—and much, much more.

"It's a very difficult room to explain if you don't feel it," says Molyneux. "This combination of things shouldn't match, but they do. Why? That is what we don't know." Molyneux has a favorite word he uses to describe his process: heterotopic. "It means choosing things from different sources and combining them in a way that produces a new reality."

His goal, he says, is to create a dialog between the architecture and the furnishings. "They tell you who the owner is and how he lives. And they talk to each other nicely—not shouting—like at a cocktail party. Together they tell a story that has a flow and harmony." Molyneux's effective but eccentric use of colors is legendary. In the library there are 17 different reds from sofa to walls to rugs. "If you put them on a board as a student they'd think you had a problem with your eyes," he laughs. And yet, somehow, they work together. "They create a sort of vibration."

Molyneux is not one to follow rules. As he is fond of explaining, all great periods of interior design have always mixed the stuff of other times and cultures—fantastic trophies from long ago and far away—in with the fashions of their own age. His is not a disregard for period purity, but rather a re-embracing of the no-rules approach of earlier eras. It's as if he were living in 18th century France, but was able to time-travel into the past or future to pick and choose the best pieces: a Roman torso here, a Giacometti sculpture there.

Nowhere is his dichotomous approach more evident than in the sitting room, where lavender tinted walls are mounted with both a Francis Bacon triptych and bronze medallions of the Roman emperors; where a framed Picasso is casually propped on an "important" table made for Louis XVI; and where a Russian constructivist painting hangs above an Aubusson rug. His contemporary flourishes are not presented to aggressively market a position, but simply because they fit into his personal aesthetic. "If I'm struck by the beauty of a piece, its age is irrelevant," he says.

Nor will he preserve the artifacts of a property merely for the sake of historical precision, but only if the elements in question are worthy of restoration. Otherwise, as he did with a house built by Addison Mizner, the legendary Palm Beach architect of the Gilded Age, Molyneux "rethought" the structure. And, though Mizner's boldness "cast a spell" on him, his successor's "mistakes" overruled. Almost recreating the house from its former shell, Molyneux made do with "reviving the spirit" of the original intent.

Another of Molyneux's hallmarks is his use of trompe l'oeil to provide a witty allusion to reality. In one house, when he couldn't produce the Caucasian carpet coveted by his client, he created instead a painted illusion of it on which he could dictate the colors and pattern and create the "tempestuous" mood he sought. Molyneux considers floors an important element on which to play out design themes, particularly in America, where ceilings tend to be low and architecturally uninteresting. In his own Manhattan dining room he commissioned a crackle glazed trompe l'oeil mural featuring assorted grotesques alongside amusing portraits of himself, his wife, and their various pets—three dogs, a horse and one very mischievous parrot!

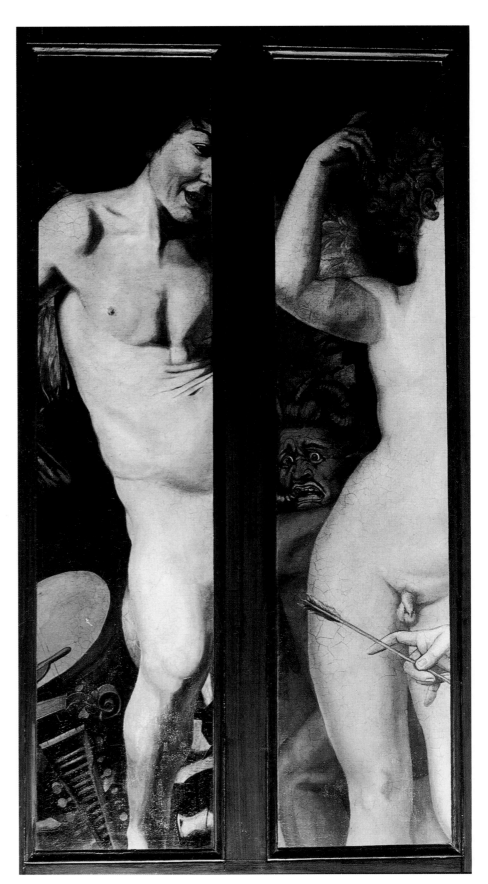

Above: Caravaggio inspired panels, in the Molyneux residence elevator.

Page 28: Drawing room overlooking Fifth Avenue. Half a Coromandal screen, early 18th century, from Pelham Galleries, London. 19th century neo-classical Gueridon from Ariane Dandois Galleries, Paris. Photo: Billy Cunningham.

Page 29:

Top left: Entrance hall with Lutyens-inspired slate floor. Photographs by Stieglitz. Sculpture by Rodin, L'Age d'Airain. Photo: Billy Cunningham.

Top right: Grotesque painted panels, including portrait of Nigel, the English Mastiff. Over the console table there are two Ming terracotta spirits. Photo: Brian Dobin.

Bottom right: Entrance Hall. Rodin's Mighty hand stands over the Italian directoire. Photo: Billy Cunningham.

Bottom left: 18th century engraving, after Le Brun Alexander's Battle of the Granites. Four Roman marble busts, 19th century Italian. Photo: Brian Dobin.

Page 30: The wall to wall carpet was designed specifically for this library. Two early 19th century German cabinets. English Regency desk with a Russian armchair. In the second image, the perspective changes, highlighting an English Regency sofa table and Charles X wall lights.

A residence designed by Molyneux and his team usually costs at least half the value of the property. "There's no limit," he says. "But the disproportion is enormous. When it's all done they can buy one painting that's thirteen inches by sixteen inches which costs double the entire project."

How does the flamboyant designer impose his highly dramatic vision on his clients? "People don't like to change their habits," he says. And when it comes to redecorating, most people know only one thing: what they don't want. Or what they think they don't want. "People can make capricious choices," he says. "For example, they will sometimes tell you that they don't like dark walls." To them he says, "You have never had the right dark walls."

Whether guiding you through his "Green Room" with its French Louis XVI bed (used as a prop in the film *Jefferson in Paris*) or through a hallway hung with Fortuny Venetian silk lanterns, Molyneux emits a childlike exuberance as he points out a table of "palatial provenance", a partial suite whose remaining parts "are in the Louvre," or a chair "that belonged to Madame Recamier."

As he ends another day by reclining on his roof-top deck with its southern views of the midtown skyline, he reflects on the fact that his passion extends to enhancing the lives of his clients. "You can change the private life of a person," says Juan Pablo Molyneux. "Sometimes you need to organize their space in order to organize their lives. My function, I suppose, is to lend focus…and a little worldliness." Ⓐ

Above: Neoclassical design for marble entrance hall, featuring an 18th century Roman bust, a George III marquetry console table and a George III armchair.

GUCCI

THE DREAM EIGHTEEN

by Tom Doak

America is home to some of the world's most challenging golf courses.
Trying to select the 18 best holes is a difficult task.
We asked Tom Doak, one of the country's most successful golf architects,
to give readers the score. Here is his Dream 18.

Attempting to choose the 18 best golf holes in America is a hopeless exercise—like trying to agree upon the perfect shade of paint for your bathroom. Today there are more than 15,000 golf courses in America, running the gamut from the hundred-year-old tree-lined fairways of New England to brand-new $30 million resort courses in Hawaii. No-one can know them all, nor produce a list free of personal bias.

But we can lay down some ground rules. Each hole was kept in its proper place in the round i.e the first hole is indeed the opening hole at Sand Hills, and the second at Pinehurst was compared against second holes throughout the USA. The combined course has four short holes and four par-5's, spaced appropriately throughout, so it would have the flow of a real 18. Individual holes were chosen based on their playing interest, challenge, beauty and historic significance. The acid test: every one of these holes would be worth the trip to play, whatever your score.

Page 34-35: No. 14th at Shinecock Hills GC, Southampton, NY

Above: No. 2 at Pinehurst CC No. 2, Pinehurst, NC

The 1st at Sand Hills Golf Club, Mullen, NE. *510 yards par-5.*

It's only been a golf course for five years, but in the classic traditions of British links golf, the first hole at Sand Hills has been sitting there for centuries among the remarkable sand dunes of northwestern Nebraska, waiting for a golfer to discover it.

With 8,000 acres on a ranch to choose from, architects Bill Coore and Ben Crenshaw were drawn to this site as the start of their course because of a large sandy blowout in front of an elevated tee. The entire hole is visible from the start, sweeping from right to left over undulating ground before rising to a green set in a saddle in the dunes, 500 yards away. With the wind at one's back, it is easily reachable in two by good players, but only after a dangerous drive past the corner of the dogleg and a long second past the yawning bunker beside the green; when the wind is opposite, anyone would be happy to have a putt for a four.

As with all good holes, the contour of the green also plays its part. The temptation is to play safely to the back of the green to avoid the bunkers and the chance that a short approach will spin back down the slope in front of the green; but the green slopes sharply from back to front, so three putts from the back are all too often needed.

The 2nd at Pinehurst Country Club (No. 2 course), Pinehurst, NC. *448 yards par-4.*

The patriarch of American golf architects is the Scotsman, Donald Ross, who emigrated from Dornoch in 1903 and established his winter residence at Pinehurst, where he lived until his death in 1948. For over thirty years, he tinkered with the design of his beloved masterpiece, the No. 2 course at Pinehurst Country Club.

In contrast to Sand Hills, Pinehurst is not immediately impressive to the eye; the wide fairways are relatively flat, and bordered by sand-and-pine needle roughs before the pines themselves. But the greens of No. 2 are the height of golfing sculpture, crowned and contoured to accept only a good shot from a certain place in the fairway, while fending off poor approaches as gracefully as a beautiful woman.

At the long second, a tee shot down the left tree line is imperative for the proper angle to the green; otherwise the second shot will have to carry a bunker at the front right corner of the green and hold an impossibly shallow target. Even then, the approach will have to be letter-perfect, or the player will face a difficult chip or putt from the apron at the back of the green. On this, like many holes at Pinehurst, the short hitter is not unduly penalized—a chip from just in front of the green on the left is the prime position— but the par-shooter is challenged to the limit.

The 3rd at Kittansett Country Club, Marion, MA. *180 yards par-3.*

The concept of an 'island' par-3 was popularized by Pete Dye's infamous 17th on the TPC at Sawgrass, but in fact many short holes are islands in theory, as the point is to hit the green on the fly.

One of the most dramatic island holes is the third at Kittansett, on the southern armpit of Cape Cod. Here, the green is an island of grass built up from the beach; at high tide the tee shot will have to carry a bit of water to get home, but sand and seaweed are even more unnerving hazards because the ball has to be played out instead of dropped.

The 4th at Spyglass Hill Golf Course, Pebble Beach, CA. *365 yards par-4.*

Robert Trent Jones is famous worldwide for bringing American golf course architecture to 50 countries, but nowhere did he have more spectacular property to work with than the first five holes at Spyglass Hill on the Monterey Peninsula, where large sand dunes are stabilized by rugged iceplant. As one of three host courses to the famed Bing Crosby Pro-Am [now the AT & T Pebble Beach Pro-Am] since it opened in 1966, Spyglass has earned its reputation as one of the most difficult courses on Tour, but its best hole is a short par-4 not beyond the reach of mortals.

From an elevated tee, the fourth doglegs sharply left through the dunes to a classic green site. The long, narrow green is hidden in a dell between the dunes, and the back half drops down onto an even lower tier than the front. Only a straight shot will do; a wide approach leaves a tricky pitch into the narrow bowl from a sandy lie.

The 5th at Merion Golf Club (East Course), Ardmore, PA. *426 yards par-4.*

For almost ninety years this compact course has been the scene of some of American golf's most dramatic moments, from Bob Jones' clinching of the Grand Slam in 1930, to Ben Hogan's epic 1951 U.S. Open triumph, completing his comeback from a near-fatal auto accident. From its wicker-basket topped flagsticks to the Scotch broom which grows out of many of its bunkers, Merion has a style like none other.

Of many great holes, one of the most intriguing is the fifth, playing up the side of a valley formed by a narrow stream which runs along the left of the fairway. The tilt of the fairway toward the stream means that the approach will have to be hit with almost a baseball swing, with the ball well above one's feet, likely to induce a hooked second. But the stream continues on to the side of the green, which also tilts dramatically from right to left, and makes chipping from the right an almost impossible proposition. The only safe way to make a four is to play the second to the left edge of the green and putt uphill at the pin; and the only reasonable way to get there is to drive along the left edge of the fairway near the stream, where a flatter stance is the reward and the approach does not have to be aimed back toward the trouble.

Ironically, it is the players trying to avoid an encounter with the stream, and a possible double bogey, who most often find themselves struggling to make their five due to the tilted green.

Below: No. 4 at Spyglass Hill GC, Pebble Beach CA.

The 6th at Apache Stronghold Golf Course, Globe, AZ. *321 yards par-4.*

The advent of modern construction techniques has made it possible for golf to flourish even in the most unlikely of places, and none is more unlikely than the rugged desert terrain of the San Carlos Apache Reservation, 90 miles east of Phoenix.

Every great course needs a handful of good short par-4 holes to allow the average player a chance for his par [or even birdie] to match a better opponent, and in recent years the concept of a drivable par-4 has become more popular. The 3,200 foot elevation of the Apache course and the elevated tee of the sixth both tempt the good player to try his luck, but there is serious risk involved; a pulled tee shot may never reach the fairway across the desert, while a blocked shot with the driver will either crash into the rocky hill above the green or carry over the ridge into fairway bunkers at the right, leaving a blind 60-yard approach from the sand.

For lesser mortals there is no need to bring out the driver. A good fairway wood or iron from the tee can be played into one of three dips in the fairway for safety, or along the ridgetop a bit more to the right to get a better view of the green. The green is a particularly shallow target with a steep fall at the back left, so even the second shot might best be played safely into the slope at the right—particularly if one's opponent is searching among the Gila monsters for his tee shot.

Above: No. 6 at Apache Stronghold GC, Globe, AZ

The 7th at San Francisco Golf Club, San Francisco, CA. *184 yards par-3.*

Every course over a hilly property should feature a short hole with a significant drop from tee to green, but none of the type is better than A. W. Tillinghast's seventh at San Francisco, which drops into a narrow valley some 60 feet below the tee. A ridge across the kidney-shaped green divides it into two definite targets—the narrow front section and a broader, bowled back pin placement—making club selection vital if one is to avoid a frightening putt over the ridge.

The hole was Tillinghast's personal favorite, not only for its testing character but for the historical significance of its location. He christened it the Duel hole because this very valley was the site of the last notable duel fought in the United States.

The 8th at Pebble Beach Golf Links, Pebble Beach, CA. *425 yards par-4.*

From its tee one cannot imagine the glories of the famous eighth at Pebble Beach. Although the tee is near the ocean's edge, the drive must be aimed up a steep hill at a large house on the horizon, with the fairway completely blinded from view. When the wind is behind, good players must lay back slightly to avoid going through the fairway, but since a shorter approach is a huge advantage, local knowledge is paramount.

Once safely in the fairway, we must calm ourselves for the most dramatic second shot in all of golf. The fairway is at the top of a 100-foot cliff, and the second shot must be played over a chasm of ocean to a tiny green set atop the far bank, which runs diagonally away to the right. Anything short or right is sucked to its destruction by the coastal winds, while a pulled or merely safe approach leaves a tricky pitch over the bunker at the left of the green.

Its eighteenth hole made Pebble Beach famous, but the eighth is clearly the best hole on the course, and often nominated as the best par-4 in America.

The 9th at Whitinsville Golf Club, Whitinsville, MA. *440 yards par-4.*

Not all great golf holes are to be found on famous courses; they are possible at even the most modest of locales whenever a great stretch of land intersects with a thoughtful design. A prime example is the finishing hole at Whitinsville, a gem of a nine-hole course between Boston and Providence.

The tee shot plays diagonally across a lily pond to a plateau of fairway some fifteen feet above the water's edge. Good players are tempted to take a bolder line toward the end of the plateau, where their drives might gain an extra thirty yards of roll down a slope. If they cannot, the approach will be at least 170 yards across a valley to a narrow green set into the slope below the small clubhouse.

Some dismiss nine-hole courses as not "real golf", but with holes this good, the prospect of a second crack in the same afternoon is an advantage rather than a detriment.

The 10th at Riviera Country Club, Pacific Palisades, CA. *311 yards par-4.*

An unassuming short par-4 which does not take kindly to impatient tactics. The fairway is flat and wide, and a sprawling fairway bunker which is easily carried on the right tempts players to drive straight toward the small green; but top professionals wisely elect to aim their tee shots over the left arm of the bunker, where an ample fairway disappears briefly behind the sand.

The reason for their caution is the green, a veritable sliver of putting surface which angles back to the right behind a narrow bunker, and tilts markedly from right to left for good measure. It's only 285 yards from the tee to the front edge of the green—reachable for many professionals today—but any shot missed to the right will leave an impossible pitch across the bunker with no chance of holding the green's counterslope.

Architect George Thomas fretted over the widening gap between professionals and club players, but this hole offers the same reward to all who think before they drive.

The 11th at Oakland Hills Country Club (South), Birmingham, MI. *385 yards par-4.*

A generation before Pete Dye became famous for his TPC at Sawgrass, Robert Trent Jones became the dean of golf architects in the postwar era with his redesign of Donald Ross' famed Oakland Hills, outside of Detroit. Asked to renovate the course to prepare for the U.S. Open Championship of 1951, Jones spent a year studying the play of the top professionals, then rebunkered the course to pinch the driving areas of nearly every par-4 and par-5. In the 72-hole event, only two players broke par for a single round, with Ben Hogan's final-round 67 taking the prize. That week, Oakland Hills became known as a 'monster', and Robert Trent Jones vaulted to the top of his profession.

The par-4 11th is one of the only holes on the course which Jones didn't change much, because its natural defenses were already quite strong. Both tee and green are set along a ridge, with the fairway starting below on the right and then swinging up through a saddle in the ridge to the left side, which the green faces. A solid drive to the left is the only shot which will do, though many slicers are lured to the right by a nest of bunkers on the side of the hill. The green is sloped sharply from back to front and always plays very fast. Professionals must take care not to put too much backspin on their approach shots, or they might well watch them spin all the way back off the front of the green.

The 13th at Pine Valley, Clementon, NJ. *446 yards par-4.*

Pine Valley is universally acclaimed as America's greatest course, and until recently, its most difficult. Each hole is an epic struggle from one 'landing area' to the next, with perfectly manicured fairways and greens guarded by fearsome native sand hazards and bushes described appropriately as 'one giant, unraked bunker.'

The thirteenth is a long par four perfectly fitting the heroic scale of the course. The drive is uphill over sandy wastes to a wide, crowned summit of fairway—a bit too far to the left, and the ball will run out of the fairway down into the sand. From the summit, the fairway sweeps around to the right, but the direct route to the large green is across the brink of a steep drop into the trees on the left, with bunkers shelved into the hillside to catch anything short. For most players, a conservative approach to the right, followed by a deft pitch, is the best chance of a four and, more importantly, of avoiding the double-digit score which threatens the golfer throughout his round here.

Below: No. 8 at Pebble Beach Golf Links, Pebble Beach, CA

Above: No. 10 at Riviera CC, Pacific Palisades, CA

Right: No. 15 at Harbour Town Golf Links, Hilton Head Island, SC

The 14th at Shinnecock Hills Golf Club, Southampton, NY.
445 yards par-4.

Set in the tony Hamptons, 100 miles east of New York City, Shinnecock's pedigree is immediately confirmed by the Stanford White-designed clubhouse, the oldest in America. The golf course was updated by Philadelphia designer William Flynn in 1927 to consolidate two eighteens into one magnificent course, which has since served as the site of two U.S. Opens.

The sandy soil and mild climate of eastern Long Island is perfect for growing the wispy knee-high rough which gives a golf course the look and feel of Scotland. At the 14th, this rough must be respected on the inside shoulder of the dogleg right. The drive is played downhill into a valley which runs back up to the right, with the green at the head of the valley after an uphill second, guarded by bunkers at both sides. The hole is named 'Thom's Elbow' after the longtime club professional, Charlie Thom, whose own elbow was bent at a similar angle.

The 15th at Harbour Town Golf Links, Hilton Head Island, SC. *588 yards par-5.*

Modern designer Pete Dye achieved infamy among the world's touring professionals for his demanding TPC at Sawgrass course, but the pros had selected Dye for the job out of their universal respect for Harbour Town, in the South Carolina lowcountry. Opened in 1969, the course turned the trend of golf architecture on its ear, stressing placement off the tee and precision iron shots to small greens instead of the long and strong designs popular in the 1950s and 1960s.

The par-5 fifteenth is the longest hole on the course, but like most true three-shotters the critical need is for accuracy rather than brute strength. A wild second shot toward the green can easily find the pond at the corner of the dogleg or be stymied behind a tree, but the key is simply to place it in the fairway. If the second shot is hit into the rough, the third has virtually no chance of holding the tiny green, and a six will be the result.

Asked about the size of the original green, which was not much more than 2,500 square feet, Dye had a simple explanation: during construction, he asked design consultant Jack Nicklaus to hit nine-irons from the second landing area, and sized the green by drawing a ring around Jack's better approaches!

The 16th at Cypress Point Club, Pebble Beach, CA. *219 yards par-3.*

This long par-3 over the edge of the Pacific Ocean is the most lusted-after hole in all of golf. Many players would give anything to finagle a way onto the ultra-private course just for the chance to hit this green with their drive, only to suffer stage fright for the whole round if the opportunity does come.

In competition the hole is more often played with a long iron out to the left onto the fatter part of the peninsula, followed by a wedge out to the green on the point; this avoids not only the obvious problem of ocean on the right, but the insidious cove on the far side of the peninsula which collects pulled drives toward the green. But to go for the green successfully can be the highlight of a lifetime in golf, and few can resist the temptation to try.

While Cypress Point is the pinnacle of Alister Mackenzie's design career, the architect admitted freely that this hole was the idea of his client, former Women's Amateur champion Marion Hollins. When told by a previous architect that it was a pity the carry was too far for a golf hole, Marion teed up a ball and drove it across to the present green site, commenting afterward that if she could do it, surely there were some men who could make the carry as well. Yes... but not many.

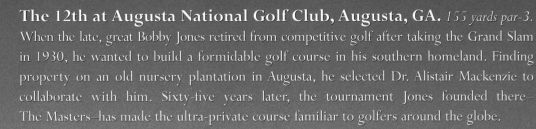

The 12th at Augusta National Golf Club, Augusta, GA. *155 yards par-3.* When the late, great Bobby Jones retired from competitive golf after taking the Grand Slam in 1930, he wanted to build a formidable golf course in his southern homeland. Finding property on an old nursery plantation in Augusta, he selected Dr. Alistair Mackenzie to collaborate with him. Sixty-five years later, the tournament Jones founded there— The Masters–has made the ultra-private course familiar to golfers around the globe.

The short twelfth hole occupies the lowest point on the course, and requires a perfect short iron across Rae's Creek in a swirling wind. The slight diagonal line of the creek and the shallowness of the green target cause every player to hesitate when the pin is set on the back right of the green, as it always is on the second Sunday in April. There are not many other holes in the game where the world's best players opt not to attack the flag, but so many contenders for the Masters title have drowned their hopes here, it is impossible not to be haunted by their memory.

The 17th at The National Golf Links of America, Southampton, NY. *368 yards par-4.*
No other club in America has so imposing a title as The National, but fittingly so, for the course was the dream of pioneer golf architect [and the first U.S. Amateur champion] Charles Blair Macdonald, who wanted to create for America a course equal to the great links of the British Isles on which he had learned the game. Macdonald made several trips abroad to study the classic links and import their best features to his own course, but the seventeenth is not a copy but Macdonald's own inspiration.

Above: No. 16 at Cypress Point Club, Pebble Beach, CA

From an elevated tee one looks down across a wasteland of sand to a fairway angling away from right to left, and then back to the right around a large sandy mound at the front of the green. Beyond, the shore of a beautiful bay runs away behind the green, making this one of the most scenic views in American golf —but we won't enjoy it unless the tee shot is played on the proper line, based upon our own strength and ability to hit solidly under the pressure imposed by such a beautiful golf hole.

To add even further character, the tee is in the shadow of the large windmill which is the signature feature of the course. Legend has it that a member of the National suggested that a windmill on this spot would be most picturesque, and Charles Blair Macdonald promptly had it erected–sending the bill for its construction to the member, of course.

The 18th at Shadow Creek Club, North Las Vegas, NV. *520 yards par-5.*
Golf architecture has changed remarkably from its origins in America to the extravagant creations of modern design, and no course better illustrates this than Shadow Creek, the opulent private playground of casino developer Steve Wynn and designer Tom Fazio. More than two million cubic yards of earth were moved in its construction, including the creation of a 3/4-mile flowing creek, and thousands of trees and shrubs were planted to transform the harsh desert site into a golfing oasis.

The climax of the round is at the eighteenth, a short par five with the man-made creek flowing from beside the green over three broad waterfalls and back to the foot of the tee. On the drive, the tee shot must be kept to the left of the water, but good players who dare to place their tee shots close to the hazard are rewarded with a chance to go at the green in two, by carrying the stream again on their second shots. For good players any score from three to seven is possible, making it the ultimate gamblers' hole; for the conservative, there is a decent prospect of a birdie or par to finish, so the customers will leave with a pleasant taste in their mouths. In this respect, at least, the course's Las Vegas roots are clearly evident. **Ⓐ**

The Carlyle

NEW YORK

THE IRISH IN AMERICA

by Thomas J. O'Gorman

*The story of the Irish in America is a poignant tale
of patriots, poets and dreamers whose exile from an island
on Europe's western edge brought them to a land
which they would, in time, come to treasure as their own.*

Out of Ireland we have come,
Great hatred, little room
Maimed us at the start.
I carry from my mother's womb
A fanatic's heart.

William Butler Yeats

Over the centuries they came, making their escape. Bold, exhausted, lifted by the wind and soaked by the sea: the Irish arrived in America with the fresh smell of promise uncovering on its shore, in every generation a Panglossian wonder. From the very beginning they had few troubles assimilating. There was an ease, a comfort that tells as much about the character of early America as it does about the Celtic wanderers who found their way to its doorstep.

Long before the half dead Irish of the Great Famine years sealed themselves into coffin ships for a macabre journey to food and freedom, the Irish knew America was a land of promise. Throughout the Eighteenth century, Irish Catholics arrived in America in modest but steady numbers, achieving success within the colonies as schoolmasters, doctors, merchants, shipbuilders, booksellers and printers. Long before the narrow bigotry of the nineteenth century Nativist persecution, the Irish knew a flamboyant America alive with the dream of the Enlightenment. The Rights of Man, expansive egalitarianism, liberty and the rich seeds of republicanism found resonance in their hearts.

As early as 1690 it is recorded that there were McCarthys from Ireland, who had arrived in Virginia after their lands had been confiscated by the Crown. They settled in Kinsale, Westmoreland County, comforted by the reminder of another Kinsale, in County Cork, one of the ancestral seats of the McCarthys in Ireland. Through this thread of McCarthys, Mary Ball, the mother of George Washington, counted many cousins.

As Commander in Chief of America's revolutionary forces, General Washington counted the Irish among his most ardent military supporters. Following the Revolution's successful outcome, many of these Irish soldiers and sailors received large land grants in Virginia for their wartime assistance. In a British parliamentary debate in 1784 it was noted that "the Irish language is as commonly spoken in the American ranks as English." Many in Britain felt that America had been lost because its military ranks were swelled by the Irish, whose valor determined the outcome of the contest.

Before the American Revolution, Daniel Carroll, one of Virginia's wealthiest landowners of Irish ancestry, had encouraged his compatriots to colonize some of his vast uncultivated land tracts. His cousin, Charles Carroll of Carrollton (who signed the Declaration of Independence) shared his zeal. Carroll even distributed handbills in Ireland, promoting emigration among the Irish. He promised land as well as religious tolerance to any Irish who would come. The proposal offered a way out for Irish Catholics, who found it impossible to prosper amid the draconian system of exactions from landlords.

The Carroll Family, whose lineage can be traced back to the Irish aristocracy, memorialized their roots by giving some of their properties in Maryland the same names as their Irish estates. History celebrates the Carrolls as America's most respected Irish Catholic patriots. In addition to Charles Carroll, who went on to outlive all other signatories of the Declaration of Independence (dying in 1832 at the age of 95) the family also numbered among their kin John Carroll, the first American Roman Catholic Archbishop.

Charles Carroll's daughter, Mrs. Richard Caton, enjoyed a position of vast social prestige in the infant Republic. She was the uncontested leader of American society, a role that would not be equaled among Americans of Irish ancestry for another century. Among her more discerning social achievements was the establishment of White Sulphur Springs, the nation's first fashionable resort. Mrs Caton's three daughters became the Duchess of Leeds, the Marchioness of Wellesley and the Baroness Stafford.

Page 45:

Top Left: President John F. Kennedy.

Top Right: The American Irish Historical Society.

Bottom Right: Grace Kelly.

Bottom Left: The 7th Regiment Irish Brigade, American Civil War.

Left: President John F. Kennedy.

Above: The Trinity Irish Dancers, Silver Medalists at the World Championships of Irish Dancing in Galway.

Above:
Two bagpipers and the sounds of Ireland.

Many Irish builders and architects were active in creating the architecture of the South. The Carroll home at Homewood in Baltimore displays many of the characteristics of Irish Georgian architecture. The architect, James Hoban from County Kilkenny in Ireland, went on to build the White House, which resembles the great Irish houses that he worked on as a young man.

Many other patriots of Irish Catholic ancestry contributed to the life of the nascent Republic: at the dawn of the Revolution, Wexford-born John Barry was a naval captain in the merchant fleet out of Philadelphia. His seamanship and military abilities made a singular contribution to the war effort against Britain. Barry earned the extraordinary sobriquet "Father of the American Navy".

In the early years of the American nation the Irish were loyal, industrious and eager to succeed. In an era defined by the philosophical sophistication of America's gentlemen farmers, their religion and customs presented little threat to the dominant Yankee population. However, within fifty years of the American Revolution both their numbers and the economic conditions affecting immigration would greatly change the prevailing image of the Irish in America.

Back in Ireland, severe economic disaster, brought about by a series of agricultural blights to the potato crop, wiped out the essential food cEommodity of the peasantry. The Great Famine that began in 1845 opened the floodgates. In the next fifteen years more than two million Irish immigrants came to America: less educated and more desperate than the Irish of earlier generations, the new immigrants came in frightening numbers, struggling to survive. Their presence soon began to worry the nation's dominant Anglo-Saxon, Protestant majority.

The America to which the new Irish came was evolving into a very different place from the land that first greeted Irish settlers a century before. Industry had begun to overshadow agriculture, and as urban centers became more congested, they proved ill—equipped for the influx of impoverished Irish immigrants. A new crisis loomed in the nation's life.

With their arrival in northeastern cities like Boston, New York and Philadelphia, a work force of cheap labor presented itself to further encourage industrial expansion. By 1850, twenty-six percent of the population of New York—133,000 out of 513,000—were Irish born. The very presence of such large numbers of Irish Catholics quickly eroded their welcome in many American communities. Strong anti-immigrant feelings provoked a backlash against immigrants in general and the Irish in particular, leading to the establishment of a political party called the Know-Nothings.

From New York to Louisville, mobs of angry Nativists (American-born citizens) swarmed the streets and back alleys of cities attacking immigrants in their tenements, often burning their hovels and Catholic churches to the ground. The intolerance of the era, characterized by such employment epitaphs as "No Irish Need Apply," galvanized the Irish for generations to come. Growing in power because of their increasing numbers, the Irish waged their own battles to defeat Nativist oppression.

Nothing permitted the Irish more success than their natural inclination toward politics and the remarkable resource of parochial education that became an extension of Catholic life in urban America. The Roman Catholic Church stood as an indelible bond among the Irish in America. Bolstered by subsequent waves of immigrants from across Europe, it became a powerful force in American cities by the 1860s.

The Catholic Church became a vehicle through which the Irish stabilized themselves in their adopted country. Its careful insistence that every parish establish a parochial school enabled continuous waves of new immigrants to have access to education denied them back in Ireland—a stepping stone to economic and political liberty.

At the latter half of the Nineteenth century, the Roman Catholic clergy of the United States found a large portion of its hierarchy and leadership among the Irish. A vast network of schools, colleges and universities emerged as the valued inheritance of this Catholic culture. Meanwhile, religious organizations like the Sisters of Mercy founded hospitals, orphanages, schools and settlement houses to combat the hardship of immigrant life.

During the American Civil War (1861-65) the Irish penchant for swashbuckling heroism became evident on each side of the Mason-Dixon line. The American South had possessed a distinctive Irish character long before Nineteenth century immigrants first arrived at the port of Charleston. By the start of the war, they had deep roots in the plantation economy. The courageous Irish lined up on both sides of the struggle, often finding themselves in battle against other Irishmen.

No single group of Irishmen demonstrate this more than the men of the Fighting 69th. This New York regiment, made up entirely of Irish troops under the command of Brigadier General Thomas Meagher, repeatedly played an extraordinary role in the war's fiercest battles—Fredericksburg, Chancellorsville, Antietam and Gettysburg. So devastating was the loss of life in defense of the Union under their battle flag of emerald green; and so critical was the effect that they had on the eventual outcome of the conflict, that almost a century later, President John Fitzgerald Kennedy presented the 69th's battle flag to the Irish Parliament on his state visit to Ireland in 1963.

The blood shed on both sides of the conflict forever changed the way the American Irish perceived themselves. Following the Civil War, they would carve out a new destiny for themselves in the land they had defended by their valor and blood. Roman Catholic parishes across the nation grew exponentially with the expansion of the Irish immigrant community in the following generations. By 1880 there were six million Catholics in America, up from a population of just more than 500,000 only 40 years before.

From New York to Chicago, from Boston to St. Paul, the Catholic Church in America was as Irish as it was Catholic. New York Archbishop John McCloskey (1810-1885) was made the nation's first cardinal in 1875, and two years later the Irish-reared Archbishop James Gibbons of Baltimore (1834-1921) also received the cardinal's red hat. Their ecclesiastical prominence as Princes of the Church was immensely significant to the Irish community, which continued to battle the familiar suspicions and intolerance of Yankee America.

Below:

Brigadier General Thomas Francis Meagher and the 69th Regiment at Antietam – America's bloodiest day, September 17, 1862

Catholic religious leaders in the Nineteenth century exercised roles far beyond the parameters of their individual clerical positions. By 1886, in the 69 Roman Catholic dioceses in the country, 39 were led by bishops of Irish birth or heritage. Their influence on the religious and cultural ethos of America redesigned the contours of urban life, while rapidly growing parishes supplanted the village identities of 'the old country'.

Above: P.J. Kennedy, father of Joseph P. Kennedy, a tavern keeper, liquor importer and banker who served in the Massachusetts state legislature for eight terms.

Right: President William Jefferson Clinton, St. Patrick's Day 1995.

The Irish clergy in America were tough potentates, builders, power-brokers, steely-eyed managers responsible for millions of Catholics, defensive of their rights and insisting on their fair share as full Americans. Often regaled in the purple robes of high Roman honor, with the title of Monsignor, they became the Irish immigrant's new-world aristocracy. And the hierarchical structure of the Roman Catholic church provided a foundation for political achievement in America.

Exiles escaping failed political insurrections in Ireland, such as the United Irishman revolt in 1848 and the Fenian Rebellion in 1867, filled Irish immigrant neighborhoods. Agitation against British rule in Ireland had given the Irish an ease with risky political adventure. The ability to band together for the common cause was a natural extension of seven hundred years of foreign occupation in their homeland. It didn't take much to redirect such inherent political skills in the fertile environment of America's big cities.

The Irish learned important political lessons in cities like Boston, where the sheer size of their numbers (and their ability to use the English language) enabled them to defend the newly arrived immigrants. Less than 40 years later, the people of Boston would elect their first Irish mayor, and before the turn of the century, the Irish achieved a majority status among the voters of Boston, promptly electing another Irish mayor, Patrick Collins. He would be succeeded, in 1901, by yet another son of Irish immigrants, John Fitzgerald, known as "Honey Fitz."

Fitzgerald launched a political dynasty that is still very much alive today. He was the grandfather of the late President John F. Kennedy, the late New York Senator Robert F. Kennedy, Massachusetts Senator Edward M. Kennedy, and former U.S. Ambassador to Ireland Jean Kennedy Smith. The enormous contributions made by Senator Ted Kennedy and his sister the Ambassador to the recent peace process in Ireland is a long thread that binds them to the immigrant Boston of "Honey Fitz." Congressman Patrick Kennedy of Rhode Island, former Massachusetts Congressman Joseph Kennedy II, Maryland Lieutenant Governor Kathleen Kennedy Townsend and Maryland State Assembly member Mark Schriver represent a new generation of political descendants among Fitzgerald's great-grand children.

As Mayor of Boston, Fitzgerald was succeeded by James Michael Curley in 1914. One of America's most controversial politicians, went on to become Massachusetts Governor and a congressman as well. In the homeland of the Yankee the Irish created a political powerbase that would, within fifty years, place a grandson of Irish immigrants in the White House.

Above: One of the Boston Irish,
Former Speaker of the House, Thomas "Tip" O'Neill.

Former Speaker of the House, Thomas "Tip" O'Neill, another Boston Irishman, once made an observation that "All politics is local." He was right, of course. Real political power had its focus in the life of the ward, the neighborhood, the parish, one's own backyard. The Irish refined the lesson that politics is at its essence concerned with the delivery of everyday service. With it they established themselves as masters of conflict resolution and brokers of community justice. In America's melting pot of cultures and languages, it was the Irish who spoke for those who had no English.

By 1900 Chicago had an Irish-born Chief of Police, Francis P. O'Neill, whose careful preservation of traditional Irish music insured its protection for future generations. Edward Dunne would shortly be elected the city's first Irish mayor, and then Governor of Illinois. The tradition in Chicago of strong Irish mayors (a product of the Cook County Democratic machine) continued throughout the century with Mayors Edward Kelly, Martin Kennelly, Richard J. Daley, Jane M. Byrne and presently, Richard M. Daley.

Machine politics—the well oiled, highly organized system of urban government, largely based on an army of patronage workers who secured high voter turnout—was not only responsible for catapulting regional politicians of Irish heritage into the national political spotlight, but also helped to shape the very character of America's national political identity. Through the system of patronage, politics became a crucial vehicle for Irish success in big cities. Police and fire departments were run by the Irish for generations. Countless Irish received employment in the intricate lattice of big city regimes. From the bottom to the top, the Irish excelled at the delivery of essential services, enhanced by their glib and easy speech.

No one characterized this more than Al Smith, Governor of New York and Presidential hopeful in the 1920s. The son of Irish immigrants, his story is like that of countless first generation Irish. His intelligence and abilities shot him to the top in New York's complex political system. He carried with him what many argue was the most important contribution by the Irish to American politics—a refined sense of the social responsibility of government. When he was denied the presidency because of his Catholicism, it was a reminder to the Irish that while they had achieved much in their new home, the familiar pattern of Yankee skepticism was still present. Much of Smith's political and social ideology found expression in the New Deal philosophy of Franklin Delano Roosevelt in the 1930s and 1940s.

The dramatic decades of gold and silver strikes in the western United States proved fruitful for some of the Irish in America. San Francisco's "Irish Big Four", William S. O'Brien, James G. Fair, John W. Mackay and James C. Flood made a fortune at the Comstock Lode in Virginia City, Nevada. This was the largest and most valuable pocket of silver ever discovered. Flood and O'Brien previously ran a local bar famous for its Irish fish chowder. When they were alerted by a miner's tip to the opportunities of the Comstock, they set off for Nevada. Mackay and Fair joined them as investment partners and they soon became four of the wealthiest men in the country. The fashionable mansion which Flood built at the top of Nob Hill still stands. Their rise from penniless immigrants to multimillionaires became the stuff of legend.

Beyond the contributions of the Irish to religious and political life, they famously enjoyed success in the world of entertainment too. In New York, young George M. Cohan, the grandson of Irish famine immigrants, became the darling of Broadway with an unbroken string of musicals. Tunes like *Yankee Doodle Dandy, You're a Grand Old Flag* and *Give My Regards to Broadway* became a part of the nation's life as it entered World War I.

The Irish also nourished a deep literary tradition among the children of the immigrant: Finley Peter Dunne began his Mr. Dooley newspaper columns in 1893, cataloging the cracker-barrel wisdom of the immigrant generation, and became one of the nation's most widely read journalists. Playwright Eugene O'Neill composed hauntingly dark portraits of Irish American family life. In the 1920s F. Scott Fitzgerald demonstrated a new literary elegance with works like *Tender is the Night* and *The Great Gatsby.* Fitzgerald, who christened the Jazz Age, created characters of great humanity and complexity before going on to Hollywood as a screen writer. James T. Farrell, whose controversial Studs Lonigan detailed the tragic self destruction of the Irish American male, faced public outrage because of his sobering characterizations of Irish family life. These artists demonstrated a coming-of-age for the second generation of the Irish in America. Their work still speaks to millions.

Nothing has helped to shape popular culture in America more than the film industry, which from its earliest days had the Irish involved on both sides of the camera. Director John Ford (born Sean O'Feeney) created dramatic images of Irish life. In 1935, Ford's production of *The Informer,* starring Irish actor Victor McLaglen, presented a tragic portrait of the conflict in Ireland's struggle for independence in the early 1920s. McLaglen would go on to become a part of Ford's large stable of Irish character actors who formed an ensemble company for many of his movies. With John Wayne (born Marion Michael Morrison) and Dublin actress Maureen O'Hara among them, Ford's ensemble would become immortal in his screen adaptation of *The Quiet Man.* This story of a Yank's return to the Ireland of his childhood is a *tour de force* of village life in rural Ireland. It garnered the Academy Award for best director in 1952.

Ford liked to say that his name at birth was Sean. And during his romance with Katherine Hepburn that is all she called him. Returning to Ireland to shoot *The Quiet Man* was an important experience for Ford, recalling the many trips he made there as a boy. Referring to the film location in Cong, County Galway, he noted, "I shot it on my native health; the actors were old family friends."

Below: American Irishman John Wayne and Dubliner Maureen O'Hara in a still from The Quiet Man, *John Ford's epic Irish tale.*

Ford's other films, like *She Wore a Yellow Ribbon, Cheyenne Autumn* and *Stagecoach,* respectively tell the story of America's settlement, its frontier character and its complex national character. As Hollywood's most dominant Irish movie maker, Ford left a lasting imprint of America with the Irish immigrant prominently on view.

The movie tastes of America were shaped by a long line of screen actors with Irish roots. Jimmy Cagney, Bing Crosby, Buster Keaton, Errol Flynn, Jackie Gleason, Grace Kelly and John Huston are just some of Hollywood's veteran actors of Irish blood. Incidentally, John Huston moved his family to Ireland in 1950 and remained there into the early 1970's. He had been smitten with the country from the first moment he saw it. "My first night in Ireland," he noted, "Ireland had me." Eventually he bought a run-down Irish estate called St. Clerans in Galway, turning it into one of the most delightful homes in Ireland. Nowadays it is owned by Merv Griffin.

Today a whole new generation of actors with strong Irish roots fill American screens. Chicago born actor Aidan Quinn spent much of his childhood back with his family in Birr, County Offaly. Sean Penn, Meg Ryan and George Clooney are just a few of the other current stars who trace their origins back to the Irish immigrant experience.

Irish assimilation into mainstream American culture was further hastened by the large number of Irish Americans who fought in World War II. Many were the children of turn-of-the-century immigrants. From Pearl Harbor to Guadalcanal, Irish Americans were proving just how American they were. Both politically and psychologically, the election of John Fitzgerald Kennedy in 1960 as President of the United States confirmed, at last, that the Irish were welcome. Kennedy's victory was a cathartic event for anyone of Irish heritage who ever felt slighted by their immigrant pedigree. The Irish had helped to transform America by their presence. They also helped to civilize its frontier, to organize its industrial labor force, to educate its citizens, and to build and staff its facilities for social service and health care. Kennedy's entrance to the White House marked the end of the old Yankee intolerance that had haunted the Irish.

The Irish contribution to American culture stemmed from their investment in every aspect of its life. They carried little with them in their exile: an ancient faith, soft talk, a strong work ethic and the eloquence of the bards. In America they reinvented themselves as writers, politicians, artists, journalists, diplomats, physicians, judges, attorneys and entertainers.

Galvanized by their devotion to faith and family, they reshaped themselves and the land that became their new home. Despite the fear of becoming second class hyphenated citizens, or the over-wrought passion of some for rapid assimilation into the larger cultural milieu, today many of the American-Irish are rediscovering their ancient roots—not in some nostalgic longing for the romantic Ireland of the past, but by engaging the Ireland of the present in supportive strategies of harmony, unity and peace. The Irish in America are tied by a thread as old as time to tribe and kin and soil and wind. As the writer John Hewitt puts it, the Irish are "like Lir's children, banished to the waters. Our hearts still listen for the landward bells." Ⓐ

Left: Grace Kelly (1928-82) Actress, Princess, Mother, Icon.

Above: With 17 best sellers to her credit, Irish-American novelist Mary Higgins Clark is known throughout the world as the "Queen of Suspense."

Experience the miracle of **La Mer**® in Cosmetics at selected stores.

Neiman Marcus

AMERICA'S
ELITE 1000

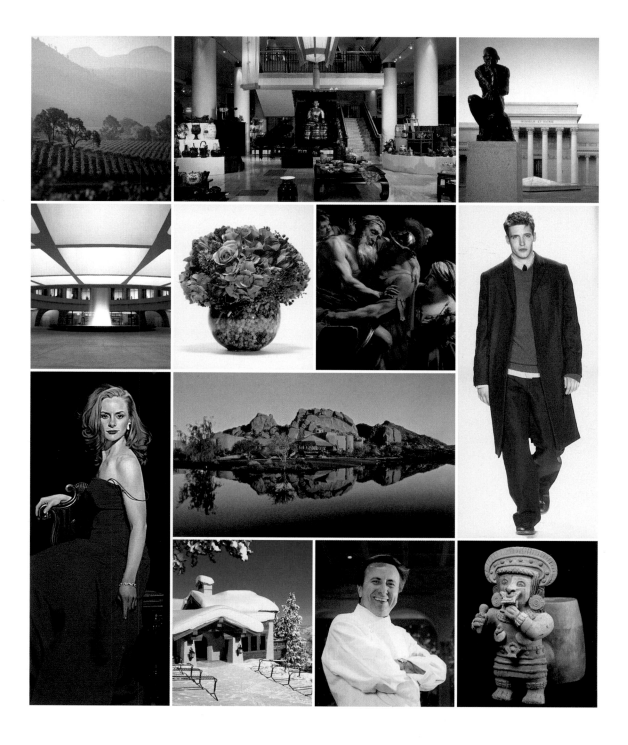

*The Best Luxury Goods, Shops and Services
in the United States of America.*

AARON BASHA
Jewelry and Watches

Aaron Basha amazed the jewelry industry with his briolette diamond, faceted like a crystal chandelier, which gives the illusion of being suspended in midair. A father of four, Basha has also captured the attention of the world's most stylish moms, from Rosie O'Donnell to Demi Moore to Melanie Griffith to Madonna, with his signature line of baby shoe charms.

Aaron Basha

680 Madison Avenue
New York, NY 10021
Phone: 212-935-1960   Fax: 212-759-8294

ABACUS SECURITY
Security Consultants

If you're a regular at top Manhattan fashion shows, you will recognize the name of this exclusive bodyguard and security service. Abacus supplies armed or unarmed New York State registered bodyguards and drivers. Run by Andrew Oberfeldt, an ex-SWAT officer, many of Abacus' security consultants are retired police officers.

Abacus Security

601 West 26th Street
New York, NY 10010
Phone: 212-727-1022

ABC CARPET & HOME
Specialty Shops

Opened in the 19th century solely to sell carpets, ABC has since grown into a ten-story market containing the best and brightest in home fashion from all over the world. Today one floor is entirely devoted to bolts of every fabric imaginable: brocades, silks, velvets and chinoiserie. Of equal renown are their extensive furniture and home furnishing collections. *Quel magasin!*

ABC Carpet & Home

888 Broadway
New York, NY 10003
Phone: 212-473-3000

HOTEL ADOLPHUS
Hotels

Built in 1912 by beer mogul Adolphus Busch, the Hotel Adolphus has become an American hotel landmark; Queen Elizabeth II, Maya Angelou, Rudolf Nureyev and presidents from Franklin D. Roosevelt through Bill Clinton are among the distinguished guests who have stayed here.

Boasting luxury on a scale befitting the Lonestar State, The Adolphus Lobby Living Room plays host to the hotel's million dollar art collection, which spills over into the guest rooms and suites. Especially prominent within The Adolphus collection are two 18th century Flemish tapestries depicting the life of Cleopatra (the other four in the series are in the Metropolitan Museum of Art) and an antique Steinway built in 1893, previously owned by Benjamin Guggenheim. The Adolphus is the perfect setting for a proper tea in the grand English tradition, uncommon in this oil-baron town. The hotel's restaurant, The French Room, offers edible artistry under the careful direction of Executive Chef William Koval.

Hotel Adolphus

1321 Commerce Street
Dallas, TX 75202
Phone: 214-742-8200   Fax: 214-651-3588

ABRAHAM MOHEBAN & SON

Antiques

If you are searching for an exquisite rug, have a look at this gallery's impressive selection of antique Oriental and European carpets. Customers often come with designers and architects to coordinate the right carpeting to suit their décor. Fashionable floor coverings include Oushaks from Turkey, Agras from India and Tabriz from Persia.

Abraham Moheban & Son

139 East 57th Street
New York, NY 10022
Phone: 212-758-3900   Fax: 212-758-3973

THE ACADEMY AWARDS

Events

The world's most celebrated exhibition of back-slapping is watched in over 150 countries, but the real fun starts after the winners and losers vacate the Dorothy Chandler Pavilion and move on to the post-Oscars parties. Graydon Carter of *Vanity Fair* hosts the best bash, which is even harder to crash than the ceremony itself.

The Academy Awards

The National Academy of Motion Picture Arts & Sciences
8949 Wilshire Boulevard
Beverly Hills, CA 90211
Phone: 310-247-3000   Fax: 310-271-3395

ACQUAVELLA GALLERIES

Art Dealers

When Steve Wynn decided to amass an art collection to rival those of the great museums, William Acquavella was the man he turned to for assistance. A specialist in 19th and 20th century art, Acquavella's extensive collection includes impressionist, cubist and surrealist masterworks. He is the exclusive agent for the paintings of British artist Lucien Freud, whose work will be honored with a retrospective in 2000.

Acquavella Galleries

18 East 79th Street
New York, NY 10021
Phone: 212-734-6300   Fax: 212-794-9394

ADDISON ON MADISON

Fashion   ***Best Kept Secret***

Addison on Madison is a smart little shirt and tie store with a huge selection of its own unique shirts and exclusively designed neckwear. There is a great sense of color and style here which truly stands out in the "basic black" world of New York. Service and attention to detail are topnotch. Ask for the Australian manager, Brian Hall, who is a real gentleman.

Addison on Madison

698 Madison Avenue
New York, NY 10021
Phone: 212-308-2660   Fax: 212-750-4444

AIDA THIBIANT
EUROPEAN DAY SPA

Spas and Clinics

For over 26 years, the Aida Thibiant European Day Spa has been the hands-down favorite of many of the local and international elite. From the moment you walk through the door, the fresh air, the trickle of a waterfall and all the elements of a world-class, state-of-the-art spa soothe your senses and restore vital energies. It is no wonder this spa has won the devotion of their well-heeled clientele. An extensive menu features many award-winning, unique services, personally developed by Madame Thibiant, an acclaimed skin care authority. Services range from energizing salt glow treatments to rejuvenating massages, skin-perfecting facials, and all the finishing touches, such as manicures, pedicures, waxing and a full-service hair salon. Let her highly trained technicians delight you with a custom facial or body treatment that will leave your skin radiant and your spirit calmed. For a sense of total renewal, try one of the Remineralizing or Detoxifying Spa Envelopments that feature powerful Marine or Rain Forest Muds enhanced with personal blends of aromatic oils. Triple-bank Vichy showers above your massage table will wash away your cares and stimulate your pulse points, leaving you ready to face the day. Don't leave the spa without a bottle of her famous Tahitian Milk Bath for at-home pampering between spa visits. This is an experience to be savored. Not to be missed.

Aida Thibiant European Day Spa

449 North Canon Drive
Beverly Hills, CA 90210
Phone: 310-278-7565   Fax: 310-278-4392

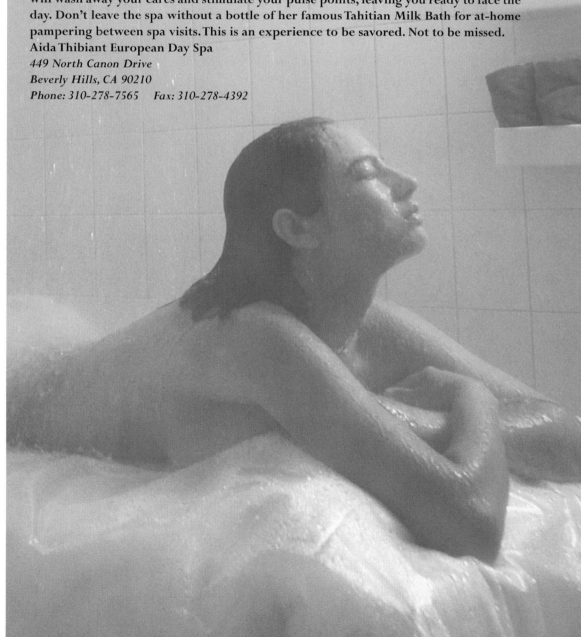

ADMIRAL LIMOUSINE SERVICE

Chauffeur Services

If you get that prized invitation to the White House, it is essential that you arrive both on time and in style. With Admiral Limousine, you can safely expect impeccable service. Drivers are well informed and professional; comfort and expedience are guiding principles of the company.

Admiral Limousine Service

1243 First Street, SE

Washington, DC 20003

Phone: 202-554-1000   Fax: 202-863-0775

AKIN, GUMP, STRAUSS, HAUER & FELD

Law Firms

This is the 10th-largest law firm in the United States, with over 850 lawyers working in offices in Austin, Brussels, Dallas, Houston, London, Los Angeles, Moscow, and New York. The firm has a diversified practice and represents regional, national, and international clients in a wide range of areas, including litigation, real estate and tax.

Akin, Gump, Strauss, Hauer & Feld

1333 New Hampshire Avenue, NW

Washington, DC 20036

Phone: 202-887-4000   Fax: 202-887-4288

ALAN FLUSSER

Fashion

One of America's best upmarket menswear designers, Alan Flusser can produce a made-to measure suit within two weeks, although bespoke suits are the mainstay of his business. He also designs dress shirts (both ready made and custom made), neckwear, hosiery, suspenders, shoes and handkerchiefs for well dressed luminaries like Bob Costas and a host of Hollywood's finest. Flusser is the author of *Style and the Man,* the definitive record of the best menswear outlets in America today.

Alan Flusser

Saks Fifth Avenue

611 Fifth Avenue, New York, NY 10022

Phone: 212-888-9494   Fax: 212-940-4849

THE ALBUQUERQUE MUSEUM OF ART & HISTORY

Museums

The purpose of this sovereign institution is to entertain visitors who are interested in learning about the history and art of the Southwest. With fine exhibitions, an art school and its charming sculpture garden, the museum has been a source of pride for the city since its establishment in 1967. A book, *Albuquerque: A Look Back* will be published later in the year, showcasing the museum's extensive photo archive spanning from 1900 to the present.

The Albuquerque Museum of Art & History

2000 Mountain Road NW

Albuquerque, NM 87104

Phone: 505-243-7255   Fax: 505-764-6546

ALDEN SHOE COMPANY

Fashion

Custom boots have never looked *this* good. Since 1884 the Alden Shoe Company of Massachusetts has designed and manufactured classic gentlemen's footwear, epitomizing the New England tradition of old-school, custom boot making at its finest. Alden's shoes are created in classic patterns with extraordinary attention to detail and their boots are made of top-grade leather from the finest tanneries in the world. Our favorites are the Traditional Saddle Oxfords, which reflect "in a quiet, sure way the solid values of the man who wears them."

Alden Shoe Company

1 Taunton Street

Middleborough, MA 02346

Phone: 508-947-3926   Fax: 508-947-7753

ALEXANDRA LIND

Fashion   *Rising Star*

Alexandra Lind started making dresses for her socialite girlfriends when she was sixteen. She has turned her passion into a thriving business, selling her line of clothing through stores in the tri-state area, and making couture for individual customers from her showroom in New York. Lind describes her style as a marriage between modern and traditional, polite and seductive.

Alexandra Lind

240 West 35th Street, Suite 800A

New York, NY 10001

Phone: 212-594-0988   Fax: 212-594-0774

ALEXIS HOTEL

Hotels   *Best Kept Secret*

Bill Kimpton's quirky hotel (located in an historic building in the heart of Seattle) is a self-styled work of art: stay in the John Lennon Suite, where the walls are lined with lithographs of lyric sheets by the great man. If you are a jazz lover you will prefer the Miles Davis Suite, which boasts Davis' own artwork. There are regular wine tastings in the Painted Table restaurant, and an ArtWalk exhibit of local artists' work. Ask for a room facing into the quiet courtyard.

Alexis Hotel

1007 First Avenue

Seattle, WA 98104

Phone: 206-624-4844   Fax: 206-621-9009

ALFRED BULLARD

Antiques

This venerable Philadelphia establishment, founded in 1924 by Alfred Bullard but owned and operated by William Bertolet since 1964, specializes in 18th and early 19th century English furniture. Bertolet exhibits pieces at the University Hospital Show in Philadelphia and New York's Winter Antiques Show at the Seventh Regiment Armory.

Alfred Bullard

1604 Pine Street

Philadelphia, PA 19103

Phone: 215-735-1879   Fax: 215-735-4820

ALGABAR

Specialty Shops   *Rising Star*

When Gail Baral moved from New York to California a few years ago, she decided to do something reflecting her love of travel. The result is Algabar, a treasure trove of furniture and decorative objects from all over the world. Asia is particularly well represented—if you are wondering where to get that antique picture frame you foolishly neglected to buy in Bali, this is the place. Gail is a warm, friendly woman whose good taste is evident throughout.

Algabar

920 North La Cienega Boulevard

Los Angeles, CA 90069

Phone: 310-360-3500   Fax: 310-360-3505

ALLURE DAY SPA & STORE

Spas and Clinics

Pamper yourself at this spa and hair design center in New York City. At the spa, try a customized acne, glycolic, or oxygen facial; a slimming anticellulite body wrap; or an invigorating algae body scrub. Talented massage therapists guarantee soothing aromatherapy deep-tissue massages and relaxing reflexology pedicures. Or let the licensed massage therapists administer painless hair removal.

Allure Day Spa & Store

139 East 55th Street

New York, NY 10022

Phone: 212-644-5500   Fax: 212-317-2445

ALONG CAME MARY!

Party Organizers and Caterers

For over 20 years Mary Micucci has staged post-Oscar parties and movie premieres–like the spectacular bash for *Titanic*–earning her the title *Party Queen of Hollywood.* Frequently plugged in lifestyle magazines, Micucci looked after Barbra Streisand's recent nuptial arrangements.

Along Came Mary!

5265 West Pico Boulevard

Los Angeles, CA 90019

Phone: 323-931-9082

TINA ALSTER, M.D.

Cosmetic Surgeons

One of the most renowned cosmetic surgeons in America today, Dr. Tina Alster, author of *The Complete Guide to Cosmetic Laser Surgery,* has been cited both on television and in countless newspapers and magazines as one of the most efficient and genial professionals in her field. Founding the Washington Institute of Dermatologic Laser Surgery in 1990, Alster dedicated it to the practice of cutaneous laser surgery and other cosmetic procedures, such as collagen injections, botox and chemical peels. Through the years, the Institute has been distinguished by clinical and technologic advances pioneered by the doctor. Her cutting edge medical practice was the first combined laser care center and skin care facility in the United States. With Dr. Alster as director, the Institute continues to explore and apply medical findings and technologies that can make a difference in people's lives. Highly recommended.

Tina Alster, M.D.
2311 M Street NW, Suite 200
Washington, DC 20037
Phone: 202-785-8855   Fax: 202-785-8858

AMANGANI

Hotels

Every item in this recent addition to the impressive chain of Aman resorts was custom-designed and built by the best stonemasons, cabinetmakers, and lighting designers. The hotel's design provides a refined contrast to the rugged Jackson Hole setting, with its breathtaking views. The Amangani feels like a particularly stylish home, free of stuffy dress codes, daunting menus and attitude.

Amangani
1535 North East Butte Road
Jackson, WY 83001
Phone: 877-734-7333   Fax: 307-734-7332

AMARYLLIS, A FLOWER SHOP

Florists

Despite its deceptively modest name, Amaryllis, A Flower Shop, is a premier floral design studio, offering unique floral arrangements and decor for all sorts of special events and private functions. Elena King's floral arrangements range from classical to European, with every elegant variation in between. Warmly recommended.

Amaryllis, A Flower Shop
303 H Street, NW
Washington, DC 20001
Phone: 202-289-8535   Fax: 202-289-8537

AMBRIA

Restaurants

Spanish Chef and owner Gabino Sotelino uses light sauces in his French nouvelle cuisine. The menu changes daily, depending on what ingredients arrive from food markets around the globe. Ambria is a big celebrity spot, but the restaurant maintains a refreshingly tight-lip stance about its clientele. Jacket is required, ties are optional, and there is absolutely no denim allowed.

Ambria
2300 N. Lincoln Park West
Chicago, IL 60614
Phone: 773-472-5959

AMERICAN ANTIQUES

Antiques

Two generations of the Miller family have been dealing American folk art from this store in Columbus since 1972. Austin Miller, the current owner, specializes in American decorative arts, painted furniture and scrimshaw. Among the more unusual pieces are a 19th century whale tooth with carvings depicting Cape Cod hero King Philip on one side and a sailing vessel on the other.

American Antiques
1631 Northwest Professional Plaza
Columbus, OH 43220
Phone: 614-451-7293   Fax: 614-459-2087

THE AMERICAN HOTEL

Hotels

Ted Conklin's American Hotel is the social center of Sag Harbor, a quaint but desperately chic 18th Century whaling village. Local artists, media bigwigs and other weary exiles from "the city" are among the devotees of this retreat, which has eight bedrooms, a cozy bar and a fine restaurant. Oenophiles will particularly appreciate the 80 page wine list, with every wine producing country in the world represented.

The American Hotel
PO Box 1349, Main Street
Sag Harbor, NY 11963
Phone: 516-725-3535   Fax: 516-725-3573

AMERICAN MUSEUM OF NATURAL HISTORY

Museums

The American Museum of Natural History houses a huge collection of fossils, specimens and artifacts, ranging from African dioramas to dinosaur eggs and embryos to Cro-Magnon cave paintings. The castle-like complex now houses over 23 buildings, including the Hayden Planetarium, which reopens in 2000.

American Museum of Natural History
79th Street & Central Park West
New York, NY 10024
Phone: 212-769-5000   Fax: 212-769-5240

AMERICAN ORIENT EXPRESS
Travel Consultants
There is a sense of nostalgia when one travels by train, a reminder of days gone by. The American Orient Express, North America's premier luxury train, preserves the relaxed, romantic feel of legendary trains from America's past on nine routes throughout the U.S. and Canada. Vintage cars from the '40s and '50s—the golden age of railroads—have been restored to their glistening, polished mahogany-and-brass best. The dining cars boast tables set with fine china, linens, and silver, while the sleeper cars complete the historic picture in all their time-honored glory.

American Orient Express
5100 Main Street
Downers Grove, IL 60515
Phone: 888-759-3944   Fax: 630-663-1595

AMERICAN SAFARI CRUISES
Hotels
Although you may be moved by views of the glaciers, icebergs, and snow-covered vistas of Alaska, your body may be moved to freezing if you gaze for too long. Enter American Safari Cruises, an upmarket entrée to the remote fjords, tiny villages, and rugged bays of America's most desolate frontier. Film stars and financial barons wax lyrical about the smart megayachts, Safari Quest and Safari Spirit.

American Safari Cruises
19101 36th Avenue West, Suite 201
Lynnwood, WA 98036
Phone: 888-862-8881   Fax: 425-776-8889

ANDOVER SHOP
Fashion
Charlie Davidson's little atelier has long attracted a steadfast bunch of devotees. Davidson is a real old-fashioned character, brimming with wit, wisdom and genuine enthusiasm for the art of creating made-to-measure suits. As Alan Flusser writes in *Style and the Man,* his superb account of the best places to buy men's clothing in America, "The Andover Shop is an esteemed institution, a museum and a place of learning in a town devoted to academia. And Charlie is its Ivy League proctor."

ANDREW & POTTER
Employment Agencies
Best Kept Secret
Heather Irena Anand has been the owner of Andrew & Potter for the past ten years. Confidentiality is the trademark of this singular boutique placement service for household professionals. Every client is treated with the greatest care and respect. Among her varied and eclectic clients, all have one thing in common: they greatly value the anonymity and consideration afforded them by Anand's careful selection process. After credentials are checked, it is all about chemistry, a vital component, since some staff will travel between residences with a family. Her bi-coastal agency specializes in placing estate and household managers, landscape gardeners, nannies, baby nurses, governesses, chefs, personal assistants, yacht staff and even flight crews in homes throughout the U.S. and the world. Much of her business is the result of word-of-mouth, as appreciative clients share their good fortune and information with friends.

Andrew & Potter
P.O. Box 50707
Santa Barbara, CA 93150
Phone: 800-800-6757   Fax: 805-565-1173

Andover Shop
22 Holyoke Street
Cambridge, MA 02138
Phone: 617-876-4900

ANDREA ROSEN GALLERY
Art Dealers
Andrea Rosen runs this gallery with great independence of mind; the pick of New York's younger artists are eager to show with her. Experimental and clever works by future stars include the installations and constructions of Andrea Zittel and the art/writings of Sean Landers. The gallery also represents the estate of Felix Gonzales-Torres, mounting occasional shows of the Cuban's complex work.

Andrea Rosen Gallery
525 West 24th Street
New York, NY 10011
Phone: 212-627-6000   Fax: 212-627-5450

ANDREW DORNENBURG PRIVATE DINING
Caterers   Best Kept Secret
Okay, so your dreaded mother-in-law is coming to dinner and she's bringing her new boyfriend, who just happens to be your biggest client, and, to make matters worse, your private chef has a case of food poisoning. Now, before jumping out the window or fleeing the country, give Andrew Dornenburg a call. Formerly a chef at restaurants like New York's Judson Grill and Boston's Biba, Dornenburg has catered for Estée Lauder, Morgan Stanley, Ernst & Young, and hordes of well-fed Ivy-Leaguers. The well-connected Dornenburg is married to Karen Page, author of a recent book on Harvard Business School's most distinguished alumni.

Andrew Dornenburg Private Dining
527 Third Avenue
New York, NY 10016
Phone: 212-642-5870   Fax: 212-682-5868

ANTHONY A.P. STUEMPFIG
Antiques
Anthony Stuempfig has sold everything from Old Master paintings to 19th century decorative and fine arts in this Philadelphia institution. He specializes in museum quality American classical and empire period furniture and decorative arts, but will deal in most antiques and fine art if they are sufficiently interesting. Stuempfig also works as an advisor to museums and does curatorial work for private collectors.

Anthony A.P. Stuempfig
2213 St. James Street
Philadelphia, PA 19103
Phone: 215-561-7191

ANTINE ASSOCIATES
Architects and Interior Designers
Anthony Antine has developed a signature style that is known worldwide. Antine trained as a couturier at the Fashion Institute of Technology and later dressed women like Barbra Streisand. For the past 18 years, he has used luxurious fabrics and rich colors to design environments for customers around the globe. Recent projects include a private residence for Robert Redford, an Adirondack-style house in the hills of Atami, Japan, and a beach house in Malibu.
Antine Associates
750 Park Avenue
New York, NY 10021
Phone: 212-988-4096

L'ANTIQUAIRE & THE CONNOISSEUR
Antiques
Enjoy a history lesson while shopping at this exquisite Upper East Side town house gallery featuring 16th to late 18th century antiques. The shop specializes in Italian and French furniture and decorative arts, but also carries other European pieces, including some of Spanish and German origin. The collection includes textiles, works on paper, paintings, sculptures, and ceramics
L'Antiquaire & The Connoisseur
36 East 73rd Street
New York, NY 10021
Phone: 212-517-9176   Fax: 212-988-5674

ANTONIO'S ANTIQUES
Antiques
Antonio and Liliane Mariani have personally selected each piece in their impressive array of 17th, 18th, and 19th century English and Continental furniture, tapestries, paintings and decorative accessories. Visitors to their San Francisco store are treated to a distinctive array of French Provincial commodes from Aix-en-Provence and Bordeaux, Tuscan Baroque walnut trestle tables, Queen Anne burr walnut secretaries and an abundance of chandeliers.
Antonio's Antiques
701 Bryant Street
San Francisco, CA 94107
Phone: 415-781-1737

ARCHITECTURAL ACCENTS
Specialty Shops
Ambitious builders and designers find original Louis XVI doors at Architectural Accents, but customers working on more modest projects will also appreciate the pilasters, pedestals and panels at this 30,000-square-foot warehouse. Charles Nevinson's company reclaims architectural antiques, refits and refurbishes them, and, in some cases, makes reproductions.
Architectural Accents
2711 Piedmont Road
Atlanta, GA 30305
Phone: 404-266-8700   Fax: 404-266-0074

ARCHITECTURAL DIGEST
Media
If you want the world to adore your breathtaking home, try sending snapshots to the editors of *Architectural Digest*. They just might come knocking. This upscale lifestyle magazine documents design around the world; each issue takes readers to stunning residences, presenting the work of leading architects and interior designers. Using topnotch writers and photographers, editor Paige Rense has created the most influential shelter magazine in the world.
Architectural Digest
6300 Wilshire Blvd., Suite 1100
Los Angeles, CA 90048
Phone: 800-365-8032

ARMFIELD, MILLER & RIPLEY
Property Consultants
Armfield, Miller & Ripley boasts the expert guidance of realtors who have worked in the luxury-homes sector for more than 20 years. An affiliate of Sotheby's, the Virginia-based company has managed many prestigious sales, including houses that belonged to Senator John Warner of Virginia and the late Pamela Harriman, the American Ambassador to France.
Armfield, Miller & Ripley
P.O. Box 1500
Middleburg, VA 20118
Phone: 540-687-6395

ART LUNA SALON
Hair and Beauty
Don't expect anything too funky from the stylish but classic Art Luna. This warm, inviting hair salon offers its clients a tasteful, secluded atmosphere with a peaceful garden in the back where you can relax and read or chat as your color is processed. Celebrities particularly appreciate the discreet staff.
Art Luna Salon
8930 Keith Avenue
West Hollywood, CA 90069
Phone: 310 247-1383   Fax: 310-247-8672

ART OF EATING
Party Organizers and Caterers
The husband-and-wife team of John Kowalenko and Cheryl Stair began catering in 1988. In the past decade they have amassed a client list of East Hampton hotshots. Singer Billy Joel books Art of Eating every Christmas, and Martha Stewart has them cater her annual summer "crab pick." Cheryl and John's artichoke-risotto cakes are especially fabulous.
Art of Eating
P.O. Box 3232
East Hampton, NY 11937
Phone: 516-267-2411

ART OF FITNESS
Fitness
Maureen O'Boyle, Ricki Lake and Debbie Matenopolous have all toned their muscles with ex-State Trooper Art Clyde. His personal training regimen includes resistance equipment, as well as cardiovascular and abdominal work, in a cutting-edge, private facility. His book, *Workout on the Go*, tells you how to take the workout home or on the road for extra maintenance.
Art of Fitness
39 West 56th Street, 5th Floor
New York, NY 10019
Phone: 212-262-4040

ARTESIA

Restaurants   *Rising Star*

Rural Abita Springs is known for its Artesian wells, which inspired the name of this restaurant, located in an historic two-story building forty minutes outside of New Orleans. Tables by one of the three fireplaces in the downstairs dining room are the most popular, and the upstairs dining room is available for private parties. Chef John Besh prepares good French cuisine with local ingredients.

Artesia
21516 Highway 36
Abita Springs, LA 70420
Phone: 504-892-1662   Fax: 504-871-9952

ASANTI FINE JEWELERS

Jewelry and Watches

Nelson Holdo, president of Asanti Fine Jewelers, brings over 20 years of experience to his charming Pasadena shop. Asanti has one of the strongest collections of colored gems in the country as well as a selection of fine timepieces. Focusing on premium stones such as emeralds, rubies and sapphires, he customizes their setting and design. Holdo is also an authorized Fabergé dealer.

Asanti Fine Jewelers
2640 Mission Street
San Marino, CA 91108
Phone: 626-403-0033

THE ASIA SOCIETY

Museums

Founded in 1956 by John D. Rockefeller III to help Asians and Americans better understand each other's cultures, The Asia Society offers a pan-Asian curriculum including all Asian arts and public affairs. Its impressive red granite building on Park Avenue houses galleries, an auditorium, a book-store, and a small but well-stocked gift shop. Exhibits include important Chinese art and porcelain from various dynasties, as well as ancient Japanese calligraphy.

The Asia Society
725 Park Avenue
New York, NY 10022
Phone: 212-517-2742

THE ASPEN CLUB & SPA

Fitness

Entrepreneur Michael Fox's club features a bewildering array of facilities: one-on-one stretching, spinning, aerobics courses, and sport-specific training all aimed at toning the overall physique, while mind/body exercises, massage therapies, and body treatments provide relaxation. The Aspen Club also houses racquetball, squash, and tennis courts, and its Sports Medicine Institute has hosted the likes of David Robinson, Kevin Costner, and the U.S. Ski Team.

AUBERGE DU SOLEIL

Hotels

Discreetly tucked away amidst the sun-dappled vineyards of Napa Valley, at the top of a gently sloping 33-acre olive grove, the "Inn of the Sun" is a Mediterranean-style villa with 50 rooms and suites located in cottages terraced on a hillside overlooking the valley.

All rooms and suites are decked out with terracotta tile, natural wood and leather furnishings and have private terraces and fireplaces. If dining on the terrace with the sun setting isn't reason enough to sojourn here, there are many ways to distract yourself during the days and evenings, including hot-air ballooning, horseback riding, tennis, swimming, mineral spas and mud baths and, of course, wine tasting in any of the 200 wineries in the vicinity.

Auberge du Soleil
180 Rutherford Hill Road
Rutherford, CA 94573
Phone: 707-963-1211   Fax: 707-963-8764

The Aspen Club & Spa
1450 Crystal Lake Road
Aspen, CO 81611
Phone: 970-925-8900   Fax: 970-925-9543

ASPEN MUSIC FESTIVAL

Events

Fifty years ago, a group of intellectuals and artists gathered in Aspen to celebrate the life of German writer and philosopher Johann Wolfgang von Goethe. Today musicians, artisans—and even humble socialites—make an annual pilgrimage to the Aspen Music Festival, which was the result of their musings. The event commemorates Goethe's tradition of fueling the mind, body, and spirit by offering fellowships to aspiring musicians through its music school.

Aspen Music Festival
Music Associates of Aspen
2 Music School Road
Aspen, CO 81611
Phone: 970-925-3254   Fax: 970-920-1643

ASSETS PROTECTION SYSTEMS

Security Consultants

Assets Protection can turn your home into a veritable Fort Knox. The company specializes in corporate security consulting, establishing and improving on-site security. President Ray Chambers served in the Army for 25 years, much of it as Deputy Chief of Staff, with responsibility for army intelligence at Fort Holabird.

Assets Protection Systems
11113 Bella Loma Drive
Largo, FL 33774
Phone: 727-596-9650

SHERRELL ASTON, M.D.

Cosmetic Surgeons

This is the man responsible for rejuvenating the famously alluring visage of the late Pamela Harriman. An expert in face and eye lifts, the chairman of the plastic surgery department at Manhattan's Eye, Ear & Throat Hospital performs the delicate feat of separating tissue layers in order to rearrange the fat beneath. Aston doesn't reveal the names of his famous clients but within the business he is regarded as a Michelangelo of surgery, reinventing faces so artfully that his work is virtually undetectable. Married to Muffie Potter, an executive at Van Cleef & Arpels, Aston travels in the same rarefied social circles as his clients.

Sherrell Aston, M.D.
728 Park Avenue
New York, NY 10021
Phone: 212-249-6000

AT HOME
Specialty Shops

When Texan socialites need one-of-a-kind table settings, they come here for handmade centerpieces from England or antique Wedgwood china; they also come for glass flowers, hand-woven baskets from China, lamps, porcelain, creamware—all of which can make your dinner party a unique experience. Can't find enough Delftware for your sideboard? At Home offers superlative new stock made with an antique process and traditional patterns.

At Home
4445 Travis Street
Dallas, TX 75205
Phone: 214-528-0400   Fax: 214-528-0492

ATLANTA ROCKS
Fitness

Atlanta Rocks has steep, gray walls and a rubber floor—actually, it sort of looks like the Batcave, but you'll be buffer than Batman after working out here. The gym provides two types of classes: an intro to gym climbing and an intensive two-hour workshop. The classes teach you both climbing techniques and knowledge about climbing equipment, such as the use of a harness.

Atlanta Rocks
4411-A Bankers Circle
Doraville, GA 30360
Phone: 770-242-7625

ATLAS FLORAL DECORATORS
Florists

In June of 1990 New Yorker Joshua Behar headed south to open Atlas Floral Decorators in Boca Raton. Since then his extravagant floral arrangements have graced innumerable parties, both private and public: Donald Trump and Marla Maples' wedding at the Plaza Hotel, The Kravis Center Ball and the Three Tenors concert were all 'designed' by Behar, and many of his clients are *Fortune 500* executives.

Atlas Floral Decorators
1060 Holland Drive
Boca Raton, FL 33487
Phone: 800-924-8710

AU BON CLIMAT WINERIES
Winemakers

Au Bon Climat ranks as one of the top wineries in the United States, offering a Pinot Noir and a Chardonnay to rival those from the best French vineyards. Jim Clendenen, who has worked in vineyards from Australia to Zacamesa, is one of winedom's brightest stars—and a real character too.

Au Bon Climat Wineries
P.O. Box 113
Los Olivos, CA 93441
Phone: 805-937-9801

AUBERGE LE GRILLON
Restaurants   Best Kept Secret

Elva Churches trained at some of France's more prestigious culinary schools but ultimately felt that her skills lay in management. Today she presides over a team of chefs at Auberge Le Grillon, where specialties include Dover sole and Chateaubriand. For a particularly romantic evening, Churches recommends table eight in the corner of this terrific little restaurant.

Auberge Le Grillon
6900 N. Federal Highway
Boca Raton, FL 33487
Phone: 561-997-6888   Fax: 561-997-6956

AUGUSTA NATIONAL GOLF CLUB
Golf Clubs

Golf writer Lorne Rubenstein notes that, with its "ample and lovely grounds," Augusta promotes the "feeling that golf should be a good walk enhanced." This esteemed home to The Masters offers a legendary expanse of perfect grass and some of the best golf worldwide. The Augusta course was laid out in 1934 by architects Bobby Jones and Alister MacKenzie on what had been a Georgian fruit tree nursery. The course features in our keynote story, "America's Dream 18."

Augusta National Golf Club
P.O. Box 2086
Augusta, GA 30903
Phone: 706-667-6000   Fax: 706-736-2321

DANIEL AUBRY
Portrait Painters and Photographers

Top Manhattan photographer and imager Daniel Aubry's work ranges from hospitality and resort photography to architecture, interior design and travel. He has exhibited in Hong Kong, Madrid, Aspen, Miami and New York. He has produced four photobooks and contributed to more than a dozen other books, including *A Day in the Life of America*, the best selling photobook of all time. Aubry's latest project is an exciting invention called the Bio.Graph. A unique gift for the CEO who has everything, it combines photos, documents and computer technology to tell the story of a person's life. The images are scanned, manipulated, compiled and transferred to a single piece of film, which is then hot laminated between two sheets of glass. When frontally lit the Bio.Graph creates its own shadow producing a holographic effect. Aubry has created Bio.Graphs for the designer Clodagh, founder of Toys R Us, Charles Lazarus and Bob Fiondella, CEO of Phoenix Home Life Insurance Company.

Daniel Aubry
100 West 23rd Street
New York, NY 10011
Phone: 212 414 0014   Fax: 212 414 0013

AUJOURD'HUI
Restaurants

The tables overlooking the Boston Public Garden are in most demand at this classy and relaxing restaurant, where sharp suits mingle with pretty faces and lady lunchers. Chef Ed Gannon prepares a menu of original American cuisine with French and Asian influences. Patrons choose from a twenty-five page wine list, which includes a 1982 Chateau Lafite Rothschild for $1500.

Aujourd'hui
200 Boylston Street
Boston, MA 02116
Phone: 617-351-2072   Fax: 617-351-2293

AUREOLE
Restaurants

This offshoot of the celebrated Aureole, which opened a decade ago in New York, is decorated by Adam Tihany and serves as the dining room for the huge Mandalay Bay resort on the Strip. Gimmicks include a four-story "wine tower," inspired by a scene in *Mission Impossible,* to which harness-wearing wine stewards gain access with mechanical hoists. But the main attraction is Charlie Palmer's stellar New American cuisine.

Aureole
3950 Las Vegas Boulevard South
Las Vegas, NV 89119
Phone: 702-632-7401

AULDRIDGE MEAD

Hotels   *Best Kept Secret*

The owner of the Auldridge Mead, Craig Mattoli, is refreshingly eccentric, and so is his historic inn, which was originally built in 1790. A physicist—turned Wall Streeter—turned woodworker and collector—Mattoli built some of the furniture in this seven-room inn, which is set on 15 acres of rolling countryside. The atmosphere is friendly and cozy—there are even cooking classes in which you can learn how to make the inn's delicious potato pancakes. An added bonus: The antiques shops of New Hope and Lamberville are only minutes away.

Auldridge Mead

523 Geigel Hill Road
Ottsville, PA 18942
Phone: 610-847-5842   Fax: 610-847-5664

AVEDA INSTITUTE

Hair and Beauty

Talk about comfort: show up for your appointment here and you will be led back into a candlelit room to relax to the sounds of soothing music and a waterfall—and this is just the waiting room. Try the comforting eye treatment, which includes a pressure-point massage designed to relieve tired eyes, or the Aveda Body Polish, an exfoliation customized with your choice of natural plant and flower essence aromas. All of Aveda's procedures are described beforehand, so you know exactly what to expect. If you plan to spend the day, you can sip tea in your robe and slippers in the waiting room or hit the steam "tent" before sampling one of the spa's make-up or skin care services.

Aveda Institute

233 Spring Street
New York, NY 10012
Phone: 212-807-1492

AVENTURA LIMOUSINES

Chauffeur Services

Aventura runs—well, drives—Miami. Guests at hotels like the Delano, the Tides, and the Casa Grande, or visitors with condos at Il Villagio, are met at the gate by a driver wearing a black suit and a tie, noticeably marked with an "A" for Aventura. Models, musicians, actors, CEOs and politicians use the company, which Neil Goodman started seven years ago.

Aventura Limousines

P.O. Box 80146
Aventura, FL 33180
Phone: 800-944-9886

AVENUE

Media

Published exclusively for residents of Manhattan's tonier neighborhoods, *Avenue* chronicles the giddy microcosm that is New York society. Editor David Patrick Columbia writes a sparkling social diary, essential reading for leading lights, bit players and audience alike. Erudite but lighthearted, *Avenue* is a useful and amusing record of life in uptown Manhattan.

Avenue

950 Third Avenue
New York, NY 10022
Phone: 212-758-9516

AXIS TWENTY

Specialty Shops

This upscale furniture store was opened 12 years ago in the fashionable Buckhead neighborhood by a native Atlantan. Axis Twenty sells the classic 20th-century design of masters like Frank Lloyd Wright and Charles Rennie Mackintosh. The store also designs and crafts custom pieces (with help from local wood carvers) in exotic woods like teak and ebony.

Axis Twenty

200 Peachtree Hills Avenue, NE
Atlanta, GA 30305
Phone: 404-261-4022

AZZURA POINT

Restaurants

Famous for the finest scenic view of Coronado Bay and the Pacific Ocean. Be sure to sit near a window and enjoy views of the sunset, Point Loma Lighthouse, and the lights of downtown San Diego. Maitre d' Sean Marron is a (charming) old hand at welcoming sports stars and Hollywood notables in town for a special evening. Azzura is also a favorite dining place for the senior officers of the nearby naval base and their families.

Azzura Point

Loews Corronado Bay Resort
4000 Coronado Bay Road
Corronado, CA 92118
Phone: 619-424-4477

THE AVON CENTRE

Spas and Clinics   *Rising Star*

Discover a new world of wellness and beauty for women and men at the Avon Center. The two-level boutique highlights long-standing favorites from Avon's popular collections and the new, innovative Avon Spa Collection for bath and body, skin, and hair, sold exclusively at Avon Centre. Above the store awaits the magnificent Spa and Salon, offering the best in beauty and personalized service. Expertly skilled professionals offer a multitude of treatments and services including hair styling and color, nearly a dozen manicure and pedicure services, specially designed facials, waxing, massage, and the latest in body treatments, including self-tanning, aromatherapy sea salt glow, paraffin body wrap, and more. For a break from the personal indulgence, have a look at the spacious and beautifully decorated Conference Centre. It is particularly suitable for private or corporate events.

The Avon Centre

Trump Tower
725 Fifth Avenue
New York, NY 10022
Phone: 212-755-2866   Fax: 212-310-6350

B & B INTERNATIONAL
Art Dealers

B & B International is run by two sets of sisters: Marisa and Berry Berenson, and Nuala (Noonie) and Anne Boylan—all capable women with sophisticated tastes. The 15,000 square foot space houses a photo studio and a gallery, which holds an unusual collection that the sisters have accumulated on their travels around the world. It includes two dozen freestanding 17th and 18th century carved wooden santos and imaginative *ex voto* pieces from Uruguay, Colombia, Ecuador and Argentina.

B & B International
601 West 26th Street, 14th Floor
New York, NY 10001
Phone: 212-243-0840   Fax: 212-645-5029

BABOR INSTITUT
Spas and Clinics

Relax from the everyday at the Babor Institut. Consultants can help you choose from a selection of treatment packages or *a la carte* services. Two to sample: the Palm Beach Retreat includes a hydrotherapy massage bath with salts from the Dead Sea, customized massage with herbal steam, and a complimentary vegetarian or Institut cuisine lunch; the Institut Escape offers a manicure, pedicure, and specialty facial.

Babor Institut
340 Royal Poinciana Plaza
Palm Beach, FL 33480
Phone: 561-832-9385

BACCHANALIA
Restaurants

Owners and chefs Ann Quatrano and Clifford Harrison prepare acclaimed contemporary American cuisine at this Victorian cottage in Georgia's capital. The *prix-fixe,* four course menu changes every day. A superb blue crab fritter, served with California citrus, avocado and Thai pepper essence, and the warm Valrhona chocolate cake are particularly popular.

Bacchanalia
3125 Piedmont Road
Atlanta, GA 30305
Phone: 404-365-0410

BADGLEY-MISCHKA
Fashion

Badgley-Mischka's hand-beaded gowns evoke images of both old-time Hollywood glamour and of modern-day stars like Ashley Judd and Winona Ryder. Classic and antique in appearance, the gowns are wearable art, with exotic materials and fabrics imported from India. Platinum line dresses make annual appearances at extravaganzas like the Academy Awards, while chic suits and daywear are available at Bergdorf Goodman and Saks Fifth Avenue.

Badgley-Mischka
525 Seventh Avenue
New York, NY 10018
Phone: 212-921-1585

DANIEL BAKER, M.D.
Cosmetic Surgeons

Daniel Baker is an Associate Professor at New York University's medical school and has written numerous articles on cosmetic plastic surgery for leading medical journals. He was responsible for the development and implementation of New York University's Facial Paralysis Clinic. Dr. Baker was recently awarded the Fairleigh Dickinson Distinguished Achievement Award and the American Academy of Achievement Award for his role in saving the severed hand of a young music student who was pushed in front of a moving subway train. He is married to socialite Nina Griscom.

Daniel Baker, M.D.
65 East 66th Street
New York, NY 10021
Phone: 212-734-9695   Fax: 212-744-5410

BAKER & MCKENZIE
Law Firms

Call it a global village of legal pros. Baker & McKenzie is a business without borders, a melting pot built upon founder Russell Baker's belief in cultural diversity and integration. Headquartered in Chicago, this multinational network of 2,400 attorneys offers clients something no other law firm can match—resources and knowledge in every area of business law in virtually every important commercial center in the world.

Baker & McKenzie
One Prudential Plaza
130 East Randolph Drive
Chicago, IL 60601
Phone: 312-861-8800

BALDWIN GALLERY
Art Dealers

This is probably the largest gallery in the Rockies, representing a cross-section of mostly American contemporary artists, including Malcolm Morley, Louise Nevelson and Robert Mapplethorpe. Harley Baldwin, the King of Aspen, shows the work of photographers like Bruce Weber, as well as painters like James Rosenquist, Jennifer Bartlett, Donald Baechler and Eric Fischl.

Baldwin Gallery
209 South Galena Street
Aspen, CO 81611
Phone: 970-920-9797

BALTHAZAR
Restaurants

Although limousines carrying the likes of Madonna, Gwyneth Paltrow and Anna Wintour still crowd the narrow street out front (much to the chagrin of local residents), Balthazar has settled down since the dizzy days of old. Londoner Keith McNally's SoHo brasserie has become a staple in the French comfort-food lexicon of well-fed New Yorkers. The steak *au poivre* is particularly good.

Balthazar
80 Spring Street
New York, NY 10012
Phone: 212-965-1414 /212-965-1785

BANK OF BOSTON
Wealth Management

The term "private banking" has become a synonym for special services provided by banks to high net worth individuals. Although any bank can now—in theory—describe itself as a private bank, there are some that stand out for the breadth of knowledge and services they provide. Bank of Boston's history and experience are considerable and its private banking arm looks set to retain its impeccable reputation well into the new century.

Bank of Boston
95 South Federal Highway
Boca Raton, FL 33432
Phone: 561-394-6664

BARBARA GLADSTONE GALLERY
Art Dealers

This Chelsea gallery represents contemporary artists in every genre, from the wooden sculptures of Stephan Balkenhol to the video installation work of Gary Hill. Barbara Gladstone has mounted complete installations by filmmaker Matthew Barney, video artist Rosemarie Trockel and Ilya Kabakov. The renowned British sculptor Anish Kapoor, a former winner of the Turner Prize, and newcomer Kcho are also among her 21 gallery artists.

Barbara Gladstone Gallery
515 West 24th Street
New York, NY 10011
Phone: 212-206-9300

BARBARA ISRAEL GARDEN ANTIQUES

Antiques

Spruce up your garden with antique fountains, furnishings and other outdoor ornamentation. Barbara Israel's vast selection includes benches, gates, urns and well heads in cast iron, wrought iron, marble and stone. Much of the collection is not only monumental in size, but also in importance: although largely 19th century Americana, some pieces date to the 17th century. There is also a considerable selection of English, French, Italian and German wares. For an expert's insight into the use of garden ornaments in America, read owner Barbara Israel's new book, *Antique Garden Ornament—Two Centuries of American Taste.*

Barbara Israel Garden Antiques
296 Mt. Holly Road
Katonah, NY 10536
Phone: 212-744-6281

BARBERA BROOKS FINE FLOWERS

Florists   Best Kept Secret

A trained horticulturist, Barbera Brooks has also worked as a stockbroker, botanist and manufacturer of decorative accessories. She established this highly regarded wire service for discerning people who want the best flowers from the United States and around the world. In the 1980s, bigger was better, but now the emphasis is on reflecting nature through fine-tuned tailoring. Responding to this fashion, her arrangements are often beautifully understated. Brooks is also the author of an impeccable guide to ordering flowers by phone. Warmly recommended.

Barbera Brooks Fine Flowers
2288 Union Street
San Francisco, CA 94123
Phone: 888-346-3356   Fax: 415-674-5590

BARCLAY REX PIPE SHOP

Specialty Shops

Founded in 1910, New York's oldest tobacco shop sells everything and anything to do with smoking. All the major brands of cigarettes, tobacco, pipes and accessories in all price ranges are available. These include sought-after lighters by Dupont and Alfred Dunhill, plus a wide selection of humidors. There are four Manhattan stores, but this Wall Street location has long been the after work pleasure stop for business tycoons.

Barclay Rex Pipe Shop
7 Maiden Lane
New York, NY 10038
Phone: 212-962-3355

BARBARA LOCKHART

Architects and Interior Designers

Barbara Lockhart is one of America's preeminent and most enduring architectural interior designers. With important projects including the new Chasen's Restaurant and Private Jockey Club in Beverly Hills, the legendary William Randolph Hearst/Marion Davies estate, the original Le Dome Restaurant and many of the world's top residential properties, fashionable restaurants and hotels, Lockhart's extraordinary talent, diversity and deft design integrity is evident throughout. The inimitable designer has been bestowed with the most coveted awards in her field, such as the S.M. Hexter Most Outstanding Interior Designer in America Award, the prestigious Beverly Hills Architectural Achievement Award and the American Society of Interior Designer's Lifetime Achievement Award for Design Excellence. Equally, Lockhart has been the honoree of many charitable organizations for the same altruistic attention and acumen that she applies to her work.

Barbara Lockhart
710 North Bedford Drive
Beverly Hills, CA 90210
Phone: 310-276-8228   Fax: 310-271-0256

BAREFOOT ELEGANCE

Architects and Interior Designers

Barefoot Elegance, which was founded by Dot Spikings and Jennifer Castle, caters to high-end clientele who want furniture, linens, dinnerware, accessories and exotic imports to add luxurious touches to their homes. Clients have included Greta Garbo, Carolina Herrera, Princess Margaret and Jackie Kennedy Onassis. One of the company's objectives is to discover and preserve local skills: they searched the jungles of Indonesia for the only tribe in the world that specializes in a specific basket weave.

Barefoot Elegance
3537 Old Conejo Road, Suite 105
Newbury Park, CA 91320
Phone: 800-834-8146   Fax: 805-499-3288

BARNARD COLLEGE

Colleges

Since Radcliffe ceded much of its independence to Harvard in the 1970s, Barnard College stands alone as the premier women's liberal arts college affiliated with a world-class research university (Columbia). As Barnard president Judith Shapiro likes to say, women come to Barnard because they can have it all. Founded in 1889, when Harlem was a small country village, Barnard was the first liberal arts college for women in New York. Its tradition of encouraging women to be independent thinkers is exemplified by a veritable army of prestigious graduates, including Jeanne Kirkpatrick, Margaret Meade, Martha Stewart and four MacArthur Award winners.

Barnard College
3009 Broadway
New York, NY 10027
Phone: 212-854-5262   Fax: 212-854-7491

BARNEYS NEW YORK

Fashion

This contemporary symbol of elegance and good taste opened in 1923, a year before its great rival, Saks Fifth Avenue. The department store for people who hate department stores hosts everything from Ralph Lauren evening wear to Cynthia Rowley dresses to Gaultier leather vests. Subsidiary stores are located throughout the country, with locations in Beverly Hills, New York and Chicago. Look out for British Creative Director Simon Doonan's celebrated window displays.

Barneys New York
660 Madison Avenue
New York, NY 10021
Phone: 212-826-8900

BARRONS
Media
A dour but incisive sister to the *Wall Street Journal*, *Barrons* has an eye on time and money, two crucial components in the world of finance. *Barrons* specializes in timely and accurate reporting of market information, steering readers through the unpredictable and often turbulent world of finance .
Barrons
Dow Jones & Company, Inc.
200 Liberty Street
New York, NY 10281
Phone: 212-416-2700   Fax: 212-416-2829

BARRY FRIEDMAN
Art Dealers
Located in a town house on Manhattan's 67th Street, just around the corner from tony Madison Avenue, lies Barry Friedman, an important presence in the world of 20th century historical works. For over 25 years, the gallery has been exhibiting and dealing in European decorative arts; avant-garde paintings from the 20s and 30s; works on paper; sculptures; vintage and contemporary photography. Over the past three years, the gallery has also moved into the field of contemporary decorative arts, with exhibitions featuring studio glass, art furniture, ceramics, and wood objects.
Barry Friedman
32 East 67th Street
New York, NY 10021
Phone: 212-794-8950   Fax: 212-794-8889

BARRY PETERSON JEWELERS
Jewelry and Watches
Barry Peterson works with some of America's top designers to produce works that are clean, simple, and original. Peterson offers customers two stunning signature pieces: the diamond sun and the diamond snowflake. The store, which specializes in yellow and white diamonds, has amassed an impressive collection of South Sea pearls, celebrated for their rarity and large size; it also provides platinum casting and works with clients to create customized pieces.
Barry Peterson Jewelers
511 Sun Valley Road
Ketchum, ID 83340
Phone: 208-726-5202

BARTRUM & BRAKENHOFF YACHTS
Yachting
David Lacz recently acquired the prestigious Bartrum & Brakenhoff Yachts brokerage from the original owners, and he plans to maintain the reputation the firm has enjoyed since 1967. Operating from its two offices in sail capitals Newport and Ft. Lauderdale, the brokerage handles everything from megayachts and custom-built yachts to vintage yachts.

Bartrum & Brakenhoff Yachts
2 Marina Plaza
Newport, RI 02840
Phone: 401-846-7355   Fax: 401-847-6329

BATH & TENNIS CLUB
Private Clubs
The name says it all at this historic Palm Beach Club, which offers members two pools and eight clay tennis courts. Tennis pro Patrick Cramer keeps the members in good form on the courts, and they can cool down at the strictly casual clubhouse, an historic landmark. Founded in 1926, the Bath & Tennis Club was incorporated in 1938 and currently has "a rather extensive" waiting list.
Bath & Tennis Club
1170 South Ocean Boulevard
Palm Beach, FL 33480
Phone: 561-832-4271

BAY CLUB
Fitness
Play racquetball, tennis or basketball at this state-of-the-art fitness facility; then work out in the cardio or free-weights room. Massage, manicures and pedicures come with the package–plus fitness evaluations to keep clients healthy and on-track. Post-workout, many unwind on the club's sun deck in a whirlpool or sauna. Staff at the Bay Club are affable and erudite.
Bay Club
150 Greenwich Street
San Francisco, CA 94111
Phone: 415-433-2550

BAY HILL CLUB & LODGE
Golf Clubs
Known as one of the toughest on the PGA Tour, Arnold Palmer's 27-hole Bay Hill course spreads out over 270 acres, next to Florida's Butler lakes. Bay Hill hosts the Bay Hill Invitational, and is home to the Arnold Palmer Golf Academy; the club also hosted the first Palmer Cup tournament in 1997.
Bay Hill Club & Lodge
9000 Bay Hill Boulevard
Orlando, FL 32819
Phone: 407-876-2429

BEACH BISTRO
Restaurants
Sean Murphy runs the small, much-praised Beach Bistro on the pearl white sands of Anna Maria Island, in intimate proximity to the surf. Chef Andrea Goyette and her team have catered to Robert De Niro, Mel Brooks and Anne Bancroft. The wine list is outstanding.
Beach Bistro
6600 Gulf Drive
Holmes Beach, FL 34217
Phone: 941-778-6444   Fax: 941-779-2308

BEACON HILL NANNIES
Employment Agencies
Although it is possible to hire good help through the classified columns of major newspapers, the fact is that nowadays the most able household managers, personal chefs and nannies are usually found through one of half a dozen topnotch agencies. Julie Pellatt's 12-year-old company is regarded by those in the know as one of the best places to find reliable domestic help.
Beacon Hill Nannies
825 Beacon Street
Newton, MA 02459
Phone: 800-736-3880   Fax: 617-630-9398

BEAUTIQUE DAY SPA AND SALON
Hair and Beauty
From basic massages to body salt glows to serious stress-relief treatments, Beautique Day Spa and Salon is *the* place for unwinding in Houston. Try the Ultimate Ultimate, which consists of a hydro-therapy bath, rub treatment with underwater massage, full-body mask, body massage, lunch, deep-cleansing facial, pedicure, manicure, hairstyling, and make-up.
Beautique Day Spa and Salon
2507 Times Boulevard
Houston, TX 77005
Phone: 713-526-1126

BEAUVAIS CARPETS
Specialty Shops
With one of the largest selections of European and Oriental carpets and tapestries in the nation, Beauvais Carpets is equipped to meet the most exacting requirements. Its client list includes a host of major fashion designers—who tend to be notoriously petulant customers, as any upscale retailer will confirm. Beauvais also offers a complete cleaning and restoration facility on the premises.
Beauvais Carpets
201 East 57th Street
New York, NY 10022
Phone: 212-688-2265   Fax: 212-688-2384

LE BEC-FIN
Restaurants
Chef and owner Georges Perrier's upscale restaurant is often cited among the best in Philadelphia. An elegant, old world ambiance and consistently terrific French cuisine keep discerning diners coming back for more. Try to snag one of the tables by the fireplace. Incidentally, if you can't get a reservation at Le Bec-Fin try Brasserie Perrier, the Frenchman's more casual restaurant just one block west. Chef Francesco Martorella prepares a modern French cuisine with Asian and Italian influences.
Le Bec-Fin
1523 Walnut Street
Philadelphia, PA 19102
Phone: 215-567-1000   Fax: 215-568-1151

BEL-AIR COUNTRY CLUB

Private Clubs

Opened in 1927, the Bel-Air Country Club was one of the first private clubs in the Los Angeles area. Primarily a golf club, there are also tennis courts, and member events are hosted throughout the year. Although located in the country's entertainment Mecca, the club's membership is highly diverse; celebrities and movie executives rub shoulders with many professionals from other fields.

Bel-Air Country Club
10768 Bellagio Road
Los Angeles, CA 90077
Phone: 310-472-9563

BELLAGIO

Hotels   *Rising Star*

Bellagio is Steve Wynn's newest addition to the Mirage Resorts lineup of super-luxurious mega-resorts. Master restaurateurs Sirio Maccioni and Jean-Georges Vongerichten have set up shop in the hotel with faithful renditions of New York mainstay Le Cirque and a steak house, Prime. Bellagio also houses one of the world's most expensive collections of art under one roof, with works by Van Gogh, Miró, and Picasso. If you're going to Las Vegas, this is *the* place to stay.

Bellagio
3600 Las Vegas Boulevard South
Las Vegas, NV 89109
Phone: 702-693-7111

HOTEL BEL-AIR

Hotels

This legendary establishment is set on 12 acres of roses, gardenias, and birds-of-paradise. There are 92 rooms and suites in Mediterranean-meets-Mission style, most of which offer complete privacy—hardly surprising, then, that the hotel has always been popular with movie stars. Grace Kelly often stayed in Suite 160, with its king-size canopy bed, wood-burning fireplace and French doors opening onto a secluded terrace and jacuzzi. Make a point of meeting General Manager Frank Bowling. He is one of the most charismatic characters in the American hotel business.

Hotel Bel-Air
701 Stone Canyon Road
Los Angeles, CA 90077
Phone: 310-472-1211   Fax: 310-476-5890

BELGHITI TAILORS

Fashion   *Best Kept Secret*

If you are in the market for a really impressive custom tailored suit, talk to Dean Belghiti. Originally from Casablanca, Belghiti worked at Barneys until three years ago, when he decided to set up shop on his own. Sonny Mehta and John Pierrepont are clients of the nimble tailor, whose modest Manhattan outlet masks a thriving business and considerable acclaim from those in the know. Ask John Malkovich.

Belghiti Tailors
127 East 69th Street
New York, NY 10021
Phone: 212-396-9266

BELL'OCCHIO

Specialty Shops   *Best Kept Secret*

There is simply no other store like this delightful treasure trove. Claudia Schwartz and her partner Toby Hanson travel frequently to Europe to pick up French and Italian ribbons (a favorite of Martha Stewart), handmade silk flowers, antique linens, unusual paper goods, novelty boxes, an exclusive range of toiletries, and a line of private-label body beauty products. If there were awards for the finest curiosity shops in America, Bell'Occhio would be a perennial winner.

Bell'Occhio
8 Brady Street
San Francisco, CA 94103
Phone: 415-864-4048

BERGDORF GOODMAN

Fashion

A longtime favorite of New Yorkers, Bergdorf Goodman offers must-haves ranging from endless collections of Chanel bags to miniature rooms filled with babies' outfits. Savvy shoppers will also find a huge selection of housewares, chic shoes and jewelry. The staff are absolutely first rate. A New York institution. Incidentally, Bergdorf Goodman's windows epitomize the art of the fashion stylist at its very best.

Bergdorf Goodman
754 Fifth Avenue
New York, NY 10019
Phone: 212-753-7300

BERINGER WINE ESTATES

Winemakers

Although this is one of the largest, most modern wineries around (producing about 16 million gallons each year), Beringer is often perceived as small and old-world. The winery, bought in 1995, offers a bewildering array of wines, but the leaders are a trio of cabernet sauvignons: Private Reserve, Knights Valley and Chabot Vineyard.

Beringer Wine Estates
P.O. Box 4500
600 Air Park
Napa, CA 94558
Phone: 707-963-7115

BERNARD & S. DEAN LEVY

Antiques

After a century spent honing their skills, the Levy family's name has become synonymous with quality among dealers and collectors of American antiques. The four generations of Levys have figured prominently in the creation of both private and museum collections of American decorative arts throughout the world.

Bernard & S. Dean Levy
24 East 84th Street
New York, NY 10028
Phone: 212-628-7088

LE BERNARDIN

Restaurants

With its high vaulted ceilings and elegant teak wood decor, this fish lover's paradise epitomizes elegance and old world charm. Sterling Maitre d' Ben Chekroun and his team of waiters take service to a whole new level, while chef Eric Ripert, whose style is firmly rooted in French haute cuisine, is acclaimed by critics and public alike. As the *Zagat's* restaurant guide put it last year: "Long reign the King of the Seas!"

Le Bernardin
155 West 51st Street
New York, NY 10019
Phone: 212-489-1515

BERRY-HILL GALLERIES

Art Dealers

Berry Of London, founded in the 17th century, was the progenitor of this resolutely uptown, old-school gallery. James and Frederick Hill are renowned authorities on 18th, 19th and early 20th century American paintings and sculpture. Berry-Hill also handles Modern European and Old Master paintings and offers estates, museums, and private collectors a discreet and confidential alternative to the public marketplace.

Berry-Hill Galleries
11 East 70th Street
New York, NY 10021
Phone: 212-744-2300

BESSEMER TRUST
Wealth Management

With one of the highest staff-to-client ratios in the business, Bessemer Trust manages $20 billion for just over a thousand clients. Established in 1907 by the heirs of steel tycoon Henry Phipps, it was originally a family office, but has served "outsiders" since 1974. The typical account size is about $20 million. Through its nationwide offices, Bessemer Trust boasts access to top venture capital, private equity, and real estate managers.

Bessemer Trust
630 Fifth Avenue
New York, NY 10111
Phone: 212-708 9100

BEST DOMESTIC SERVICES
Employment Agencies

Finding the best housekeeper to keep things running smoothly is only half the battle nowadays. When you realize that your domestic help has slowly but surely become an indispensable part of your life, the question becomes, *How on earth am I going to hold onto this gem?* Billing itself as America's premier domestic agency, Don Williams' firm specializes in supplying "keepers"—the maids, housekeepers, nannies, and chefs who are looking for long-term positions in the country's most affluent homes.

Best Domestic Services
9107 Wilshire Boulevard, #675
Beverly Hills, CA 90210
Phone: 310-205-3100

THE BEVERLY HILLS HOTEL
Hotels

Glamour, wealth, and romance, anyone? They're all here at the historic Beverly Hills Hotel. Built in 1912 on 12 lush acres of gardens, the hotel soon began attracting stars from the growing neighborhood—including Charlie Chaplin and Rudolph Valentino. Indeed, it was Marlene Dietrich who changed the no-slacks-for-ladies rule one day, when she came to the Polo Lounge in pants. Ask to stay in one of the completely private luxury bungalows, each one created as an elegant individual residence.

The Beverly Hills Hotel
9641 Sunset Boulevard
Beverly Hills, CA 90210
Phone: 310-281-2958   Fax: 310-281-2989

BIBA
Restaurants

In conjunction with Susan Regis, owner and chef Lydia Shire prepares a cuisine which she calls American eclectic, based on ideas from around the world. Biba's upstairs dining room, which was designed by Adam Tihany, accommodates 150 guests for "upscale casual dining." Especially popular are the tables near the windows overlooking the Boston Public Garden.

Biba
272 Boylston Street
Boston, MA 02116
Phone: 617-426-5684

BIGSBY & KRUTHERS
Fashion

In its comfortable, masculine store, Bigsby & Kruthers offers only designer merchandise such as Giorgio Armani and Donna Karan. The classic boutique provides the best tailors and salespeople, plus a touch of R&R. There is a bar, lots of couches and chairs, and several big-screen TVs to satisfy stars like Joe Montana, Gary Sinise and Michael Jordan.

Bigsby & Kruthers
1750 North Clark Street
Chicago, IL 60614
Phone: 312-440-1750

BESTSELECTIONS
Specialty Shops

The first Web site of its kind, launched in 1998, BestSelections.com elevates on-line shopping to the highest possible level–it aims to showcase the best selections from the best stores around the world, whether on Madison Avenue, Bond Street, Rue Montaigne or off-the-beaten-track. Its swelling roster of shopping categories runs from couture to caviar, candles to candelabras, cigars to cutlery, antiques, jewelry, electronics, toys, clothing and everything in between. Whether a price tag reads $5 or $77,000, each item represents the very best in its category. The site evolved in order to fill three major voids: to make the Web accessible to high-quality retailers who may not have an Internet presence; to sell unique, sophisticated and interesting merchandise; to attract discriminating shoppers. Its groundbreaking retail concept–a unique galleria-style approach that gives each store its own custom storefront while at the same time allowing it to benefit from proximity to other high-caliber retailers–also lets shoppers browse in an atmosphere so relaxed they might as well be on vacation.

BestSelections
350 Seventh Avenue
New York, NY 10001
Phone: 212-465-9797   Fax: 212-465-9444
Website: BestSelections.com

BIJAN
Fashion

With its by-appointment-only approach, Bijan has gained unprecedented access to royalty, presidents and heads of state. One of the more expensive and exclusive men's salons, Bijan's custom-made clothing is produced in a numbered series to ensure individuality. While the three boutiques are usually reserved for fitting the rich and powerful in fine couture, Bijan's designers once outfitted the interior of a train car for a client who refused to travel by plane.

Bijan
Penthouse Suite
421 North Rodeo Drive
Beverly Hills, CA 90210
Phone: 310-271-1122

BILLY BLANKS' WORLD TRAINING CENTER
Fitness   *Best Kept Secret*

An inspirational motivator, Billy Blanks specializes in exercising the mind *as well as* the body. Brooke Shields, Magic Johnson, Paula Abdul, Brandy and Carmen Electra are among the adoring fans who sing the praises of his "spiritual" exercising program. Tae-Bo is a bewildering mixture of tae kwan do, boxing and ballet done to hip-hop music. Strange indeed! But the plaudits come thick and fast.

Billy Blanks' World Training Center
14708 Ventura Boulevard
Sherman Oaks, CA 91403
Phone: 818-906-8528   Fax: 818-906-8031

BINION'S HORSESHOE
Casinos

One of the very last family-owned and operated Las Vegas casinos, Binion's Horseshoe is a downtown landmark. Far from a 1990s mega resort, the "Shoe" is more of the salty old 1970s-style casino: Players' comfort is top priority, especially if they know you (we know one lucky guest whose jet fuel was paid for in cash–prior to play). With the World Series of poker held here since 1952, the Horseshoe has the highest limits on its tables *in the world*. "Money plays, sir, we'll tally it all later."

Binion's Horseshoe
128 East Fremont Street
Las Vegas, NV 89101
Phone: 800-622-6468

LAWRENCE BIRNBAUM, M.D.
Cosmetic Surgeons

Dr. Lawrence Birnbaum specializes in breast augmentation, liposuction, face-lifts, and upper and lower eyelid surgery–basically, most of your plastic surgery needs. Men often visit for liposuction, abdominal-plasty, face-lifts and eyelid surgery to eliminate those not-so-distinguished fine lines. Dr. Birnbaum has two surgical suites, a pre-surgical area, and a private post-op room.

Lawrence Birnbaum, M.D.
153 South Lasky Drive, Suite 1
Beverly Hills, CA 90212
Phone: 310-556-5663

BLACK DIAMOND RANCH
Golf Clubs

Stan Olsen's objective when he designed the Black Diamond Ranch was to honor the natural features of this very private West Florida residential community. Homes are dotted among oaks, azaleas, and crepe myrtles. The golf club at Black Diamond includes two courses, Ranch and Quarry, designed by Tom Fazio, who returned in 1997 to add nine more holes to the Ranch course. The club hosts the Dodge Shootout celebrity tournament every June.

Black Diamond Ranch
2600 West Black Diamond Circle
Lecanto, FL 34461
Phone: 352-746-7400

BLACKBERRY FARM
Hotels

Often described as a "Ritz in the woods," this delightful bastion of Southern style and charm is tucked away at the foot of the Great Smoky Mountains–making it one of America's more exclusive getaways. The 44-room country hotel is furnished throughout with fine English and French antiques, personally chosen by owners Kreis and Sandy Beall; service is superb and the surroundings are sublime. Blackberry Farm is Tennessee at its best.

Blackberry Farm
1471 West Millers Cove Road
Walland, TN 37886
Phone: 423-984-8166   Fax: 423-983-5708

BLACKBIRD
Restaurants   *Rising Star*

This architecturally stunning West Loop restaurant, which Donald Madia opened in December of 1997, is named after the French slang for a plump Merlot grape. Chef Paul Kahan–who trained with Rick Bayless at Topolobampo–prepares signature dishes like wood grilled sturgeon with braised oxtail, caramelized root vegetables, curry oil and oxtail jus, for the likes of Mayor Daley, Oscar de la Renta and Michael Jordan. Spare but sophisticated.

Blackbird
619 West Randolph
Chicago, IL 60606
Phone: 312-715-0708   Fax: 312-715-0774

BLISS
Spas and Clinics   *Rising Star*

At Bliss, don't be surprised if you look up from your magazine in the waiting room and find Oprah sitting beside you. Opened in July 1996, the spa is known for its celebrity clientele and high-quality treatments. From the fully loaded facials to the hot milk–and–almond pedicure, Bliss leaves even the most harried New Yorker feeling somewhat refreshed. As we went to press the spa had just been sold to LVMH, the leading luxury goods conglomerate. Big plans are rumored to be in the pipeline.

Bliss
568 Broadway, 2nd Floor
New York, NY 10012
Phone: 212-219-8970
Fax: 212-965-1433

BLOCKHEADIA RINGNOSII
Winemakers   *Best Kept Secret*

This winery makes minuscule amounts of Sauvignon Blanc, Zinfandel and Petite Syrah. Although winemaking is something of a hobby for owner Michael Ouellette (he is also a partner in Mustard's Grill), these are absolutely outstanding wines. Ouellette already counts some of the top restaurants in the country among his clients, and Blockheadia Ringnosii looks set to grow exponentially over the next few years.

Blockheadia Ringnosii
1764 Scott Street
St. Helena, CA 94574
Phone: 707-963-8593   Fax: 707-967-9548

BLACK PEARL ANTIQUES & FINE ARTS

Antiques

Fans of this Connecticut gallery say that it is so like a museum, the owners should charge admission. The collection includes period furniture, paintings from the Renaissance through American impressionism, sculpture and Asian antiquities. Black Pearl specializes in tomb pieces from ancient dynasties—like this pair of extremely rare, unglazed red pottery polo players from the seventh-century T'ang Dynasty.

Black Pearl Antiques & Fine Arts

2217 Main Street
Glastonbury, CT 06033
Phone: 860-659-3601   Fax: 860-659-2387

BOCA RATON RESORT AND CLUB

Hotels

Rich in lush foliage and sparkling fountains, the Boca Raton Resort and Club has a private beach and beautiful ocean views. The original core of the hotel, known as The Cloister, dates back to 1926 and is decorated in a Spanish/Mediterranean style. Nick Nicholas offers fine northern and southern regional cuisine at the Top of the Tower restaurant.

Boca Raton Resort and Club

501 East Camino Real
Boca Raton, FL 33431
Phone: 561-447-3000   Fax: 561-447-3183

BONITA BAY CLUB

Golf Clubs   ***Rising Star***

Arthur Hills designed three courses on the western portion of Bonita Bay between 1985 and 1994. The last of his creations, the Bay Island course, is considered one of the toughest in the country. The ninth hole overlooks Estero Bay from the highest point on the grounds. At Bonita Bay East, Tom Fazio designed the Sable and Cypress courses as part of a nature preserve, where wild boars, turkeys and deer are frequent guests

Bonita Bay Club

26660 Country Club Drive
Bonita Springs, FL 34134
Phone: 941-495-0200

BLOOM

Florists

Situated in the heart of New York, Bloom has quickly established itself as one of the city's premier florists. A favorite of the publishing, fashion and entertainment set, the firm has a reputation for classic, freestyle garden arrangements that capture the city's creative zeitgeist, offering a profusion of sophisticated flower varieties. "If it takes a special effort, we'll do it," says owner Lesly Zamor, whose work has been featured in *Vogue, The New York Times, W* and *Harpers Bazaar.* Bloom's florists have decorated everything from celebrity dining tables at Lincoln Center to elaborate events in the Hamptons. And the firm's converted 1920s parking garage is an ideal venue for hosting chic cocktail parties, receptions, photo shoots and special events.

Bloom

16 West 21st Street
New York, NY 10010
Phone: 212-620-5666

THE BOULDERS

Hotels

Lavish casitas follow the colors and contours of the land here in the foothills of the Sonoran Desert's Bradshaw Mountains. Already established as one of the country's premier golf resorts, The Boulders now boasts hiking, mountain biking, and rock climbing. If you'd rather have a hot-rock massage, head for the spa. Devised by a Tucson massage therapist, it mixes traditional Swedish techniques with the therapeutic powers of local smooth volcanic stones, heated in water and placed on key muscles.

The Boulders

34631 North Tom Darlington Drive
Carefree, AZ 85377
Phone: 480-488-7337   Fax: 480-488-9428

BRANDEIS UNIVERSITY

Colleges

Located just outside Boston, Brandeis University is one of the nation's top private research universities. With a student-to-faculty ratio of just nine to one and a median class size of 17, personal attention between faculty and students is a key Brandeis principle. Most notable of the university's five academic components are the Graduate School of Arts and Sciences, offering master's and doctoral degree programs in 29 fields, and the Graduate School for International Economics and Finance.

Brandeis University

P.O. Box 9110
Waltham, MA 02454
Phone: 781-736-2000   Fax: 781-736-3536

THE BREAKERS
Hotels
The century-old Breakers resort recently underwent a $75 million renovation. The elegant "old lady" offers a vast selection of recreational activities to satisfy every whim, including two 18-hole golf courses, tennis and spa facilities. One of the most famous hotels in America, the Breakers is set on its own private beach—perfect for spending the day enjoying surf and sand.

The Breakers
One South County Road
Palm Beach, FL 33480
Phone: 561-655-6611

BREEDER'S CUP
Events
For the past 16 years, the Breeder's Cup has been the world's richest day in thoroughbred racing. Held in early November, the race offers $13,000,000 in purse money to the sport's most distinguished equine athletes. Hardly surprising, then, that it attracts owners and breeders ranging from the oil-rich sheiks of Saudi Arabia and the high living Irish to the entertainment moguls of California.

Breeder's Cup
2525 Harrodsburg Road
Lexington, KY 40504
Phone: 606-223-5444   Fax: 606-223-3945

BRIDGEHAMPTON POLO CLUB
Polo Clubs
Matches are a major social event here, attracting many of New York's society and fashion gangs to the grounds of Two Trees Farm in Bridgehampton. Founded in 1995 by Neil Hirsch and Peter Brant, the Mercedes-Benz Polo Challenge and The Hamptons Cup are battled out over six consecutive weekends during July and August. There is a huge tent that holds 600 VIPs attending cocktail parties. This is high-goal polo at its most glamorous, with a slew of international players and regular bystanders like Donald Trump, Julianne Moore, Sean "Puffy" Combs and Cindy Crawford.

Bridgehampton Polo Club
c/o 40 East 52nd Street, Floor 23
New York, NY 10022
Phone: 212-421-1367 or 212-759-2800
Fax: 212-906-9096

BRILL'S CONTENT
Media   Rising Star
This self-styled watchdog has quickly become an indispensable guide to the American media. Editor in Chief Stephen Brill has been lambasted in some quarters for self-righteously trying to bring the media "into line," but the fact is that his detractors read this first-class insider's guide to the fourth estate just as avidly as his fans. If you want the story behind the story, look no further.

Brill's Content
521 5th Avenue
New York, NY 10175
Phone: 212-824-1900   Fax: 212-824-1950

BRINSMAID
Jewelry and Watches
Brinsmaid produces hand-tailored and designed jewelry, characterized by sleek and simple lines, engraving, multiple metals and a cutting-edge look. Co-owner Susan Range and her brother Scott specialize in blending innovative design with impeccable workmanship. Look particularly for the work of award-winning designer Henry Dunay.

Brinsmaid
35 Elm Street
New Canaan, CT 06840
Phone: 203-966-8654   Fax: 203-966-5588

THE BROADMOOR
Hotels
Built at the foot of the Rockies, the Broadmoor was founded in 1918 by Spencer and Julie Penrose, who made their fortune in gold and copper mines. After traveling all over the globe, they decided to bring the world of opulence and elegance that they had experienced in Europe and Asia to the city they called home. The resort has grown into a grand old lady indeed, offering every imaginable service from a round of golf to a day at the spa.

The Broadmoor
One Lake Avenue
Colorado Springs, CO 80906
Phone: 800-634-7711   Fax: 719-577-5700

THE BROOK
Private Clubs
One of the most exclusive gentleman's clubs in the United States, The Brook's priority is social over business; briefcases are checked at the door and conversation is supposed to focus on more lofty subjects than the day's Dow Jones. Membership includes international heavy hitters as well as a long list of powerful Americans: this was FDR's club of choice. Meals are served at common tables and the food is exceptionally good, especially for a club.

The Brook
111 East 54th Street
New York, NY 10022
Phone: 212-753-7020   Fax: 212-753-7486

Ram's Head, by Georgia O'Keeffe

BROOKLYN MUSEUM OF ART
Museums
An outpost of refined culture in an urban jungle, the Brooklyn Museum of Art hosts varied collections spanning many different eras. The Egyptian, classical and Middle Eastern art collections are generally acknowledged as some of the most impressive in the world. Highlights include a portion of an eighth-century Theban tomb. The Asian collection, begun in 1903, houses the only complete set of polychrome woodblock prints by Utagawa Hiroshige in America.

Brooklyn Museum of Art
200 Eastern Parkway
Brooklyn, NY 11238
Phone: 718-638-5000   Fax: 718-638-5931

BROWN BROTHERS HARRIMAN & CO.
Wealth Management
Like most of the private banks featured in this directory, Brown Brothers Harriman boasts intimate relationships with its clients. But it seems unlikely that many

institutions go to such extraordinary lengths to please the customer: this, after all, is the firm that once famously arranged for one of its managers to help a client put up his Christmas tree. Incidentally, President Bush's father was a partner in BBH.

Brown Brothers Harriman & Co.

50 Milk Street

Boston, MA 02109

Phone: 617-742-1818

BROWN UNIVERSITY

Colleges

Founded in 1764, Brown is a long-standing member of the fabled Ivy League. The university is renowned for its eclectic undergraduate curriculum, which gives talented, self-motivated students an opportunity to carve their own education. Brown's seven libraries house over three million volumes and are some of the best college research libraries in existence. The late John F. Kennedy, Jr. was a graduate of Brown.

Brown University

Box 1920

Providence, RI 02912

Phone: 401-863-1000   Fax: 401-863-3700

BROWNES' & CO. APOTHECARY

Hair and Beauty

Rustic and natural, this English-style store and salon has earned its position on pedestrian-filled Lincoln Road. A fabulous scent wafts continuously from the store, where more than 50 hard-to-find lines of beauty and skincare products are housed. Overlooking the store, the loft contains a salon, Some Like It Hot, as well as treatment rooms for massages and facials. A champion of the local art scene, Brownes' & Co. rotates its displays of up-and-coming area artists.

Brownes' & Co. Apothecary

841 Lincoln Road

Miami Beach, FL 33139

Phone: 305-532-8703   Fax: 305-532-7752

BROWNS

Specialty Shops

Possibly America's most exclusive hand dry-cleaning service, proprietor Lois Von Morganroth's Los Angeles firm specializes in the cleaning of beaded gowns and retailoring where necessary to clean separate garment parts. Demi Moore, Michelle Pfeiffer and Madonna frequent the premises, as do clients from around the world—some ship their treasures via Federal Express from Paris, London and Hong Kong.

Browns

1223 Montana Avenue

Santa Monica, CA 90403

Phone: 310-451-8531

BROWN-DAVIS INTERIORS

Architects and Interior Designers

American designers Robert Sidney Brown and Todd Dyer Davis joined forces and talents to found Brown-Davis Interiors in 1992. Since then, the focus has been on creating beautiful, world-class designs for both residential and commercial clients. They are currently working with Ambassador Christopher Meyer and Lady Catherine Meyer in the re-design of the British Embassy in Washington, D.C., the premier residence of Britain's Ambassador to the United States. The selection of an American firm for this high-profile project is unprecedented. *Architectural Digest* will feature the Embassy and has published features on other projects by Brown-Davis Interiors. The team has also completed important projects in New York, Washington, D.C., Palm Beach and Miami Beach. Their sophisticated designs include custom-designed furniture, interior architecture, carpets, fabrics and trims. The principals strictly limit the number of commissions so that clients receive the highest level of personal attention. Each design is custom-tailored to the client's specific needs and geographic location. Interiors designed by the company have been featured in *Architectural Digest, Maison Francaise-Russian Edition, Southern Accents, Veranda, Traditional Home-Showhouse* and *The Washington Post.* They have also been seen on the television show *Interiors by Design.* Recently completed projects by Brown-Davis include a private residence in New York, featuring one of the world's finest private art collections, a prestigious country club in Maryland and a modernist yacht in Miami.

Brown-Davis Interiors

1617 29th Street NW

Washington, DC 20007

Phone: 202-333-5883

BROWN'S RESTAURANT

Restaurants   *Rising Star*

Busy bees and idle WASPs have turned Taylor Stein's French-American bistro into a hive of pinstriped debauchery. The service is slow and Adrien Barrow's cooking has some way to go, but that's not really the point. This is a pick-up joint for the 21st century, where your fellow diners will meet your eye and smile sheepishly before getting back to the serious business of sizing you up with 'nary a thought for discretion. Exhilarating and bemusing.

Brown's Restaurant

33 East 61st Street
New York, NY 10021
Phone: 212-888-9127   Fax: 212-751-9829

BRYAN CAVE

Law Firms

This law firm, which ranks among the 25 largest in the country, offers legal counsel and advice in virtually every area of interest to business and entrepreneurial clients. With 550 lawyers in nine offices in the U.S. and seven overseas, Bryan Cave is one of the leaders in the fields of corporate, transaction, and litigation law.

Bryan Cave

One Metropolitan Square
211 North Broadway, Suite 3600
St. Louis, MO 63102
Phone: 314-259-2000

BRYN MAWR COLLEGE

Colleges

Bryn Mawr College was founded in 1885 to provide women with an education modeled on Oxford, Yale and Princeton. Today there are 1,200 female undergrads and 500 grad students of both genders. Alumni include actress Katherine Hepburn and Alice Rivlin, who recently retired from the Federal Reserve.

Bryn Mawr College

101 North Merion Avenue
Bryn Mawr, PA 19010-2899
Phone: 610-526-5000   Fax: 610-526-7471

BUMBLE & BUMBLE

Hair and Beauty

With its young, hip clients and industrial decor, Bumble & Bumble has brought a distinctly downtown feel to its midtown salon. The funky salon concentrates on modern, editorial-friendly haircuts for clients like Naomi Campbell and Jennifer Lopez. Metal and glass furnishings offer a cool backdrop to the company's chic product line.

Bumble & Bumble

146 East 56th Street
New York, NY 10022
Phone: 212-521-6500

BUNNY WILLIAMS

Architects and Interior Designers

For all her years spent working in New York, Bunny Williams is still a soft-spoken Virginian. Like her predecessor, Nancy Lancaster, who influenced generations of decorators in Britain as the doyenne of Colefax & Fowler, she grew up in Albermarle County, Virginia. With this strong tradition of gracious Southern living, coupled with a knowledge of English antique furniture, Williams has carved out a remarkable career. A member of the Interior Design Hall of Fame, her elegant work is regularly featured in *Architectural Digest, House and Garden, House Beautiful,* and *Elle Décor.* Williams has had design projects in New York, California, Texas, Florida, Maine and even the South of France, with homes varying from a penthouse to a ranch. Along with interior design, Williams has a great passion for gardening. She is a partner in Treillage, a garden furniture shop in Manhattan, and is the author of the book *On Garden Style,* which won Williams the 1999 "Quill and Trowel" Award.

Bunny Williams

306 East 61st Street, 5th Floor
New York, NY 10021
Phone: 212-207-4040   Fax: 212-207-4353

BURGER BOAT COMPANY

Yachting

The Burger Boat Company custom-designs luxury yachts ranging from 80 to 140 feet for people obsessed with quality. In a fast-moving industry, the firm keeps up with changing technology while also being environmentally conscious and consistent with the company's 136-year history. Yachts feature sound systems from Holland that minimize noise, steam rooms, whirlpools, generators, water converters—everything to ensure self-sufficiency and comfort.

Burger Boat Company

1811 Spring Street
Manitowoc, WI 54220
Phone: 920-684-1600   Fax: 920-684-6555

THE BURGUNDY WINE COMPANY

Wine Merchants   *Best Kept Secret*

This exceptional merchant carries the wines of Burgundy and the same grape varieties (like Pinot Noir and Chardonnay) as found in California and Oregon. Albert Hotchkin and Geraldine Tashjian ensure that only those wines which genuinely impress them are stocked in the shop. Clients are sent a regular newsletter which includes totally objective tasting notes—not the opinions or scores of assorted "experts." Warmly recommended.

The Burgundy Wine Co.

323 West 11th Street
New York, NY 10014
Phone: 212-691-9092   Fax: 212-691-9244

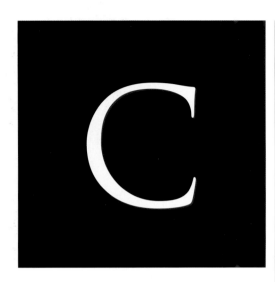

CACHAREL
Restaurants

Hans Bergmann presides over the kitchen at this penthouse restaurant, which has been serving French-American cuisine since 1986. Patrons vie for the corner table next to the window overlooking a roller coaster in neighboring Six Flags, and finish off their meals with Bergmann's famous filo layers, filled with white chocolate mousse. Cacharel was recently voted one of the top 50 restaurants in the country by *Condé Nast Traveler*.

Cacharel
2221 East Lamar Boulevard
Arlington, TX 76006
Phone: 817-640-9981   Fax: 817-633-5737

CAESARS PALACE
Casinos

After massive ($250 million plus) renovations, Caesars Palace has emerged better than ever—with magical aura intact, instead of neon cheesiness. Two huge new towers, with unmatched top-floor mega suites, a spa, Prada, Gucci, and even a branch of Caviarteria, the New York bacchanalian delight, round out this landmark resort.

Caesars Palace
3570 Las Vegas Boulevard South
Las Vegas, NV 89109
Phone: 800-634-6661

CAFÉ ALLEGRO
Restaurants

Diversity is the theme of this upscale bistro in Kansas City. Chef Ted Habiger, in conjunction with owner and fellow chef Stephen Cole, prepares an ethnically varied menu. A superb tuna tartare is hand cubed and tossed with ginger, scallions, cilantro and fried capers. The 35-page wine list includes a number of impeccable French clarets, including a 1982 Chateau Mouton Rothschild for $900.

Café Allegro
1815 West 38th Street
Kansas City, MO 64111
Phone: 816-561-3663   Fax: 816-756-3265

CAFÉ DES AMIS
Restaurants

Dennis Baker's intimate spot has just 13 tables; there is no best table here and, conversely, no Siberia. The kitchen is small too, thus avoiding the institutional assembly line routines of larger restaurants. There are no special dishes. What the chef wants to cook is what you get. If it happens to be on the menu, don't miss the filet of beef with port-garlic sauce, an outstanding example of what can be done to improve a choice cut of steak.

Café des Amis
1987 NW Kearney Street
Portland, OR 97209
Phone: 503-295-6487   Fax: 503-722-5392

CAKEBREAD CELLARS
Winemakers

Cakebread is a feast for the eyes and the palate. Drive through the colorful gardens framing the entrance, passing rows of stately olive trees and then park by Jack Cakebread's award-winning redwood winery. The vineyards themselves feature breathtaking views of the mountains—a perfect prelude to tastings of crisp, clean, perfectly balanced whites and premium cabernet sauvignons.

Cakebread Cellars
8300 St. Helena Highway
Rutherford, CA 94573
Phone: 707-963-5221   Fax: 707-963-1067

CALABRIA
Florists

Denise Spatafora has designed Emmy parties, movie openings, and major events for clients such as the American Ballet Theatre, Condé Nast, Gucci, and the Grammy Awards. A full-fledged lifestyle diva, Spatafora has a philosophy on everything, from aesthetics (flowers, linens, colors, space) to whom to invite to your home.

Calabria
216 West 18th Street
New York, NY 10011
Phone: 212-675-2688

C & M ARTS
Art Dealers

Situated in a Georgian-style townhouse on the Upper East Side of Manhattan, C&M Arts was inaugurated in 1992 and has created a new standard for visually exciting and scholarly exhibitions. The gallery exhibits and sells paintings, drawings and sculpture by world-renowned 20th century artists including Pablo Picasso, Henri Matisse, Mark Rothko, Jackson Pollock and Willem de Kooning. The gallery additionally represents the Estate of Joseph Cornell, whose box constructions and collages are internationally admired. C & M Arts was awarded First Place Best Art Gallery Show 1997-1998 by the International Association of Art Critics, for its exhibition featuring Picasso's portraits of his lover, Dora Maar, alongside de Kooning representations of women.

C & M Arts
45 East 78th Street
New York, NY 10021
Phone: 212-861-0020   Fax: 212-861-7858

CALIFORNIA CULINARY ACADEMY
Culinary Schools

Located in San Francisco, where the year-round Mediterranean climate is ideal for growing and producing fine foods, the California Culinary Academy has thrived on its "from the farm to the table" philosophy for 20 years. Renowned as one of the best cookery schools in the Americas, the CCA also caters weddings, garden parties and gala black-tie benefits.

California Culinary Academy
625 Polk Street
San Francisco, CA 94102
Phone: 800-229-2433 or 415-771-3500

CALLAHAN CATERING
Party Organizers and Caterers

The dashing Peter Callahan is caterer of choice for many Upper East Side socialites. He offers the ultimate in haute cuisine and thoughtful service: Callahan is the man who uses vinaigrettes instead of herbs in his canapés, to save guests from having herbs caught between their teeth. There is a strong emphasis on design and concept–the influence of Callahan's fashion designer wife, Josephine Sasso, perhaps–that is evident in soirées on Hampton beaches, like the one for Pia Getty, and at hip downtown events in Manhattan. Callahan Catering is based in New York, with a second operation in Philadelphia.

Callahan Catering
205 East 95th Street
New York, NY 10028
Phone: 212-327-1144   Fax: 212-327-1096

CAFÉ L'EUROPE
Restaurants

Café L'Europe is a fine dining Mecca for celebrities, corporate bigwigs, socialites, civic leaders and people who simply love good food. Owners Norbert and Lidia Goldner have carved themselves a reputation as the most celebrated restaurateurs in Palm Beach– a considerable feat given the number of smart eateries in this affluent enclave.

Guests enjoy the restaurant's award-winning cuisine and wines either in the elegant flower-filled Dining Room, or the more casual bistro with its popular Piano Bar. Behind the Dining Room is the new Wine Room which is the *in* place these days for private parties up to 40 guests. The main attraction of the Wine Room is the handsome temperature-controlled Wine Cellar with antique beveled Belgian windows housing several thousand bottles of the finest imported and domestic wines.

Café L'Europe was recently inducted into the prestigious "Fine Dining Hall of Fame," an honor bestowed on only 200 restaurants nationwide over the past 20 years. The award is

presented annually to 10 restaurants who "meet and exceed the highest standards of the restaurant industry in food quality, service, ambiance and staff training." The same attributes led readers of *Palm Beach Illustrated* to vote Café L'Europe the "Best Restaurant Under the Sun." In the same poll Maitre D' Bruce Strickland won top honors as Best Maitre D' in Palm Beach and "Under the Sun." This has been an award-winning year for Café L'Europe–a Palm Beach tradition for 19 years.

Café L'Europe
331 South County Road
Palm Beach, FL 33480
Phone: 561-655-4020   Fax: 561-659-6619

CALLIGRAPHY STUDIOS
Specialty Shops

This personalized calligraphy service in Manhattan's TriBeCa painstakingly produces custom, hand-written material for any event. Specializing in designing personal monograms for stars like Quincy Jones, Calligraphy Studios creates entire stationery wardrobes which include business cards, personalized letterheads, envelopes, calling cards and note cards. The shop also designs bar and bat mitzvah invitations and centerpieces for parties, as well as projects requiring exquisite gold engraving.

Calligraphy Studios
100 Reade Street
New York, NY 10013
Phone: 212-964-6007   Fax: 212-964-9170

CALVERT WOODLEY
Wine Merchants

Calvert Woodley specializes in Bordeaux wines and wine futures. The store holds an extensive inventory of virtually every classified American and Australian wine and rare French wines such as Romanée Conti. Customers enjoy personalized service offered by the store's small staff of seven, each of whom has worked in the industry for up to 25 years. These experts travel to the wine areas of the world in search of savory finds and hold wine tastings every week.

Calvert Woodley
4339 Connecticut Avenue NW
Washington, DC 20008
Phone: 202-966-4400   Fax: 202-537-5086

CALVIN KLEIN

Fashion

Ambitious, shrewd and publicity savvy, Calvin Klein has always had a knack for knowing and creating the "next big trend," from jeans to underwear. Klein's lines range from fragrance and pantyhose to women's and men's ready-to-wear. He particularly excels in the use of natural fabrics such as leather and suede with colors in down-to-earth tones.

Calvin Klein

654 Madison Avenue
New York, NY 10022
Phone: 212-719-2600

CAMBERLEY BROWN

Hotels

This legendary hotel in Theater Square has been at the center of Louisville's social life since it was built in 1923. The interior is sumptuous, with a marble-accented grand lobby, antique furnishings and intricate plaster moldings. High ceilings and stained glass lend it the air of a grand old house. Enjoy complimentary *hors d'oeuvres* in the Club Room, or a cocktail in the stylish Grand Lounge. Incidentally, the Hot Brown was invented here.

Camberley Brown

335 West Broadway
Louisville, KY 40203
Phone: 502-583-1234   Fax: 502-587-7006

THE CAMBRIDGE SCHOOL OF CULINARY ARTS

Culinary Schools

Years ago, Roberta L. Dowling's love of cooking inspired her to give occasional cooking classes from her home. Response to the classes grew and grew, until she decided to find a better location. Today, that site is the renowned Cambridge School of Culinary Arts, which emphasizes the tenets of cooking established by Auguste Escoffier, the father of classical cuisine. Mrs. Dowling has taught French and Italian cuisine to professional chefs and restaurateurs around the country, and has catered private parties for Princess Grace of Monaco, Julia Childs, and Senator Edward Kennedy, among others.

The Cambridge School of Culinary Arts

2020 Massachusetts Avenue
Cambridge, MA 02140
Phone: 617-354-3836

CAMPAGNE

Restaurants

Owner Peter Lewis leaves the kitchen entirely to Jim Drohman at this small (seating for forty people) and intimate waterside Seattle eatery. Guests vie for window tables that look out over Pike Place Market and Elliot Bay. The unapologetically French cuisine includes a sublime *foie gras* terrine. Expensive but worth every cent.

Campagne

Pike Place Market
87 Pine Street
Seattle, WA 98101
Phone: 206-728-2800   Fax: 206-448-7740

CAMPANILE

Restaurants

Husband and wife owners Mark Peel & Nancy Silverton met in the kitchen of Wolfgang Puck's Spago. They opened Campanile & La Brea Bakery in 1989. The Campanile itself was built by Charlie Chaplin in the 1920s, for his office; before it was completed he lost it in a divorce settlement to his first wife, Lita Grey. Serving Californian and Mediterranean fare in a chic venue, Campanile is consistently acclaimed as one of the best restaurants in L.A. Peel trained at two French three-star establishments, La Tour d'Argents and Moulin de Mougins.

Campanile

624 S. La Brea Avenue
Los Angeles, CA 90036
Phone: 323-938-1447   Fax: 323-938-5840

CAMPBELL, DETTMAN & PANTON REALTY

Property Consultants

For distinctive waterfront communities in the Fort Lauderdale area, Campbell Dettman & Panton is *the* real estate company. In fact, owner Barbara Campbell was vice president of a company that developed one of these communities, Harbor Beach, before she purchased her own real estate firm in 1992. Homes in Harbor Beach have ocean views, private beaches, access to a private marina that can accommodate yachts, and 24-hour security.

Campbell, Dettman & Panton Realty

2228 SE 17th Street
Fort Lauderdale, FL 33316
Phone: 954-525-2170

CANNON/BULLOCK INTERIOR DESIGN

Specialty Shops   ***Rising Star***

If you are serious about finding the best handmade wallpaper you should probably talk to Richard Cannon and Richard Bullock, two partners who make it their exclusive business. Cannon/Bullock Interior Design serves a high-end clientele, primarily residential, through 18 showrooms in cities like New York, Chicago, Washington, D.C., Seattle and San Francisco.

Cannon/Bullock Interior Design

612 Moulton Avenue
Los Angeles, CA 90031
Phone: 323-221-9286   Fax: 323-221-9287

CANYON RANCH

Spas and Clinics

Enjoy the romance of the Old West and the luxuries of the new at this impressive health resort. The 20-year-old Canyon Ranch has a rich tradition of healing, recreation, and healthy living. Dotted with fountains and haciendas, the 70-acre property features a luxury hotel and 65,000 square feet of spa, offering more than 200 activities and services daily.

Canyon Ranch

8600 East Rockcliff Road
Tucson, AZ 85750
Phone: 520-749-9000

CARAPAN

Spas and Clinics

When choosing a term to describe this urban spa and store, look no further than the name. *Carapan* is a Pueblo Indian word meaning "a beautiful place of tranquillity where one comes to restore one's spirit." Appropriate, no? This seriously mellow salon makes you feel like you have been transported to another place, far from the hustle and bustle of New York City. The massage treatments are legendary, but we are particularly fond of Carapan's aromatherapy rituals and reflexology.

Carapan

5 West 16th Street
New York, NY 10011
Phone: 212-633-6220   Fax: 212-633-6719

CAREY INTERNATIONAL

Chauffeur Services

Political leaders, sports players, and CEOs rely on Carey International; the company's cars are spotted at NFL games, the Grammy's, and many illustrious events. Operating in 420 cities in 65 countries, Carey always provides an English-speaking driver.

Carey International

4530 Wisconsin Avenue NW
Washington, DC 20016
Phone: 202-895-1200   Fax: 202-895-1251

CARIBOU CLUB

Private Clubs

The name is not on the door. Look for the lantern a few short steps down Caribou Alley, which quietly signals the entrance to Aspen's most alluring private club. One of the town's great movers and shakers, owner Harley Baldwin hosts the best party in town. Like Annabel's in London or Castel's in Paris, the Caribou Club is the sort of place where you know you will meet old friends.

Caribou Club
411 East Hopkins Avenue
Aspen, CO 81611
Phone: 970-925-2929

CARLYLE WINES

Wine Merchants

Kevin Bacon is a regular customer at this smart little wine store, which boasts an impressive array of wines, brandies and spirits. Each bottle has been personally selected by proprietor David Oei, whose expertise and commitment to service make this a must-stop destination for wine lovers. The store is particularly strong on burgundies, which is unusual for New York. Woody Allen and Sharon Stone are also frequent customers.

Carlyle Wines
997 Madison Avenue
New York, NY 10021
Phone: 212-744-1028

CAROL DOPKIN REAL ESTATE

Property Consultants

Carol Dopkin has specialized in selling and managing luxurious homes in Aspen since 1979. She and her ten agents have a personal approach to the business, often showing clients the spectacular countryside on horseback and taking them on culinary tours of their favorite restaurants. The firm also offers services that range from hiring household help to getting telephones installed and cars serviced.

Carol Dopkin Real Estate
122 West Main Street
Aspen, CO 81611
Phone: 800-920-1186

CAROLINA HERRERA

Fashion

A prominent figure in New York social circles, "La Bombe" was in her forties when she launched her first exquisite line of women's wear. The typical Herrera client mixes and matches opulence and glamour to create a picture of radiant confidence. Fox wraps, stretchy wool fabrics, and rich colors like camel, chocolate brown, and butterscotch dominate the collection for autumn and winter. Available at Saks Fifth Avenue, Bergdorf Goodman, and Neiman Marcus, Herrera's elegant clothes are perfect for both day and evening wear.

Carolina Herrera
501 Seventh Avenue, 17th Floor
New York, NY 10018
Phone: 212-575-0557

CARROLL & CO.

Fashion

Startled to find in 1949 that a man would have to travel across town to buy a good suit, Richard Carroll began his custom-tailoring business on Rodeo Drive. Today, Carroll & Company has moved from this shopping Mecca to a freestanding building, but still carries the finest in updated traditional menswear from Europe and America. Among the products on the dark green carpeted floors of this well-lit, brass-accented store, shoppers will find Carroll's top-selling item, a cashmere sweatshirt.

Carroll & Co.
425 North Canon Drive
Beverly Hills, CA 90210
Phone: 310-273-9060   Fax: 310-273-7974

CARSWELL RUSH BERLIN

Antiques   ***Best Kept Secret***

This highly specialized private dealer features American formal antique furniture of the period 1800 to 1840 including dining tables, worktables, breakfast tables, sofa tables, card tables, side chairs, armchairs, mirrors, sofas, stools, benches, secretaries, desks, bookcases and period lighting. Each piece represents one of three styles within the classical rubric: Sheraton, Empire, or French Restoration, as interpreted by American cabinet-makers. Berlin caters primarily to major American museums and collectors, by appointment only.

Carswell Rush Berlin
P.O. Box 0210, Planetarium Station
New York, NY 10024
Phone: 212-721-0330

CARTER LANDSCAPING

Landscape Architects

Richard and Shirley Carter, along with their daughter and son, form the team which makes Carter Landscaping, the company responsible for much of the tamed beauty you will see en route from New York City to the Hamptons. With high standards of design and maintenance, they have a string of loyal clients on Long Island.

Carter Landscaping
16 Vail Avenue
East Quogue, NY 11942
Phone: 516-653-5361   Fax: 516-653-8042

CARLETON VARNEY DESIGN GROUP

Architects & Interior Designers

Carleton Varney Design Group is a division of Dorothy Draper & Company, America's oldest established interior and industrial design firm. The group has designed properties all over the world, including the Greenbrier at White Sulphur Springs, West Virginia; the Grand Hotel on Mackinac Island, Michigan; and The Breakers at Palm Beach, Florida. Varney has designed glass for Galway Irish Crystal, as well as fashion and home furnishings. A new "Favorite Things Collection" for Kindel of Grand Rapids, Michigan, is now being created. Varney was the White House designer in the Carter Administration and is the author of some 20 books, including two novels.

Carleton Varney Design Group
60 East 56th Street
New York, NY 10022
Phone: 212-758-2810   Fax: 212-759-0739

THE CASTLE AT TARRYTOWN
Hotels

Set high on a bluff overlooking the Hudson River, the Castle at Tarrytown's 31 exquisitely furnished suites induce fantasies of another time and place. Recently inducted into the prestigious Relais & Chateaux group, the Castle is a particularly fine place for a romantic rendezvous. The cuisine in the renowned Equus restaurant is splendid.

The Castle at Tarrytown
400 Benedict Avenue
Tarrytown, NY 10591
Phone: 914-631-1980   Fax: 914-631-4612

CENTURY HOUSE ANTIQUES
Specialty Shops

People tell Katherine Danielson that getting to her antiques shop is half the experience. The picturesque brick building at the end of an alleyway overlooks the Thomas Elfe House gardens. Danielson caters to a nationwide clientele who collect 18th and 19th century English and Chinese export porcelain, as well as maps and prints from earlier periods. If you cannot make it to the store, Danielson will send you photos via e-mail.

Century House Antiques
56 1/2 Queen Street
Charleston, SC 29401
Phone: 843-722-6248

CESSNA
Airplanes

With a total of eight light to mid-sized business jets, Cessna is the world leader in this category. If you can call any jet "an entry-level" aircraft, the Cessna cj1 is just that. The cj1 is single-pilot certified and a natural step up from turbo props for the amateur pilot—plus, at $3.5 million, it won't break the bank. But if speed and cutting-edge technology are what you're after, Cessna's flagship, the Citation 10, is calling your name.

Cessna
One Cessna Boulevard
Wichita, KS 67215
Phone: 316-517-6000 or 800-423-7762

THE CARLYLE
Hotels

One of the most impressive addresses in New York, The Carlyle guest list reads like a who's who of world affairs, business and entertainment. Renowned among discerning Europeans as an exquisite retreat from the frenetic pace of life in New York, it is a legend among Manhattan hotels. Most of the lavishly appointed bedrooms and suites boast bathrooms with Jacuzzis and many have views of Central Park. Each room is individually designed, with delicate accessories such as chintz coverlets, antique satin boudoir chairs, or porcelain vases. The strong art deco influence has been painstakingly maintained; The Carlyle is a hotel with charm and serenity, amply reflected in James Sherwin, its celebrated English General Manager. Understated elegance is the theme throughout—wonderful Gobelin tapestries, architectural renderings by Piranesi, museum-quality antiques, spectacular floral displays and priceless pictures are complemented by an

attentive, discreet staff. The Carlyle Restaurant is one of the most comfortable dining rooms in New York. Its pillow-sprinkled banquettes focus on a sumptuous floral arrangement, evoking a sense of quiet, understated luxury. After dinner, guests enjoy a drink in the elegant Bemelmans Bar or finish the night at the Café Carlyle, listening to the magical sounds of Bobby Short or Eartha Kitt.

The Carlyle
35 East 76th Street
New York, NY 10021
Phone: 212-744-1600   Fax: 212-744-2819

CHAIKEN AND CAPONE
Fashion

Catering to the chic, urban woman who understands fashion and luxury, Chaiken and Capone offers classic styling with an urban edge. The company's meticulous attention to detail has earned it worldwide recognition in the fashion industry; look for Chaiken and Capone collections in Barneys and Harvey Nichols.

Chaiken and Capone
580 Broadway, Suite 400
New York, NY 10012
Phone: 212-334-3501   Fax: 212-334-3504

CHALONE VINEYARD
Winemakers

Chalone is in John Steinbeck country, east of Salinas and is located 2000 feet up in the rugged Gavilan Mountains. Around the turn of the century a Frenchman ventured up there to plant vines in the limestone rich soil, but the winery did not come to fruition until Richard Graff took over in the 1960s. Graff established strict Burgundian growing rules which remain in place today. Chalone mainly produces award-winning Chardonnay, but look out for their well priced, well made Pinot Noir.

Chalone Vineyard
PO Box 518
Soledad, CA 93960
Phone: 831-678-1717   Fax: 831-678-2742

CHARLES NOB HILL
Restaurants

With its old-European feel and abundance of flowers, Charles Nob Hill has become a favorite for the romantic reveler and the distinguished diner alike. Ron Siegel, formerly of French Laundry and Restaurant Daniel, deftly combines a background in French cuisine with a penchant for contemporary American flavors. The result is a rewarding experience which appeals to epicureans like George Schultz and Charles Schwab.

Charles Nob Hill
1250 Jones Street
San Francisco, CA 94109
Phone: 415-771-5400   Fax: 415-771-3542

CHARLES PERRY-CHINESE EXPORT PORCELAIN
Antiques

A favorite way for the English aristocracy of the 18th century to present their coats of arms was on Chinese porcelain. Collecting these exquisite pieces was a hobby for Charles Perry before he launched this business in 1982. Perry principally deals with private collectors, but has also sold items to institutions like the Du Pont Winterthur Museum and the High Museum of Art in Atlanta.

Charles Perry-Chinese Export Porcelain
P.O. Box 12468
Atlanta, GA 30355
Phone: 404-364-9731

CHARLIE TROTTER'S
Restaurants

Owner Charlie Trotter's cooking is rooted in the classic French tradition, but influenced by American ingenuity and Asian minimalism. This was one of the first restaurants in America to feature a table in the kitchen—reservations need to be made six months in advance. Beware: *Food and Wine* magazine recently awarded Trotter's its "most overpriced restaurant in Chicago" award.

Charlie Trotter's
816 W. Armitage Avenue
Chicago, IL 60614
Phone: 773-248-6228   Fax: 773-248-6088

CHASE INTERNATIONAL
Property Consultants

Having built her reputation on selling exclusive homes in Lake Tahoe, Nevada and California, Shari Chase is opening an office in London, which will represent buyers purchasing upmarket properties throughout Europe. Her customers, who include Jack Dreyfus, Jr. of the Dreyfus Fund and casino developer Steve Wynn, often return to buy other luxury homes, which can cost up to $50 million. In 1996 Shari sold the highest residential sale in America, a lakefront home which sold for $28 million.

Chase International
195 Highway 50, Suite 201
Lake Tahoe, NV 89448
Phone: 775-588-6130   Fax: 775-588-1206

CHASE MANHATTAN PRIVATE BANK
Wealth Management

"Put not your trust in money, but your money in trust," wrote Oliver Wendell Holmes, Sr. He was right, of course. However, you will still need at least a million dollars to convince Chase Manhattan that you are up to snuff as a private banking client. Since the Rockefeller era, this bank has emphasized its "integrated approach to entrepreneurship and wealth management," and has long boasted a strong reputation within the industry.

Chase Manhattan Private Bank
205 Royal Palm Way
Palm Beach, FL 33480
Phone: 561-838-8700

CHARLESTON GRILL
Restaurants

From the gastronomic point of view, Charleston is…well…Charleston. As a city of gracious good living and sumptuous eating it needs no introduction. Bob Waggoner's superb example of the regional cuisine includes a famous fish soup, crammed with scallops, mussels and garlic croutons, accompanied by oysters, crayfish and soft-shelled crabs brought in the same day by the fishing boats in the harbor. Justly acclaimed.

Charleston Grill
Charleston Place
224 King Street
Charleston, SC 29401
Phone: 843-577-4522

CHATEAU MONTELENA WINERY
Winemakers

By California standards this is an old winery (founded in 1882), but Montelena fell on lean times until 1972, when Jim Barrett bought it and followed a simple philosophy: "Make the best, period." His Montelena Estate Cabernet Sauvignon is justly renowned and the winery also produces some excellent Chardonnays. Today, Jim's son Bo is the winemaker. Ralph Hersom, Wine Director at *Le Cirque 2000,* describes Montelena as "one of the all time great Cabernets–in any vintage."

Chateau Montelena Winery

1429 Tubbs Lane
Calistoga, CA 94515
Phone: 707-643-1981

CHÂTEAU MARMONT
Hotels

This deliciously decadent landmark has always been a home away from home for movie stars and entertainment honchos. When the hotel opened in 1929, its design was based on the Château Amboise on the Loire. Several renovations later, it is more evocative of Hollywood's own glamorous past. Dorothy Parker and Errol Flynn were frequent guests. The lobby emanates the 1920s, while the suites echo the looks of the 1940s and 50s.

Château Marmont

8221 Sunset Boulevard
Hollywood, CA 90046
Phone: 323-656-1010

CHARLOTTE MOSS INTERIOR DESIGN
Architects and Interior Designers

Charlotte Moss is an interior designer, lecturer and author. Moss spent a successful decade on Wall Street before launching a career in the world of interiors. Her design installations have appeared in *Architectural Digest, House Beautiful,* and British *House and Garden* among numerous other magazines. Moss designs furniture and decorative accessories under license and produces her own home fragrance. She creates interiors that reflect the lifestyles of her clients by emphasizing the basic elements of comfort, practicality, and hospitality to produce surroundings that are at once elegant, distinctive, personal and functional.

Charlotte Moss Interior Design

16 East 65th Street
New York, NY 10021
Phone: 212-772-6244
Fax: 212-734-7250

CHEF ALLEN'S
Restaurants

With none of the glitz or glare of the usual suspects in Miami dining, Chef Allen's is a haven for epicures. Opened 20 years ago by Allen Susser, who trained at the Bristol Hotel in Paris and the Turnberry Country Club in Florida, this intimate bistro claims to be the originator of "New World" cuisine, combining flavors only available in the surrounding areas of southern Florida and the Caribbean. Keep an eye out for Pat Riley and the Miami Heat, and actors like Jack Nicholson.

Chef Allen's

19088 NE 29th Avenue
Aventura, FL 33180
Phone: 305-935-2900

CHEF RETO'S RESTAURANT
Restaurants

A veteran of Four Seasons hotels around the world before striking out on his own, chef-owner Reto Demarmels prepares what he describes as "Geo-classical cuisine" at this unusual restaurant, which he has been running with his wife Lynne since 1991. Try his walnut and garlic roasted clams; they are outstanding. Like many a good Swiss chef, Demarmels has a passion for patisserie.

Chef Reto's Restaurant

41 E. Palmetto Park Rd.
Boca Raton, FL 33432
Phone: 561-395-0633   Fax: 561-395-5074

CHEZ FRANÇOIS
Restaurants

Chez François is located in a 19th century historical landmark building; the dining room is appropriately French, with dark wooden beams and brick walls. A magnificent wine cellar boasts, among other treasures, a 1945 Romanée Conti. Owner Matthew N. Mars and Chef John M. D'Amico often throw special wine dinners. Ask for table 21—it's the best in the house, overlooking the Vermilion River.

Chez François

555 Main Street
Vermilion, OH 44089
Phone: 440-967-0630

CHEZ PANISSE
Restaurants

As a student in France, the teenage Alice Waters developed a passion for fresh and unusual ingredients which were unavailable in her native California. That passion grew into a lifelong interest in food which led her to found the now legendary Chez Panisse in 1971. The restaurant has played a formative role in the development of California cuisine. For instance, asking a friend in Nice to send her mesclun seed which she planted and served, Waters single-handedly introduced Americans to the tasty mixture of baby greens. In developing a local farming system that produces fresh, local ingredients Waters has become a prime mover in the national movement of artisan food growers. Waters has an in-house "forager" whose job is to ensure that local farmers supply only the highest quality ingredients for her healthy, Mediterranean-inspired food.

Chez Panisse

1517 Shattuck Avenue
Berkeley, CA 94709
Phone: 510-548-5525   Fax: 510-548-0140

CHINESE PORCELAIN COMPANY
Antiques

One of the major dealers of Asian art in the United States, the Chinese Porcelain Company has consistently been expanding its inventory since Khalil Rizk and Conor Mahoney opened it in 1984. The company sells a wide range of Chinese ceramics and works of art, Tibetan, Indian, Khmer and Vietnamese sculpture, as well as French furniture and decorations. Major private and institutional investors are among the company's clientele, including the Metropolitan Museum of Art, the Freer Gallery, the Brooklyn Museum of Art and the Peabody and Essex Museum in Salem, Massachusetts.

Chinese Porcelain Company

475 Park Avenue
New York, NY 10022
Phone: 212-838-7744   Fax: 212-838-4922

CHINOIS ON MAIN
Restaurants

Austrian-born Wolfgang Puck serves up French-Asian cuisine, which includes his signature sizzling catfish and Cantonese duck dishes, in this small Santa Monica restaurant which he opened in 1993. Barbara Lazaroff designed the Asian-inspired interior at Chinois, in which Billy Crystal, Lauren Bacall and Quincy Jones are regulars.

Chinois on Main

2709 Main St.
Santa Monica, CA 90405
Phone: 310-392-9025   Fax: 310-396-5102

CHISHOLM GALLERY
Art Dealers

Polo enthusiasts will find a trove of images and memorabilia to admire and collect in Jeanne Chisholm's gallery. Chisholm has amassed a large collection of polo paintings, prints, watercolors, sculpture and rare books. She is a tremendous resource for collectors and decorators and her holdings include paintings of general sporting interest from the 18th and 19th centuries.

Chisholm Gallery

Palm Beach Polo and Country Club
13368 Polo Road West, La Quinta C-202
Wellington, FL 33414
Phone: 561-791-8607   Fax: 561-798-4582

THE CHOPRA CENTER FOR WELL BEING
Spas and Clinics

Through educational, medical and spa services, the Chopra Center emphasizes healing on all levels and from all different angles. Guests feel nurtured by the excellent massage, meditation and ayurvedic treatments, obtaining a base of knowledge to take home and implement in a basic routine. No matter what your spiritual beliefs, this is an interesting way to get to know yourself on a more intimate basis.

The Chopra Center for Well Being

7630 Fay Avenue
La Jolla, CA 92037
Phone: 888-424-6772

CHATEAU DU SUREAU
Hotels

The closest thing to the French countryside near one of the most stunning destinations in North America—Yosemite National Park, Chateau du Sureau is a small, intimate hotel that reflects another time. The grounds include a koi pond, statuary and a giant-sized checkers and chess board. The ten rooms in this Relais & Chateaux, five star, five diamond dream spot are each named after a different herb or flower to reflect their uniquely opulent and dramatic qualities, including canopy beds, wood-burning fireplaces, antique furnishings and views of the garden and the magnificent Sierra Nevada. In the estate's nature park, Villa Sureau, a luxurious two bedroom, turn-of-the-century style Parisian villa awaits the most discriminating guests. The restaurant at Chateau du Sureau, Erna's Elderberry House, reflects Erna Kubin-Clanin's love of the French countryside of Provence. James Overbaugh, Executive Chef since 1995, prepares a prix fixe six course menu that changes nightly, and educates future chefs at the restaurant's cooking school, which takes on twelve students for three-day sessions four times a year.

Chateau du Sureau

48688 Victoria Lane
Oakhurst, CA 93644
Phone: 559-683-6860   Fax: 559-683-0800

CHRISTIE'S

Auction Houses

The recent unveiling of its huge new headquarters in Rockefeller Center provides the clearest indication yet of the importance of the American market to Christie's, one of the most acclaimed and prestigious fine art auctioneers in the world. Over 80 collecting fields are represented, including paintings, furniture, decorative arts, photographs, books, wine and even pop memorabilia—for instance, 100 of Eric Clapton's personal guitars fetched over $5 million at a recent auction. The 315,000 square foot premises, which is more than twice the size of the company's former space on Park Avenue, houses auction rooms, exhibition galleries, on-site storage and offices at one of the most famous addresses in the world. The new headquarters features a soaring triple-height entranceway with a specially commissioned mural by minimalist artist Sol LeWitt and a main salesroom with dramatic double height ceilings. Christie's looks set to prosper in its new home.

Christie's

20 Rockefeller Plaza
New York, NY 10020
Phone: 212-636-2679
Fax: 212-636-4951

CINDY GRIEM FINE JEWELS

Jewelry and Watches

It is rare that one gets to shop in such surroundings. Using luxurious Fortuny fabrics and lamps, Cindy Griem has created an intimate and inviting boutique-style jewelry salon. This designer showroom features an incredible array of designers and styles. From Donna Vock's luscious Tahitian and South Sea pearls, melded with platinum, gold and diamonds, to Elizabeth Locke's sumptuous neoclassical made-to-be-worn gold pieces, featuring Venetian glass intaglios, precious and semiprecious stones, pearls and little pieces of antiquity, there is something for everyone. In such a conducive environment, you will quickly be in the mood to splurge in a grand style. The architecturally

and archeologically-inspired designs make mere browsing a sheer delight. With no counters to separate the buyers from the seller, it is like being in a private livingroom, although few livingrooms exhibit such dazzling displays. Christopher Walling's unique designs incorporate beautiful and unusual stones to create to-die-for pieces. The result lures even the most timid jewelry buyer. A very hard worker and big supporter of the local community, Cindy is also the exclusive dealer of silk Fortuny lamps of Venice, Italy.

Cindy Griem Fine Jewels

112 South Mill Street
Aspen, CO 81611
Phone: 970-925-3800   Fax: 970-925-1800

CHRISTIE'S GREAT ESTATES

Property Consultants

Christie's Great Estates, owned by the world's oldest auction house, offers an international selection of estates, mansions, and country retreats. Under the helm of President and CEO, Kay Coughlin, it is comprised of over 120 real estate firms with more than 400 office locations and 12,000 agents all over the world. Great Estates, whose affiliates' annual sales total more than $35 billion, recently sold the Doris Duke estate, and a home in Beverly Hills built by Rudolph Valentino.

Christie's Great Estates

1850 Old Pecos Trail, Suite D
Santa Fe, NM 87505
Phone: 505-983-8733   Fax: 505-982-0348

CHUBB GROUP OF INSURANCE COMPANIES

Art Consultants

With vast experience in appraising and insuring fine art, jewelry and furniture, Chubb offers itemized policies that cover even the largest, most valuable collections. An international guarantee of your prized possessions can be arranged, either listing pieces individually or providing blanket insurance. Chubb is among the best art insurers in business today.

Chubb Group of Insurance Companies

15 Mountain View Road
Warren, NJ 07059
Phone: 908-903-2000

CIGAR AFICIONADO

Media

Big, flashy, brash—a little, in short, like the inimitable Marvin Shanken. It does seem unlikely that a European publication could succeed on such a flimsy premise. Having said that, *Cigar Aficionado* is beautifully produced and has single-handedly revived the noble art of cigar smoking.

Cigar Aficionado

M. Shanken Communications
387 Park Avenue South
New York, NY 10016
Phone: 212-684-4224   Fax: 212-684-5374

THE CIGAR BOX

Cigar Bars

After dinner in East Hampton, members of this private club pop in to relax with a fine smoke and a drink. With about 50 members (artists, entertainers, lawyers, doctors, and business moguls among them) the club features lockers and periodic wine tastings. Members regularly often host their own dinner and cocktail parties.

The Cigar Box

10 Main Street
East Hampton, NY 11937
Phone: 516-324-8844   Fax: 516-324-9532

CIPRIANI

Restaurants

Harry Cipriani (*the* Harry Cipriani) offers fine Italian fare at this Sherry Netherland institution, where middle aged playboys, French movie stars, Wall Street tycoons and glamorous *belles* come to see and be seen. The tables are far too small, lending the experience an air of desperation which seems strangely appropriate. If you have trouble securing a reservation ask for the affable Sergio Vacca.

Cipriani

781 Fifth Avenue
New York, NY 10022
Phone: 212-753-5566

DENNIS CIRILLO, M.D.

Cosmetic Surgeons

Focusing on plastic and reconstructive surgery, Dennis Cirillo's facility offers up-to-the-minute treatments and technology, including "every laser known to man." He specializes in innovative techniques such as vein laser treatments and Parisian peels. Dr. Cirillo is a member of the American Society for Aesthetic Plastic Surgeons. Incidentally, his wife, Dexter, is one of the foremost authorities on native American arts and crafts.

Dennis Cirillo, M.D

400 West Main Street, Suite 100
Aspen, CO 81611
Phone: 970-544-0500

LE CIRQUE 2000

Restaurants

A *macedoine* of old New York money, presidents of the United States and bejeweled overseas tourists, this most aristocratic of restaurants, based in an historic landmark town house, is very special indeed. There are no good or bad tables. You will sit where the legendary Sirio Maccioni chooses to seat you, probably between a great American fortune and the Secretary-General of the United Nations, but if you can, sit in the back, away from the brouhaha of the table-hopping regulars. Some say this incarnation is not as good as the original Le Cirque, but they are wrong: it is better. Incidentally, the Maccionis have recently opened a new branch of Le Cirque in the Bellagio Hotel, the flagship of Steve Wynn's Las Vegas empire. If early reports are accurate, it looks set to enjoy a very long life indeed.

Le Cirque 2000

455 Madison Avenue
New York, NY 10022
Phone: 212-303-7788   Fax: 212-303-7788

CITIBANK PRIVATE BANK
Wealth Management

When CitiGroup was founded in 1998, it combined the banking, securities and insurance businesses of Citibank, Salomon Smith Barney, and Travelers, respectively. It is now the prototype for the one-stop financial supermarkets springing up across the banking landscape, luring clients who want the convenience of all their financial services under one roof. Citibank's Private Bank unit is a prime beneficiary of the merger. It now oversees more than $100 billion in assets and the company believes it may reach $1 trillion by 2010. The minimum requirement for a private banking account is $3 million.

Citibank Private Bank
153 East 53rd Street
New York, NY 10043
Phone: 212-627-3999

CLEVELAND MUSEUM OF ART
Museums

Designed by famed Cleveland architects Hubbell and Benes in 1916 in elegant beaux-arts fashion, the Cleveland Museum of Art houses more than 30,000 works spanning 5,000 years, from Ancient Egypt to the present. The museum is set within the 15 acre fine arts garden in the midst of Cleveland's University Circle, a concentrated grouping of museums, schools, and performing arts facilities. The collection of American and Mayan art is among the finest in the United States.

Cleveland Museum of Art
11150 East Boulevard
Cleveland, OH 44106
Phone: 216-421-7340   Fax: 216-229-5095

CLAREMONT RUG COMPANY
Specialty Shops

The artwork hanging on these walls is suitable for stepping on for those who are fortunate enough to live with them. The Claremont Rug Company, founded in 1980, offers a creative and often under-appreciated art form. President and founder Jan David Winitz, who has taught courses on antique rugs at the University of California at Berkeley, recently furnished a house whose art collection included works by several master painters. "I put an antique camelhair carpet beneath a Picasso," he says. Then the customer "leaned over and whispered, 'Between you and me, the impact of the rug is greater than the Picasso.'" Incidentally, Claremont Rug Company's investment quality 19th century rugs apparently appreciate up to 20 percent annually. One of a handful of major companies in North America dealing exclusively in art-level antique rugs, Winitz accepts only carpets of rare beauty, whose colors come exclusively from pure natural dyes. The company's San Francisco area gallery complex offers rugs of quality rarely seen outside of museums. Executives of Fortune 500 firms, top fine art buyers, movie stars and royalty have been acquiring these carpets with ravenous abandon, at an average of $50,000 a piece. A charming satellite store located in Berkeley, Claremont II, stocks an exquisite selection of Persian tribal rugs and flatwoven kilims.

Claremont Rug Company
6087 Claremont Avenue
Oakland, CA 94618
Phone: 800-441-1332 or 510-654-0816 Fax: 510-654-8661

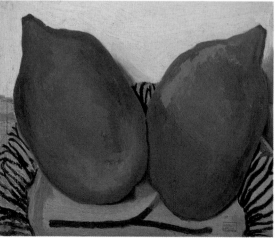

Lemons, by Joseph Stella.

CLINE FINE ART GALLERY
Art Dealers

Located in Santa Fe, a major art travel destination, Cline Fine Art Gallery has attracted a particularly cosmopolitan clientele. The gallery represents estates and individual works of important 20th century American painters and sculptors, with a focus on early American Modernism. Recent exhibitions have highlighted the works of de Kooning, Joseph Stella and Louis Ribak.

Cline Fine Art Gallery
526 Canyon Road
Sante Fe, NM 87501
Phone: 505-982-5328   Fax: 505-982-4762

CLODAGH DESIGN
Architects and Interior Designers
Clodagh is one of America's leading interior designers. Her company pursues "total design," involving all the senses and all the elements. Renowned for inventive and sensitive use of materials, Clodagh and her young, affable team have a true understanding of their clients' needs and a refreshingly quirky attitude—there may be talk of astrological signs or energy fields during a planning session. This divine Irishwoman's mantra is, "contemplate, cleanse, clarify and then create." Warmly recommended.
Clodagh Design
670 Broadway, 4th Floor
New York, NY 10012
Phone: 212-780-5300   Fax: 212-780-5755

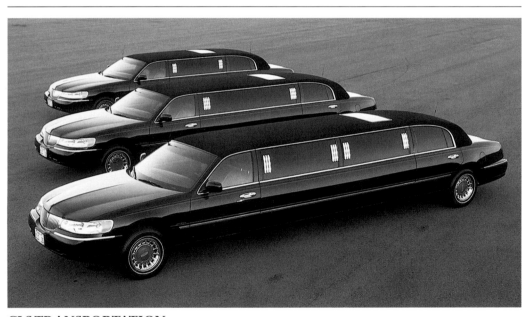

CLS TRANSPORTATION
Chauffeur Services
At CLS, the mission statement is simply: "To extend to our clients the highest degree of service possible, without intrusion." This blue-chip limousine company succeds admirably, providing exceptional service, whether in a town car, a stretch limousine, or a corporate aircraft. CLS has more than 300 vehicles between its Los Angeles, San Francisco, Las Vegas, Aspen and New York offices. In addition, the company maintains a network of affiliates throughout the States and abroad to afford its clients great service *literally* anywhere in the world.
CLS Transportation
6341 Arizona Circle
Los Angeles, CA 90045
Phone: 800-266-2577   Fax: 310-417-4189

CLUB COLETTE
Restaurants
Daniel Ponton opened his private dinner club in Palm Beach 17 years ago, and he recently launched a second location in Southampton. Open only to members and their guests, this tony club is apparently besieged by requests for membership. Several high-profile socialites held "intimate" dinner parties in the Hamptons outpost last summer.
Club Colette
215 Peruvian Avenue
Palm Beach, FL 33480
Phone: 561-659-0537

CLUB MACANUDO
Cigar Bars
Edgar M. Cullen, Jr., built on the success of his Upper East Side establishment when he opened Club Macanudo in Chicago's Gold Coast a few years ago. It offers 130 varieties of cigars (Macanudo, Partagas, Ramon Allones), cuisine and signature desserts by Jason Paskewitz, and 600 personal mahogany humidors, lined with Spanish cedar, for lease. Only humidor holders are guaranteed a reservation.
Club Macanudo
60 East Walton Street
Chicago, IL 60611
Phone: 312-642-4200

COATES, REID & WALDRON
Property Consultants
A full-service real estate brokerage, Coates, Reid & Waldron specializes in the sale of luxury homes in Aspen. The company, which recently sold a custom-built log home for $12 million, also offers upscale vacation rentals and property management services. A small firm with 13 agents and two offices, it has the annual sales of a much larger firm: $163 million.
Coates, Reid & Waldron
720 East Hyman Avenue
Aspen, CO 81611
Phone: 970-920-0565   Fax: 970-925-2895

COEUR D'ALENE
Spas and Clinics
Nestled among the evergreens that hem the Rocky Mountains, the picturesque Coeur d'Alene overlooks one of 50 lakes that decorate the Idaho region. This full service European day spa offers head to toe services, from facials and manicures to hydrotherapy, body exfoliation, and hot rock treatments. The lakefront meditation room is a favorite among celebrities like Pierce Brosnan, Linda Hamilton and John Travolta. In addition to the day spa, Coeur d'Alene also houses a luxury hotel and America's only floating golf green.
Coeur d'Alene
115 South Second Street
Coeur d'Alene, ID 83814
Phone: 800-688-5253

COLIN COWIE LIFESTYLES

Party Organizers and Caterers

This versatile designer runs a multifaceted business that caters to luminaries, socialites and corporate clients. Cowie plans Elton John's Oscar party each year and has designed weddings for Kenny G, Hugh Hefner and Lisa Kudrow. Besides events, Cowie has written two coffee table books (a style guide for brides and grooms is due in January of 2000), and has his own television show called *Everyday Elegance with Colin Cowie*.

Colin Cowie Lifestyles

8439 Sunset Boulevard, Suite 406
Los Angeles, CA 90069
Phone: 323-462-7183

THE COLONY CLUB

Private Clubs

This ladies-only Park Avenue institution, once a rest stop for socially elite shoppers, has since become a bastion of power and influence, playing a major role in the business and politics of the city—although discussion of business remains forbidden. Members include women from the oldest families in New York.

The Colony Club

564 Park Avenue
New York, NY 10021
Phone: 212-838-4200

COLONY SURF HOTEL

Hotels

The Colony Surf has hosted many notables over the past four decades (it was a favorite of Frank Sinatra and Lana Turner) and since its renovation last year, the hotel has wowed many more. The interior resembles a Balinese-type retreat, with the lobby offering a particularly lush, tropical landscape. Chef David Paul Johnson creates food infused with flavors and techniques from his travels around the globe.

Colony Surf Hotel

2885 Kalakaua Avenue
Honolulu, HI 96815
Phone: 808-924-3111   Fax: 808-791-5110

LES CONCIERGES

Specialty Shops

There is no specific category for Les Concierges within our directory, because this San Francisco based company is a self-styled panacea for all ills. For instance, if you have lost half of a one-of-a-kind set of cufflinks, the staff will find you a replacement; if your overbearing mother-in-law shows up on your doorstep, they will reserve her a suite at even the most overbooked hotel. This ingenious outfit will even remind you of your wife's birthday, along with supplying you with a bottle of her favorite perfume.

Les Concierges

100 Bush Street, Suite 300
San Francisco, CA 94104
Phone: 415-291-1165   Fax: 415-291-0190

COMMANDER'S PALACE

Restaurants

Commander's Palace is the spiritual home of contemporary Creole cuisine, which it helped to create: chef Jamie Shannon's turtle soup, smoked fish cakes, veal chop *Tchoupitoulas* and bread pudding soufflé are all superb. Housed in a Victorian building complete with turrets, columns and gingerbread, the restaurant is owned and operated by the Brennan family, who have won innumerable awards for their legendary hospitality. For a taste of quite how exotic New Orleans can be, let bartender Linda Smith choose your aperitif.

Commander's Palace

1403 Washington Avenue
New Orleans, LA 70130
Phone: 504-899-8221
Fax: 504-891-3242

CONGRESSIONAL COUNTRY CLUB

Golf Clubs

Devereaux Emmett, Donald Ross, Rees Jones and Robert Trent Jones Sr. all had a hand in designing the Congressional Country Club Blue and Gold courses. Members' guests are permitted on one course at a time, which alternates daily between Blue and Gold. Those seeking a challenge come for the notorious Blue Course, with its rigorous par fours and the rolling hills that almost defeated Ken Venturi when he won the Open here in 1964.

Congressional Country Club

8500 River Road
Bethesda, MD 20817
Phone: 301-469-2000

CONOVER REAL ESTATE

Property Consultants

Conover Real Estate specializes in luxury waterfront properties on Martha's Vineyard, an island famous for its diversity, history and carefully protected natural environment. Five sales associates and two brokers assist clients to acquire properties which range from $500,000 to $6 million. Owners Gerret C. Conover and Thomas E. LeClair founded the firm in 1988.

Conover Real Estate

20 South Summer Street
Edgartown, MA 02539
Phone: 508-627-3757   Fax: 508-627-8617

CONTINENTAL LIMOUSINE

Chauffeur Services

Continental specializes in catering to a wide array of entertainment and corporate clients. Each car is impeccably maintained and both the office staff and the chauffeurs go out of their way to satisfy clients' personal requests. If you are heading to Michigan and need to be pampered, these are the people you will be talking to first.

Continental Limousine

37689 Schoolcraft Road
Livonia, MI 48150
Phone: 248-626-8282

MICHELLE COPELAND, M.D.

Cosmetic Surgeons

While many doctors are running to and from the hospital to perform surgery between patient consultations, Dr. Michelle Copeland never has to leave her private practice. With her own operating room on site, patients come right to the office to have their surgery, without having to deal with all the red tape a trip to the hospital involves. Whether you are scheduling a liposuction, face-lift, breast augmentation, or any other form of reconstructive surgery, you will feel at home throughout your stay.

Michelle Copeland, M.D.

1001 Fifth Avenue
New York, NY 10028
Phone: 212-452-2200   Fax: 212-452-2200

THE COOPER-HEWITT NATIONAL DESIGN MUSEUM

Museums

Part of the Smithsonian Institution since 1967, the National Design Museum has one of the largest collections of design related material in the world. The collections are broken up into several categories: industrial design, textiles, wall coverings, drawings and prints, which include graphic design, architecture, interior and environmental design. With over 50,000 volumes of design related reference material, and 5000 rare books, its new library is unparalleled. The museum also offers lectures, seminars and tours.

The Cooper-Hewitt National Design Museum

2 East 91st Street
New York, NY 10128
Phone: 212-849-8420   Fax: 212-849-8401

LE COQ AU VIN

Restaurants

Louis Perrotte has been the chef and owner of this casual, French country restaurant since it opened 16 years ago. The menu changes every two months, switching its emphasis to different regions in France with the seasons. Some of the more popular dishes include the restaurant's namesake, a braised chicken with red burgundy wine, and a salmon with horseradish sauce on braised cabbage. Perrotte, whose wife Magdalena is the hostess, recommends the corner tables in each of his restaurant's three dining rooms.

Le Coq au Vin

4800 S. Orange Avenue
Orlando, FL 32806
Phone: 407-851-6980   Fax: 407-248-0658

CORCORAN GALLERY OF ART

Museums

The oldest museum in the capital, the Corcoran Gallery of Art has been housed in a *beaux arts* building designed by Ernst Flagg since 1897. A new extension designed by Frank Gehry will be ready early in the next century. This delightful institution showcases the best American painting, with the prestigious Corcoran School of Art situated on-site. The current president, David Levy, has increased the museum's endowment from $8 million to $29 million in less than a decade.

Corcoran Gallery of Art

500 17th Street, NW
Washington, DC 20006
Phone: 202-639-1700

THE CORCORAN GROUP

Property Consultants

Specialists in the sale and rental of luxury co-ops, condominiums, townhouses and lofts in New York City. With 440 real estate brokers, 10 offices and $1.5 billion in annual sales and rental transactions, the firm ranks among the largest in Manhattan. Owner Barbara Corcoran has been showered with awards, including the prestigious Realty Foundation Golden Apple Award and *Crain's* All Star Award.

The Corcoran Group

660 Madison Avenue
New York, NY 10021
Phone: 212-355-3550   Fax: 212-223-6381

COSENTINO

Winemakers   *Best Kept Secret*

Owner Mitch Cosentino is an innovator. He was the first to use the term Meritage (wine made with Bordeaux-type grapes) on a label and has returned to punched cap fermentation for most red wines. Production varies based on the availability of good grapes. "The goal," he says "is to make the best wine, not the best wine to fit a certain number of cases." The M Coz is particularly worth hunting out.

Cosentino

7415 St. Helena Highway
PO Box 2818
Yountville, CA 94599
Phone: 707-944-1220

LA COSTA

Spas and Clinics

A world-class spa, championship golf course, and 21-court racquet club—all packaged into 75,000 square feet in Carlsbad, California. La Costa serves up a mixture of recreation and indulgence. Savvy clients choose the spa service called La Costa Glow; this specialized treatment is an hour and a half of pampering, including a combination of exfoliation, wrap, and massage.

La Costa

2100 Costa Del Mar Road
Carlsbad, CA 92009
Phone: 800-854-5000

COVINGTON & BURLING

Law Firms

This law firm, founded in 1919, has developed a nationwide reputation for superior standards of quality and efficiency in legal practice. Based in Washington, D.C., thorough research and meticulous drafting are its hallmarks. When it comes to pro bono work, the firm consistently ranks at the top of the pack.

Covington & Burling

1201 Pennsylvania Avenue, NW
Washington, DC 20044
Phone: 202-662-6000

COVE LANDING

Antiques   *Rising Star*

Soaring above the Connecticut River's southern shores, Cove Landing is a newly constructed antiques gallery voted "Best Retail Project" by *Interiors Magazine* in 1999. Architect and interior designer L.A. Morgan co-owns the business with respected author and antiques dealer Angus Wilkie, who honed his eye at Christie's. Cove Landing's spare presentation and unique surroundings echo the quality, scale and integrity of superb objects and furniture. An unusual selection chosen from diverse periods includes examples of Ming Dynasty, Irish Regency, Biedermeier, and contemporary Twentieth century design.

Cove Landing

Route 156, Lyme
Hadlyme, CT 06439
Phone: 860-526-3464   Fax: 860-434-3103

CRAIG F. STARR ASSOCIATES

Art Dealers

Craig Starr has been selling 19th and 20th century American art to both institutions and individuals from his Upper East Side establishment since the 1980s. With an inventory strong on Jasper Johns and Edward Hopper, Starr does business with many of the nation's more affluent art lovers.

Craig F. Starr Associates

30 East 85th Street
New York, NY 10028
Phone: 212-570-1739   Fax: 212-570-6848

CRAVATH, SWAINE & MOORE

Law Firms

Measured by sheer number of lawyers, this firm is not among the largest in the United States, but its lawyers have certainly been involved in some of the nation's more important cases. Attorneys are trained within one of four departments—corporate, litigation, tax, or trusts & estates. Each associate rotates among the firm's partners, gaining experience in all aspects of their practice area. The purpose is to develop lawyers as generalists, bucking the trend toward narrow specialization favored by most of the other major law firms. A report in *The New York Observer* last year described Cravath, Swaine & Moore as a "stiff-jawed old-world firm."

Cravath, Swaine & Moore

Worldwide Plaza
825 Eighth Avenue
New York, NY 10019
Phone: 212-474-1000

CRAIN'S NEW YORK BUSINESS

Media

Devoted to the movers and shakers of New York, this magazine is a premium source of information on local business news for its readers, 40 percent of whom are millionaires. Top-level executives turn to *Crain's* for its attention to smaller and midsize companies that the national publications don't cover. List lovers, take note—*Crain's* is renowned for its rankings of companies in many industries, including advertising, accounting, media and much more.

Crain's New York Business

Crain Communications Inc.
220 East 42nd Street
New York, NY 10017
Phone: 212-210-0259   Fax: 212-210-0499

CROUCH & FITZGERALD

Fashion

Since 1839 this elegant luggage store has been the suitcase buyer's Mecca for leather goods, including the store's chic private label. High-quality services include monogramming and repairs, and salespeople who rarely have less than 10 years of experience. The three floors of luxury traveling goods are made mostly in the United States, but unusual accessories from Germany, England, and Italy complete this impressive selection.

Crouch & Fitzgerald

400 Madison Avenue
New York, NY 10017
Phone: 212-755-5888

THE CULINARY INSTITUTE OF AMERICA

Culinary Schools

The Culinary Institute of America is the only residential college in the world devoted solely to culinary education. It offers acclaimed degree programs in culinary arts, baking, and pastry arts, as well as bachelor's degree programs in culinary arts management and baking and arts management. Located on the east bank of the Hudson River, the CIA is situated on a 150-acre campus replete with rolling hills and springtime vegetation. The school employs more than 120 instructors from 15 countries and trains students in a highly professional environment.

The Culinary Institute of America

433 Albany Post Road
Hyde Park, NY 12538
Phone: 914-452-9600

CULLMAN & KRAVIS

Architects and Interior Designers

Cullman & Kravis, founded in 1984 by Elissa Cullman and the late Hedi Kravis, is known as "the interior decorator for collectors of fine art and antiques." The company is known for its broad versatility of design in traditional and modern aesthetics. True to its excellent reputation, Cullman & Kravis' clients have included the CEOs of Philip Morris, Paramount Communications, Salomon Brothers and Goldman Sachs.

Cullman & Kravis

790 Madison Avenue
New York, NY 10021
Phone: 212-249-3874   Fax: 212-249-3881

CYPRESS POINT CLUB

Golf Clubs

Working its way through the Del Monte forest on California's Monterey Peninsula, the Cypress Point course is, according to experts Robert Graves and Geoffrey Cornish, "one of the world's greatest layouts." Designed in 1928 by Alister MacKenzie, the course is unique, with its consecutive par threes and par fives. Players need to take the ocean into account on holes 15, 16 and 17. A very small, very private club, Cypress Point hosts no major tournaments, although it was the site for the AT&T Pebble Beach National Pro-Am through 1990.

Cypress Point Club

17 Mile Drive
Pebble Beach, CA 93953
Phone: 831-624-6444

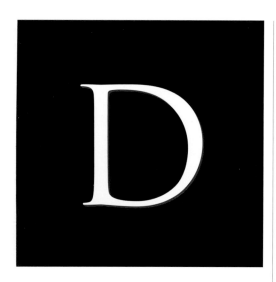

D & M CHAMPAGNE

Wine Merchants

D & M Champagne has labored for three generations to accumulate an extensive collection of wines, Armagnac, Calvados and 300 types of Single Malt Scotch. Through the years, the store has fostered relationships with wine lovers around the country and now boasts a huge customer base. Owners Mike and Joe Politz have a combined 79 years of experience in the wine business.

D & M Champagne

2200 Fillmore Street
San Francisco, CA 94115
Phone: 415-346-1325

D'AMICO CUCINA

Restaurants

D'Amico Cucina joined the growing coterie of topnotch Midwestern Italian restaurants in 1987. The atmosphere is at once dynamic, urbane and comfortable at this stunning Butler Square eatery, where Chef J.P. Samuelson serves up his signature butternut squash *cappelletti* with pistachio and sage, and a *pangrattato* crusted pork tenderloin with soft polenta. Service is superb.

D'Amico Cucina

Butler Square, 100 North Sixth Street
Minneapolis, MN 55403
Phone: 612-338-2401   Fax: 612-337-5130

DA SILVANO

Restaurants

Owner Silvano Marchetto oversees the cuisine at this small West Village Italian—whether you order basic spaghetti and lasagna, or esoteric dishes from little-known provinces. Lauren Bacall or Rupert Everett might be sitting two tables away. Best to book in advance; tables are hard to come by at the last minute.

Da Silvano

260 Sixth Avenue
New York, NY 10014
Phone: 212-982-2343

DALLAS MUSEUM OF ART

Museums

The Dallas Museum of Art boasts a collection as diverse as the community it serves, with ancient American artifacts and masterpieces by Georgia O'Keeffe happily residing side by side. But we are particularly fond of the Wendy and Emery Reves Collection, which re-creates the idyllic lifestyle enjoyed by this remarkable couple at their home, Villa La Pausa, in the South of France. The Reveses were revered for both their social prowess and their fine art collection; guests at Villa La Pausa included Winston Churchill, Albert Einstein, and Noel Coward. The Reves Collection includes art by impressionist masters like van Gogh, Manet, Renoir, Gauguin and Monet.

Dallas Museum of Art

1717 North Harwood
Dallas, TX 75201
Phone: 214-922-1200   Fax. 214-954-0174

DALLAS POLO CLUB

Polo Clubs

Renowned arena player Bill Walton presides over a bracing year-round schedule of competitive polo at the Bear Creek Polo Ranch. The Dallas Polo Club maintains two full fields, and a third has been planted and growing as this book goes to press. Grooms care for more than 100 member and pro thoroughbreds. Membership has three levels, descending from VIP to corporate to social. The club continues to breed new fans of the game through its prestigious polo school.

Dallas Polo Club

2906 Maple Avenue, Suite 204
Dallas, TX 75201
Phone: 214-979-0300   Fax: 214-979-0849

DALVA BROTHERS

Antiques

When Louis XIV was fitting out Versailles, the best craftsmen of Europe were drawn to Paris. The fruits of their labor are on show in Manhattan, where the Dalva brothers' collection of French furniture from the 17th and 18th centuries fills a five-story townhouse. The Dalvas have helped the Getty and the Metropolitan Museums build public collections of some of the most beautifully built furniture ever made.

Dalva Brothers

44 East 57th Street
New York, NY 10022
Phone: 212-758-2297

DANA BUCHMAN .

Fashion

A businesswoman, wife and mother, Dana Buchman has used her life as inspiration for her sophisticated suits and polished career looks. Ornamented with beads and embroidery, her new luxe collection includes the season's chicest must-haves and was created for the top tier of her customer base. Look for the company's clothing, eyewear and accessories at Neiman Marcus, Saks and Hudson's.

Dana Buchman

65 East 57th Street
New York, NY 10022
Phone: 212-319-3257

DANIEL

Restaurants

The latest triumph of indefatigable French super-chef Daniel Boulud, his namesake restaurant blends sublime cuisine with one-of-a-kind touches, like personalized napkins with your name woven into them. Boulud blends simple, strong flavors into masterpieces of powerhouse flavor. Order the signature sea bass with red wine sauce or the spit-roasted guinea hen and anything that includes *foie gras*. Call at *least* two weeks in advance to make reservations.

Daniel

60 East 65th Street
New York, NY 10021
Phone: 212-288-0033   Fax: 212-737-0612

DANIELS, DANIELS & DANIELS

Antiques

The Daniels brothers sell a diverse array of 19th century French and English antiques from their stores in Hallandale, Florida and Aspen, Colorado, from furniture that formerly graced the interiors of royal palaces, to that with a slightly less aristocratic past. The firm exhibits at most of the country's more prestigious antique shows.

Daniels, Daniels & Daniels Antiques

2520 SW 30th Avenue
Hallandale, FL 33009
Phone: 954-454-1395   Fax: 954-454-6452

DARRELL SCHMITT DESIGN ASSOCIATES

Architects and Interior Designers

With projects like a royal residence in Saudi Arabia and two Four Seasons Hotels under his belt, Kansas native Darrell Schmitt has become a key player in the interior design world. Along with his small group of talented and experienced design professionals, Schmitt particularly enjoys challenging projects; the enduring quality of his work ensures a loyal clientele.

Darrell Schmitt Design Associates

6399 Wilshire Boulevard, #1010
Los Angeles, CA 90048
Phone: 323-951-9283   Fax: 323-951-9231

DARTMOUTH COLLEGE

Colleges

Founded in 1769, Dartmouth was the last college established under colonial rule. Its original mission was to educate and instruct the "youth of the Indian Tribes in this Land…and also English youth and any others." Dartmouth established the first professional school of engineering in the United States and the first graduate school of management in the world. Today, this Ivy League institution admits over a thousand new undergraduates each year. Historian James Wright was recently elected president of the school.

Dartmouth College

Pikehouse
38 N. Main Street
Hanover, NH 03755
Phone: 603-646-3661

DAV EL

Chauffeur Services

Scott A. Solombrino, president and CEO of Dav El, saw a good deal when the opportunity to own this limousine service arose. Once the sole Boston franchisee for Dav El, Solombrino eventually snatched the company up from David Klein, who founded it in 1966. Dav El now has a massive network in 350 cities around the world, and its vehicles are supplied with state-of-the-art equipment and luxurious features.

Dav El

200 Second Street
Chelsea, MA 02150
Phone: 617-887-0900   Fax: 617-884-2707

DAVID ANTHONY EASTON

Architects and Interior Designers

David Easton is renowned for recreating the sumptuous gentility of English country houses, although he is equally capable of working in other styles. For 25 years this trained architect has designed homes for a very select clientele: Easton is the man who built John Kluge's massive house on a 12,000 acre Virginia estate from its humble beginnings as a sketch on the back of a napkin. His headquarters have recently moved from the Upper East Side to SoHo. Recommended.

David Anthony Easton

72 Spring Street
New York, NY 10012
Phone: 212-334-3820   Fax: 212-334-3821

DAVID JONES

Florists

A veteran florist, David Jones—who has lectured at the Smithsonian—lists the Reagans, Bloomingdales, Mehtas and Annenbergs among his clients. His personal arrangements are invariably distinctive and delightful, and Mr. Jones is an old-fashioned character in the best sense of the term. One could not produce a list of America's best florists without including this fabulous man.

David Jones

450 North Robertson
Los Angeles, CA 90048
Phone: 310-659-6347

DAVID LAVOY

Florists

David LaVoy turned his interest in flowers into a thriving business, focusing on weddings and other gala events throughout the South. His style is best described as classical and opulent, with a heavy emphasis on roses. Atlanta institutions like the Cherokee Country Club and the Piedmont Driving Club retain LaVoy for their weekly flower arrangements and Christmas decorations.

David LaVoy

2126 Faulkner Road
Atlanta, GA 30324
Phone: 404-320-6677   Fax: 404-320-7788

DAVID WEBB

Jewelry and Watches

Founded in 1948 by David Webb and Nina Silberstein, David Webb Inc. has established itself as the standard-bearer of American jewelry. Bold design, exotic animals, striking enamels, and exciting colors, combined with impeccable craftsmanship, have long been the trademarks of this 57th Street landmark. Though based in New York, the firm has always enjoyed a large international following. Clients are known to gravitate to Webb's salons from all over the world and across America. For the future, the company promises to continue the tradition it has established for design, workmanship, and service. The key trend in jewelry these days is wearability, and Webb's experienced staff is always available to assist and guide one through the plethora of fun, exciting, and wearable jewels in the salons. In addition to its locations at Park Avenue and 57th Street in New York, and the Pavilion in Houston, David Webb is in the Regent Beverly Wilshire Hotel in Beverly Hills. All pieces continue to be crafted in their workshops in New York under the watchful eye of Chairwoman Nina Silberstein and President Stan Silberstein.

David Webb

445 Park Avenue
New York, NY 10022
Phone: 212-421-3030   Fax: 212-758-7827

DAVID STERN DESIGNER JEWELERS

Jewelry and Watches

David Stern brings a personal touch to every piece he creates, establishing a rapport with his customers and designing jewelry that meets their exacting standards. He labors to bring his clients jewelry that is functional, easy to wear and timeless. Stern specializes in gold and platinum and has been stunning women for years with items like a white-gold custom necklace, a sublime combination of Brazilian green tourmaline and beautiful white diamonds.

David Stern Designer Jewelers

3013 Yamoto Road, Suite B20
Boca Raton, FL 33434
Phone: 561-994-3330

DAVIS, POLK & WARDWELL

Law Firms

Clients rely on Davis, Polk & Wardwell lawyers for their ability to create practical, innovative solutions to difficult problems in the business sector and to manage highly complex transactions and cases. The New York-based firm serves clients in the U.S. and abroad, with international centers thriving in Europe, Asia and Latin America. The lawyers work within 20 major areas of practice, under the umbrellas of corporate law, litigation, tax law, trusts and estates.

Davis, Polk & Wardwell

450 Lexington Avenue
New York, NY 10017
Phone: 212-450-4000

DEBORAH KOEPPER

Hair and Beauty

When she worked for the late Robin Weir, Nancy Reagan's personal stylist at the White House, Deborah Koepper did the makeup for Indira Ghandi and Princess Diana. Now in business for herself in Palm Beach, Koepper's seaweed facials and deep tissue massage are popular with clients like Brooke Shields. The salon also offers hairstyling and manicures.

Deborah Koepper

215 Sunset Avenue
Palm Beach, FL 33480
Phone: 561-833-6561   Fax: 561-659-9805

DE VERA

Specialty Shops   ***Rising Star***

Owner Federico de Vera's San Francisco galleries are a showcase for the designer's furniture in glass, metal and wood, though you will also find exquisite jewelry and *objets d'art* from all over the world. A native of the Philippines, de Vera moved to California in the 1980s, where he worked for several art galleries and museums, soaking up the local color before opening the first of his three shops in 1991.

De Vera

580 Sutter Street
San Francisco, CA 94102
Phone: 415-989-0988   Fax: 415-989-0468

DEERFIELD ACADEMY

Schools

Founded in 1797 in a rural Western Massachusetts village, Deerfield Academy today enrolls students for four years of secondary education and one year of postgraduate study. During their Junior years, students have the option of attending the Mountain School in Vermont, where they assist in maintaining a farm in addition to their academic pursuits. Opportunities for studying abroad include unique programs in Switzerland, South Africa, France, Spain and Germany. The quality of the faculty and a 1:6 faculty-student ratio draws approximately 135 students to the Deerfield campus each Fall. Dr. Eric Widmer, former Dean at Brown University, was appointed headmaster in 1994.

Deerfield Academy

Main Street
Deerfield, MA 01342
Phone: 413-774-1425

DEER VALLEY RESORT

Hotels

Deer Valley has almost single-handedly reinvented the upscale American ski resort. Just 39 miles from Salt Lake City airport, its superb lodging and truly memorable service (when was the last time you said *that* about a ski resort?) have basically given affluent snow lovers a good reason not to fly to the Alps. But what about the skiing? The slalom events in the 2002 Winter Olympics will be held at the resort.

Deer Valley Resort

PO Box 1525
Park City, UT 84060
Phone: 435-649-1000   Fax: 435-645-6939

DE PASQUALE, THE SPA

Spas and Clinics

Enjoy a soak in an authentic Japanese steaming tub, an Italian "rainshower" and then a candlelit massage. Or try the De Pasquale Experience, which takes place in two adjoining suites and can be experienced alone or with one other person. De Pasquale, The Spa, is a total sensory experience—everything from the architectural design to the decor to the aromas in the air are designed to exhilarate the mind and body.

De Pasquale, The Spa

Rt. 10 East, Powder Mill Plaza
Morris Plains, NJ 07950
Phone: 973-538-3811

DEGUSTIBUS COOKING SCHOOL

Culinary Schools

Held at Macy's Herald Square location in New York, this 19-year-old cooking program is the one to which most other programs in the field are compared. Under the watchful eye of director Arlene Feltman Sailhac (whose husband, Alain, was the Executive Chef at Le Cirque for many years), top chefs and cookbook authors reveal their culinary insights. Degustibus is considered a rite of passage for many up-and-coming cooks.

Degustibus Cooking School

343 East 74th Street, Suite 14A
New York, NY 10021
Phone: 212-439-1714

DELANO HOTEL
Hotels
A haven of relaxation in Miami's chic South Beach, where an indoor/outdoor lobby creates the feeling of an interwoven village, with a seamless walk from the street into the hotel. High ceilings and flowing curtains extend this European-style "village" from the lobby to the water's edge, with tents, cabanas, and whimsically designed wooden buildings along the way. Try to snag one of the eight poolside bungalows, with floor-to-ceiling marble bathrooms.

Delano Hotel
1685 Collins Avenue
Miami Beach, FL 33139
Phone: 305-672-2000   Fax: 305-532-0099

DELAWARE RIVER TRADING COMPANY
Specialty Shops   Rising Star
Jon Carloftis is the young designer behind some of the smartest penthouse gardens on the Upper East Side of Manhattan. Delaware River Trading is an acclaimed garden business that he set up with Willis Watts in 1995. Together they sell a host of stylish garden "accessories," like wrought iron chairs and benches, stainless steel flower-pots and architectural fragments.

Delaware River Trading Company
47 Bridge Street
Frenchtown, NJ 08825
Phone: 800-732-4791   Fax: 908-996-7642

DELLA FEMINA
Restaurants
Caricatures of celebrity patrons like Billy Joel, Martha Stewart and Christie Brinkley line the walls of ad man Jerry Della Femina's East Hampton mainstay, where seeing and being seen are an integral part of the package. Executive Chef Kevin Penner's contemporary American cuisine includes an excellent tartar of Hawaiian tuna appetizer, and halibut served with wild mushroom broth.

Della Femina
99 North Main Street
East Hampton, NY 11937
Phone: 516-329-6666

DELMONICO
Restaurants
Under the new direction of Emeril Lagasse, Delmonico has become a tribute to classic Creole cuisine. Tableside service and preparation are reminiscent of a bygone era; *Trout Meunière* and *Chicken Clemenceau* are classics dating back to the restaurant's 1895 opening. Designed by Holden & Dupuy, the restaurant has an elegant, understated charm in keeping with the historic nature of the building which it occupies.

Delmonico
1300 St. Charles Avenue
New Orleans, LA 70130
Phone: 504-525-4937   Fax: 504-525-0506

DEMPSEY & CARROLL
Specialty Shops
In a world overwrought with e-mail and cellphones, Dempsey & Carroll are a welcome reminder of a more refined method of communication. For over 100 years, the firm has been supplying stationery and writing tools to presidents, royalty and dignitaries from all over the world. Be it a business note, a quick thank-you or a romantic poem, the firm's engraved cotton paper turns the job of writing into a fanciful art form.

Dempsey & Carroll
110 East 57 Street
New York, NY 10022
Phone: 212-486-7526   Fax: 212-486-7523

DEPARTURES
Media
Under the brilliant editorship of Gary Walther, *Departures* has become arguably the best travel magazine in the United States. Unlike many of its competitors, one gets the distinct impression that the editors have actually grasped the essence of the places they feature, without kowtowing to special interests. Really well-researched information, incisive writing and superb photography; enough, in short, to make any sensible person sign up for an American Express Platinum Card.

Departures
American Express Publishing Company
1120 Avenue of the Americas
New York, NY 10036
Phone: 212-382-5600   Fax: 212-382-5878

DESIGN ASSOCIATES
Architects and Interior Designers
Design Associates has been providing comprehensive architectural services for construction, restoration, and renovation work throughout New England since 1979. The company's projects are conceived and designed in a restorative manner, using siting, massing, and period details to create buildings that are sympathetic to a site, its context, and its architectural style.

Design Associates
432 Columbia Street
Cambridge, MA 02141
Phone: 508-228-4342

DESPOS
Fashion   Best Kept Secret
Chris Despos offers 19 years of experience in family-run custom tailoring. Suiting, shirting and trousers are the specialties; all products are made in-house. The Chicago branch is housed in an architecturally classic structure with a sleek, contemporary interior.

Despos
34 East Oak Street, Suite 300
Chicago, IL 60611
Phone: 312-944-8833

DEVON YACHT CLUB
Private Clubs
The Devon Yacht Club was incorporated in 1916 and had its first season in 1917, with 46 members. Today, its 350 members keep approximately 30 yachts in the marina, and races are scheduled every Saturday. Besides yachting, the club offers tennis on eight clay courts, with instruction by pro Tim Snell. Lunch at the clubhouse is casual, but dinner requires a jacket and tie.

Devon Yacht Club
P.O. Box 2549
Amagansett, NY 11930
Phone: 516-267-6340

DIA CENTER FOR THE ARTS
Museums
This four-story warehouse is dedicated to the presentation and preservation of art in almost every medium. Among its permanent installations are Dan Graham's roof pavilion and Walter De Maria's *The Lightning Field* (1977), located in New Mexico—overnight visits can be scheduled. Largely responsible for launching the Chelsea art district, the Dia Center was also involved in the establishment of The Andy Warhol Museum in Pittsburgh and The Cy Twombly Gallery in Houston.

Dia Center for The Arts
548 West 22nd Street
New York, NY 10011
Phone: 212-989-5566

DIAMOND CREEK WINERY
Winemakers

Al Brounstein, owner of Diamond Creek, is a very colorful guy—an aviator, skier and marvelous storyteller; apparently he once smuggled first growth cuttings from Bordeaux through Mexico and into California. Al and winemaker Bill Steinschrieber only produce wines from their own grapes. Their Cabernets are a story in themselves, possibly the best in Napa—which is saying magnums—and they get better with age.

Diamond Creek Winery
1500 Diamond Mountain Road
Calistoga, CA 94515
Phone: 707-942-6926

DIDIER AARON
Antiques

Immerse yourself in a world of luxury as you meander through this town house gallery on the tony Upper East Side. 18th and 19th century European furniture and interior decorations are elegantly displayed on two floors, accented by 19th century drawings and paintings hanging on the walls.

Didier Aaron
32 East 67th Street
New York, NY 10021
Phone: 212-988-5248   Fax: 212-737-3513

DILLINGHAM & COMPANY
Antiques

This gallery in the Jackson Square antiques district carries an exquisite line of primarily English furniture from the 17th, 18th and early 19th centuries. Some European furniture is also represented. Pieces in the collection are vetted for quality and execution of design. The shop also carries a smattering of period paintings and objects, including pottery, porcelain, snuffboxes and curiosities of all sorts.

Dillingham & Company
700 Sansome Street
San Francisco, CA 94111
Phone: 415-989-8777

DHS DESIGNS
Specialty Shops

DHS Designs offers full-service interior design to a discerning clientele, from financial figures to sports personalities, who appreciate the art of incorporating fine antiques with comfortable furnishings. The company's signature look has been featured in *House Beautiful, Interior Design, Traditional Home* and *Veranda.* Owner/designer Darryl Savage scours the French countryside to bring back the best of these treasures.

DHS Designs has two unique shops in Maryland which offer a complete array of fine antique Continental furniture from the 18th and 19th centuries as well as decorative arts, and specialize in antique garden appointments and exquisitely carved French limestone mantelpieces, which range from ornately carved Renaissance pieces to the simple clean lines of the 18th-century Neoclassical style. These works of art come from the Loire Valley, and are the handiwork of artisans of the courts, who flourished from the 16th–18th centuries, and are for a select few who want to share a part of history and will not settle for reproductions. With their great style and beauty, these treasures will bring lasting satisfaction to any home.

DHS Designs
86 Maryland Avenue
Annapolis, MD 21401
Phone: 410-280-3466   Fax: 410-280-8729

DIMSON HOMMA
Specialty Shops

Unlike any other store in the world! That's what visitors say about this shop, where the eclectic mix of goods for sale can be grouped only under the category "Fabulous Things." Among the spectacular offerings: Chinese Ming Dynasty furniture, African sculptures, antique Turkish rugs, French porcelain, vintage crystal, George Jenson sterling silver, 1,200-year-old gold jewelry, and first-edition books. Oh, and those colorful live birds that look like they were painted by Mondrian are for sale, too! They are Lady Gouldian finches—Queen Victoria thought they were the most beautiful birds in the world.

Dimson Homma
20 East 67th Street
New York, NY 10021
Phone: 212-439-7950   Fax: 212-439-7960

DISTINCTIVE BOOKBINDING & STATIONERY

Specialty Shops   *Best Kept Secret*

Bringing the glamour of the fashion world to stationery is a tall order, but one that is met with ease by Distinctive Bookbinding and Stationery. Their fine bookbinding services, handmade stationery and distinctive desk sets borrow the best of Milanese and Florentine design and tradition, offering a refreshingly sophisticated take on the business of writing.

Distinctive Bookbinding & Stationery

1003 North Rush Street

Chicago, IL 60611

Phone: 312-867-7474   Fax: 312-867-7157

DIVA LIMOUSINES

Chauffeur Services

Established by one person with one car and a good driving record, Diva Limousines has multiplied its business exponentially in only a few years. Bijan Zoughi established Diva in 1986; his firm now has over 150 vehicles nationwide, exclusive accounts with Paramount and Fox and top-name clients like Condé Nast, where the caliber of your car is almost as important as the make of your shoes.

Diva Limousines

1670 North Sycamore Avenue

Los Angeles, CA 90028

Phone: 310-278-3482   Fax: 323-962-3803

DIXON AND DIXON OF ROYAL

Antiques   *Rising Star*

The romantic opulence of the French Quarter and the never-ending charm of the South go hand in hand with Dixon and Dixon of Royal. The company's lifetime guarantee of an annual five percent appreciation in value takes southern hospitality to a new level. Specializing in 18th and 19th century furnishings, the Dixon family entered the world of antiques after traveling extensively throughout Europe and America. This worldly influence is apparent throughout some 20,000 square feet of gallery space.

Dixon and Dixon of Royal

237 Royal Street

New Orleans, LA 70130

Phone: 504-524-0282   Fax: 504-524-7378

DOMINUS ESTATES

Winemakers

This is the brand produced by the wine marriage of the family of John Daniel, Jr. and Christian Moueix, who owns Chateau Pétrus in Bordeaux. Red wines dominate with Cabernet Sauvignon and Merlot prominent; unlike most California wineries, you will not find Chardonnay here. The wines are powerful, intense, tannic and designed for the long haul.

The key is to wait until the winemaker wants you to drink it, not before. The Pétrus connection lends particular appeal for Europeans.

Dominus Estates

2570 Napnook Road

Yountville, CA 94599

Phone: 707-944-8954

DONALD YOUNG GALLERY

Art Dealers

Donald Young worked for 10 years in Paris before opening this large Chicago gallery, which represents artists like Richard Long and Rosemarie Trockel. Young has shown large-scale video installations by Bruce Nauman, Gary Hill and Bill Viola. His other areas of expertise include American minimal, formal and conceptual artists from the 1960s and 70s.

Donald Young Gallery

933 West Washington Boulevard

Chicago, IL 60607

Phone: 312-455-0100   Fax: 312-455-0101

DONNA KARAN

Fashion

A key player in the fashion world of the nineties, Donna Karan's acclaimed designs have redefined style for women and men across the United States. Since her first collection in 1983, Karan's empire has consistently expanded. Nowadays her name can be found on clothes, accessories, skin care products, hosiery and thousands of other staples. Along with her children and husband, sculptor Steve Weiss, Karan lives in Manhattan, where she has just opened a 17,000 square foot 'lifestyle emporium' on Madison Avenue at 60th Street. Ilse Crawford, the stylish Briton who founded *Elle Decoration,* commissioned the home furnishings for sale in the new store.

Donna Karan

550 Seventh Avenue

New York, NY 10018

Phone: 212-789-1500   Fax: 212-354-4005

DORAL GOLF RESORT & SPA

Golf Clubs

Accompanied by a four-star resort and the only five-diamond spa in the United States, the Doral has five championship courses, including the notorious Blue Monster, site of the Doral-Ryder Open. Signature holes on the Blue Monster include the par-three 9th and the par-four 18th. Billy Casper, Jack Nicklaus, Lee Trevino, Hubert Green, Raymond Floyd, Tom Kite, Ben Crenshaw, and Greg Norman have all tasted victory here. Master PGA professional Jim McLean runs the prestigious Doral Golf Learning Center.

Doral Golf Resort & Spa

4400 NW 87th Avenue

Miami, FL 33178

Phone: 305-592-2000

DORMEUIL PERSONAL TAILORING

Fashion

Founded in 1842, Ashley Dormeuil's family business has provided exclusive custom tailoring for more than 150 years. Clients have whirlwind lifestyles, so fittings are usually made at their convenience. Custom shirts, suits and English bench-made shoes by Edward Green hark back to the golden days of Savile Row.

Dormeuil Personal Tailoring

21 East 67th Street

New York, NY 10021

Phone: 212-396-4444   Fax: 212-396-0599

DOUBLES

Private Clubs

A not-so-secret door in the lobby of the Sherry Netherland hotel leads down to Wendy Carduner's cavernous private dining club, where junior members of New York society—and delirious wannabes—gather after work or shopping for dinner. If Doubles were in London it would probably be populated by a host of struggling novelists and resident alcoholics. But New York breeds a different clubber: investment bankers, short skirts and buckets of Coke (diet).

Doubles

783 Fifth Avenue

New York, NY 10021

Phone: 212-751-9595

JEFFREY DOVER, M.D.

Cosmetic Surgeons

A hodgepodge of plastic surgery treatments, you can get any image-improving technique here—from tattoo removal and vein work to full facial resurfacing, liposuction, and laser hair removal. Although the practice is essentially part of a major local hospital, its off-site venue makes patients feel like they're in a private practice.

Jeffrey Dover, M.D.

Cosmetic Surgery and Laser Center

25 Boylston Street, Suite 104

Chestnut Hill, MA 02467

Phone: 617-738-4222

DOWNTOWN

Specialty Shops

Downtown is a stylish haven for sybarites in search of mid-20th century furniture. Here you will find some of the finest pieces by Wormley, Knoll, Probber and Wegner. The firm regularly works with leading designers, collectors and architects throughout the United States and Europe. If vintage is not for you, see their line of original designs inspired by the classic modernists.

Downtown

719 North La Cienega Boulevard

Los Angeles, CA 90069

Phone: 310-652-7461   Fax: 310-652-4916

DUCKHORN VINEYARDS

Winemakers

If you like Merlot, Duckhorn is for you. It was not always that way, but starting with their 1978 vintage, the Merlots have been among the best in the state, almost up in First Growth territory. Duckhorn produces other wines (including an excellent Sauvignon Blanc), but most of their 30,000-bottle annual production is red.

Duckhorn Vineyards

1000 Lodi Lane
St. Helena, CA 94574
Phone: 707-963-7108

DUKE UNIVERSITY

Colleges

Known as the Harvard of the south, Duke University, located in Durham, North Carolina, is one of America's leading research universities; the medical center, for instance, has achieved international prominence for its cutting edge medical research. Founded in 1924 by James Duke, of the Duke tobacco dynasty, the school is deeply rooted in Southern tradition. Duke has nine colleges supporting over 6000 undergraduate students and 5400 professional students.

Duke University

Box 90586
Durham, NC 27708
Phone: 919-684-8111

DUNEMERE ASSOCIATES REAL ESTATE

Property Consultants

Searching for the perfect getaway in the Hamptons? Look to Dunemere Associates, recognized authorities in renting and selling luxury properties all over Long Island. The agency maintains a sales staff of 25 experienced, full-time brokers, dedicated to the luxury real estate business in one of the most competitive markets in the country today.

Dunemere Associates Real Estate

37 Newtown Lane
East Hampton, NY 11937
Phone: 516-324-6400   Fax: 516-324-6343

DUNTON HOT SPRINGS

Hotels   ***Best Kept Secret***

Dunton Hot Springs is a 19th century mining town, situated near Telluride, deep in the San Juan Mountains of Southern Colorado, offering the highest standards of mountain resort living. Dunton consists of 20 period guest cabins, a chapel, a library, and other historic buildings, which have been painstakingly restored. Other guest facilities, with views of El Diente peak, include a barn-style bath house, a 26-foot Indian teepee with the hot springs shooting into its own private wooden tub, and the Dunton Bar and Saloon, where Butch Cassidy and the Sundance Kid could have quenched their thirst. Dunton Hot Springs is the ultimate in a wilderness retreat—remote, but never boring, offering gourmet dining, riding, hiking, ice-climbing, snow shoeing, cross-country skiing, and heli-skiing in a joint venture with Helitrax of Telluride. Dunton is not open to the general public; instead, the resort specializes in customizing its services to select groups ranging from 8 to 24 guests. Highly recommended.

Dunton Hot Springs

P.O. Box 818
Dolores, CO 81323
Phone: 970-882-4800   Fax: 970-882-7474

E

EAST BANK CLUB
Fitness

It's difficult to find a single amenity that this club doesn't have: there are outdoor and indoor pools, two tracks, nine indoor tennis courts, two basketball courts (which can also be used for volleyball), an indoor driving range, a unisex hair salon, a tanning booth, two restaurants, a sundeck, cardio and nautilus rooms, children's activities, parking and—if none of that takes your fancy— 155 aerobics classes to whip you into shape. Oprah Winfrey is a member.

East Bank Club
500 North Kingsbury
Chicago, IL 60610
Phone: 312-527-5800

EAST HAMPTON GYM
Fitness

Unfortunately, watching the waves is not really a sufficient workout during your summer weekends at the beach. Instead, sign up for a three month membership at the no-nonsense East Hampton Gym, where Cybex equipment, cardio machines with a cardio theater and an Olympic weight room will keep you in shape. Look out for Cindy Crawford and Martha Stewart, whose daughter, Alexis, owns the gym.

East Hampton Gym
P.O. Box 234
2 Fithian Lane
East Hampton, NY 11937
Phone: 516-324-4499

EAST & ORIENT COMPANY
Specialty Shops

Antiques from the 17th, 18th and 19th centuries adorn this enormous 18,000-square-foot store. Although in the past most of the pieces came from Asia, today the mainly English, Italian, and French items originate in Europe and are shipped to Dallas. The salons where the antiques are displayed are elegant and sophisticated, with an appropriate air of grandeur. The store also boasts a lecture hall for talks on specialties such as porcelain or silver. Actress Connie Stevens has bought furniture here.

East & Orient Company
1123 Slocum Street
Dallas, TX 75207
Phone: 214-741-1191   Fax: 214-741-2192

EDENHURST GALLERY
Art Dealers

Edenhurst is a reputable source for important paintings by the Early California impressionists, and for fine American and European modern art. The gallery routinely displays work by notables like Payne, Rose, Wendt and Redmond, as well as American and European artists from 1850-1950. Edenhurst is within a few blocks of the Pacific Design Center and the antiques and design quarters of West Hollywood and Beverly Hills.

Edenhurst Gallery
8920 Melrose Avenue
Los Angeles, CA 90069
Phone: 310-247-8151   Fax: 310-247-8167

EDWARD CARTER GALLERY
Art Dealers

After spending many years collecting the photographs of Ansel Adams and other favorite artists, Edward Carter founded his Gallery in 1991 for private collectors in Europe and the United States. It was opened to the public for the first time in 1997. Carter now has the world's largest available collection of Adams' work.

Edward Carter Gallery
560 Broadway, 4th Floor
New York, NY 10012
Phone: 212-966-1933   Fax: 212-966-2145

EDWARD LEE CAVE
Property Consultants

Edward Lee Cave was a senior vice president at Sotheby's before he founded this upmarket real estate brokerage. The company's average sale price is $2.2 million but large, unusual homes command up to $15 million. The apartments and single-family homes which Cave handles typically come with staff quarters, libraries, ballrooms, gymnasiums and

other old-world *accoutrements*. He also negotiates the sale of international properties, including Hever Castle for the Astor family and the Chateau de Menars for the St. Gobain Corporation. Cave's ability to find the right luxury properties for clients is well known. A client once wanted a dry place to walk her dog on rainy days—Cave found her a Manhattan apartment with a covered terrace.

Edward Lee Cave
790 Madison Avenue, Suite 405
New York, NY 10021
Phone: 212-772-8510

ELEVEN MADISON PARK
Restaurants   Rising Star

Kerry Heffernan of Bouley and Mondrian fame prepares seasonal New York cuisine with a French accent in Danny Meyer's new restaurant on Madison Square Park. With its elegant art deco interior and sublime service, Eleven Madison Park provides further evidence that Meyer—who owns Gramercy Tavern and Union Square Café—knows a thing or two about pleasing the public.

Eleven Madison Park
11 Madison Avenue
New York, NY 10010
Phone: 212-889-0905

ELINOR GORDON
Antiques

Elinor Gordon and her late husband, Horace, began their personal collection of Chinese porcelain in the 1940s, and Mrs. Gordon became a dealer in the field soon thereafter. A prolific author and frequent consultant to such institutions as the State Department's Fine Arts Committee, the White House and the Blair House, Gordon is recognized as one of the leading experts on Chinese porcelain in America today.

Elinor Gordon
22 Wistar Road
Villanova, PA 19085
Phone: 610-525-0981   Fax: 610-525-1451

ELIZABETH ARDEN RED DOOR SALON & SPA

Spas and Clinics

Unwind in style at this impressive spa. Options include manicures and pedicures, salt glow treatments and Swedish massages. For a special treat, try the Reiki, the Craniosacral, or the Desert Stone. For perfect skin, make an appointment for a special Skin Illuminating Anti-Oxidant Treatment or the Millennium Moisture Renewal. Expert localized treatments can help to cure tough problem areas, like stretch marks and varicose veins.

Elizabeth Arden Red Door Salon & Spa

3822 East University Drive

Phoenix, AZ 85034

Phone: 602-864-8191 or 800-592-7336

Fax: 602-437-4220

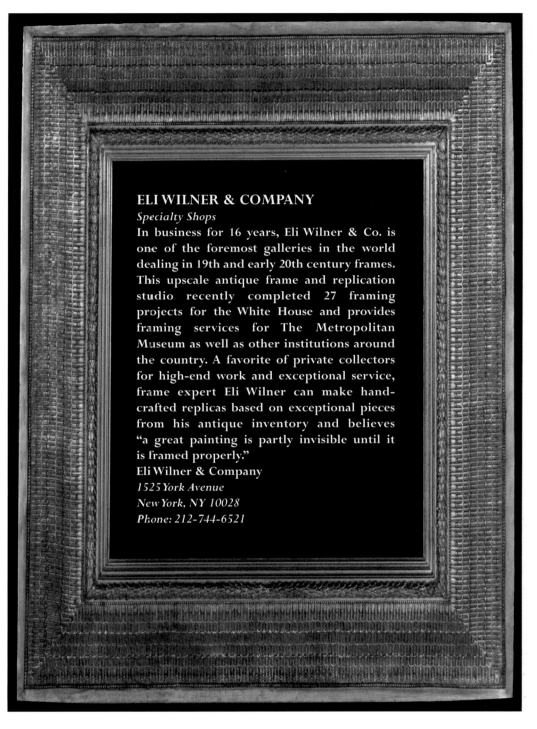

ELI WILNER & COMPANY

Specialty Shops

In business for 16 years, Eli Wilner & Co. is one of the foremost galleries in the world dealing in 19th and early 20th century frames. This upscale antique frame and replication studio recently completed 27 framing projects for the White House and provides framing services for The Metropolitan Museum as well as other institutions around the country. A favorite of private collectors for high-end work and exceptional service, frame expert Eli Wilner can make hand-crafted replicas based on exceptional pieces from his antique inventory and believes "a great painting is partly invisible until it is framed properly."

Eli Wilner & Company

1525 York Avenue

New York, NY 10028

Phone: 212-744-6521

ERIC JAVITS

Fashion

Although he is still a young man, this debonair milliner has been adorning the heads of ladies who lunch for many years. Inspired by both his love of art and his indomitable grandmother Lily, Javits' creations have given elegant women a reason to cherish hats again. His *chapeaux* have many celebrated admirers—including Hillary Rodham Clinton, Blaine Trump and Elizabeth Taylor. America's answer to the brilliant Philip Treacy.

Eric Javits

406 West 31st Street

New York, NY 10001

Phone: 212-967-8410   Fax: 212-967-8571

L'ERMITAGE BEVERLY HILLS

Hotels

L'Ermitage has finally reopened after four-and-a-half years of extensive renovations. If you shun pampering, stay elsewhere: each guest is assigned a personal valet before arriving, employees never use the same routes as guests and your room is a nest of tranquility. The décor is sleekly modern and understated to a fault; the best rooms, to the rear of the upper floor, offer breathtaking views of the Santa Monica mountains.

L'Ermitage Beverly Hills

9291 Burton Way

Beverly Hills, CA 90210

Phone: 310-278-3344   Fax: 310-278-8247

L'ESPALIER

Restaurants

Among the quaint brick townhouses that comprise the Back Bay is L'Espalier on Gloucester Street, where Frank McClelland's savory specialties include a grilled juniper spiced elk tenderloin with Canadian wild rice and tri-colored orzo. This elegant restaurant, which opened in 1978, played a formative role in the introduction of haute cuisine to Boston. It is a favorite of Beantown's old-money set.

L'Espalier

30 Gloucester Street

Boston, MA 02115

Phone: 617-262-3023   Fax: 617-375-9297

EUPHEMIA HAYE
Restaurants
Chefs Raymond and D'Arcy Arpke have won countless accolades and their beautifully named restaurant, Euphemia Haye, has long been a favorite of winter visitors and cruising celebrities, playing host to Robert DeNiro, Mel Brooks and Anne Bancroft, as well as the late Audrey Hepburn and writer Stephen King. Sit downstairs to enjoy the Gulf view, and don't miss the signature roast duckling with blackberry sauce.
Euphemia Haye Restaurant
5540 Gulf of Mexico Drive
Longboat Key, FL 34228
Phone: 941-383-3633

ESTATE ANTIQUES
Antiques
Southern antiques are the specialty at Jim and Harriet Pratt's showroom. Located in Charleston's antiques quarter, it features pre-1820 American furniture, with an emphasis on southern decorative arts. Each piece is meticulously scrutinized to meet strict criteria before being put up for sale. That goes not only for the furniture, but also for the shop's paintings, maps, prints, porcelain and brass.
Estate Antiques
155 King Street
Charleston, SC 29401
Phone: 843-723-2362   Fax: 843-723-2363

EVELYN POOLE
Antiques
Want to make a statement with a piece of furniture? Evelyn Poole's 5,000-foot showroom deals in fine 17th, 18th and 19th century furniture, works of art, silver, porcelain and other decorative accessories. Most of the pieces are of French and Italian origin, but the collection also includes English and Russian works. If you share Ms. Poole's passion for all things Napoleonic, you will particularly enjoy this shop.
Evelyn Poole
3925 North Miami Avenue
Miami, FL 33127
Phone: 305-573-7463   Fax: 305-573-7409

EVENTQUEST
Party Organizers and Caterers
In the increasingly competitive world of upscale event management, Mark Veeder and John Schwartz are self-styled "visionaries." Their attention to detail is the secret behind successful events for corporate clients like Disney, Microsoft and Mercedes Benz, as well as a host of leading figures in New York society. Warm ambience, impressive lighting, exotic imagery and unusual locations are EventQuest hallmarks.
EventQuest
568 Broadway, #507
New York, NY 10012
Phone: 212-966-3146   Fax: 212-966-3295

EVEREST
Restaurants
Everest is perched on the 40th floor of a Chicago skyscraper, with breathtaking views in every direction. Elegantly decorated, the restaurant features the "personalized" service of owner Jean Joho, who seems to be on hand to greet diners every day. A filet of beef poached with *foie gras* is superb, and the wine cellar is famous for its Alsatian vintages.
Everest
One Financial Place
440 South LaSalle Street
Chicago, IL 60605
Phone: 312-663-8920   Fax: 312-663-8802

EVERGLADES CLUB
Private Clubs
Architect Addison Mizner opened this club in 1919; the clubhouse that he designed still stands today. The Everglades Club offers golf, tennis and dining. Admittance is reserved strictly to the approximately 1100 members and their guests. The club hosts black tie parties every Saturday night during February and March. The waiting list for membership is at least five years.
Everglades Club
356 Worth Avenue
Palm Beach, FL 33480
Phone: 561-820-2620

FAO SCHWARZ
Specialty Shops
The moment a toy soldier opens the door, FAO Schwarz reveals itself as a place where more is *definitely* more and no one leaves empty handed. Kids of all ages love this epic homage to the serious business of having fun. Who can blame them? For eleven months of the year it offers clean, cheerful, candy filled respite from the harshness of midtown Manhattan. December, however, is quite a different story.
FAO Schwarz
767 Fifth Avenue
New York, NY 10153
Phone: 212-644-9400

FAR NIENTE VINEYARDS
Winemakers
Far Niente ("Without Care" in Italian) winery goes back to 1885, but nothing much happened until it was bought by race-car enthusiast Gil Nickel in 1978. Nowadays the vineyard's Chardonnay, Cabernet, Semillon and Dolce have become so popular that they are strictly allocated. Nickel certainly helped with the growth of the Napa Valley. Ashley Heisey is now Far Niente's official winemaker.
Far Niente Vineyards
PO Box 327
Oakville, CA 94562
Phone: 707-944-2861   Fax: 707-944-2312

LEWIS FEDER, M.D.

Cosmetic Surgeons

Lewis M. Feder, M.D. is a prominent New York City dermatologist and cosmetic plastic surgeon whose pioneering techniques have received considerable acclaim. His specialties include facial and body rejuvenation, facial resurfacing and total body liposculpture. As a full-service cosmetic plastic surgeon in practice for over 20 years, Dr. Feder performs corrective procedures for all beauty, aesthetic and cosmetic surgical problems in his Fifth Avenue offices and on-premise operating facility. Dr. Feder manufactures treatment products for therapy, prevention and maintenance, and has published a book, *About Face*, on cosmetic surgery, beauty and skincare. He is also the host of a television show, *Here's Looking at You!* which discusses cosmetic surgery, beauty and lifestyle.

Lewis Feder, M.D.

965 Fifth Avenue
New York, NY 10021
Phone: 212-535-8700

FENTON & LANG

Property Consultants   **Best Kept Secret**

Fenton & Lang specializes in luxurious seasonal homes on Jupiter Island, which enjoyed a certain notoriety last year when *Worth* magazine reported that it had the highest median property prices in the country. President Graeme Lang, a modest, low profile figure, has seen the price of top homes rise from $300,000 25 years ago to $15 million today. His 12 realtors treat their clients with great sensitivity and considerable charm.

Fenton & Lang

Beach & Bridge Roads
Jupiter Island
Hobe Sound, FL 33455
Phone: 800-587-4753   Fax: 561-546-2381

FELIDIA RISTORANTE

Restaurants

Lidia Mattichio Bastianich opened Felidia in 1981 in a converted old brownstone. This cozy restaurant is dotted with wine bins and shelves of crystal, elegant mahogany wood-paneled walls, rough white plaster walls trimmed with brick, and terracotta floors. Sicilian-born Executive Chef, Fortunato Nicotra, creates Felidia's signature dishes which include octopus, potato and red onion salad, homemade stuffed pastas, and special tasting menus centered around seasonal produce. During the fall, these include mushroom and game menus, and for winter, Fortunato creates a tasting menu highlighting white truffles. Felidia was named one of the Top Ten Italian Restaurants in the U.S. by *Wine Spectator*, among many other honors. Lidia's other restaurants include Frico Bar and Becco, both in New York, and Lidia's in Kansas City.

Felidia Ristorante

243 East 58th Street
New York, NY 10022
Phone: 212-758-1479

FERRARI CARANO WINERIES

Winemakers

Certainly one of the standout vineyards of Sonoma. Ferrari Carano is out to make the best wine possible: the Chardonnay and Fumé Blanc are outstanding. It is hypothesized that the owners parlayed their winnings at the casinos of Reno into choice vineyard land in California, which with a little luck and an imaginative host yielded a selection of very fine wines indeed.

Ferrari Carano Wineries

8761 Dry Creek Road
Healdsburg, CA 95448
Phone: 707-433-6700   Fax: 707-431-1742

FERRÉE FLORSHEIM CATERING

Party Organizers and Caterers

Partners Susan Florsheim and Anne Ferrée are renowned for their innovative catering of events, from intimate dinners and corporate shindigs to high-profile celebrity weddings. Providing whimsical dishes like mashed potatoes topped with caviar in martini glasses, they have garnered an enviable reputation as *the* caterers to Chicago's smart set.

Ferrée Florsheim Catering

5080 North Kimberly
Chicago, IL 60630
Phone: 773-282-6100

15 DEGREES

Restaurants   *Rising Star*

Boulder, Colorado, is better known for its outdoor sports than its dining, but 15 degrees offers a "new school" of fine dining. The menu features classic comfort food with lots of eclectic, ethnic accents. Executive Chef James Mazzio is justly renowned for his innovative blend of classic French, robust Italian, and flamboyant American cuisine.

15 degrees

1965 15th Street
Boulder, CO 80302
Phone: 303-442-4222   Fax: 303-444-1812

FIELD MUSEUM OF NATURAL HISTORY

Museums

Chicago's Field Museum of Natural History was founded to house the biological and anthropological collections assembled for the world's Colombian exposition of 1893. The objects in the original collection form the core of the more than 20 million specimens in the permanent collection. The Field Museum is home to "Sue," the largest and most complete Tyrannosaurus rex in the world. It also has an active staff of scientists who conduct research in evolutionary biology, anthropology and paleontology in conjunction with local universities.

Field Museum of Natural History

1400 South Lakeshore Drive
Chicago, IL 60605
Phone: 312-922-9410

FIORIDELLA

Florists

For twenty years, immaculate presentation (most recently, flowers blossoming from thick, straight-cut glass cylinders or orchids neatly wrapped in burlap) has been the big draw at this chic floral designer. Stunning window displays draw admirers in to peruse the handmade, cement tables bearing exotic delights like Ecuadorian roses, French tulips, tobacco boxes from India and Moroccan screens.

Fioridella

1920 Polk Street
San Francisco, CA 94109
Phone: 415-775-4065   Fax: 415-775-6396

FELISSIMO

Specialty Shops

Felissimo New York strives to be more than a store. Since its inception, the Felissimo message and mission have been the pursuit of a better world for all people through innovative and socially-minded business ventures. The name itself, a fusion of Latin terms meaning "ultimate happiness," is synonymous with its corporate vision: Felissimo was conceived as an urban oasis, a life-enhancing space designed in accord with Feng Shui principles and constructed in materials compatible with nature. Its collection of innovative products and designs was created with a global sensibility meant to complement and inspire a holistic and harmonious lifestyle.

The Felissimo Group have re-opened their New York store after re-imagining and re-inventing its space, using designer Clodagh's celebrated style: a blend of minimalism and Feng Shui done in earth-friendly materials of maximum luxe, minimum waste. Start at *threshold,* the luminous mirrored foyer, strewn with a changing sample of Felissimo's best items, then flow up to *ch'i* and choose a talisman from the Feng Shui collection. *Dreamgrounds,* with its fountain sounds mixed with floral smells, will reveal a melange of everything for the dreamer: candles, journals, writing and gardening tools. For the perfect accessory or gift, visit *idiosyncrasies.* At *r.e.m.,* you'll find home and personal care products. From *pedigree,* you can take home a book on Feng Shui for Cats, or other non-essentials for your pet. And don't leave without sampling a cup of Felissimo's renowned Haiku tea in *the tearoom.* Get a glimpse of the experience at *www.felissimo.com.*

Felissimo

10 West 56th Street
New York, NY 10019
Phone: 212-956-4438 or 800-565-6785
Fax: 212-956-0081

FINE ARTS MUSEUM OF SAN FRANCISCO

Museums

The Fine Arts Museum of San Francisco was created in 1970 from the merging of two well-known collections, the M. H. De Young Memorial Museum and The California Palace of the Legion of Honor. The De Young Museum houses primarily American art from all periods, while the Legion of Honor's collection–a gift to the city from Alma de Bretteville Spreckels–displays a huge selection of early 20th century art, including over 80 sculptures by Auguste Rodin.

Fine Arts Museum of San Francisco

233 Post Street
San Francisco, CA 94108
Phone: 415-863-3330

FIRESTONE AND PARSON

Antiques

Edwin Firestone, who founded this store with the late Kenneth Parson in 1946, claims that Firestone and Parson has sold more silver by Paul Revere than all other antique dealers and auction houses in the United States combined. Besides Revere's silver, the store's main business is antique and period jewelry, ranging mostly from the 19th century to the art deco and art nouveau periods. Firestone and Parson exhibits at only one show: The International Art and Antique Dealers Show, held at the Seventh Regiment Armory in New York every October.

Firestone and Parson

8 Newbury Street
Boston, MA 02116
Phone: 617-266-1858   Fax: 617-266-0117

FIRST UNION NATIONAL BANK

Wealth Management

"More than just a bank," First Union also offers investment banking and asset management services such as trust and estate planning, tax advantage strategies and business valuations. The Private Client Group is designed to serve the investment and financial planning needs of individuals with $1 million or more in investable assets. A relationship manager operates as an individual liaison between First Union and these "very special" clients.

First Union National Bank

First Union Corporation
301 South College Street
Charlotte, NC 28288
Phone: 704-374-6161   Fax: 704-383-0699

FISH & NEAVE

Law Firms

Ideas are the business of this law firm, which prides itself on representing leaders in technological innovation. With offices in New York and California, Fish & Neave's practice focuses on patent, trademark, copyright and intellectual property law. Founded in Boston in 1878, the firm has been a leader in its field ever since, representing such pioneers as the Wright Brothers, Thomas Edison and Alexander Graham Bell. Fish & Neave lawyers represented Polaroid in its suit against Kodak involving patents on instant photography, arguing successfully for an injunction that shut down Kodak's instant photography business and obtained for Polaroid a judgment of nearly $1 billion, the largest amount ever awarded for patent infringement.

Fish & Neave

1251 Avenue of the Americas
New York, NY 10020
Phone: 212-596-9000

FISHER TRAVEL

Travel Consultants   *Best Kept Secret*

Bill Fisher used to book Club Med vacations for a living. But this Brooklyn-born travel consultant has now carved a lucrative niche for himself as travel agent to the stars. Tom Cruise, Diane Sawyer and Calvin Klein are among the oh-so chic 500 who can claim that "Bill does my booking." To utter those words with any conviction you will need to stump up $10,000.

Fisher Travel

200 East 42nd Street, Suite 1411
New York, NY 10017
Phone: 212-867-4040

FISHER ISLAND SPA

Spas and Clinics

Discerning residents and smart visitors enjoy a seemingly endless list of options at Fisher Island. The resort, set around the Vanderbilt family's winter escape, houses a deluxe inn, five restaurants, a nine-hole golf course, 18 tennis courts, and a highly regarded spa. Fisher Island Spa, which stretches across 22,000 square feet, boasts exceptional treatments and a topnotch beauty salon.

Fisher Island Spa

1 Fisher Island Drive
Fisher Island, FL 33109
Phone: 305-535-6000   Fax: 305-535-6036

FISHERS ISLAND COUNTRY CLUB

Golf Clubs   *Best Kept Secret*

This summer-home community on the Long Island Sound includes a 1920 vintage Seth Raynor golf course which encompasses the east end of the island. Dramatic elevation changes afford views of the Long Island and Connecticut shorelines, while water is in play on eight holes. Fishers Island is the only course rated among America's 100 Greatest which has asked to be excluded from the list. Not for the rabbit or the socially insecure.

Fishers Island Country Club

Fishers Island, NY 06390
Phone: 516-788-7221

FLEET BANK

Wealth Management

Individualized portfolio and investment advice and a high staff-to-client ratio are the big draws here, earning Fleet considerable kudos within the industry. Each new Fleet Bank client is assigned a personal relationship manager and an investment officer. Integrated solutions and a full range of services are also key features.

Fleet Bank

One Federal Street
Boston, MA 02110
Phone: 617-346-4537

FLEUR DE LYS
Restaurants

Fleur de Lys was originally opened in 1958; Hubert Keller and Maurice Rouas have owned the restaurant since 1970. Keller's traditional French cuisine includes superb signature dishes like a corn pancake appetizer, stuffed with fresh salmon and topped with caviar, and squab in a port wine sauce. Mayor Willie Brown and Senator Diane Feinstein are regulars. Warmly recommended.

Fleur de Lys
777 Sutter Street
San Francisco, CA 94109
Phone: 415-673-7779

FLEXJET
Airplanes

The horses you ride on the polo grounds may be your own, but more often than not you won't be the one cleaning the stables or changing the shoes. This is the principle behind FlexJet's fractional aircraft ownership, which lets you enjoy all the advantages of owning a private jet without the common hassles of operating one. In fact, the only difficulty you will face is choosing one of Bombardier's impeccable aircraft—a Challenger, Global Express or LearJet. FlexJet provides you with the pilot and maintenance, and will even pick you up from the polo field

FlexJet
14651 Dallas Parkway, Suite 600
Dallas, TX 75240
Phone: 972-720-2536   Fax: 972-720-2435

FLIGHT OPTIONS
Airplanes

Flight Options, a new kid on the block in the fractional ownership program, operates fifty jets from its operations center in Ohio. Available aircraft include Citation 2, Beechjet 400a, Hawker 800—and the top-of-the-line jet, the Challenger 601, which brings European and Caribbean destinations within easy reach of New York or Chicago. Planes are interchangeable and guaranteed anywhere in the U.S. within four to eight hours, depending on the percentage owned. Limousine transportation is provided with all flights. Flight options also guarantee immediate liquidity on ownership shares if a quick sale becomes necessary.

Flight Options
Corporate Wings
26180 Curtiss Wright Parkway
Richmond Heights, OH 44143
Phone: 216-261-3500

FLORAL EVENTS UNLIMITED
Florists

Planning a gala or wedding in Washington, D.C.? If you have a large budget then you might as well use the floral designer who dressed both of Clinton's last inaugural balls. Often cited as one of the most successful florists in the area, Angelo Bonita's company receives frequent accolades from wedding and party planners. Senator and Mrs. Jay Rockefeller are regular customers.

Floral Events Unlimited
2700 Garfield Avenue
Silver Spring, MD 20910
Phone: 301-585-2772

FLOWERS
Winemakers   Rising Star

Walt and Joan Flowers, former nursery owners, recognized the potential of Camp Meeting Ridge, less than two miles from the Pacific and at an elevation of 1300 feet, for growing Pinot Noir and Chardonnay. Their 1996 Camp Meeting Ridge Pinot Noir was served at the White House for the 50th Anniversary of NATO, reputedly causing a few explosions among the French contingent.

Flowers
28500 Seaview Road
Cazadero, CA 95421
Phone: 707-847-3661

THE FORD MONTREUX DETROIT JAZZ FESTIVAL
Events

The Ford Montreux Detroit Jazz Festival is the largest festival of its kind in North America, where legends Miles Davis, Sonny Rollins, Betty Carter and Carmen McRae have all performed. With more than 100 acts performing every Labor Day weekend, the festival attracts hundreds of thousands of music fans. The festival draws a smart set (as well, of course, as some not-so-smart people!) who like to groove to musicians like Dave Brubeck, Joe Henderson and Kenny Burrell.

The Ford Montreux Detroit Jazz Festival
The Music Hall
350 Madison Avenue
Detroit, MI 48226
Phone: 313-886-9074

PETER B. FODOR, M.D.
Cosmetic Surgeons

Dr. Peter B. Fodor is a leader in the field of Aesthetic Plastic Surgery and is highly respected by the profession as a teacher, surgeon and author. His residency training at Columbia University in New York was followed by his obtaining board certification in general surgery as well as plastic surgery. All of the surgeries are performed exclusively by Dr. Fodor, who prefers the safe setting of a hospital. Despite professional accolades and awards for his leadership in the field of Aesthetic Plastic Surgery, Dr. Fodor receives greatest satisfaction from the effect his work has on his patients and on their lives.

Peter B. Fodor, M.D.
2080 Century Park East, #710
Los Angeles, CA 90067
Phone: 310-203-9533
Fax: 310-203-9798

FORTUNE
Media

Fortune offers indispensable advice on stocks you can love forever, top mutual funds that have staying power, and tips from the millionaire next door. The bimonthly magazine presents potential formulas for improving business and personal managing skills while reporting on investment trends and analyzing developments in business. Strong profiles and good investigative business stories keep executives reading. The *Fortune 500* has become synonymous with major American corporations.

Fortune
Time & Life Building
Rockefeller Center
New York, NY 10020-1393
Phone: 212-522-7636   Fax: 212-765-2699

FORTUNOFF

Jewelry and Watches

The 77-year-old Fortunoff has grown from a neighborhood housewares store in Brooklyn to a ritzy department store on Manhattan's Fifth Avenue, housing impressive antique and estate silver. Specialists at the store find unique jewelry, magnificent tea sets, estate flatware, and sterling silver home accessories that make lifelong treasures.

Fortunoff

681 Fifth Avenue
New York, NY 10022
Phone: 212-758-6660

FOUNTAIN PEN HOSPITAL

Specialty Shops

This high-tech store has stocked the largest selection of new and vintage pens in the world for the past 54 years. The 5000 or so pens include limited edition models—particularly pleasing to devout collectors—spread over 2500 square feet. Owner Terry Wiederlight counts actor Bill Cosby as a friend and one of Fountain Pen Hospital's best customers; Cosby even appears in the store's catalog.

Fountain Pen Hospital

10 Warren Street
New York, NY 10007
Phone: 800-253-7367   Fax: 212-227-5916

FOUR SEASONS BOSTON

Hotels

Since opening in 1985, the Boston Four Seasons has consistently been ranked one of the top hotels in the world. Even at its young age, the hotel looks and feels as if it has always been part of Beantown. Blending the history and spirit of the city, the hotel's public spaces and 288 guest rooms and suites reflect the style of a traditional Beacon Hill home. The hotel is centrally located, just minutes from the city's renovated Theater District, where you can enjoy plays, symphonies, and the Boston Ballet.

Four Seasons Boston

200 Boylston Street
Boston, MA 02116
Phone: 617-338-4400   Fax: 617-423-0154

FOUR SEASONS LAS VEGAS

Hotels   Rising Star

Far from the madding crowds, the rattling of machines and the revelry of boisterous gamblers, the Four Seasons Las Vegas is an oasis of serenity and understatement in a city not renowned for either. Upon entering the cool, marble-decked lobby with huge vases of fresh flowers, guests are struck by the hotel's tranquility. A grand staircase leads to the second and only other floor of the main hotel; guest rooms begin on the 35th floor of an adjoining tower, where floor-to-ceiling windows offer breathtaking views.

Four Seasons Las Vegas

3960 Las Vegas Boulevard South
Las Vegas, NV 89119
Phone: 702-632-5000

FOUR SEASONS NEW YORK

Hotels

Manhattan's Four Seasons Hotel is just what you'd expect: sleek, chic, and very sophisticated. This is the only hotel in the Western hemisphere designed by I. M. Pei, and it shows. Big and beautiful bedrooms have wide-ranging views of the Manhattan skyline. The marble bathrooms have fast flooding tubs—thirty-seconds and you're over the top. Spectacular public spaces give the impression of being in a mini-Grand Central Station, with all the grandeur that implies, but without the tour groups—unless you mean aging rock stars. Best of all: the legendary Four Seasons service. If you are hip, cool, demanding or discerning—a Gucci, Prada, Armani or Paul Smith aficionado—this place is for you. Warmly recommended.

Four Seasons New York

57 East 57th Street
New York, NY 10022
Phone: 212-758-5700
Fax: 212-758-5711

FOUR SEASONS PALM BEACH

Hotels

Palm Beach's Four Seasons is the highest-rated hotel in the state of Florida. In just nine years it has made its mark as the area's most elegant and sophisticated retreat. The entrance, flanked by palm trees and tropical flowers, is a prelude to the interior's understated elegance. Most of the lavishly appointed, spacious rooms and suites offer spectacular ocean views. And executive chef Hubert Des Marais is widely celebrated—sample his cuisine in three smart dining areas.

Four Seasons Palm Beach

2800 South Ocean Boulevard
Palm Beach, FL 33480
Phone: 561-582-2800

FOUR SEASONS RESTAURANT

Restaurants

Diane Sawyer, Barbara Walters and Henry Kissinger are among hundreds of high profile regulars at this New York landmark. Even the nonagenarian Philip Johnson, who designed the restaurant, has a corner table reserved for him every day. Signature dishes by Executive Chef Christian Albin include Crisp Farmhouse Duck and the Seared Abalone with Sea Beans, while the wine list includes arguably the country's largest selection of Brunello di Montelcino wines. If you want to impress someone bring them to the Four Seasons: the term "power lunch" was invented in reference to this extraordinary establishment.

Four Seasons Restaurant

99 East 52nd Street
New York, NY 10021
Phone: 212-754-9494   Fax: 212-754-1077

FOX RESIDENTIAL GROUP

Property Consultants

Fox Residential Group sells and leases upscale cooperative and condominium apartments and townhouses throughout New York. Barbara Fox's ten-year-old company has handled the sale of homes worth up to $20 million. Recent clients include Walter Cronkite and theater producer Harold Prince.

Fox Residential Group

1015 Madison Avenue
New York, NY 10021
Phone: 212-772-2666

FRAENKEL GALLERY

Art Dealers

For over 20 years Jeffrey Fraenkel has placed numerous photographs of the 19th and 20th century in prominent international museums, as well as private and corporate collections. Under director Frish Brandt, the gallery continues to offer the work of photographers like Paul Strand, Robert Mapplethorpe, Diane Arbus, Man Ray, and Irving Penn.

Fraenkel Gallery

49 Geary Street
San Francisco, CA 94108
Phone: 415-981-2661   Fax: 415-981-4014

FRAMED ON MADISON

Specialty Shops

There was a time when antique picture frames could be found discarded in the trash, but in the past decade, these treasures have started to fetch high prices. Framed on Madison has been acquiring frames at auction or from private collectors around the world since 1942. Owner Daniel Koren now offers an astonishing selection of really outstanding frames in many materials.

Framed on Madison

740 Madison Avenue
New York, NY 10021
Phone: 212-734-4680   Fax: 212-988-0128

FRANK & BARBARA POLLACK

Antiques

Naïve paintings are the specialty of Frank and Barbara Pollack, who also carry 18th and 19th century antiques and furniture. Most of the works originated in New England, with some from Pennsylvania. Paintings of people, scenes and still lifes are created in various media, including watercolor on paper, oil on canvas and oil on panel. Make an appointment to view the collection, which also boasts American textiles, pottery, toleware (decorated tin), folk art, carvings and first edition books.

Frank & Barbara Pollack

1214 Green Bay Road
Highland Park, IL 60035
Phone: 847-433-2213

FRANCISCAN ESTATES

Winemakers

Cuvée Sauvage, a big, oaky, rich Chardonnay, is what first earned a reputation for Franciscan Estates. The Quintessa, in a Meritage blend, is the one to look out for. Ralph Hersom, Wine Director at Le Cirque 2000, says "they set out to make one wine which stands comparison with their French cousins. They have succeeded." Limited quantities, lots of money invested in the property: truly an elite wine.

Franciscan Estates

1178 Galleron Lane
St. Helena, CA 94574
Phone: 707-963-7112

FRASER YACHTS

Yachting

A global yacht brokerage with six worldwide offices, Fraser Yachts specializes in the sale, purchase, charter, management and new construction of 100-foot and up mega-yachts. With headquarters in Fort Lauderdale and several other nationwide offices, including San Diego and Seattle, Fraser can handle any manner of marine needs. Clients range from captains of American industry to some of the world's most accomplished yachtsmen.

Fraser Yachts

2230 SE 17th Street
Fort Lauderdale, FL 33316
Phone: 954-463-0600   Fax: 954-763-1053

FRÉDÉRIC FEKKAI BEAUTÉ

Hair and Beauty

A perfect juxtaposition of the old and new, Frédéric Fekkai's parlor houses a sunny southern terrace potted with French cypress and evergreen. Inside, the gorgeous details—textured limestone floors, custom-made sinks cast in terra-cotta, walls sponged in warm ochre—create a serene ambiance that embodies all the warmth and beauty of Southern France, where Fekkai hails from. In addition to specialized hair care, facial, and body treatments, his store also offers an in-house café, an elegant boutique, and a top-floor sanctuary. Last year Fekkai launched a new accessories collection, which includes handbags and eyewear.

Frédéric Fekkai Beauté

15 East 57th Street
New York, NY 10022
Phone: 212-753-9500

FREEDMAN JEWELERS

Jewelry and Watches

Maurice Freedman, along with his father and his grandfather, have been designing important and exquisite pieces of jewelry from their store in Huntington since 1936, although the Freedmans have been involved in the jewelry business for over a century. The family specializes in using exotic diamonds and large colored stones to make special and original pieces, but they also sell designer pieces from the likes of Mikimoto and Tiffany.

Freedman Jewelers

345 New York Avenue
Huntington, NY 11743
Phone: 516-423-2000   Fax: 516-673-4466

FREER GALLERY OF ART

Museums

An Italian Renaissance-style building of granite and marble designed by Charles Platt, the Freer Gallery was the first museum of fine arts within the Smithsonian Institution when it opened in 1923. In conjunction with the Sackler Gallery, the Freer is home to the Smithsonian's collection of Asian art. The Freer also has a collection of 19th and early 20th century American art, featuring the largest selection of James McNeill Whistler's work in the world.

Freer Gallery of Art

12th Street & Jefferson Drive
Washington, DC 20560
Phone: 202-357-2700

THE FRENCH CULINARY INSTITUTE
Culinary Schools
The preeminent American training school for classic French cooking models its program on that of France's official training school. Instructors include local gastronomic legends like Alain Sailhac of Le Cirque, and former chef-owner of Lutèce, André Soltner. The Institute is open to amateurs for a 22-week Saturday program, *La Technique*.
The French Culinary Institute
462 Broadway
New York, NY 10013
Phone: 212-219-8890   Fax: 212-431-3054

THE FRENCH LAUNDRY
Restaurants
Celebrated chef-owner Thomas Keller has just released his first cookbook, which showcases his French-American cuisine. Truffles in season and a classic *pot au feu,* plus a selection of more than 300 French and Californian wines, help to make his award-winning restaurant a Napa Valley treasure—and a Mecca for wine lovers. If the weather is nice ask for a table in the garden of this rustic stone house.
The French Laundry
6640 Washington Street
Yountville, CA 94599
Phone: 707-944-2380   Fax: 707-944-1974

FRENCHWAY TRAVEL
Travel Consultants
In the busy exchange of fashionistas between New York, Paris and London, outfits like Madison Models and *Harper's Bazaar* use Frenchway to organize exotic excursions. The firm will also arrange adventure tours and honeymoons. Alec Baldwin, Kate Moss and Mira Sorvino have relied on Frenchway for personal vacations.
Frenchway Travel
11 West 25th Street
New York, NY 10010
Phone: 212-243-3500   Fax: 212-243-3535

FRICK COLLECTION
Museums
Housed in the Gilded Age mansion of the late Henry Clay Frick, this is one of the most important private collections of Western fine and decorative arts in the world. Paintings by El Greco, Rembrandt, Titian, Turner, Vermeer and Whistler mingle with fine French furniture and Chinese porcelain. Europeans love the Frick, which feels like a palazzo or a chateau and yet remains quintessentially American. Formal but intimate, grand but inviting.
Frick Collection
1 East 70th Street
New York, NY 10021
Phone: 212-288-0700   Fax: 212-628-4417

THE FRENCH ROOM
Restaurants
The Hotel Adolphus has long been recognized as one of the country's leading hotels and its restaurant, The French Room, is equally feted among people who love good food. Satisfied critics and customers— like Billy Joel, Oscar de la Renta, Gloria Vanderbilt and Julia Childs—refer to this French eatery as one of the best dining experiences in the United States.

Executive Chef William Koval's distinctive cuisine includes specialties like a fresh cremini and roasted Maine lobster risotto with a sorrel and chive oil, a sweet white miso marinated Alaskan halibut with baby shiitake spinach, and honey soy-seared duckling with garlic whipped potatoes, baby bok choy and a lemon grass demi.

When arriving at the French Room, patrons walk through The Adolphus' multi-million dollar art collection in the lobby and on into the dining area, with its hand-blown glass chandeliers from Murano, marble floors and murals of cherubs. Under the careful direction of Maitre d'Hotel Jim Donohue and his assistant Cesar De Los Reyes, customers are assured of a memorable experience. Warmly recommended.
The French Room
Hotel Adolphus
1321 Commerce Street
Dallas, TX 75202
Phone: 214-742-8200
Fax: 214-651-3588

G. RAY HAWKINS
Art Dealers

G. Ray Hawkins opened the first photography gallery in L.A. 25 years ago with shows of Man Ray, Edward Curtis and James Van Der Zee and has matured with the photography market into a celebrated dealer of both vintage and contemporary prints. He moved the gallery to Santa Monica in 1990 when he put together a show of Alexander Rodchenko years before the museums started to take an interest. He is often the first to show local photographers and bring international talent to Los Angeles and also finds time to raise money for AIDS research.

G. Ray Hawkins
908 Colorado Avenue
Santa Monica, CA 90401
Phone: 310-394-5558   Fax: 310-576-2468

GA GA GIFTS OF WHIMSY
Specialty Shops   ***Rising Star***

New mothers and babies often need a little pampering, and this enchanting store offers just that. Crammed with delightful items for mom and irresistible presents for baby, it attracts stylish shoppers like Jennifer Aniston, Tatum O'Neal and Tori Spelling, who come in search of feather slippers and tiny towels. Our favorite gift for weary moms? A five-step kit for rejuvenation and relaxation in a box.

ga ga gifts of whimsy
8362 West Third Street
Los Angeles, CA 90048
Phone: 323-653-3388

GAGOSIAN GALLERY
Art Dealers

Larry Gagosian opened a gallery in 1980 in Los Angeles and has built up an empire of three large gallery spaces that show mostly contemporary and Modern works. This world-class networker has the resources to attract and keep the best contemporary artists. His Beverly Hills gallery was designed by Richard Meier and has shown Warhol, Basquiat, Picasso and Cy Twombly amongst others since it opened in 1995. Gagosian's stable includes blue chip artists like Richard Serra and Francesco Clemente, as well as more controversial figures like Damien Hirst. As we went to press Gagosian announced plans to open a huge new gallery in Chelsea. So long, SoHo?

Gagosian Gallery
980 Madison Avenue
New York, NY 10021
Phone: 212-744-2313

GALERIE MICHAEL
Art Dealers

No great art collection is complete without at least one Rembrandt; Galerie Michael has the largest collection of etchings by the artist in the United States. Specialists in building and curating private collections for over twenty years, the Beverly Hills gallery has amassed art portfolios for some of the entertainment industry's most prominent players. A large Rembrandt retrospective is slated for the millennium.

Galerie Michael
430 North Rodeo Drive
Beverly Hills, CA 90210
Phone: 310-273-3377   Fax: 310-273-3452

GALILEO
Restaurants

Chef Todd Gray keeps the capital's elite clamoring for authentic northern Italian cuisine. Off the main dining room are two private cellars that are perfect for private gatherings, as well as a large terrace for dining outside in the summer. Try for the chef's table; it seats up to eight and is nestled in the corner of the kitchen. Galileo's owner, Roberto Donna, has successfully launched 11 other restaurants in the Washington area since Galileo's opening in 1984. But this is still his best.

Galileo
1110 21st Street, NW
Washington, DC 20036
Phone: 202-293-7191   Fax: 202-331-9364

GALLERY PAULE ANGLIM
Art Dealers

With a remarkable eye and a personality to match, Paule Anglim is one of the strongest women in the Bay Area art scene today. Born in Quebec, Anglim grew up longing to become an artist, taking classes and hoping to one day attend the Beaux Arts school. While the dream of art school didn't come true, she wound up art consulting and eventually opened her own gallery. Today, the gallery, one of the most successful and oldest in town, represents artists like William Tucker, Louise Fishman, Deborah Butterfield and Paul Kos.

Gallery Paule Anglim
14 Geary Street
San Francisco, CA 94108
Phone: 415-433-2710

GALPER/BALDON ASSOCIATES
Landscape Architects

Galper/Baldon Associates is a landscape architectural firm with offices on the boardwalk in Venice, California. In designing thousands of pools, the firm pioneered trends like raised pools, lap pools, infinity edges, natural settings and invented contour spa seating. Recent projects include a koi pond for Sharon Stone and a garden pavilion for Leonard Nimoy.

Galper/Baldon Associates
723 Oceanfront Walk
Venice, CA 90291
Phone: 310-392-3992   Fax: 310-392-9858

GAME CREEK CLUB
Private Clubs   ***Rising Star***

Envisioned many years ago by Vail founder Pete Seibert and inspired by similar private clubs in Europe, Game Creek Club opened its doors in 1996. Located on Vail Mountain, it has already become one of the more prestigious ski clubs in America. Members are invited annually to ski in Gstaad, scuba dive in Bora Bora or go helicopter skiing in Canada. Director Lita Hitchcock manages to make this private club feel just like home.

Game Creek Club
278 Hanson Ranch Road
Vail, CO 81657
Phone: 970-479-4280   Fax: 970-479-8010

GARDELLA'S ELITE LIMOUSINE SERVICE

Chauffeur Services

Established in 1984, Gardella's Elite Limousine Service discreetly serves celebrities and wealthy individuals who value their privacy. Operating principally in the New York tri-state area, the company's clients have included Shania Twain, Bruce Springsteen, Nile Rogers, and Paula Abdul.

Gardella's Elite Limousine Service

264 Main Avenue
Norwalk, CT 06851
Phone: 800-659-5466 or 203-846-6949
Fax: 203-840-6632

GARDEN GATE

Florists

In her capital guide to ordering flowers by phone, Barbera Brooks offers the following distinction between florists and floral designers: "an ability to arrange flowers in a way that celebrates flowers as opposed to shouting the human ego behind the scenes." Husband and wife co-owners Maria and Junior Villanueva belong firmly to the former camp. Their work on the annual Beaux Arts Ball, benefiting the Dallas Museum of Art, provides a good illustration of their talents.

Garden Gate

2615 Roth Street
Dallas, TX 75201
Phone: 214-220-1272

THE GARDENER

Specialty Shops

When it opened in 1984, The Gardener revived interest in gardening among many smart Californians. Alta Tingle's Berkeley store continues to sell an eclectic mixture of furniture, tools and every conceivable *accoutrement* for both budding and veteran green thumbs. Nowadays, there is also another branch of the operation in Healdsburg.

The Gardener

1836 Fourth Street
Berkeley, CA 94710
Phone: 510-548-4545

GARDNER COLBY GALLERY

Art Dealers

Nancy Winch opened her Martha's Vineyard gallery in 1988 after leaving the advertising rat race. A lifelong art lover (Winch was an art history major in college), her collection includes only living American artists and sculptors who are specialists in the fields of still life, portraiture and landscapes.

Gardner Colby Gallery

27 North Water Street
Edgartown, MA 02539
Phone: 508-627-6002 or 888-969-9500
Fax: 508-627-8296

GAZELLE BEAUTY CENTER AND DAY SPA

Hair and Beauty   *Rising Star*

Clients are invariably struck by the atmosphere of serenity and relaxation at Gazelle Beauty Center and Day Spa, on New York's Madison Avenue. Owner Patricia French originally launched this innovative business in 1986 at the Galeries Lafayette department store in Paris. Her credo is simple: to honor not only the physical body, but the mind and soul as well. Devotees include Whitney Houston and Elizabeth Diouf, the First Lady of Senegal. Gazelle also offers a wonderful skin care line, specifically created for women and men of color.

Gazelle Beauty Center and Day Spa

509 Madison Avenue
New York, NY 10022
Phone: 212-751-5144   Fax: 212-751-5145

GARY E. YOUNG

Antiques

Gary Young's business, which he took over from his father in the early 1970s, focuses on 18th century English and Irish furniture, known particularly for its fine patina and colors. In addition, Young sells portrait miniatures on ivory. Located on Maryland's Eastern Shore, Young has sold to most of the major museums over the years. In addition to a large private clientele, he works with a number of East Coast interior decorators.

Gary E. Young

128 South Commerce Street
Centreville, MD 21617
Phone: 410-758-2132   Fax: 410-758-8755

GEARYS OF BEVERLY HILLS

Specialty Shops

This specialty store has been running a bridal registry longer than anyone in Southern California. The salespeople are trained in giving one-on-one attention to customers, ensuring that every experience, from registering through returning gifts post-honeymoon, is nothing but a pleasure. The store is filled with luxurious fine linens, china, silver, jewelry, and glass.

Gearys of Beverly Hills

351 North Beverly Drive
Beverly Hills, CA 90210
Phone: 310-273-4741   Fax: 310-858-7555

GAVERT ATELIER

Hair and Beauty   *Rising Star*

Master colorist Stewart Gavert offers sleek weaves and baliage treatments (a highlighting technique) in this unusual Beverly Hills hair salon. Eyebrow shaping, eyelash tinting and makeup lessons are also available for dramatic details. Five stylists and colorists work under Gavert's direction; he also performs his magic at New York's Peter Coppola salon and teaches a class in Japan during bi-annual visits. Clients include Kurt Russell and Christina Applegate.

Gavert Atelier

9666 Brighton Way
Beverly Hills, CA 90210
Phone: 310-858-7898   Fax: 310-858-7216

GENE & GEORGETTI
Restaurants

The quintessential Chicago steak house has real old-fashioned character and considerable style, complete with guests clad in finest Armani. In business for almost 60 years, Gene & Georgetti is famous for its blood-rare strip steaks, Shrimp de Jonghe, the world's best martinis and a curious seating policy: if you arrive underdressed, be prepared for Siberia.

Gene & Georgetti
500 N. Franklin Street
Chicago, IL 60610
Phone: 312-527-3718   Fax: 312-527-2039

GENE JUAREZ SALON & SPA
Spas and Clinics

Gene Juarez Salon & Spa features three hydrotherapy rooms with 17 shower heads, European hydro-tubs, and three eucalyptus steam and Swiss shower rooms— enough to lure Gwyneth Paltrow, Josie Bisset and Bianca Jagger across the street from Seattle's Pacific Place. Salon employees make home visits, but enjoying the spa's mosaic tiles, velvet drapes, fireplaces, grand piano and private pedicure suites is half the fun.

Gene Juarez Salon & Spa
1661 East Olive Way
Seattle, WA 98102
Phone: 206-323-7773

GENMAR HOLDINGS
Yachting

One of the major players in the design of mega-yachts and luxury boats, Genmar Holdings has long been a favorite of seamen and landlubbers alike. Genmar consists of 12 different boating companies manufacturing a wide range of vessels, from Scarab sport boats for weekend warriors, to family cruisers for *Mayflower* descendants, to 140-foot mega-yachts for the rest of us.

Genmar Holdings
100 South Fifth Street, Suite 2500
Minneapolis, MN 55402
Phone: 612-339-7600

GENOA
Restaurants

One of the greatest Italian cooks, Marcella Hazen, has called Genoa "the best Italian restaurant in America," an opinion backed by superlatives from food guides ranging from the *Mobil Travel Guide* (four stars) and *Gourmet* to *Zagat*. This Mediterranean treasure has only 10 tables, so be sure to book early. For a quarter of a century it has offered colossal seven-course dinners of superb quality.

Genoa
2832 SE Belmont Street
Portland, OR 97212
Phone: 503-238-1464

GEOFFREY BRADFIELD
Architects and Interior Designers

Geoffrey Bradfield has designed palatial residences, private jets, yachts and "unique office environments" for a clientele whose identities are as guarded as their names are well-known. Bradfield, whose original partner was the late Jay Spectre, describes his style as "functional opulence" that draws its inspiration from the Orient, African Primitivism and Art Deco.

Geoffrey Bradfield
105 East 63rd Street, 1B
New York, NY 10021
Phone: 212-758-1773

HOTEL GEORGE
Hotels   *Rising Star*

The Hotel George is within walking distance of the U.S. Capitol, the National Gallery and the Smithsonian Institution. Washington's first really stylish boutique hotel has attracted guests like Alanis Morissette and John Malkovich. There is a fitness center with steam rooms, a 24-hour concierge and twice-daily maid service. The lobby exudes a sleek, contemporary feel, with vast expanses of glass and steel.

Hotel George
15 E Street, NW
Washington, DC 20001
Phone: 202-347-4200

GEORGE L. JEWELL CATERING
Party Organizers and Caterers

George is a Chicago party planning institution and a genius at venue scouting. For over 20 years he has organized galas, weddings and parties for big (and not so big) groups. Regularly throwing private and corporate parties at museums, historic mansions and galleries, he is known for producing the same exceptional quality food and service for every client, regardless of the size of the party.

George L. Jewell Catering
424 North Wood Street
Chicago, IL 60622
Phone: 312-829-3663   Fax: 312-829-9791

GIBSON, DUNN & CRUTCHER
Law Firms

With 15 offices situated in most of the hubs of international business activity, Gibson, Dunn & Crutcher is one of the largest law firms in the world. For more than a century the firm has proven its ability to deliver quality and creativity in its legal services. Its lawyers' expertise encompasses virtually every area of the law.

Gibson, Dunn & Crutcher
333 South Grand Avenue
Los Angeles, CA 90071
Phone: 213-229-7000

GILMARTIN STUDIOS
Specialty Shops

If you want to order a new mission-style bench for your mud-room, contact this custom fitted wood furniture manufacturer. Michael Gilmartin is one of the few artisans today still using traditional joinery techniques and hand rubbed finishes on each piece.

Gilmartin Studios
1385 English Street NW
Atlanta, GA 30318
Phone: 404-351-7886

MARY GINGRASS, M.D.
Cosmetic Surgeons

"Some people come in weighing 250 pounds and think they'll walk out looking like a *Victoria's Secret* model. Unfortunately that's not the case," says Mary Gingrass, who has a strong conviction that the well-informed patient will have a better attitude towards cosmetic surgery and an easier recovery period. Dr. Gingrass' experience includes specialty training in breast and aesthetic surgery, including body contouring and ultrasonic liposuction.

Mary Gingrass, M.D.
2021 Church Street, Suite 806
Nashville, TN 37203
Phone: 615-340-4500

GIOIA
Jewelry and Watches

Walking into Gioia is like stepping into the glamour and luxury of an 18th century private salon. The jewelry, made by its own atelier in Paris, is equally exquisite with designs that artistically combine unusually colored diamonds and stones with a classical but unique sensibility. This store is definitely for the jewelry connoisseur who prizes unique, high quality individual pieces that are destined to become collectible.

Gioia
485 Park Avenue
New York, NY 10022
Phone: 212-223-3146   Fax: 212-223-0294

GIOVANNI'S
Restaurants

Even the pots and pans speak Italian here, according to Giovanni Gabriele, who opened this establishment 27 years ago. Frank Paul, Giovanni's son and a third-generation Italian chef, has now taken over the kitchen. Signature dishes include a *pappardelle con porcine*. The restaurant boasts an extensive wine list, including special vintages of Gaja Barolo and Barbaresco. Giovanni's was the spot where Dick Gephardt endorsed Al Gore for his presidential bid.

Giovanni's
5201 Shaw Avenue
St. Louis, MO 63110
Phone: 314-772-5958   Fax: 314-772-0343

GUMP'S
SAN FRANCISCO
1.800.766.7628

LYNN NAKAMURA
TAHITIAN CULTURED PEARLS, BAMBOO AND WOVEN SILK CORD

GIVENCHY HOTEL & SPA

Spas and Clinics

In recent years, American spas have become increasingly sophisticated, offering a host of new treatments for discerning customers. Givenchy Hotel & Spa is no exception. Modeled after the Givenchy Spa at the Hotel Trianon in Versailles, it provides relaxation and rejuvenation in a temple of beauty. The emphasis is on relentless pampering, with extensive spa treatments tailored to clients' specific needs and wants.

Givenchy Hotel & Spa

4200 East Palm Canyon Drive
Palm Springs, CA 92264
Phone: 800-276-5000

GLADSTONE ANTIQUES SHOW

Events   *Best Kept Secret*

This annual event brings 50 of the better antique dealers in the country together for one delightful weekend. Situated on the grounds of the U.S. Equestrian Team Headquarters and Olympic Training Center in Gladstone, New Jersey, the show turns horse stalls into mini-galleries where collectors can view 17th, 18th and 19th century collectibles. Visitors are also invited to watch daily equestrian demonstrations. Antique collectors usually leave Gladstone with a newfound passion for horses!

Gladstone Antiques Show

c/o U.S.E.T. Pottersville Road
Gladstone, NJ 07934
Phone: 908-234-0555

GLEN GATE

Landscape Architects

A winner of countless international design awards, Glen Gate is unique in its full service approach to high-level residential design, construction and in-house maintenance of the total landscape environment. Their plantsmen, trained horticulturists and landscape designers all know the power of the right plantings to lay open the spirit of the land.

Glen Gate

644 Danbury Road
Wilton, CN 06897
Phone: 203-762-2000   *Fax: 203-762-9070*

GLORIOUS FOODS

Party Organizers and Caterers

This full-service catering company, which Sean Driscoll and Jean-Claude Nedelec started in 1971, is one of the top caterers in New York City. They have worked for every major cultural institution in Gotham, including the New York Public Library, The Metropolitan Museum of Art and Lincoln Center. Glorious foods catered Ronald Reagan's second inaugural luncheon in 1985, the reopening of the Statue of Liberty in 1986, where they served over 7000 people within a 24-hour period, and they cater Michael Bloomberg's 4400-person Christmas party each year.

Glorious Foods

504 East 74th Street
New York, NY 10021
Phone: 212-628-2320

GOLDEN BEAR

Jewelry and Watches

Situated in the affluent resort community of Vail, Colorado, The Golden Bear deals in high end distinctive jewelry. The firm's trademark is the signature of Vail Valley, the bear-handcrafted in sterling silver or yellow gold. In addition to their Bear collections, the Golden Bear offer a variety of fine jewelry collections by well known designers, and a line of clothing and accessories.

Golden Bear

286 Bridge Street
Vail, CO 81657
Phone: 970-476-4082

GOLDEN DOOR

Spas and Clinics

The only American facility to receive the highest spa rating by the Condé Nast reader service, Golden Door is unparalleled in following the mind-body-spirit path to complete relaxation. Japanese Gardens, waterfalls, meandering streams, hiking trails and outdoor pavilions provide serenity outside, while inside unobtrusive staff help guests achieve "quiet of mind" through massage and meditation. Recommended.

Golden Door

777 Deer Springs Road
San Marcos, CA 92069
Phone: 760-744-5777

GOLDEN NUGGET

Casinos

To the casual observer, it would appear that Steve Wynn's Mirage Resorts owns *all* of Las Vegas. The only place Mirage didn't have its hands on was old downtown Vegas–until now. Recently, Wynn purchased "The Nugget," which remains a true player's casino with lots of table game action, double-deck 21, and almost no table limits for high rollers. The Golden Nugget's suites have been renovated and now offer amazing views–if you are in your room long enough to look.

Golden Nugget

129 East Fremont Street
Las Vegas, NV 89101
Phone: 800-634-3454

GOLDEN WEST INTERNATIONAL

Wine Merchants

Golden West has stocked top rated vintage Port, Bordeaux, Sauternes and Champagne for over twenty years. With the use of temperature controlled storage and a strict selection criteria, this San Francisco based mail-order merchant has become a top supplier to wine lovers around the world.

Golden West International

2443 Fillmore Street
San Francisco, CA 94115
Phone: 800-722-7020   *Fax: 415-931-3939*

GOLDMAN, SACHS & CO.

Wealth Management

Edith Wharton wrote that "the only way not to think about money is to have a great deal of it." But how do you manage such wealth? That is where Goldman, Sachs comes into the picture. Principally a brokerage rather than a private bank, this blue-chip firm dabbles in private-client services–but even great novelists will need a minimum of $5 million in investable assets.

Goldman, Sachs & Co.

85 Broad Street
New York, NY 10004
Phone: 212-902-5400

GORDON
Restaurants
Gordon Sinclair opened his pioneering restaurant 23 years ago in an underdeveloped area of Chicago, between a currency exchange and a dirty bookstore; it is now a vibrant district called River North. *Bon Appetit* recently voted Gordon one of the "10 best tried and true restaurants in America." Chef Don Yamauchi offers "solid edge rather than cutting edge" New American cuisine with global influences.
Gordon
500 North Clark Street
Chicago, IL 60610
Phone: 312-467-9780

LA GOULUE
Restaurants
Along with the other ladies who used to lunch at Mortimer's, society mavens like Nan Kempner and Nina Griscom have moved to La Goulue. This New York version of a Paris sidewalk café is on the Upper East Side, among great shops and very expensive homes. The cuisine is French—and excellent from beginning to end. If you cannot secure a reservation, ask for Craig, the superb Scottish Manager. La Goulue will particularly appeal to Milanese and Parisians who enjoy smoking after dinner.
La Goulue
746 Madison Avenue
New York, NY 10021
Phone: 212-988-8169   Fax: 212-396-2552

GRAMERCY TAVERN
Restaurants
Danny Meyer is one of the more amiable restaurateurs in Manhattan. This establishment and its sister, Union Square Café, are widely praised for genuinely friendly service and high-quality food. The excellent tavern cuisine and unpretentious atmosphere are pleasant surprises in a city not renowned for either. Sit toward the front for less-formal dining, or in the back if you're looking for (more expensive) intimacy. Either way, you will be treated like royalty.
Gramercy Tavern
42 East 20th Street
New York, NY 10003
Phone: 212-477-0777   Fax: 212-477-1160

GRAND HAVANA ROOM
Cigar Bars
Cigars, martinis, and contented smiles are the order of the day at this civilized retreat from the artifice of life in Hollywood. Arnold Schwarzenegger, George Clooney, and Tom Cruise have their own humidors here. You, too, can have a private humidor, not to mention the best cigars, drinks, and good company—if, that is, you enjoy the company of matinée idols.
Grand Havana Room
301 North Cannon Road
Los Angeles, CA 90210
Phone: 310-247-2900

GREEN CLASSIC LIMOUSINES
Chauffeur Services
Jeff Green's limousine company serves the Atlanta area; he is the exclusive limousine provider for the Ritz Carlton and Four Seasons hotels. When the likes of Elton John and Michael Jordan are in town, they are chauffeured in one of Green's vehicles, which are also a regular presence at 1 Coca Cola Plaza. A trade magazine recently rated Green Classic in the nation's top three limousine companies.
Green Classic Limousines
2330 Defoor Hills Road
Atlanta, GA 30318
Phone: 404-875-3866

GREENBERG VAN DOREN GALLERY
Art Dealers
St. Louis native Robert Greenberg opened his gallery in 1972 and John Van Doren joined him shortly after. Located in the Central West End, Greenberg Van Doren specializes in the blue chips among modern and contemporary artists, including the likes of Andy Warhol and Roy Lichtenstein.
Greenberg Van Doren Gallery
44 Maryland Plaza
St. Louis, MO 63108
Phone: 314-361-7600

THE GREENBRIER HOTEL
Hotels
Nestled in the Allegheny Mountains of West Virginia, the Greenbrier has pampered, renewed and restored its patrons since the early 19th century. In the beginning, the social set were drawn to the healing properties of the local sulfur waters, and although research suggests that it has no wondrous powers, people still flock to this mountain oasis, enjoying the spa, tennis, rafting, billiards and hiking. But golf reigns supreme: Dwight Eisenhower, the Prince of Wales and Bob Hope have enjoyed the Greenbrier's courses. Incidentally, a huge nuclear bunker, built by the U.S. government during the Cold War, lies under the hotel, enhancing its appeal for travelers who need something to worry about.
The Greenbrier Hotel
300 West Main Street
White Sulfur Springs, WV 24986
Phone: 304-536-1110   Fax: 304-536-7818

GREENHOUSE GALLERY OF FINE ART
Art Dealers
Jim Janes opened this Alamo Heights gallery 18 years ago to provide local art collectors with a new outlet for contemporary art. The gallery shows mostly realist and impressionist landscapes, still lifes and figurative pieces by artists such as Mian Situ and Frederick Hart. Janes sells principally to private collectors, although he has also helped several museums to enhance their collections.
Greenhouse Gallery of Fine Art
2218 Breezewood
San Antonio, TX 78209
Phone: 210-828-6491   Fax: 210-828-6669

THE GREENHOUSE GROUP
Spas and Clinics
With a world-renowned full service destination spa and day spas strategically located throughout the country, the Greenhouse Group pampers thousands of spa-goers nationwide with its innovative spa treatments and cutting-edge techniques. At the Greenhouse destination spa in Texas, sign up for an exclusive week of r&r, chock full of facials, massages, manicures, pedicures, body wraps, hair and make-up services, a personal fitness consultation and other holistic options.
The Greenhouse Group
7 East Skippack Pike
Ambler, PA 19002
Phone: 215-643-2954

GREENLEAF & CROSBY
Jewelry and Watches
As the oldest jeweler in Palm Beach, Greenleaf & Crosby understands the importance of blending quality with service. No request is too unusual

and no suggestion too difficult to implement. The signature Riviera necklace, a row of diamonds in shining splendor, is particularly desirable. Designer jewelry as well as clocks and frames are also stocked.

Greenleaf & Crosby

236 Worth Avenue
Palm Beach, FL 33480
Phone: 561-655-5850

LA GRENOUILLE

Restaurants

Enjoy the atmosphere of yesterday's glory at this Manhattan landmark, now finely aged but still impressive. Originally a watering-hole for artists, such as Charlie Chaplin, Greta Garbo, Marlene Dietrich, and Jean Gabin, it still retains an air of faded glamor. This is where Truman Capote sipped his Roederer Cristal and wrote devastating gossip about his friends. Flawless French cuisine.

La Grenouille

3 East 52nd Street
New York, NY 10021
Phone: 212-752-1495 or 752-0652

GRGICH HILLS CELLARS

Winemakers

It was enough to give one goose bumps when California's 1973 Chateau Montelena beat the best French white Burgundies in the 1976 Paris tasting. The man who was responsible for that coup, Croatian Mike Grgich, still makes complex and exquisite Chardonnays. A charismatic and utterly dedicated winemaker, Grgich has said "I was taught to treat grapes and wines as if they were living things—our children. Each vintage brings a new challenge to create the best wines of the future." Hear, hear!

Grgich Hills Cellars

1829 St. Helena Highway
Rutherford, CA 94573
Phone: 707-963-2784   Fax: 707-963-8725

THE GRILL ON THE ALLEY

Restaurants

Part celeb hangout, part bar next door, The Grill on the Alley has long been a watering hole for those who require civility and charm, with a side order of favoritism. This Beverly Hills bar and grill offers five-star martinis and discreet but super-attentive service. Mikhail Baryshnikov and Barbra Streisand find the Grill's out-of-the-way location appropriate for their very private lives, and even former President Ronald Reagan has sampled the exquisite all-American desserts.

The Grill on the Alley

9560 Dayton Way
Beverly Hills, CA 90210
Phone: 310-276-0615   Fax: 310-276-0284

GREENBAUM INTERIORS

Specialty Shops

"Home is the center of civilization," says David Greenbaum, Design Director of Greenbaum Interiors. The philosophy is evident throughout this family-run business, which is at once an interior design firm, a vast showroom and a producer of finely crafted custom furniture, in the European tradition. Greenbaum's 30 member design staff and 35 artisans collaborate under one roof, offering many advantages. The custom workrooms—including cabinet, upholstery and finishing shops, along with a hand decorating studio—afford a profound synthesis of creative talents between designer and artisan. These extraordinary capabilities allow Greenbaum Designers to conceive, customize and interpret pieces for client's site specific projects. Each of the showroom's 125 unique settings are fully dressed, appointed and accessorized with an array of magnificent objets d'art. They showcase a selection of fine pieces drawn from Greenbaum's extensive international collection of antique, custom, and imported furnishings. For nearly 50 years this acclaimed institution has been of service to a distinguished clientele and their families, including leaders of *Fortune 500* companies, celebrated athletes and performance artists, distinguished professionals and entrepreneurs. The Greenbaums pride themselves on craftsmanship and connoisseurship, and are adept at satisfying a broad range of tastes and budgets. Warmly recommended.

Greenbaum Interiors

101 Washington Street
Paterson, NJ 07505
Phone: 973-279-3000
Fax: 973-279-3006

GULFSTREAM AEROSPACE CORPORATION

Airplanes

Founded in 1958 and known as the Rolls-Royce of jets, Gulfstream continues to excel under the direction of its CEO, Teddy Fortsmann, a legendary Wall Street tycoon. The latest innovation is the Gulfstream 5, cruising at 51,000 feet, with a 6500-mile range. The GS5 is the world's first ultra-long-range jet, flying travelers from New York to Tokyo nonstop. Onboard voice and data satellite communications ensure that business can be conducted *en route*.

Gulfstream Aerospace Corporation

P.O. Box 2206

Savannah, GA 31402

Phone: 912-965-3000   Fax: 912-965-3775

GWATHMEY SIEGEL & ASSOCIATES

Architects and Interior Designers

Charles Gwathmey and Robert Siegel came together 31 years ago to form this prestigious architecture and interior design firm, which uses a modernist vocabulary in designing private residences, art museums and corporate interiors, including the Zumikon residence in Switzerland and the 1992 addition to the Guggenheim in New York. Gwathmey and Siegel designed Quelle Barn, Steven Spielberg's compound in the Hamptons, as well as homes for Jerry Seinfeld and David Geffen in Manhattan.

Gwathmey Siegel & Associates

475 Tenth Avenue

New York, NY 10018

Phone: 212-947-1240

GUMP'S

Specialty Shops

Gump's is a unique specialty store of engaging galleries featuring advanced, classic and custom jewelry, Asian and American art objects, mastercrafts, gifts and decorative home accessories. The world's best crystal and china (formal and casual), a vast collection of silver, and bed, bath and fragrance selections complete this East/West emporium's offerings.

Founded in this city by the bay in 1861–like cablecars and the Golden Gate Bridge, Gump's symbolizes San Francisco–its provenance and always-current-panache make it a must stop on every traveler's list. Gump's remains an iconic shopping experience for natives and newcomers alike.

Gump's

135 Post Street

San Francisco, CA 94108

Phone: 415-982-1616   Fax: 415-984-9379

GROTON SCHOOL

Schools

Located in Massachusetts on a 300-acre campus, this venerable bastion of Anglo-Saxon privilege has been honored with countless awards over its 115 year history. A co-educational, primarily residential school, Groton is renowned for promoting high standards in academic achievement, intellectual growth, ethical awareness and behavior, sportsmanship, athletic endeavor, and service to others.

Groton School

Farmers Row

PO Box 991

Groton, MA 01450-0991

Phone: 978-448-3363   Fax: 978-448-3100

THE GROVE PARK INN RESORT

Hotels

This historic resort becomes The Grove Park Inn Resort *and Spa* in the summer of 2000, when it opens its $13 million, 40,000-square foot spa in a rooftop-landscape setting in the heart of the hotel complex. General Manager Jim France promises "the finest resort spa in the United States." Even without this addition, Grove Park is one of America's better mountain golf resorts. With its balmy climate and panoramic views of the Blue Mountains, the inn's Sunset Terrace restaurant offers spectacular outdoor dining.

The Grove Park Inn Resort

290 Macon Avenue

Asheville, NC 28804

Phone: 800-438-5800

GUARISCO GALLERY

Art Dealers

This large Washington gallery is run by Laura Guarisco & Jane Studebaker, who have been collecting 19th and early 20th century European and American paintings, sculpture and watercolors for 19 years. A recent show highlighting the work of impressionist and postimpressionist painters was particularly well received. They are equally strong on the Academic school of the same period.

Guarisco Gallery

2828 Pennsylvania Avenue, NW

Washington, DC 20007

Phone: 202-333-8533

H. M. LUTHER ANTIQUES
Antiques

H. M. Luther, in New York's East Village, caters to an international clientele of collectors and designers seeking the superlative and the rare. It boasts a large stock of European and Asian furniture, chandeliers, and decorations from the 17th to the 20th centuries. Director Daniel Harrison says what they look for is not determined by period or style, but something much harder to define: "You know what it is when you see it, but you have to see it to know it."

H. M. Luther Antiques
61 East 11th Street
New York, NY 10003
Phone: 212-505-1485   Fax: 212-505-0401

H. S. TRASK & CO.
Fashion

These men's hand-crafted shoes are constructed exclusively of America's original leathers: bison, elk, and longhorn. Deceptively soft, they wear like iron and will probably be your favorite shoes from the moment you put them on. Check out H.S. Trask's collection nationwide at upscale footwear retailers.

H. S. Trask & Co.
685 Old Buffalo Trail
Bozeman, MT 59715
Phone: 888-218-7275

HALL AND HALL RANCH BROKERS
Property Consultants

Handling over $50 million in rural property sales annually, Hall and Hall specializes in large ranches, farms and luxury homes in the Rockies. The firm, owned by Jim Taylor and his seven partners, sold $115 million worth of real estate in 1998, with an average sale price of $3 million. Hall and Hall has six offices in Montana, Wyoming, Idaho and New Mexico, and is planning to open two others in Colorado and Nebraska.

Hall and Hall Ranch Brokers
P.O. Box 1924
Billings, MT 59103
Phone: 406-656-7500

HAMILTON CIGAR BAR
Cigar Bars

Opened in January 1997 as part of the New York, New York Hotel and Casino, Gotham is the theme at the Hamilton Cigar Bar, owned by actor George Hamilton. With no restaurant or other accessories, Hamilton is a pure upscale cigar bar, with a VIP room and a rear entrance. Among the 30 varieties of cigars available are Monte Cristo, Macanudo, and Tartagus. Approximately 100 humidors are available for lease.

Hamilton Cigar Bar
3790 South Las Vegas Boulevard, Suite 6
Las Vegas, NV 89109
Phone: 702-740-6400

HAMILTON JEWELERS
Jewelry and Watches

For three generations this family owned firm has been wowing customers with superb traditional and modern jewelry. Founded in Trenton, Hamilton now has four stores throughout New Jersey and Florida. Its flagship store in Princeton boasts in-house boutiques for jewelry and watch designers like Mikimoto, David Yurman and Rolex.

Hamilton Jewelers
92 Nassau Street
Princeton, NJ 08542
Phone: 609-683-4200   Fax: 609-771-8250

HAMMER GALLERIES
Art Dealers

Art lovers will adore the collection of works by 19th and early 20th century European and American masters. Impressionist, postimpressionist and early modern paintings, including pieces by Renoir and Monet, are among Hammer's specialties. The gallery, which was founded in 1928, also shows contemporary art by realists. And if Picasso is your pleasure, you will doubtless appreciate a collection of over 40 ceramics, straight from the master's estate.

Hammer Galleries
33 West 57th Street
New York, NY 10019
Phone: 212-644-4400   Fax: 212-832-3763

HAMPTON COUNTRY REAL ESTATE
Property Consultants

Established in 1989, Hampton Country Real Estate represents top properties on Eastern Long Island. The firm specializes in prime building sites and waterfront land. It draws an international clientele, ranging from European and Asian buyers and sellers to entertainment industry celebrities to Wall Street attorneys. The firm's 10 agents also sell and rent contemporary and turn-of-the-century farmland and woodland homes.

Hampton Country Real Estate
19 Corwith Avenue
Bridgehampton, NY 11932
Phone: 516-537-2000

HAPA
Restaurants   Rising Star

This small restaurant, run by a young husband and wife team of chefs, James & Stacey McDevitt, offers one of the more memorable culinary experiences in Arizona. Hapa—the Hawaiian term for half—refers to James' Asian-American background as well as the cuisine, which gleefully borrows from both culinary traditions. The McDevitts look set to enjoy lasting success.

Hapa
6204 North Scottsdale Road
Scottsdale, AZ 85253
Phone: 602-998-8220   Fax: 602-998-2355

HARBOUR TOWN GOLF LINKS
Golf Clubs

The most famous of the courses at the Sea Pines Resort, the Harbour Town Golf Links was designed by Pete Dye and Jack Nicklaus and finished in 1969. *Golf Magazine* has ranked this course 36th in the world and 29th in the United States. The signature 18th hole, which runs along the Calibogue Sound and plays out to the lighthouse at the harbor, is one of the most photographed holes in golf.

Harbour Town Golf Links
11 Lighthouse Lane
Hilton Head Island, SC 29928
Phone: 843-842-8484

HARGRAVE YACHTS

Yachting

Hargrave has designed Hatteras sport fishing yachts for nearly three decades. Recently adding manufacturing to their design capabilities, its new line, Hargrave Yachts, ranges from 40-200 foot, composite and steel hulls. Anglers in search of offshore big game will love the new 41-foot Express Sport-Fisher that boasts a 1000 gallon fuel capacity and a 50-mph top speed.

Hargrave Yachts

901 SE 17th Street
Fort Lauderdale, FL 33316
Phone: 954-463-0555   Fax: 954-463-8621

HARLAN ESTATE

Winemakers

Small wonder that Cabernet Sauvignon is the main grape grown here: the great Bordeaux winemaker Michel Rolland has been working with Robert Levy for years. The grapes are hand-picked, hand sorted and fermented in small lots, then aged in French oak barrels for two years. After rigorous selection the wine is bottled unfiltered. It was first released in 1990—just 300 cases—but production has risen modestly since then. Annual production now averages about 1000 cases. Ralph Hersom, Wine Director at Le Cirque 2000, says "if you can get hold of Harlan, call me—I'll buy it!"

Harlan Estate

P.O. Box 352
Oakville, CA 94562
Phone: 707-944-1441   Fax: 707-944-1444

HARRISON K-9 SECURITY

Security Consultants

Alarm systems are great for the house—when they are on. But there is no substitute for protection from the vigilant eyes of a precision-trained guard dog. Harrison K-9 provides German shepherds from European bloodlines. Whether you opt for a puppy or a fully trained adult, all of Harrison's dogs are unconditionally guaranteed for suitability. An optional two-day training course is available at the company's South Carolina facility.

Harrison K-9 Security

P.O. Box 1620
Aiken, SC 29802
Phone: 803-649-5936

HARRY WINSTON JEWELERS

Jewelry and Watches

Harry Winston Jewelers, founded in New York City in 1920, has been installed at the same Fifth Avenue location for 45 years. One of the best wholesale, manufacturing and retail jewelers in the world, the firm is renowned for cutting rare, large diamonds—like the famed Hope Diamond, now on display at the Smithsonian—although it has an extensive inventory of jewels for all tastes.

Harry Winston Jewelers

718 Fifth Avenue
New York, NY 10019
Phone: 212-245-2000

HARTMANN LUGGAGE & LEATHER GOODS

Specialty Shops

Founded by Joseph Hartmann 120 years ago with the intention of manufacturing luxury steamer trunks for wealthy travelers, Hartmann produces a signature square leather briefcase that's a favorite among CEOs. Hartmann also sells business and personal travel accessories, make-up cases, large suitcases on wheels, garment bags and casual computer cases.

Hartmann Luggage & Leather Goods

1301 Hartmann Drive
Lebanon, TN 37087
Phone: 800-621-5293

HARVARD UNIVERSITY

Colleges

Named after John Harvard, a clergyman who left half of his estate to the school in 1638, this venerable institution has built prodigiously upon that original gift to amass an endowment of $13 billion. The oldest institution of higher learning in the United States has graduated six presidents including Theodore and Franklin Delano Roosevelt and John Fitzgerald Kennedy. Its schools of business, law and medicine have produced more than 30 Nobel laureates and a slew of prominent graduates including T.S. Eliot, Leonard Bernstein and Vice President Al Gore. *Phantom Menace* star Natalie Portman recently picked Harvard over Yale as her college of choice.

Harvard University

Glass Hall
8 Garden Street,
Cambridge, MA 02138
Phone: 617-495-1000   Fax: 617-495-8821

HAVANA STUDIOS

Cigar Bars

The humidors at Havana Studios hold between 75 and 100 cigars from around the world, and members can have their own humidors and lockers. Needless to say, Nick Nikkah's upmarket smokery is a favorite of Hollywood executives and other cigar snobs; Walt Disney Studios, among others, holds a party here every few months.

Havana Studios

245 East Olive Avenue
Burbank, CA 91502
Phone: 818-557-7600

THE HAY-ADAMS HOTEL

Hotels

Situated across Lafayette Square from the White House, the historic Hay-Adams Hotel was built in the Italian Renaissance style, in the mid 1920s. For years the epicenter of polite society, The Hay-Adams attracted such guests as Charles Lindbergh, Amelia Earhart, Sinclair Lewis and Ethel Barrymore. Today it continues this long standing tradition by housing celebrities, dignitaries and discerning visitors from around the world. The elegant guest suites are handsomely furnished; many offer grand views of the White House or St. John's Church. What finer way to top off an afternoon of sightseeing or shopping than to indulge in the hotel's exquisite High Tea, complete with Devonshire cream, jam and scones.

The Hay-Adams Hotel

One Lafayette Square
800 16th Street, NW
Washington, DC 20006
Phone: 202-638-6600
Fax: 202-638-2716

HAVERFORD COLLEGE
Colleges
Haverford College is one of the top five liberal art schools in the nation. A small, tightly knit community (there are only 1100 students), all senior faculty live on campus, which means they are available to students. The college's strong Quaker roots are still evident in the practice of an honor code and focus on group discussions.
Haverford College
370 Lancaster Avenue
Haverford, PA 19041
Phone: 610-896-1037

KIM HEIRSTON
Art Consultants   Rising Star
"They want edgy stuff that is relevant to their lives," says art adviser Kim Heirston of her Wall Street clientele. The Yale graduate, who cut her teeth at the Pace, Robert Miller and Stux galleries, steers investment bankers to artists such as Robert Gober, Jenny Holzer, Cindy Sherman, Julian Schnabel and Chris Wool. With an average of four invitations a night, *Harper's Bazaar* has called this affable young woman "one of New York's most sought-after guests."
Kim Heirston
44 East 65th Street
New York, NY 10021
Phone: 212-734-0464   Fax: 212-734-0607

HEITZ WINE CELLARS
Winemakers
The joke goes that if you stand still long enough in the Napa Valley someone will start a vineyard on you, although it was not that way when former teacher Joe Heitz and his wife Alice arrived in 1961—there were fewer than a dozen. Their 1968 and 1974 Cabernet Sauvignons are some of the finest ever produced in California.
Heitz Wine Cellars
500 Taplin Road
Saint Helena, CA 94574
Phone: 707-963-3542   Fax: 707-963-7454

HELENA LEHANE
Florists
On an impulse 16 years ago, Helena Lehane asked Elio Guatolini if she could do the flowers for his New York restaurant, Elio's. Her deliciously decadent floral designs have won many admirers since then, including Bijan and Carly Simon. Nowadays Helena enjoys all aspects of event planning. If you wanted to throw a particularly successful dinner, for instance, she would meticulously organize the evening in conjunction with Daniel Boulud.
Helena Lehane
Phone: 212-888-7763   Fax: 212-888-9755

HELMUT LANG
Fashion
It is an understatement to say that the fashion world took notice when Helmut Lang moved from Vienna to New York in 1997, but understatement is definitely this reticent designer's style. Lang's collection, which successfully blends casual and formal, basic and luxurious, has been aptly described as "cool for grown-ups." From his headquarters on Greene Street in SoHo, the 44-year old is single-handedly rewriting the rules of fashion—including, most famously, the order of the international shows. His recent alliance with Prada promises to expand the empire further.
Helmut Lang
80 Greene Street
New York, NY 10012
Phone: 212-334-1014

THE HESS COLLECTION WINERY
Winemakers
Swiss-American entrepreneur Donald Hess has combined his two passions in life by opening a winery and an art gallery in the same building, located on the top of Mount Zeeder in the Napa Valley. Hess makes three tiers of wine, Select, Collection and Reserve. Many of the excellent Reserves, such as a 1990 Cabernet Sauvignon, are available only at the winery.
The Hess Collection Winery
4411 Redwood Road
Napa, CA 94558
Phone: 707-255-1144   Fax: 707-253-1682

HICKOX SALON AND SPA
Spas and Clinics
At this full-service day spa, clients are pampered from head to toe. Whether you opt for an hour long facial or massage or stop by for a manicure, pedicure and waxing, you will be well taken care of. Complete your visit with a cut or color treatment in the salon and emerge with a whole new look.

Hickox Salon and Spa
711 Southwest Alder Street
Portland, OR 97204
Phone: 503-241-7111   Fax: 503-241-1908

HIGH MUSEUM OF ART
Museums
The High Museum of Art, founded in 1905 as the Atlanta Art Association, is one of the South's premier fine art museums. The permanent collection is noted for its 19th and 20th century American art, including the comprehensive Virginia Carroll Crawford collection of American Decorative Arts. The Frances and Emory Cocke collection of English ceramics and an ever-growing assortment of American folk art—including the recently acquired collection of T. Marshall Hahn, Jr.—also draw crowds.
High Museum of Art
1280 Peachtree Street, NE
Atlanta, GA 30309
Phone: 404-733-4400

HIRSCHL & ADLER GALLERIES
Art Dealers
Hirschl & Adler specializes in American and European paintings, watercolors, drawings and sculpture from the 18th through the early 20th centuries; American prints of all periods; and American decorative arts from 1810 to 1910. Hirschl & Adler's modern section shows American and European art from the postwar period. Each year, the gallery assembles about a dozen special exhibitions exploring historical and contemporary themes, or examining the work of individual artists. The gallery maintains an active group of clients, including private collectors, museums, architects, interior designers, art consultants and other dealers.
Hirschl & Adler Galleries
21 East 70th Street
New York, NY 10021
Phone: 212-535-8810   Fax: 212-772-7237

HIRSHHORN MUSEUM AND SCULPTURE GARDEN

Museums

Businessman Joseph Hirshhorn donated his collection of 19th and 20th century art to the federal government in 1966. It now forms the core of this unusual collection, which is housed in a concrete, donut-shaped building that surrounds a sculpture garden, all designed by Gordon Bunschaft. The Hirshhorn is the only museum in Washington, D.C. devoted exclusively to modern art. Its 6000 works include masterpieces by Picasso and Matisse.

Hirshhorn Museum and Sculpture Garden

Smithsonian Institution
Independence Avenue at Seventh Street, SW
Washington, DC 20560
Phone: 202-357-3091   Fax: 202-786-2682

HOKANSON

Specialty Shops

Hokanson custom-designed and produced the rug for the White House's Oval Office during George Bush's administration. For 12 years this manufacturer of hand-tufted rugs has specialized in thin, tightly woven floor coverings with the fastest production time in the business. It is known for its high-quality, 100 percent wool or 100 percent silk rugs custom-made to any size, color, or design.

Hokanson

5120 Woodway
Houston, TX 77056
Phone: 713-621-6609

THE HOTCHKISS SCHOOL

Schools

In 1891, Yale president Timothy Dwight convinced Maria Bissell Hotchkiss to found a school that would prepare young men for study at his university. Today's graduates choose from a wider array of colleges; they are a significant presence at all of the Ivy Leagues. Located on a 520-acre campus bordered by two lakes in Northwestern Connecticut, the school now accepts both young men and women for grades 9-12, as well as for a year of postgraduate study. A full-time faculty of 109 members for approximately 550 students assures that each student gets close attention.

The Hotchkiss School

11 Interlaken Road
Lakeville, CT 06039
Phone: 860-435-2591

THE HOTEL

Hotels   *Rising Star*

Color: that is the first thing you will notice at Tony Goldman's 52-room hotel, the Miami Beach hot spot custom-designed by fashion guru Todd Oldham. From the lobby's sparkling mosaic walls, to the emerald-cut roof pool, to the hand-blown glass lamps illuminating *Wish* restaurant, Oldham has infused every inch of the former Tiffany Hotel with color. The result is a veritable feast for the eyes.

The Hotel

801 Collins Avenue
Miami Beach, FL 33139
Phone: 305-531-2222
Fax: 305-531-3222

HOUSTON POLO CLUB

Polo Clubs

With the largest membership in Texas, Houston's Polo Club is the capital of the game in the Lonestar State. Located inside the loop near the old money haven of River Oaks, the club hosts the Texas Open, now in its third year, and the Silver Cup, which is celebrating its centennial year. Big social events accompany the club's Paella Festival and Dominican Cup tournaments. The Isla Carrol team, past winners of the U.S. Open and the Gold Cup, are based at the club, and Texan Tommy Lee Jones plays here regularly.

Houston Polo Club

8552 Memorial Drive
Houston, TX 77024
Phone: 713-622-7300

THE HOUSE ON BAYOU ROAD

Hotels   *Best Kept Secret*

A warm and genuinely hospitable character, Cynthia Reeves welcomes all her guests personally to this *petite* Creole plantation just minutes from the French Quarter. With the intimacy of a small B&B, her charming inn has many of the facilities of a hotel. Four of the eight rooms in the house (which was built in 1798) are suites, with double Jacuzzis and working fireplaces. Unusual and elegant.

The House on Bayou Road

2275 Bayou Road
New Orleans, LA 70119
Phone: 504-945-0992   Fax: 504-945-0993

HOWARD KAPLAN ANTIQUES

Antiques

Make a splash in your home with an antique bathroom basin. From formal to country, this dealer specializes in 19th century French and English furniture, with an accent on beautiful bathroom sinks and accessories. The collection is on display at the Manhattan shop, which also carries a full line of custom tables, including dining consoles and side tables, as well as chandeliers, armoires, chests, lamps, and more.

Howard Kaplan Antiques

827 Broadway
New York, NY 10003
Phone: 212-674-1000

HR BEAUTY GALLERY

Spas and Clinics   *Rising Star*

Although it has only been open for a few months, the HR Beauty Gallery has already established itself as one of the most innovative spas in the United States. Its 8000-square foot space in SoHo houses cutting edge technologies for skin care, including the corneometer, which tests the skin's hydration, sebum, and pH levels. For women on the go, the "HR Express" offers a manicure, pedicure and facial in 60 minutes.

HR Beauty Gallery

135 Spring Street
New York, NY 10012
Phone: 212-343-9966

HUGH NEWELL JACOBSEN
Architects and Interior Designers

Hugh Jacobsen's credo is simple: "Good architecture never shouts: it is like a well-mannered lady who is polite to her neighbors." The Yale-trained architect's sparse and linear designs have earned him enormous acclaim, including, most recently, the Virginia Society's Inform Award, for the Forbes residence and garden in Michigan and the McKinney residence in North Carolina. A good-humored and very approachable figure, Jacobsen has been in practice since 1958. At the time of writing, the National Building Museum had a retrospective exhibition of his work on display.

Hugh Newell Jacobsen
2529 P Street NW
Washington, DC 20007
Phone: 202-337-5200

THE HUNTINGTON HOTEL
Hotels

Celebrating its 75th anniversary in 1999, the Huntington Hotel is all about high standards, gracious service, and quiet, understated luxury. The crown jewel of Nob Hill was once a resting place for luminaries like Princess Grace, Claudette Colbert, and the Vanderbilts, while in recent years this exquisite reminder of the past has also played host to stylish personalities like Paloma Picasso and Alistair Cooke.

The Huntington Hotel
1075 California Street
San Francisco, CA 94108
Phone: 415-474-5400   Fax: 415-474-6227

HUNTINGTON PRIVATE FINANCIAL GROUP
Wealth Management

"If you would know the value of money," wrote Benjamin Franklin, "go and try to borrow some." On the other hand, if you have lots of money to invest in a broad array of financial instruments—and if you particularly enjoy being pampered—then we cannot recommend the good people at Huntington highly enough. They have a superb reputation within the industry.

Huntington Private Financial Group
8889 Pelican Bay Boulevard
Naples, FL 34108
Phone: 941-594-5900   Fax: 941-594-8330

HYDE PARK ANTIQUES
Antiques

Founded in 1965, Hyde Park Antiques has been a leading source for the finest late 17th, 18th and early 19th century British furniture. The extensive collection, with its variety of style and form, allows both the first time buyer as well as the experienced connoisseur the opportunity to select from a vast inventory. The experienced staff have supplied an international client base with everything from Queen Anne and Georgian pieces to excellent examples from the Regency period. Rare and important items have been acquired for major museums, including the Carnegie Museum in Pittsburgh and the DeYoung Museum in San Francisco, as well as Spencer House and Kenwood House in England. Whether destined for a public property or a private home, the furniture at Hyde Park will make a wonderful addition to any environment.

Hyde Park Antiques
836 Broadway
New York, NY 10003
Phone: 212-477-0033   Fax: 212-477-1781

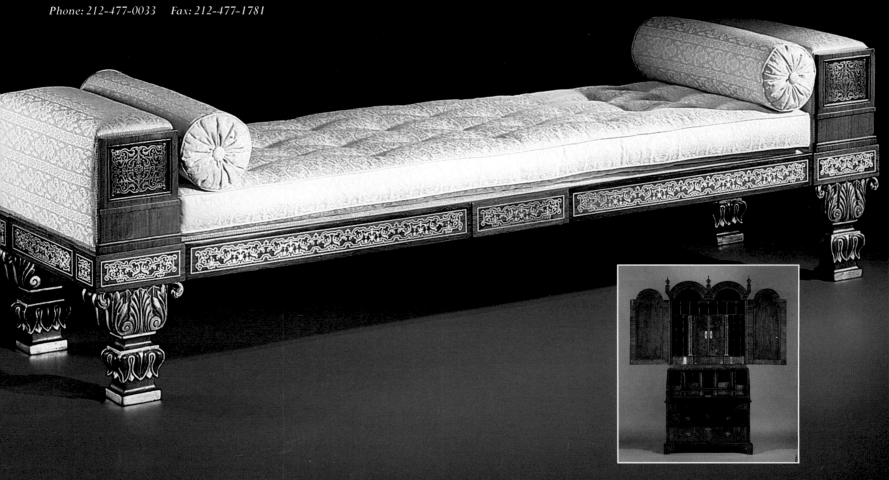

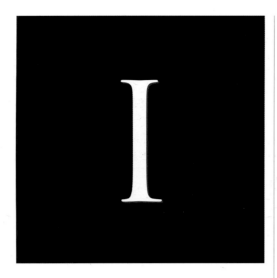

GERALD IMBER, M.D.
Cosmetic Surgeons

Board-certified in plastic surgery, Gerald Imber, M.D., has performed more than 5,000 facial operations. Well known as a leading face-lift surgeon, he is also the author of an acclaimed book, *The Youth Corridor*. Dr. Imber is particularly noted for his pioneering work in anti-aging and youth-maintenance procedures.

Gerald Imber, M.D.
1009 Fifth Avenue
New York, NY 10028
Phone: 212-472-1800

INCREDIBLE ADVENTURES
Travel Consultants

Want to fly a late-model Mig fighter over Moscow at Mach 1.5? Or try the zero-gravity parabolic maneuvers in a specially modified military cargo plane? Adrenaline junkies, in particular, love Incredible Adventures. In addition to the Moscow trips, the company runs another program in Cape Town, South Africa, featuring British Lightning jets capable of Mach 2 at 60,000 feet. Or, if fighter jets make you dizzy, the company also operates a one-week covert operations program in Arizona that is half-Rambo, half-Bond. The instructors are all ex-Green Beret types. You'll learn combat pistol shooting, *real* defensive driving (hooking and ramming), and anything else necessary to diffuse your average terrorist, hostage, or bank robbery situation.

Incredible Adventures
6604 Midnight Pass Road
Sarasota, FL 34242
Phone: 800-644-7382

INTERIEURS
Specialty Shops

A Normandy native, the owner of this furniture and design store in SoHo carries mainly French lines such as Nord Sud and Modenature, throwing in some Provençal antiques for good measure. Regularly traveling to Europe, she offers new lines of contemporary furnishings. Many of the city's

THE INN AT LITTLE WASHINGTON
Hotels

This elegant hotel is nestled in the foothills of the Blue Ridge Mountains, in the tiny town of Washington, Virginia. The Inn has won almost every culinary and hospitality award, year after year. One feels truly pampered there, like staying in a lavish yet comfortably appointed home of a consummate host, with all the services of a world class hotel. The internationally famous restaurant is Chef Patrick O'Connell's platform to showcase the bounty of the Virginia countryside in a setting of elegance and perfect service. Patrons of this property include Barbra Streisand, Paul Newman, Al Gore and Alan Greenspan.

The Inn at Little Washington
Middle Main Street
Washington, VA 22747
Phone: 540-675-3800   Fax: 540-675-3100

leading interior designers are customers here: they come in search of the clean and modern look which clients are clamoring for these days.

Interieurs
114 Wooster Street
New York, NY 10012
Phone: 212-343-0800

THE INN AT SPANISH BAY
Hotels   **Best Kept Secret**

Situated on the famous 17-mile Drive, the Inn at Spanish Bay is a quiet enclave that offers the Pebble Beach experience in considerable comfort. The California dunes, cliffs, and trees outside inspired the elegant interiors; the suites come with balconies and patios offering views of the ocean or the forest. Golfers will appreciate the friendly golf staff and the preferred tee times at the Pebble Beach, Spyglass Hill and Del Monte Golf Clubs.

The Inn at Spanish Bay
2700 17-Mile Drive
Pebble Beach, CA 93953
Phone: 831-647-7500   Fax: 831-644-7955

INTERMARINE YACHTING
Yachting

Although it started out as a military contractor, Intermarine now specializes in building large composite and fiberglass yachts in the 80-200 foot range. Projects currently under construction include 95 and 142 foot tri-deck yachts. Intermarine also repairs and refurbishes all yachts—especially private yachts—at their 535 foot Savannah drydock facility.

Intermarine Yachting
301 North Lathrop Avenue
Savannah, GA 31415
Phone: 912-234-6579   Fax: 912-236-8887

THE INTERNATIONAL FINE ART AND ANTIQUE DEALERS SHOW
Events

As Brian and Anna Haughton's "International Show" enters its second decade at the Seventh Regiment Armory, its reputation as the preeminent showcase for art and antique dealers looks secure. Strict vetting ensures that only top dealers are represented at the October Fair. New exhibitors last year included the furniture and decoration specialist, Carlton Hobbs of London, and Kenneth Rendell, the popular autograph and manuscript dealer from New York. The Gala preview (which Nan Kempner co-chaired with Mrs. Daisy Soros in 1999) is usually one of the more glittering events of the year.

The International Fine Art Show
Seventh Regiment Armory
643 Park Avenue
New York, NY 10021
Phone: 212-877-0202

INN AT THE MARKET

Hotels   ***Best Kept Secret***

In the heart of Seattle's historic Pike Place Market is a small luxury hotel, tucked away like undiscovered treasure, yet in the heart of the action. As you approach the Inn at the Market through its ivy-covered courtyard, if the weather is cool enough, you will be greeted by a blazing fire in the lobby hearth, the smell of freshly brewed coffee and the lure of comfortable sofas and chairs. During 1999, sixty guestrooms underwent a transition from the traditional French floral motif to a more sophisticated

European design combining the practical requirements of the modern traveler with elements of the Biedermeier style; simple elegant lines accented by color and texture. Chenille, silk and cotton in shades of blue, beige and taupe create a warmth and sophistication. Especially favored are the waterview rooms. Parlor and Townhouse Suites retain the more traditional taste. Guests enjoy their morning coffee or tea by the fireplace, but some may prefer to begin the day on the fifth-floor arbored terrace, which offers panoramic views of Puget Sound, the islands and mountains. This award-winning hotel is the perfect place from which to explore Seattle's museums, shopping, theater and symphony.

Inn at the Market

86 Pine Street
Seattle, WA 98101
Phone: 206-443-3600   Fax: 206-448-0631

THE INTERNATIONAL FINE ART FAIR

Events

Held at the Seventh Regiment Armory in May of each year, this younger sibling to the Fine Art and Antique Dealers show is a platform for European and American paintings, drawings and sculpture. The gala dinner and preview for last year's fair, which was hosted by Mrs. Martin Gruss and Mr. Thompson Dean III and benefitted the Lenox Hill Neighborhood House, was one of the highlights of Manhattan's social calendar.

The International Fine Art Fair

Seventh Regiment Armory
643 Park Avenue
New York, NY 10021
Phone: 212-879-9713

INTERNATIONAL HOUSE

Hotels   ***Rising Star***

This beautifully designed hotel is a haven of tranquillity. As the name suggests, International House evokes the medley of cultures that have shaped New Orleans, represented by French colonial cuisine at the Lemongrass restaurant or voodoo roots at the candlelit bar. Guests are welcomed with heavy, decorative rugs during the winter, or soft white linens during the summer. Exotic and charming–a little, in short, like New Orleans itself.

International House

221 Camp Street
New Orleans, LA 70130
Phone: 504-553-9550   Fax: 504-553-9560

IRON HORSE VINEYARDS

Winemakers

The location of Iron Horse, 65 miles north of San Francisco and 10 miles from the Pacific coast, provides sunny days with fog-cooled nights and mornings, the ideal growing season for Chardonnay and Pinot Noir. Iron Horse's sparkling and still wines are traditionally served at White House state dinners and events of the past three administrations; the White House recently commissioned a special Cuvée for all of its millennium events. Iron Horse also produces several Cuvées for some of America's top chefs—Charles Palmer of Aureole in New York, Guenter Seeger in Atlanta, and Roy Yamaguchi in Hawaii—and special Cuvées for favorite customers, including Barbra Streisand.

Iron Horse Vineyards

9786 Ross Station Road
Sebastopol, CA 95472
Phone: 707-887-1507   Fax: 707-887-1337

ISLAND WEISS GALLERY

Art Dealers

Island Weiss has been supporting and promoting artists through galleries for more than 25 years. Set high above the bustle of city life, in a penthouse apartment, Weiss' eponymous gallery, which is open by appointment only, sets the standard in nontraditional exhibition space. With a collection of rare and extraordinary paintings discreetly installed throughout the luxurious living space, Weiss has created what he considers "a true environment rather than an imagined one," making the experience more realistic and enjoyable for patrons. Weiss is a leading dealer of 19th and 20th century American paintings, contemporary representational works and fine portraiture. Actively involved in artist representation and art brokerage, he also organizes museum and fine art exhibitions worldwide.

Island Weiss Gallery

201 East 69th Street, Penthouse M
New York, NY 10021
Phone: 212-861-4608   Fax: 212-861-0093

ISABELLE GREENE & ASSOCIATES

Landscape Architects

Isabelle Greene's designs are among the most photographed landscapes in the country. Transforming and reconfiguring existing gardens, she specializes in creating mature and settled looking landscapes out of brand new sites. With a degree in botany and post-graduate work in studio art, she is particularly influenced by Japanese garden design.

Isabelle Greene & Associates

2613 De La Vina Street
Santa Barbara, CA 93105
Phone: 805-569-4045

ISRAEL SACK

Antiques

Integrity is the motto of this prestigious firm, which principally deals in authentic American antique furniture. The specialty is 18th century merchandise, but you can find unusual pieces from the 17th through the early 19th centuries. A family owned business, Israel Sack has had a strong reputation within the trade for almost a century. Recommended.

Israel Sack

730 Fifth Avenue
New York, NY 10019
Phone: 212-399-6562   Fax: 212-399-9252

THE IVY

Restaurants

Reservations do not come easy at this celebrity hangout where Chef Richard Irving assembles an eclectic menu of international fare. Crab cakes, fish and chips and the grilled vegetable salad are all particularly good, as are the tarte tatin and key lime pie. The heated patio is popular, but the inside dining room is preferable for an intimate meal. Beware the abundance of poseurs.

The Ivy

113 North Robertson Boulevard
Los Angeles, CA 90048
Phone: 310-274-8303   Fax: 310-274-8170

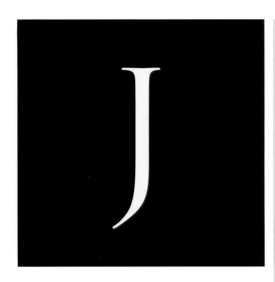

J. C. DE NIRO
Property Consultants

Jack De Niro specializes in opulent oceanfront and waterfront estates and other luxury properties in southern Florida. He attracts an international clientele through a worldwide marketing campaign and handles a wide variety of residential properties, with prices ranging from $100,000 to $39 million. With two offices and 30 agents, the company sold $60 million worth of property in just one month last year. Incidentally, Jack's nephew is actor Robert De Niro.

J. C. De Niro
407 Lincoln Road
Miami Beach, FL 33139
Phone: 561-278-7370

THE J. PAUL GETTY MUSEUM
Museums

In order to compete with the view and the architecture, the art at the Getty Museum needs to be special. And it is: the six-building complex houses the late J. Paul Getty's massive collection of Greek and Roman artifacts, European old-master paintings, and royal French furniture from the 17th and 18th centuries, as well as rotating exhibits of photography and other modern art. Set on 750 acres in Malibu overlooking the Sepulveda Pass, the Getty is the biggest, most expensive museum to be built in America since The Metropolitan Museum in New York City. Its genesis is outlined in one of our keynote features, *The Modern Acropolis*.

The J. Paul Getty Museum
1200 Getty Center Drive
Los Angeles, CA 90049
Phone: 310-440-7330

JAMES DANZIGER GALLERY
Art Dealers

This large Madison Avenue photo gallery was opened 10 years ago by James Danziger, who exclusively represents 22 photographers and estates, from Annie Leibovitz and Cecil Beaton to Henri Cartier-Bresson. Danziger was the features editor of *Vanity Fair* under Tina Brown and photo consultant to *The New Yorker*. He mounts consistently interesting shows which have attracted buyers from MOMA, the Whitney and Metropolitan museums. The Danziger Gallery was recently hailed by *The Wall Street Journal* as one of the three finest galleries in New York.

James Danziger Gallery
851 Madison Avenue
New York, NY 10021
Phone: 212-734-5300

THE JACK S. BLANTON MUSEUM OF ART
Museums

Boasting one of the nation's largest assortments of Latin American art and an extensive offering of 20th century art, this is one of the leading university museums. Its permanent collection includes over 12,000 works, spanning the history of Western culture, from ancient Mesopotamia to modern-day American technology. The Mari and James A. Michener Collection of 20th century art is one of the most comprehensive in the country, with works by Hans Hofmann, Alice Neal and Thomas Hart Benton.

The Jack S. Blanton Museum of Art
University of Texas Austin
23rd and San Jacinto
Austin, TX 78712
Phone: 512-471-2005   Fax: 512-471-7023

JAMES KIERAN PINE
Architects and Interior Designers

James Kieran Pine has worked in both residential and commercial design for clients around the world. The designer began his career in the office of Carleton Varney at age sixteen, where he came to appreciate the benefits of marrying design sense with business savvy. After several years of art and design education in Italy, Pine joined Smallbone, where he was named one of *Town and Country's* Top Ten Kitchen Designers in America. Later, as design assistant to Juan Pablo Molyneux, Pine broadened his exposure to very high-end residential interiors from Palm Beach to New York, including architectural work as well as landscape and garden design. Today, Pine owns the acclaimed Pennsbury Inn in Pennsylvania. This 18th-century farmhouse provides an ever-changing showcase for his design business, as well as for his retail store, Trade Secrets, dedicated to high-end residential furnishings. His projects span New York City, Bridgehampton, Southampton, East Hampton, Lighthouse Point, Chadds Ford, Princeton, Philadelphia, London and Saudi Arabia.

James Kieran Pine
880 Baltimore Pike
Chadds Ford, PA 19317
Phone: 610-388-8491   Fax: 610-637-3836

JACQUELINE JASPER PORTRAITS
Portrait Painters and Photographers

Jacqueline Jasper's background in the fashion world brings a classic sense of style to her work as a portrait artist. As a result, she has a strong reputation, especially in the south, where classic portraiture has long been appreciated. Specializing in painting children, she has an uncanny knack of capturing the personality as well as the likeness of her subjects. Jasper is a founding member of the American Society of Portrait Artists.

Jacqueline Jasper Portraits
360 Penn Estates
East Stroudsburg, PA 18301
Phone: 570-420-9752

JAMES ROBINSON
Antiques

James Robinson moved from England to New York City in 1912 and established his antique business there that same year. Today, Robinson's great-niece, Joan Boening, is president of the firm, which specializes in French, English and American jewelry from the 1840s to the 1950s. Among their current delights are an art deco diamond and emerald bracelet from the mid-1920s, selling for $200,000 and a Tiffany diamond and amethyst suite for $55,000.

James Robinson
480 Park Avenue
New York, NY 10022
Phone: 212-752-6166

JANOS
Restaurants

Featuring traditional southwestern American with a French touch, Janos also boasts fresh seafood flown in from the Sea of Cortez. French cooking techniques blended with local vegetables, seasonings, and herbs result in cuisine cited for excellence by the *Mobil Travel Guide* (four stars) and the James Beard Foundation.

Janos
3770 East Sunrise Drive
Tucson, AZ 85718
Phone: 520-615-6100   Fax: 520-615-3334

JANIS ALRIDGE
Antiques

If your heart is set on mechanical, architectural and natural-history engravings from the 17th through the 20th centuries, you have found the right place—with three different venues. You can stop into the store year-round in Washington, D.C.; view by appointment in New York; or browse seasonally on Nantucket Island. Expert presentation, framing and matting lend this dealer its impeccable reputation. The collection also comprises English School paintings, 18th and 19th century European antiques and a fabulous selection of hand-blown, hand-etched crystal lamps and English shades.

Janis Alridge
2900 M Street, NW
Washington, DC 20007
Phone: 202-338-7710

JAPONESQUE
Specialty Shops

Japonesque is a gallery which specializes in showcasing the Japanese aesthetic: from antiques to contemporary artwork and furnishings. Owner Koichi Hara also displays his own architectural yet organic designs and tables. In the annex, Japonesque on the Pier, there is a comprehensive selection of large stoneworks by Izumi Masatoshi, Noguchi's collaborator for over two decades.

Japonesque
824 Montgomery Street
San Francisco, CA 94133
Phone: 415-391-8860   Fax: 415-391-3530

JARDINIÈRE
Restaurants   *Rising Star*

After an inspiring evening of music at Davies Symphony Hall, discerning San Franciscans stroll across to this youthful supper club, where the orchestrations of Traci Des Jardins combine French and Californian cuisine with considerable aplomb. The marble and mahogany interior, which was designed by co-owner Pat Kuleto, complements the food with its good taste and sophistication.

Jardinière
300 Grove Street
San Francisco, CA 94102
Phone: 415-861-5555   Fax: 415-861-5580

JEAN GEORGES
Restaurants   *Rising Star*

The latest addition to the restaurant empire of the surprisingly modest Jean-Georges Vongerichten and partners Phil Suarez and Bob Giraldi. This one is in the new Trump International Hotel, a short stroll from Lincoln Center for opera, concert, and drama lovers. The dining room is a bit more formal than the Nougatine café, but the place to be is the terrace on a pleasant evening. Service is excellent, the decor is dazzling and Vongerichten's food—as always—is wonderful. Looks like another winner.

Jean Georges
Trump International Hotel
One Central Park West
New York, NY 10023
Phone: 212-299-3900

JEFFREY BILHUBER
Architects and Interior Designers

In addition to teaching at the Parsons School of Design and mounting a major photography exhibition at the Metropolitan Museum of Art, Jeffrey Bilhuber is, at the time of writing, handling ten interior design projects. In the past he has decorated homes for Paul Wilmot, Peter Jennings and Randolph Duke. Bilhuber describes his style as "American Classicism."

Jeffrey Bilhuber
330 East 59th Street
New York, NY 10022
Phone: 212-308-4888

JENSEN-SMITH
Property Consultants

Between them, co-owners Betty Jensen and Melanie Smith know every inch of prime real estate in the Connecticut area. Their territory begins at water's edge and extends into the rolling countryside of Fairfield County. Jensen-Smith specialize in the sale of outstanding historic homes; some of them are less than fifty miles from Manhattan.

Jensen-Smith
411 Pequot Avenue
Southport, CT 06490
Phone: 203-255-1001   Fax: 203-255-2330

HOTEL JEROME
Hotels

Established in the heart of Aspen in 1889, the Hotel Jerome is famous for its old-world ambiance. A member of *The Leading Hotels of the World*, meticulous attention to detail is evident throughout, and the Jerome is widely renowned for offering quiet elegance, gracious hospitality and unobtrusive pampering. A stunning tribute to the charm of a bygone era.

Hotel Jerome
330 East Main Street
Aspen, CO 81611
Phone: 970-920-1000

JERRY DILTS AND ASSOCIATES
Party Organizers and Caterers

Not your regular cookie-cutter caterer, Jerry Dilts has been concocting exclusive private parties and upscale soirées for the past 30 years. His expert team can accommodate crystal and china service for up to 500 people. Dilts works in many of the more elegant homes in Atlanta, including the Governor's mansion. Some of his staff have been on board for over 15 years, consistently providing the sort of service one expects from an experienced team.

Jerry Dilts and Associates
500 Bishop Street, NW
Atlanta, GA 30309
Phone: 404-352-0611

JETSOURCE
Airplanes

JetSource provides private jet charters out of Carlsbad Airport, in Southern California. The firm has two Lear 35s for short trips to Las Vegas or Dallas and one Challenger 601, which has full international capabilities. JetSource can also out-source any plane for mission-specific requirements. Client confidentiality is a priority.

JetSource
2036 Palomar Airport Road
Carlsbad, CA 92008
Phone: 760-804-1500   Fax: 760-804-1515

JFA DESIGNS
Jewelry and Watches

The rings, bracelets, pendants, necklaces, earrings and cufflinks which bear his name distinguish Jean-Francois Albert among contemporary jewelry designers as a leader and innovator. Born in Lausanne, Switzerland, Albert's big break came when he was hired by the house of Piaget in his early twenties. Today his focus on colored gemstones and pearls is challenging the centuries long dominance of diamonds as the most prized of stones.

JFA Designs
17791 Fitch
Irvine, CA 92614
Phone: 949-263-9909   Fax: 949-263-9910

THE JOCKEY CLUB
Private Clubs

The only private dining, smoking and dancing club in Beverly Hills, The Jockey Club's membership includes studio heads, agents and, of course, the requisite movie stars. Just east of Rodeo Drive, the Barbara Lockhart–designed space holds one of the finer restaurants in the area, Chasen's, where Chef Andreas Kisler helps members wind down after a long, hard day of filming. Poor dears.

The Jockey Club
246 North Cannon Drive
Beverly Hills, CA 90210
Phone: 310-858-3060

JOEL SOROKA GALLERY
Art Dealers

Native New Yorker Joel Soroka moved to Aspen to open this intimate fine art photo gallery. Soroka's inventory includes works by early 20th century artists (Man Ray, Edward Weston) and he also represents contemporary photographers like Beatrice Helg and Josef Sudek. Well worth investigating when you tire of all that snow.

Joel Soroka Gallery
400 East Hyman Avenue
Aspen, CO 81611
Phone: 970-920-3152   Fax: 970-920-3823

JOHN BARRETT SALON
Hair and Beauty

Haircuts, color and blow-dries are not the only services available at this state-of-the-art salon on the ninth-floor penthouse of the Bergdorf Goodman empire in New York. Schedule an appointment for a manicure, pedicure, or waxing treatment as a respite from your shopping spree. Clients range from uptown madams to international guests seeking John Barrett's talents.

John Barrett Salon
754 Fifth Avenue
New York, NY 10019
Phone: 212-872-2700   Fax: 212-872-2709

JOHN BARTLETT
Fashion   Rising Star

A new hero in the fashion industry, John Bartlett received the 1994 CFDA Award for new fashion talent and the 1997 CFDA award for best menswear designer. Recognized for their edgy quality and funky, downtown style, Bartlett's clothes are elegant but casual, created from cashmere and the finest Italian materials. He has dressed Cindy Crawford, Julianne Moore and Ashley Judd; Janet Jackson wore one of his shirts to last year's Grammy Awards. Bartlett's day and evening wear can be found in Barneys, Neiman Marcus, Saks, Ultimo, and Bloomingdale's.

John Bartlett
650 Fifth Avenue
New York, NY 10019
Phone: 212-245-6750

JOHN BERGGRUEN GALLERY
Art Dealers

After a training that included a stint in his father's gallery on Paris's Left Bank, John Berggruen moved on to the Brook Street Gallery in London, New York's Perls Galleries and finally opened up his own space in San Francisco in 1970. Highly regarded within the trade, Berggruen specializes in modern and contemporary art; works by Picasso and Matisse are frequently in stock and the gallery also represents contemporary artists like Squeak Carnwath and David Bates.

John Berggruen Gallery
228 Grant Avenue
San Francisco, CA 94108
Phone: 415-781-4629

JOHN DAUGHERTY, REALTORS
Property Consultants

An affiliate of Sotheby's International Realty and Leading Estates of the World, John Daugherty specializes in luxury estates in the most prestigious neighborhoods of Houston. His properties range from French-style estates with marble columns, fountains and lush gardens to Mediterranean-style homes on large, landscaped lots. Owner John A. Daugherty, Jr. founded the firm in 1967.

John Daugherty, Realtors
520 Post Oak Boulevard
Houston, TX 77027
Phone: 713-626-3930   Fax: 713-963-9588

JOHN H. SUROVEK GALLERY
Art Dealers

John Surovek's impressive gallery has dealt for 30 years in 19th and early 20th century works by artists like John Singer Sargent, van Gogh, Andrew Wyeth and Childe Hassam. Surovek deals world-wide, exclusively representing Stephen Scott Young and the estate of William Glackens; his range also extends to Peale and Bellows. Well worth a detour.

John H. Surovek Gallery
349 Worth Avenue, #8 Via Parigi
Palm Beach, FL 33480
Phone: 561-832-0422

JOHN & PAUL HERRING & CO.
Art Consultants   Best Kept Secret

The Herring twins, Paul and John, enjoy considerable renown among the art-world cognoscenti in New York, London and Paris. For many years they have shuttled between the three cities, acting as private art dealers to a highly select group of connoisseurs. A few years back, for instance, they famously acquired a $50 million Cézanne still life for cosmetics heir Ronald Lauder. But the majority of their business is conducted behind firmly closed doors. With impeccable aesthetics and an old-world disdain for indiscretion, the Herring twins have quietly built a reputation for themselves as the art dealer's art dealer.

John & Paul Herring & Co.
10 East 68th Street
New York, NY 10021
Phone: 212-628-5763

THE JOHN SAHAG WORKSHOP
Hair and Beauty

The inimitable John Sahag had his first foray into the hair world when at six years of age he began working in a salon. At the ripe old age of 16, he earned his first major editorial feature. Nowadays his client roster includes royalty, supermodels, business titans and a host of Condé Nasties. It was Sahag who took the long, golden tresses of Gwyneth Paltrow and, well, cut them off.

The John Sahag Workshop
425 Madison Avenue
New York, NY 10017
Phone: 212-750-7772   Fax: 212-750-7494

JORDAN VINEYARD & WINERY
Winemakers

Jordan is one of the most beautiful vineyards in the world–Lafite for the Alexander Valley! The facilities are ultra modern, yet the wine produced at Jordan (mostly Cabernet Sauvignon) has an old world flavor. Visit the winery if you have an opportunity, but remember to call ahead.

Jordan Vineyard & Winery
1474 Alexander Valley Road
Healdsburg, CA 95448
Phone: 707-431-5250   Fax: 707-431-5259

JOHN'S ISLAND CLUB
Golf Clubs

Located on a barrier island between the Atlantic Ocean and Indian River, this "very private" club maintains three courses, identified by points on the compass North, South and West. Tom Fazio made something of a stylistic departure in designing the unusually hilly West course; its 18th is one of the truly great holes in golf. The North and South courses were designed by Pete Dye in the late 1960s and early 70s, although they are currently being redesigned by Craig Schreiner and should be completed in 2000. The club is not currently taking new members.

John's Island Club
3 John's Island Drive
Vero Beach, FL 32963
Phone: 561-231-1700

JONES, DAY, REAVIS & POGUE
Law Firms

Among the world's largest and most geographically diverse law firms, Jones Day encompasses more than 1100 lawyers in 20 offices spanning the globe and incorporating all the major centers of business and finance. The firm has been engaged for legal practice by more than half of the *Fortune 500* companies and also serves smaller companies, foundations, educational institutions and individuals.

Jones, Day, Reavis & Pogue
North Point
901 Lakeside Avenue
Cleveland, OH 44114
Phone: 216-586-3939

JOSEPHINE SASSO
Fashion   *Rising Star*

Josephine Sasso has a big future in the fashion business. Her unique custom ordering system enables the client to create countless looks based on her own needs and tastes. There are forty basic silhouettes, each one available in a wide array of fabrics, which mix and match in multiple combinations, allowing chic, discerning women to build their own personalized wardrobes.

Josephine Sasso
93 East Lancaster Avenue
Paoli, PA 19301
Phone: 610-408-8599   Fax: 610-408-8717

JOSEPH A. BANK CLOTHIERS
Fashion

Every product designed by Joseph A. Bank Clothiers is backed by an unconditional guarantee. And it is no wonder: since 1905, the company has provided the business world with exceptional quality and value as well as timeless styling. This line of men's classic, tailored and casual clothing is available at over 100 stores nationwide.

Joseph A. Bank Clothiers
500 Hanover Pike
Hampstead, MD 21074
Phone: 410-239-2700   Fax: 410-239-5700

JOSEPH PHELPS
Winemakers

In the 1970s Joe Phelps came to California seeking to expand his Colorado construction firm and inadvertently got hooked on the wine business. Ever the experimenter, he has a number of "Firsts" to his credit, including the 1978 release of his 1974 Insignia, the first Bordeaux-style blend in America: Cabernet Sauvignon, Cabernet Franc and Merlot. Produced in California under a proprietary label, Phelps was the first American winery to offer a true Syrah wine.

Joseph Phelps
200 Taplin Road
St. Helena, CA 94574
Phone: 800-707-5789

JOSHUA & COMPANY
Property Consultants

Many of the most luxurious residences in Aspen, Colorado are sold by this boutique real estate firm. Properties range from elegant country homes with magnificent mountain views to contemporary ranches to remodeled duplexes in Mountain Valley. Properties handled by the five-agent company are seldom publicly advertised. Instead, they are "quietly for sale." Prices range from $500,000 to $12.5 million with an average exceeding $3 million. Owner Joshua Saslove, who founded the company in 1976, has sold homes to numerous celebrities, including diet guru Jenny Craig and actor George Hamilton.

Joshua & Company
300 South Hunter Street
Aspen, CO 81611
Phone: 970-925-8810

JOSIE NATORI
Fashion

Established as a manufacturer of lingerie, Natori recently launched its signature evening wear collection. Sculpted into simple, architectural shapes, the line is structured around lean, kimono-inspired jackets and silk-lined tunics, fluid trousers, envelope-neckline dresses, bias skirts, and gently fitted sweaters. Fine European fabrics ranging from delicate wool, lace and beaded knits to double faced wools, dense jerseys, viscose crepes and cashmeres provide a lush, textural dimension to their stunning collection. Look for the collection at Bergdorf Goodman, Saks and Neiman Marcus.

Josie Natori
40 East 34th Street
New York, NY 10016
Phone: 212-532-7796

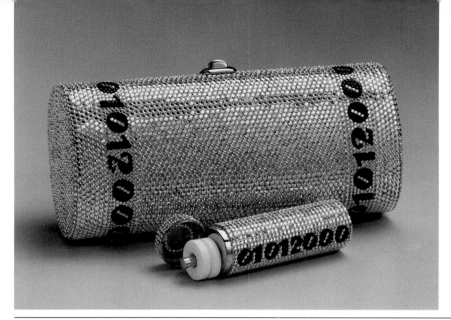

JUDITH LEIBER
Fashion
Judith Leiber has been designing her full line of timeless collectibles since the 1960s. Austrian crystal beading decorates her exclusive pillboxes, change purses and handbags, which come in all shapes and sizes. Cats, dogs and polar bears make up only a few of the animal-shaped bags; other nature-inspired designs include tomatoes, eggs, and roses. Leiber's uniquely funky bags have accessorized Naomi Campbell, Hillary Rodham Clinton and Rosie O'Donnell.

Judith Leiber
20 West 33rd Street
New York, NY 10001
Phone: 212-736-4244

JP KING AUCTION COMPANY
Auction Houses
JP King keeps its sales–and they are *big* sales–in the family. Over the past 84 years, four generations have run the celebrated auction house, which is the oldest specializing in the sale of luxury properties and ranches. Calumet Farms, one of the nation's leading studs, sold at JP King Auction Company a few years ago for more than $20 million. So it is no surprise that the new generations stay in this lucrative family business.

JP King Auction Company
108 Fountain Avenue
Gadsden, AL 35901
Phone: 256-546-5217

JP MORGAN
Wealth Management
Warren Buffett once averred that Wall Street is the only place where people visit in a Rolls Royce to get advice from people who take the subway. Mr. Buffett, as usual, was right on the money. JP Morgan is the archetype for Wall Street operations that boast high-flying clients. Nowadays the investment house offers integrated wealth management for private clients. Although there are no formal minimum account requirements, you will probably need at least $1 million in investable assets; with that sort of money you will have access to some of the best advisors in the land.

JP Morgan
60 Wall Street
New York, NY 10260
Phone: 212-483-2323

JUAN JUAN SALON
Hair and Beauty
Do not let the earthy ambiance, aromatherapy scents and unique architecture fool you. This Wilshire Boulevard star has all the comforts of a New Age retreat with the cutting edge technology of an innovative, upscale salon. Colorist Jonathan Gale is renowned for bringing "fried and dyed" hair back to life. Uma Thurman and Diane Keaton are fans of Juan Juan.

Juan Juan Salon
9667 Wilshire Boulevard
Beverly Hills, CA 90210
Phone: 310-278-5826

JUPITER HILLS
Golf Clubs
Tom Fazio and his uncle, George Fazio, collaborated in designing the two courses at this popular club, which Bob Hope and William Clay Ford founded. The Hills course has been ranked among the top 100 courses in the country since it was finished in 1970. The signature ninth hole is all carry over sand. The Village course was completed in 1979. Of special note are the par threes and the unforgiving, fluffy sand.

Jupiter Hills
11800 South East Hill Club Terrace
Tequesta, FL 33469
Phone: 561-746-5151

JUST ASK PETER
Party Organizers & Caterers
Best Kept Secret
Word of mouth is all that Peter Helburn needs to keep clients clamoring for his services. For ten years he has organized weddings, galas and parties for some of the most demanding clients in the United States. Trained by the legendary Fairmont Hilton, Helburn was part of the opening team of the Little Nell Hotel. William F. Macy, Felicity Huffman and Hollywood moguls beckon Helburn to produce their soirées. Between parties, he donates his time by serving on the boards of The Aspen Ballet Company and School, The Aspen Valley Medical Foundation, and Les Dames d'Aspen. Warmly recommended.

Just Ask Peter
608 West Hopkins Avenue, #2
Aspen, CO 81611
Phone: 970-925-3351   Fax: 970-544-0086

JUDITH RIPKA
Jewelry and Watches
First Lady Hillary Clinton commissioned Judith Ripka to design an historic pin for the Presidential Inauguration in 1997. Ripka has also designed pins for the Long Island Philharmonic, the United States Holocaust Museum's fifth anniversary and numerous charity organizations. She is well known for her signature PN1, a strand of pearls with an 18-karat gold loop and toggle closure that can be used to create endless design possibilities–you can even add rare stones, clip-on pendants and intricate metal work.

Judith Ripka
21 West 46th Street
New York, NY 10036
Phone: 212-391-2340   Fax: 212-644-5936

FRANK KAMER, M.D.

Cosmetic Surgeons

While other doctors can perform face-lifts, liposuction, breast augmentations, and other commonly requested procedures, Dr. Kamer specializes in everything from the neck up, including face-lifts, nose jobs, and brow work.

Frank Kamer, M.D.

201 South Lasky Drive
Beverly Hills, CA 90212
Phone: 310-556-8155

KAY LEDBETTER & ASSOCIATES

Property Consultants

Kentucky's bluegrass region is known for its horse farms that raise thoroughbreds for the likes of the Kentucky Derby. When these farms, or other residential properties worth over $1 million, go on the market, Kay Ledbetter is invariably on the short list of realtors who represent them. With her aggressive marketing style, the Lexington area's big landholders have access to a market that spans the entire United States.

Kay Ledbetter & Associates

3138 Custard Drive
Lexington, KY 40517
Phone: 606-273-2825

KEMBLE INTERIORS

Specialty Shops

One of the more endearing characters in Palm Beach owns this successful interior design practice; Mimi Kemble's eclectic and whimsical style is complemented by impeccable taste. Kemble has been in business for over 30 years. She works for a host of celebrities and corporate bigwigs (discreetly refusing to divulge their names), while her daughter, Celery, takes care of younger clients–many are based in Los Angeles.

Kemble Interiors

294 Hibiscus Avenue
Palm Beach, FL 33480
Phone: 561-659-5556   Fax: 561-833-3476

KENNEDY GALLERIES

Art Dealers

One of the oldest and most respected dealers in American art, Kennedy Galleries has been going strong since 1874. The erudite staff at this prestigious Fifth Avenue space have remarkable enthusiasm for 18th, 19th and 20th century masters. Look out for their collection of Hudson River School works.

Kennedy Galleries

730 Fifth Avenue
New York, NY 10019
Phone: 212-541-9600   Fax: 212-977-3833

KENNEDY & VIOLICH

Architects and Interior Designers

Sheila Kennedy and Frano Violich own one of the largest and most influential architectural firms in the Boston area. It was one of 12 firms included in last year's "Fabrications" exhibition, co-sponsored by three American museums, including the Museum of Modern Art. Kennedy is also an associate professor at the Harvard Graduate School of Design.

Kennedy & Violich

160 North Washington Street
Boston, MA 02114
Phone: 617-367-3784

KENSINGTON COUNTRY CLUB

Private Clubs

Only residents of Kensington, a private, gated community centrally located in the Naples area, have the privilege of joining the Kensington Country Club, which boasts a golf course designed by Robert Trent Jones, Jr., a tennis center with seven courts and a clubhouse that offers a fitness center, semi-casual dining and pool facilities. At the time of writing a few properties were still available at Kensington.

Kensington Country Club

2700 Pine Ridge Road
Naples, FL 34109
Phone: 941-649-4440   Fax: 941-649-0427

KENT SCHOOL

Schools

Founded in 1906 by the Reverend Frederick H. Sill, the Kent School has maintained its strong affiliation to the Episcopal church; students are required to take two term courses in theology before they graduate. Sill's intention was to teach students "the value of physical labor," and, with six days of classes per week and five courses per term, they do maintain a rigorous schedule. Students at Kent enjoy a diverse array of extracurricular activities, from assisting the Kent volunteer fire department to running the school's radio station to playing in one of the Dixieland bands at the school.

Kent School

PO Box 2006
One Macedonia Road
Kent, CT 06757
Phone: 860-927-6000

KENTSHIRE GALLERIES

Antique Dealers

The 59 year old Kentshire Galleries specializes in 18th and 19th century English furniture and antique jewelry. Known especially for its Georgian and Regency period furniture, Kentshire's clients include most of the leading interior decorators and architects in the United States, Europe and South America. Bergdorf Goodman's seventh floor jewelry and antiques shop is Kentshire's exclusive outlet.

Kentshire Galleries

37 East 12th Street
New York, NY 10003
Phone: 212-673-6644

KENTUCKY DERBY

Events

For over 100 years the first Saturday in May has been known as Derby Day; on this day each year, three-year old thoroughbreds have raced into history at Churchill Downs, home of the Kentucky Derby. For the two weeks leading up to the Derby, the entire town of Louisville is caught up in the festivities, which is no wonder, since only Ascot can compete.

Kentucky Derby

Churchill Downs Derby Office
700 Central Avenue
Louisville, KY 40208
Phone: 502-584-6383

KERRY JOYCE

Architects and Interior Designers

Kerry Joyce, long renowned for his love for detail and fine materials, deftly creates interiors that reflect a broad range of styles and personalities. "I reject trend or fad," states Joyce, "creating a timeless, enduring interior is very important to me." Some of Joyce's recent projects include remodeling a 1930s Southampton beach house for Ian Schrager and the L.A. and Manhattan homes of MTV CEO, Tom Freston.

Kerry Joyce

115 North La Brea Avenue
Los Angeles, CA 90036
Phone: 323-938-4442   Fax: 323-938-0484

KEY LIME PIE SALON AND WELLNESS SPA

Hair and Beauty

With its abundance of fresh flowers, scented candles, family heirlooms and natural sunlight,

KARL KEMP & ASSOCIATES

Antiques

New York's leading dealer of neoclassical furniture has been in business since 1987, selling the finest quality European neoclassical and Biedermeier furniture and decorative objects. German-born Kemp came to New York in the 1970s, where he began collecting exquisite antique furniture. In his early career, Kemp bought antiques on his many shopping trips to Europe and stored them in his home in New York, until visiting friends, recognizing his flair for quality, purchased them. Later, his keen eye was noticed by the late Urs Christen, whose New York gallery was known for the finest neoclassical antiques. Christen persuaded Kemp to manage his gallery and it is under his mentor that Kemp acquired the necessary skills to operate a successful gallery, becoming one of Christen's greatest discoveries. Today you can visit his gallery and browse the elegant mixture of early neoclassical antiques from the late 18th and early 19th centuries at his showroom in downtown Manhattan, where you will also find a stylish collection of fine French art deco from the 1920s—architectural, clean and streamlined, with an emphasis on beautiful wood.

Karl Kemp & Associates

36 East 10th Street
New York, NY 10003
Phone: 212-254-1877   Fax: 212-228-1236

Key Lime Pie is not therapeutic so much as downright spiritual! Aromatherapy sessions, full body massages and hydrotherapy treatments are a few of the indulgences provided by the spa, while the salon, which uses all natural cleansers and styling agents without animal byproducts, offers extensive hair and scalp treatments. Elton John, Natalie Merchant and Monica Seles have enjoyed "sensory journeys" in this cozy but chic retreat.

Key Lime Pie Salon and
Wellness Spa

806 North Highland Avenue
Atlanta, GA 30306
Phone: 404-873-6512   Fax: 404-873-0386

THE KEYES COMPANY

Property Consultants

A mega-brokerage company located in Florida, The Keyes offers a large array of services to its clients, including home sales, title insurance, financing, property management, commercial investment property and extensive relocation services. Exclusive residences handled by the firm include unique homes on private islands, luxury condos on Miami Beach and restored older houses.

The Keyes Company

1023 Lincoln Road
Miami Beach, FL 33139
Phone: 305-531-5803   Fax: 305-531-5883

KIAWAH ISLAND GOLF & TENNIS RESORT

Hotels

This award-winning resort offers five championship golf courses, fashioned by greats like Jack Nicklaus and Clyde Johnston. Exceptional dining and tennis, and ten miles of pristine beach lend it further appeal among sybarites and athletes alike. Guests can stay at the newly renovated Kiawah Island Inn, or in one of many villas.

Kiawah Island Golf & Tennis Resort

12 Kiawah Beach Drive
Kiawah Island, SC 29455
Phone: 843-768-2121   Fax: 843-768-6828

KIESELSTEIN-CORD
Fashion
Barry Kieselstein-Cord created his first jewelry collection for Georg Jensen back in 1972. By the early 80s, his gold and silver designs were turning heads across the country. Nowadays he also creates handbags, belts, luggage, small leather goods, eyewear, gloves and home furnishings. His pieces are signed, dated and copyrighted, and are collected by people like Steven Spielberg and Oprah Winfrey. Kieselstein-Cord will open a flagship store on Madison Avenue in April of 2000.

Kieselstein-Cord
132A East 65th Street
New York, NY 10021
Phone: 212-288-0200   Fax: 212-288-3438

KIMBELL ART MUSEUM
Museums
This museum, which bears the name of founder Kay Kimbell, boasts a diverse collection, including works by El Greco, Velazquez, Cézanne, Picasso, Matisse and Mondrian. Besides European works, the museum also has the largest collection of Asian arts in the Southwestern United States, as well as fine collections of African and Mediterranean antiquities.

Kimbell Art Museum
3333 Camp Bowie Boulevard
Fort Worth, TX 76107
Phone: 817-654-1034

KING & SPALDING
Law Firms
In its mission statement, this premier law firm cites quality legal work, client service and community stewardship as its three fundamentals. In 1998, the firm unveiled its on-premises courtroom—a state of the art facility designed to give attorneys a preparatory edge in litigation.

King & Spalding
191 Peachtree Street, NE
Atlanta, GA 30303
Phone: 404-572-4600

KINGSMILL RESORT
Spas and Clinics
Cradled by the oaks, hardwoods, and dogwoods that border the James River, the stately Kingsmill Resort is sculpted into the rolling hills of Virginia. Williamsburg's only spa offers facials, massages, and body treatments; more action-minded guests can visit the state-of-the-art fitness center. In addition to the spa, the resort also features three PGA-level golf courses.

Kingsmill Resort
1010 Kingsmill Road
Williamsburg, VA 23185
Phone: 800-832-5665

Courtesy of The Jack S. Blanton Museum of Art.

KINSEY MARABLE BOOKSELLERS
Specialty Shops
This former Wall Street honcho has translated his love of the printed word into a thriving business which caters to budding bibliophiles. Marable's store, which was designed by Charlotte Moss, positively beckons one to nestle into a comfortable corner with a good book. Marable designs personal libraries for many clients, specializing in first edition or out of print gardening, design, architecture and society books.

Kinsey Marable Booksellers
18 East 67th Street
New York, NY 10021
Phone: 212-717-0342

KITTANSETT CLUB
Golf Clubs
Designed by Frederick Hood in 1922, the course at "Kitty" is known for its treacherous 215-yard, par three 11th hole, its classic old school design and the signature third hole, whose green is surrounded by sand. The course itself is located on a small point of land in Buzzards Bay at the southern end of the Cape Cod Canal, and has water on three sides. Membership is currently full, as is the waiting list.

Kittansett Club
11 Point Road
Marion, MA 02738
Phone: 508-748-0148   Fax: 508-748-0518

KINDEL FURNITURE

Specialty Shops

The woodworkers of Grand Rapids have been crafting traditionally designed furniture at Kindel since 1901, and the original casegoods plant is still open today. Although no longer owned by the Kindels, this old-line furniture maker is still a family company; just this year CEO Robert Fogarty named his daughter Paula as President. The Fogartys have presided over a fourfold growth of Kindel's business, marked in 1982 by their exclusive agreement with the Winterthur Museum to make reproductions of some of the objects in Henry Francis du Pont's famed collection. Kindel does not so much reproduce furniture as bring back to life the entire production process from the 18th and 19th centuries, to create objects at unrivaled standards of excellence. Copying the detail work found in the best 18th century American furniture at the level of accuracy demanded means that it must be hand carved. All the original primary materials, including mahogany, walnut and cherry, are used in the "line for line" reproductions, which vary in their dimensions from the originals by less than one thirty-second of an inch. Two years after Kindel was awarded the license to reproduce furniture from the Winterthur Museum, it became the exclusive licensee to the Irish Georgian Society. Today, shoppers in Ireland can browse through Kindel's collection of Irish Georgian furniture at Leixlip Castle, County Kildare, home of the Society's founder, the Honorable Desmond Guiness. In 1995 Paula Fogarty developed The Neoclassic Collection of furniture and this year she is introducing a collection for Carleton Varney and Sons, entitled "The Varney's Present: Our Favorite Things."

Kindel Furniture

100 Garden Street, PO Box 2047
Grand Rapids, MI 49501
Phone: 616-243-3676   Fax: 616-243-6248

THE KNICKERBOCKER CLUB

Private Clubs

This exclusive club is a favorite of transplanted French and old New York families. Its patio overlooking Central Park is the best breakfast venue in Manhattan. The gentleman's-only bar seems to have been removed cleanly from the last century, complete with formidable French barmen. The mixed drawing room is a pleasant respite from busy Madison Avenue, particularly during the winter when a fireplace is lit.

The Knickerbocker Club

2 East 62nd Street
New York, NY 10021
Phone: 212-838-6700

KNIGHT SECURITY SYSTEMS

Security Consultants

The premier designer and installer of high end home and corporate security systems in Texas, Knight Security Systems keep the Dallas offices of Fidelity Investments safe and sound. Knight does not sell packages; all work is customized to site specific requirements. In addition to design and installation, Knight will monitor systems anywhere throughout the Southwest.

Knight Security Systems

11056 Shady Trail
Dallas, TX 75229
Phone: 214-350-1632

KROLL ASSOCIATES

Security Consultants

When you need to know *exactly* who you're up against, talk to Kroll. If a company suspects that employees are embezzling funds, absconding with proprietary information, or even if an executive is in danger of being kidnapped and held for ransom, its highly-trained team of investigators are often brought in to handle the situation. Founded in New York in 1972, Kroll now has offices located throughout the Americas, Europe and Asia. Specializing in financial fraud, corporate investigations, litigation intelligence, monitoring services and asset searching and analysis, the firm's clients have included the governments of Russia, Kuwait and the United States.

Kroll Associates

900 Third Avenue
New York, NY 10022
Phone: 212-593-1000   Fax: 212-593-3509

KRONISH, LIEB, WEINER & HELLMAN, L.L.P.

Law Firms

This New York based firm has been providing legal services around the world since 1958. The diverse client base includes many high-net worth individuals as well as insurance companies, commercial and investment banks, media and telecommunications businesses, high-technology corporations, property owners and developers. Through its system of lean and cost-effective staffing, clients gain direct access to the firm's highly skilled senior attorneys.

Kronish, Lieb, Weiner & Hellman, L.L.P.

1114 Avenue of the Americas
New York, NY 10036
Phone: 212-479-6000

KURT E. SCHON

Art Dealers

If art is where your heart is, you will love this New Orleans gallery, which specializes in 18th and 19th century French and English paintings, but also includes modern works. Among the magnificent pieces are portraits from the Court of Louis XIV and paintings once exhibited at London's Royal Academy and the Paris Salon.

Kurt E. Schon

510 St. Louis Street
New Orleans, LA 70130
Phone: 504-523-5902

L.A. LOUVER GALLERY
Art Dealers

The L.A. Louver Gallery, which Peter Goulds opened in 1975, is committed to showcasing the best contemporary art, exemplified by current and upcoming exhibitions of work by Dale Chihuly, David Hockney and Tony Berlant. For its museum quality exhibitions, the gallery recently built a new three-story, 8,000 square foot building, which was designed by Frederick Fisher.

L.A. Louver Gallery
45 North Venice Boulevard
Venice, CA 90291
Phone: 310-822-4955   Fax: 310-821-7529

LAGOS
Jewelry and Watches

Steven Lagos' award-winning collections exude a classic signature style, designed for comfort, versatility and flexibility. The Lagos collection of over 1000 pieces in 22-karat gold, 18-karat gold and platinum with precious stones has garnered worldwide attention.

Lagos
1735 Walnut Street
Philadelphia, PA 19103
Phone: 215-567-0770

LAKE PLACID LODGE
Hotels   ***Best Kept Secret***

The 19th century lodge which is the centerpiece of Christie and David Garrett's seductive resort is a classic example of the Adirondack style. Tall stone fireplaces, rough-hewn cedar, pine and handmade twig furniture offer guests a frontier experience amidst the pristine beauty of Great Lakes wilderness, but with all the amenities of a full-service resort. The lakefront cabins are beautifully decorated and offer great privacy.

Lake Placid Lodge
Whiteface Inn Road, P.O. Box 550
Lake Placid, NY 12946
Phone: 518-523-2700   Fax: 518-523-1124

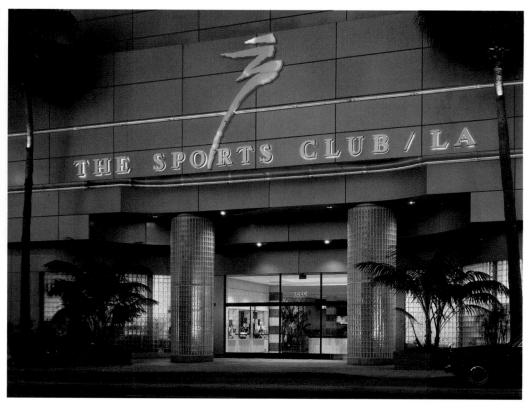

THE L.A. SPORTS CLUB
Fitness

With over 100,000 square feet at its disposal, this luxury athletic club can afford to be comprehensive. Attractions in the $35 million complex include two restaurants, a clothing store, a hair salon, a massage area, an entire floor devoted to weights, a basketball court, a pool, a cardio floor, daily classes and private trainers. Among the 400 employees, there is a nutritionist and dietitian on board to help balance your workout routine with a healthy intake of food. Members include Madonna and Princess Stephanie of Monaco. Two new Sports Clubs are scheduled to open in New York in early 2000.

The L.A. Sports Club
1835 Sepulveda Boulevard
Los Angeles, CA 90025
Phone: 310-477-7799

LAKESIDE GOLF CLUB
Golf Clubs

Along with the Bel-Air, Riviera and Los Angeles Country Clubs, Lakeside was among the first wave of important golfing enclaves founded in the Los Angeles area in the 1920s. Members Bing Crosby, Dean Martin and Bob Hope played on its undulating course, which runs along the "L.A. River Bed," opposite Universal Studios, in Toluca Lake. Although it is a short course, Lakeside demands great accuracy. The club still caters to celebrities and other show business bigwigs.

Lakeside Golf Club
4500 Lakeside Drive
Burbank, CA 91505
Phone: 818-984-0601

LAKEVIEW INN
Restaurants

Alain Sailhac of Le Cirque and "21" fame oversees the menu at Doug and Dorothy Hamilton's upscale country restaurant on Lake Waramaug. Dining areas include an outdoor deck, a garden room and a private dining room which has been decorated with memorabilia from the nearby Kent School. Jasper Johns, Kathleen Turner and Henry Kissinger are frequent guests. Five deluxe suites are available for overnight lodging. The Hamiltons also own the French Culinary Institute in New York.

Lakeview Inn
107 N. Shore Road
New Preston, CT 06777
Phone: 860-868-1000   Fax: 860-868-2595

LAMBERTSON TRUEX
Fashion   ***Rising Star***

Longevity and style are keywords at this young firm, where accessory designers Richard Lambertson and John Truex have already created a modern classic in their signature Box Car Tote. Alexandra von Furstenberg, Sharon Stone and many of New York's more prominent socialites are among their clients. Look for beautifully produced leather bags and attaché cases by Lambertson Truex in Bergdorf Goodman and Neiman Marcus.

Lambertson Truex
19 West 21st Street
New York, NY 10010
Phone: 212-243-7671

THE LARK
Restaurants
Diners' polls in *Condé Nast Traveler* and *Gourmet* have voted The Lark, located in a high-income suburb of Detroit, one of the best restaurants in the United States. Situated in a walled garden filled with flowers and wild birds, it is the quintessential country inn, transplanted to an upscale community of automobile-manufacturing aristocracy. Sit in the main dining room near a window to enjoy the landscape, or find a seat in the more intimate café.

The Lark
6430 Farmington Road
West Bloomfield, MI 48322
Phone: 248-661-4466

LATHAM & WATKINS
Law Firms
Latham & Watkins is one of the top business law firms in the world, with more than 950 attorneys in nine U.S. and five international offices. Lawyers are well versed in a broad range of business-related matters and trained to apply practical tactics to resolve a case or close a deal, without being derailed by legal obstacles. Teamwork is the underlying strategy for tackling solutions, with the client always the leader and decision-maker. Meantime, the collective experience of the firm's lawyers and all its resources are available at the drop of a hat through a labyrinthine communications system. Latham & Watkins has been called the "best managed firm in the legal profession" by the *Sloan Management Review* and *The American Lawyer*.

Latham & Watkins
633 West Fifth Street, Suite 4000
Los Angeles, CA 90071
Phone: 213-485-1234

LAURELS
Florists
Legend has it that when Rob Smith opened Laurels he was besieged by architecture students, demanding to know how this unusual studio was actually built. The hype about Laurels has quietened down since those heady days, when valet parking and an unlisted phone number had the Hollywood hostesses clamoring for Smith's services, but his floral arrangements are more ambitious than ever.

Laurels
7964 Melrose Avenue
Los Angeles, CA 90048
Phone: 213-655-3466

THE LAWRENCEVILLE SCHOOL
Schools
The Lawrenceville School was established in 1810 with the purpose of educating the sons of church elders in what was then a small village in New Jersey. In 1885, Lawrenceville introduced its distinctive House System, which today divides the students into 19 separate houses that each maintain their own sports teams and dining facilities. With approximately 780 students in four grades and one year of postgraduate study, the House System enables Lawrenceville to maintain the same sense of community that might be found at a much smaller school. Lawrenceville maintains 31 major buildings on its 500-acre campus. The school became co-educational in 1987.

The Lawrenceville School
Route 206 (Main Street)
Lawrenceville, NJ 08648
Phone: 609-896-0400

LAZZARA YACHTS
Yachting
Vincent Lazzara and his two sons have been building composite yachts (40-foot and over) since the late 1950s. Personalized interiors, the quietest ride in the industry and high resale values ensure an enjoyable investment. Lazzara yachts can be built with one of several different cockpit configurations: for fishing, diving or, for pleasure seekers, with a "sky lounge."

Lazzara Yachts
5300 West Tyson Avenue
Tampa, FL 33611
Phone: 813-835-5300   Fax: 813-835-0964

LEADING ESTATES OF THE WORLD
Property Consultants
Leading Estates of the World is an international organization for luxury real estate brokerage companies. Its highly regarded eponymous magazine highlights estates for sale around the world. Nearly 3.3 million copies are distributed in the United States, Canada and 60 other countries. The magazine has a star-studded list of estate owners whose property has been featured, including Barbra Streisand and Jacqueline Kennedy Onassis. If you are in the market for a really distinctive property, the magazine is a good first step.

Leading Estates of the World
1801 Avenue of the Stars
Los Angeles, CA 90067
Phone: 800-525-1122   Fax: 805-686-2086

LEE EPTING
Party Organizers and Caterers
This upscale catering company has organized 3,000-person events, specializing in theme parties including southern plantation dinners, jungle dances and period soirées. Epting takes care of everything from the food to the flowers and some elaborate props in-between. Kenny Rogers, Ted Turner & Jane Fonda have hired him to throw big bashes. Although he provides mostly southern food, Epting will cater to any taste.

Lee Epting
2425 Jefferson Road
Athens, GA 30607
Phone: 706-353-1913

LEHMAN BROTHERS PRIVATE CLIENT SERVICES
Wealth Management
Through Lehman Brothers' Private Client Services (PCS) group, high net worth individuals gain access to a range of financial services usually available only to large institutions. The PCS group operates in the United States, Europe, Latin America and the Middle East. Representatives of this eminent Wall Street investment house often become trusted confidantes of their affluent clients.

Lehman Brothers Private Client Services
Three World Financial Center
New York, NY 10285
Phone: 212-526-7000

LEO CASTELLI GALLERY
Art Dealers
It is difficult to describe Leo Castelli without using the word legend. The 91 year old, who recently moved his fabled operation from SoHo to the Upper East Side, represents artists—like Johns, Rauschenberg, Serra, Lichtenstein and Judd—who are truly icons. It seems unlikely that one man will ever again exercise quite as much influence in the market for American 20th century art. But for all his power Castelli remains delightfully unpretentious. Last year he told *Vanity Fair* magazine that his most treasured possession is his cat.

Leo Castelli Gallery
59 East 79th Street
New York, NY 10021
Phone: 212-249-4470   Fax: 212-431-5361

LEONARD N. STERN
SCHOOL OF BUSINESS
Colleges

This top tier business school integrates general management theory, case studies, and hands-on experience into the curriculum. Part of New York University, its student community is truly multicultural, hailing from more than 60 foreign countries.

Leonard N. Stern School of Business

New York University
44 West 4th Street
New York, NY 10012
Phone: 212-998-0600

LESLIE & CO.
Fashion

Ball-and-claw leg tables, antique trunks, and oriental rugs comprise the hand-picked decor of Houston's Leslie & Co., an independent men's and women's specialty store targeted to consumers who are more clothes-oriented than price-oriented. A refreshing escape from modern consumerism, this high-end custom-tailoring shop does not have a cash register and refrains from checking identification.

Leslie & Co.

1749 Post Oak Boulevard
Houston, TX 77056
Phone: 713-960-9113

LESPINASSE
Restaurants

Several critics have described this classic French treasure as the "best restaurant in New York." Those who have their own favorites may disagree, but best or not it is certainly way up there. There was some uneasiness among fans when chef Grey Kunz left, but his replacement, Christian Delouvrier, has kept up the high standards. And the service is as wonderful as ever. Warmly recommended.

Lespinasse

The St. Regis Hotel
2 East 55th Street
New York, NY 10022
Phone: 212-339-6719   Fax: 212-350-8738

LESPINASSE
Restaurants

This Washington institution—a sister restaurant to New York's Lespinasse—is the epitome of upscale elegance in a city which is blessed with many pretenders to that crown. The recent appointment of Sandro Gamba, who trained with Alain Ducasse at *Le Bastide de Moustiers,* as head chef ensures that the Provencal cuisine continues to draw plaudits from locals and visiting luminaries alike.

Lespinasse

923 16th Street, NW
Washington, DC 20006
Phone: 202-879-6900

THE LEVISON & CULLEN GALLERY
Antiques

A premier expert in the field of American antiques, The Levison & Cullen Gallery focuses on consulting to museums and private collectors of American 18th and 19th century furniture, decorative arts and art. Deanne Levison, who owns the gallery with her daughter, Suzanna Cullen, is known worldwide for her attention to authenticity. The retail shop in Atlanta boasts mostly American pieces, but occasionally offers works of English or Continental origin or early 20th century objects. The Federal period is a specialty of the gallery, as is the strong representation of Southern pieces. Like a scholar, Levison knows the history of American furniture, the regions and the craftsmen, and like a businesswoman, she knows the market. This winning combination puts her in the forefront of antique dealers in the U.S. Levison has been in the business for over 37 years and has worked hard to promote her love of furniture and decorative arts. An all-women enterprise, Levison & Cullen Gallery is a member of the prestigious National Antique & Art Dealer's Association of America.

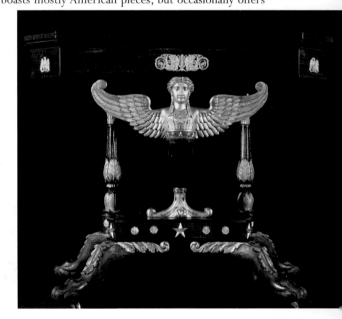

The Levison & Cullen Gallery

Suite C-102
2300 Peachtree Road
Atlanta, GA 30309
Phone: 404-351-3435   Fax: 404-351-5443

CAP B. LESESNE, M.D.
Cosmetic Surgeons

A board certified plastic surgeon and Instructor of Plastic Surgery at two medical schools, Dr. Cap Lesesne heads International Cosmetic Surgery, located on New York's Park Avenue. Educated at Princeton, Duke Medical School, Stanford Hospital and Chief Resident at Cornell, Lesesne has performed over 10,000 procedures. Models and fashion photographers swear by his "minimal bruise" rapid recovery liposuction techniques. He has performed facial cosmetic surgery on a multitude of actors, socialites and even two queens, all wanting an excellent result with an attention to detail. 50% of the clients of ICS come from around the world. Dr. Lesesne has been listed as a top U.S. plastic surgeon by the *London Observer, New York* magazine and *Town and Country* magazine. *The New York Times* recently labeled Lesesne a "special doctor." He has been quoted by many major magazines and is a consultant to the NBC National News.

Cap B. Lesesne, M.D.
International Cosmetic Surgery
620 Park Avenue
New York, NY 10021
Phone: 212-570-6318

LEXINGTON BAR AND BOOKS
Cigar Bars

This elegant, upscale cigar bar (which also has a downtown branch) is a favorite rendezvous for weary investment bankers and corporate honchos, who drop in on their way home from the office. Our European readers will agree that nestling into a leather armchair with a glass of vintage port and a Montecristo is a far more civilized way to greet the evening than sweating it out in the gym. Here you will find people who share your good sense.

Lexington Bar and Books
1020 Lexington Avenue
New York, NY 10021
Phone: 212-717-3902   Fax: 212-355-1316

LIGHTHOUSE POINT YACHT & RACQUET CLUB
Fitness

Tucked away in a prestigious residential area, the family-oriented Lighthouse Point offers a multitude of fitness options in a clean, comfortable, upscale environment. The saunas, jacuzzis and steam rooms are favorites among adults, while children enjoy training for the club's summer swim team in the outdoor Junior Olympics-sized lap pool. Staff members circle the one-floor gym every 15 to 20 minutes to clean the free weights and universal equipment.

Lighthouse Point Yacht & Racquet Club
2701 Northeast 42nd Street
Lighthouse Point, FL 33064
Phone: 954-942-3524   Fax: 954-942-3565

LILLY PULITZER
Fashion

When Lilly Pulitzer retired from the fashion business in the early 1980s, the Palm Beach set went into mourning. Now Lilly is back as the chief designer and consultant for her eponymous company. Pulitzer, who describes her designs as "timeless, feminine and fun," has maintained her signature pink and greens; a welcome comeback for chic women of a certain age.

Lilly Pulitzer
500 American Avenue
King of Prussia, PA 19406
Phone: 610-878-5550   Fax: 610-878-5555

LING SALON
Hair and Beauty

Elegant but simple decor makes Ling Chow's salon a minimalist's dream. With 20 high-tech styling stations, the salon offers top-quality cuts, color and manicures for celebrities and mortals alike. Ling's personable stylists and exclusive use of high-end products by René Furterer ensure that clients like Scottie Pippin and Jennifer Flavin keep coming back.

Ling Salon
3390 Mary Street, Suite 202
Miami, FL 33133
Phone: 305-444-1444

LING SKIN CARE
Hair and Beauty

The Oxygen Organic Sulfur Serum was once a top-secret military formula, but can now be found here for use on sunburn, acne, and hyperpigmentation. If it is good enough for Naomi Campbell and Rosie Perez, it is probably good enough for the rest of us. This holistic facial palace prides itself on being specifically geared to upscale clients who yearn for fine skin care products and cutting-edge treatments.

Ling Skin Care
128 Thompson Street
New York, NY 10012
Phone: 212-982-8833

THE LINKS CLUB
Private Clubs

If the Brook is the top gentleman's social club in New York, the Links is its business counterpart. Although members are required to check brief cases at the cloakroom, the luxurious halls, decorated in an old-English style, are filled with whispered business deals that cannot be read about in *The New York Times:* this is where the power elite belong.

The Links Club
36 East 62nd Street
New York, NY 10021
Phone: 212-838-8181

LISA LINDBLAD TRAVEL DESIGN
Travel Consultants

For two decades, Lisa Lindblad has been making contacts all over the world: artisans, hotel operators, guides, shopkeepers, traveling companions—each with his or her own intimate knowledge of exotic locations around the globe. Once the customer's destination and tickets are set, Lisa adds her very personal touch. The result is an impeccable vacation that unfolds like a theatrical production. Lisa's fee-based service extends the concept of luxury to include local insights into the destination through the use of guides and "friends," opening up new worlds. Her out-of-the-ordinary services include travel designs devoted to women, family ventures and artisan-focused trips; Lindblad can also customize the vacation of your dreams.

Lisa Lindblad Travel Design
27 East 95th Street
New York, NY 10128
Phone: 212-876-2554
Fax: 212-722-2797

THE LITTLE NELL

Hotels

This is one of the truly great ski hotels of the world. Nestled in the heart of the Colorado Rockies, The Little Nell blends naturally into the landscape, giving the appearance of being carved into the mountain. A haven of comfort, style and elegance, this is the resort of choice for the likes of Arnold Schwarzenegger, Christie Brinkley, Jane Fonda and Ted Turner; guests feel as if they are spending a weekend in their own country home. No two rooms are alike although all have outstanding views of either the town of Aspen or Aspen Mountain. The most luxurious suite is the 2,500 square foot Elizabeth Paepcke Suite on the top floor of the hotel, with its private keyed entrance.

One of the highlights of this resort is the ski concierge: your ski equipment is whisked away on your return from the slopes, and your skis waxed and boots warmed overnight. Unwind in the bar, known as *the* aprés-ski spot in Aspen, and enjoy live jazz nightly. In the unlikely event that you want a day off from the slopes, the heated outdoor pool and Jacuzzi might be just the thing. Set in the privacy of the hotel's courtyard, they are surrounded by a waterfall and landscaped gardens. In case you are not getting enough exercise, try working out in the fully equipped exercise center, then pamper yourself in the indoor spa with its steam room and three massage rooms.

The Little Nell

675 East Durant Avenue
Aspen, CO 81611
Phone: 970-920-4600   Fax: 970-920-6328

LONDON JEWELERS

Jewelry and Watches

From its humble roots as a local watch shop in Glen Cove, Long Island, London Jewelers has become one of the bigger names in jewelry in America. One of the first to showcase big-name designers in small, personalized collections, the company features Tiffany, Bulgari, Cartier and Mikimoto in-store boutiques. With new shops in East Hampton and Manhattan and a new platinum-and-diamond line of its own, London looks set to continue prospering.

London Jewelers

2046 Northern Boulevard
Manhasset, NY 11030
Phone: 516-627-7475

LOS ANGELES TIMES

Media

With 22 Pulitzer prizes to its name, an editorial staff of 1000 and over one million copies sold every day, *The Los Angeles Times* is among the most respected and influential papers in the United States. When it was founded by Colonel Harrison Gray Otis in 1881, Los Angeles was nothing more than a desert site on the Pacific. Otis' descendants still control the publishing empire.

Los Angeles Times

Times Mirror Square
Los Angeles, CA 90053
Phone: 213-237-5000   Fax: 213-237-5493

LOUIS, BOSTON

Fashion

With its exclusive fabrics, erudite staff and artisan vendors, the homogenization that has infiltrated many menswear boutiques is clearly spurned at Louis, Boston. Murray Pearlstein and Debra Greenberg buy only three or four of the same article from designers like Brioni and Kiton.

Louis, Boston

234 Berkeley Street
Boston, MA 02116
Phone: 617-262-6100

LUCQUES

Restaurants   Rising Star

Owners Suzanne Goin and Caroline Styne opened this comfortable carriage-house restaurant as a rendezvous for young opinion makers and Hollywood players. They come for Suzanne's outstanding California-influenced French cuisine: try her grilled sea bass with lemons. On a typical evening you might find stars like Cameron Diaz or Jodie Foster ensconced on the sofa beside you. Mellow, homey, hip.

Lucques

8474 Melrose Avenue
Los Angeles, CA 90069
Phone: 323-655-6277   Fax: 323-655-3925

THE LODGE ON LITTLE ST. SIMONS ISLAND

Hotels   *Best Kept Secret*

Little St. Simons Island is the northernmost of Georgia's beautiful Golden Isles and the most secluded. A 10-minute boat ride on a private ferry transports guests to this exclusive paradise. Nature rules the roost here, where 10,000 perfectly preserved acres are shared by no more than 30 overnight guests. Seven miles of secluded, shell-strewn beaches and many recreational activities, such as birding, boating, horseback riding, bicycling, hiking, wildlife observation and naturalist programs beckon guests to explore. Gracious accommodations, gourmet cuisine and a knowledgeable staff provide all the creature comforts needed. Exclusive full-island reservations for up to thirty people are perfect for family or friend's reunions or the ultimate private getaway.

The Lodge on Little St. Simons Island
P.O. Box 21078
St. Simons Island, GA 31522
Phone: 888-733-5774   Fax: 912-634-1811

LOWRANCE INTERIORS

Architects and Interior Designers

Lowrance Interiors uses grade-A materials and furnishings, including many museum-quality antiques, in the creation of homes for its tony clientele. Jack Lowrance, president and owner, and Richard Gaz, senior designer, work together to create acclaimed contemporary spaces without sacrificing the lessons of classic interior design theory. Working on only about a dozen projects a year, the firm has the ability to focus on even the smallest of details. Such precision will be applied to a new line of furniture to be produced in 2000.

Lowrance Interiors
707 North Alfred Street
Los Angeles, CA 90069
Phone: 323-655-9713
Fax: 323-655-0359

LUTSKO ASSOCIATES

Landscape Architects

Based in San Francisco, Lutsko Associates have worked on public and private projects from California to Pennsylvania; this is the firm behind many of the country's most elaborate botanical gardens. Ron Lutsko's work can be seen in the book, *Breaking Ground: A Portrait of Ten Garden Designers.*

Lutsko Associates
Pier One 1/2 Embarcadero
San Francisco, CA 94111
Phone: 415-391-0777

LUXURYFINDER.COM

Specialty Shops   *Rising Star*

This interesting new venture from James Finkelstein and his wife, Pamela Gross, is one of only two web-based companies in our directory. Luxuryfinder.com is a newfangled shopping assistant for America's most affluent consumers. Amusing features and interviews with taste makers like Sirio Maccioni ensure that the site has a lot more punch than one might expect of an on-line shop. Well worth investigating.

Luxuryfinder.com
55 East 59th Street
New York, NY 10022
Phone: 212-308-8500

LYMAN PERRY

Architects and Interior Designers

A finalist in the 1960 Olympics for rowing, Lyman Perry now applies the same tenacious determination he once used for athletics to his architectural creations. Perry and his design teams have created acclaimed homes from Maine to Virginia for, among many others, top executives at Goldman Sachs and IBM.

Lyman Perry
42 Cassatt Avenue
Berwyn, PA 19312
Phone: 610-889-9966   Fax: 610-889-9969

LYNN JACHNEY CHARTERS

Yachting

Over 30 years ago Lynn Jachney knocked on the cockpit of her first yacht and started Lynn Jachney Charters. Now she tours the globe from the Caribbean to Alaska to the Mediterranean, looking for the perfect charter for her clients. A board member of the San Remo Yacht Show, Jachney's impeccable taste and tireless attention to detail are legendary within the industry. Warmly recommended.

Lynn Jachney Charters
Two Market Square
Marblehead, MA 01945
Phone: 800-223-2050   Fax: 617-639-0216

LOU MAROTTA, INC.
Antiques

If paint is your passion and the natural world your niche, you'll feel like a kid in a candy store at this Manhattan gallery. Lou Marotta specializes in painted surfaces in original condition—nothing is restored. The collection includes French, Italian, Swedish and Spanish furniture, ranging from the 17th to the 20th century. He selects pieces that are a little bit off, things that bring out a smile when you see them, such as a John Dickinson-designed limited-edition table of galvanized steel bent to look like a draped tablecloth. Other unusual furniture includes pieces with natural shapes derived from plants and animals, blending form and function in head-turning ways—witness the tables that look like tree branches or chairs with goat legs. Natural and primitive on the one hand, sophisticated and rich on the other, his singular collection begs to be seen. Also reflected in his collection is Marotta's own penchant for 18th century French, Italian and Swedish antiques. Of his more unusual pieces, even the owner admits "they're not for everybody, though they should be!"

Lou Marotta, Inc.
243 East 60th Street
New York, NY 10022
Phone: 212-223-0306
Fax: 212-223-4744

M. FINKEL & DAUGHTER
Antiques

M. Finkel & Daughter specializes in American decorative and folk arts. For example, at the time of going to press the firm had just acquired a sampler, made in 1824 by an important Quaker elder in Burlington County, New Jersey, distinctive for its high-quality needlework.

M. Finkel & Daughter
936 Pine Street
Philadelphia, PA 19107
Phone: 215-627-7797   Fax: 215-627-8199

M. PENNER
Fashion

A favorite among Houston's top business executives, this store is located in the River Oaks area. The floor space is open, airy, and modern. Its strictly European selection, which emphasizes Italian menswear, features the Zegna line, as well as Comali and Keron. "We're not overloaded with merchandise," says one salesman, "we just carry the diamonds."

M. Penner
2950 Kirby Drive
Houston, TX 77098
Phone: 713-527-8200

M. S. RAU ANTIQUES
Antiques

The family run business has been around since 1912 and the collection amassed includes antique canes, music boxes, medical antiques, important silver, American cut glass, porcelain, chandeliers, fine paintings and furniture. As you weave through the antique pool tables and suits of armor, look out for the treasure chest used by Spanish *conquistador* Francisco Pizarro to send Peruvian gold back to his homeland after conquering the Incas in 1520.

M. S. Rau Antiques
630 Royal Street
New Orleans, LA 70130
Phone: 504-523-5660   Fax: 504-566-0057

MADISON AVENUE BOOKSHOP

Specialty Shops   *Best Kept Secret*

This is Alistair McAlpine's favorite shop in New York: "a place where I can spend time with wonderful books when the weather is inclement." Lord McAlpine is one of many fans of this utterly enchanting little store in the heart of Manhattan's Upper East Side. The staff are genuinely interested in the world of books (an increasingly rare phenomenon) and the obscure gems on offer are enough to keep any bookworm happy for weeks.

Madison Avenue Bookshop

833 Madison Avenue
New York, NY 10021
Phone: 212-535-6130   Fax: 212-794-5231

MAGNUM MARINE

Yachting

When Don Aronow sold Donzi, he took his love for high speed to the next level: Magnum Marine. Magnum's new line of boats feature a body designed by Pininfarina in Italy, and a hand laminated kevlar hull that is as light as fiberglass, but as strong as metal. The new Magnum-Pininfarinas come in 80 and 90 foot versions, with the 80 foot topping out at over 70 mph—as fast as many 38 foot super boats. The interiors are designed in Italy to spec, with the finishing touches done in Miami.

Magnum Marine

2900 NE 188th Street
Aventura, FL 33180
Phone: 305-931-4292   Fax: 305-931-0088

LA MAISONETTE

Restaurants

A classic French restaurant, La Maisonette is the only establishment in the Mobil Travel Guide to have received the coveted five-star award for 35 years in a row in its 50 years of existence. It is a favorite among Cincinnati's power elite, as well as visiting media, VIPs, political figures, corporate CEOs, and celebrities—from President Clinton all the way down (or across) to Larry Flynt.

La Maisonette

114 East Sixth Street
Cincinnati, OH 45202
Phone: 513-721-2260   Fax: 513-287-7785

MALCOLM FRANKLIN

Antiques

Ever wondered where the White House buys its antiques? Several pieces come from this family-owned third generation dealer, which specializes in 17th and 18th century English furniture and accessories, including clocks, mirrors, globes and porcelain. The gallery has also sold a dining table to Colonial Williamsburg and various pieces to Governors' mansions around the country. There is a particularly impressive selection of walnut veneer pieces from the late 17th and early 18th centuries.

Malcolm Franklin

34 East Oak Street
Chicago, IL 60611
Phone: 312-337-0202   Fax: 312-337-8002

MANHATTAN ANTI-AGING CLINIC

Cosmetic Surgeons

Dr. Adrienne Denese treats hormonal deficiencies with supplemental dosages, and prescribes anti-oxidants and skin care regimens to help patients through mid-life changes. Her colleague Julian Henley, who is on the teaching staff at the Yale School of Medicine, can perform a variety of rejuvenation surgeries.

Manhattan Anti-Aging Clinic

330 Orchard Street
New Haven, CT 06511
Phone: 203-787-4647

MANSION ON TURTLE CREEK

Hotels

This elegantly restored Italian Renaissance–style mansion was originally built in the 1920s for a wealthy cotton baron. Its many personal touches will make you feel like you are staying at the home of a particularly tasteful friend. Try to snag Terrace Suite 907, a favorite of Ted Turner and Jane Fonda; this top-floor retreat features a king-size canopy bed sprinkled with gardenia petals and a separate servants' entrance so you can relax, completely uninterrupted.

Mansion on Turtle Creek

2821 Turtle Creek Boulevard
Dallas, TX 75219
Phone: 214-559-2100

MANSOUR

Specialty Shops

With an incredible top-quality antique rug inventory, this showroom specializes in rare pieces, supplying decorators and individuals across the U.S. Mansour's twenty buyers search worldwide for unique pieces from Persia, Europe, and the Far East. The store also sells period tapestries, with many dating back to the 16th century.

Mansour

8600 Melrose Avenue
West Hollywood, CA 90069
Phone: 310-652-9999

MARC FRIEDLAND

Specialty Shops

In smart social circles, where the quality of an invitation often determines how many people accept or decline, hosts like Oprah Winfrey, Tom Hanks and Kate Capshaw turn to Marc Friedland for assistance. Friedland creates singular invitations which are cherished as mementos long after the events they flag.

Marc Friedland

4988 Venice Boulevard
Los Angeles, CA 90019
Phone: 213-936-9009   Fax: 213-935-8299

MARC MAGNUS

Jewelry and Watches

Marc Magnus creates fine jewelry by combining various precious stones in unique settings. Magnus, who is Swiss, uses only high quality stones and the best European workmanship. All items are set either in platinum or 18-karat gold, creating one of a kind conversation pieces, which are worn by moguls, professionals and celebrities. The Upper East side store also carries its own timepieces.

Marc Magnus
41 East 78th Street
New York, NY 10021
Phone: 212-585-3976   Fax: 212-327-1861

MARC JACOBS
Fashion

In 1987, Marc Jacobs was the youngest designer to be awarded one of the fashion industry's highest tributes: The Council of Fashion Designers of America Award for New Fashion Talent. Since winning the award, Jacobs has made tremendous strides, first joining Perry Ellis in 1989, then launching his own signature line in 1994. Today, his SoHo boutique showcases an acclaimed line of outerwear, furs, fine jewelry, scarves and shoes.

Marc Jacobs
163 Mercer Street
New York, NY 10012
Phone: 212-343-1490

MARGUERITE RIORDAN
Antiques

Marguerite Riordan has been selling New England High Country antiques for some 40 years. She also sells American primitive paintings by artists such as Ammi Phillips, John Brewster and Joseph Whiting Stock along with all other types of American decorative arts. Mrs. Riordan has been exhibiting at the Armory's Winter Show for many years.

Marguerite Riordan
Eight Pearl Street
Stonington, CT 06378
Phone: 860-535-2511

MARIAN GOODMAN GALLERY
Art Dealers

A 57th Street institution, Marian Goodman's gallery specializes in contemporary conceptual paintings, sculpture, photography, installations, film and video. Artists represented include Gerhard Richter, Tony Cragg, Juan Muñoz and Thomas Schütte. Goodman's clientele includes museums, corporations and a sprinkling of jet-set notables.

Marian Goodman Gallery
24 West 57th Street
New York, NY 10019
Phone: 212-292-8530   Fax: 212-581-5187

MARIO BUATTA
Architects and Interior Designers

The 'prince of chintz' has unmistakable style, both personally and in his work. Buatta uses a maximum of comfort and a balance of contemporary and antique furnishings set against a fabulous sense of color. Barbara Walters, Henry Ford II and the late Malcolm Forbes, have all used this style star to decorate their homes. Buatta was also responsible for the renovation of Blair House, the White House guest house.

Mario Buatta
120 East 80th Street
New York, NY 10021
Phone: 212-988-6811

MARK HAMPTON
Architects and Interior Designers

Mark Hampton was the decorator of choice for some of the country's most prominent families. Many European readers will be familiar with his work on the opulent interior of New York's Carlyle Hotel. Since the beloved decorator passed away, Hampton's business has been carried forward in the competent hands of his wife Duane and daughter Alexa.

Mark Hampton
654 Madison Avenue, 21st Floor
New York, NY 10021
Phone: 212-753-4110   Fax: 212-758-2079

MARK'S GARDEN
Florists

Mark's Garden is often cited as one of the top florists in the United States. The largest flower shop in Los Angeles creates floral designs for the Governor's Ball after the Academy Awards, for the Los Angeles Philharmonic's opening season, and for countless film premieres and weddings. Those who value discretion will appreciate the firm's refusal to release the names of its celebrity clients.

Mark's Garden
13838 Ventura Boulevard
Sherman Oaks, CA 91423
Phone: 818-906-1718   Fax: 818-386-2693

THE MARK
Hotels

Affluent Europeans flock to this chic uptown haven, where former guest requests and preferences are recorded to ensure their comfort on future stays. A member of *The Leading Hotels of the World,* The Mark was aptly described in a British magazine last year as "discreet enough for the Earl of Snowdon, smart enough for Sharon Stone and hip enough for Bruce Springsteen." It is owned by Monte Carlo-based Georg Rafael. If dropping his name does not get you a good table or open the right doors just ask Giorgio, the head concierge. He can make pigs fly.

The Mark
25 East 77th Street
New York, NY 10021
Phone: 212-744-4300   Fax: 212-744-2749

MARK'S LAS OLAS
Restaurants

Mark's Las Olas is ideal for a late-night rendezvous or a formal business lunch, but whatever time you go, be prepared to brave the crowds. Chef/owner Mark Militello has created a raucous yet refined restaurant where the cuisine and the atmosphere battle for attention. At the time of writing, Militello was planning to open a new restaurant in Palm Beach. He clearly has a big future, despite one review which claimed that "at the age of 38, Militello is one of the grand old men of New Florida cuisine."

Mark's Las Olas
1032 East Las Olas Boulevard
Fort Lauderdale, FL 33301
Phone: 954-463-1000   Fax: 954-463-1887

MARLBOROUGH

Art Dealers

Originally founded in London in 1946 by Frank Lloyd and Harry Fischer, Marlborough Fine Arts now has galleries in Madrid, Santiago, London, Boca Raton, and two in New York—one downtown in Chelsea and another one on 57th Street. Artists represented in the New York galleries include Fernando Botero, John Alexander, Grisha Bruskin, Red Grooms and Tom Otterness. The uptown gallery tends to have more established artists in its inventory.

Marlborough
40 West 57th Street
New York, NY 10019
Phone: 212-541-4900

MARTIN KATZ

Jewelry and Watches

Michael Katz was the youngest manager at Laykin et Cie, the jewelry salon at I. Magnin in Beverly Hills, and later served as the company's vice president. In 1988 Katz went into business for himself, working with clients such as Anjelica Huston, Emma Thompson, Nicole Kidman and Angela Bassett to match their unique tastes to exquisite pieces of vintage and contemporary jewelry. His collection focuses primarily on platinum pieces of art deco and Edwardian origin.

Martin Katz
P.O. Box 10658
Beverly Hills, CA 90213
Phone: 310-276-7200   Fax: 310-276-3775

MARVIN ALEXANDER

Antiques

Entering the Marvin Alexander store is like walking into a glass menagerie. This lighting specialist and decorative accessories resource has been selling mostly European merchandise for the past 40 years. One-of-a-kind antique furniture, ranging from the late 17th century to the 1920s, vies for space with the shop's ever-growing reproduction line, including copies of antique Louis XIV, Regency, Louis XVI and Second Empire—plus anything exquisite that can be converted into a lamp! Don't be surprised to see top international decorators and architects on site.

Marvin Alexander
315 East 62nd Street
New York, NY 10021
Phone: 212-838-2320   Fax: 212-754-0173

MARTEL PRODUCTIONS

Party Organizers and Caterers

For the past nine years Simone Martel has exercised her own brand of event planning in the worlds of finance, fashion, film, media, charities, corporate events and private parties. With a prominent social and hospitality network in place, she has produced over 1000 events ranging from 20 to 2000 guests. As President of Martel Productions, she has capitalized on her strengths in actualizing ambitious projects with great panache, using great creativity and vast resources. Martel's expertise extends but is not limited to invitation design, supervision of catering, decoration and lighting design, booking entertainment, managing security and coordination of guest speakers. Martel has worked closely with and orchestrated unforgettable fundraisers for founders and chair-people such as Marty Richards, Arnold Schwarzenegger, Steven Spielberg, Edgar Bronfman, Charles Bronfman, and Academy Award winner, Frances McDormand. Martel's client list extends to a field in which she is most passionate; the perfect execution of exclusive private parties. With an impressive track record behind her, any client can relax enough to be a guest at their own party.

Martel Productions
10 East 53rd Street
New York, NY 10022
Phone: 212-753-3999   Fax: 212-753-4329

MARY BOONE GALLERY

Art Dealers

With her remarkable ability to discover new talent, Mary Boone has long been one of the most celebrated art dealers in New York City. While her recent move from SoHo up to Midtown sent shockwaves through the industry, the gallery has maintained a strong sense of continuity, perhaps most evident in the fact that both spaces were designed by Richard Gluckman. Boone represents artists like Barbara Kruger, Eric Fischl and Inka Essenhigh. Michael Ovitz is one of many prominent clients.

Mary Boone Gallery
745 Fifth Avenue
New York, NY 10151
Phone: 212-752-2929   Fax: 212-752-3939

MARY ELAINE'S

Restaurants

In an atmosphere of sophisticated elegance, award-winning chef de cuisine James Boyce presents his signature modern French cuisine at Mary Elaine's. This romantic rooftop restaurant also offers a strong wine list (featuring Californian gems), a top jazz vocalist and breathtaking views of Scottsdale. Try to get in before sunset.

Mary Elaine's
Phoenician Resort
6000 East Camelback Road
Scottsdale, AZ 85251
Phone: 602-423-2530

MARY McFADDEN

Fashion

Manufacturing her couture since 1976, the inimitable Mary McFadden gears her evening gowns and dresses to those who aim to master the art of dressing beautifully. Inspired by ancient cultures and world travel, McFadden's two annual collections are perfect for country club dances, galas and charity events. Consistently on the cutting edge of fashion, she has created a fetching hand-painting technique for jackets and gowns. She has also developed Marii pleating, a mushroom pleating reminiscent of Fortuny that is adorned with embroidery on Charmonse fabric. Mary McFadden boutiques are located in both Bergdorf Goodman and Saks Fifth Avenue.

Mary McFadden
240 West 35th Street
New York, NY 10001
Phone: 212-736-4078

ALICE F. MASON
Property Consultants

Alice F. Mason has been working in real estate for over 40 years. One of the top residential brokers in New York, Mason—who is ably assisted by her daughter, Dominique Richard—specializes in the sale of luxury co-ops, condominiums and town houses. This real estate doyenne, who has strong links to the Democratic Party, is also renowned for her aplomb as a hostess.

Alice F. Mason
635 Madison Avenue
New York, NY 10022
Phone: 212-832-8870   Fax: 212-832-7634

MASON & MORSE
Property Consultants

Mason & Morse sells premier ranches and homes set in some of the nation's most spectacular countryside. Its ranch division has over 133 years of experience in Western real estate sales, selling properties in Colorado, Montana, Wyoming, Idaho, Arizona, California, Nevada, Oregon, Texas, Nebraska and Kansas. Recent sales include the 25,000 acre Sun Ranch in Montana's Madison Valley for $25 million.

Mason & Morse
514 East Hyman Avenue
Aspen, CO 81611
Phone: 970-544-9700   Fax: 970-925-7027

MASTERS TOURNAMENT
Events

One of the most prestigious events in sport today, the Masters was founded in 1934 by Bobby Jones and Cliff Roberts. Those lucky few who manage to secure tickets have the pleasure of watching some of the biggest names in the game battle it out for a total purse of over $4 million. Jack Nicklaus has won the tournament, which is held at Augusta National Golf Club, six times—last year it was won by José Maria Olazabal.

Masters Tournament
2604 Washington Road
Augusta, GA 30903
Phone: 706-667-6700   Fax: 706-731-0611

MARTHA ANGUS
Architects and Interior Designers

With a training that ranged from the École des Beaux Arts in France, to Sotheby's in New York, to the Wharton School in Philadelphia, Martha Angus's handiwork has been in heavy demand since she started doing interiors in the 1970s. With a headquarters recently moved from New York City to San Francisco, major clients have included Saks Fifth Avenue, Ralph Lauren and Estée Lauder, for whom she has decorated both stores and private residences. Angus believes in an elegant, comfortable approach with emphasis on fine art and interior design.

Martha Angus
1177 California Street
San Francisco, CA 94108
Phone: 415-931-8060
Fax: 415-931-8095

ALAN MATARASSO, M.D.
Cosmetic Surgeons

Like most of the individuals featured in our selection of the nation's leading cosmetic surgeons, Alan Matarasso is Board-certified. Catering to the whims and aspirations of socialites, professionals and a bevy of other creatures from all walks of life, Dr. Matarasso handles his difficult role with admirable aplomb. He specializes in body contouring and abdominoplasty.

Alan Matarasso, M.D.
1009 Park Avenue
New York, NY 10028
Phone: 212-249-7500

MATSUHISA
Restaurants

Chef and owner Nobu Matsuhisa designed this small and intimate seafood restaurant himself. Opened in 1987, it was the precursor to the fabled Nobu empire. Matsuhisa's experience as a Japanese chef who worked for many years in Peru is evident in signature dishes like new style sashimi, cooked slightly in hot olive oil for people who don't eat raw fish; with jalapeños and cilantro it achieves a blend of Caribbean and Japanese flavors. This is the only restaurant in the United States which serves the exquisite Hokusetsu sake, served cold in bamboo bottles. Highly recommended.

Matsuhisa
129 North la Cienega Boulevard
Beverly Hills, CA 90211
Phone: 310-289-4925   Fax: 310-659-0492

MATTHEW MARKS GALLERY
Art Dealers

With two impressive Chelsea spaces, the Matthew Marks Gallery has the room and the resources to represent a veritable who's who of contemporary art. Paintings by Lucien Freud, Brice Marden, Terry Winters and Ellsworth Kelly contend with the photographs and slide shows of Nan Goldin and the breathtaking sculptures and installations of Katarina Fritsch. The gallery currently represents 22 artists; many garner consistently glowing reviews.

Matthew Marks Gallery
523 West 24th Street
New York, NY 10011
Phone: 212-243-0200

MAURICE BADLER FINE JEWELRY
Jewelry and Watches

Maurice Badler has been faithfully outfitting Americans in luxurious jewelry for over 40 years, from rare South Sea pearls to classic diamond chokers. Jeff Badler, the president, trains his staff so that every Badler customer is treated like family—for example, they keep a wish list of jewelry certain customers have marveled at while visiting the store. Then, they call those customers' loved ones before anniversaries or birthdays to suggest items on the list, all done with the subtlety necessary to surprise the unsuspecting recipient.

Maurice Badler Fine Jewelry
578 Fifth Avenue
New York, NY 10036
Phone: 800-622-3537

THE MAUNA LANI BAY
Hotels

Kevin Costner stayed in one of Mauna Lani Bay's exclusive Bungalows while shooting *Waterworld*. Indeed, water is a central theme at Mauna Lani, a Five Diamond resort between two white sand beaches on the Big Island of Hawaii's Kohala Coast. Unique events at Mauna Lani Bay include "Turtle Independence Day," every July 4th, when the hotel releases some of the Hawaiian green sea turtles (an endangered species) that are raised in the hotel ponds. Many of the turtles remain in the ocean fronting the hotel, where they are a delight to snorkelers. Everything at Mauna Lani speaks of the island paradise of Hawaii. The two championship golf courses are carved from ancient lava flows; a startling contrast of emerald green fairways against black lava. Mauna Lani Bay's signature restaurant, The CanoeHouse, offers the finest in Pacific Rim cuisine in a beautiful oceanfront setting.

The Mauna Lani Bay
68-1400 Mauna Lani Drive
Kohala Coast, HI 96743
Phone: 808-885-6622   Fax: 808-885-1483

MAURICE BONAMIGO

Hair and Beauty   Best Kept Secret

The self-styled *Grand Master of Color* is known for the sophisticated styles he creates for clients like Sean Penn and Julia Childs. Bonamigo, who claims that he has received special CIA clearance to "do" Mrs. John Major, works between Chicago and Kalamazoo, Michigan.

Maurice Bonamigo
67 East Cedar Street
Chicago, IL 60611
Phone: 312-664-6353

MAXFIELD
Fashion

Based in a former warehouse in Beverly Hills, Maxfield's 10,000 square foot store is shopping bliss. While contemporary designers and European fashion collections fill the ample floor space, *objets d'art* frame the store's edges. For instance, antique display cases are chock-full of vintage jewelry and accessories.

Maxfield
8825 Melrose Avenue
Los Angeles, CA 90069
Phone: 310-274-8800

MAURICE JENNINGS AND DAVID McKEE

Architects and Interior Designers

The legendary Fay Jones, who was an apprentice of Frank Lloyd Wright, won the American Institute of Architect's gold medal in 1990. Jones retired in 1997, but his longtime associates Maurice Jennings and David McKee maintain this firm's organic style, utilizing refined, milled woods to create homes of distinction. The firm specializes in chapels and private residences, including the Roy Reed house in Hog Eye, the Edmondson residence in Forrest City and the Thorncrown Chapel in Eureka Springs.

Maurice Jennings and David McKee
619 West Dickson
Fayetteville, AK 72701
Phone: 501-443-4742   Fax: 501-443-0637

MAXWELL GALLERIES
Art Dealers

This San Francisco Gallery was founded in 1940. In the ensuing years it has become one of the largest and most extensive independent galleries in the city, renowned for its collection of fine 19th and 20th century American and European paintings and sculpture. Particular attention is given to early Californian landscape and *plein air* paintings. Owner Mark Hoffman also represents several leading contemporary artists.

Maxwell Galleries
559 Sutter Street
San Francisco, CA 94102
Phone: 415-421-5193   Fax: 415-421-4858

THE MAYFLOWER INN
Hotels

In 1920 Harry van Sinderen converted this former schoolhouse into The Mayflower Inn, which soon become a discreet retreat for some of America's most distinguished families. After years of ghostly neglect, The Mayflower was brought back to life, thanks to Adriana and Robert Mnuchin, proprietors as of 1992. This country house of splendid proportions now offers comfort, luxury and exquisite attention to detail on 28 acres of century-old rhododendrons and stately maples.

The Mayflower Inn
118 Woodbury Road
Washington, CN 06793
Phone: 860-868-9466   Fax: 860-868-1497

MAYLE

Fashion   *Rising Star*

When Jane Mayle was modeling, fashion editors and photographers often asked her where she bought her own exotic clothes. After several years in the business she realized that maybe there was something special about her taste. Mayle and her then boyfriend, Christopher Jarvis, started to design their own clothes, and a shop called Phare was the result. They have now split up and the shop's name recently changed to Mayle. She does a bustling business in super-trendy NoLIta, rivaling Garment Center designers with her fresh take on sleek women's wear. Incidentally, Mayle's father, Peter, is the best-selling author of *A Year in Provence*.

Mayle
252 Elizabeth Street
New York, NY 10012
Phone: 212-625-0406

McCARTY POTTERY

Specialty Shops   *Best Kept Secret*

The husband and wife team of Lee and Pup McCarty opened their pottery studio back in 1954. Since then the amiable couple have been designing stoneware and porcelain pieces which have found their way across the country and around the world. With true Southern charm, many of the pieces are what Manager Stephen Smith calls "flights of fancy," often because people can't figure out what they're supposed to represent! A vase could turn out to be an owl face, a water pitcher might be a duck. Whatever the outcome, these backroad wares are reason enough to visit this Merigold hideaway.

McCarty Pottery
101 St. Mary Street
Merigold, MS 38759
Phone: 601-748-2293

McMILLEN

Architects and Interior Designers

When you hire America's first full-service interior design firm, it will probably be the beginning of a long relationship. Since its foundation in 1924, McMillen has developed a reputation for representing the same client through every phase of his or her life. Gregory Smith, one such client, eventually had more than 12 residences decorated over the course of 30 years. As endorsements go, that is hard to beat.

McMillen
155 East 56th Street
New York, NY 10022
Phone: 212-753-6377

MECOX GARDENS

Specialty Shops

Mecox Gardens' emphasis on simplicity is reflected in elegant but well constructed pots, dishes, and furniture, whether brand-new or centuries old. There are beautifully rich and intricate textures that work in any discerning client's garden, be it on a rooftop or by the sea. Mecox have an outlet in Manhattan (managed by the wonderful Britta) and at the time of writing the company was planning to open a store on the west coast.

Mecox Gardens
257 County Road, 39A
Southampton, NY 11968
Phone: 516-287-5015   Fax: 516-287-5018

MEDFITNESS

Fitness

At this private, personal training gym, trainers are professionally certified and recommended by members of the medical community. With no more than five clients in the gym at one time, trainers take you through a series of weight training and cardiovascular regimens but you can also try yoga, kickboxing and plyometric workouts outdoors or schedule an appointment with the nutritional consultant on staff. Clients have access to the gym 24 hours a day.

MedFitness
12 East 86th Street
New York, NY 10028
Phone: 212-327-4197

MELLON BANK

Wealth Management

A staggering increase in demand for personalized and consolidated services has caused Mellon Bank's private banking division to blossom in the last few years. With an excellent reputation and seven branches spread across the country, it is particularly well equipped for handling the wealth of America's emerging affluent. You will need at least $250,000 on deposit, plus at least two of the following: investable assets of $500,000, net worth of $1 million, or a minimum annual income of $150,000.

Mellon Bank
1 Mellon Bank Center
Pittsburgh, PA 15258
Phone: 412-234-5000   Fax: 412-236-1662

MEADOWOOD NAPA VALLEY

Hotels

To find a place which reflects the grace and beauty of California's extraordinary wine country, look to Meadowood Napa Valley, an exquisite property reminiscent of a grand country estate. Meadowood offers eighty-five cottages, suites and lodges, nestled among the oaks and pines of the property's very private setting. Discriminating travelers will find the amenities, activities and services consistent among Relais & Chateaux properties. Enjoy croquet, tennis, golf, swimming, a complete health spa, and fine dining in The Restaurant at Meadowood.

Meadowood Napa Valley
900 Meadowood Lane
St. Helena, CA 94574
Phone: 707-963-3646   Fax: 707-963-3532

MERCER HOTEL

Hotels   *Rising Star*

A newcomer from André Balazs, *eminence grise* of Château Marmont in L.A. Christian Liaigre's minimalist decor is breathtaking and there are a variety of rooms to choose from, including large courtyard lofts with exposed brick and arched windows. Bathrooms are positively elephantine. Room service from the Mercer Kitchen, overseen by Jean-Georges Vongerichten, is a good way to avoid the masses: for every star there are a hundred wannabes in the basement restaurant.

Mercer Hotel

147 Mercer Street
New York, NY 10012
Phone: 212-966-6060

MERION GOLF CLUB

Golf Clubs

Merion's short but difficult East Course has been the scene of some of American golf's most dramatic moments, including the last leg of Bobby Jones' Grand Slam at the 1930 U.S. Amateur, and Ben Hogan's play-off victory in the 1950 U.S. Open, less than two years after his near-fatal automobile accident. Club member Hugh Wilson designed the course in 1911 after a six-month tour of the great British links, and his "white faced" bunkers and undulating greens still provide a fascinating test, though it is generally thought that the course plays too short today to add to its five U.S. Opens.

Merion Golf Club

450 Ardmore Avenue
Ardmore, PA 19003
Phone: 610-642-5600

THE MERCURY

Restaurants   *Rising Star*

Executive chef and part owner Chris Ward prepares excellent "cross-cultural cuisine" at this sleek, minimalist Preston Hollow eatery. Lone star luminaries get the best of both worlds at the VIP room in the back, which offers seclusion and a view of the rest of the restaurant through a closed circuit TV. Try the pepper-crusted rare tuna on a cranberry corn galette with a chanterelle mushroom sauce.

The Mercury

11909 Preston Road
Dallas, TX 75230
Phone: 972-960-7774   *Fax: 972-960-7988*

MERRILL LYNCH FINANCIAL SERVICES

Wealth Management

We have always sympathized with the wag who observed that a broker is called a broker because after dealing with him…you are. Of course, that is *not* the reason Merrill Lynch decided to become one of the most aggressive competitors in the new arena of wealth management. The leading investment house now offers private advisory services for its most valuable clients. How valuable? You will need a seven-figure sum to invest, although just $250,000 earns clients a "priority" status that gives them access to perks like lower lending rates.

Merrill Lynch Financial Services

World Financial Center
250 Vesey Street
New York, NY 10281
Phone: 212-449-1000

METROPOLITAN LIMOUSINE

Chauffeur Services

This 25-year-old company hand-picks its drivers, checking that they are informed, knowledgeable, and well trained, with impeccable appearances, personalities, and service habits. The vehicles are always fresh, the driver always speaks your language, and he or she will settle you in with your favorite drink and music—and safely take you anywhere around the Windy City.

Metropolitan Limousine

845 North Michigan Avenue, 1B
Chicago, IL 60611
Phone: 800-437-1700

METROPOLITAN MUSEUM OF ART

Museums

At over two million square feet, with more than three million pieces of art, The Met has something for everyone. Spanning over four city blocks on upper Fifth Avenue, the museum is divided into three floors, with everything from arms and armor, Egyptian, Greek and Roman art, European paintings and sculptures to 20th century art. Incidentally, if you positively *need* to socialize among the upper echelons of American society, beg, borrow or steal a ticket to the annual Costume Institute Gala: it's one of the biggest nights in Manhattan's social calendar.

Metropolitan Museum of Art

1000 Fifth Avenue
New York, NY 10028
Phone: 212-650-2911   *Fax: 212-650-2170*

CRÈME DE LA MER

Hair and Beauty

It might take a bit of effort (not to mention money) to find this exclusive moisturizing cream, but more than a generation of enthusiasts have found it worth their while. Through a unique biofermentation process that takes up to four months, sea kelp, calcium, magnesium, potassium, iron, lecithin, Vitamins C, D, E and B12, as well as oils of citrus, eucalyptus, wheat germ, alfalfa and sunflower are transformed into a singular and magical elixir that many have claimed has restorative powers.

NASA aerospace physicist Max Huber created La Mer after he suffered facial chemical burns from an experiment gone awry. The formula took twelve years to perfect, but when Huber passed away at the age of 65, his scars were hardly visible. Other notables have found the cream to their liking; Austrian Countess Lucienne von Doz swears that she has found the Fountain of Youth in the two-ounce jars. Leonard Lauder was also attracted to the cream because of its homemade roots, similar to the one with which his mother Estée launched her business.

Leonard Lauder was in fact so attracted to the formula that he acquired the company after Max Huber's death. The product continues to be made in the exact same way as day one, and still maintains its low-key marketing approach. It is available at Neiman Marcus, Bergdorf Goodman and Saks Fifth Avenue. A face serum, cleansing lotion, gel, tonic, oil absorbing tonic, mist, body serum and body lotion are now also available.

Crème de la Mer

767 Fifth Avenue
New York, NY 10153
Phone: 212-572-4322   *Fax: 212-572-4040*

THE METROPOLITAN OPERA

Events

For over 100 years, the Metropolitan Opera has been the gold-standard in American opera houses. While it may not have the intimacy or charm of Milan's La Scala, the Met has taken its production values well into the 21st century—and the music is certainly on a par with the best that Europe has to offer. Every diva from Callas to Te Kanawa has performed here. Opening nights are particularly glamorous.

The Metropolitan Opera
Lincoln Center for the Performing Arts
New York, NY 10023
Phone: 212-362-6000

MEURICE GARMENT CARE

Specialty Shops   *Best Kept Secret*

Giorgio Armani and Calvin Klein use Meurice to freshen up clothes after trunk shows. These dry cleaners to the stars have customers as far away as Europe and throughout America. As owner Wayne Edelman puts it: "We have more dirt on our celebrity clientele than the *National Enquirer!*" To his credit, Edelman refuses to name names, preferring to keep his reputation...spotless.

Meurice Garment Care
20 Park Avenue
Manhasset, NY 11030
Phone: 516-627-6060   *Fax: 516-627-2943*

MGM GRAND

Casinos

With over 5,000 rooms, the MGM Grand certainly does not conjure images of intimacy. What this Vegas landmark does deliver is pure sensory excitement. In addition to its huge casino, with all the standard games offered, the MGM is best known for its fights—in the ring, that is. Suites are hard to come by on fight nights, with regulars such as Jerry Seinfeld and Andy Garcia quickly snatching suites on the top floor.

MGM Grand
3799 Las Vegas Boulevard South
Las Vegas, NV 89109
Phone: 702-891-1111

MICHAEL GRAVES & ASSOCIATES

Architects and Interior Designers

For over 30 years, this Indiana native has been inspiring others in and out of his field with his accessible, figurative designs. A winner of over 130 prestigious awards for his work in architecture, interiors, products and graphics, Graves enjoys a prestigious international reputation. With acclaimed homes and buildings from Japan to Ohio, he is one of the most original voices in contemporary American design.

Michael Graves & Associates
341 Nassau Street
Princeton, NJ 08540
Phone: 609-924-6409

MICHAEL TAYLOR DESIGNS

Specialty Shops

While most interior designers were following the futurist trend of the 1950s, making extensive use of formica and chrome, Michael Taylor was using white slipcovers, neutral colors, limestone and marble to create what has become known as the "California look." Today the firm that Taylor established is an upscale furniture manufacturer, probably best known for its fabulous stone tables.

Michael Taylor Designs
1500 Seventeenth Street
San Francisco, CA 94103
Phone: 415-558-9940   *Fax: 415-558-9770*

MICHAEL WERNER GALLERY

Art Dealers

This New York and Cologne based gallery represents a wide range of the best modern and contemporary artists. The emphasis is on German and European post-WWII paintings, drawings, photography and sculpture. Works by Sigmar Polke, Georg Baselitz, Per Kirkeby, Eugène Leroy, Marcel Broodthaers, A.R. Penck, Jörg Immendorff and Don Van Vliet regularly line the walls here. Michael Werner Gallery represents the estate of the remarkable James Lee Byars and also offers the intriguing possibility of viewing contemporary artists alongside the work of their major influences, for example, the late Joseph Beuys alongside Wilhelm Lehmbruck. Exhibitions of 20th century masters like Francis Picabia, Hans Arp and Kurt Schwitters are typical.

Michael Werner Gallery
21 East 67th Street
New York, NY 10021
Phone: 212-988-1623   *Fax: 212-988-1774*

MICHAEL'S

Restaurants

Michael McCarty's restaurant is renowned both for top-class service and Sang Yoon's innovative mixture of French and Californian cuisine. McCarty, who also has a New York branch, clearly has impeccable taste; patrons dine among a large and impressive collection of contemporary art. The restaurant's sculpture garden is absolutely idyllic.

Michael's
1147 Third Street
Santa Monica, CA 90403
Phone: 310-451-0843   *Fax: 310-394-1830*

MILLE FLEURS
Restaurants

Chef Martin Woesle, one of the James Beard Foundation's "great regional chefs of America," prides himself on not having a signature dish, since everything is special in this cozy, elegant restaurant (ask for a table in the charming Spanish garden). Service may be a bit slow, but only because everything is freshly prepared and well worth waiting for. Try the outstanding rabbit in aspic.

Mille Fleurs

Country Squire Courtyard
6009 Paseo Delicias
Rancho Santa Fe, CA 92067
Phone: 619-756-3085

MILWAUKEE ART MUSEUM
Museums

20,000 works of art in Milwaukee? It's true—and this museum is getting bigger, with a $50 million expansion set for the near future. Formed by an alliance of the Layton Art Gallery and The Milwaukee Art Institution in 1957, the private, nonprofit Milwaukee Art Museum exhibits 15th to 20th century European and American paintings, sculptures, prints, drawings, photographs, and folk art. Highlights include the Bradley Collection of modern and contemporary expressionists, Pablo Picasso, Andy Warhol, and Georgia O'Keeffe.

Milwaukee Art Museum

750 North Lincoln Memorial Drive
Milwaukee, WI 53202
Phone: 414-224-3220

MINDY WEISS PARTY CONSULTANTS
Party Organizers and Caterers

This Beverly Hills based wedding and event planner has helped dozens of celebrities to throw their dream soirée. With close ties to celebrity Chef Wolfgang Puck, her parties are often catered by the maestro and his team. Producer Steve Tisch used her services in planning his high profile nuptials, as did Billy Crystal and his wife when throwing a 25th wedding anniversary party to renew their vows.

Mindy Weiss Party Consultants

232 South Beverly Drive
Beverly Hills, CA 90212
Phone: 310-205-6000   Fax: 310-205-6005

THE MIRAGE
Casinos

The original crown jewel in Steve Wynn's extensive cadre of resorts, The Mirage still rates as one of Las Vegas' top properties. From its incredible aqua-scape dolphin habitat to smart two-bedroom suites, The Mirage continues to deliver. Incidentally, late February's Chinese New Year celebrations at the hotel are rivaled only by those in Hong Kong.

The Mirage

3400 Las Vegas Boulevard South
Las Vegas, NV 89109
Phone: 800-627-6667

MIRAVAL
Spas and Clinics

Miraval is a vacation destination specializing in stress reduction. The Zen theory of mindfulness, which basically means being fully present in the moment and aware of what you are doing, is threaded throughout all of the treatments. The spa offers over 120 activities and treatments including (believe it or not) classes in "journal writing" and Hot Stone Massage, where instead of human touch the stones massage your aches, pains and worries away.

Miraval

5000 E. Vía Estancia Miraval
Catalina, AZ 85739
Phone: 520-825-4000   Fax: 520-825-5199

MITCHELL-INNES AND NASH
Art Consultants

This complementary partnership handles 19th and 20th century fine art from two Madison Avenue galleries. Lucy Mitchell-Innes focuses on masterworks by contemporary artists on the secondary market and David Nash represents impressionist and modern artworks. They co-represent the estate of William de Kooning with the Matthew Marks Gallery and often present exhibitions of his work. Mitchell-Innes and Nash also operate a full-service art consultancy for private clients.

Mitchell-Innes and Nash

1018 Madison Avenue
New York, NY 10021
Phone: 212-744-7400   Fax: 212-744-7401

MLS LIMOUSINES
Chauffeur Services

The business of getting from A to B has changed in recent years, with a new generation of topflight limousine firms plying their wares from coast to coast. MLS Limousines, based in Los Angeles, opened a branch in New York three years ago, with plans for additional expansion. MLS provides luxurious, reliable service and is the sole transporter for the New York Palace Hotel.

MLS Limousines

9641 Sunset Boulevard,
Beverly Hills, CA 90210
Phone: 800-310-1980   Fax: 310-271-8979

MINARDI SALON
Hair and Beauty

When Beth and Carmine Minardi opened their doors in 1986, their goal was to create contemporary hair design and fabulous hair color that is better than natural. All in an attitude-free environment with an unparalleled level of service and attention. Thirteen years later, Minardi Salon remains ahead of its time. Currently the salon boasts nine artistic colorists and nine stylists who cater to a discerning clientele which trusts the Minardi's and their dedicated staff. Celebrities like Rene Russo, Julianna Moore, Brad Pitt and Matt Dillon are among the VIPs who have slipped into these experts' chairs and put their famous locks into skillful hands.

Minardi Salon

29 East 61 Street
New York, NY 10021
Phone: 212-308-1711   Fax: 212-753-6831

MONTRACHET
Restaurants
Robert De Niro's frequent visits to this sparse French eatery convinced him to get into the restaurant business. Chef Remi Lauvand, who cut his teeth at Le Cirque, prepares a menu of modern French cuisine that changes with the seasons. The restaurant's impressive wine list has been voted one of the 10 best in the country by *Wine Spectator*. White burgundies, as one would expect, are well-featured.
Montrachet
239 West Broadway
New York, NY 10013
Phone: 212-219-2777   Fax: 212-274-9508

MONTREUX GOLF & COUNTRY CLUB
Golf Clubs
Jack Nicklaus calls Montreux "one of my top four or five," hardly surprising given its spectacular European architectural style and beautiful Lake Tahoe location. About 25 minutes drive from Reno,

the club is truly incorporated into the lush landscape which surrounds it. One of the finest private mountain golf communities, Montreux is home to the latest PGA tour event, the Reno-Tahoe Open. The clubhouse is an incredible 34,000 square feet and a new fitness center is to be added later this year.
Montreux Golf & Country Club
16475 Bordeaux Drive
Reno, NV 89511
Phone: 775-849-9444   Fax: 775-849-3130

MOORE BROTHERS WINE COMPANY
Wine Merchants
As the sommelier at Le Bec-Fin for some 20 years, Gregory Moore developed a loyal following of customers, which make up a large part of the clientele at his present store. A true democrat, Moore's employees must all agree on a wine before they will stock it, so there is not a single bottle in store which does not come recommended. The emphasis is on lesser-known regions of Italy and France.

Moore Brothers Wine Company
7200 North Park Drive
Pennsauken, NJ 08109
Phone: 609-317-1177

Life Mask of George Washington, Jean Antoine Houdon.

THE MORGAN LIBRARY
Museums
Originally the private library/palazzo of financier J. Pierpont Morgan, New York's Pierpont Morgan Library now hosts one of the world's finest collections of rare books and manuscripts. Highlights include the ninth century *Lindau Gospels,* a rare vellum copy of the Gutenberg Bible, the Hours of Catherine of Cleves, Albrecht Dürer's *Adam and Eve* and drawings by Rembrandt and Leonardo da Vinci. Visitors can also see original letters from George Washington and Thomas Jefferson.
The Morgan Library
29 East 36th Street
New York, NY 10016
Phone: 212-685-0610   Fax: 212-481-3484

MORGAN STANLEY DEAN WITTER
Wealth Management
The 400,000 high net worth households in America (those with $5 million or more to invest) are increasingly turning to old-fashioned investment houses like Morgan Stanley Dean Witter to look after their money. With a minimum investment of $5 million, the private wealth management division of this bluest of blue-chip firms will provide you with one of the more comprehensive packages in the business. Personal contact and customized service at the highest possible level are the big draws.
Morgan Stanley Dean Witter
1585 Broadway
New York, NY 10036
Phone: 212-761-4000

JUAN PABLO MOLYNEUX
Architects and Interior Designers
Although he is now an American citizen, Juan Pablo Molyneux was born in Chile to an affluent family of partly English heritage. He was trained, as he puts it himself, "in rigid modernism before rebelling against that minimalist doctrine" by enrolling at the École des Beaux-Arts, where he formed his lifelong passion for the neoclassical. Despite his latter-day affection for the Greco-Roman tradition, the Versailles aficionado still retains a place in his oeuvre for modern touches. Let's call it Palladio meets Le Corbusier– by way of South America. For a comprehensive account of this remarkable designer's career, have a look at our keynote feature, *A Life of Style.*
Juan Pablo Molyneux
29 East 69th Street
New York, NY 10021
Phone: 212-628-0097   Fax: 212-737-6126

MUSEUM OF CONTEMPORARY ART SAN DIEGO

Museums

Founded in 1941, the Museum of Contemporary Art hosts 3,000 works from 1950 to the present. This small but influential museum recently received a significant boost when the late Lela and Rea Axline left it $30 million, placing MCA's endowment among the top five for contemporary art museums in the United States. Since the 1970s the museum has hosted the black-tie Monte Carlo Ball at the end of each summer: it is San Diego's most elegant gala.

Museum of Contemporary Art San Diego

1001 Kettner Boulevard
San Diego, CA 92101
Phone: 619-234-1001

MORGENTHAL FREDERICS OPTICIANS

Specialty Shops

With the opening of a new location in Bergdorf Goodman in fall 1999, this high end full service eyewear company will offer cutting edge styles and high quality service in four Manhattan stores. Offering unusual, whimsical, colorful glasses, Morgenthal is a trend setter's haven for comfortable, elegant prescription lenses and sunglasses. Clients include Eric Clapton and Robin Williams.

Morgenthal Frederics Opticians

685 Madison Avenue
New York, NY 10021
Phone: 212-838-3090

MORRISON & FOERSTER

Law Firms

Wealthy individuals, small businesses in emerging industries and major international corporations alike turn to Morrison & Foerster. One of the nation's largest law firms, its attorneys are renowned for being on the cutting edge of new developments. Last year a mergers and acquisitions team represented Clorox in its $2 billion acquisition of First Brands and also Intel in its acquisition of Shiva Corporation.

Morrison & Foerster

425 Market Street
San Francisco, CA 94105
Phone: 415-268-7000   Fax: 415-268-7522

MURAD SPA

Spas and Clinics

The Murad Spa health center offers not only massages, facials and body treatments, but also hosts a medical center, a full-time certified nutritionist, and an elixir bar. Friendly, competent staff work with clients' inner and outer beauty and health, relieving everyday stress, strengthening a sense of self and teaching clients to value time. The clear, light and airy health center draws both men and women seeking peace and harmony in their lives.

Murad Spa

2141 Rosecrans Avenue
El Segundo, CA 90245
Phone: 310-726-0470   Fax: 310-726-3216

MUSEUM OF FINE ARTS, BOSTON

Museums

Boston's venerable museum of Fine Arts is renowned for its 19th century European paintings, Japanese art collection, and its John Singer Sargent murals. The museum has undergone a host of changes in recent years, including the restoration of the Norma Jean Calderwood Courtyard, and the new Claire and Richard Morse Study Room. Additionally, new permanent exhibitions opened in the Brown and Carter Galleries, featuring the arts of Africa, Oceania, and the ancient Americas.

Museum of Fine Arts, Boston

Avenue of the Arts
465 Huntington Avenue
Boston, MA 02115
Phone: 617-267-9300

MUSEUM OF MODERN ART

Museums

The 1.5 million people who visit MoMA each year must be onto something—perhaps they're attracted by the museum's unparalleled collection of 20th-century modern art. Or its unique focus on film and photography. Or its forward-looking shows, which never shy from the avant garde. From an initial gift of eight prints and one drawing in 1929, the museum's collection has flourished to include more than 100,000 works of art in various media.

Museum of Modern Art

11 West 53rd Street
New York, NY 10019
Phone: 212-708-9400

MYOTT STUDIO WORKSHOP

Specialty Shops

America's Prince of picture framing is the artist currently known as Myott. His hand-carved, custom designed gilded frames have been popular in Atlanta for two decades, although Myott's business now spans the nation, catering to clients like Ted Turner, Jane Fonda and Elton John. He also does conservation work and art consulting.

Myott Studio Workshop

30 East Andrews Drive
Atlanta, GA 30305
Phone: 404-233-2063   Fax: 404-841-9653

NANCY GOSLEE POWER & ASSOCIATES

Landscape Architects

Formerly an interior designer, Nancy Goslee Power now concentrates on designing exteriors. Her California based firm has worked closely with architects like Frank Gehry, Steve Ehrlich and the Office for Metropolitan Architecture, among many others. Having traveled extensively, Power's various influences mixed with her design sense and horticultural knowledge invariably bring landscapes and gardens to exuberant life. Her work has been published in *Breaking Ground: Portraits of Ten Garden Designers* and she has written a book, *The Garden of California*.

Nancy Goslee Power & Associates

1660 Stanford Street
Santa Monica, CA 90404
Phone: 310-264-0266

NAOMI LEFF & ASSOCIATES

Architects and Interior Designers

One of America's premier interior designers, Naomi Leff is noted for her innovative imagery, which has been widely copied. As the creator of retail outlets for the likes of Giorgio Armani, Ferragamo and Gucci, Leff has set a precedent for "listening to the clients, seeing their vision and then interpreting it into reality." Her work on the homes of Tom Cruise and Nicole Kidman, and Steven Spielberg and Kate Capshaw (in East Hampton) has further cemented Leff's reputation as one of the most accomplished decorators working in the United States today.

Naomi Leff & Associates

12 West 27th Street
New York, NY 10001
Phone: 212-686-6300

NATHAN LIVERANT AND SON ANTIQUES

Antiques

This renowned antiques shop in Connecticut has put the unassuming town of Colchester on the map. According to the owners, "there's probably no reason in the world to come here except to see us—oh, and a world-famous hot dog stand." This third generation business specializes in 18th and 19th century American furniture, paintings, silver, pottery, and accessories, including mirrors, baskets and other decorative items.

Nathan Liverant and Son Antiques

168 South Main Street
Colchester, CT 06415
Phone: 860-537-2409

NATALIE GERSCHEL KAPLAN

Party Organizers and Caterers　　*Rising Star*

Although this smart, high profile, twenty-something New Yorker has only organized a handful of important events she is constantly cited as someone to look out for in the future. And besides, as any seasoned partygoer will confirm, it is quality rather than quantity which really counts. On that basis this consultant to Christie's is already in the top tier; she produced the President's Hamptons parties last summer.

Natalie Gerschel Kaplan

Phone: 212-772-7458　　Fax: 212-772-7463

NATIONAL AIR AND SPACE MUSEUM

Museums

The Smithsonian Institution's National Air and Space Museum maintains the largest collection of historic air and space crafts in the world. Some of the permanent displays include the *1903 Spirit of St. Louis,* the original Wright Brothers' flyer, the *Apollo 11* command module, and an actual lunar rock that visitors can touch. The collections include thousands of space and air artifacts, from jet engines to manuscripts.

National Air and Space Museum

601 Independence Avenue
Washington, DC 20560
Phone: 202-357-1300

NATIONAL GALLERY OF ART

Museums

The National Gallery of Art was created in 1937 through a gift from financier and art collector Andrew J. Mellon. The original Mellon collection forms the nucleus of the museum, but numerous additions from private gifts have considerably increased the museum's holdings. The permanent collection includes a vast array of American, British, Dutch, Flemish, Spanish and assorted 20th century art.

National Gallery of Art

Constitution Avenue at 6th Street NW
Washington, DC 20090
Phone: 202-737-4215

NATIONAL GOLF LINKS OF AMERICA

Golf Clubs

Charles Blair McDonald designed this course amid the robber baron's Long Island estates in 1908; in doing so he established a new standard of excellence that influenced the design of courses both in the United States and Europe. With its place in history secure, the club has done little to alter McDonald's original design. Deceased members' name plates, including those of Henry Clay Frick and Dwight Eisenhower, are kept on the lockers. The 18th hole provides an especially dramatic view of the Taconic Bay.

National Golf Links of America

Sebonac Inlet Road
Southampton, NY 11968
Phone: 516-283-0410　　Fax: 516-283-0424

NEAL AUCTION COMPANY

Auction Houses

John Neal, a collector of 19th-century Americana, founded Neal Auction Company in 1984. Both museums and private collectors flock to New Orleans for the auction of fine arts, decorative arts, and paintings. The October Louisiana Purchase Sale is highly regarded. The company has secured record prices for a Louisiana armoire and many of the local artists.

Neal Auction Company

4038 Magazine Street
New Orleans, LA 70115
Phone: 504-899-5329

NEIMAN MARCUS

Fashion

To consumers throughout the world the name Neiman Marcus conjures up images of high fashion apparel, world famous designers and flamboyant, fun-filled gifts. Since Neiman Marcus' founding over 90 years ago, the specialty retailer has established a rich history of innovation and has developed a legacy of pioneering new retail concepts such as the fabled "His And Hers" Christmas gifts, The Christmas Book, the Neiman Marcus Fortnight celebrations, and InCircle, Neiman Marcus' customer loyalty program. Today, Neiman Marcus has millions of customers throughout the United States, both in its 34 stores nationwide and through the mail with NM Direct.

Neiman Marcus

1618 Main Street
Dallas, TX 75201
Phone: 214-741-6911　　Fax: 214-742-4904

Because some flights are inherently fancy.

Neiman Marcus

NELSON & NELSON ANTIQUES
Antiques

While Steve and Marge Nelson search for new acquisitions, Pat Nelson stays in New York to manage this impressive store on Park Avenue. The Nelsons specialize in American overlay and French doré bronze antiques. Overlay was an exclusively American craft which became extinct in the 1920s when the recipe for the epoxy used in these silver and glass pieces was lost.

Nelson & Nelson Antiques
445 Park Avenue
New York, NY 10022
Phone: 212-980-5825

NEMATI COLLECTION
Antiques

Sift through this glorious field of one-of-a-kind, rare and antique European and Oriental carpets and tapestries. The pieces, dating from the 16th through the 19th centuries, are on display in a spacious gallery in New York's renowned Art and Design Building. The luxurious, $8 million collection of art lies at your feet, but your designer can arrange for selected pieces to be hung on the walls for viewing.

Nemati Collection
1059 Third Avenue
New York, NY 10021
Phone: 212-486-6900

NETJETS
Airplanes

"Not your average fractional ownership service" is a good way to describe Executive Jet and its European subsidiary, owned by Warren Buffett's Berkshire Hathaway. Join ranks with Tiger Woods, Pete Sampras, Michael Mondavi, Bobby Rahl, and other high-profile celebs in NetJets' fractional ownership. The product line includes the Cessna Citation 10, the fastest executive jet available, and the Boeing Business jet, a 737-based custom corporate long-range jet with bedrooms and offices. Jets are also available throughout Europe via the NetJets program.

NetJets
Executive Jet
625 North Hamilton Road
Columbus, OH 43219
Phone: 800-821-2299

NEW LIFE CLINIC
& THERAPY SPA
Spas and Clinics

Tired of your typical aromatherapy massage and standard facial? Try the eclectic treatments offered at New Life. An oxygenating or deep-hydrating facial, a therapeutic massage, or an algae body scrub featuring marine sediments all come highly recommended, while the spa's signature body treatment will send you into a sedated bliss for at least a few hours. It includes a moor mask, deep water soak, lymphatic drainage and an alpha capsule aromatherapy massage to reduce stress, detoxify and improve your metabolism. Sounds like hard work to us!

New Life Clinic & Therapy Spa
Bay Harbor Island
1065 Kane Concourse, Suite 201
Miami Beach, FL 33154
Phone: 305-865-6265   Fax: 305-864-0633

NEVADA WINE CELLAR
& SPIRITS
Wine Merchants   *Rising Star*

Nevada Wine Cellar has rapidly established a reputation for its enviable stock of California boutique wines. Caviar, truffles, cigars, and some 300 types of beer are also stocked at the store, which is down the road from André Agassi's Vegas base. Partners Thomas Llamas, Jeff Schauer and Sonny Ahuja are courteous, erudite and enthusiastic.

Nevada Wine Cellar & Spirits
8665 West Flamingo Road
Las Vegas, NV 89147
Phone: 702-222-9463   Fax: 702-222-9763

NEW ORLEANS AUCTION
GALLERIES
Auction Houses

When auction deadline occurs, New Orleans Auction is one busy place. People come to Louisiana for this auction house, which offers a slew of categories. Jean Vidos owns and runs the operation with flair and passion; she is hugely enthusiastic about the future of auctions and the role her ambitious company will play.

New Orleans Auction Galleries
801 Magazine Street
New Orleans, LA 70130
Phone: 504-566-1849

NEW ORLEANS JAZZ
& HERITAGE FESTIVAL
Events

No city is more closely associated with jazz than New Orleans, so it is fitting that no music festival draws more devotees than the New Orleans Jazz & Heritage Festival. Held every April until early May, this 10-day, all-out jam session draws thousands of musicians and artisans to its famed tents and stages. From Santana to B. B. King to Chick Corea, Jazz Fest is known for its eclectic musical styles; even an eight-year-old Harry Connick, Jr. performed here. Although the temperatures can be overpowering and the crowds overzealous, no other festival stands out more for its love of the harmony of sound. And for a real down-South spiritual encounter, check out the gospel tent.

New Orleans Jazz & Heritage Festival
336 Camp Street, Suite 250
New Orleans, LA 70130
Phone: 504-522-4786

NEW ORLEANS
MUSEUM OF ART
Museums

Founded in 1910 as a 'temple of art for rich and poor,' the New Orleans Museum of Art boasts a fine selection of European art including 17th century Dutch, 18th century French and impressionist paintings. Among the Museum's more unusual holdings are beautiful jewel-like watercolor miniature portraits, a stunning Fabergé collection of imperial Easter eggs and a gallery devoted to the works of African-American and Louisiana artists.

New Orleans Museum of Art
One Diboll Circle
New Orleans, LA 70124
Phone: 504-488-2631   Fax: 504-484-6662

NEW YORK AVIATION
Airplanes

Jack Gentile has owned and operated New York Aviation from La Guardia Airport for 22 years. His chartered planes are used by the Saudi Arabian Royal Family and many top dogs in film, music, and Wall Street. "Money is not a concern for our clients; speed, service, and quality are," Gentile says. The company specializes in "short-notice situations": a Gulfstream with a full tank and stocked galley can be ready with just four hours notice.

New York Aviation
P.O. Box 438
La Guardia Airport
Flushing, NY 11371
Phone: 718-279-4000   Fax: 718-279-3814

NEW YORK BOTANICAL GARDEN
Museums

Set on 250 acres of perfectly manicured gardens, this celebrated refuge is home to America's largest Victorian glasshouse, 40 acres of a forest which once covered all of New York City, 16 specialty gardens and a 19th century snuff mill. "When you walk mostly on concrete sidewalks, work in rooms with blinds and fluorescent lights, and descend into the underworld to roar through tunnels to your home," wrote Anne Raver in *The New York Times* recently, "a place like the Botanic Garden becomes a haven like the ancient Persian gardens that were linked to Paradise."

New York Botanical Garden
200th Street and Kazimiroff Boulevard
Bronx, NY 10458
Phone: 718-817-8700

Because you can make a statement,
and still keep the peace.

NeimanMarcus

www.neimanmarcus.com

NEW YORK PALACE HOTEL
Hotels

Staying at the Palace is like stepping back into a more sophisticated and elegant era, with all the amenities of the modern age. The hotel unites the landmark Villard Houses with a sleek 55 story tower. A wonderful 7000 square foot gym overlooks St. Patrick's Cathedral, and the guest rooms are among the largest in New York. For serious luxury and *serious* views, try the Triplex Suites.

New York Palace Hotel
455 Madison Avenue
New York, NY 10022
Phone: 212-888-7000

THE NEW YORK OBSERVER
Media

This irreverent weekly covers the driving industries in Manhattan: Wall Street, entertainment, fashion, publishing and property. Look out for brilliant writing and incisive criticism by Frank DiGiacomo, Michael Thomas, Billy Norwich and Terry Golway.

The New York Observer
54 East 64th Street
New York, NY 10021
Phone: 212-755-2400

THE NEW YORK TIMES
Media

The largest seven-day newspaper in the United States is an indispensable tool for anyone who wants to make sense of America today. With a record 77 Pulitzer prizes for its reporting, the Gray Lady maintains its reputation as the pre-eminent paper of record in part by noting the errors of the previous edition each day. Our favorite writers? William Safire, Max Frankel and Maureen Dowd.

The New York Times
229 West 43rd Street
New York, NY 10036
Phone: 212-556-1234

NEW YORK YACHT CLUB
Private Clubs

The preeminent yacht club in the United States accepts reciprocity from only two clubs: the St. Francis in San Francisco and the Royal Thames in London. Yachts are kept in Newport, Rhode Island. The historically listed building is a prominent feature on club row. Its facade is carved to resemble the front side of a galleon; the walls and ceiling of the dining room create the effect of dining in the hull of a boat, with their dark curved oak. The club now admits lady members despite the loud protest of some of the older, saltier members who lived out their last days in the upstairs bedrooms and enjoyed coming down for drinks dressed only in robe and slippers.

New York Yacht Club
37 West 44th Street
New York, NY 10036
Phone: 212-382-1000

FREDERICK A. NEWMAN, M.D.
Cosmetic Surgeons

Certified by the American Board of Plastic Surgery, a member of the American Society for Aesthetic Plastic Surgery, and one of the first physicians in the country to perform liposuction, Dr. Frederick A. Newman offers his patients an extensive menu of surgical options. His skills stem from his training at Yale, Harvard, and the Institute of Reconstructive Plastic Surgery at New York University Medical Center. He specializes in facial and breast cosmetic and reconstructive surgery. Newman's endearing bedside manner illustrates genuine care and concern for his patients.

Frederick A. Newman, M.D.
2 Overhill Road
Scarsdale, NY 10583
Phone: 914-723-0400   Fax: 914-723-0404

NEWPORT ART MUSEUM
Museums

In 1916 a group of artists and friends purchased the home of railroad mogul John Griswold. Several renovations later, the Griswold House contains six galleries that focus primarily on the past and present art scene of Newport and Rhode Island. Highlights in the collection include works by Fitz Hugh Lane, George Inness and Howard Gardiner Cushing. The museum hosts an annual Summer Gala and an Artists' Ball every Spring. Artists donate a work of art in lieu of purchasing a ticket, and the works are sold at a silent auction during the ball.

Newport Art Museum
76 Bellevue Avenue
Newport, RI 02840
Phone: 401-848-8200

NEWPORT MUSIC FESTIVAL
Events

Set in a town transformed by the great robber barons of the 19th century, Rhode Island's Newport Music Festival has made use of the former palaces of the Vanderbilts and their friends, turning them into elegant concert halls, for more than 30 years. Some of the greatest classical artists and ensembles perform to the delight of thousands during the two-and-a-half-week season, held in mid-July. Director Mark Malkovich runs the whole affair with the easy charm of a modern-day Gatsby.

Newport Music Festival
P.O. Box 3300
Newport, RI 02840
Phone: 401-846-1133   Fax: 401-849-1857

NEWSEUM
Museums   Best Kept Secret

Under the auspices of Al Neuharth's Freedom Forum, the Newseum offers visitors a fascinating account of how news is created in America. The flagship facility in Virginia includes a theater, cyber café and an interactive News Room on the lower level, where visitors can be a newscaster or an editor for the museum's fictitious newspaper, *The Daily Miracle*. The New York branch of the Newseum holds an outstanding series of talks, exhibitions and seminars throughout the year.

Newseum
1101 Wilson Boulevard
Arlington, VA 22209
Phone: 888-639-7386

NEWTON VINEYARDS
Winemakers

Dramatic wines in a dramatic setting on the slopes of the Maya Camas mountains. Peter Newton and wife, Dr. Su Hua, have created a monumental 560-acre estate. With superb Japanese temple gardens, it is truly a place to visit. Call ahead for a tour and tasting. Newton's unfiltered Chardonnay is among the top five Chardonnays produced in California, and their Merlot and Viognier are both excellent.

Newton Vineyards
P.O. Box 540
2555 Madrona Avenue
St. Helena, CA 94574
Phone: 707-963-9000

NIALL SMITH ANTIQUES
Antiques   *Best Kept Secret*

This ebullient Irish antiques dealer has traded in New York City for nearly three decades. Smith has a discerning eye for quality, which shows in his eclectic assortment of neoclassical furniture, Grand Tour objects, boldly carved English and Irish Georgian pieces (spanning the Regency and William IV periods) and unusual Victorian trinkets. Smith's winning personality complements an impressive inventory.

Niall Smith Antiques
96 Grand Street
New York, NY 10013
Phone: 212-941-7354   *Fax: 212-925-1395*

NICK AND TONI'S
Restaurants

When husband and wife team Jeff Salaway and Toni Ross opened this restaurant in 1988 they hardly knew that it was going to become a Hamptons institution within a few years. Its incredible popularity throughout the last decade is due in large part to the upscale Mediterranean cooking, although a high celebrity quotient has certainly done no harm either. Salaway also co-owns a Manhattan branch of Nick and Toni's.

Nick and Toni's
136 North Main Street
East Hampton, NY 11937
Phone: 516-324-3550   *Fax: 516-324-7001*

NIEBAUM COPPOLA
Winemakers

When Oakville Estates went bankrupt in 1975 moviemaker Francis Ford Coppola made the sellers an offer they couldn't refuse, buying the estate, formerly owned by Gustave Niebaum, to make "just enough wine to drink." With the legendary André Telitscheff as advisor, Coppola created a red with a blend of Cabernet Sauvignon, Merlot and Cabernet Franc. Called Rubicon, it is aged 6 years (3 years in oak barrels, 3 years in the bottle) before release. Back in the 1980s it was rather rustic, although the 1994 has 14% alcohol and is full, well rounded with a spicy finish.

Niebaum Coppola
1991 St. Helena Highway
Rutherford, CA 94573
Phone: 707-968-1100

NINA HOVNANIAN COUTURE
Fashion   *Best Kept Secret*

This amiable New Yorker used to be the Director of Development for the Princess Grace Foundation. Nowadays she has two roles: Cultural Ambassador at large for Armenia and designer of clothes for discerning women. Hovnanian's feminine, timeless, one of a kind pieces are made with fine materials—cashmere, for instance, from Loro Piana. Her hand painted velvets are particularly coveted by stars like Uma Thurman and Joan Rivers.

Nina Hovnanian Couture
The Aspen Grove Mall
525 East Cooper Avenue
Aspen, CO 81611
Phone: 970-948-1188

NO. 9 PARK
Restaurants   *Rising Star*

Owner and chef Barbara Lynch prepares highly acclaimed "European country fare" in this 1940s-style restaurant in Boston's historic Beacon Hill. No. 9 Park, which opened in July of 1998, includes two formal dining rooms and a bistro-style bar and café with a separate menu. The most popular tables are those near the windows overlooking the Boston Common. Casually elegant.

No. 9 Park
9 Park Street
Boston, MA 02108
Phone: 617-742-9991   *Fax: 617-742-9993*

NOBU
Restaurants

Robert De Niro is a partner with chef and owner Nobu Matsuhisa and Drew Nieporent at this incredibly popular TriBeCa restaurant. It has spawned a veritable empire, with offshoots in New York, Las Vegas, London and Tokyo. The cuisine is Japanese, although Matsuhisa adds South American touches that he picked up in Peru. Signature dishes include a sublime black cod marinated in miso paste. Architect David Rockwell has compared the interior to a "whimsical Japanese forest."

Nobu
105 Hudson Street
New York, NY 10013
Phone: 212-219-0500   *Fax: 212-219-1441*

NORTHERN TRUST
Wealth Management

Northern Trust boasts 110 years of private banking experience and $120 billion in private banking assets, making it one of the oldest and largest U.S. institutions in the business of managing wealth. The firm provides clients with almost every financial option available: basic money-market checking accounts; proprietary mutual funds; investment advice and portfolio management; risk management; access to hedge funds; specialized loans for art, securities and real estate—and even private jets. The wealth management group serves about 150 families with minimum assets of $100 million per family. If you're in that sort of league, chances are you know all about Northern Trust already.

Northern Trust
50 South La Salle Street
Chicago, IL 60675
Phone: 312-630 6000

NOVA LIMOUSINE SERVICE
Chauffeur Services

Nova keeps an updated profile on its customers, outlining their personal preferences—down to nitty-gritty such as how they like their coffee or which paper they want to read. Special requests such as fresh flowers, dinner reservations, and gift delivery are welcomed and handled with grace. The company offers a modern fleet of impeccably maintained automobiles.

Nova Limousine Service
15201 Dallas Parkway
Dallas, TX 75001
Phone: 972-490-3333   *Fax: 972-233-8125*

NURSERY LINES
Specialty Shops

Head here for the ultimate in simple, elegant baby clothing, accessories and nursery furnishings. Most items have an Italian flavor; sizes on clothing like hand knitted sweaters and J.P. Tods go to infants and toddlers. Custom interior design services include faux finishing, window treatments and custom sewn linens. TV Anchor Al Roker and Madonna shop here.

Nursery Lines
1034 Lexington Avenue
New York, NY 10021
Phone: 212-396-4445

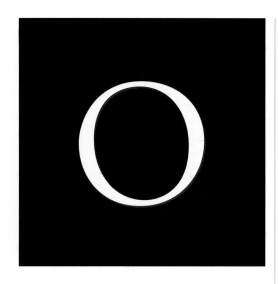

OAKLAND HILLS COUNTRY CLUB
Golf Clubs

The famous South course (known as The Monster) at the historic Oakland Hills Club was designed by Donald Ross and finished in 1918. Television cannot capture the subtle treachery that lies within the rolling terrain of this Midwestern classic. The 16th hole is often described as a masterpiece, and the 18th green is notoriously tough.

Oakland Hills Country Club
3951 West Maple Road
Bloomfield Hills, MI 48301
Phone: 248-258-1698

OAKMONT COUNTRY CLUB
Golf Clubs

With 200 bunkers and the slickest putting surfaces in America, Henry Fownes' diabolical design near Pittsburgh has been considered one of the country's toughest championship tests since it opened in 1903. In the 1935 U.S. Open, Club member Sam Parks was the only player in the field to break 300 over 72 holes, but since then the course has produced champions like Hogan and Nicklaus, and in 1973 a miraculous final-round 63 catapulted Johnny Miller to the National Championship.

Oakmont Country Club
1233 Hulton Road
Oakmont, PA 15139
Phone: 412-661-2360

OBER, ONET & ASSOCIATES
Party Organizers

Polly Onet is one of the more successful young event planners in New York, but one rarely reads about the glittering soirées she organizes in the gossip columns. Why? Because most of her customers are in the mega-wealthy category. They are the sort of people who would prefer to be in the front line of a nuclear war than the dizzy heights of *Page Six*. Onet's more visible clients include John Kluge, George and Susan Soros, and David and Julia Koch.

Ober, Onet & Associates
205 East 95th Street
New York, NY 10128
Phone: 212-876-6775

OJAI VALLEY INN AND SPA
Spas and Clinics

The 31,000 square foot Ojai Valley Inn and Spa has the charm and ambiance of a thriving Mediterranean village. Ojai's 28 treatment areas feature decorative tiles and hand-stenciled walls painted in warm shades. Try a couples' massage in a decidedly romantic room featuring a fireplace, private terrace and whirlpool, then retreat to your own penthouse, complete with a private elevator, a treatment room, a sauna, and sunrise/sunset terraces with outdoor whirlpools.

Ojai Valley Inn and Spa
905 Country Club Road
Ojai, CA 93023
Phone: 800-422-6564   Fax: 805-640-0305

OLD LOUISVILLE INN
Hotels   **Best Kept Secret**

God, as they say, is in the details: at the Louisville Inn there is always a jigsaw in progress in the downstairs parlor. This stately 1901 Inn, located on one of the town's loveliest streets, has only ten bedrooms, each adorned with antique quilts, Victorian furniture, bay windows and working fireplaces. Many of the bathrooms even have their original fixtures. This is a warm and charming retreat where guests are treated like royalty by owner Marianne Lesher.

Old Louisville Inn
1359 South Third Street
Louisville, KY 40208
Phone: 502-635-1574

L'OLIVIER FLORAL ATELIER
Florists

Once you start speaking with Olivier Guini, you will never want to stop. And once you have purchased one of his floral creations, you will want to be constantly surrounded by them. Years ago, the designer Pierre Cardin wanted to open a floral design shop and he chose the exuberant young Frenchman to help him. Today Guini runs his own studio, which is renowned for creating unusual living sculptures in vibrant colors.

L'Olivier Floral Atelier
19 East 76th Street
New York, NY 10021
Phone: 212-774-7676   Fax: 212-774-0058

OLD CHATHAM SHEEPHERDING COMPANY INN
Hotels

Like a relaxing visit to a friend's elegant country home, staying at this luxurious yet informal inn is both serene and satisfying. With just 14 individually decorated bedrooms and four intimate dining rooms, guest privacy is assured. Listed on the National Historic Register, the 1790 Georgian colonial manor house rests gracefully on a gentle rise overlooking ancient maples, pastoral hills and, of course, sheep grazing on rolling pastures. The courteous, friendly staff take care of your every need, in a manner that reminds one of a bygone era; and American regional cuisine from the award winning kitchen features homegrown produce and sheep's milk cheeses and lamb from the farm. The Old Chatham Sheepherding Company Inn, a Relais & Chateaux property, is a sumptuous way to spend a weekend or extended holiday in the country.

Old Chatham Sheepherding Company Inn
99 Shaker Museum Road
Old Chatham, NY 12136
Phone: 518-794-9774   Fax: 518-794-9779

ONE PICO

Restaurants

One Pico offers a winning combination of terrific cuisine, soothing atmosphere, attentive service and extraordinary views. A floor to ceiling limestone fireplace, amber-colored wood floors, clean, contemporary lines and breathtaking sunset views provide a stunning backdrop for Jeff Littlefield's impressive Californian cooking.

One Pico

Shutters at the Beach
1 Pico Boulevard
Santa Monica, CA 90405
Phone: 310-587-1717

OPUS ONE WINERY

Winemakers

Wine legends Robert Mondavi and Philippe de Rothschild created the stunning Opus One winery and in 1979 brought forth their first wine. It won high praise, but at the time it was the most expensive wine in California. Still, it succeeded and continues to succeed, although much of it is sold by the glass in restaurants. Opus One makes only one red wine, a Cabernet Sauvignon with a little Cabernet Franc and Merlot. Its price is not unrelated to the glamour of Mondavi and Rothschild affiliations.

Opus One Winery

7900 St. Helena Highway
Oakville, CA 94562
Phone: 707-944-9442

OREGON BACH FESTIVAL

Events   ***Best Kept Secret***

The Oregon Bach Festival, led by artistic director and conductor Helmuth Rilling, presents masterworks for chorus and orchestra in the Pacific Northwest. The festival brings together new artists, intimate chamber concerts, talks, master classes and family events. *The Los Angeles Times* has described it as "a musical enterprise virtually without equal in America."

Oregon Bach Festival

1257 University of Oregon
Eugene, OR 97403
Phone: 541-346-5666

OUTSIDE

Specialty Shops   ***Rising Star***

This purveyor of "mid-century modern" exterior furniture offers a lavish selection of meticulously restored vintage pieces by designers like van Keppel Green, Walter Lamb and Richard Neutra. The furniture here is equally at home inside or out, depending on your taste.

Outside

442 North La Brea
Los Angeles, CA 90036
Phone: 323-934-12547

L'ORANGERIE

Restaurants

For 'a trip to Paris by way of La Cienega,' Gerard Ferry's L'Orangerie offers a sophisticated dining experience, dazzling flowers and excellent cuisine. Chef Ludovic Lefebvre's menu offers dishes that are faithful to the principles of simplicity, freshness and flavor, created with the passion of an artist. Savor the crispy polenta pancake with foie gras, banyuls, green cabbage and curry complemented by a fine Californian or French wine. Service here is surprisingly friendly for a restaurant of this stature, where wealth, power and pretty faces meet to wine, dine and deal.

L'Orangerie

903 North La Cienega Boulevard
Los Angeles, CA 90069
Phone: 310-652-9770   *Fax: 310-652-8870*

OSTERIA DEL CIRCO

Restaurants

Osteria del Circo is the latest creation of Sirio Maccioni, proprietor of Le Cirque; his wife Egidiana, the supervising chef and their sons, Mario, Marco and Mauro, who combined make up the owners, hosts and ringmasters of this sophisticated big top restaurant in the heart of New York City. Designed to be as exciting as a European carnival tent, the colorful décor is innovative, whimsical and vibrant and the atmosphere electric. A bright blue circus ring is hung with gold stars, sculptures of monkeys swing near the striped pole, a clown peeps down from over the kitchen door and a trapeze sails above the bar. But despite the playfulness, sitting down to eat you will soon discover how serious the menu is. Executive Chef Alessandro Giuntoli creates dishes that taste divine and look as beautiful as a Cézanne still life. Like the Tuscan countryside where he grew up, his rustic cuisine is elegantly simple and beautiful, a style he describes as "real Tuscan food with a New York dress." His creations are festive reinventions of traditional soups, pastas, risottos, fish, poultry and meat dishes that Tuscan families might enjoy for Sunday dinner. Incidentally, the sovereign Maccioni clan have recently launched an Osteria del Circo in Las Vegas. Given the increasing sophistication of Las Vegas and the local penchant for all things exotic, the new restaurant looks like a sound investment.

Osteria del Circo

120 West 55th Street
New York, NY 10019
Phone: 212-265-3636

PACE WILDENSTEIN
Art Dealers

From its original New York location on 57th Street, Pace Wildenstein has represented such artists as Jim Dine, Jean Dubuffet, Louise Nevelson and Lucas Samaras, as well as the estates of Alexander Calder, Henry Moore, Pablo Picasso and Mark Rothko. Today, the gallery also has exhibition spaces in SoHo and Beverly Hills and features, within its inventory, contemporary artists like Elizabeth Murray and Robert Rauschenberg. Pace Wildenstein is, in short, a super-power of the modern and contemporary art world.

Pace Wildenstein
32 East 57th Street
New York, NY 10022
Phone: 212-421-3292

PACIFIC TALL SHIP COMPANY
Specialty Shops

This is one of the few firms which produces miniature reproductions of famous ships from around the world. An in-house master craftsman builds each one by hand, hence no two are exactly alike; these unusual works of art have been presented to 17 different presidents and the British Royal Family. Pacific Tall Ship also produce canned cigars (packaged this way so they will never spoil), and can custom make private labels for special clients.

Pacific Tall Ship Company
106 Stephen Street
Lemont, IL 60439
Phone: 800-690-6601

THE PACIFIC-UNION CLUB
Private Clubs

In 1889, the Pacific Club and the Union Club consolidated to form the Pacific-Union Club, which is now the fifth oldest city club in the United States. After the earthquake and fire of 1906, this distinctly private entity purchased what remained of the Flood Mansion on Nob Hill for its clubhouse, which today houses a dining room, bar, reading rooms, private dining rooms, a formal library, squash courts, a swimming pool, Masseur's station, dry sauna and sixteen bedrooms.

The Pacific-Union Club
1000 California Street
San Francisco, CA 94108
Phone: 415-775-1234   Fax: 415-673-0104

PACIFIC WESTERN TRADERS
Specialty Shops

Situated in the historic American River Gold Rush town of Folsom, California, Pacific Western Traders fosters the creation of traditional and contemporary Native American arts. Many of the artists, including Maidu traditionalist, Frank Day, still use ancient tribal techniques in their pottery, basketry and carvings. Institutions like the Smithsonian, Yosemite National Park and the National Museum of American Art have bought from the firm.

Pacific Western Traders
305 Wool Street
Folsom, CA 95630-2550
Phone: 916-985-3851   Fax: 916-985-2635

PAHLMEYER
Winemakers

Pahlmeyer was catapulted to stardom in 1991 when its Chardonnay was ranked best in the nation. Its fame wasn't damaged either by being imbibed in the movie *Disclosure,* starring Michael Douglas and Demi Moore. Colorful owner, Jayson Pahlmeyer (a qualified attorney), describes the wines as "industrial strength" to convey their abundance of viscous fruit flavors, creamy oak and intense aromas. The red Bordeaux Blend is incredibly concentrated.

Pahlmeyer
P.O. Box 2410
Napa, CA 94558
Phone: 707-255-2321   Fax: 707-255-6786

LE PALAIS
Restaurants

Critics adore this French restaurant located in Atlantic City's first gaming establishment, the Resorts. With the culinary skills of chef, Carl Colucci, the charm and professionalism of Maitre d', Glenn Lamison and the musical virtuosity of chanteuse, Kitt Moran, Le Palais certainly offers better cuisine, service and ambiance than most restaurants along the Jersey shore.

Le Palais
Resort Casino Hotels
1133 Boardwalk
Atlantic City, NJ 08401
Phone: 609-340-6400

PALM BEACH INTERNATIONAL ART & ANTIQUE FAIR
Events

Connoisseurs and collectors pour in from around the world for this prestigious event, a veritable who's who of the arts and antiques world. In 2000, the fourth-annual Palm Beach fair runs from February 3rd to 13th. Meander through the 55,000-square-foot International Pavilion and inspect the wares offered by more than 80 top dealers, including furniture, paintings, Asian art, jewelry, carpets, tapestries, books, and manuscripts.

Palm Beach International Art & Antique Fair
3725 South East Ocean Boulevard
Sewalls Point, FL 34996
Phone: 561-220-2690   Fax: 561-220-3180

PALM BEACH POLO AND COUNTRY CLUB
Polo Clubs

This winter headquarters for international high-goal players—all 14 polo fields of it—also offers one of the finest golf courses in the area. The polo club regularly hosts the prestigious U.S. Open Championship, and equestrians enjoy a world-class winter festival that attracts sponsorship from heavyweights like Revlon, Cadillac and Ralph Lauren. The club has a high social cachet—Prince Charles has played in a Rolex Gold Cup tournament here, and regular spectators include Calvin Klein and Jimmy Buffett.

Palm Beach Polo and Country Club
11199 Polo Club Road
Wellington, FL 33414
Phone: 561-798-7110   Fax: 561-798-7125

PALMER JOHNSON YACHTS
Yachting
For more than 80 years, Palmer Johnson has set the standard for luxury mega-yachts. The world's largest builder of all-aluminum, high-end private yachts makes hulled boats that are as strong as steel, and as light as fiber glass. Their shallow draft and hull strength allow them to carry additional fuel and navigate shallow waters. A recent project, the 195-foot *Baronessa,* commissioned by a high-profile Asian businessman, demonstrates the firm's ability to produce luxurious, seaworthy mega-yachts.
Palmer Johnson Yachts
61 Michigan Street
Sturgeon Bay, WI 54235
Phone: 920-743-4412   Fax: 920-743-3381

PAMELA DENNIS
Fashion
Pamela Dennis was 'discovered' when she designed a dress to wear to a friend's wedding. She now designs evening wear for the likes of Jamie Lee Curtis, Joan Rivers, Geena Davis and Liv Tyler. Her signature style, on view at Bergdorf Goodman, Barneys, Saks Fifth Avenue and boutiques across the country, has been described as "glamorous, sexy and wearable."
Pamela Dennis
550 Seventh Avenue
New York, NY 10018
Phone: 212-354-2100   Fax: 212-354-2244

PASCAL
Restaurants
Who would think that in a quiet little area of California's Orange County lies a culinary jewel reminiscent of the finest restaurants in the Cote d'Azur? For the last decade, chef/owner Pascal Olhats has been bringing his classic, spirited aesthetic to every dish (try the sautéed *foie gras*—it is simply heaven). This charming restaurant, decked out in a profusion of multicolored roses, is a French oasis in Newport Beach.
Pascal
1000 North Bristol Street
Newport Beach, CA 92660
Phone: 949-752-0107   Fax: 949-752-4942

PATINA
Restaurants
Simple elegance both in cuisine and in ambiance are the trademarks of this award-winning French-Californian restaurant, which invariably features in lists of the most popular restaurants in Los Angeles. Owned and operated by Joachim and Christine Splichal, their catering offshoot, Patina Catering, offers a full party-planning service for everything from quiet dinners to lavish film premieres—like *The X-Files* and *Pleasantville*. The Splichals have catered private dinners in honor of President Clinton.
Patina
5955 Melrose Avenue
Los Angeles, CA 90038
Phone: 323-467-1108
Fax: 323-467-0215

PAUL, HASTINGS, JANOFSKY & WALKER
Law Firms
Founded in 1951, this international law firm has more than 600 attorneys practicing in seven domestic and two overseas offices. Major practice areas include business law, employment law, litigation, real estate and tax law.
Paul, Hastings, Janofsky & Walker
555 South Flower Street
Los Angeles, CA 90071
Phone: 213-683-6000

PAUL KASMIN GALLERY
Art Dealers
Son of the London art dealer John Kasmin, Paul Kasmin has made his own international reputation in the art world with his downtown New York gallery. Representing artists like Donald Baechler, Alessandro Twombly (son of Cy Twombly), Nancy Rubins and Aaron Rose, the younger Kasmin's clients include architect Alan Wanzenberg and real estate developer Arthur Fleischer.
Paul Kasmin Gallery
74 Grand Street
New York, NY 10013
Phone: 212-219-3219

PAUL STUART
Fashion
Family-owned for over 60 years, Paul Stuart produces some of the finest private-label suits in the world. This full-service men's store, which also offers some women's goods, provides one-stop shopping. American with a European twist, Paul Stuart's suits, sportswear and accessories are made to measure. The firm's designers, who pride themselves on catering to the needs of even their most demanding customers, recently created $12,000 worth of ties from a client's design for his employees.
Paul Stuart
Madison Avenue & 45th Street
New York, NY 10017
Phone: 212-682-0320

PAULINE POCOCK ANTIQUES
Antiques
Browse through nine fully decorated rooms in this elegant gallery, which specializes in 18th century American and English furniture, as well as impressionist and post-impressionist American paintings. Another highlight is the collection of silver and porcelain accessories that predate 1820.
Pauline Pocock Antiques
607 East Las Olas Boulevard
Fort Lauderdale, FL 33001
Phone: 954-525-3400

PAVILLION AGENCY
Employment Agencies   Best Kept Secret
Whether it is a nanny for the kids or a butler for your good self, this small family-run company is all about discretion. For 38 years, co-owners Keith & Clifford Greenhouse have served the needs of the influential and high profile, providing sevices from nannies, housekeepers and chefs, to butlers, chauffeurs and personal assistants.
Pavillion Agency
15 East 40th Street, Suite 900
New York, NY 10016
Phone: 212-889-6609

PEABODY MUSEUM OF NATURAL HISTORY

Museums

Founded in the 18th century as a miscellaneous assortment of artifacts, typical of that era's college collections, Yale's Peabody Museum is now a leading paleontology and geology research museum. The museum's best-known exhibits are a 110-foot-long mural, *The Age of Reptiles* and a mounted giant "brontosaurus"—if those don't appeal, there are another 11 million objects to inspect.

Peabody Museum of Natural History

Yale University
170 Whitney Avenue
New Haven, CT 06520
Phone: 203-432-5050   Fax: 203-432-9816

PEBBLE BEACH RESORTS

Golf Clubs

Site of the AT&T Pro-Am, in which Samuel L. Jackson, Clint Eastwood and President George Bush have all participated, the famous Pebble Beach Golf Links course is considered among the top five in the world. Jack Nicklaus, Tom Kite and Tom Watkins have all made history here. Reputations are made on the par three 17th and par five 18th holes. Almost as famous as the course, the pub at Pebble Beach, the Tap Room, has won various awards for its French cuisine.

Pebble Beach Resorts

2700 Seventeen Mile Drive
Pebble Beach, CA 93953
Phone: 800-654-9300   Fax: 831-644-7960

THE PENINSULA BEVERLY HILLS

Hotels

Secluded behind high walls and designed around a cobblestone courtyard, the Peninsula feels like a grand estate or palazzo. All the rooms are impressive, but for something special, stay in one of the 16 villas, which are set in a tropical garden with imported plants from the Amazon and Hawaii. The pool is heated to 84 degrees and the poolside cabanas come with fresh fruit, TV, and even fax facilities.

The Peninsula Beverly Hills

9882 Little Santa Monica Boulevard
Beverly Hills, CA 90212
Phone: 310-551-2888   Fax: 310-788-2319

PERFORMANCE SKI

Specialty Shops   Best Kept Secret

Energetic young husband and wife team, Lee Keating and Tom Bowers (he is a former skiing champion), run this small shop adjacent to the Gondola in the heart of Aspen. It is packed to the rafters with all the top names in skiwear like Prada and Armani. Incidentally, Lee's brother, Michael, is equally at home with designer comfort—he runs the town's Gucci store.

Performance Ski

408 South Hunter Street
Aspen, CO 81611
Phone: 970-925-8657

JON PERLMAN, M.D.

Cosmetic Surgeons

Specializing in breast augmentation, implants, lifts, reductions, tummy tucks, liposuction, and face-lifts, Dr. Jon Perlman is a leading member of the American Society for Aesthetic Plastic Surgeons. His surgical schedule is invariably pretty full, though Perlman's staff will certainly try to accommodate patients at short notice. Botox, collagen and skin resurfacing are other frequently requested procedures.

Jon Perlman, M.D.

414 North Camden Drive, Suite 800
Beverly Hills, CA 90210
Phone: 310-854-0031

THE PERLMAN MUSIC PROGRAM

Events

Formerly known as the Hamptons Summer Music Program, The Perlman Music Program is a highlight of the summer in this quaint enclave on Long Island. Organized by Toby Perlman, wife of famed violinist, Itzak Perlman, the focus of the program is to allow gifted students to escape for two weeks into a world filled with the joys of music. The program attracts top musicians from across the globe (like Billy Joel and Mr. Perlman) performing and teaching master classes.

The Perlman Music Program

P.O. Box 4163
East Hampton, NY 11937
Phone: 516-329-7405

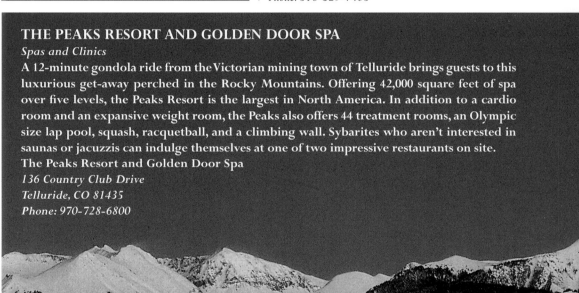

THE PEAKS RESORT AND GOLDEN DOOR SPA

Spas and Clinics

A 12-minute gondola ride from the Victorian mining town of Telluride brings guests to this luxurious get-away perched in the Rocky Mountains. Offering 42,000 square feet of spa over five levels, the Peaks Resort is the largest in North America. In addition to a cardio room and an expansive weight room, the Peaks also offers 44 treatment rooms, an Olympic size lap pool, squash, racquetball, and a climbing wall. Sybarites who aren't interested in saunas or jacuzzis can indulge themselves at one of two impressive restaurants on site.

The Peaks Resort and Golden Door Spa

136 Country Club Drive
Telluride, CO 81435
Phone: 970-728-6800

THE PENINSULA NEW YORK

Hotels

The Peninsula adds its own belle époque touch to the cosmopolitan flavor of Fifth Avenue. The two large outdoor roof-terraces of the cocktail lounge provide impressive views up and down the Avenue, and are among the few places in Midtown offering a skyline perspective. The hotel's tri-level spa and fitness center provides stress-relieving therapies and alternative healing methods. Each of the 55 suites in the hotel are now brighter and grander than before. The Peninsula Suite, with its spectacular views, large parlor and separate 'his and hers' vanity areas, is without a doubt the loveliest of them all.

The Peninsula New York

700 Fifth Avenue
New York, NY 10019
Phone: 212-956-2888   Fax: 212-903-3949

PERNA LUXURY REAL ESTATE

Property Consultants

Perna Luxury Real Estate is a provider of real estate services for the owners of multiple homes. Working with 27 hand-chosen national real estate brokers and 11 international brokerage firms, Perna counsels its high-end clients from offices in Arizona, Colorado and Austria. The company's owners, Lou and Jane Perna, are a dynamic couple; in another life Lou spent 27 years as a *Fortune 500* Executive.

Perna Luxury Real Estate

8787 East Pinnacle Peak Road
Scottsdale, AZ 85255
Phone: 602-515-0100   Fax: 602-515-0200

PETE DYE GOLF CLUB

Golf Clubs

In designing this course, the legendary Pete Dye transformed a reclaimed coal mine into one of the most visual and satisfying golf experiences in the world. If, as some members claim, walking the course is a religious experience, then approaching the tough 17th hole is like coming face to face with the creator. The club is currently accepting members, although by invitation only. The Pittsburgh Open, which has one of the largest purses in professional golf, was held at the Pete Dye Club last July.

Pete Dye Golf Club

Aaron Smith Drive
Bridgeport, WV 26330
Phone: 304-842-2801

PETER COPPOLA SALON

Hair and Beauty

Despite its size–there are 31 stylists and colorists, two nail technicians, one aesthetician and a waxing specialist–this salon is as intimate as it gets on Madison Avenue. Exposed brick walls and slate floors give it a laid-back, unintimidating look. Stop by for a sleek new image overhaul with a cut, color, style, manicure, pedicure and waxing treatment.

Peter Coppola Salon

746 Madison Avenue
New York, NY 10021
Phone: 212-988-9404

PETER CUMMIN & ASSOCIATES

Landscape Architects

Peter Cummin ensures that landscape and architecture are in perfect harmony. Starting work in the pre-construction phase, Cummin continues long after construction is final, the garden is complete and land has settled. Whether an adobe house in New Mexico or a New England shingle house, his designs grow and mature with the home, complementing its particular style.

Peter Cummin & Associates

39 Prentice Williams Road
Stonington, CT 06378
Phone: 860-572-4111

PETER MARINO & ASSOCIATES

Architects and Interior Designers

Peter Marino creates opulent interiors for discerning clients, often mixing antiques and artworks from several different centuries. Marino originally made his name as an architect, working on big retail projects like the Giorgio Armani store on Madison Avenue. His firm also maintains offices in London, Philadelphia and East Hampton.

Peter Marino & Associates

150 East 58th Street, 36th Floor
New York, NY 10022
Phone: 212-752-5444   Fax: 212-759-3727

PETER MICHAEL

Winemakers

In 1982, Briton Sir Peter Michael bought over 600 acres in the hills north of Knights Valley. Originally he made his wine from purchased grapes, but eventually decided to produce his own under the guidance of legendary winemaker, Helen Turley. Michael's Chardonnay and Cabernet Sauvignon are both world class. His Sauvignon Blanc, L'Après Midi, is also outstanding.

Peter Michael

12400 Ida Clayton Road
Calistoga, CA 94515
Phone: 707-942-4459

PHILIP BALOUN

Florists

When Lincoln Center celebrated its 40th Anniversary, the mood, look and ambiance of the event was orchestrated by Philip Baloun, who is principally regarded as an event producer and manager rather than simply a florist. Born and raised in Chicago, Baloun has been creating memorable atmospheres for 20 years. He has produced events for almost every bigwig on the east coast, including Alfred Taubman and George Soros.

Philip Baloun

340 West 55th Street
New York, NY 10019
Phone: 212-307-1675

PETERSEN AVIATION
Airplanes
If you're in the Los Angeles area and have a sudden need to be whisked to Tokyo or London in a Gulfstream G4SP, this full-service aviation company will accommodate you with little notice. On board you are treated with all jet services including important passenger amenities like Krug and beluga-and-buckwheat blinis! With twin-engine jet helicopters for local service, light jets for trans-continental jaunts and a 1998 Pilots Choice Award, Petersen also sells and manages personal aircraft for private clients.
Petersen Aviation
7155 Valjean Avenue
Van Nuys, CA 91406
Phone: 800-451-7270   Fax: 818-902-9386

PHILIP H. BRADLEY
Antiques
One of the largest antiques shops in the country, Philip H. Bradley sells 18th and early 19th century American furniture and decorative arts, including silver, brass, pewter, glass, pottery, porcelain and needlework. The erudite staff, carefree layout, hands-on philosophy and old-time Pennsylvania setting lend the experience of browsing here real charm. Incidentally, the shop has an outstanding collection of fireplace equipment.
Philip H. Bradley
1101 East Lancaster Avenue
Downingtown, PA 19335
Phone: 610-269-0427

PHILIP JOHNSON/ALAN RITCHIE ARCHITECTS
Architects and Interior Designers
One of the most recognizable and influential architects of the 20th century, Philip Johnson and his partner, Alan Ritchie, head a firm that offers design excellence, vast knowledge and technical experience. Johnson pioneered and championed the two movements that have most affected the urban landscape during the last 60 years: the international style and postmodernism. The bespectacled builder created both the Seagram Building and the AT&T Corporate Headquarters. Among many other achievements, the Johnson/Ritchie team recently created the Trump International Hotel and Tower in New York City and a new chapel for the University of St. Thomas in Houston.
Philip Johnson/Alan Ritchie Architects
375 Park Avenue
New York, NY 10152
Phone: 212-319-5880   Fax: 212-319-5881

PHILIP PRESS
Jewelry and Watches
Philip Press works only in platinum, creating extraordinary jewelry that is emboldened by the medium. Press designs each piece himself, blending the old world tradition of hand made jewelry with new age technology to create ornate art deco rings, brooches, and necklaces. His opulent line of wedding and engagement rings are encased in handmade lacy metal work, engraved and fitted with fine diamonds.
Philip Press
Sunset Plaza
8601 Sunset Boulevard
Los Angeles, CA 90069
Phone: 310-360-1180

PHILIPS EXETER ACADEMY
Schools
John Irving's *alma mater* is one of the top prep schools in the country. A sprawling 640-acre campus, located in New Hampshire, provides the backdrop for a highly diverse, international student body. Small class sizes place students at the center of the learning process. An endowment of $334 million makes Philips Exeter one of the wealthiest secondary schools in the country.
Philips Exeter Academy
20 Main Street
Exeter, NH 03833
Phone: 603-772-4311

PINE VALLEY GOLF CLUB
Golf Clubs
Designed by George Crump, Pine Valley is known to those lucky few who have played it as one of the best courses in the country. Open to the public one day a year, the only other way to get on the course is to be asked by a member. The club currently hosts no major competitive events, although it has twice hosted the Walker Cup tournament in the past.
Pine Valley Golf Club
East Atlantic Avenue
Pine Valley, NJ 08021
Phone: 609-783-3000

PHILADELPHIA MUSEUM OF ART
Museums
The Philadelphia Museum of Art's collection spans over 2000 years, with a comprehensive range of fine and applied arts from the U.S., Europe and Asia. One of the most notable features of this museum, founded in 1876, is the building itself; a striking, Greek temple—like vision. Featured pieces include *Sunflowers* by Vincent Van Gogh and *Woman in Blue* by Henri Matisse.
Philadelphia Museum of Art
26th Street & Benjamin Franklin Parkway
Philadelphia, PA 19130
Phone: 215-684-7500

PINEHURST POLO CLUB

Polo Clubs   *Best Kept Secret*

This small, casual club boasts only a dozen members, who enjoy from two to eight ponies a piece. Spectators are always welcome and matches can turn into 100-strong social gatherings. Because the players are all amateurs, there are no high-goal egos here. Pinehurst is managed by octogenarian Bob Johnson; he has been playing the game since 1934.

Pinehurst Polo Club

56 Pinelake Drive
Whispering Pines, NC 28327
Phone: 910-949-2106

PINEHURST RESORT & COUNTRY CLUB

Golf Clubs

Pinehurst, which hosted last year's U.S. Open, is a golfing superpower. Donald Ross designed its first four courses between 1898 and 1914. The next four courses were designed by Ellis Maples, Rees Jones, and Tom and George Fazio between 1961 and 1996. The Number Two course has been ranked among the top ten courses in the country. Its crowned greens and tightly mowed chipping areas make it much more difficult to stay on the greens than to hit them.

Pinehurst Resort & Country Club

Carolina Vista Drive
Pinehurst, NC 28374
Phone: 910-295-6811

PLANTATION

Specialty Shops   *Rising Star*

Mark Cole and Craig Olsen's furniture and accessories shop has garnered considerable praise from savvy shoppers since opening two years ago. Cole describes their self-designed pieces as "clean and modern, combining various styles from Biedermeyer to Mission with a sprinkling of far eastern decor." This melange of tastes has attracted high profile patrons like Rachel Hunter, George Michael and Tori Spelling.

Plantation

144 South La Brea Avenue
Los Angeles, CA 90036
Phone: 323-932-0511   Fax: 323-932-0485

PNC ADVISORS

Wealth Management

PNC Advisors is the fourth largest money manager for the high net worth market. Financial solutions are offered through a one-on-one version of traditional and investment banking, tailored to clients' specific investing history.

PNC Advisors

3305 Flamingo Drive
Vero Beach, FL 32963
Phone: 561-231-6300

PRIVATE CHEFS, INC.

Employment Agencies   *Best Kept Secret*

Flying in from Zurich after a hard day's banking, there is no finer way to end the day than by walking into your home to the aroma of one of your personal chef's creations. If you are clever enough to have hired one of Christian Paier's Private Chefs, you will always have a master of international cuisine at your disposal. Paier has brought some of the most renowned chefs from around the world to work their culinary magic. Clients such as Prince Charles, the Royal Family of Saudi Arabia, Tom Cruise, and Janet Jackson have all used Private Chefs, Inc. to hand pick their own personal chef.

Private Chefs, Inc.

204 South Beverly Drive, Suite 105
Beverly Hills, CA 90211
Phone: 310-278-4707   Website: www.privatechefsinc.com

POST RANCH INN

Hotels   *Best Kept Secret*

Built on a ridge overlooking Big Sur, Post Ranch Inn has a wood-and-glass design inspired by the nearby California redwoods. The guest rooms, all freestanding structures, are named for their views and angular architectural designs—such as the Tree House, shaped like a triangle and perched on 9-foot stilts. Our favorite is Ocean House, with its curved beamed roof covered with a soft carpet of grass and wildflowers. It offers unobstructed ocean views from every angle of the house and terrace. Warmly recommended.

Post Ranch Inn

Highway One
Big Sur, CA 93920
Phone: 831-667-2200   Fax: 831-667-2512

PRINCETON UNIVERSITY

Colleges

As many European readers (and 99% of our American audience) already know, Princeton is one of the top schools in America. Established in 1746, it was the product of a theological dispute among the Presbyterians at Yale University. Current graduates include MCA Chairman and CEO Frank Biondi, presidential candidates Bill Bradley and Steve Forbes and actors David Duchovny and Brooke Shields. Albert Einstein lectured at the school, where the Department of Physics has counted 18 Nobel laureates among the ranks of its faculty from 1927 to 1998.

Princeton University

Stanhope Hall
Princeton, NJ 08544
Phone: 609-258-3000

PRINCE DIMITRI
Fashion
Prince Dimitri of Yugoslavia designs and manufactures an exquisite range of cufflinks, which are available in stores like Bergdorf Goodman. This talented young man may become America's answer to David Linley, Queen Elizabeth's nephew, whose furniture pops up in 'all the right places' in England.

Prince Dimitri
400 East 52nd Street
New York, NY 10022
Phone: 212-606-7168   Fax: 212-606-7014

PRIVÉ
Hair and Beauty
Laurent Dufourg's Privé offers fine hair care and make up at its locations in Los Angeles, Las Vegas (at Bellagio) and New York (at the SoHo Grand), each of which manages to be cozy and intimate, yet stylish and sleek. Laurent's wife, Fabienne, played an important role in designing the salons, which are popular with stars like Elisabeth Shue and Shannon Doherty.

Privé
8458 Melrose Place
Los Angeles, CA 90069
Phone: 323-651-5045   Fax: 323-651-0509

PROFESSIONAL NANNIES INSTITUTE
Employment Agencies
Owner Denise Kapelus, former director of the Mother and Child Center, is actively involved in all aspects of the screening and placement process. With a professional background in counseling and education, she ensures all the nannies selected are suitable and able care givers, and she also provides ongoing support both to families and nannies.

Professional Nannies Institute
501 Fifth Avenue, Suite 908
New York, NY 10017
Phone: 212-692-9510   Fax: 212-692-9835

PUCCI
Fashion
One of Chicago's most exclusive menswear boutiques, Pucci has been in business for more than 70 years. Dedicated to elegant custom tailoring, the staff call themselves "architects of fashion," catering to living legends and emerging luminaries. Dean Martin and Jerry Lewis are among the clients who have visited this image-maker over the years.

Pucci
333 North Michigan Avenue
Chicago, IL 60601
Phone: 312-332-3759

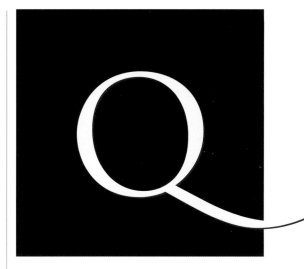

QUEST
Media
If you want to know who's who on Manhattan's Upper East Side, turn to this urbane but resolutely cheerful guide to the good life. Kristina Stewart, the ambitious young editor, knows many key players in the city and her well produced magazine provides an insider's look at the smartest of the smart.

Quest
100 Avenue of the Americas
New York, NY 10013
Phone: 212-334-1212

LA QUINTA
Golf Clubs
Pete Dye designed three courses for La Quinta in the 1980s: Citrus, Dunes and Mountain. While the Dunes and Mountain courses are open to all guests of La Quinta resort, Citrus is maintained strictly for club members. Beware of the treacherous 433-yard, par-four 17th hole on the Dunes course; the Mountain course is known for its signature 16th hole and a deep rough. Both courses provide striking views of the Santa Rosa mountains. Celebrities are particularly fond of this secluded resort.

La Quinta
49-499 Eisenhower Drive
La Quinta, CA 92253
Phone: 800-598-3828

THE POINT
Hotels
If you are not lucky enough to have a mountain retreat in the family, you will certainly enjoy this former home of the Rockefeller clan, which bills itself as "the ultimate civilized wilderness experience." Nestled in the heart of the Adirondack Mountains at the upper end of Saranac Lake, the Point's balsam clad luxury and exclusive house-party ambiance are reminders of the opulence of a bygone era. Guests come together for an evening cocktail at the Elco Lake Launch, and gather for dinner at the Great Hall's round tables.

The Point
Beaverwood Road
Saranac Lake, NY 12983
Phone: 800-255-3530   Fax: 518-891-1152

RABBIT RIDGE VINEYARDS
Winemakers

In his school days, Eric Russell was a long distance runner known as 'The Rabbit.' When he and partner Darryl Simmons bought this property in 1979, choosing a name did not pose problems. Today, Russell and Simmons have 35 acres under vine and with purchased grapes in the Dry Creek and Carneros, Rabbit Ridge turn out roughly 70,000 cases of wine a year. Most of it is top notch. Their single vineyard Zinfandels are particularly worth hunting for.

Rabbit Ridge Vineyards

3291 Westside Road
Healdsburg, CA 95448
Phone: 707-431-7128

RACQUET & TENNIS CLUB
Private Clubs

Housed in a brick and limestone Florentine Renaissance style building with a loggia on the second floor, where afternoon tea and muffins are served in the warmer months, the Racquet & Tennis club is a dramatic architectural outpost amidst its glass and steel neighbors. Founded in 1890, the club moved to its current residence in 1916 when members complained that larger buildings were blocking sunlight from the skylight-lit indoor courts. Traditionally an institution for the Ivy League members of the New York Stock Exchange, this gentlemen-only club now attracts, above all, sportsmen: this is where George Plimpton keeps fit and up to date. The club also houses a world class collection of sports paintings and sculpture as well as a sports library decorated with portraits of former members, such as Charles Scribner, who published, amongst other sportsmen, Fitzgerald and Hemingway.

Racquet & Tennis Club

370 Park Avenue
New York, NY 10022
Phone: 212-753-9700

R.H. LOVE GALLERIES
Art Dealers

R.H. Love Galleries, flanking Chicago's Magnificent Mile, is housed in an opulent Italianate mansion built for Samuel M. Nickerson, president of the First National Bank in Chicago, in 1883. This was, coincidentally, about the time French impressionism was introduced to the American public, and the gallery's collections correspond to the major art movements that began with the Colonial period and later ones that were popular at the time of the house's construction. Since about 1970, art historian, art dealer and artist, Richard H. Love has specialized in American art from about 1785-1940, an intriguing and diverse period that encompasses portraiture, the Hudson River School, romanticism, tonalism, impressionism, postimpressionism, and even early modernism: art for just about everyone. The public is encouraged to stroll through the sumptuous marble and alabaster halls with rich

My Dollies, by Joseph Henry Hatfield, Oil on canvas.

handsomely carved woodwork and intricately patterned parquet floors. Here one can admire exceptional works by outstanding American artists, including Gilbert Stuart, Asher B. Durand, Theodore Earl Butler, William Merritt Chase, Childe Hassam, George Inness, Lawton Parker, Theodore Robinson, John Twachtman and countless others. You will also have the opportunity to see works of lesser-known American artists, many of whom were award-winners and famous in their own time, but who went out of fashion, suffering from the forces of the European-oriented modernist movement. Don't pass by the Bookshop or the Prints and Drawings Room, which is equally enjoyable to visit.

R.H. Love Galleries

40 East Erie Street
Chicago, IL 60611
Phone: 312-640-1300   Fax: 312-640-5435

RANDOLPH DUKE

Fashion   *Rising Star*

Randolph Duke is one of Hollywood's newly-celebrated style makers. Duke's inimitable designs have become media events on the likes of Sharon Stone, Celine Dion, Mariah Carey, Tyra Banks, Heidi Klume, Angie Harmon and Cindy Crawford. In February 1999, Duke presented his first show under his own label at the Seventh on Sixth Fashion Show, which was critically acclaimed by the fashion press. He has appeared on numerous television shows and has received several awards acknowledging his influence in the industry. He was the media darling of the 1999 Oscar ceremonies with Minnie Driver, Geena Davis, Kim Basinger, Lisa Kudrow, Laura Linney and Rita Wilson all wearing Randolph Duke Designs.

Randolph Duke

260 West 39th Street, 19th Floor
New York, NY 10018
Phone: 212-768-1730

RADU PHYSICAL CULTURE

Fitness

Romanian-born fitness guru Radu Teodorescu is a graduate of the University of Bucharest, one of the most prestigious physical fitness schools in the world. Radu heads a staff of nine highly-trained fitness professionals who practice the combination of athletic training, gymnastics, track and field, karate, soccer, muscle physiology and weight training which comprise the Radu method. Devotees include Cindy Crawford and Jennifer Lopez.

Radu Physical Culture

24 West 57th Street
New York, NY 10019
Phone: 212-581-1995

RALPH LAUREN

Fashion

You have to hand it to Ralph Lauren. Although many of his lines have become increasingly mass-market, Lauren's clothes still appeal to the sophisticated shopper. A mixture of good design and brilliant marketing have seen to that. Lauren's Madison Avenue flagship is one of the most lavish stores in America today—although it inadvertently epitomizes the gaudiness of new money rather than the stodginess of the British upper class (to which it pays homage).

Ralph Lauren

650 Madison Avenue
New York, NY 10021
Phone: 212-318-7000

RANCHO VALENCIA RESORT

Hotels

Located on 40 acres in a private canyon near Douglas Fairbanks' and Mary Pickford's old ranch, this 15-year old resort is a favorite among top Hollywood executives, politicians and other power brokers. Governor Gray Davis of California and Microsoft's Bill Gates have both enjoyed the facilities, which include a regulation croquet lawn, a host of tennis courts and the full range of spa and body care treatments.

Rancho Valencia Resort

5921 Valencia Circle
Rancho Santa Fe, CA 92067
Phone: 619-756-1123

RAYTHEON

Airplanes

Raytheon has a fractional ownership program designed to meet the personal travel needs of corporations and high net worth individuals. What separates this company from others with fractional ownership programs, is the choice of three aircraft: Beech-King Air twin turboprop, Beechjet 400a light jet, or Hawker 800 midsize jet, allowing the fractional owner to choose an aircraft as needed.

Raytheon

101 South Webb Road
Wichita, KS 67201
Phone: 888-824-6359   Fax: 316-676-8867

REBECCA MOSS

Specialty Shops

Pen aficionados like Daniel Day Lewis haunt this specialty pen boutique which stocks its own brands, fine stationery and every major luxury gift pen. To mark Rebecca Moss' 10th anniversary, Mont Blanc, Omas, Visconti, Stipula and Fabergé are all making limited editions of 100 pens exclusively.

Rebecca Moss

510 Madison Avenue
New York, NY 10022
Phone: 800-465-7367

THE REDFERN GALLERY

Art Dealers

Ray Redfern has specialized in the work of the Californian *plein air* impressionists for 25 years. The quality and variety of these painters, some trained in Europe and some locally, is a Californian secret that the rest of the world has just started to discover.

The Redfern Gallery

1540 South Coast Highway
Laguna Beach, CA 92651
Phone: 949-497-3356   Fax: 949-497-1324

REEBOK SPORTS CLUB

Fitness

Try classes like Power Play, Cycle Reebok Plus, Reebok City Jam and Fired Up to get your adrenaline pumping and your fat burning at this Mecca for fitness fans. Serious fitness buffs can practically live here.

Reebok Sports Club

160 Columbus Avenue
New York, NY 10023
Phone: 212-362-6800

REGEN-LEIGH ANTIQUES

Antiques

Bobbie Culbreath specializes in English and Continental furniture, silver and *objets d'art* from 1730 to 1840. Culbreath, who trained at London's Royal Society of Arts and Christie's, works with interior designers like Victoria Hagen, building neo-classical collections for *beau monde* luminaries.

Regen-Leigh Antiques

3140 East Shadowlawn Avenue NE
Atlanta, GA 30305
Phone: 404-262-9303   Fax: 404-816-6463

JOHN REILLY

Portrait Painters and Photographers

John Reilly's studio is filled with exemplary photos of stylish belles in pretty dresses, famous men in formal poses, and of course, blushing brides. Reilly was once a professor of history at the University of Illinois. For the past 25 years he has been snapping pictures of Chicago's most prominent individuals and families.

John Reilly

Phone: 312-266-2550   Fax: 312-266-2519

RENAISSANCE

Restaurants   *Rising Star*

When Charles Dale opened this restaurant on a fringe block of downtown Aspen, it seemed unlikely that Renaissance would soon become one of the hardest restaurants to secure reservations for in the tony resort. Dale's innovative New American cuisine, a stunning view of the Aspen Mountains and sommelier Steve Humble's inspiring respect for good wine have all contributed to its success.

Renaissance

304 East Hopkins Avenue
Aspen, CO 81611
Phone: 970-925-2402

RENNY

Florists

Frederick Reynolds got his start as a celebrity florist doing the decorations for parties at Studio 54. Now favored by a host of bigwigs (like the Clintons) his signature designs feature tight, English-style floral arrangements and suspended candle balls. Reynolds has a perennial farm in Pennsylvania, a store on Park Avenue and a small outlet at the Carlyle Hotel.

Renny

505 Park Avenue
New York, NY 10022
Phone: 212-593-3688

RIALTO

Restaurants

Michela's has moved to the edge of Harvard Square, a million miles away from the obscure office complex it once inhabited. The name has changed, of course, there is a new partner in the venture, and chef Jody Adams has gone from offering straight Italian to "Mediterranean fare with a Latin influence." But the Michela's magic is still there: warm ambiance, affable staff and fabulous food.

Rialto

Charles Hotel
1 Bennett Street
Cambridge, MA 02138
Phone: 617-661-5050   Fax: 617-661-5053

RICHARD ANDERSON FINE ARTS

Art Dealers

A decade ago, banker Richard Anderson decided to indulge his passion for art; his downtown gallery now represents the likes of Adam Cvijanoviz and Marco Breuer, as well as the estate of Hugh Steers. Anderson also started an innovative program at his gallery called "Multiple Choice," where established artists make pieces within emerging collectors' budgets.

Richard Anderson Fine Arts

453 West 17th Street
New York, NY 10011
Phone: 212-463-0970

THE REGENT BEVERLY WILSHIRE

Hotels

The Regent Beverly Wilshire is located in a large corner lot of a charming neighborhood, offering exquisite bedrooms and master suites. Many of the rooms offer sweeping views of the city or the mountains. Managed by the mighty Four Seasons Group, the Beverly Wilshire has personal attendants who cater to the most demanding customers. The shops on Rodeo Drive and Wilshire Boulevard, which are top notch, are steps away.

The Regent Beverly Wilshire

9500 Wilshire Boulevard
Beverly Hills, CA 90212
Phone: 310-275-5200   Fax: 310-275-5986

RICHARD J. FISHER TINWORK

Specialty Shops   *Best Kept Secret*

When 99% of your business comes from word of mouth recommendations you must be doing something right. Tinsmith Richard Fisher has hand produced interior furnishings like sconces, tin ceilings, brass beds and mirrors for the past 15 years. Often applying metal on metal and adding patina after patina in an intricate, painstaking process, Fisher takes the old Northern New Mexican style of tinwork and combines it with an avant-garde approach to create enduring, hand stamped classics.

Richard J. Fisher Tinwork

9 Griegos Arroyo Road
Tesuque, NM 87574
Phone: 505-989-4227   Fax: 505-989-3336

RICHARD GOULD ANTIQUES

Antiques

Studio honchos and mere mortals flock to this well-established antique business, founded by Richard Gould and his wife in 1955. Gould's specialty is traditional English and American pieces from the 18th and early 19th centuries, although his total inventory ranges from $35 teacups to $30,000 bookcases. The Winterthur, Williamsburg and L.A. County museums have all purchased from Richard Gould.

Richard Gould Antiques

808 North La Cienega Boulevard
Los Angeles, CA 90069
Phone: 310-657-9416   Fax: 310-657-9416

RICHARD HAYNES & ASSOCIATES

Security Consultants

If you suspect that someone is ripping you off, talk to Richard Haynes. His comprehensive approach to security encompasses its physical, procedural and human aspects. Clients include affluent individuals as well as companies in fields as varied as petrochemicals, mining, banking and retail. Investigators review the entire operations of the company to identify key areas of vulnerability and weakness.

Richard Haynes & Associates

1021 Temple Street
Charleston, WV 25312
Phone: 304-346-6228

RICHARD KEITH LANGHAM

Architects and Interior Designers

After stints at Mark Hampton and Irving and Fleming, Richard Keith Langham set out on his own in 1990. His distinctive style, which "flirts with the ill-defined border between tasteful and over-the-top," has won him admirers (and customers) across the country, including the late Jackie Onassis, who used him to design the interiors of her cottage in Virginia.

Richard Keith Langham

153 East 60th Street

New York, NY 10022

Phone: 212-759-1212   Fax: 212-759-5151

RICHARD L. FEIGEN & COMPANY

Art Dealers

Richard L. Feigen & Company specializes in paintings, drawings and sculpture from the 13th through the 20th centuries, while its Chelsea affiliate, Feigen Contemporary, concentrates on contemporary pieces. It has many museum clients, as well as private clients for whom it acts as auction adviser, agent and principal.

Richard L. Feigen & Company

49 East 68th Street

New York, NY 10021

Phone: 212-628-0700   Fax: 212-249-4574

RICHARD YORK GALLERY

Art Dealers

Richard York represents American artists from 1750 to 1950 and deals in paintings, drawings and watercolors. His shows draw on a rich inventory which includes the work of Georgia O'Keeffe, Joseph Stella, Mary Cassatt and the estate of John Marin. York's holdings reflect two centuries of change and growth: early landscapes and nature paintings of Audobon; the evolution of the portrait; the first spark of modernism in Stuart Davis and the many strands of 20th century art.

Richard York Gallery

21 East 65th Street

New York, NY 10021

Phone: 212-772-9155

RIDGE VINEYARDS

Winemakers

In the late Fifties, three Stanford research scientists bought this property, located in the Santa Cruz Mountains, for recreational purposes—and then discovered the three-tier Monte Bello Winery on the property which had been shut down during Prohibition. The temptation to make wine proved irresistible. The fruits of their labor are a Cabernet Sauvignon of First-Growth quality and an unusual Zinfandel.

Ridge Vineyards

17100 Monte Bello Road

Cupertino, CA 94014

Phone: 408-867-3233

RICHARD GRAY GALLERY

Art Dealers

Stop by this prestigious gallery in the John Hancock Building when you are in the mood for modern masters like Picasso, Warhol and Alberto Giacometti. A trained architect, Richard Gray was in the manufacturing business before he opened the gallery as a sideline in 1963. President of the Art Dealers Association of America, Gray now represents contemporary giants like Roy Lichtenstein, David Hockney and Jim Dine. He recently opened another gallery on New York's Upper East Side.

Richard Gray Gallery

875 North Michigan Avenue

Chicago, IL 60611

Phone: 312-642-8877   Fax: 312-642-8488

THE RIENZI HOUSE MUSEUM

Museums   *Rising Star*

This neo-Palladian house, which was bequeathed to Houston's Museum of Fine Arts by the late Harris Masterson III, is an unusual marriage of Texan exuberance and English restraint. Masterson began to amass his impressive collection of Worcester soft-paste porcelain when he was stationed with the American Army in England during the Second World War. Rienzi also features paintings by artists like George Romney, Bartolomé Murillo and the great 17th century Italian master, Guido Reni.

The Rienzi House Museum

1406 Kerby Drive

Houston, TX 77019

Phone: 713-639-7300

RIO

Casinos

The Rio is one of only four or five Vegas properties that still welcome what the casino industry calls "big fish," or even the occasional "whale" i.e. someone playing with over $1 million. In addition to the casino's spectacular high-limit area, featuring all the requisite games (including double-deck games for serious 21 players), the Rio also offers exclusive private baccarat rooms ($1000 to $5000 minimum per hand) replete with white-gloved personal butlers.

Rio

3700 West Flamingo Road

Las Vegas, NV 89103

Phone: 702-252-7777

RITZ-CARLTON HOTEL

Hotels

If you're looking for the largest single malt Scotch collection in the United States, come to this opulent 91-year old Nob Hill landmark, which is consistently rated one of the best hotels in the world. The Ritz-Carlton is renowned for outstanding service, luxuriously appointed bedrooms, terrific leisure facilities and a dining room which readers of *Gourmet* magazine have voted the best restaurant in San Francisco.

Ritz-Carlton Hotel

600 Stockton Street

San Francisco, CA 94108

Phone: 415-296-7465   Fax: 415-291-0147

RITZ-CARLTON, BUCKHEAD

Restaurants

Joel Antunes and his staff prepare meals in an open kitchen at the five-diamond Dining Room in Atlanta's Ritz-Carlton Hotel. Antunes prepares French dishes with Thai accents in his daily-changing menu. Mahogany walls and soft lighting provide a cozy but elegant atmosphere—perfect for clinching deals with Coca Cola executives.

Ritz-Carlton, Buckhead

3434 Peachtree Road

Atlanta, GA 30326

Phone: 404-237-2700   Fax: 404-239-0078

RITZ-CARLTON, LAGUNA NIGUEL

Hotels

At this classic Mediterranean villa, guest rooms open onto private balconies overlooking tiled courtyards with fountains, landscaped gardens and spectacular ocean vistas. Best rooms are the corner suites, with views of both the ocean and the coastline's bright nighttime lights. Activities include tennis, swimming, spas, Jacuzzis and a gorgeous expanse of beach.

Ritz-Carlton, Laguna Niguel

1 Ritz Carlton Drive

Dana Point, CA 92629

Phone: 949-240-2000   Fax: 949-240-0829

RIVIERA COUNTRY CLUB
Golf Clubs

Tom Cruise has recently become a member of the Riviera, where he can join Sylvester Stallone and Michael Keaton on the green. Located in the Santa Monica Valley, the course is known for inventive bunkering and its kikuyu grass rough. The signature hole is the par three sixth, but the 18th is also memorable for its length and panoramic amphitheater finish.

Riviera Country Club
1250 Capri Drive
Pacific Palisades, CA 90272
Phone: 310-454-6591   Fax: 310-454-8351

RL
Restaurants   Rising Star

Evidently bored of the Fashion Café, Ralph Lauren teamed up with Nino Esposito to open this new Italian restaurant in Chicago. The clubby interior, with black and white photos lining the walls, is *very* Ralph. Chef Giancarlo Gottardo prepares a steak from cattle raised on the designer's ranch in Telluride. Oprah Winfrey, a fan of Nino's restaurants in New York, has already commandeered RL twice for special events. One assumes she resisted the beef.

RL
115 East Chicago Avenue
Chicago, IL 60610
Phone: 312-475-1100   Fax: 312-266-9853

ROBERT A.M. STERN ARCHITECTS
Architects and Interior Designers

Robert Stern is well known for the shingle style that he developed in designing homes on the east coast. This Yale-trained protégé of Robert Venturi was one of the first architects to use the term "post modern" and today he is regarded as something of a titan. Stern was recently appointed Dean of the Yale School of Architecture.

Robert A.M. Stern Architects
460 West 34th Street
New York, NY 10001
Phone: 212-967-5100   Fax: 212-244-2054

THE RITTENHOUSE HOTEL
Hotels

This ninety-eight room boutique hotel is described as a refined second home by many of its distinguished guests. It is located on exclusive Rittenhouse Square, close to cultural attractions, fine dining and part of the prestigious Rittenhouse Row retail district. The Rittenhouse Hotel has received the coveted AAA Five-Diamond Award for nine consecutive years and is often rated as one of the top hotels in the world. Guests arrive to a private courtyard of Belgian stone with a fountain centerpiece, surrounded by lush manicured gardens. The wood-columned and inlaid marble foyer leads to the elegantly furnished lobby where guests are greeted by exceptional staff. Fancy a spot of tea? The Cassatt Tea Garden is the perfect place for a secret rendezvous or a meeting of heads-of-state. Regally appointed oversized guest rooms are complemented with extravagant marble baths and the luxury suites with their whirlpool tubs are the favorite of celebs Tom Hanks, Luciano Pavarotti and former president George Bush. The Adolf Biecker Spa and Salon offers state-of-the-art fitness equipment, an indoor pool with skylights, sauna, aromatherapy and massage to help the busy or leisurely traveler unwind at the end of a long day.

The Rittenhouse Hotel
210 West Rittenhouse Square
Philadelphia, PA 19103
Phone: 215-546-9000   Fax: 215-546-9858

ROBERT ISABELL
Florists

"Oh, so and so is the Robert Isabell of Pasadena..." Isabell has become *the* point of reference in a hugely competitive business. He famously creates entire environments with lighting, sets, entertainment, floral designs and anything else an event may need. He has designed weddings for Caroline Kennedy, Whitney Houston and the Miller sisters. A Royal wedding in Saudi Arabia is next on the agenda.

Robert Isabell
410 West 13th Street
New York, NY 10014
Phone: 212-645-7767

ROBERT LONG

Florists

In Atlanta they are coming out with Robert Long; every year he creates the floral designs for the city's Debutante ball. Long's business takes him between Atlanta, New York and London. Flowers are flown from all over the world to serve clients who pay up to $400,000 for a particularly extravagant reception.

Robert Long

3181 Roswell Road
Atlanta, GA 30305
Phone: 404-365-0500

ROBERT MANN GALLERY

Art Dealers   *Rising Star*

With the recent move of the New York art world from SoHo to Chelsea, many of the established galleries have faded, but the Robert Mann Gallery remains one of the leading sources of museum-quality fine art photography. With extensive holdings of 20th century luminaries like Ansel Adams, Man Ray, and Aaron Siskind, the gallery's new 6,000 square foot space hosts six to eight exhibitions a year.

Robert Mann Gallery

210 Eleventh Avenue
New York, NY 10001
Phone: 212-989-7600   Fax: 212-989-2947

ROBERT MONDAVI WINERY

Winemakers

Though known as a great winemaker, Robert Mondavi is also a great promoter. No one has done more to publicize Napa Valley wines. From the winery that bears his name, he produces over 650,000 cases of wine a year. Production is mostly Chardonnay and Cabernet Sauvignon, but he also produces a variety of others include a Fumé Blanc, a term invented by Mondavi to describe dry, oak-aged Sauvignon Blancs.

Robert Mondavi Winery

7801 St. Helena Highway
Oakville, CA 94562
Phone: 800-228-1395

ROBERT TALBOTT SHIRTS

Fashion

This 50 year old, family owned firm creates shirts which are designed and crafted with the utmost attention to detail. With two California outlets (in Pebble Beach and Carmel) and a Madison Avenue showcase in New York City, Robert Talbott has carved a reputation as the premium purveyor of hand-tailored shirts in America today. We particularly like the limited edition state shirt ($340), which honors the unapologetically masculine style of matinée idols like Clark Gable and Spencer Tracy.

Robert Talbott Shirts

Talbott Studio
Carmel Valley, CA 93924
Phone: 831-624-6604   Fax: 831-649-4244

THE RIVER CAFÉ

Restaurants

Buzzy O'Keeffe's waterfront restaurant is popular among native New Yorkers as well as foreign dignitaries, heads of state and celebrities. Renowned for its extraordinary views of Manhattan, this may be the most romantic setting in New York. Unusually for a destination restaurant, the River Café has always had decent chefs at the helm. Indeed, it has been described (a little generously, perhaps) as the Harvard Business School of the culinary world.

The River Café

One Water Street
Brooklyn, NY 11201
Phone: 718-522-5200   Fax: 718-875-0037

THE ROCKWELL GROUP

Architects and Interior Designers

For David Rockwell, all the world's a stage—and every restaurant, hotel, and even zoo should be constructed accordingly. The Rockwell Group focuses on using custom-made materials—like laminated seaweed wallpaper and pressed ginkgo leaves—to create a sense of drama at New York hotspots like Nobu, the Monkey Bar and the W Hotel. The 43-year-old specializes in designing commercial spaces rather than homes, but everything has its price...

The Rockwell Group

5 Union Square West
New York, NY 10003
Phone: 212-463-0334

RON HERMAN L.A.

Fashion

Don't leave L.A. before you hit this inimitable department store, the place for scoping out everything from denim to couture to vintage. Ron Herman L.A., formerly Fred Segal, specializes in spotting—and selling—trends long before they hit the mainstream. Prices vary almost as much as the clientele: look for pieces in cotton, linen, silk, and blended polyester fabrics which range in price from $20 to $5000.

Ron Herman L.A.

8100 Melrose Avenue
Los Angeles, CA 90046
Phone: 323-651-4129   Fax: 323-651-5238

RON HERMAN LANDSCAPE ARCHITECT

Landscape Architects

When Oracle CEO Larry Ellison decided to build a lake at his Japanese style country retreat he turned to Ron Herman, the gentle 58 year old landscape architect who created a garden for I.M. Pei's east wing of the National Gallery in Washington. Herman's Asian-influenced designs are in hot demand across the country, although you would never know it from talking to this modest master craftsman.

Ron Herman Landscape Architect

261 Joaquin Avenue
San Leandro, CA 94577
Phone: 510-352-4920

ROSE TARLOW – MELROSE HOUSE

Architects and Interior Designers

Rose Tarlow has said that she became a decorator because she needed venues in which to place her finds. In the 1970s, long before Aaron Spelling discovered Melrose Place, Tarlow opened her stuff-of-dreams antiques shop there. The store, Rose Tarlow–Melrose House, sells both the real thing (mainly 19th century antiques) and her own designs, including a rustic Tuscan walnut table, a gorgeous ebony lamp and a Louis XVI desk.

Rose Tarlow – Melrose House

8454 Melrose Place

Los Angeles, CA 90069

Phone: 323-651-2202   Fax: 323-658-6548

ROSENBERG & STIEBEL

Art Dealers

This gallery handles a huge range of European art and has sold more than 300 works to the Metropolitan Museum. With a heavy emphasis on 18th century France, Rosenberg & Steibel sell period furniture and *objets d'art* – as well as old master paintings, drawings, and sculptures – to many of the world's great museums and private collectors.

Rosenberg & Stiebel

32 East 57th Street

New York, NY 10022

Phone: 212-753-4368   Fax: 212-935-5736

ROYAL FIESTA CATERERS

Party Organizers and Caterers

Elegantly styled with hardwood floors, glass sculptures and crystal chandeliers, Royal Fiesta's Banquet rooms are famous for their exclusive service and unapologetically 'posh' food. The company has catered wedding receptions and corporate parties, with staples like grilled salmon and prime rib, for 12 years.

Royal Fiesta Caterers

1680 South East Third Court

Deerfield Beach, FL 33441

Phone: 954-570-9422   Fax: 954-570-9833

ROYAL GARDEN AT WAIKIKI

Hotels

This perfectly located "garden" is nestled between the mountains and the ocean in Waikiki. Inspired by Hawaii's natural beauty, the interior and guest amenities are relaxing and beautiful. Both the Cascada, offering exquisite Mediterranean cuisine with a Hawaiian flair, and the Shizu, serving unique Japanese dishes in an Oriental atmosphere, are superb.

Royal Garden at Waikiki

440 Olohana Street

Honolulu, HI 96815

Phone: 808-943-0202

RUDOLF STEINER SCHOOL

Schools

This is the flagship for an international group of institutions which espouse the eminently sensible notion that education is an artistic process. The Waldorf philosophy promotes unconventional learning techniques which stimulate the intellect and the imagination. For example, first grade students will run in the pattern of a pentagon to understand and feel geometry in a more physical sense.

Rudolf Steiner School

15 East 79th Street

New York, NY 10021

Phone: 212-535-2130   Fax: 212-744-4497

RUGGLES GRILL

Restaurants

Creativity is the key at this Houston restaurant, where husband and wife team Bruce and Susan Molzan specialize in producing southwestern cuisine that transcends the normal barriers in grill fare. Desserts like a sublime White Chocolate Bread Pudding have also ensured acclaim for Ruggles since it opened in 1986. Incidentally, Bruce's Club Flamingo, right beside Ruggles, is a Latin Hotspot.

Ruggles Grill

903 Westheimer

Houston, TX 77006

Phone: 713-524-3839   Fax: 713-524-7396

ROY'S

Restaurants

Hollywood refugee Roy Yamaguchi offers creative, fusion-based cuisine at his eponymous Honolulu gem. Following the success of this restaurant (and Yamaguchi's stature as the "King of Pacific Rim cuisine") he has now launched a small culinary empire on the west coast.

Roy's

6600 Kalanianaole Highway

Honolulu, HI 96825

Phone: 808-396-7697   Fax: 808-396-8706

THE RYLAND INN

Restaurants

Distinctly American, but with the feel of a fine French restaurant, The Ryland Inn has become a pinnacle of fine dining in the Garden State. Chef and co-owner Craig Shelton has turned this 200-year old country house into a haven for sybarites who enjoy exquisite *foie gras* and ethereal baby lamb. A Yale graduate in biophysics, Shelton has also amassed a prize winning wine collection.

The Ryland Inn

PO Box 284, Route 22 West

Whitehouse, NJ 08888

Phone: 908-534-4011   Fax: 908-534-6592

S. BERNSTEIN & CO.
Antiques

Fine Chinese jade antiquities, from the Neolithic period through the 18th century, are the specialty at this gem of a gallery. Sam Bernstein boasts more than 20 years of expertise in his roles as a dealer of jade, metalwork, and ancient sculpture and as a scholar who guides and educates collectors interested in becoming connoisseurs. Bernstein pieces can be found in museums and private collections around the world.

S. Bernstein & Co.
950 Mason Street
San Francisco, CA 94108
Phone: 415-421-3434

S.J. SHRUBSOLE
Antiques

The oldest antiques store on 57th Street, this lavish gallery boasts what may be the country's largest selection of antique Georgian silver. Other collectibles include Sheffield plate and glass from the Georgian period. The dealer also features early American silver and fine antique jewelry ranging from Victorian to Art Deco. This family owned business was founded in London in 1912.

S.J. Shrubsole
104 East 57th Street
New York, NY 10022
Phone: 212-753-8920   Fax: 212-754-5192

SAFRA BANK
Wealth Management

Safra bank has a private banking program aimed at an international clientele of family-owned businesses, which are offered both traditional services and investment opportunities. Clients are attracted by the reputation that the Safra family cultivated in terms of service, privacy and a concern for safety.

Safra Bank
546 Fifth Avenue
New York, NY 10036
Phone: 212-704-5500

SAKS FIFTH AVENUE
Fashion

Horace Saks and Bernard Gimbel opened this audacious challenge to New York's retail establishment in 1924. Their dream was to construct a unique specialty store that would become synonymous with gracious living. Saks and Gimbel succeeded, of course, in considerable style and to great acclaim: within a year of its opening Saks had 60,000 charge account customers. In addition to the famous flagship there are now stores in 23 states across the country, quite a feat when most large retailers are downsizing. In promoting the best European and American designers—Gucci, Prada, Armani, Klein, Lauren—and supporting the stars of tomorrow, the future of this venerable institution looks secure.

Saks Fifth Avenue
611 Fifth Avenue
New York, NY 10022
Phone: 212-753-4000   Fax: 212-940-4239

SALANDER-O'REILLY GALLERIES
Art Dealers

This impressive partnership has mounted over 300 exhibitions of American and European painting and sculpture. American modernists like Stuart Davis and Marsden Hartley are well represented, as are social realists like Peter Blume, Robert Gwathmey and Ben Shahn. The unusual collection of work by German Expressionists—from Emil Nolde to Gustav Klimt, Max Beckmann to Egon Schiele—also make this gallery a compelling stop on the Upper East Side.

Salander-O'Reilly Galleries
20 East 79th Street
New York, NY 10021
Phone: 212-879-6606

SALLEA ANTIQUES
Antiques

Sally Kaltman's unusual gallery specializes in decorative containers of all sorts. Delight in the assortment of scrumptious 18th and early 19th century English tea caddies, many of them wooden, some tortoiseshell or ivory. The collection also features French and English jewelry boxes, work boxes, glove boxes, watch holders, card holders and other "smalls," like silver cigar cutters, brass scales and early English cribbage boards.

Sallea Antiques
66 Elm Street
New Canaan, CT 06840
Phone: 203-972-1050

SALON AKS
Hair and Beauty

Far from impersonal (like many of the quick service salons around) Salon AKS offers clients a warm, inviting and comfortable ambiance in which to relax. With an excellent staff and hair services that include cuts, coloring and styling as well as waxing, manicures and pedicures, this is a good place to go when you need a little refurnishing.

Salon AKS
694 Madison Avenue
New York, NY 10021
Phone: 212-888-0707

SALON CRISTOPHE
Hair and Beauty

Tint your lashes, wax your bikini line, condition your scalp and trim your brows at this full service hair salon. Most clients stop by for the wash, haircut, color and styling treatments but many add body wraps and makeup lessons to their list once they have seen the extensive list of services that are offered here. Try the *Sur Le Pouce:* 90 minutes with an expert hairdresser and a quick stop at the manicurist's table—all while you enjoy a delectable lunch.

Salon Cristophe
348 North Beverly Drive
Beverly Hills, CA 90210
Phone: 310-274-0851

SALON D'ARTISTE
Spas and Clinics

Not just your run of the mill day spa: try a cleansing facial with an eye zone treatment designed to soothe fine lines, an algae facial exfoliation treatment or a Murad Environmental Shield Vitamin C treatment for a really unique experience. Body massages, body spa treatments, hair cut and color options, waxing and tweezing services and manicures and pedicures complete your full or half day of beauty.

Salon d'Artiste
503 West Lancaster Avenue
Strafford, PA 19087
Phone: 610-687-2020

SALTS
Restaurants   Rising Star

Harvard dignitaries often complain that there are few restaurants in the Cambridge area which offer good food in a hospitable setting. Steve Rosen and Lisa Mandy-Rosen have come to the rescue in this interesting new venture, which showcases distinctive, delicious entrées like a lavender glazed duckling with rhubarb preserves and "long baked" flageolet. Steve was recently named one of the ten best new chefs in America by *Food and Wine* magazine. Salts looks set to prosper.

Salts
798 Main Street
Cambridge, MA 02139
Phone: 617-876-8444   Fax: 617-876-8569

SAN DIEGO MUSEUM OF ART

Museums

Inspired by a selection of modern artworks from the Paris Luxembourg Gallery, Mr. and Mrs. Appleton Bridges opened the doors of the Fine Arts Gallery of San Diego in 1926. The name remained until 1978 when it was changed to The San Diego Museum of Art. In its permanent collection, European paintings include a core of important works by the Spanish artist Juan Sanchez. The Asian collection includes Chinese, Japanese and Korean decorative arts, sculpture and paintings.

San Diego Museum of Art

Balboa Park

1450 El Prado

San Diego, CA 92112

Phone: 619-232-7931   Fax: 619-232-9367

SAN DIEGO POLO CLUB

Polo Clubs

Located 25 miles north of San Diego, in Rancho Santa Fe, The San Diego Polo Club is spread across 78 acres of rural California countryside, with five playing fields and a training ground. Membership is limited to 35 founding members, each of whom can recommend one sponsored member. While all of these slots are currently filled, polo enthusiasts new to the area may take solace in the fact that there are an unlimited number of social memberships. The 70 founding and sponsored members keep approximately 650 thoroughbreds at the club, each with a private staff of groomers and trainers. Tommy Lee Jones and Sylvester Stallone have been known to drop in for a game.

San Diego Polo Club

14555 El Camino Real

Rancho Santa Fe, CA 92067

Phone: 619-481-9217   Fax: 619-481-2247

SAN FRANCISCO GOLF CLUB

Golf Clubs

Designed by A.W. Tillinghast and finished in 1917, the course at the San Francisco Golf Club is a bit hilly on its front side and partially forested. Playing in the fog that so often envelops this bay city is a memorable experience. The signature par three seventh hole was the site of the historic 1859 Terry-Broderick duel, the last of its kind before the practice was outlawed. This small, very private club is like a sister to the legendary Cypress Point.

San Francisco Golf Club

Junipero Serra Blvd. & Brotherhood Way

San Francisco, CA 94132

Phone: 415-469-4100

SANTA BARBARA POLO AND RACQUET CLUB

Polo Clubs

The Santa Barbara Polo Club hosts the finals of the Pacific Coast Open at the end of every summer. With three fields of its own, the picturesque club keeps stabling facilities for eight full teams. Glen Holden, Sr., the Jamaican Ambassador, keeps his Gehacag team at the club, and Andrew Busch of the Budweiser family keeps his Grants Farm Manor team there as well. The Polo Black Tie Gala is the social highlight of the year.

Santa Barbara Polo and Racquet Club

3375 Foothill Road

Carpinteria, CA 93013

Phone: 805-684-6683

SAN YSIDRO RANCH

Hotels

Nestled on 500 wooded canyon acres above Santa Barbara, San Ysidro Ranch offers its guests luxurious accommodations in a beautiful countryside setting. The quaint cottages have recently been renovated and offer the richest of interiors and the romance of a country getaway. The privacy sought by Hollywood luminaries in the 1930s and 40s is still here, along with the tranquility that inspired writers from Somerset Maugham to Sinclair Lewis. The San Ysidro Body Works program offers an extensive range of Ayurvedic treatments, massage, and a beauty and wellness program. The stunning views of the gardens and the majestic Santa Ynez Mountains are enough to make you want to permanently take up residence.

San Ysidro Ranch

900 San Ysidro Lane

Santa Barbara, CA 93108

Phone: 805-969-5046   Fax: 805-565-1995

SANTA FE HORSE PARK AND POLO CLUB

Polo Clubs

On the edge of New Mexico's adobe city, amid the harsh desert terrain, the Santa Fe Horse Park and Polo Club houses two full-size polo fields and one training arena on 27 acres of Kentucky bluegrass, not to mention a state-of-the-art hunter, jumper, and dressage facility. The polo grounds are maintained for 50 playing members.

Santa Fe Horse Park and Polo Club

460 St. Michael's Drive, Building 1000
Santa Fe, NM 87501
Phone: 505-424-7400

SANTA FE OPERA

Events

Up until architect James Polshek added a ceiling and adobe walls in 1997, The Santa Fe Opera was housed in a modern open-air amphitheater. Carved into the Sangre de Cristo Mountains, the distinctive building is one of the city's visual and artistic triumphs, showcasing some of the greatest voices and one of the best symphony orchestras in the country.

Santa Fe Opera

Taos Highway
Santa Fe, NM 87500
Phone: 505-986-5900

JULIAN SCHNABEL

Portrait Painters and Photographers

There was a time when the mere mention of Julian Schnabel's name was enough to send art-world types into flustered fits of hyperbole. But his profile has died down considerably since the heady days of the late 1980s. His recent exploits include producing movies and recording a country music album. But Schnabel still accepts occasional commissions.

Julian Schnabel

c/o Pace Wildenstein Gallery
32 East 57th Street
New York, NY 10022
Phone: 212-421-3292

SCHRAMSBERG VINEYARDS

Winemakers

Famed for its sparkling wine, Schramsberg got a jump start in 1972 when then President Nixon took a bottle with him on an official visit to China. The vineyard was founded way back in the 1800s, but was sold before Prohibition and fell on hard times, until being revitalized in 1965 by Jack Davies. Today its premium wine is bottled on the J. Schram label.

Schramsberg Vineyards

1400 Schramsberg Road
Calistoga, CA 94515
Phone: 707-942-4558   Fax: 707-942-5943

THE SCHWEBEL COMPANY

Antiques

Tailor-made "couture" for the home is the focus of this antiques dealer and interior designer. Historic buildings all over the country are embellished with the Schwebel touch, which strives to inject a period feel into everything from gardens to doorknobs. If you dream of turning your home into, say, an 18th century Victorian mansion and are prepared to wait up to two years for completion, talk to Schwebel. The firm also deals in 19th century American furniture of neoclassical, Gothic and other revival styles.

The Schwebel Company

311 West Superior Street
Chicago, IL 60610
Phone: 312-280-1998

SCOTT SNYDER

Architects and Interior Designers

Scott Snyder is one of the most accomplished young interior designers on the east coast. An immensely stylish figure, Snyder began his career as the owner of an upscale home furnishings store in 1979. Since then, he has worked for an eclectic array of discerning clients. Recent projects include waterfront homes in Palm Beach, an estate in Greenwich, a Texas ranch and a resort in Antigua.

Scott Snyder

42 Via Mivner
Palm Beach, FL 33480
Phone: 561-659-6255   Fax: 561-832-5946

SCOTTSDALE MUSEUM OF CONTEMPORARY ART

Museums   *Rising Star*

Four local philanthropists each contributed over $1 million to the founding of this exemplary new institution, which was the first public museum to open in the city. Upcoming exhibits include large-scale sculptures and paintings by Keith Haring. The museum hosts an Art-rageous Ball each February.

Scottsdale Museum of Contemporary Art

7374 East Second Street
Scottsdale, AZ 85251
Phone: 480-994-2787

SCREAMING EAGLE VINEYARDS

Winemakers

It is famously difficult to find the little barn in which Heidi Barret makes her $1000 bottle of Cabernet Sauvignon based red wine. Try a bottle of the 1992, rated one hundred points. With one taste you will know why. A heavenly experience, and worth every cent of the equally stratospheric price.

Screaming Eagle Vineyards

P.O. Box 134
Oakville, CA 94562
Phone: 707-944-0749   Fax: 707-944-9271

SCULLY AND SCULLY

Specialty Shops

Several generations of New York's socially prominent families have made Scully and Scully their headquarters for gifts and home furnishings. Founded by a husband and wife team in 1934 (whose son Michael is now company president) the store carries Herend porcelain, Lynn Chase china, Baccarat crystal, Halcyon Days English enamel and Limoges porcelain boxes, among many other items.

Scully and Scully

504 Park Avenue
New York, NY 10022
Phone: 212-755-2590

SEATTLE ART MUSEUM

Museums   *Rising Star*

The Seattle Museum of Art offers something for every art lover, from Asian to Native American to African art. The museum is well known for its comprehensive modern American art collection, including artists such as Mark Rothko, Frank Stella, Roy Lichtenstein, Robert Rauschenberg, Julian Schnabel, and Willem de Kooning. The five-story building was designed by Robert Venturi.

Seattle Art Museum

100 University Street
Seattle, WA 98101
Phone: 206-625-8900

SEA ISLAND
Golf Clubs
Built on an 18th century cotton plantation, Sea Island boasts 54 holes of championship golf along the coast of Georgia on St. Simons Island. When he's not touring, Davis Love III lives at the club, which has hosted seven USGA championships in its history and is hosting the U.S. Women's Senior Amateur Tournament in September 2000. Golfers staying at The Cloister Hotel may use the course, but the club is not currently taking new members.

Sea Island
100 Hudson Place
Sea Island, GA 31561
Phone: 912-638-3611

SEAMAN SCHEPPS
Jewelry and Watches
Seamen Schepps' imagination and chutzpah have served him well on both coasts: his witty and flattering jewelry is coveted by lady lunchers and movie stars alike. Today, the company Schepps founded in 1904 continues to approach jewelry making with precision and flair, specializing in dressy, design-oriented pieces—even though the Schepps family no longer owns the business. Look out for the trademark shell earrings, a stunning combination of 18-karat gold and beautiful gemstones.

Seaman Schepps
485 Park Avenue
New York, NY 10022
Phone: 212-753-9520   Fax: 212-753-9531

SEAN KELLY GALLERY
Art Dealers   Rising Star
Prominent collectors from all over the world come to this minimal powerhouse to see the best of contemporary art. Sean Kelly, formerly a museum curator and director, represents a group of leading contemporary artists including Ann Hamilton, Laurie Anderson, Callum Innes, Joseph Kosuth, Lorna Simpson, James Casebere and Christine Borland. They are represented in high caliber museum collections worldwide.

Sean Kelly Gallery
43 Mercer Street
New York, NY 10013
Phone: 212-343-2405   Fax: 212-343-2604

SHAPUR MOZAFFARIAN
Jewelry and Watches
Shapur Mozaffarian's jewelry store on Post Street in San Francisco houses a wealth of traditional and unique artistry. Each of Shapur's one-of-a-kind pieces carries the mark of generations of expertise and superior craftsmanship. The business originated in Persia in 1883, but his family's tradition of jewelry-making dates back even further. They were among the first to manufacture enamel *objets d'art*, a tradition Shapur upholds and one which has earned him his reputation and popularity for creating custom-made pieces and for an outstanding selection of fine Swiss timepieces. Shapur brought his business to San Francisco in 1970 where he opened his shop off Union Square, an area now regarded as San Francisco's jewelry district. He travels the globe in search of the most spectacular stones to adorn the jewelry which he designs himself. The appeal of his designs is evidenced by celebrity testimonials which are tucked among the *objets d'art* throughout his Post Street shop. Shapur has opened two other boutiques in San Francisco to accommodate his many loyal customers.

Shapur Mozaffarian
245 Post Street
San Francisco, CA 94108
Phone: 415-392-1200   Fax: 415-392-6660

SEMINOLE
Golf Clubs

Designed by Donald Ross and completed in 1929, members of "The Nole" play among palm trees, sea-grape bushes and over 200 bunkers on a course that extends to the Atlantic Ocean. Of special note is the sixth hole, Ben Hogan's favorite, and the view from the 18th green. Only a lucky few have had the privilege of playing golf at this exclusive club.

Seminole Golf Club

901 Seminole Boulevard
North Palm Beach, FL 33408
Phone: 561-626-1222

77 MAIDEN LANE
Spas and Clinics

Enjoy an extensive menu of spa pampering in the heart of San Francisco's historic Union Square. Owner Sherlee Rhine gives clients the chance to spend all day immersed in bliss, or briefly dip in during their lunch breaks. The spa's hair styling department features acclaimed colorists, and masseuse Therese Cunningham is renowned in the Bay Area.

77 Maiden Lane

77 Maiden Lane
San Francisco, CA 94108
Phone: 415-391-7777

SHADOW CREEK
Golf Clubs   Rising Star

"Yes, but is it worth paying a thousand dollars for a round of golf?" There is no simple answer, but the consensus suggests that Shadow Creek is eminently playable as well as delicious to behold. That $1000 green fee includes a suite at the fabled Mirage, which begins to make the proposition look like good value.

Shadow Creek

The Mirage Hotel
3400 Las Vegas Boulevard
Las Vegas, NV 89109
Phone: 888-778-3387   Fax: 702-692-8193

SHAFER
Winemakers

Former Publishing executive John Shafer planted 65 acres of vineyards, mostly Cabernet Sauvignon, in the old Batista Scansi ranch under the Stag's Leap Palisades in 1972. The 75-year-old's first two vintages were 1978 and 1979. The 1978 catapulted to fame when it beat 71 other vineyards in blind tastings held in San Francisco. Shafer has increased his acreage to about 140 and today all his wines are good, with the Hillside Select Cabernet leading the way.

Shafer

6154 Silverado Trail
Napa, CA 94558
Phone: 707-944-2877

SHARON SACKS PRODUCTIONS
Party Organizers and Caterers

Ideas guru Sharon Sacks and her staff of 14 manage the logistics and design of everything from meeting planning, destination management, and large and small fund raisers ranging from the Revlon Run Walk, involving 50,000 people, to the celebrity studded Fire & Ice Ball. From expert handling of the lights, sound and show elements to events like post-Grammy parties, to a very small number of select weddings–like that of Rebecca Romajin to John Stamos, for which Sharon was featured on Oprah–this company takes service and the wishes of their international client list to the highest level. More often than not, local experts Patina and Wolfgang Puck handle the catering for Sharon's events.

Sharon Sacks Productions

6934 Canby Avenue, Suite 103
Reseda, CA 91335
Phone: 818-996-9655   Fax: 818-996-9654

SHEARMAN & STERLING
Law Firms

Founded in 1873, this law firm is rooted in American history of the late 19th and early 20th centuries. Shearman & Sterling saw the inception of the U.S. financial markets, beginning its path on the frontier of development–in business and law– with early clients including the railroads, industrial companies and financial institutions. The firm now represents clients in a broad range of business activities under the umbrella of several major practice areas—corporate, litigation, property, tax, antitrust, and compensation and benefits.

Shearman & Sterling

599 Lexington Avenue
New York, NY 10022
Phone: 212-848-4000

SHELLY ZEGART QUILTS
Specialty Shops

Nothing evokes nostalgia for the pastoral lifestyle more than the great American quilt. Shelly Zegart is an expert on the subject. The author of *American*

Quilt Collections: Antique Quilt Masterpieces has built many private and corporate collections. Her selection of antique quilts attracts clients from all over the world, who come to Kentucky for a generous slice of pure Americana.

Shelly Zegart Quilts

300 Penruth Avenue
Louisville, KY 40207
Phone: 502-897-7566   Fax: 502-897-3819

SHERRY LEHMANN
Wine Merchants

Sherry-Lehmann has been family operated from day one. Today it is heralded as one of the chicest wine shops in the world. Offering more than 4000 rare and older vintages, its collection of Bordeaux and Port is one of the finest in America. Commendable service and extensive catalogue promotions lend this Madison Avenue institution further appeal.

Sherry Lehmann

679 Madison Avenue
New York, NY 10021
Phone: 212-838-7500   Fax: 212-838-9285

SHINNECOCK HILLS GOLF CLUB

Golf Clubs

Tooney and Flynn redesigned the Shinnecock Hills course in 1931. It remains a classic of natural beauty, most challenging in a strong wind. The course has been the site of the U.S. Open three times in the last century, most recently in 1995. With 325 members, this prestigious club is currently full, although it does have a ten year waiting list.

Shinnecock Hills Golf Club

200 Tuckahoe Road
Southampton, NY 11968
Phone: 516-283-1310

SHIPMAN HOUSE

Hotels   ***Best Kept Secret***

Built by local rancher Willie Shipman at the turn of the century, Shipman House is now a five-room inn owned and operated by his great-granddaughter, Barbara Ann Anderson, who has included contemporary art works by Hawaiian artists among the family mementos that fill the elegant Victorian interior. If you want to see Hawaii without "doing" a resort this may be the place for you.

Shipman House

131 Kaiulani Street
Hilo, HI 96720
Phone: 800-627-8447

SHREVE & CO.

Jewelry and Watches

Located since 1852 in San Francisco's Union Square, Shreve & Co. has catered to many luminaries, including several European kings (and, of course, their queens). Shreve carries a full range of jewelry, including diamonds, watches and precious stones, and has an in-house Mikimoto pearl boutique. One of only a few in the United States, the Mikimoto boutique showcases a dazzling array of large black Tahitian South Sea pearls and cold-water akoyas.

Shreve & Co.

200 Post Street
San Francisco, CA 94108
Phone: 415-421-2600   Fax: 415-296-8187

SHREVE, CRUMP & LOW

Antiques

This Boston shop began selling jewelry back in 1796 and launched its antiques department in the 1850s, making it one of the oldest dealers in America. Shreve, Crump & Low's collection features 18th and 19th century English and American antiques, prints and paintings. Many of the better pieces relate to New England's history, especially from the China Trade period.

Shreve, Crump & Low

330 Boylston Street
Boston, MA 02116
Phone: 617-267-9100

SHUTTERS ON THE BEACH

Hotels

Located on the beach of Santa Monica bay, Shutters on the Beach is designed to exude the feeling of a sumptuous, yet unpretentious 1920s beach house. And it has that lived-in feeling of a private residence: guest rooms have candles in the bathroom, potted plants, framed photographs, VCR with movies and a selection of magazines. The lobby lures guests and local residents alike to share a bottle of wine while watching the sun set over the Pacific Ocean. Its fireplaces, plush sofas, parquet floors and leather club chairs add to the intimate and elegant atmosphere. Difficult to leave—even for the beach.

Shutters on the Beach

One Pico Boulevard
Santa Monica, CA 90405
Phone: 310-458-0030
Fax: 310-458-4589

SIDLEY & AUSTIN

Law Firms

This full-service business law firm has represented some of the nation's most powerful corporations and individuals. Sidley & Austin's 900 attorneys have experience handling even the most complex litigation. Published reports regularly rank the firm among the leaders in representing corporate and financial clients. Billion-dollar assignments are not out of the ordinary in transactional matters.

Sidley & Austin

One First National Plaza
Chicago, IL 60603
Phone: 312-853-7000   Fax: 312-853-7036

SILVER OAK CELLARS

Winemakers

The story begins in 1972 when Ray Duncan met Justin Meyer, a Christian brother wine maker, who had just left the order. For ten years Ray and Justin bought and sold land in their quest for ideal Cabernet producing conditions. Only making Cabernet Sauvignon allows them to concentrate their energies on the creation of a single excellent wine. The 1992 is particularly outstanding.

Silver Oak Cellars

24625 Chianti Road
Geyserville, CA 95441
Phone: 707-857-3562

SILVER SCREEN SECURITY

Security Consultants

Frank Sinatra didn't compromise when it came to his personal security in New York City. He used Silver Screen Security's highly trained personal bodyguards. They are just as comfortable "shadowing" tourists while shopping. All male and female bodyguards are New York State registered, and many of them are former or current (off duty) N.Y.P.D. Officers.

Silver Screen Security

P.O. Box 140939
Staten Island, NY 10314
Phone: 212-415-9125

SILVERADO VINEYARDS

Winemakers

Walt Disney grew up on a farm. His widow Lillian, daughter Diane and her husband continue the tradition with Silverado. The trio started by selling grapes from vineyards they had bought in 1976 and then built their own winery in 1981. They now get their grapes from four different vineyards; nothing goofy about the results, particularly the Merlots and Cabernet Sauvignon.

Silverado Vineyards

6121 Silverado Trail
Napa, CA 94558
Phone: 707-252-9658

SKADDEN, ARPS, SLATE, MEAGHER & FLOM

Law Firms

This prestigious law firm has 1300 attorneys in 21 offices worldwide. 37 Skadden partners were selected for inclusion in the 2000 edition of *The Best Lawyers in America*. In 1998, the *National Law Journal* cited three of the firm's women lawyers on its list of the 50 most powerful women attorneys in the country. Last year the firm moved its headquarters to a Times Square skyscraper, which is shared with Condé Nast, the magazine publishing company behind titles like *Vogue* and *Vanity Fair*. A report in *The New York Observer* concluded by asking whether the firm has "unwittingly arranged its own downfall by moving in with Condé Nast? What effect will being surrounded by 6-foot-tall beauties have on the Skadden lawyers' self-confidence?"

Skadden, Arps, Slate, Meagher & Flom

4 Times Square
New York, NY 10036
Phone: 212-735-3000

VICTOR SKREBNESKI

Portrait Painters and Photographers

Orson Welles, Bette Davis and Vanessa Redgrave have all been photographed by this gifted Chicagoan, who made his name by shooting editorials for some of the greatest names in fashion. A personal friend of Hubert de Givenchy, Skrebneski has worked with everyone from Lacroix to St. Laurent. But mere mortals can also secure a Skrebneski portrait. Look out for a new book, *Skrebneski: The First 50 Years*, which documents his extraordinary career.

Victor Skrebneski

1350 North Lasalle
Chicago, IL 60610
Phone: 312-944-1339

SOKOLIN WINES

Wine Merchants

Bill and Dave Sokolin, a father and son team, are among the largest importers of Bordeaux wines. They also control a chunk of the nation's supply of Dom Perignon. Recently moved from Manhattan to the East End of Long Island, they are looking with keen interest at the rapid developments in the neighborhood: Bill devoted a section of his last book, *The Complete Wine Investor*, to the investment potential of Long Island wine. One of the great characters of the American wine business, Bill Sokolin once played baseball for the Brooklyn Dodgers.

Sokolin Wines

25 North Sea Road
Southampton, NY 11968
Phone: 516-283-0505   Fax: 516-287-3739

SONIAT HOUSE

Hotels   ***Best Kept Secret***

In the heart of the New Orleans French Quarter, Rodney and Frances Smith have filled their circa 1830 Creole town house with French antiques, offsetting them with splendid carpets and contemporary paintings. Of the thirty-three rooms, no two are alike, but all have one thing in common: a luxurious, yet personal touch. Four-poster beds with French 19th century crewel-embroidered panels are just some of the highlights of this alluring hotel. Foreign imports and high-tech bathrooms notwithstanding, the leisured intimacy of the shady fountain courtyard remains true to its French Quarter setting. So many guests requested to purchase their fine antiques and furnishings, that Soniat House opened two antique galleries, specializing in, among other things, French Decorative Arts. For a taste of times past with all the conveniences of a modern hotel, Soniat House is the place to stay, and for many antiques-hunters, it is first and often the only stop in New Orleans.

Soniat House

1133 Chartres Street
New Orleans, LA 70116
Phone: 800-544-8808   Fax: 504-522-0570

SOLE BY SOLEDAD TWOMBLY

Fashion   *Rising Star*

Soledad Olivera Twombly's line of eastern-inspired women's wear has made this native of Buenos Aires the toast of the Garment District. Her simple credo, that the fine details—like a pair of shoes from Afghanistan, a Moroccan necklace, a scarf from Punjab—are what make an ensemble, has helped the thirty-something designer become a high-priestess of continental-couture. Her husband, Alessandro, is a promising painter and sculptor.

SOLE by Soledad Twombly

611 Broadway, Suite 841
New York, NY 10012
Phone: 212-477-2005   Fax: 212-674-8617

SOOLIP PAPERIE & PRESS

Specialty Shops   *Best Kept Secret*

This zen-like boutique offers a discerning selection of the finest papers and inks from Europe and Asia. Husband and wife owners Grant Forsberg and Wanda Wen use a 15th Century printing technique; the subtle texture and characteristics of the paper produced in their letterpress evokes a bygone era. Soolip devotees include Jodie Foster and Keanu Reeves.

Soolip Paperie & Press

8646 Melrose Avenue
West Hollywood, CA 90069
Phone: 310-360-0545   Fax: 310-360-0548

SOTHEBY'S

Auction Houses

One of the world's premier auction houses, Sotheby's has sold everything from the complete remains of a Tyrannosaurus rex to personal items from the estate of former First Lady Jacqueline Kennedy Onassis. Established in London in 1744, the firm is now owned by Alfred Taubman.

Sotheby's has made history many times, most recently with Paul Cézanne's *Rideau, Cruchon et Compotier,* which sold for $60.5 million.

Sotheby's

1334 York Avenue
New York, NY 10021
Phone: 212-606-7000

SOTHEBY'S INTERNATIONAL REALTY

Property Consultants

Sotheby's has set the pace for luxury real estate brokerage around the globe since 1976. Clients enjoy an unparalleled level of service, taking advantage of a prestigious network of more than 200 affiliates from England to South Korea to Australia. Leaders in their respective markets, these associates are selected for their record of excellence in serving clients; combined with Sotheby's expertise in real estate and the firm's impeccable reputation, it is hardly surprising that the alliance has prospered.

Sotheby's International Realty

980 Madison Avenue
New York, NY 10021
Phone: 212-606-7660   Fax: 212-606-4199

SOUCHI

Fashion   *Rising Star*

While a student at the San Francisco Academy of Art, Suzi Johnson took a class in knitting to fill a graduation requirement; it soon became her *métier.* Her line of luscious mohair and cashmere tops, turtlenecks and dresses have become the preferred pullover for the likes of Claire Danes and Demi Moore. Recently, Johnson started a line of baby wear, complete with vintage buttons and gingham bows which can be found on Alexandra von Furstenburg's little girl. Look for the new luxe label, Souchi Red.

Souchi

150 Powell Street, #311
San Francisco, CA 94102
Phone: 415-397-5254

SPYGLASS HILL GOLF CLUB

Golf Clubs

Designed by Robert Trent Jones, Sr., and finished in 1966, the demanding Spyglass Hill course runs through Del Monte forest, and includes lakes at the 12th, 14th and 15th holes. The greens are noted for being deceptively slick. The par four fourth hole is one of the most famous holes in golf, and the 464-yard par four 16th is the toughest hole on the PGA Tour.

Spyglass Hill Golf Club

Stevenson Drive / Spyglass Hill Road
Pebble Beach, CA 93953
Phone: 831-647-7500   Fax: 831-625-8592

SPAGO HOLLYWOOD

Restaurants

Meeting place of Hollywood movers and shakers and flagship of Wolfgang Puck's empire, Spago was where the superagent Swifty Lazar hosted his legendary Oscar parties for film royalty. Now called Spago Hollywood to avoid confusion with Spago Beverly Hills, it is luxurious without being stodgy. But even Puck classics like pan-roasted black sea bass with succotash and grilled garlic chicken take second place to star-watching. Sit in the front if you want to see bad singers being *prima donnas.*

Spago Hollywood

1114 Horn Avenue
West Hollywood, CA 90069
Phone: 310-652-4025   Fax: 310-657-0927

ST. GEORGE'S SCHOOL

Schools

This small school in Newport, Rhode Island, was founded in 1896 by the Reverend John Diman. It is situated on one of the most breathtaking ocean bluffs in New England. With only 325 students, St. George's has average class sizes of seven or less students. Geronimo, a 69-foot cutter, is used as a school at sea during the academic year. Graduates include retired Senator Clairborne Pell, and current Vermont Governor, Howard Dean.

St. George's School

P.O. Box 1910
Newport, RI 02840
Phone: 401-847-7565   Fax: 401-842-6677

ST. JOHN KNITS
Fashion

St. John Knits is the nation's premier designer, manufacturer and marketer of fine women's apparel. Showcased in upscale specialty stores and St. John boutiques, these timeless, classic collections are treasured for their high quality and design integrity. Marie Gray, co-founder and Chief Designer, demonstrates a sensitivity to the needs of women and a passion for quality that are evident throughout St. John's evening wear, sportswear, accessories, jewelry, timepiece, eye wear and fragrance lines. Kelly Gray, president and signature model for St. John, has achieved high acclaim in the industry, winning the 1996 Cadillac Award for Excellence in American Design and being featured in *Vanity Fair's* "200 Legends, Leaders and Trail Blazers." Kelly Gray has become a symbol for the company and its classic elegance. Whether in couture evening designs, accessories or fragrance, St. John Knits offer exacting standards, unique style and, above all else, understated elegance.

St. John Knits

2382 Morse Avenue
Irvine, CA 92614
Phone: 949-863-1171

ST. MARK'S SCHOOL
Schools

This outstanding Episcopal boarding school has a faculty-student ratio of 1:5. Joseph Burnett founded St. Mark's in 1865 to provide young men with a classic liberal arts education. The school has maintained Burnett's original vision, although it has been accepting young women since 1977, when it merged with the Southborough School for Girls.

St. Mark's School

25 Marlborough Road
Southborough, MA 01772
Phone: 508-786-6000

ST. PAUL'S SCHOOL
Schools

Founded by Dr. George Cheyne Shattuck in 1856, St. Paul's maintains a strong sense of community on its sprawling 2,000-acre campus by taking in only boarding students. Juniors and Seniors have the opportunity to study abroad in Japan or France. All 100 full-time faculty members live on campus. The school's ballet company has produced dancers for the Chicago City Ballet, the Royal Ballet of Flanders, and the New York City Ballet.

St. Paul's School

325 Pleasant Street
Concord, NH 03301
Phone: 603-225-3341

ST. REGIS
Hotels

The beaux-arts St. Regis Hotel, smack in the heart of midtown Manhattan, has the look and feel of a European hotel, with crystal chandeliers, marble floors, and antique tapestries. Peruse a collection of 3000 leather-bound classic and contemporary books, or stop by the King Cole Bar and enjoy a Bloody Mary, which was the creation of a St. Regis bartender.

St. Regis Hotel

2 East 55th Street
New York, NY 10022
Phone: 212-753-4500   Fax: 212-787-3447

STAG'S LEAP WINE CELLARS
Winemakers

This winery put California on the world wine map. In the Paris tastings held in May 1976, its Cabernet Sauvignon won first place, beating Chateau Mouton-Rothschild by, as it were, a nose. Stag's Leap (which should not be confused with neighboring Stag's Leap Winery) today produces Chardonnay, Merlot and other wines but its Cabernet Sauvignon is still the star attraction, with "Cask 23" its premier wine.

Stag's Leap Wine Cellars

5766 Silverado Trail
Napa, CA 94558
Phone: 707-944-2020

STANFORD UNIVERSITY
Colleges

Seven years after its founding, Stanford suffered severe structural damage from the San Francisco earthquake of 1906, and the university is still recovering from the more recent earthquake a decade ago. Philip Knight of Nike, Charles Schwab and Tiger Woods claim Stanford as their *alma mater*. Other graduates include men and women at the helm of Silicon Valley giants like Cisco, Hewlett-Packard, Varian and Yahoo!

Stanford University

Stanford, CA 94305
Phone: 650-723-2489

STARKEY INTERNATIONAL
Employment Agencies

A founder of the International Nanny Association, Mary Louise Starkey has been placing household managers in the nation's more affluent homes for over 16 years. Eight-week intensive training programs in a 13,000 square foot Georgian manor ensure that Starkey graduates (there are over 400 of them working throughout the U.S.) shine in even the most demanding American households.

Starkey International

1350 Logan Street
Denver, CO 80203
Phone: 800-888-4904

STEINWAY & SONS

Specialty Shops

For pianos, Steinway is the only name you need to know. This 145-year-old institution is still the place for hand-crafted instruments. Steinways have been endorsed by music greats ranging from Rachmaninov to Billy Joel: in fact, 97 percent of the world's piano soloists perform exclusively on a Steinway. In the ever-increasing world of mass production, these instruments stand apart for their superior quality. The Steinway flagship showroom is appropriately situated opposite Carnegie Hall on 57th Street in Manhattan. For a complimentary color catalog on Steinway pianos and for the nearest exclusive Steinway dealer showroom, call 1-800-345-5086 or visit the Steinway web site at www.steinway.com.

Steinway & Sons

One Steinway Place
Long Island City, NY 11105
Phone: 800-345-5086

STELLA SALONS

Hair and Beauty

Stars like Mariah Carey and Madonna have used the VIP room at this 3000 square foot South Beach hair and beauty salon. The Guinot facial, in which an electrocurrent infuses moisturizer and essential oils into the skin, is especially popular. Also on the menu at colorist Johanna Stella's self-styled oasis for the 'tressed-out' are manicures, pedicures, and massages.

Stella Salons

404 Washington Avenue
Miami Beach, FL 33139
Phone: 305-532-0024   Fax: 305-535-8323

STEVE MARTINO & ASSOCIATES

Landscape Architects

Incorporating native Arizona vegetation into their designs, Steve Martino & Associates' create interesting and dynamic relationships between exteriors and interiors. Recent landscape projects include the Scottsdale Museum of Contemporary Art. Their work has been featured in *House Beautiful*, *Landscape Authority* and in the book, *Breaking Ground: Portraits of Ten Garden Designers*.

Steve Martino & Associates

3336 North 32nd Street
Phoenix, AZ 85018
Phone: 602-957-6150   Fax: 602-224-5288

STEVEN HOLL ARCHITECTS

Architects and Interior Designers

The prolific principal of this New York firm has published some 150 articles since 1978, and his designs have been exhibited at the Walker Art Center in Minneapolis and the Henry Art Gallery in Seattle. Recent works of note include the Texas Stretto House in Dallas and the Chapel of St. Ignatius in Seattle, both winners of the National AIA Honer Award for Excellence in Design.

Steven Holl Architects

435 Hudson Street, 4th Floor
New York, NY 10014
Phone: 212-989-0918   Fax: 212-463-9718

STRATEGIC CONTROLS

Security Consultants

Gerald O'Rourke's security philosophy is one of "total control." A former state trooper, Deputy U.S. Marshal and security manager of Flying Tiger Airways, O'Rourke acts as an independent security consultant to large institutions and private clients. He often reevaluates and redesigns problematic security situations for prominent individuals who do not employ a full time security management team.

Strategic Controls

244 Madison Avenue, Suite 147
New York, NY 10016
Phone: 888-206-8325

STRIBLING & ASSOCIATES

Property Consultants

This boutique brokerage firm lists and sells family homes in the most exclusive areas of Manhattan. The company handles a wide variety of townhouses, condominiums and cooperative apartments up to $20 million, average sale price is above $1 million. Elizabeth Stribling describes her business as large enough to list distinctive properties but small enough to maintain quality control.

Stribling & Associates

924 Madison Avenue
New York, NY 10021
Phone: 212-570-2440

STUDIO SOFIELD

Architects and Interior Designers

Moving on from the ivy-covered walls of Princeton University to his current headquarters in downtown Manhattan, William Sofield has designed the interiors of upscale retail stores, corporate headquarters and private residences in the United States and abroad. Clients have included Gucci, Donna Karan, the SoHo Grand Hotel and Sean "Puffy" Combs.

Studio Sofield

380 Lafayette Street
New York, NY 10003
Phone: 212-473-1300

STYLINE FURNITURE
Specialty Shops

This trendsetting furniture store in the Los Olas art district of downtown Fort Lauderdale is dressed up more like a gallery than a furniture store; the artistic showroom houses the best in cutting-edge contemporary style, catering both to the public and to designers.

Styline Furniture

116 South Federal Highway
Fort Lauderdale, FL 33301
Phone: 954-523-3375   Fax: 954-525-3375

SULLIVAN & CROMWELL
Law Firms

Many of America's more prominent moguls turn to this establishment law firm for representation, trusting its renowned responsiveness to client needs and its expert understanding of the business world. Established in the 19th century, Sullivan & Cromwell has slowly but steadily grown over the years; the firm currently has 478 lawyers.

Sullivan & Cromwell

125 Broad Street
New York, NY 10004
Phone: 212-558-4000

SUMPTER PRIDDY III
Antiques

Sumpter Priddy was the curator at Colonial Williamsburg before going into business for himself in the early 1980s. Focusing on American 18th century furniture and fine arts, he has a particularly good eye for unusual, high quality Southern furniture. Clients include the Philadelphia Museum of Art, the Art Institute of Chicago and the White House.

Sumpter Priddy III

601 South Washington Street
Alexandria, VA 22314
Phone: 703-299-0800   Fax: 703-299-9688

SUNDANCE HOTEL
Hotels

Film legend Robert Redford's rustic yet elegant mountain resort is set on the edge of a 12,000 foot canyon, with its own stream running through 5000 acres of open terrain. Furnished in a Native American and Western style, its Wild West cottages offer top of the line amenities as well as good riding, skiing, hiking and fishing nearby. Sundance is also home to a film festival, which Redford started in order to showcase young directors making movies without the help of the major studios. It is now one of the biggest events in the film world.

Sundance Hotel

North Fork Provo Canyon
Sundance, UT 84604
Phone: 801-225-4107   Fax: 801-226-1937

STEMS
Florists

The name Stems has become synonymous with beautiful, stylish floral designs—no run of the mill arrangements here. Owner Maggie Oyen and her capable staff have done everything from decorating lavish weddings in Nantucket and Martha's Vineyard, to corporate and private events for Bear Stearns and American Express. Recently, Stems has begun to branch out, keenly pursuing a floral shipping service, so that you no longer have to worry about the sort of floral designs being sent blindly to friends and family. From Philadelphia to New York, Greenwich to the Hamptons, indeed anywhere nationwide, with Stems you can be confident that what is sent will fully represent your taste and intentions—and then some.

Stems

98 Elizabeth Street
Redhook, NY 12571
Phone: 914-758-8080
Fax: 914-758-8082

SUE FISHER KING
Specialty Shops

Sue Fisher King has one of the most exclusive and unique selections of Italian sheets and bed coverlets in the United States from Anichini, Frette, Catherine Memmi and their own exclusive sources. Agnona, a famous name in Italian textiles, weaves their stunning cashmere, alpaca and silk blankets and throws. The shop imports sumptuous hand blocked velvets and Fortuny silk lamps from Venice, "chateau" pottery from France, and gutsy Palio dinnerware from Sienna. Sue Fisher King has specially selected a large collection of French flatware, bath linen and table linens which can be custom ordered from a large selection of samples or chosen from an eclectic mix available immediately. Whether you are selecting home furnishings for a new dwelling, or looking to add a soupcon of panache to an existing decor, you will discover a plethora of exciting choices at either of their San Francisco locations.

Sue Fisher King

3067 Sacramento Street
San Francisco, CA 94115
Phone: 415-922-7276
Fax: 415-922-9241

SUMMIT AVIATION

Airplanes

If you need a Hawker to hightail it to Hong Kong, or a Boeing to blast off to Belgium, Summit Aviation will make it happen. This industry leader offers a full line of transportation services, catering to the needs of active, quality-conscious executives and professionals. Whether you need to travel 40 or 4000 miles, Summit's jets, helicopters, and limousines are on the job...worldwide.

Summit Aviation

7144 Republic Airport
East Farmingdale, NY 11735
Phone: 516-756-2545   Fax: 516-756-0809

SUNSET BEACH

Hotels

For a taste of the French Riviera in New York, venture to Shelter Island. Only a couple of hours drive from Manhattan, it can be reached by ferry from Long Island or by seaplane from anywhere you please. André Balazs operates this chic boutique hotel. Calvin Klein and Cindy Crawford often stop by for dinner in the outdoor waterfront restaurant. Journalist Lucy Sykes recently told *New York* magazine that she had nicknamed some of the restaurant customers "the boat people, because they all come over on their incredible boats, and they leave $300 tips."

Sunset Beach

35 Shore Road
Shelter Island, NY 11965
Phone: 516-749-2001

SUNSET COTTAGE

Architects and Interior Designers

Sunset Cottage's clients include Goldie Hawn, Bette Midler, and Ted Danson; Mollie Mulligan's interior design company is a favorite of discerning celebrities seeking style and comfort for their retreats. Her team work on homes in upscale locales nationwide, including Aspen, Jackson Hole, Vail, Martha's Vineyard, and Nantucket.

Sunset Cottage

8157 Sunset Boulevard
Los Angeles, CA 90046
Phone: 323-650-8660   Fax: 323-650-8662

SUSAN CIMINELLI DAY SPA

Spas and Clinics

Adhering to the idea that the best deserve the best, Susan Ciminelli Day Spa uses only the finest botanicals, exotic essential oils and natural seaweed from France. Although the spa menu includes New Age treats like Reiki and Amma for relaxation, Susan Ciminelli also offers traditional and alternative therapies. Clients looking for a rare combination of conventional and singular treatments come back time and again to this smart little spa, tucked away on the ninth floor of Bergdorf Goodman.

Susan Ciminelli Day Spa

Bergdorf Goodman
754 Fifth Avenue
New York, NY 10019
Phone: 212-872-2650   Fax: 212-872-2655

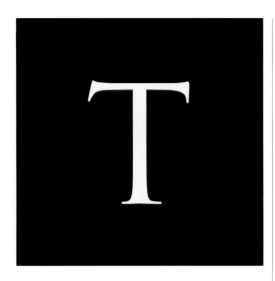

THE TAFT SCHOOL
Schools

Horace Dutton Taft founded this non-denominational school in 1890 and served as its Headmaster for 46 years. Lance Rue Odden, the third Headmaster since Taft, now presides over 540 students on the school's 220-acre campus. Study programs are offered in subjects as diverse as short-story writing, play production and computer programming. Taft has been co-educational since 1971.

The Taft School
110 Woodbury Road
Watertown, CT 06795
Phone: 860-945-7777

TALBOTT
Winemakers

The Talbott family started making wine in Carmel in 1983, using grapes from the Salinas area. Impressed with the quality of the fruit, they increased production and bought acreage there themselves. Today they are famed for their Chardonnay, under the labels Monterey County and Diamond T; they also produce some fine Pinot Noir.

Talbott
P.O. Box 776
Gonzalez, CA 93926
Phone: 831-675-3000

TANGLEWOOD MUSIC FESTIVAL
Events

For a week every summer, the Boston Symphony Orchestra hosts a very social festival of classical music in historic Lenox, the jewel of Berkshire County. The festival, which runs on a schedule of up to three concerts a day, includes orchestral, vocal and multimedia events and features a variety of guest conductors and soloists. Many concerts are held in the 2000-seat Seiji Ozawa Hall.

Tanglewood Music Festival
297 West Street
Lenox, MA 01240
Phone: 413-637-1666

THAD HAYES DESIGN
Architects and Interior Designers

Thad Hayes is one of the youngest of the big-name interior decorators. Along with Victoria Hagan, Hayes' expertise is in especially heavy demand among the younger members of Manhattan society. His relatively simple, elegant style is often described as "classic contemporary."

Thad Hayes Design
90 West Broadway
New York, NY 10007
Phone: 212-571-1234

THEA WESTREICH ART ADVISORY SERVICES
Art Consultants

Thea Westreich's scholarship and connections are impressive and her team of advisers are eminently qualified to counsel even the most discerning collector. With a 5000 volume art library, housed in a huge SoHo loft, Westreich helps her clients to acquire "works of the highest quality, beauty and import."

Thea Westreich Art Advisory Services
114 Greene Street, 2nd Floor
New York, NY 10012
Phone: 212-941-9449   Fax: 212-966-0174

THERIEN & COMPANY
Antiques

In two locations, a Continental-style townhouse in San Francisco and the galleries that enclose an olive tree-bedecked courtyard in Los Angeles, Therien and Company maintains a rigorous standard of excellence in both its own collection and in the evaluation services it offers to clients. Therien discourages clients from purchasing antiques solely as a financial investment, and will happily exchange any piece purchased from its inventory.

Therien & Company
716 North La Cienega Boulevard
Los Angeles, CA 90069
Phone: 310-657-4615

THIERRY DESPONT
Architects and Interior Designers

Frenchman Thierry Despont is the man responsible for the remarkable galleries at the Getty Center in California, illustrated in our feature on the museum, *The Modern Acropolis*. The hugely successful architect, whose attention to detail is legendary, has been working in New York for 15 years. His business is mostly high-end residential interior design; Despont has designed homes for Bill Gates and Calvin Klein.

Thierry Despont
335 Greenwich Street
New York, NY 10013
Phone: 212-334-9444   Fax: 212-334-1847

THUNDERBIRD PRODUCTS
Yachting

Although Thunderbird carries a full line of boats, from runabouts to offshore cruisers, it is best known for high-performance offshore models. The company has replaced the standard v-hull in its flagship, the 43-foot 419 Fasttech, with a newly designed hull based on the tri-hull design found in seaplane pontoons, called Steptall. The new hull reduces drag, makes for smoother reentry into the water, self-corrects pitch, and is 14 times stronger. All of this, of course, is very important when you are sailing open-throttle on triple 500-horsepower engines. And creature comforts are not sacrificed for high performance: a full cabin with galley, electric head, and an impressive entertainment system completes the package.

Thunderbird Products
2200 West Monroe Street
Decatur, IN 46733
Phone: 800-736-7685

THE TIDES
Hotels

Owned by Island Records founder, Chris Blackwell, The Tides offers considerable comfort and what regulars describe as "a good vibe." The open and generous feel of the lobby extends to the rooms with their soft tones of beige, white and sand accented with bright, vibrant colors. Each of the 45 rooms has an oceanfront view and a telescope (aimed at the beach) for the curious stargazer. The Firefly and Goldeneye penthouses have terraces and expansive views.

The Tides
1220 Ocean Drive
Miami Beach, FL 33139
Phone: 305-604-5070   Fax: 305-604-5180

TIFFANY & CO.
Jewelry and Watches

Whether it is for a milestone in the life of a company, a family member or a friend, each Tiffany gift, wrapped in the signature blue box, symbolizes the rich heritage and reputation of a firm which has truly become an American icon. Tiffany's china sets the tables at White House dinners, and its jewels have been worn by icons like Grace Kelly, Jacqueline Kennedy Onassis, Babe Paley and Diana Vreeland. In addition to its signature line, the firm—which now has more than a hundred stores and boutiques worldwide—offers a dazzling array of watches, clocks, china, crystal and silverware. Tiffany's is the last word in American luxury.

Tiffany & Co.
727 Fifth Avenue
New York, NY 10022
Phone: 212-755-8000   Fax: 212-605-0465

Roses, by Tina Modotti

THROCKMORTON FINE ART

Art Dealers

Discerning collectors adore the contemporary and classic Latin American photography that Spencer Throckmorton has been collecting for 20 years. He moved his gallery to the former home of Peggy Guggenheim in 1993, and has never been busier. His vast inventory includes high quality vintage images as well as conceptual contemporary images. Throckmorton also has a comprehensive selection of Pre-Colombian artifacts and textiles. "Everything south of the border" is his enthusiastic cry, and museums have been lining up to borrow and buy from his vast collection. Throckmorton is the main lender to Tina Modotti's European retrospective exhibition "Tina Modotti and the Mexican Renaissance," which is showing in Sweden, Finland, Switzerland and France from Spring 2000 to Winter 2001. He has also lent many images to the Montreal Museum of Fine Arts and the National Gallery of Canada for the exhibition "Mexican Modern Art, 1900-1950." In addition, Throckmorton will curate a traveling exhibition called "Frida Kahlo Unmasked: Portraits by various photographers" for San Antonio Museum of Art in Texas and the Flint Institute of Art, Michigan.

Throckmorton Fine Art
153 East 61st Street
New York, NY 10021
Phone: 212-223-1059

Middle: Frida Kahlo Rivera. Bottom: Standing Musician, c. 500B.C.-500A.D., ceramic.

TIMBERHILL RANCH

Hotels

Dwarfed by 6000 acres of California Redwoods, Timberhill is a luxurious country retreat 20 minutes walk from the Pacific ocean. Its 15 cottages all have wood-burning fireplaces. Facilities include a Jacuzzi, championship tennis courts and a swimming pool heated to a perfect 84 degrees. There are also many miles of excellent hiking on the estate. Cottages 11 and 14 have the best views of the surrounding forests and offer the most privacy.

Timberhill Ranch
35755 Hauser Bridge Road
Cazadero, CA 95421
Phone: 1-800-847-3470   Fax: 707-847-3342

TIME WILL TELL

Jewelry and Watches

Vintage watches are good investments: they are useful, beautiful to look at and their value is soaring. This small store specializes in unusual and unique examples by the world's great makers, including Audemars, Cartier, Patek Philippe and Tiffany. Owner Stewart Unger is the co-author of a book called *American Wristwatches*. Unger also offers fine straps and an excellent service and repair operation.

Time Will Tell
962 Madison Avenue
New York, NY 10021
Phone: 212-861-2663

TIMOTHY EATON FINE ART

Art Dealers

Eaton Fine Art hosts exhibitions and sales of important 19th and 20th century and contemporary American and European painting, sculpture, photography and decorative art. Museum quality exhibitions are complemented by academic programs, including lectures and tours. Exhibitions are documented in catalogs written by noted art historians and authors.

Timothy Eaton Fine Art
435 Gardenia Street
West Palm Beach, FL 33401
Phone: 561-833-4766   Fax: 561-833-3134

TOCCA

Fashion   Rising Star

This promising young company, founded by Gordon Finkelstein and Edoardo Mantelli in the early 1990s, produces fashions that abound with color and distinctive embroidery. Finkelstein and Mantelli sell their clothes through department stores and specialty boutiques across the world. Helena Christiansen, Naomi Campbell, Drew Barrymore and Gwyneth Paltrow are all fans.

Tocca
161 Mercer Street
New York, NY 10012
Phone: 212-343-3912   Fax: 212-343-3913

TODD OLDHAM

Fashion

Todd Oldham's boutiques marry *nonpareil* merchandise with out-of-this-world decor. The combination can be overwhelming, but look past the fun, brightly colored floor tiles and tie-dyed velvet curtains: Oldham's clothes are fabulous. His boutiques carry everything from jeans to sequined gowns, but they also offer such oddities as dog dishes, which promote Oldham's fight for animal rights. Justly acclaimed as an innovator.

Todd Oldham

123 Wooster Street
New York, NY 10012
Phone: 212-226-4668

TONY SHAFRAZI GALLERY

Art Dealers

Tony Shafrazi has played a vital role in the development of contemporary American art. His gallery opened publicly in the early eighties and soon represented several young artists who would become synonymous with the decade: Keith Haring, Jean-Michel Basquiat, James Brown and Kenny Scharf. Shafrazi has recently shown important work by Andy Warhol and Francis Bacon.

Tony Shafrazi Gallery

119 Wooster Street
New York, NY 10012
Phone: 212-274-9300   Fax: 212-334-9499

TOWN & COUNTRY

Media

This ancient bastion of wedding and party coverage has recently become something with a little more import. Nowadays the profiles hail accomplishment, not just entitlement; after all, the magazine's mission is to document the nation's "style *and* substance." Deputy Editor John Cantrell is one of the more charming figures in American journalism.

Town & Country

1700 Broadway
New York, NY 10019
Phone: 212-903-5332   Fax: 212-977-7277

TOM MATHIEU & COMPANY

Florists

A floral designer for over twenty-five years, Tom Mathieu started his own company a little over three years ago to wide acclaim. Catering to the *crème de la crème* of Palm Beach society, Mathieu is known for being able to create a floral fantasy with only a moments notice. He is renowned throughout the design community for his style and good taste. And often, whether it is a corporate client, U.S. Trust Bank or, say, the chic Club Colette, Mathieu is trusted enough to let his vision come through.

Tom Mathieu & Company

312-D Worth Avenue
Palm Beach, FL 34480
Phone: 561-655-5880   Fax: 561-655-5803

ADELAIDE ALTHIN TOOMBS SUNDIN

Portrait Painters and Photographers

Adelaide Toombs Sundin has created nearly 100 bas-relief portraits of children in the du Pont family and is now into the third generation. Her charmingly old fashioned plaques become family heirlooms. The delicacy of the artwork and the translucency of Parian Porcelain give an exquisite quality to these unusual sculptures.

Adelaide Althin Toombs Sundin

132 Hedgeapple Lane
Greenville, DE 19807
Phone: 302-998-6466   Fax: 302-999-0047

TOTAL TRAVEL & TICKETS

Travel Consultants

This travel business is devoted exclusively to the most spectacular and exclusive events in the world of sports, music and the theater. Bill Germaine's company will put together a total travel package for almost any major event, taking away all the worries that so frequently attend such outings. Total Travel can get clients into the likes of the U.S. Open, Wimbledon or popular Broadway shows with little advance notice, because they keep a stock of tickets on hand, and can tap into an extensive and international network of brokers. Highly personalized service and attention to detail resulted in the company's business doubling every year for the first four years that it was in operation; they have recently opened a new office in Tampa.

Total Travel & Tickets

6250 North Andrews Avenue, Suite 205
Fort Lauderdale, FL 33309
Phone: 954-493-9151   Fax: 954-493-8195

TOWN & COUNTRY NANNIES & MOTHERS IN DEED

Employment Agencies

If you are looking for a full-time nanny, or even just for someone reliable to pick up the kids after soccer practice, this is the place to start looking. Town & Country recently joined forces with Mothers In Deed to form the Bay Area's leading agency. After an extensive screening process and placement, the agency provides follow-up services and guidance to both families and nannies.

Town & Country Nannies & Mothers In Deed

425 Sherman Avenue, Suite 130
Palo Alto, CA 94306
Phone: 650-614-0276   Fax: 650-326-1556

TRIPLE CREEK RANCH

Hotels **Best Kept Secret**

Amid millions of acres of pristine wilderness lies this mountain hideaway where one can truly escape the daily rigors of junk bonds, cell phones and the like. The Triple Creek Ranch offers cabins that are equipped with fireplaces, data ports, and best of all–fresh baked cookies delivered daily. And to ensure maximum privacy, they are nestled among the dense pines. With all the luxury of an urban resort in the middle of the Rocky Mountains you can go for a massage, take a ride on the trail, enjoy the rewarding fly fishing on the many nearby alpine lakes, or simply relax in a hammock–the way nature intended.

Triple Creek Ranch
5551 West Fork Road
Darby, MT 59829
Phone: 406-821-4600   Fax: 406-821-4666

TRACEY ROSS

Fashion *Rising Star*

Tracey Ross not only offers everything from Chloé to Tocca, but also the most wonderful service in her L.A. boutique. Ross will select items for busy celebrities and movie executive clientele, send them on location and allow the clients to keep what they like and send back the rest. This Sunset Boulevard luminary is destined to become an enduring success.

Tracey Ross
8595 Sunset Boulevard
Los Angeles, CA 90069
Phone: 310-854-1996

TRACY FEITH

Fashion

SoHo, which was once a hotbed of creative activity in the art and fashion worlds, has now been colonized by big-name fashion retailers, squeezing the smaller, more bohemian designers into NoLIta (North of Little Italy). At the vanguard of this movement is Texan designer Tracy Feith, whose delightful dresses are afforded ample space in this chic Mulberry street store.

Tracy Feith
209 Mulberry Street
New York, NY 10012
Phone: 212-334-3097

TRINITY SCHOOL

Schools

Henry C. Moses now presides over New York City's venerable Trinity School, which was founded in 1709. More than 10% of the faculty at this powerhouse of elementary and secondary education have doctorates. Approximately 58% of the prospective students who applied for admission to the 1997 freshman class of the upper school were accepted, although those spurned may console themselves in the knowledge that preference is given to the children of faculty and alumni. The diverse course offerings include marine biology, ethics, computer programming, Latin and Greek. Graduates go on to many of the leading colleges in the country.

Trinity School
149 West 91st Street
New York, NY 10024
Phone: 212-873-1650

TROON GOLF & COUNTRY CLUB

Golf Clubs

Designed by Tom Weiskopf and Jay Moorish and completed in 1985, the course at Troon is best described as "demanding desert golf." Most memorable is the 13th hole, "Postage Stamp," which mirrors the famous hole in Scotland of the same name. The 14th and 15th holes, "The Cliff" and "Troon Mountain," complete the signature triumvirate. With 390 members, Troon is currently full. Prospective members have to wait for a current member to resign, although the nonrefundable, $65,000 membership fee reduces that likelihood.

Troon Golf & Country Club
25000 North Windy Walk Drive
Scottsdale, AZ 85255
Phone: 602-585-4310

TROQUET

Restaurants *Rising Star*

Opened just a couple of years ago by top chef Tim Goodell (who also owns Aubergine) this Costa Mesa bistro serves terrific French cuisine with California accents in a somewhat unlikely location. Signature dishes include *Veal en Cocotte,* served with vegetables and black truffles. In the summer, ask for a table in the garden patio.

Troquet
S. Coast Plaza
3333 Bristol Street
Costa Mesa, CA 92626
Phone: 714-708-6865   Fax: 714-708-6869

TRUMP INTERNATIONAL GOLF CLUB

Golf Clubs *Rising Star*

Jim Fazio, brother of Tom Fazio, is designing a brand-new golf club of truly Trump proportions—the par-72 course will include lakes, a running stream, a two-tiered waterfall and an 18th hole on a 45-foot-high plateau. Other signature holes will include a 596-yard par five at the 12th hole, a 458-yard par four at the 13th, and a par-three 17th hole with an island green.

Trump International Golf Club
3505 Summit Boulevard
West Palm Beach, FL 33406
Phone: 561-832-2600   Fax: 561-832-2669

TRUMP INTERNATIONAL HOTEL

Hotel

When approaching this Philip Johnson–designed monolith, one cannot imagine that beyond the mirrored facade lies one of the world's more discreet boutique hotels. While there is hardly anything subtle about its ubiquitous promoter, here one is taken by the serene ambiance. Each of the 168 rooms feature breathtaking views of Manhattan's Central Park—why leave them when your room service comes from four-star restaurant Jean Georges, located on the ground floor?

Trump International Hotel

One Central Park West
New York, NY 10023
Phone: 212-299-1000   Fax: 212-299-1150

TULEH

Fashion   *Rising Star*

According to co-founder and co-designer Josh Patner, he and partner Bryan Bradley started Tuleh about a year and a half ago because they knew a lot of pretty girls in need of pretty clothes. Cameron Diaz and Jennifer Lopez are fans of their romantic, slightly frivolous clothes, which are available at Bergdorf Goodman and selected Neiman Marcus stores around the country.

Tuleh

175 West 81st Street, 5C
New York, NY 10024
Phone: 212-595-3879   Fax: 212-595-3879

TURLEY WINE CELLARS

Winemakers

Dr. Larry Turley was an emergency room medical physician for 20 years before he opened this winery in 1993. In just six years of operation, Turley has carved a place for himself in the history of Californian Zinfandels. He produces more varieties than any other wine maker in the region, most of which are rated in the 90s—and he also makes a superb Petite Syrah. The winery produces between five and six thousand cases per vintage.

Turley Wine Cellars

3358 St. Helena Highway
St. Helena, CA 94574
Phone: 707-963-0940

20/20 WINES

Wine Merchants

The Golbahar family turned a high-end liquor store into a fine wine shop that lures celebrities and movie executives. In addition, they ship wines to collectors around the country. Specializing in obscure Californian, French and Italian gems, the store has approximately 5000 different wines in its inventory. 20/20 also rents out wine lockers to oenophiles whose collections are bulging at the seams.

20/20 Wines

2020 Cotner Avenue
Los Angeles, CA 90025
Phone: 310-447-2020   Fax: 310-475-2836

TWIN FARMS

Hotels   *Best Kept Secret*

Since opening in 1993, this luxurious 300-acre woodland estate has been managed by Shaun and Beverly Matthews, the young British couple who formerly managed Richard Branson's Necker Island in the Caribbean. Guests report that Twin Farms feels like the home of a wealthy friend; instead of check-in, for instance, you will be greeted by the family Labrador and a blazing fire. During the summer there is canoeing, cycling and fishing, while winter offers skiing, skating or snowshoeing. Evenings are best spent relaxing in the Japanese furo bathhouse, followed by intimate dinners in the wine cellar.

Twin Farms

P.O. Box 115
Barnard, VT 05031
Phone: 802-234-9999   Fax: 802-234-9990

TWO DESIGN GROUP

Florists

Two Design Group, an event workshop specializing in the creation of extraordinary events, works in the corporate and social markets across the country and overseas. TDG features impressive linens, large scale decor, floral designs in exquisite fixtures and tabletop accoutrements unlike other event suppliers. A talented group of designers and staff, led by Creative and Sales Director Todd Fiscus, they are focused on perfection for every event. *Town and Country* named Two Design Group a top design firm for 1999. In fact Condè Nast, *Elegant Bride, House Beautiful, Southern Accents* and *Traditional Home* have all raved about his Dallas-based firm. Two Design Group creates everything from the menu to the parting gifts with perfection in mind.

Two Design Group

1113 Dragon Street
Dallas, TX 75207
Phone: 214-741-3145

U.S. OPEN POLO
Events

The U.S. Open Polo tournament draws players like Amateur champion Peter Brant, Tim Gannon, the proprietor of Outback steakhouses and actor Tommy Lee Jones. A 5000 seat stadium provides spectators with sweeping views of the matches and heavyweight sponsors like Rolex and Louis Vuitton ensure that the event boasts a lively social scene.

U.S. Open Polo Tournament
13420 South Shore Boulevard
Wellington, FL 33414
Phone: 561-793-1440   Fax: 561-790-3872

U.S. OPEN TENNIS
Events

Tennis fans like Brooke Shields and Bill Cosby flock to the courts at Flushing Meadows Corona Park on the Monday before each Labor Day weekend for the United States Tennis Open, one of the most fabled tournaments in the game. For extra points try to get hold of a courtside box.

U.S. Open Tennis
Flushing Meadows Corona Park
Flushing, NY 11368
Phone: 914-696-7000   Fax: 914-696-7027

U.S. SECURITY
Security Consultants

Leading consultants for special events and executive residences. Jack Smith and J. Peter Rush worked on President Clinton's inauguration in 1993. They have also consulted many of the *Fortune 500* on the security of their residences. Their firm employs former U.S. Secret Service agents.

U.S. Security
10480 Little Patuxent Parkway
Columbia, MD 21044
Phone: 410-442-1756   Fax: 410-489-3669

ULTIMO
Fashion

Joan Weinstein's Ultimo is a premier source for the best in international fashion, offering a great array of designer clothing and accessories. This fashion-forward retailer brought designers like Issey Miyake, Jean-Paul Gaultier, Giorgio Armani and Jean Muir to the U.S. In *Style and the Man,* Alan Flusser describes Ultimo as "the hippest store in the heartland." There are also branches in San Francisco and Dallas.

Ultimo
114 East Oak Street
Chicago, IL 60611
Phone: 312-787-1171

THE UNION CLUB
Private Clubs

On any given night the Union Club's grand dining room is inhabited by people whose surnames are etched into the cornerstones of New York's greatest public buildings. The club features squash courts as well as bedrooms, which seem to be plucked from the English country homes of the last century; appropriate enough, as overnight guests are often reciprocals from the top clubs in London. This is one of the few old-school clubs in which children are found "at table."

The Union Club
101 East 69th Street
New York, NY 10021
Phone: 212-734-5400

UNIVERSITY OF PENNSYLVANIA
Colleges

Founded by Benjamin Franklin in 1740 as a children's charity school, UP's 12 graduate and professional schools include the Wharton School of Business, routinely rated the best in the nation; graduates include Donald Trump and Ivan Boesky.

University of Pennsylvania
Walnut Street
Philadelphia, PA 19104
Phone: 215-898-5000

URBAN EPICURIA
Specialty Shops   *Rising Star*

When Alan and Gail Baral moved out to Los Angeles from New York three years ago, they soon realized that Hollywood executives and movie stars would appreciate a gourmet deli. So they teamed up with Christophe Bergen and Wayne Davis to open this upscale godsend. Do not be surprised if this cornucopia of culinary delights goes nationwide: the concept is sound and the people behind it are smart and ambitious.

Urban Epicuria
8315 Santa Monica Boulevard
West Hollywood, CA 90069
Phone: 323-848 8411   Fax: 323-848 8416

US TRUST
Wealth Management

John Paul Getty said "if you owe the bank $1 million, that's your problem. If you owe the bank $100 million, that's the bank's problem." It seems unlikely that the venerable US Trust has ever had to address such a misfortune, as its clients come from the ranks of the *seriously* rich. Established way back in 1853, it is one of those fabled old-school wealth managers who have acquiesced to chase new money. The company manages $75 billion in assets.

US Trust
114 West 47th Street
New York, NY 10036
Phone: 212-852-1000

ULTRAMARINE
Yachting

Ultramarine founder and CEO Cindy Brown, the broker-cum-concierge of high-end yacht charters, knows her clients' needs. Brown's focus is on hospitality. No request is too difficult: Egyptian cotton linens, organic fruit, and restaurant reservations are all par for the course. Ultramarine specializes in megayachts, but Brown can also get you a charter on the elegantly refurbished 130-foot J-class America's Cup sloop, *Endeavor.*

Ultramarine
200 East 90th Street
New York, NY 10128
Phone: 212-423-9280   Fax: 212-289-0844

VALENTINO
Restaurants
Piero Selvaggio came to the United States from Sicily in his early twenties. With more than 130,000 bottles and 1300 different varietals, his restaurant has one of the most extensive wine lists in the world, and is well-known for its homemade pastas, risottos and sea bass imported from the Mediterranean. Selvaggio has recently opened up three new restaurants in Las Vegas.
Valentino
3115 Pico Boulevard
Santa Monica, CA 90405
Phone: 310-829-4313

VALLEY CLUB OF MONTECITO
Golf Clubs   Best Kept Secret
Even members of exclusive L.A. clubs like Bel Air and Riviera speak in hushed tones about the Valley Club, set in a peaceful valley overlooking the Pacific just a few miles from Santa Barbara. Jigsaw-puzzle bunkers and an outstanding quartet of par-3 holes distinguish the design, but its secluded setting is what sets the Valley Club apart from anything else in busy southern California.
Valley Club of Montecito
1901 East Valley Road
Santa Barbara, CA 93108
Phone: 805-969-2215

VANITY FAIR
Media
Canadian Graydon Carter rules the roost in the seven chambers that constitute HQ at one of the world's most influential magazines. Brilliant writing by the likes of Christopher Hitchens, Bob Colacello and Amy Fine Collins and superb photography by Annie Leibovitz and Michael O'Neill light up the pages of this iconoclastic publication.
Vanity Fair
4 Times Square
New York, NY 10036
Phone: 212-880-8800

VARIETY
Media
When you want to know which movies are going to make it big in the coming months, turn to this industry bible. The show business trade publication since 1905, *Variety* delivers unmatched global coverage spanning the entire entertainment world.
Variety
5700 Wilshire Boulevard, Suite 120
Los Angeles, CA 90036
Phone: 323-965-4467   Fax: 323-857-0494

VASSAR COLLEGE
Colleges
Brewer Matthew Vassar founded this college in the Hudson Valley in 1861, in order to provide women with an education equal to that which men were receiving at the time. Today it is the only one of the Seven Sisters colleges that accepts men. The first African-American woman sworn in as a United States attorney (Vicki Miles-La Grange) and the first woman to head the National Institute of Health (Dr. Bernadine Healy) were both Vassar graduates.

Vassar College
124 Raymond Avenue
Poughkeepsie, NY 12604
Phone: 914-437-7000

VERA WANG
Fashion
A popular figure on the Manhattan social circuit, Vera Wang opened her first boutique on Madison Avenue in 1990, after working as an editor at *Vogue* for 17 years and as design director of Ralph Lauren for two years. She expanded her successful wedding finery into a less expensive line of ready-to-wear bridal and evening dresses in 1992 and 1993, respectively. Wang's profile was raised in 1994, when she designed stylish costumes for figure skater Nancy Kerrigan to wear in the Winter Olympics. In 1968 she herself had almost qualified for the Olympics—as a figure skater.
Vera Wang
225 West 39th Street, 9th Floor
New York, NY 10018
Phone: 212-575-6400

VALERIE WILSON TRAVEL
Travel Consultants
Valerie Wilson Travel stands above its competition by providing the ultimate in customer service. Founded in 1981 by Valerie Ann Wilson, the primary philosophy of this privately owned and family managed company is to provide the highest level of personal service and knowledge to leisure and business travelers. Ranked as the 41st largest US Travel Agency, this core principal remains undaunted. Valerie Wilson is regularly named one of the 200 Most Powerful Women in Travel. Wilson and her daughters (Jennifer Wilson-Buttigieg and Kimberly Wilson Wetty) not only run the day-to-day operations of this 175 person company, but continually explore and develop innovative ways to better influence the travel industry and serve the traveling consumer.
Valerie Wilson Travel
475 Park Avenue South
New York, NY 10016
Phone: 212-532-3400
Fax: 212-779-7073

VERITAS

Restaurants   *Rising Star*

Park Smith and Steve Verlin have one of the largest wine collections in the country. In conjunction with Gino Diaferia and Executive Chef Scott Bryan, they recently opened this small, tastefully decorated restaurant across the road from Danny Meyer's Gramercy Tavern. A brave move, certainly, but Veritas looks set to prosper. Service is impeccable and the food is unusually impressive for a restaurant which emphasizes the strength of its wine list—1400 selections from every wine country in the world. Try Bryan's signature seared halibut.

Veritas

43 East 20th Street
New York, NY 10003
Phone: 212-353-3700

VICTORIA HAGAN

Architects and Interior Designers

A native New Yorker who studied at the Parsons School of Design, Victoria Hagan's style is classical yet very comfortable. Her work is distinguished by the effective use of beautiful antiques. Like her contemporary, Thad Hayes, Hagan does a lot of work for the younger set.

Victoria Hagan

654 Madison Avenue, Suite 2201
New York, NY 10021
Phone: 212-888-1178   Fax: 212-888-0974

A LA VIEILLE RUSSIE

Antiques

Founded in Kiev in 1851, A La Vieille Russie moved to Paris during the Russian revolution before transferring to New York. The firm specializes in European and American antique jewelry, gold snuffboxes and *objets de vertu*. Russian paintings, icons, and decorative arts—including silver, porcelain, and enamel—are also specialties.

A La Vieille Russie

781 Fifth Avenue
New York, NY 10022
Phone: 212-752-1727

THE VIRGINIAN GOLF CLUB

Golf Clubs

In the rolling hills of the Southern Highlands, only a few miles from the highest mountains, and one of the largest and most breathtaking lakes, The Virginian Golf Club is a 538-acre private residential community with a Tom Fazio-designed golf course as its centerpiece. The community is rated in the "Top Five Places to live in America."

The Virginian Golf Club

22512 Clubhouse Ridge
Bristol, VA 24202
Phone: 800-452-8065   Fax: 540-645-7055

Portrait of Miss Helen Durham, by John Singer Sargent.

VANCE JORDAN FINE ART

Art Dealers

Vance Jordan Fine Art is one of the country's leading galleries, dealing primarily with 19th and early 20th century American paintings, as well as important European—especially Italian—paintings of the same period. As part of an ongoing commitment to American art scholarship, the gallery also regularly organizes museum quality exhibitions and publications, featuring artists such as John La Farge, H.R. Newman, Richard Miller, Childe Hassam and other major American impressionist painters. Whether assisting new or veteran collectors, the aim of the gallery is to educate and counsel, ensuring that the client's experience is an exciting and richly rewarding one.

Vance Jordan Fine Art

958 Madison Avenue
New York, NY 10021
Phone: 212-570-9500   Fax: 212-737-1611

VISION AIRE

Airplanes

You'll have to wait until 2002 to take a ride on the new Vantage, the world's first all-composite construction single-engine personal/business jet, and Vision Aire's first entry in the personal jet market. It can operate on as little as 2,500 feet of runway, but will cruise at 350 knots at 41,000 feet. Its spacious interior seating for five is unheard of in the super-light jet category.

Vision Aire

595 Bell Avenue
Chesterfield, MO 63005
Phone: 314-530-1007   Fax: 314-530-0005

VOSE GALLERIES OF BOSTON

Art Dealers

The oldest art gallery in the United States originally opened in Rhode Island in 1841. Today it is owned and operated by the fifth generation of the Vose family. The specialty is 18th, 19th and early 20th century American paintings, although a limited number of French and English works are also carried. Painters like John Singer Sargent and Frank Benson are particularly well represented.

Vose Galleries of Boston

238 Newbury Street
Boston, MA 02116
Phone: 617-536-6176

W

Media

The brainchild of John Fairchild (who is profiled in our *Amazing Americans* feature), *W* is arguably the most glamorous women's magazine in America. Editorial Director Patrick McCarthy and a talented staff continue in Fairchild's inimitable fashion, offering sophisticated, trendsetting readers an oversize glimpse of the fashion world in all its well-heeled finery.

W

7 West 34th Street
New York, NY 10001
Phone: 212-630-4900

WAGWEAR

Specialty Shops

Wagwear is the last word in canine couture—from the sheepskin collar which Rupert Everett's dog is wearing, to the ultimate status symbol for your rebel without a bone, a hooded leather jacket lined with quilted satin. Fighting Fido doesn't even have to fret if Wagwear is a bridge too far: just order from the colorful catalog.

Wagwear

4 East 10th Street
New York, NY 10003
Phone: 888-924-9327   Fax: 212-375-8106

THE WALL STREET JOURNAL

Media

In a land where the dollar is king it is entirely appropriate that one of the largest selling quality newspapers is *The Wall Street Journal,* the bible of investors—big and small—across the nation. Superb investigative financial writing, coupled with strong news features and impeccably researched investment counsel.

The Wall Street Journal

Dow Jones & Company
200 Liberty Street
New York, NY 10281
Phone: 212-416-2000

WALTERS ART GALLERY

Museums

One of only a few museums in the world to present a comprehensive history of art from the third millennium B.C. to the early 20th century, the Walters Art Gallery has an impeccable reputation among art historians. Diverse public programs coupled with an historic commitment to conservation and scholarship enable the gallery to serve an audience of specialists and students without sacrificing its appeal among the general public.

Walters Art Gallery

600 North Charles Street
Baltimore, MD 21201
Phone: 410-547-9000   Fax: 410-783-7969

WARREN-TRICOMI SALON

Hair and Beauty   ***Best Kept Secret***

"A salon is for the cultivation of beauty so it should be a beautiful place," says stylist Edward Tricomi of his salon, which is bedecked with hand-carved Moroccan doors, plush feather filled sofas, Venetian-style blown glass chandeliers, slate floors and stained glass windows. Celebrities like Demi Moore, Raquel Welch and Rachel Hunter flock to the salon, where Warren-Tricomi's staff create chic *coifs* in cutting edge styles. Manicures and pedicures are also available at this beauty haven.

Warren-Tricomi Salon

16 West 57th Street
New York, NY 10014
Phone: 212-262-8899

WEISBROD CHINESE ART

Antique Dealers

It was a medical doctor and art collector who founded this gallery in Toronto, and his son Michael Weisbrod moved it to Manhattan back in the 1970s. Weisbrod Chinese Art is an exclusive and elegant gallery offering some of the highest quality Chinese Art to collectors and museums around the world. Specialists for almost 30 years, the gallery carries fine Chinese art from the Neolithic period to the turn of the 20th Century and presents seasonal exhibitions, as well as displaying an array of rare Chinese ceramics, jades, Buddhist sculpture, cloisonné, lacquer, bronzes and paintings of exceptional quality. Amongst the fine collection is a Very Rare Massive Imperial Blue and White Porcelain Dish from the Ming Dynasty, which once graced the walls of The Victoria and Albert Museum in London.

Weisbrod Chinese Art

36 East 57th Street
New York, NY 10022
Phone: 212-319-1335   Fax: 212-319-1327

THE WASHINGTON POST

Media

With the help of its five national offices and 20 news bureaux around the world, *The Washington Post* promises its readers incisive, well-researched stories—and it usually delivers the goods. Katharine Graham, one of the most influential women in America, ran the Post with great flair for many years, defying the unions and her begrudgers to create a paper which smart people inside the Beltway just cannot do without. Graham's son, Donald, is now at the helm, although she still has considerable clout.

The Washington Post

1150 15th Street, NW
Washington, DC 20071-0070
Phone: 202-334-6000   Fax: 202-334-6664

WAYNE PRATT ANTIQUES

Antiques

Wayne Pratt keeps his collection of 18th and 19th century American furniture and accessories in the Marshall Mansion, located in the antiques Mecca of Woodbury, Connecticut and in a second store in Nantucket. Recognized as an authority on antiques for over thirty years, Pratt regularly appears on the *Antiques Road Show,* where he has focused his discussions on American folk art. Among his more exciting recent acquisitions, Pratt picked up a parringer-top tea table in pristine condition at a New England auction.

Wayne Pratt Antiques

346 Maine Street South
Woodbury, CT 06798
Phone: 203-263-5676   Fax: 203-266-4766

WELLESLEY COLLEGE
Colleges
No longer a school of white gloves and etiquette studies, Wellesley has become one of the top five liberal arts colleges in the United States. A leader in the education of women for over 120 years, its commitment to excellence is evident in the superb facilities and laboratories on a 500 acre campus near Boston. First Lady Hillary Rodham Clinton has long credited Wellesley for helping to shape her life.

Wellesley College
106 Central Street
Wellesley, MA 02481
Phone: 781-283-1000

WENDY KRISPIN
Party Organizers and Caterers
Wendy Krispin caters parties on the social scene in Dallas, either in private homes, public spaces or one of her two restaurants in the Design Center. Particularly popular with doyennes of design, her food has multi-ethnic influences, including Thai, French, Italian and Mexican. She also does Texan-chic or upgraded Southern recipes and famously caters lavish fund raisers, including a star-studded AIDS benefit earlier this year. Ranch weddings are another specialty. An affable and enthusiastic figure, Wendy Krispin will happily arrange events throughout the state of Texas.

Wendy Krispin
Dallas Design Center
1025 North Stemmons Freeway
Dallas, TX 75207
Phone: 214-748-5559   Fax: 214-748-4022

PATRICIA WEXLER M.D.
Cosmetic Surgeons
While other cosmetic surgeons may jump to put you under the knife, Pat Wexler's specialty is non-scalpel rejuvenation of the face and body. For the past eight years, she has been injecting Botox into forehead lines, furrows, crows feet and lax necks. She is also known for performing liposuction on her patients and recycling their fat by injecting it into their hollowed undereye areas, sunken cheeks and nasal labial folds to resculpt these areas. With fellowships in the American Academies of Dermatology, Dermatologic Surgery and Cosmetic Surgery, Wexler's expertise draws patients to her inviting, European-style office, decorated with black leather Italian armchairs and black and white photography.

Patricia Wexler M.D.
Wexler Dermatology
145 East 32nd Street
New York, NY 10016
Phone: 212-684-2626
Fax: 212-684-6906

WHITINSVILLE GOLF CLUB
Golf Clubs
A classic completed by Donald Ross in 1925, *Sports Illustrated* recently selected Whitinsville's nine-hole course as the second best in the country. The signature four par ninth hole, 440 yards long from the back tee, was named by *Golf Digest* as one of the top hundred holes in the country.

Whitinsville Golf Club
179 Fletcher Street
Whitinsville, MA 01588
Phone: 508-234-6210

WILDENSTEIN & CO.
Art Dealers
This family of dealers has been in the fine art business since 1875, acquiring major collections of impressionist, Renaissance and 18th century paintings and sculpture. Behind the stately doors of their 1932 townhouse are old master treasures that many museums have borrowed and most would be lucky to own. An international institution which has worked with some of the most important collectors of this century, Wildenstein remains one of the key players in the world art market.

Wildenstein & Co.
19 East 64th Street
New York, NY 10021
Phone: 212-879-0500   Fax: 212-517-4715

WILL ROGERS POLO CLUB
Polo Clubs
The last remaining grass polo field in Los Angeles County was originally the private estate of Will Rogers, where stars like Spencer Tracy and Clark Gable tacked up in the 1950s. The Ronald Reagan tournament in May of each year is particularly good fun.

Will Rogers Polo Club
12100 Wilshire Boulevard, 15th Floor
Los Angeles, CA 90025
Phone: 310-573-5000   Fax: 310-207-3230

WILLIAM A. KARGES FINE ART
Art Dealers
William Karges serves the high end of the market for California art from 1880 to 1940, including artists such as Guy Rose, William Wendt, Granville Redmond and Armin Hansen. Karges is the largest dealer of early California artists in the country and, rare among dealers, he publishes his own monographs. Now that greater interest is developing in California artists who were contemporaries of the East Coast impressionists, Karges' clientele is becoming ever more eclectic.

William A. Karges Fine Art
P.O. Box 222091
Carmel, CA 93922
Phone: 831-625-1025

WILLIAM B. MAY

Property Consultants

William B. May first opened its offices in 1866, selling to New York's most prominent families, and through various land deals and sales, spearheaded the opening up of 57th Street. Today, it has grown to seven offices and some 150 salespeople, serving all of Manhattan, Westchester's River Towns, and Brooklyn's historic brownstone neighborhoods, brokering the sale and rental of townhouses, co-operatives and condominiums from $100,000 to $21 million.

William B. May

575 Madison Avenue
New York, NY 10022
Phone: 212-872-2200

WILLIAM CALVERT

Fashion   *Rising Star*

"Beauty," wrote John Milton, "hath strange power." He may have been referring to the designs of William Calvert, the modest but talented young designer whose enchanting ready to wear collections are already stocked at Bergdorf Goodman, Barneys and Ultimo. A former apprentice to Balenciaga and Diane von Furstenburg, Calvert looks set to become one of the more celebrated designers of the next decade.

William Calvert

29 West 57th Street
New York, NY 10019
Phone: 212-888-8808

WILLIAM DOYLE GALLERIES

Auction Houses

William Doyle Galleries, owned by Kathleen M. Doyle, is one of New York's preeminent boutique auction galleries. Known for paintings, furniture, jewelry and estates, the company's spectacular couture sales attract stars, models, and designers; at the last sale one celebrity walked away with her dress for the Emmy Awards.

William Doyle Galleries

175 East 87th Street
New York, NY 10128
Phone: 212-427-2730

WILLIAM PITT REAL ESTATE

Property Consultants

This firm sells country estates, waterfront homes with spectacular views of Long Island Sound, horse farms and other prestigious properties in Fairfield County, Connecticut. A full-service, 50-year old brokerage, William Pitt sells estates for as high as $18 million, although its average sale is $1.3 million. The firm's web site will take you on a room-by-room "virtual tour" of their properties for sale.

William Pitt Real Estate

1266 East Main Street
Stamford, CT 06902
Phone: 203-327-5353

WILMINGTON TRUST–FSB

Wealth Management

One of the top ten trust companies in the U.S., Wilmington Trust–FSB boasts an intensely dedicated staff who are invariably cited by clients as one of the hardest-working teams in the industry, with family relationships spanning five generations. For high-end financial services and comprehensive wealth management, the company enjoys a superb reputation.

Wilmington Trust–FSB

1100 North Market Street
Wilmington, DE 19890
Phone: 302-651-1000   *Fax: 302-651-1458*

WILSON SONSINI GOODRICH & ROSATI

Law Firms

The largest law firm in Silicon Valley has been used by some of the world's leading companies in technology, science and consumer products. WSGR's practice covers a broad range of corporate and litigation services; the firm is renowned as a leader in public and private offerings of equity and debt securities, mergers and acquisitions, securities class action litigation and intellectual property litigation.

Wilson Sonsini Goodrich & Rosati

650 Page Mill Road
Palo Alto, CA 94304
Phone: 650-493-9300

WILKES BASHFORD

Fashion

Wilkes Bashford is one of the finest luxury retailers for men and women in America. San Franciscans describe him as the man "who made Sutter Street." The Bashford touch is certainly evident from the moment one steps into the subdued yet inviting ambiance of his flagship store, which houses a lavish array of hand tailored clothing and upscale fashions for men and women on seven floors. The 33-year old firm, which also sells an impressive selection of imported home furnishings, recently expanded from its original San Francisco location, opening mens and womens shops in Mendocino, St. Helena, and Mill Valley, where they feature a new line of sportswear. Bashford's legion of faithful customers can now enjoy a signature fragrance; look for the bottles that simply say Wilkes on the label.

Wilkes Bashford

375 Sutter Street
San Francisco, CA 94108
Phone: 415-986-4380   *Fax: 415-956-3772*

WINDOWS ON THE WORLD WINE SCHOOL

Culinary Schools

There is not a vine in sight on the 107th floor of the World Trade Center, but if you want to take an intensive course without traveling to France, Kevin Zraly's World Wine School is the place for you. The man who made drinking American wines cool became obsessed with wine as soon as he could legally drink it. Students rave about this course—Zraly rarely fails to instill an enthusiasm for the noble grape.

Windows on the World Wine School

One World Trade Center, 107th Fl.
New York, NY 10048
Phone: 914-255-1456

WINDSOR COURT HOTEL

Hotels

The Windsor Court Hotel adds a stiff upper lip to often raucous New Orleans. Among its celebrated features is a magnificent collection of art and antiques, which, like the style and décor of the hotel itself, is distinctly British. Built by James Coleman, Jr. in 1974, the 324-bedroom property caught the eye of another Anglophile, James Sherwood, chairman of Orient Express Hotels, under whose management it has been since 1991. Sovereign attention to detail is evident throughout. For instance, the Grill Room wine cellar is built on springs, so the bottles will not be disturbed in an earthquake.

Windsor Court Hotel

300 Gravier Street
New Orleans, LA 70130
Phone: 504-523-6000   Fax: 504-596-4513

WINDSOR VILLAGE

Property Consultants

Windsor Village and Orchid Island are two private golf communities which are being developed in Vero Beach, Florida. The European-style Windsor Village offers luxury homes with sweeping ocean views, a concierge department, new fitness center, a beach club and a golf club. Of the 350 homes planned for the village, 100 are completed or under construction. Prices range from $750,000 to $4 million. Owner Galen Weston started developing the communities in 1999.

Windsor Village

3125 Windsor Boulevard
Vero Beach, FL 32963
Phone: 561-388-8400

THE WINE CASK

Wine Merchants

Doug Margerum's commitment to excellence has ensured that his restaurant, wine store and catering company has grown exponentially over the past 18 years. The Wine Cask now stocks the largest collection of Santa Barbara wines in America, and a healthy smattering of New World treats among an inventory of 3500 wines.

The Wine Cask

813 Anacapa Street
Santa Barbara, CA 93101
Phone: 805-966-9463

WINTERTHUR MUSEUM, GARDEN AND LIBRARY

Museums   Best Kept Secret

Henry Francis Du Pont's magnificent collection of American decorative arts from 1640 to 1860 is exhibited on his former estate, which also boasts a 60 acre garden and a research library for the study of American art and material culture. The Campbell collection of soup tureens was recently donated by the Campbell Museum. Winterthur hosts an annual crafts festival and academic conferences on a regular basis.

Winterthur Museum, Garden and Library

Route 52 & Old Kennett Road
Winterthur, DE 19735
Phone: 302-888-4600   Fax: 302-888-4700

WINGED FOOT GOLF CLUB

Golf Clubs

A.W. Tillinghast designed a West course and an East course for "The Foot" in 1921. The West course is consistently ranked as one of the most challenging American courses, although the East course probably has more variety.

Winged Foot Golf Club

Fenimore Road
Mamaroneck, NY 10543
Phone: 914-698-8400

WOMEN'S CENTER FOR PLASTIC AND RECONSTRUCTIVE SURGERY

Cosmetic Surgeons

Dr. Diane Gibby founded this center as an oasis for women created *by* women. Dr. Gibby sees many types of patients, from women who need breast reconstruction following mastectomies to young mothers who want to improve their figures after having children.

Women's Center for Plastic & Reconstructive Surgery

7777 Forest Lane, Suite 820
Dallas, TX 75230
Phone: 972-566-6477

THE WOODS

Florists

Tables full of lush flowers adorn this bright, airy Brentwood store. It was opened seven years ago by husband and wife team Wayne and Yvonne Woods, who actually met each other in a flower shop. Wayne's background in fashion design imbues his arrangements with an extravagant, collection-like spirit, and his occasional classes on floral design are very popular. Drew Barrymore and Glenn Close are frequent visitors.

The Woods

11711 Gorham Avenue
Los Angeles, CA 90049
Phone: 310-826-0711   Fax: 310-826-0652

WHISTLING STRAITS

Golf Clubs

Whistling Straits stands out among North American golf courses. Its designer, Pete Dye, says he has "never seen anything like it. Anyplace. Period." In style and character, it emulates the great seaside courses of Ireland, and as a walking-only course, honors the game's origins. Sculpted along two miles of Lake Michigan's shoreline, vistas of the great lake are offered from each of the 18 holes. Look for the Irish course, a second 18-hole championship course, scheduled to open soon.

Whistling Straits

1111 West Riverside Drive
Kohler, WI 53044
Phone: 800-618-5535   Fax: 920-565-6055

YACHTSCAPE

Yachting

It was only a matter of time before the yacht industry caught on to the "fractional ownership" concept pioneered by private jet manufacturers. Yachtscape takes the lead with its Hatteras Yachts fractional program. Owners can buy a one-third or one-sixth share in a convertible sport fisher or a two-deck motor yacht. A one-third share entitles owners to 84 days a year on the water, with two to three crew members and a loaded galley. The boats are currently stationed on the East Coast from Newport to the Bahamas and are scheduled to hit the West Coast next year.

Yachtscape

110 North Glenburnie Road, P.O. Box 199
Newbern, NC 28560
Phone: 800-871-5440

YALE SCHOOL OF MANAGEMENT

Colleges

The Yale School of Management has been a major innovator in graduate business education since its inception over 21 years ago. Its early emphasis on teamwork and using business skills for leadership across the public and private sectors is now being emulated by business schools throughout America. The two year Masters in Business Administration program is among the best in the world.

Yale School of Management

135 Prospect Street
New Haven, CT 06511
Phone: 203-432-6035

YALE UNIVERSITY GOLF COURSE

Golf Clubs

An intrinsic part of campus life at one of the country's oldest institutions of higher learning, Yale's golf course is open to students, alumni, faculty and their guests. Designed by the venerable Charles Blair McDonald and completed in 1926, the most memorable hole is the ninth, with a drop in the middle of the green in which a grown man could hide from players at the tee. Yale's course is the site each August for the Dock Rivers Invitational, a favorite for celebrities and professional athletes from other sports.

Yale University Golf Course

200 Conrad Drive
New Haven, CT 06515
Phone: 203-432-0895

YEAMANS HALL CLUB

Golf Clubs   ***Best Kept Secret***

This exclusive golfing plantation includes a 1926 Seth Raynor golf course and a small housing development planned by Olmstead Brothers. The club was founded by a group of wealthy New Yorkers, who chose Charleston because it was precisely an overnight train journey from the city—but the magnificent live oaks around the course and clubhouse, and the secluded site surrounded by river on three sides, didn't hurt either.

Yeamans Hall Club

900 Yeamans Hall Road
Charleston, SC 29401
Phone: 843-744-5555

YORK FURRIER

Fashion

This full-service furrier opened on York Road in 1931. The salon provides a warm and friendly atmosphere for its discerning customers. Celebrated fur coats, in a variety of designs and colors, are exhibited on the sales floor. The boutique also offers a range of fashions in leather, cashmere, and precious fiber, among other fabrics.

York Furrier

107 North York Road
Elmhurst, IL 60126
Phone: 630-832-2200   Fax: 630-832-2321

ZACHY'S

Wine Merchants

With the use of temperature-controlled storage, strict selection criteria and a reputation for affable service, Zachy's has prospered since 1946. Topnotch Bordeaux, Burgundy, Californian and Italian wines are offered by Jeff Zacharia's well-regarded retail and mail order outfit, which also enjoys a partnership with Christie's, one of the most reputable auction houses in the country.

Zachy's

16 East Parkway
Scarsdale, NY 10583
Phone: 914-723-0241

Since 1952

The Fine Art

of

Custom Interior Design

and Decoration

FROM

the WORKROOMS *and* SHOWROOMS

of

GREENBAUM
INTERIORS

DESIGN SERVICES • FURNITURE, CARPETS & ACCESSORIES

ANTIQUES & FINE ART • CUSTOM SHOPS

Presenting the World's Largest Selection of Extraordinary Home Furnishings

BANKING FOR BILLIONAIRES

by Robinson G. Clark

*There was a time, not so long ago, when the term 'private banking' suggested images
of secretive institutions in the Swiss Alps. But, as Robinson Clark discovers,
the business of managing the money of the rich has changed forever.*

Just off the shores of a famous lake in a famous city, a bank caters to some of the world's wealthiest people, offering highly personalized, ultra-confidential, fully comprehensive accounts designed to meet a client's every need—from basic checking and savings to high-tech investing in options and offshore hedge funds, from tax and estate planning to financing that getaway mountain home or latest addition to a budding art collection.

This isn't Lac LeMan in Geneva, where ancient institutions offer fabled Swiss bank accounts—the kind that conjure up images of wood-paneled, teller-less offices, hush-hush, well-connected account executives and the ill-gotten loot of dictators and drug barons being stashed in secretive vaults. This is Northern Trust, not far from the water's edge of Lake Michigan in downtown Chicago. And this is just one symbol of how far the business of private banking—banking geared strictly to the super wealthy—has come in the U.S.

Northern Trust boasts 110 years of private banking experience and $120 billion in private banking assets, making it one of the oldest and largest U.S. institutions in the game. Although it will never have the cachet of its Swiss counterparts like Pictet & Cie, Northern Trust does resemble a financial Swiss Army knife. The bank provides clients with almost every financial option available: basic money-market checking accounts; proprietary mutual funds; investment advice and portfolio management; risk management; access to hedge funds; specialized loans for art, securities and real estate—and even private jets.

Beyond the range of capabilities that make these accounts so alluring are the intensely personal relationships that private banks develop with their clients. Northern Trust clients are assigned a "relationship manager" who quarterbacks a team of specialists. Together, they oversee a client's every need, from creating an investment and retirement strategy to establishing a trust and planning an estate. Do account executives ever walk their clients' dogs, as the cliché about the highly personalized service of private banking goes? "Let's just say that in an era of 1-800 banking, private banking still makes significant investments in being a high-touch business," says Philip A. Delaney, who heads the firm's private banking business.

Until the 1970s, private banking existed only in name in the U.S. In reality, banks were engaged largely in "private lending"—the business of making large loans to wealthy people. That's because Depression-era banking laws prohibited banks from managing their clients' investments, which was and still is the core of their European predecessors' business. However, with the deregulation of the banking and brokerage industries that began in 1975, banks have been increasingly involved in money management and other financial services.

Nowhere in the U.S. is that deregulation-spurred consolidation of businesses more visible than in the creation of CitiGroup in 1998, which combined the banking, securities and insurance businesses of Citibank, Salomon Smith Barney and Travelers, respectively. At the time of the merger an editorial in *The New York Times* wrote of financial Goliaths who can "touch any American who buys a house, saves for retirement, insures a car or uses a credit card." CitiGroup is the prototype for these one-stop financial supermarkets, luring clients who want the convenience of having all their financial services under one tent. And Citi's Private Bank unit was a prime beneficiary of the merger: it now oversees more than $100 billion in assets and predicts $1 trillion by 2010.

The ranks of the world's wealthy are swelling, thanks to soaring stock markets and vibrant economies around the world. High net-worth individuals—those who have investable assets of more than $1 million—boasted $17 trillion in cumulative wealth in 1997, and the figure is expected to reach almost $23 trillion by the end of the year 2000. More than $5 trillion of that current wealth is in the United States, which in 1998 boasted some 2.5 million households with $1 million or more in investable assets. Some experts claim that the ranks of the country's millionaires are growing 10 times as fast as the overall population.

Managing those vast sums is an incredibly complex task, which is why the world's wealthy are increasingly turning to private bankers. And banks, eager to add higher-margin, less-volatile businesses to their mix, are all too happy to lend a hand. Global private banking revenue now totals more than $100 billion a year, and according to a recent report from Merrill Lynch, pre-tax returns on equity are typically two to three times higher than they are on retail banking. U.S. Trust, one of the biggest and oldest private banking institutions in the U.S, saw fee revenue from its personal wealth management services business grow at a compound rate of 20 percent since 1996 to $256.4 million last year.

Private banks in the U.S. are usually divided into three categories. The first tier consists of the likes of J.P. Morgan, Bankers Trust, U.S. Trust and Bessemer Trust. The second tier includes firms like Northern Trust, Wells Fargo and Citibank. And the third tier is made up of so-called super-regional banks such as Bank One and Fleet.

Why does that matter to you? Such fat returns are drawing more and more competitors into the private banking arena, meaning more competition. In the U.S. alone, there are hundreds of institutions offering private banking services, from the 'big boys' like Bankers Trust, J.P. Morgan and Northern Trust, to newly-acquired firms like Safra, whose honorary chairman, the legendary Edward J. Safra, brought an unprecedented level of personal service to his super-affluent clientele.

Competition, both from other banks and brokers, investment houses and independent financial advisers, is forcing the key players in the industry to be more aggressive about luring clients and meeting their needs. In March 1999, for example, J.P. Morgan, the whitest of the "white shoe" U.S. banks, began its first-ever direct mail campaign, inviting potential clients for free consultations about the bank's "private client services." Noticeably absent from the ads were the bank's former appeals to individuals with $5 million in investable assets. "There is no minimum requirement," says Bridget Smith, a spokeswoman for the bank. "We're reaching out to new prospective clients."

Other banks and institutions also stress that there are no minimums *per se.* Northern Trust demands just $100,000 in investable assets for private bank accounts, while at Merrill Lynch $250,000 earns clients a "priority" status that gives them access to perks like lower lending rates. As Dan Rottenberg, a journalist at *Bloomberg Personal Finance,* put it recently: "legendary old-money wealth managers are now chasing new money, and have lowered their entrance requirements accordingly."

That's not the only good news for investors. Banks are more customer-oriented than ever, a response, in part, to the fact that private banking clients are more informed about the choices available to them. "A big shift away from old traditional family wealth/passive investors to new money/active investors is expected in all countries," said a survey this year from Pricewaterhouse Coopers. And there is a continuing shift away from lower-yielding fixed-income investments to the higher returns being posted by equities.

These changes have forced banks to respond in more sophisticated ways to the complex challenges their clients' enormous wealth poses. They can customize each clients' portfolio to take into account needs for growth, stability, diversification and tax efficiency. They make loans so that their clients can meet the high minimums required by hedge funds. They offer hedging and risk management tools such as futures and options to help protect investments and enable them to take advantage of certain market conditions. Merrill Lynch tells of structuring swaps and collars for executives who are paid disproportionately in stock or stock options, and thus need liquidity and hedging. And the banks do all of this with an eye toward minimizing their clients' tax hit.

Private banks are taking increasingly comprehensive approaches to serving their clients needs. But this sophistication doesn't end with the financial markets. It extends to every other fiscal realm, from insurance to advising on charitable giving. Citibank, for example, has a specific team that helps advise clients on art collecting. It boasts an in-house staff of art history professionals. It even allows art objects to be used as an asset to secure funds as collateral for other investments.

Banks provide assistance with valuing properties such as real estate, oil fields, and private businesses. They help raise money for starting or buying businesses, and they advise on private placements and divestitures. Many will even advise clients on creating their own bank, known as family offices, in order to better serve their needs. What's more, estate planning is being increasingly customized as baby boomers prepare for the largest intergenerational transfer of wealth in the history of the world (they stand to inherit almost $10 trillion within the next four decades).

Page 202: Bessemer Trust, New York City.
Photo: John Earle

Above: The New York Stock Exchange, where 200,000,000 shares are traded every day.
Photo: John Naughton

How much does all this know-how cost? Private banking clients usually pay an annual fee based on a percentage of their assets. That fee averages about 1.5 percent a year. But it varies from institution to institution and it tends to drop as the assets grow. At Northern Trust, for example, a client with $1 million or $2 million in investable assets would be charged roughly 1 percent. But the client would enjoy "substantial discounts" as the account's size increased from there. And Merrill Lynch lets customers shop á la carte, paying per service used.

Despite the increased competition within the industry, there are still operations whose services lag far behind those included in our directory listing of the best private banks in America. Many banks are still so new to the field of money management that they "don't have their act together," says John DeMarco of PSI Global, the Florida based consulting firm. After visiting institutions under the guise of a potential client, DeMarco found that many banks still weren't comfortable with their role as a money manager, even though many boasted performance records that rivaled their brokerage brethren.

"Some banks weren't nearly as smooth, confident or polished as their competitors," he says. "Brokerages would listen to my spiel about my investing, tax and estate needs and then tell me what they could do for me. The banks were more sales-oriented. They were trying to sell me things more than they were trying to figure out what my needs were. There's a lot of variance across the banks. Some are much better than others."

DeMarco recommends that potential customers pay more attention to the people they'll be dealing with than to the institution itself. "The old distinctions are rapidly breaking down, so shop for the people who will be serving you," he says. Two quick pointers he offers: steer clear of any banker who immediately makes sales pitches about specific products; and "no one's good at everything, so be wary if they tell you they are."

The role of private banks has changed enormously in the last few years, with a dazzling array of services to entice the burgeoning number of new millionaires. The pace of change within the financial world suggests that this is only the tip of the iceberg. Within the next few decades the business of wealth management looks set to change just as dramatically as it has done in the nineties. The watchword, as always, is caution. As even a banker will confirm, the safest way to double your money is to fold it over once and put it in your pocket. ⒶA

The ranks of the world's wealthy are swelling, thanks to soaring stock markets and vibrant economies. Individuals with investable assets of more than $1 million boasted $17 trillion in cumulative wealth in 1997, and the figure is expected to reach almost $23 trillion by the end of 2000.

BE YOUR OWN BANK

Some of the world's wealthiest individuals and families take private banking one step further: They become their own private bank by establishing a "family office"—essentially a self-contained private bank that deals just with your own finances. Bessemer Trust is the largest "family office" in the U.S. with $24 billion in assets. Henry Phipps, a partner of Andrew Carnegie in the Carnegie Steel Co., started the trust in 1907, when his wealth totaled about $50 million. Why? The same reason why some individuals and families do so today: to ensure that their financial affairs are given the utmost attention and care.

"The advantages of starting or having a family office is that you get a dedicated group of individuals focused exclusively on your family's financial affairs, so you get a higher level of attention and service," says Robert C. Elliott, senior executive vice president of Bessemer Trust, which is based in New York. Bessemer offers the same range and quality of services that the big-name banks do. Elliott says that today, a family office requires assets of $100 million or more to achieve what he calls "critical mass." Those who do and are interested can then work with consultants, such as Family Office Exchange in Chicago, Institute for Private Investors in New York, or even banks like U.S. Trust. They specialize in helping clients figure out the costs, regulatory requirements and staffing and equipment needs of setting up a family office.

A word of caution: "It's expensive if you're only dealing with one family," says Elliott at Bessemer, which itself began accepting "non-owner" clients in 1974. "I may be biased, but what somebody with $100 million or $50 million could do is go to a family office like ours and for much less money get similar service," he says. "Probably, the breadth of expertise is going to be even better because it's easier to attract and maintain high-quality people when you're larger."

The Maccioni Family Presents

Le Cirque 2000
455 Madison Avenue
New York, NY 10022
Tel 212 303 7788
Fax 212 303 7712

Le Cirque at Bellagio
3600 Las Vegas Boulevard South
Las Vegas, NV 89109
Tel 702 693 8100
Fax 702 693 8500

Osteria Del Circo
120 West 55th Street
New York, NY 10019
Tel 212 265 3636
Fax 212 265 9283

Osteria Del Circo
3600 Las Vegas Boulevard South
Las Vegas, NV 89109
Tel 702 693 8150
Fax 702 693 8500

THOSE AMAZING AMERICANS

*Style, energy, creativity and, above all else, a sense of the possible are what make
the United States such a powerful influence on the world today.
Here, Debra Scott and Kevin Kelly profile one hundred outstanding Americans.*

ALTSCHUL

Serena Altschul is a Christiane Amanpour for the twenty-something set: articulate, charming, tenacious and as stunning in the flesh as she is on screen. In her short career—first at Channel One News, and now at MTV—she has covered subjects as diverse as the Middle East peace treaty, heroin abuse among teenagers and the death of rap artist Notorious B.I.G.

A New Yorker, Altschul first hit the headlines with *The Last Party*, a documentary she co-produced about the 1992 Presidential Election that was shown in theatres nationwide. Interviewing key figures, from Oliver North to G. Gordon Liddy, Altschul succeeded in measuring the pulse of the nation at a time when many young people wondered whether it had any political life at all.

Nowadays she presents hourly news bulletins on MTV, but her principal focus is on producing documentaries on issues which directly concern her viewers, like hate crimes against gay people, homelessness and internet crime. Altschul is defiantly optimistic about the future of America, in stark contrast to many of her peer group. But her apparent idealism is tempered by a sharp tongue and a keen intelligence. Altschul looks set to become one of the more influential personalities in the American media.

ANGELOU

When Maya Angelou was a child in rural segregated Arkansas her grandmother regaled her with stories, the kind that teach life lessons, and the kind that the poet now imparts back to the world. "The honorary duty of a human being is to love," she says.

Last year the multitalented writer—besides poetry, she writes plays, songs, and prose—realized her dream of directing a feature film with the release of *Down in the Delta,* a Southern family saga starring Alfre Woodard, Al Freeman Jr., and Wesley Snipes. Viewed round the world when she read her poem *On the Pulse of Morning* at President Clinton's 1993 inauguration (the first poet to do so since Robert Frost 32 years earlier), the self-described "Southern black lady" had been known to her countrymen since 1970 with the publication of *I Know Why the Caged Bird Sings,* the first volume of her autobiography, in which she confessed a childhood rape and its ramifications. The book has been in print ever since. Angelou has received both Pulitzer and National Book Award nominations.

Her rich cultural background includes stints as a dancer, actress, editor and teacher. Active on the board of the American Film Institute, the scriptwriter-director-producer is one of the few female members of the Director's Guild. A former civil-rights activist, Angelou holds a lifetime chair at Wake Forest University in North Carolina, where she teaches philosophy, French and Spanish.

ASTOR

In 1783 John Jacob Astor came to the United States and promptly launched one of the most successful dynasties in the history of the modern world. Five generations later, Vincent Astor's wife, Brooke, began contributing the interest as well as some of the principal of the Astor fortune to New York's most important cultural institutions.

John Jacob might have frowned upon spending principal, but with this money, Brooke Astor has become one of Gotham's greatest benefactors. A trustee emeritus of the Metropolitan Museum of Art and the Pierpont Morgan library, and a supporter of innumerable good causes, she is most closely associated with the New York Public Library. Mrs Astor played a crucial role in helping that institution through the city's fiscal crisis in the 1970s and she has continued to support it with donations totaling $25 million. In 1997, for instance, the Vincent Astor Foundation, which she heads, committed $5 million to establish an endowment for the purchase of books. This gift alone resulted in the additional purchase of 140,000 new books.

In 1998 *The New York Times* reported that she has "been honored at or chairwoman of no fewer than 19 benefits this year." Put simply, Brooke Astor is the *grande dame* of New York Society—a remarkable philanthropist whose name alone is enough to lend dignity and value to even a weary endeavor. Her late husband used to say that among the reasons for the various Astors' success was that they always married above themselves. In his case he was not only doing himself a favor: Astor's marriage has benefited the entire population of the largest city in the United States.

AVEDON

In the summer of 1931, nine year old Richard Avedon spent a day at the beach with his father, receiving his first rudimentary lesson in the power of the sun to burn through a negative and make a positive image. It was a day that opened his eyes "to the wonder of photography." By 1945, after honing his craft in the Merchant Marines, the store owner's son convinced the powers that be at *Harpers Bazaar* to let him try his hand at fashion photography. During this early period, while shooting the work of couturiers like Chanel, he developed his signature stark black and white compositions with minimal backgrounds and a crisp texture that seemed to expose the soul of the subject. The 1957 movie *Funny Face* starring Fred Astaire as "Dick Avery" was based on his early career.

A chronicler of the late century's zeitgeist, the legendary lensman subsequently turned his photojournalistic talents to the American West with its rugged oil riggers and forlorn drifters, followed by political epiphanies from the civil rights movement and anti-war protests, through to the dissembling of the Berlin Wall. But Avedon's most memorable images are provocative portraits of international celebrities, from the Duke and Duchess of Windsor to Marilyn Monroe and Samuel Beckett.

Despite the documentary style, Avedon is not beneath artifice. He will flatter and cajole, take multiple shots, and crop and retouch until the final product meets his precise vision. He lives between New York and a cliff-side compound of cedar-shingled houses in Montauk—with his family, caretakers, four horses, four goats, chickens, and an 800-pound Duroc pig named Serena.

Photo: Steve Sands

BACALL

At the age of 20 Lauren Bacall played opposite Humphrey Bogart in *To Have and Have Not,* the film in which she uttered the line that only the whiskey-voiced screen goddess could have mouthed: "You know how to whistle, don't you? You just put your lips together—and blow." A year later, Bacall, the star of classics like *The Big Sleep* and *Key Largo,* married her leading man, the legendarily pugnacious 45-year-old Bogart, and relegated her career to a back burner. Shortly after Bogie died of cancer in 1957, the sultry siren became engaged to Frank Sinatra. The couple never tied the matrimonial knot, although she eventually married (and later divorced) actor Jason Robards, Jr.

Despite reaching a "certain age," Bacall has always refused to slow down. In the seventies she won Tony's for two Broadway musicals: *Applause* and *Woman of the Year.* The author of two autobiographies, the still eye-catching grande dame played Barbra Streisand's vainglorious mother in *The Mirror Has Two Faces,* a performance which garnered her a Golden Globe Award and an Oscar nomination. Although, in her own estimation she was never "thought of as much of an actress," this seasoned diva is every inch an American icon.

BALAZS

After a much publicized gestation of eight years, the sublimely laid-back Mercer Hotel finally opened its doors in SoHo in 1998. An instant hit, it has attracted a wide and unlikely array of bedfellows: Rupert Murdoch, Calvin Klein and a young man called Leonardo have all called the place home. And The Mercer Kitchen, with its stone floors, 12-seat communal tables and four-star executive chef Jean-Georges Vongerichten, is the most fashionable restaurant in a city which boasts many pretenders to that title.

The clientele of The Mercer at times seem to reflect the eclectic interests and career of its entrepreneurial owner, André Balazs. Born and raised in Cambridge, Massachusetts by Hungarian parents—his father, a scientist, his mother, a jazz pianist—Balazs published a newspaper before co-founding and running a biotechnology company called Biomatrix, Inc. It is now listed on the New York Stock Exchange.

His introduction to the hospitality business came via an investment in M.K., a Fifth Avenue night club which was hot, in his own words, "for four or five years during the late 1980s." Balazs raised eyebrows when he bought the notorious Chateau Marmont hotel in Hollywood, but he has upgraded and repositioned the hotel without sacrificing its fabled character. Earlier this year he launched The Standard in Hollywood, an inexpensive hip hotel, with plans to replicate it across the country. Don't be too surprised if he succeeds: his partners include Chase Manhattan and Leonardo DiCaprio. He also owns the Sunset Beach hotel on Shelter Island.

A trustee of the New York Academy of Art and the Boston Biomedical Research Institute, Balazs enjoys a reputation as an approachable and amiable figure. His extracurricular passion is skiing, both on water and snow. Balazs lives with his wife, Katie Ford, CEO of Ford Models, and their two daughters in SoHo and Shelter Island.

BERGEN While her first on-screen performance was in the 1966 motion picture *The Group,* actress Candice Bergen remembers playing the human counterpart to her father's ventriloquist dummy at a much earlier age. This former fashion model, who was brought up in Beverly Hills, was born into entertainment. As a photo journalist for over twenty-five years, however, she has had success in more than one professional field.

Life has not always been kind to Bergen. Her husband of fifteen years, the great French director Louis Malle, died of lymphoma in 1995, and after successful performances in films like *Starting Over* (1979), she experienced something of a career slump in the 1980s. The inveterate performer bounced back with an award-winning role in the long-running CBS sitcom *Murphy Brown,* which aired its final episode on May 18, 1998. But even in this celebrated role she was not without detractors; playing a seasoned journalist who becomes an unwed mother, Bergen crossed swords with Vice President Dan Quayle. We cannot help suspecting that history will be kinder to this intelligent and vivacious beauty.

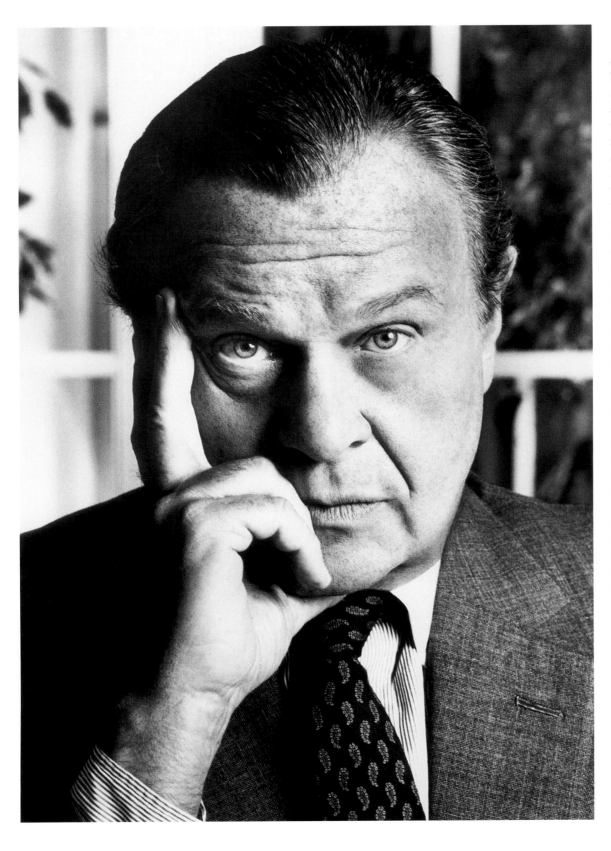

BLASS For half a century, Indiana-born couturier Bill Blass has helped define both fashion and style. One of the first American designers to have his name appear on a label—it is now licensed out to 56 licensees worldwide—his moniker is synonymous with upper crust taste and panache. In a recent stint as Guest Editor of *Civilization* magazine, he wrote that "style should not be confused with glamour, and certainly not with clothes. It's evident in the way one enters a room, in one's speech, in one's movements and one's standing still." But wearing his feminine and tailored daytime apparel or his glamorous evening wear, known for its exotic and spare elegance, can't hurt the society dames aspiring to achieve the style he so articulately characterizes. Among his many clients are Anna Wintour, Brooke Astor, Susan Soros, Katharine Graham and Nina Griscom. In 1997 he even created a gown especially for Barbie.

One of the founders of the influential Council of Fashion Designers of America (CFDA), the 77-year old Blass is a member of both its Executive Committee and Board of Directors. An active philanthropist, he has contributed much to AIDS care and was commemorated with the Bill Blass Public Reading Room at the New York Public Library after donating $10 million to the institution.

BOWES

In the Bay Area an invitation to one of John and Frances Bowes' soirées is as coveted as stock options in The Gap. In fact, John was an initial investor in the retail chain and served on its board for 25 years. He also founded Kransco, the largest privately owned toy company in the world.

Both San Francisco natives, the Bowes' are avid collectors of contemporary art and their party guest lists are filled with names from the international art community. Collecting mostly minimalist art from the sixties, the pair own works by artists like Brice Marden, Richard Serra, Robert Ryman, and Donald Judd. John sits on the international committee of London's Tate Gallery and for many years the couple were actively involved with San Francisco's Museum of Modern Art.

In keeping with their international lifestyle, the Bowes have several homes: a house in San Francisco (designed by the architect of the Golden Gate Bridge) with panoramic views of the bay; a retreat in Sonoma; an apartment on New York's Fifth Avenue; and a new home they're currently building in the heights of St. Bart's—all reachable in their own plane.

BRANT

52-year old Peter Brant, the owner and CEO of Brant-Allen Industries, a manufacturer of newsprint in Bear Island, Virginia, counts *The Wall Street Journal* and *The New York Times* among his biggest clients. As the co-owner of Brant Publications, he is the publisher of the magazines *Art in America* and *Interview*, which he originally established with Andy Warhol. A trustee of the Solomon R. Guggenheim Foundation, his contemporary art collection is regarded by many as one of the finest in America. Brant is also the highest ranked amateur polo player in the country. And he is married to Victoria's Secret model Stephanie Seymour.

However, the native New Yorker has not always had it so good. In 1990 he served an 84-day sentence for failing to keep proper records in relation to entertainment and travel expenses. Last year he told *Polo* magazine that "it was the end of the '80s, and I'm sure with everything everyone was doing they wanted to make an example of someone, which turned out to be me." Brant can afford to be philosophical about the experience. A stylish, well traveled and popular figure, he has bounced back with typical gusto. In recent years he has devoted considerable energies to the Brant Foundation. Based in Greenwich, Connecticut, its primary mission is to promote American art of the last half of the 20th century.

Left: Peter Brant with Stephanie Seymour.
Photo: Patrick McMullan

BRAVO

Two years ago, when Burberry, the upscale London haberdashers with annual sales of $425 million, came to the conclusion they needed a younger and cooler image, they chose to import a Stateside lifesaver. In a surprise coup, the venerable old firm seduced one of retail's brightest stars, Saks Fifth Avenue president Rose Marie Bravo, who was responsible for giving the upscale department store a hipper image.

As the CEO of Burberrys Worldwide, Bravo's daunting assignment was to create a new luxury market while maintaining a solidly British sensibility—akin to transforming the Queen into a Spice Girl. Approaching the task with her customary élan, Bravo streamlined the 150-year old company's logo, introduced a new high-end label called Burberry *Prorsum* (Latin for "future"), modified the famous plaid, and hired Mario Testino to compose ads that featured gabardine clad models straddling motor cycles.

Eighteen months after her appointment Bravo showed off the work of her import, Italian designer Roberto Menichetti (a former assistant to Jil Sander) who, in his first full collection for the company, garnered the cover of *Women's Wear Daily* where he was lauded for the "high note" he struck at the otherwise "dull" London shows. The sporty collection wowed fashion editors with its modern Italian lines, its unexpected layering and (gasp!) its garments of black. *Bravo, Bravo!*

BRENNAN GLUCKSMAN

Though Loretta Brennan Glucksman was raised by first generation Irish parents, it is ironic that the formidable philanthropist was introduced to the mystical terrain of her ancestral homeland by her Jewish husband, Wall Street whiz Lew Glucksman. The future English teacher learned prayers and poems in Irish from her paternal grandfather growing up in the blue-collar enclave of Allentown, Pennsylvania.

For years an award-winning television producer of news and public affairs, her passion for the country of her roots took hold in 1987 when her husband, an Irish scholar, took her to Ireland for the first time. Shortly thereafter the Glucksmans circled the area within an hour of Shannon airport to find a Hibernian retreat. In 1993 the Glucksmans donated Glucksman Ireland House, a cultural center, to New York University. Located in an atmospheric Greenwich Village mews house across the street from the Glucksman's own New York residence, the cottage feels so authentically Celtic, with its sculptures depicting Ireland's great writers, its paintings by Jack B. Yeats, and its steaming pots of Barry's Tea, that one of the university's Irish literature teachers insists on holding his classes there.

As president of the American Ireland Fund, a celebrated network of wealthy descendants raising funds to support programs of peace, culture and community development in Ireland, Glucksman has used her elegance and charm to raise millions of dollars from admirers such as Liam Neeson, Gregory Peck and Paul Newman. The Glucksmans have donated over $11 million to the American Ireland Fund.

BROWN

Among the 17th century settlers of New England was one Chad Brown, who made his way from Boston to Rhode Island in the late 1630s. Like other patrician families, the Browns found their niche in trade, railroads and banking. J. Carter Brown is one of several eminent Americans who claim descent from the bold Chad. Graduating first in his class from Groton at age 16, he was a leading member of the Harvard Glee Club, both as an undergraduate and during his two years in the business school there. Brown left his doctoral program at New York University's Institute of Fine Arts to become John Walker's assistant at the National Gallery of Art in 1961. When Walker retired in 1969, Brown took over as Director of the Capitol Museum at the age of 34.

At the National Gallery, Brown served as a magnet for talent, and worked prodigiously to build up the museum's collection of drawings and 20th century art. During his tenure, the Gallery constructed its East Building, designed by I.M. Pei. Brown also expanded the special exhibitions program, and his "African Sculpture" show was a hallmark of the adventurous direction that museums were moving in the late 1960s and early 1970s. Brown's last major show was "Circa 1492," a monumental tribute to the 500th anniversary of Columbus' discovery of America. When he abruptly resigned in 1992 a report in *The International Herald Tribune* concluded that "the quiet gallery he took over has become a strutting giant on the international stage...he has closed a chapter in the evolution not only of his own institution but of all American museums."

This unflappable and hugely energetic sexagenarian, whom *The New York Times* describes as a "Washington Institution," chairs the Leadership Council and the jury of the Pritzker Prize in Architecture. Among many other interests, he is Chairman of the U.S. Commission of Fine Arts, a Fellow of the American Academy of Arts and Sciences, and a key investor in Ovation, a television arts network.

BROWN

Passions run high in San Francisco, where the residents have a suitably enthusiastic mayor. Regarded as a brilliant politician by friends and enemies alike, Willie Brown certainly knows how to wield his power; if you want to run for office in San Francisco, you had better talk to the mayor first.

Brown's famous charisma, which explains much of his enduring popularity, is countered by a Quaylian tendency to open his mouth a bit too soon; like the impulsive campaign pledge to fix San Francisco's ailing bus system in the first hundred days of his mayoralty. However, with city coffers benefiting from the current economic boom, Brown has been able to promise more money for several key program areas, including police, parks, public transportation and the public health system.

Born in Texas, Brown spent much of his early life in Sacramento as the longest serving Speaker of the State Assembly in the history of California. In a state where anti-immigrant sentiment runs high, Speaker Brown was a staunch advocate of immigrants' rights, affirmative action and gay rights. As mayor of San Francisco, a city suffering from a long-standing housing shortage, he has supported tight landlord controls and has been very supportive of tenants' rights. Willie Brown, who has been married since 1958, is passionate about cars, clothes and football.

BUSH George W. Bush, 53, son of former President George Herbert Walker Bush, wants America to be prosperous in the 21st century "so people can realize their entrepreneurial dreams." To achieve that, the 46th Governor of the State of Texas (now in his second term), would like to get a promotion–to President of the United States. And the native Texan just might. At press time, the "compassionate conservative" is the current front-runner for the Republican Presidential nomination in 2000. With his war chest and family connections, the sky's the limit for his political aspirations. Having enacted the largest tax cut in Texas history, a $1 billion school property tax cut, Bush's primary goal is to overhaul the sluggish state educational system, making it his priority that every child learn to read by the third grade.

A Yale graduate like his father, the F-102 pilot got his MBA from Harvard before founding an oil and gas exploration company. After helping his father win the Presidency in 1988, he served as managing general partner of the Texas Rangers. Committed to strong families and an active member of the Methodist Church, Bush lives with his wife, Laura, a former teacher and librarian, in the historic Governor's Mansion in Austin with their teenage twin daughters, Barbara and Jenna; their dog, Spot; and their three cats, India, Cowboy and Ernie.

CHILDS Back in 1961, as America nibbled happily away on Fluffernutter sandwiches (peanut butter and Marshmallow Fluff) and tuna casseroles (don't ask), a fifty year old former OSS operative published her first cook book and was launched as the country's gastronomic grande dame. With publication of *Mastering the Art of French Cooking*, the artistry of "foreign foods" like soufflés became available to every dinette set-owning housewife across the land. Since then, in her mission to democratize haute cuisine, the familiar 6'2" figure with her high-pitched schoolmarms' voice has hosted a series of television cooking shows, penned nine cook books, and tested thousands of recipes.

Now nearly 90, the nation's unofficial ambassador of good dining spends two to three days writing a recipe because, as she says, "Any book that I do is only as good as its worst recipe." Still answering all the mail she receives at her Cambridge home, Childs thrives on a very simple diet: toast and coffee (Gevalia) for breakfast and a piece of cold roast chicken with commercial mayonnaise and white bread for lunch. America's first lady of cuisine, who says she "won't touch trendy food" and "doesn't like low fat or low-cholesterol stuff," eats dinner while watching her favorite TV shows. Julia Childs co-founded The American Institute of Wine and Food.

COPPOLA One of the most dynamic and accomplished filmmakers in the world, Francis Ford Coppola has ridden personal highs and lows as radical as those in his widely acclaimed films. Surviving a childhood bout of polio (during which he amused himself by making an 8mm film), he went on to win six Oscars by the time he was 36. But in 1983, after struggles with the Hollywood studio system, the bearded and bespectacled auteur was forced to sell his beloved American Zoetrope Studio which he had founded in 1969 with the backing of Warner Brothers. Despite predictions to the contrary, that was the not the end of the maverick's directorial career. His subsequent commercial successes include *Peggy Sue Got Married, Bram Stoker's Dracula* and, more recently, *The Rainmaker,* based on the novel by John Grisham.

After a stint as an apprentice to low-budget cult director Roger Corman, Coppola won his first Oscar for his screenplay of *Patton*. His stature rose a year later with the release of *The Godfather*. One of the highest-grossing movies in history, it garnered an Oscar for Best Picture and a Best Director nomination. Coppola took home a statue for best screenplay adapation which he shared with novelist Mario Puzo. A sequel, *The Godfather II,* is one of the best American films ever made.

In the late seventies, Coppola invested $16 million of his own money to make the overblown, pretentious but occasionally brilliant epic, *Apocalypse Now,* based on Joseph Conrad's *Heart of Darkness*. Plagued by illnesses, typhoons, and the near destruction of his marriage, it remains one of the most controversial films of all time. Though many of his later films have not fulfilled his early promise, Coppola has certainly managed to introduce a multitude of talents to the silver screen: Matt Dillon, Tom Cruise, Patrick Swayze, Rob Lowe, Emilio Estevez, and his own nephew, Nicolas Cage. When not making films, the opera-lover runs a magazine, a restaurant, a mountain resort in Belize, and the largest contiguous vineyard in America.

COX CHAMBERS With a combined net worth of more than $10 billion (and rising) Anne Cox Chambers and her younger sister Barbara Cox Anthony are America's richest women. Heirs to the fortune accrued by their media tycoon father, James M. Cox–a former three-term Ohio governor and 1920 Democratic nominee for President whose running mate was Franklin Roosevelt–the two were ranked No. 19 on *Forbes* magazine's most recent list of America's 400 richest people.

Principal owners of both the Atlanta-based Cox Enterprises (the 12th largest media conglomerate in the U.S. with 18 daily newspapers, seven weekly papers, $3 billion in annual revenues, and 37,000 employees) and Cox Communications (the third largest cable provider in the country, with 40 cable TV systems and 3.1 million subscribers), the sisters also own six TV stations, 14 radio stations, and the world's largest auto auction company. In a $1.2 billion deal in the mid-80s, the sisters returned the company, which had begun publicly trading on the New York Stock Exchange in the mid-60s, to its private status.

Chambers' generous donations to fellow Georgian Jimmy Carter helped land him in the White House. In 1977, President Carter appointed her ambassador to Belgium. The twice-divorced octogenarian flits around the globe on a Gulfstream IV, alternating between an Atlanta estate, a 17th century farmhouse in Provence, a duplex on Sutton Place, and her 12,000 acre plantation in South Carolina.

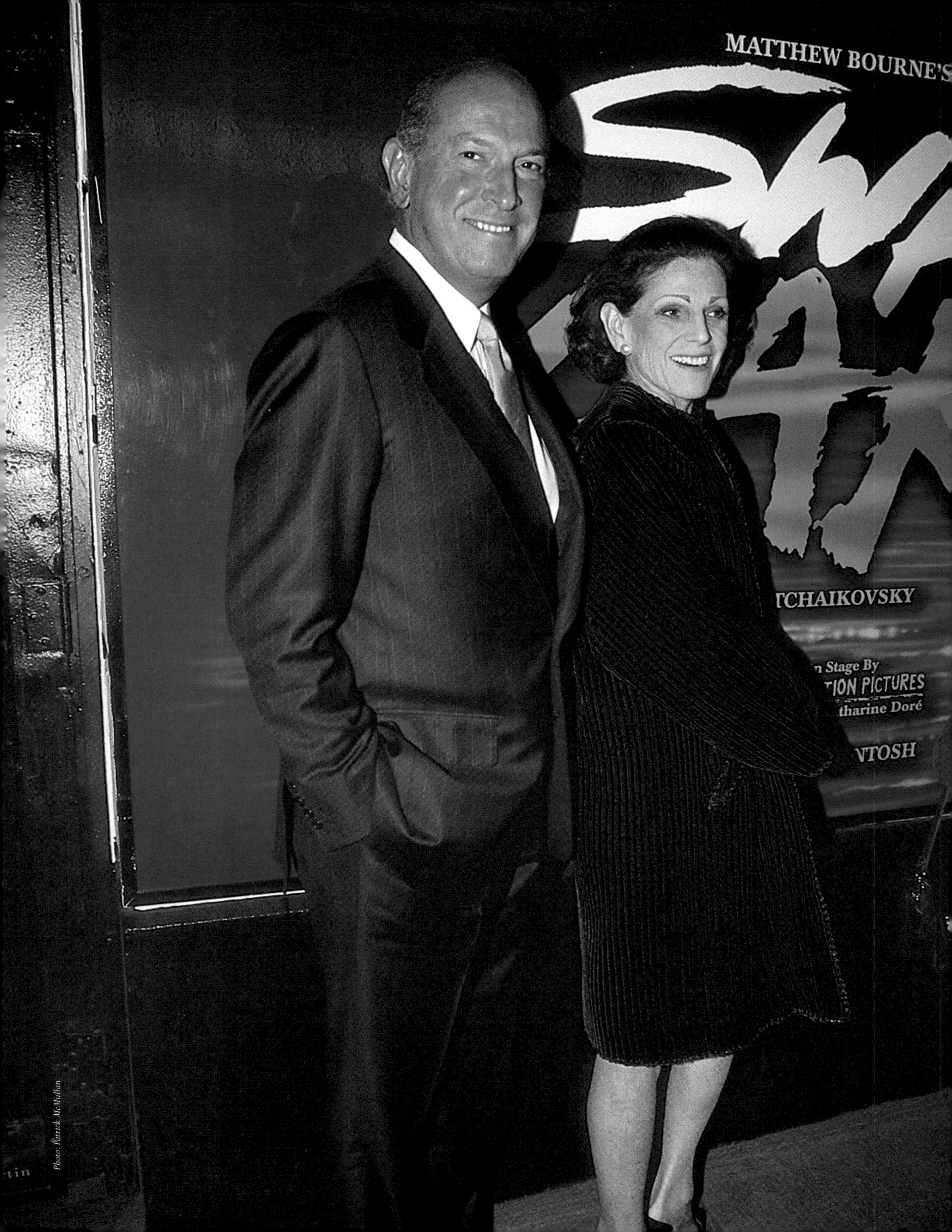

Photo: Patrick McMullan

de la RENTA

Couturier Oscar de la Renta, who designed for Balenciaga, Lanvin and Elizabeth Arden before establishing his own label in the sixties, has dressed the likes of Princess Diana, Nancy Reagan and Hillary Clinton in his elegantly understated frocks. De la Renta, who reads poets Robert Browning and Emily Dickinson, is highly active in the affairs of his homeland, the Dominican Republic, where he keeps an estate in Punta Cana, a fishing village which he and an investment group, including his pal Julio Iglesias, plan to develop into the "greatest destination in the Caribbean."

His wife, Annette, heiress to the Engelhard metals fortune, is known for her outspoken wit and seemingly contradictory shyness. A passionate gardener who reigns over an abundant horticultural Eden at the couple's Connecticut home, Brook Hill Farm, the head of the Engelhard Foundation also raises ornamental poultry.

One of New York society's more ubiquitous couples, the de la Rentas count among their friends notables like Philip Johnson, Barbara Walters, and the two Henrys and their wives—Kissinger and Kravis. Mrs. de la Renta recently co-chaired the prestigious Costume Institute benefit gala with Clarissa Bronfman and *Vogue* editor Anna Wintour. "She's already the next Brooke Astor," columnist Liz Smith recently told *New York* magazine.

de MONTEBELLO

The Metropolitan Museum of Art's director for the past 21 years is an avowed elitist who, ironically, has managed to raise the institution's attendance to more than five million visitors per year. De Montebello, who traces his lineage back to one of Napoleon's marshals and the Marquis de Sade, was promoted to CEO last spring after sharing the operational duties in an odd two-head system that had been instituted after predecessor Thomas Hoving's much maligned tenure. Celebrated for maintaining the integrity of the permanent collections while affixing such additions as the Milton Petrie Sculpture Court and the Lila Acheson Wallace Wing, the French-born American citizen has steered the Metropolitan to its status as the world's most comprehensive museum. De Montebello has said that its 17 curatorial departments cover "every category of art in every known medium from every part of the world during every epoch of recorded time."

The magisterial voice behind the Acoustiguide tours, this sartorially splendid blue blood, who spoke little English when he emigrated Stateside from France at age 14, is a dapper figure at museum soirées, although de Montebello is vociferous about his disdain for black tie events, which he equates with an eternity spent in hell. A grandfather, de Montebello lives with his wife Edith, a financial aid officer at leading prep school Trinity, whom he met in a poetry course while they both were at Harvard.

DELL

By his last year in high school, Michael S. Dell had sold enough papers to pay cash for a BMW. At the University of Texas, in Austin, he began selling IBM PCs from his dorm, hiding them in a bathtub when his family came to visit. By 1984, this dorm-room business became Dell Computer Corporation. With the brilliant and unprecedented idea of selling computers directly to users, he set new standards in the PC industry. By 1986, Dell had 250 employees. Today his company is one of the top vendors of personal computers worldwide, employing more than 26,000 people and serving customers in more than 170 countries. In the 15 years since its inception, company sales have grown from $6 million to $19.9 billion, with most *Fortune 500* companies among its clients.

Nowadays Dell is redefining the role of the world wide web in delivering faster, better and more convenient service to customers. His company sells about $18 million worth of computers online every day. Dell has been honored many times for his visionary leadership, earning titles like "Entrepreneur of the Year" from *Inc.* magazine, "Man of the Year" by *PC Magazine,* "CEO of the Year" by *Finance World* and *Industry Week* magazines. In 1997, 1998 and 1999, he was included in *Business Week's* list of the top 25 Managers of the Year. At 34-years old, Michael Dell is one of the richest people in the world.

DOWD

Although *New York Times* columnist Maureen Dowd defies political categorization, she is anything but neutral. The scathing wit for which she is both revered and feared is an equal-party annihilator. The woman who James Carville described as a "professional wiseass" (in *Brill's Content*) has called Bill Clinton a "letter-sweater smoothie," while branding right wing Pat Buchanan the "class bully." Her provocative and highly entertaining bi-weekly (Wednesdays and Sundays) column has given the "Gray Lady" a healthy dollop of razzle dazzle. Aside from her amusing attacks on politicians and matters of serious national concern, the 47-year old equally skewers pop culture, from television's "screwball litigator" *Ally McBeal* to that "emporium of hip couture, Barney's."

Starting her journalistic career in 1974 with *The Washington Star,* Dowd rose through the ranks to become a sports columnist, metropolitan reporter and feature writer. After a stint at *Time,* she joined *The New York Times* as a metropolitan reporter in 1983. From 1986 until her appointment to Op-Ed page columnist in 1995, she served as a correspondent in the broadsheet's Washington bureau, gaining a reputation for her barbed and uncompromising commentary on the capitol's nabobs.

It is telling that the journalist whose pen is truly mightier than many a sword, does not grant interviews of herself. Celebrated for her "novelist's eye" and attention to personal detail, Dowd won a (long overdue) Pulitzer Prize last year. The Irish-American, Washington, D.C. native still lives in the city of her birth.

DUCHIN

In an era when dance bands have gone the way of the foxtrot, Peter Duchin—society's favorite band leader—heads an orchestra that plays for inaugural balls, debutante dances, charity balls, state dinners, museum openings and movie premieres. Much of the music, of course, is the big band swing and standards of yore, hearkening back to an era of tinkling highball glasses and cotillions, the era in fact when the dashing pianist's parents met.

Duchin's mother, who hailed from a socially prominent Newport and New York family, was struck off the social register in 1935 when she married band leader Eddie "The Magic Fingers of Radio" Duchin, who was so famous Cole Porter wrote "Night and Day" for him to play. The feisty Mrs. Duchin responded, "Who cares? It's only a phone book." She passed away six days after giving birth to Peter. Her friends, Marie and Averill Harriman, took little Peter, who'd been born with a collapsed lung and was expected to perish, home with them to die. To escape his grief, Eddie took his band off to Rio from where they exported the Samba back stateside. But Duchin prospered in the Harriman's palatial residence. The story of his early years is depicted in the Hollywood heartbreaker *The Eddie Duchin Story* and in his own memoir, *Ghost of a Chance,* published in 1996.

In his twenties, the privileged son slid effortlessly into his father's shoes. Duchin, by the way, doesn't always play old fogey standards. The recording artist, who has produced 26 albums, has kept up with the times and is the first to incorporate a new Eric Clapton or Bruce Spingsteen number into his routine. Duchin is married to the writer Brooke Hayward, daughter of Hollywood agent Leland Hayward and movie star Margaret. They live between Washington, Connecticut and Manhattan.

DUNNE

After a career producing films like *Panic in Needle Park* and *Play It As it Lays,* Dominick Dunne reinvented himself in his fifties by chronicling the antics of his privileged social peers in best-selling *romans a clef,* many of which have been made into television mini-series. His *Two Mrs. Grenvilles,* for example, was based on the 1950s' society scandal in which Ann Woodward was accused of killing her socially prominent husband.

Dunne's journalism–he is a contributing editor for *Vanity Fair*–has followed the sensational trials of the present day. After the murder trial of the abusive boyfriend accused of strangling his daughter, actress Dominique Dunne, he went on to cover the trials of Claus von Bulow, the Menendez Brothers, and O.J. Simpson. Dunne's Hollywood connections and publishing stature have also won him audiences with elusive Hollywood legends like Ava Gardner. Elizabeth Taylor granted him an interview after she was released from the Betty Ford clinic because Dunne, a self-confessed former hard-drinker and cocaine abuser, shared her experience of drying out: he famously spent six months in an Oregon cabin going cold turkey and writing a novel.

A former friend of Truman Capote, Dunne is welcome at A-list parties from New York to Tinseltown. During the Simpson trial, when Dunne, wearing his signature horn-rim glasses, was viewed daily by the world as he scribbled notes in Judge Ito's courtroom, he performed his "O.J. Simpson floor show" for the likes of Nancy Reagan, Elizabeth Taylor, the late Princess of Wales, and Princess Margaret, who pronounced, much to his dismay, that the trial was "a bore." That could certainly not be said for Dunne's recounting of it. And his coverage of President Clinton's impeachment hearings was equally impressive. Dunne's son, Griffin, has taken over where his father left off–as an actor and film producer.

EASTON

Don't ask David Easton to decorate your home in blue–it is the architect, interior designer, landscaper and furniture maker's least favorite color. And please don't utter the dreaded phrase "postmodernism." Though he will adapt to most styles, he would never "stick a classic pediment" on top of a "modern box." Easton is renowned for recreating the sumptuous gentility of English country houses, although the former Parish-Hadley assistant claims that his style is quintessentially American. Ideally involved in every aspect of a house's design, from choosing the land to the bed linen, he has built or renovated such diverse properties as a farm compound in Maryland, a pool pavilion in Virginia and a ski lodge in Colorado. But his true calling is the stately home. It was Easton who built John Kluge's house, chapel, and other outbuildings on a 12,000 acre Virginia estate from its humble beginnings as a sketch on the back of a napkin.

The "gentleman decorator" believes in "living with a client" so that he can assess their needs for both comfort and style. The approach of this latter day Stanford White is not about imposing his ego, but rather, "to integrate the triumvirate of landscape, architecture and decor." His client list reads like a who's who of the plutocracy: the Martin Rayners, William Crockers, Henry Ford IIs and Richard Swigs among others. A decorators' decorator, his name appears regularly in the 'top ten' interior designer lists of shelter magazines. The two time recipient of the Arthur Ross Award for architectural design and the Hall of Fame Design Award, he lives between a Manhattan apartment and an enchanting cottage in New York State.

ERTEGUN

Mica Ertegun is the wife of Ahmet Ertegun, the legendary founder of Atlantic Records, who reputedly wooed her by hiring a five-piece band to emerge from a box playing "Puttin' on the Ritz" at the Ritz-Carlton. Ertegun is the man who signed, among many others, Aretha Franklin and Whitney Houston to his record label.

In 1967 Mica Ertegun established the interior design firm MAC II with her friend, the late Chessy Raynor. Romanian-born Ertegun continues to create homes for clients who appreciate uncluttered interiors. The best example of her style is probably her own elegant summer home on Shinnecock Bay, where the super-social designer has created a veritable dacha, with an element of Mount Vernon thrown into the mix. Striving "to achieve a sense of serenity" in her rooms, Ertegun is said to loathe "overdone" furnishings or "extravagant" trimmings. The keynotes of her spaces are comfort, understatement, refinement. But they brim with personality and often offer an original surprise.

Currently on the board of The World Monuments Fund, Ertegun has served on the boards of the New York City Ballet and the Archives of American Art. An immensely civilized and very stylish figure, she is often described as one of New York's best hostesses.

FAIRCHILD

Consummate journalist, formidable businessman, terrifying editor. When John Fairchild ruled his fashion publication empire no one—neither his reporters, nor the society dames he celebrated and denigrated, nor the couturiers he helped launch to super stardom—dared incur his wrath. Before retiring as publisher of *Women's Wear Daily* and *W* in 1997, "Mr. Fairchild" was a force to be reckoned with on both sides of the Atlantic.

In the 1950s, despite early ambitions to be a doctor, Fairchild assumed control of *WWD*, one of the papers in the stable of rag-trade organs his grandfather had founded at the turn of the century. With a formula of hard hitting journalism coupled with a nose for gossip and a propensity for star-making, he turned the ingloricus trade journal into a glamorous, tell-all must-read. Cozying up to Coco Chanel and the like, he managed to scoop such venerable papers as *The New York Times* on fashion stories. His editorial mantra always remained: "Get the story first!" And the story to him was less about hemlines than the personalities behind them: a new chef at Le Cirque was as important as a changing of the guard at Sak's; getting Jeane Kirkpatrick's recipe for salad dressing was an urgent assignment. He once ordered a reporter to run through the lavender fields in the Abbey of Senanque and write about it.

A dapper Yankee fond of Lobb shoes, Fairchild made news as much as broke it when he coined such terms as "Jackie O", "hot pants" and "fashion victim" in his pages. A family-oriented grandfather, Fairchild now lives in London with his wife.

Left: "Portrait of the Artist", Eric Fischl 1998; Oil/Linen.

Right: "April Changing", Eric Fischl 1993; Oil/Linen.

FISCHL

Eric Fischl and April Gornik are leading lights of the contemporary American art world. Their paintings—his are provocative, often sexually charged narratives of suburbia gone awry, hers are serene, enigmatic landscapes—are in the permanent collections of such institutions as the Museum of Modern Art and the Whitney Museum of American Art.

Now represented by the prestigious Mary Boone Gallery, Fischl made his mark in the early 1980s with the psychologically confessional "The Bad Boy," a provocative rendering of a little boy watching a woman in erotic repose (based on childhood memories of being raised in an alcoholic household). A realist sometimes compared to Sargent and Hopper, the boyishly handsome artist has been described by *Time* art critic Robert Hughes as "the painter laureate of American anxiety in the eighties." Another critic, Mario Naves of *The New York Observer,* was a little less ambiguous when he concluded "that a painter, and a figurative one at that, should be so lacking in the fundamentals of art makes Mr. Fischl one of the more prominent casualties of our conceptualist age."

Fischl, whose works are owned privately by collectors such as Condé Nast's S.I. Newhouse, is such a tennis fiend that he has traded drawing lessons for coaching with John McEnroe. Meanwhile, Gornik's easy-on-the-eye, large format paintings reflect her own taste in art—that which is emotionally moving, intuitive and "vulnerable to interpretation." The couple live between New York and the Hamptons.

FLAHERTY

The glass ceiling is no obstacle for Tina Santi Flaherty. From the 1960s through the 1980s she rose to the top of three major U.S. corporations: Grey Advertising, Colgate-Palmolive and GTE. Nowadays she is president and CEO of Image Marketing International, which trains high-level executives and political candidates in effective speaking. As an author she has published *The Savvy Woman's Success Bible*, which was named one of the top five motivational books, and *Talk Your Way to the Top*. This former television journalist, who arrived in New York with a hundred dollars to her name, certainly managed to do that.

In her latest tome Flaherty argues that a woman's personal image is as important as business acumen in the corporate world. She ought to know. Early in her career she found she wasn't getting invited into the boardroom because she dressed "like a Russian folk dancer." Named "one of the country's top corporate women" by *Business Week*, she is featured in the book *Powerchicks: How Women Will Dominate America*. She married William Flaherty, president and CEO of Horsehead Industries, a leading world producer of zinc, 23 years ago. The couple live with their three dogs in New York City (above the old Jackie Onassis apartment), and commute by private jet between homes in the Hamptons, Palm Beach and Pebble Beach.

FORBES

When billionaire Malcolm Forbes died, his four sons inherited the patriarch's vast fortune, including a string of domiciles scattered far and wide by the extravagant publisher: the Palais Mandoub in Tangier, the Chateau de Balleroy in Normandy, a ranch in Colorado, a castle in the Scottish highlands, and an English home where Christopher "Kip" Forbes and his family oversee an incredible collection of Victoriana.

While still in school, the young aesthete informed his father that hundreds of Victorian paintings could be purchased for the price of one Impressionist, such as the Monet that hung in the progenitor's office. As an author, Forbes has published numerous tomes including *Victorians in Togas* and *Fabergé Eggs* (with Armand Hammer) now in its fourteenth printing. Incidentally, the Fifth Avenue headquarters of *Forbes* houses 12 Fabergé eggs, one more than the Kremlin.

Forbes, who is Vice Chairman of Forbes, Inc., sits on the boards of The New York Historical Society, The Business Committee for the Arts, and The Victorian Society in America. His club memberships include the Grolier, Knickerbocker and National Arts Clubs in New York. Kip Forbes lives with his wife and their daughter in New Jersey.

FRAWLEY BAGLEY

From 1994 to 1997 Elizabeth Frawley Bagley served as the United States Ambassador to Portugal, the first woman to hold that post. Not bad for the former French and Spanish major who was 41 when she entered the post. Bagley has always been busy: as a student in France, Spain, and Austria, she studied international trade law and public international law. At the Department of State during the Carter Administration, she acted as congressional liaison for the Panama Canal treaty, and as special assistant to Ambassador Sol Linowitz during the Camp David Accords' negotiations over Palestinian autonomy.

The smooth talking and amiable diplomat continues to wield considerable clout at the State Department, where she is a senior advisor to the Secretary of State. She oversees the media programming acquisition project for Serbia. And, as an Irish citizen, she has long been active in promoting the cause of peace in Northern Ireland. Indeed, it is often predicted that she will one day serve as Ambassador to Ireland.

A mother of two young children, her husband, Smith Bagley, is heir to a tobacco fortune and a heavy-hitting fundraiser for Democratic Presidential and Senatorial campaigns. In the tradition of the fabulous Fourth of July party for 2000-plus guests they hosted at the American embassy in Portugal, the Bagley's Georgetown home is the venue for many of Washington's more memorable parties. In her spare time, Ambassador Bagley loves skiing and swimming, and has "seen every Broadway play that there ever was."

FORD There was a time, not so long ago, when the 'G' in Gucci signified gaudy. Its over-licensed initials appeared on everything from coffee mugs to fake versions of its handbags. Enter Tom Ford, the Texan designer who was appointed the company's creative director in 1994 at the age of 34. Ford put the famous GGs out to pasture, and revitalized the ailing fashion house by introducing seductive finery like backless shoes, velvet hip-huggers and satin shirts.

His audaciously sexy duds brought in customers like Madonna, Gwyneth Paltrow and Helen Hunt, who wore her Gucci frock to the Oscars. But Ford, who has homes in Paris, Santa Fe, London and Bel-Air, clearly refuses to stand still. Veering away from his winning sleek look, last spring he introduced more romantic Gucci menswear: pink shirts, hip-hop drop-crotch pants as well as a sequined khaki shirt.

When we told people that we were compiling a list of the most stylish and creative Americans, Ford's name was mentioned with most frequency. The man who recently announced that fur, smoking and gold Rolexes are "what's now" as opposed to "what's over" is, it seems, the epitome of good taste in America today.

von FURSTENBERG

In 1976 Diane von Furstenberg triumphed over President Gerald Ford to land the cover of *Newsweek*. At the age of 29, the socialite who designed the wrap dress was, after all, "the most marketable female in fashion since Coco Chanel."

A fashion icon, the body-hugging knit dress, whose dozen prototypes the Studio 54 habitué manufactured at a cost of $1000, in some prophetic way seemed to point to her future "pack and go" life. The leonine seductress has had almost as many lovers (Richard Gere, Ryan O'Neal, and of course, her husband Egon von Furstenberg "who gave me the children and the name") as careers: designer (first time around), cosmetics queen, author, designer (second time around).

A couple of years ago, after a "Bohemia Luxuria" period in Bali and an intellectual residence in Paris, the doyenne of self-reinvention cashed in on the 70s revival by relaunching the wrap dress. On a recent outing on the Home Shopping Network, she sold over a million dollars worth of clothes in three hours. With her daughter-in-law Alexandra (née Miller) in tow, and a new label, Diane by Diane von Furstenberg, she introduced her latest line on the internet. But it is not as a businesswoman that the native Belgian is most remembered. She is an icon of her generation: entrepreneurial, social, glamorous, Diane von Furstenberg was with the right people (Marisa Berenson, Barry Diller) and in the right places (at the signing of the Camp David peace accord) in a decade when pedigree still meant something.

GANZ COONEY

The lively and vociferous Muppets, who have now entertained and educated kids in more than 140 countries for more than 30 years, may be the brain children of late Muppet creator Jim Henson, but they wouldn't be a fixture in the collective unconscious if it weren't for Joan Ganz Cooney, the creator of *Sesame Street*. Figuring that children respond to plenty of action, music, and cartoons, in 1968 she sought private and public funding for a show that would employ these ingredients to teach. At the time, the idea of educational TV was a stretch. Two generations and 71 Emmy Awards later, 14 million preschoolers tune into television's most celebrated neighborhood to laugh at a math-loving vampire and learn Spanish from Rosita. Guest stars have included Ray Charles (singing *It's Not Easy Being Green* with Kermit), the rock group REM and Rosie O'Donnell.

Along with her colleagues, Cooney created several other educational programs for public television, including *The Electric Company* and *3-2-1 Contact*. Still active in children's programming, Cooney has recently launched Noggin, a .24-hour cable children's channel with educational programming, in collaboration with Nickelodeon. The "lady from *Sesame Street*" came up with the idea while watching the paltry offerings on TV with her granddaughter. Aside from leaving the Big Bird legacy, Cooney, who is married to Chairman of The Blackstone Group and former U.S. Secretary of Commerce, Peter Peterson, is a trustee of both the National Child Labor Committee and the Museum of Television and Radio. She was recently awarded the nation's highest civilian honor, the Presidential Medal of Freedom. "I wish I could tell you that the Children's Television Workshop and *Sesame Street* were thanks to my genius," she has said with typical modesty, "but it really was a lucky break."

GEHRY

Finally recognized as one of the century's major architects, Frank Gehry has built his *piece de résistance*–the Guggenheim Museum in Bilbao, Spain, an architectural Mecca that draws lowbrows and highbrows to bear witness to Getty's newfangled cathedral. The building is such a profound triumph that the sight of it reduced Gehry's friend and mentor Philip Johnson to tears.

After a career spent struggling to freely express his idiosyncratic vision, America's most visible architect is currently the recipient of numerous commissions including a vaporetto terminal in Venice, a wing for the Corcoran Gallery of Art in Washington D.C., a bank in Berlin, and the Walt Disney Concert Hall in his hometown of Los Angeles. He was recently awarded the American Institute of Architects Gold Medal.

Gehry, now 70, shaped his unconventional sensibility through his friendships with such quintessentially L.A. artists as Ed Moses. The first project to bring him wide recognition, both positive and negative, was the conversion of his own house, a suburban "Cape Cod" style bungalow in Santa Monica, which he wrapped with chain link, corrugated metal and glass. Progressing from its boxy and raw beginnings, his architectural vernacular has morphed into more fluid and sculptural lines. Despite occasional complaints that his work is unappreciated in Los Angeles, Gehry continues to work from his Santa Monica office.

GILBERTSON

Mark Forrest Gilbertson occupies a unique position in New York society. The boyish 40-something from Rumson and Palm Beach acts as a consultant for high profile charities and luxury goods companies (like Asprey and Garrard and Lilly Pulitzer), discreetly ensuring that their civic liaisons are mutually beneficial. Gilbertson also raises funds for many philanthropic endeavors, though he is probably best known as the founding Chairman of the Director's Council of the Museum of the City of New York. He has been credited with enhancing the image of this once sedate institution, and, in the process he has helped to raise several million dollars.

In private Gilbertson is "just another guy," as he puts it himself, but the truth is somewhat different. A key player in the social whirligig of uptown Manhattan, this archetypal WASP knows just about everyone who is anyone in the city's top ranks, and he is not afraid to involve them in a bewildering array of good causes. A recent profile in *The New York Times* winningly described him as "the Pied Piper of New York's blueblood families and many of their not-so-blueblood friends. Anyone between 20 and 45 with an active social life in the Anglo-Saxon bastion of the Upper East Side has probably been introduced to Mr. Gilbertson."

In the same article David Patrick Columbia, the editor of *Avenue* magazine, called him a "social impresario," and in some respects this is the most appropriate moniker for a man who has seemlessly blended his private and professional lives. In person—at, say, Doubles or La Goulue, two of his favorite stomping grounds—he seems like a welcome relic from a former age, in which charm and etiquette were indispensable rather than merely cute. But Gilbertson can also be refreshingly wicked to those who assume, as arrivistes often do, that old money means old fogey. You have been warned.

GRAHAM

A debutante who attended finishing school before pursuing a more serious education at Vassar College and the University of Chicago, Katharine Graham grew up to run *The Washington Post,* the most powerful newspaper in the nation's capital. Bought for a song at a 1933 bankruptcy sale by her father, Eugene Meyer, the paper was published by Graham's husband, Washington attorney Philip L. Graham, until he committed suicide in 1963. Graham's definition of journalism as a "first draft of history" is still quoted.

Despite the fact that women were still "second class citizens," it was time, as she wrote in her Pulitzer Prize-winning 1997 memoir *Personal History,* that she "went to work." Rather than using the organ to support her political agenda as her patriarchal predecessors had, the fearless publisher hired tough investigative journalists and let them dig—even if it meant that the muck splattered on some of her own cohorts. It was under Graham's dominion that Woodward and Bernstein broke the Watergate story, even while she entertained Nixon's aides at her celebrated dinner parties. It was around this time that a cabinet member famously warned that her "tit would get caught in a big wringer" if she went to press with a certain story. Having relinquished the title of publisher to her son Donald, Graham maintains her place as chairman of the executive committee of The Washington Post Company, a diversified media organization whose holdings include broadcast stations and magazines such as *Newsweek*.

GUTFREUND

New York socialite Susan Gutfreund is the wife of Wall Street czar John Gutfreund, the former CEO of Salomon Brothers.

Gutfreund's father's work with NATO brought her to England at a young age, where she remained throughout her school years. Completing high school in Virginia, Washington and Louisiana, she began a degree at the University of Texas, but later transferred to the Sorbonne in Paris, where she studied French civilization. Introduced to John Gutfreund on a blind date, the couple have been married for twenty years and have one son.

Susan Gutfreund is a Trustee at the Museum of American Folk Art, a Council Member of the National Academy of Design and a member of the Chairman's Council of Lincoln Center for the Performing Arts. Keenly interested in vintage couture, she is also on the Committee of the Costume & Textiles Department at the Philadelphia Museum of Art and has written for Sotheby's on the subject.

The Gutfreunds entertain in style at their Fifth Avenue apartment, which Susan Gutfreund decorated in collaboration with the late, great French decorator Henri Samuel. At their dinner table you might rub shoulders with Lord McAlpine, the Knight of Glin, or the owner of Christie's, Francois Pinault.

The Gutfreunds spend weekends in Villanova, Pennsylvania; they also have a home in Paris' seventh arrondissement. A Francophile, Susan Gutfreund enjoys life in New York, which she compares to champagne: "if you linger too long over a glass, it will lose its bubbles." Paris, on the other hand, "is like a fine bottle of Chateau Latour, to be savored, not rushed."

HEPBURN

With her plummy New England accent, tomboy manner, and Bryn Mawr attitude, Katherine Hepburn has always embodied the spirit of a well-bred rebel. The daughter of a wealthy surgeon and a suffragette mother, the blue-blood maverick favored forward-looking feminist roles: a feisty lawyer in *Adam's Rib*, a woman who poses as a man in *Sylvia Scarlett*, and a "lady athlete" in *Pat and Mike*. The only actor or actress nominated for twelve Academy Awards and the only woman to win four as Best Actress (three of them after the age of 60), her career wasn't always so peachy. After a successful spell in the 1930s when she made such classics as *Little Women* and the greatest screwball comedy of all, *Bringing Up Baby*, her unglamorous offstage mien—she insisted on wearing slacks—and disdain for playing the publicity game, hurt her popularity and she was labeled "box-office poison." Offered a part in a B-movie, Hepburn bought out her RKO contract and decamped to MGM, where she resurrected her star status as a witty heiress (what else?) in *The Philadelphia Story*.

Rich fodder for the gossip columns, Hepburn's romantic exploits with the likes of superagent Leland Hayward, moneyed recluse Howard Hughes, and her 25-year liaison with Spencer Tracy, kept the tabloids well oiled. Never one to hide her feelings, she spat in the face of Joel Mankiewicz, her director in *Suddenly Last Summer*, for his bad behavior toward her co-star Montgomery Clift. In the view of her biographer, Barbara Leaming, because the young Hepburn suffered the tragedy of the suicide of her grandfather, two uncles, and her own brother (whom she found hanging from a rafter), she feared committing to a permanent bond with a man. Despite nearly being killed in a 1984 auto accident, the inimitable Ms. Hepburn continues to take her famous icy showers and indulge her passion for chocolate. There are few more amazing Americans than Katherine Hepburn.

HILL The queen of hip-hop, rapper-singer-actress Lauryn Hill commands the throne of the country's most profitable music genre. Once called a fad, rap music (from which hip-hop is derived) is currently celebrating its 20th anniversary and boasts an audience that is 70 percent white. In the tradition of many a diva before her–Diana Ross, Tina Turner, Stevie Nicks–superstar Lauryn Hill emerged from the shadows of a group to claim her place as a formidable solo artist. As lead singer of *The Fugees,* she helped infuse hip-hop with the soul of predecessors like Aretha Franklin and Nina Simone.

Hill's funky version of the Roberta Flack standard *Killing Me Softly* helped the trio's second album *The Score* to sell more than 8 million copies worldwide, and created a diverse crossover audience. But it is with the 24-year-old's 1998 debut solo album, the multi-platinum selling *The Miseducation of Lauryn Hill,* an amalgamation of soul, R&B, reggae and hip-hop, that the superstar has truly begun to shine. Winner of five Grammies, the critically and commercially triumphant masterpiece has been called one of the most important albums of the decade by many industry players. Hill has two children with her boyfriend Rohan Marley, son of reggae icon Bob Marley.

Photo: Steve Sands

JONES

Everybody knows who Quincy Jones is. It's harder to define what he is. Musician, composer, producer, stage performer, arranger, conductor, record company executive, filmmaker, magazine founder, multimedia entrepreneur…the list goes on. Fusing pop, soul, hip-hop, jazz, classical, African and Brazilian music into unique hybrids that span the charts, this extraordinary musician is the most nominated Grammy artist of all time, with an astounding 76 nominations.

In his teens Jones played wedding gigs with a local Seattle singer-pianist named Ray Charles, but was first recognized in the 1950s post-swing era as a trumpeter with Lionel Hampton and Dizzy Gillespie. In the 1960s he became the first African-American to hold a top level position in a white-owned record company. Soon thereafter he was asked by director Sidney Lumet to compose music for the film *The Pawnbroker*. It was the first of Jones' more than 50 major motion pictures (for which he has garnered seven Oscar nominations) and television scores including those for *In Cold Blood*, *The Bill Cosby Show*, and *Roots* (for which he won an Emmy).

In the 80s the social activist, known to his friends as "Q", earned international acclaim as producer of *We Are The World* and Michael Jackson's *Thriller*, the best-selling album in the history of the recording industry, selling 30 million copies around the globe. Among his many awards and honors, he has been bestowed with France's Legion d'Honneur. Incidentally, Jones' daughter, Kidada (whose mother is actress Peggy Lipton), is a Tommy Hilfiger model.

JONES

As publisher of Esquire, Randy Jones was the youngest ever head of a major American magazine. Now, as founder and CEO of Capital Publishing, a seven year old magazine empire, he creates magazines exclusively for the top 5% of the demographic pyramid. Among the titles are *Worth*, which advises readers how to create, invest, protect and live well with their wealth. The *American Benefactor* encourages America's richest citizens to make a social difference with their wealth, while *Civilization*, the official magazine of the Library of Congress, features renowned guest editors such as Martin Scorcese, Vaclav Havel and Kofi Annan in each issue. Jones' most recent magazine launch is *Equity*–a magazine designed specifically for affluent women with a keen interest in money and business.

Jones was born to cattle ranchers and clothing manufacturers near Atlanta, Georgia. The family of his wife, Connie Cole, who was his childhood sweetheart, has interests in banking, real estate and insurance. Chairman of the Magazine Publishers of America's Annual Magazine Conference, Jones is also a member of the Creative Coalition and the Young President's Organization and sits on numerous other charitable boards. Impeccably mannered and well dressed–on casual Fridays he is rarely seen in anything other than a three piece suit–Jones moves with ease in eclectic circles throughout Europe and America. In New York, for instance, he numbers among his friends Joan Collins, Peter Jennings, Walter Annenberg, Anne Slater and Brooke Astor. The 43-year-old has a penchant for collecting old Steuben crystal animals.

KELLEY

A decade ago he was a young Boston attorney. These days the prolific television producer-writer David Kelley is heralded as the Charles Dickens of TV writers. Creating unconventional, dramatic series with medical and, of course, legal themes, he has earned critical acclaim, high ratings and numerous Emmy Awards. Defying formula, his shows portray multilayered characters grappling within intensely paced plots–serious in tone, but leavened with his peculiar brand of humor and frenetic dialogue. His rich themes encompass of-the-moment issues which present more questions than answers, reflecting the ambiguity of real life.

The visionary who has helped reshape the face of television broke into the medium writing for the 1980s mega hit *L.A. Law.* Since then Kelley has created, produced and written groundbreaking shows including *Picket Fences* (about a struggling, almost surreal midwestern town), *The Practice* (about a struggling young law firm), *Chicago Hope* (about a struggling hospital staff), and *Ally McBeal* (about a struggling young female attorney). Known to be fiercely private, he is married to movie star Michelle Pfeiffer, with whom he has two children.

KEMPNER

Without women like Nan Kempner, *haute couture* would be dead. For the industry that thrives on deep-pockets, the New York socialite is one of the only 300 or so women who keeps their bounty flowing, in her case for almost five decades. A regular in the front rows of the Paris collections, this striking San Franciscan started her sartorial love affair at nineteen, when her mother, Irma Schlesinger, took the only child on a trip to Paris to "treat" her to some appetizers from the likes of Balenciaga and Chanel. Shortly thereafter Kempner discovered a Dior sheath dress (from the hand of Yves St. Laurent) that came with a coat and a smattering of luxe trimmings: she was hooked.

Crediting part of her famous style sense to the influence of Lauren Bacall, whom she met when she was 13, the 68-year-old grandmother of six (whose husband, Tommy, is a banker) has always worked hard at "being noticed." Dinner at the glamorous hostess' apartment is one of the most coveted invitations in Manhattan. Her knack for entertaining is attributed to her eclectic mix of guests and her own gustatory passion. She also knows when to skimp: Kempner admits that she would rather spend on food and wine than flowers, so she reuses the same porcelain bird arrangements. And, my dear, she mostly purchases couturier "models"—at half the price. If all this suggests that Nan Kempner is even remotely difficult, it should also be stressed that she is one of the most charming women in New York. Look out for *RSVP*, her new book on entertaining, the proceeds of which will benefit Memorial Sloan-Kettering Hospital.

KLEIN Described as 'Calvin the Conqueror' by *Women's Wear Daily* and listed as one of America's 25 most influential people by *Time,* Calvin Klein, 57, who taught himself how to sew as a boy, is one of the fashion industry's biggest names with an annual turnover of around $5 billion.

Prospering on the seventies Studio 54 designer jeans craze, Klein went on to create a minimalist, all-American niche in the casualwear industry. Starting with a nubile Brooke Shields purring, "Nothing comes between me and my Calvins," the Klein image has been shaped by erotically provocative and controversial ad campaigns. His predilection for gaunt models, such as British waif Kate Moss, who appeared in ads for the unisex fragrance cK one, inspired the term "heroin chic." Mark Wahlburg shot to Hollywood stardom after baring his backside in beefcake billboards for Klein boxer shorts.

The recipient of many industry awards, including America's Best Designer in 1993, Klein sits on numerous committees, including the Council of Fashion Designers of America. Recently separated from socialite and photographer Kelly Klein, he has a daughter, Marci. Klein lives between Manhattan and his retreat on Georgica Pond.

KRAMER With West End and Broadway hits such as *Sugar Babies, Me and My Girl* and *Nick & Nora* under her belt, Terry Allen Kramer is a successful theater producer. But her most visible achievement is La Follia, a controversial 46,000 square-foot oceanfront palazzo in Palm Beach.

La Follia is one of the largest homes in Palm Beach, which is why—along with its estimated $27 million price tag—it has inspired tongues (especially local ones) to wag. The house was conceived to follow in the Mediterranean tradition of Addison Mizner, the 1920s architect whose arched doorways, marbled floors and palatial ceilings define the upscale town's architectural vernacular. Located on a coveted "ocean to lake" property, like the famous Mar-a-Lago, the manse, designed by architect Jeffrey Smith, boasts vaulted ceilings, coral-veneered facades, a 106-foot central hall, niches filled with Roman busts, artwork such as Picasso's *Buste Homme,* and untold antiques (many of which came from the Henry Ford estate). Interior designer Pauline Boardman was hired to imbue the house with youth and levity. Landscape architect Mario Nievera created a lush garden out of a blank terra firma. House guests at the Kramers' include many Britons, like Sean Connery, Ned Ryan and the Duke of Marlborough. The daughter of Wall Street tycoon Charles Allen, Terry Allen Kramer has been married to financier Irwin Kramer for 41 years.

KRAVIS They called J.P. Morgan, John D. Rockefeller and his ilk robber barons. Today's financial titans are celebrated only slightly ironically as masters of the universe. And the biggest one of them all is Henry Kravis. Financier, investor, dealmaker par excellence, Kravis, 55, is still going strong, but in a quieter fashion than in the heyday of the leveraged buyout, which he pioneered.

A founding partner of Kohlberg, Kravis, Roberts, he is responsible for some of the biggest corporate takeovers in history, including household brands like Safeway, Playtex, Samsonite and Texaco. In all, the dreaded triple initials with Henry K. at the helm, have spent more than $73 billion acquiring more than 45 companies. Kravis is often assumed to be the model for Oliver Stone's rapacious Gordon Gekko, played by Michael Douglas in *Wall Street,* who justified his insatiable appetite for purchasing undervalued companies with his famous "Greed is good" speech. Unlike the fictional Gekko, Kravis is a renowned philanthropist; he has made contributions as large as $10 million to New York's Mount Sinai Medical Center and the Metropolitan Museum of Art. Kravis, who claims his mission is "to show the rest of corporate America how they can become more competitive," has admitted that "maybe we've made too much money, but it's a way to keep score, that is all." His third wife, Marie-Josée Drouin, is an elegant French-Canadian economist.

LANSING

When Sherry Lansing was named production chief at Twentieth Century Fox in 1980, she made history as the first female to head a Hollywood studio. Almost 20 years and a slew of hit films later, she is one of the most influential women in America. As chairman of Paramount Pictures' Motion Picture Group, where she reigns supreme behind the famous Melrose gates, she has been called "Hollywood's No. 1 studio boss" by *Fortune* magazine and inhabits 11th place (climbing ten notches from last year) on *Entertainment Weekly's* prestigious list of Tinseltown's most powerful honchos. The ranking was not entirely surprising to insiders: the studio which Lansing has ruled since 1992 was responsible for what has been called the "deal of the century." As co-financier of the film *Titanic,* Paramount received almost 40 percent of the blockbuster's staggering profits in return for its $65 million wager. Continuing its co-production schedule, the studio last year reaped further rewards with its share of the proceeds from *Deep Impact* and *Saving Private Ryan* (co-produced with Dreamworks).

Before taking the reins at the legendary studio, she and partner Stanley Jaffe originated such hits as *Fatal Attraction.* Renowned for creating blockbusters on a sane budget, the striking powerhouse has overseen Paramount as it launched contemporary classics like *Forrest Gump, Braveheart* and *The Truman Show.* Under her guidance, the studio has won the Oscar for Best Picture three times. Lansing lives in Bel Air with her husband, director William Friedkin.

LAUREN

"The first image-maker," according to *New York* magazine. Ralph Lauren is one of the fashion industry's heaviest hitters. Born Ralph Lipschitz in 1939, he changed his name in the 1960s when he founded a tie shop. Despite no formal design training, Lauren triumphed as a designer and manufacturer of menswear that emulated the casual uniform of the Northeastern Establishment WASP—making the navy blue blazer, chino pants, and Oxford shirt accessible to men who'd never heard of Brooks Brothers. Branching into womenswear and home furnishings, the guru of prep has built one of the most impressive fashion and lifestyle empires in the world. Employing 3000 people and boasting such brands as Polo Ralph Lauren, Polo Sport and the Ralph Lauren Collection, the fashion king's signature style has pervaded homes nationwide in the form of richly patterned sheets, seasoned leather sofas, handsome dinner plates and decorative paints. Lauren's personal wealth is estimated at more than a billion dollars. He lives with his wife Ricky in Bedford, Connecticut.

Ralph and Ricky Lauren.
Photo: Patrick McMullan

LEGUIZAMO

This dynamic actor has moved from playing Latino junkies in way off Broadway productions to starring in Hollywood feature films like Spike Lee's *Summer of Sam*. He first became a mainstream success when he co-starred with Patrick Swayze and Wesley Snipes in *To Wong Foo, Thanks for Everything, Julie Newmar*, a road picture about a trio of drag queens who head west in the Cadillac they won in a beauty contest. On the boards of Broadway, the Bogota-born Leguizamo wrote and starred in his own one-man show, *FREAK*, chronicling his early street and family life growing up in a tough New York neighborhood. Splendidly outrageous and hilariously entertaining, *FREAK* was nominated for two Tony Awards: best play and best actor. Besides creating brilliant character-studies, Leguizamo also probed the pain of his own troubled relationship with his father—a figure he portrays as both terrifying and sympathetic.

Relying on his wits from the get-go, the young Leguizamo would disarm potential assailants by breaking into a sort of self-invented Tourette's Syndrome. In other words, he would spout a series of off-putting obscenities at would-be attackers. Before his name was emblazoned on a Broadway marquee, the comedic talent gained a following with other critically acclaimed shows that plumbed the depths of his past: *Mambo Mouth* and *Spic-O-Rama*. In 1995, he starred in the first Latin comedy-variety show, the Emmy Award-winning *House of Buggin* for Fox-TV.

LORING
Design Director of Tiffany & Co. for the past two decades, this accomplished designer, artist, and author is one of America's most celebrated collectors. Among his numerous collections of 20th-century decorative arts, the graduate of Yale and the École des Beaux Arts owns one of the world's largest collections of 30s, 40s and 50s Swiss product posters. Some of his prints and paintings, which have been widely exhibited, are in the permanent collections of museums such as the Museum of Modern Art and the Whitney Museum of American Art.

A true pioneer, Loring contributed to the gentrification of New York's Hell's Kitchen neighborhood by carving a splendid personal residence from a multiple dwelling in the former slum near Times Square. As an author, six of his books on entertaining, taste and decor were published at Doubleday by his longtime friend, the late Jacqueline Kennedy Onassis. Under the Tiffany name, Loring has penned eight books including 1997's *Tiffany's 20th Century: A Portrait of American Style,* chronicling the history of the premier American design house from the Victorian era to the mid-century designs of Jean Schlumberger and the contemporary triumphs of Elsa Peretti and Paloma Picasso. In addition to his various book projects and speaking engagements, the aesthete contributes to such magazines as *Architectural Digest, Metropolitan Home,* and *Art in America.* His latest tome, *Tiffany Jewels,* will be published this fall.

Above: Mario and Lauren Maccioni with their children Luc, Olivia and Nicolas.
Right: Sirio and Egidiana Maccioni with sons Marco and Mauro.

MACCIONI
A global status symbol on a par with Belgian chocolate and Italian motor cars, Sirio Maccioni's Le Cirque 2000 is the world's number one restaurant in which to see and be seen. Michael Douglas, Diana Ross, Bill Cosby, Barbara Walters and Woody Allen are among the celebrities who regularly eat there. Since Le Cirque first opened in 1974, every U.S. President has dined in the restaurant, as well as countless foreign dignitaries including King Juan Carlos of Spain, the President of Italy, and Princess Margaret of England.

The charismatic creator of this culinary and social phenomenon has reigned over the front of the house since opening in its original location on Park Avenue and 65th Street in 1974. Two years ago, the ringmaster reinstated its successor in the Villard House, the anchor of the Royal Family of Brunei's New York Palace Hotel. Adam Tihany's theatrically futuristic design gives the feeling of a sleek Ferrari parked in Versailles and Sottha Khunn's cuisine is equally dazzling.

The Italian-born Maccioni has launched many of today's culinary stars into orbit as well as his own three sons, Mauro, Marco and Mario, whom he set up in Osteria del Circo. A colorful restaurant that features the food of their beloved Tuscany, Circo, as it is referred to, has become the setting for New York's younger social set. Sirio's three charming sons, with their mother Egidiana at the helm, are fluent in Italian, French, Spanish, German and English, which is hardly surprising, given their pedigrees: Mario trained with Roger Vergé at the famous Moulin de Mougins, while both Marco and Mauro worked in the three-star Boyer Le Crayères in the heart of Champagne country. In October 1998, the Maccionis opened Le Cirque and Circo at Bellagio in Las Vegas. The cook in the family is Egidiana, Sirio's wife, whose good humor, insight, and quiet strength have propelled this extraordinary clan into the front rank of American restaurateurs.

McDONALD On July 12, 1986, while on routine patrol in Central Park, Police Detective Steven McDonald was shot in the back by 13-year old Savod Jones. Paralyzed and confined to a wheelchair, this third generation Irish-American has spent the subsequent 13 years preaching the forgiveness that he offered his assailant. Teaching school children his "peace pledge," the power of compassion, and the need to turn away from violence, the unsung hero has had a lasting and profound effect on many of them.

Last year, a week after the Omagh bombing, one of the worst tragedies in the history of the Troubles, McDonald made a visit to Ireland that he'd planned for his whole life. Sponsored by the Hibernian Civil Rights Coalition, McDonald's mission was to deliver his courageous message of reconciliation. Among the notables from opposing sides to whom he brought his extraordinary expression of humanitarianism were the British Ambassador to Ireland, the Irish Prime Minister, injured Royal Ulster Constabulary officers and IRA members. It was said at the time that he brought "more to the healing process in ten days than many politicians have in three decades."

MERRILL Socialite turned actress Dina Merrill was born Nedenia Hutton in 1925. The daughter of cereal scion Marjorie Merriweather Post and stockbroker Edward F. Hutton, she grew up in Mar-a-Lago, the celebrated 118-room Palm Beach estate, where her bedroom was a veritable fortress against kidnappers.

Merrill's much married mother, the queen of Palm Beach society, oversaw construction of the 58-bedroom residence, while the young Dina was tutored in her own private schoolroom on a 350-foot yacht. Though her parents tried to dissuade her from a career in acting, the budding thespian prevailed. A star of more than 20 feature films (including *Butterfield Eight* with Elizabeth Taylor), the courtly actress has appeared on Broadway (*Angel Street, On Your Toes*) and many television shows, including hosting a syndicated interior design series.

Merrill's theatrical foray was never fully embraced by society. Her name was dropped from the Social Register in 1966 after her marriage to actor Cliff Roberston. Merrill and her third husband, investment banker and movie producer Ted Hartley, bought RKO Pictures (a legendary studio in Hollywood's Golden Age) in 1991, along with remake and sequel rights to 650 of the former behemoth's motion pictures. The couple, who enjoy playing golf and tennis, live between Los Angeles, New York City, East Hampton, Vail and Palm Beach where, these days, Merrill keeps a mere pied-à-terre.

MILLER What do Crown Princess Marie-Chantal of Greece, Alexandra von Furstenburg, and Pia Getty have in common? Answer: their parents. Not since the Edwardian heyday of "dollar princesses" marrying European aristocracy has such a triumvirate of triumphant marriages been made.

Collectively known as the "Miller sisters" (not to be confused with the 1950s country duo), the multilingual heiresses are betrothed respectively to royalty, royalty, and oldish American money. Of course, in Hong Kong, where the girls grew up, they are still known as the "Miller daughters" in deference to their parents, American duty-free mogul Robert Miller and his Ecuadorian wife Chantal, who spent much of the 1970s and 1980s entertaining in lavish style. Lavish? Caviar, junks, hot air balloons, elephants and helicopters. The daughters have clearly inherited their parents' genius for over-the-top amusement. The Hamptons is still recovering from the Tarzan soirée Pia threw at her Southampton estate, which featured prominent members of New York society in leopard print and skimpy suede sheaths.

Not just pretty faces, each has found a niche for herself. Pia, a former art historian, is now American spokeswoman for Sephora, the French cosmetics chain owned by her father. Alexandra, who studied costume design and history at Brown University, is the creative director of Diane von Furstenberg Studio, where she was a significant influence in refining and marketing her mother-in-law's reborn wrap dress, sartorial emblem of the 1970s working woman. And Marie-Chantal has set up a charitable foundation for nature preservation.

MARTINS Danish-born Peter Martins has honored the legacy bequeathed to him by choreographer extraordinaire George Balanchine, co-founder of the New York City Ballet. Before Balanchine's death in 1983, the former dancer with the Ballet Russe trained his young prodigy to take over the most prestigious post in dance.

Currently celebrating its 50th anniversary, the NYCB was created to allow American audiences to watch their own native dancers (schooled by foreign ballet masters), rather than continuing to import European companies. Martins oversees the largest dance organization in the country with some 90 dancers and a repertory of more than 150 works mostly choreographed by himself, Balanchine, and Jerome Robbins.

Starting his career with the company as a principal dancer in 1970, the bravura performer has gone on to choreograph over 60 ballets known for their intense drama, starting with his 1978 debut of the abstract-expressionist *Calcium Light Night*. Three years ago, when he turned 50, the ballet master says he considered returning to his roots at the Royal Danish Ballet, but his sense of commitment prevailed and he has stayed on to create material for the next generation of dancers, providing them with an impressive post-Balanchine repertory. Married to principal dancer Darci Kistler since 1991, they have a daughter, Talicia.

MORRISON

Novelist Toni Morrison credits her parents with instilling in her the drive that contributed to her winning the Nobel Prize for Literature in 1993. Morrison's mother, who died three months after her daughter was awarded the accolade, was delighted but "not surprised" that her daughter had become the first native-born American winner since John Steinbeck in 1962. Not to mention that she was a black woman, giving her forgotten sisters their rightful place in the American literary pantheon.

Often compared to Faulkner, another Southerner given to mesmerizing, incantatory rhythms, Morrison explores issues of race, gender and class in lyrical prose, which jumps between stylized and magical metaphor to the plain-speak of jus' folks. *Song of Solomon*, the 1977 novel that helped launch her career, rediscovered an audience of over a million readers in 1996 when Oprah Winfrey chose it for her book club—much to the astonishment of Morrison, a TV-illiterate who was unaware of the daytime TV titan's vast influence. Winfrey also bought the screen rights to Morrison's novel *Beloved* (for which she won a Pulitzer prize). A child of the Depression, the avid reader and gardener feels secure maintaining multiple residences: a Manhattan triplex, a Princeton apartment near the university where she has held a seat since 1989, a stone house in Rockland County, and a Hudson River house that burned down in a Christmas Day fire six years ago. The Nobel laureate and grandmother, who has lived contentedly alone since her marriage ended in 1964, says that now that she can call the shots she refuses to appear on morning TV shows with their trite sound bites. A snob of the right sort.

MOYNIHAN

Scholar and gentleman, public servant and statesman, former ambassador and soon to be former senator (four-term Democrat from New York)–Daniel Patrick Moynihan has cruised the corridors of academia and government with great aplomb. Translating intellectual thought into political action, the former Harvard professor has made his mark on issues from public architecture to international relations. As the only American in history to serve in four successive administrations, Moynihan held court in Camelot as assistant secretary of labor under President Kennedy. He kept that position under Lyndon Johnson. Under Nixon, he acted as an urban affairs specialist. President Ford gave him ambassadorships to both India and the United Nations. After studying the potential impact of Y2K on society's vital sectors, Moynihan was the first national politician to warn the President that "we have cause for fear."

The author or editor of 18 books and the recipient of 62 honorary awards, Moynihan is one of the most respected public figures in America today. His wife of 44 years, Elizabeth Brennan Moynihan, an architectural historian with a special interest in 16th century Mughal architecture, is the author of *Paradise as a Garden: In Persia and Mughal India*.

NEGROPONTE

Dr. Nicholas Negroponte is a refreshingly old-fashioned spokesman for the future. This visionary teacher and author is the co-founder and director of the Media Laboratory at Massachusetts Institute of Technology—where he has been a member of the faculty since 1966. The Media Lab has long been on the cutting edge of development in areas such as digital video and multimedia. Negroponte and his colleagues conduct advanced research into a broad range of technologies, including digital television, holographic imaging, computer music, computer vision, electronic publishing and artificial intelligence.

He believes that the digital age can neither be denied nor stopped. His vision of the future, which he describes in his best-selling book, *Being Digital,* portrays a world in which we will all have private multimedia "butlers" to screen our calls, schedule our days and select and arrange our entertainment. The stream of information that enters our homes will be converted into customized newspapers, featuring weather reports, sports results, our favorite columnists, converted into a printout chart, a verbal report, a video picture or a miniature re-creation in our living rooms. All entertainment and data will be available on demand and tailored by "intelligent agents," ultimately providing increased autonomy and opportunity for the busy individual.

Born the son of a ship owner on New York's Upper East Side, Negroponte trained to be an architect before turning his talents to the development of technology. The product of an elite European and American education, he is a patrician who cares about mass culture, an academic who keeps the company of the world's major CEOs and a professor whose wardrobe is tracked by *W* magazine.

NICHOLSON In retrospect it hardly seems surprising that a man with this much charisma has become one of the world's most popular celebrities. But the actor whose lovable but morally dubious characters have enthralled cinemagoers for the past three decades got his big break by chance. When actor Rip Torn dropped out of *Easy Rider* in 1969, Jack Nicholson, who had spent the 1960s playing in low budget horror flicks and Westerns, tuned in and turned on. In *One Flew Over the Cuckoo's Nest*, his tour de force performance as a psychiatric inmate put an Oscar on his mantelpiece. Nicholson's devilish charm, killer smirk and jaded drawl, combined with a series of larger than life roles—a burned out private eye in *Chinatown*; an aging astronaut in *Terms of Endearment*; a towering military commander in *A Few Good Men*—has gained him a place in American hearts as the nation's favorite bad boy. His role as *Batman's* Joker earned him a whopping $50 million in pay and merchandising profits. In 1998 he charmed audiences as the obsessive-compulsive romance novelist in *As Good as It Gets*, a role director James Brooks created for him. During shooting, Nicholson moved Jill, the dog that plays his onscreen nemesis, into his Hollywood Hills home.

The actor with a talent for making abhorrent characters endearingly sympathetic has been romantically linked over the years with some of the most beautiful women in America: Faye Dunaway, Candice Bergen, Jessica Lange, Meryl Streep and Angelica Huston, with whom he had a 17-year relationship. When his daughter's best friend, Rebecca Broussard, became pregnant with his child, he married her and moved mother and child into a separate house on his property. Jack Nicholson, who discovered late in life that the woman he thought was his older sister was actually his mother, has three kids of his own.

NORMAN   Throughout her childhood Jessye Norman was sure she would grow up to be a psychiatrist. But fate intervened when she accidentally turned the radio dial to a live broadcast from the Metropolitan Opera. She was transfixed. "Opera," says the diva, "is life blown up really big. It's soap opera."

Her career as a singer began officially in 1968 when she won a voice competition in Munich. A year later she made her operatic debut as Elizabeth in *Tannhäuser*, a role she admits is "about as Aryan as you can get." The inspiration for Jean-Jacques Beineix's film *Diva*, about a young Parisian postman who falls in love with a black opera singer, she says that "being big and black" has never presented any problems. Proud that she's never sung *Porgy and Bess*, it is the strong, sexually dominating characters such as Salomé that appeal to her.

Norman is renowned for her stage presence, her ability to convey emotional intensity and for the opulent timbre of her "oceanic" voice with its vast scale that rises from contralto and mezzo to high soprano. In 1985 the woman who has an orchid named after her was given an ovation in Tokyo for 47 minutes and a year later her ovation in Salzburg lasted 55 minutes.

A civil rights activist and former ambassador to the UN, she gives frequently to educational causes, dance companies and AIDS research. She has received honorary doctorates from universities such as Cambridge, Harvard, and Yale. Jessye Norman lives alone in London, in an antique-filled mews house.

OVITZ

It is difficult to keep track of Michael Ovitz: by the time you read this potted biography he may well be representing Martian "talent." In the interim, however, it is fair to say that in the feudal society that is Hollywood, Michael Ovitz is the once and future king.

The deal-maker *non pareil* abandoned his castle to co-rule the Walt Disney Company with one of the most powerful dukes in the land, his childhood friend Michael Eisner. Promised that he would inherit Eisner's fiefdom upon his semi-retirement, Ovitz soon realized that the coronation was not about to transpire. After a mere 14 months on the job, Ovitz left, taking with him an astonishing $128 million or so in severance pay. The press gloated at how the mighty potentate had fallen. "Twenty-five years of building CAA— it's as if I was never there," he told a *Fortune* magazine reporter after the Disney debacle.

The former Universal Studios guide had risen to Tinseltown heights through a combination of hype and his practice of "packaging" producers, directors, and writers in order to attract actors to a project. Representing talent like Tom Cruise, Tom Hanks, Kevin Costner, Sean Connery, and Sylvester Stallone, Creative Artists Agency became so powerful that people forgot that only a decade before agents had been mere lackeys in the Hollywood hierarchy.

Last year Ovitz took over Livent, the Toronto-based theatrical colossus whose Broadway hits included *Ragtime* and *Kiss of the Spiderwoman.* But soon thereafter he filed for bankruptcy and initiated a $225 million fraud suit, claiming that the company had cooked its books and was in deep financial straits. In a career that reads like the plot points in a screenplay, Ovitz is ready for the third act. Returning to the agency trenches early this year, he founded Artists Management Group and has been raiding agencies to woo the kind of talent that graces the covers of *Vanity Fair:* Leonardo DiCaprio, Claire Danes, Cameron Diaz, Samuel L. Jackson. This is Hollywood. The protagonist must make a comeback.

PALTROW

As she was growing up in New York and Los Angeles, Gwyneth Paltrow nurtured thespian aspirations—much to her mother's chagrin. Peculiar, since her mother, Tony-Award winner Blythe Danner, is one of the most well-respected actresses of stage and screen (remember *The Prince of Tides?*). But Danner, who sacrificed her own career to raise a family, felt her promising daughter was too smart to chase the acting bug. Envisioning her as an anthropologist, she was not amused when the golden girl cut classes to attend Hollywood auditions. One day, while hanging with family friend Steven Spielberg, he offered her the part of young Wendy in his big-budget Peter Pan-spinoff, *Hook* (1991). But it wasn't until her father, TV writer-producer Bruce Paltrow, gave her the go-ahead to relinquish her education, that her career began to take off.

Paltrow gained attention early on playing James Caan's smart-alecky girlfriend in *Flesh and Bone*. After playing opposite Brad Pitt in the thriller *Seven,* she gained more notoriety from her well-publicized love affair with the hunk of the moment than for her diminutive role. With her subsequent relationship with Ben Affleck, the serious actress was in danger of finding fame more by association than in her own right. But with a series of high profile parts—the title role in *Emma;* opposite Michael Douglas in *A Perfect Murder;* and her courtly performance in *Shakespeare In Love* (for which she won a best actress Oscar)—the ethereal beauty finally came into her own. Admired for her grace, the swanlike actress, who is arguably the most eligible woman in America, lives alone (at the time of writing) in a small New York townhouse.

Liv Tyler with Gwyneth Paltrow.
Photo: Patrick McMullan

PECK

Even in Hollywood's golden era of dominating leading men, Gregory Peck, stood out as a beacon of style, heroism and decency. One of the big screen's most enduring and beloved leading men, he began life as a shy and inarticulate boy whose divorced parents left him to be raised by his grandmother in San Diego. Excelling as an oarsman for the U.C. Berkeley crew team, the handsome 6' 3" pre-med student made a beeline for a stage career the moment he graduated in 1939. Arriving in New York with $160 in his pocket and a new name (he changed his given name Eldred to his middle name Gregory), the pharmacist's son waited on tables, conducted tours through Rockefeller Center for $40 a week, and modeled before being accepted into the legendary Neighborhood Playhouse.

Peck's Broadway debut was in Emlyn Williams' *The Morning Star* in 1942. A year later he moved back to Southern California where his first starring film role, in *The Keys of the Kingdom,* earned him an Oscar nomination. After three more Oscar nods (*The Yearling, Gentleman's Agreement, Twelve O'Clock High*), he finally won an Academy Award for probably his most memorable role, as Atticus Finch, the humane small town trial lawyer who defends a black man falsely accused of raping a white woman, in *To Kill a Mockingbird* (1962). Of all his 55 films, the Harper Lee adaptation is Peck's favorite. One of America's most distinguished and admired superstars, the 83-year old has received many honors, including the American Film Institute's Life Achievement Award and the Presidential Medal of Freedom.

PEI

Born in China in 1917 (his name Ieoh Ming means "to inscribe brightly"), the son of a prominent banker, I.M. Pei's life has made an indelible mark on architecture. As the jury that awarded him the Pritzker Architecture Prize in 1983 commented, the naturalized American citizen "has given this century some of its most beautiful interior spaces and exterior forms."

Gaining kudos with his East Building of the National Gallery of Art in Washington (1968-78), Pei and his firm have gone on to design many of the most important buildings on the globe, often accompanied by the controversy that follows innovative design. Artfully marrying manmade structures with their environment and contemporary form with classical theory, he has faced and conquered—always with his famous smile—some of his field's greatest challenges: from his expansion of the crumbling Louvre (accompanied by xenophobic Gaulic harumphing: French women actually spat at his feet) to his less than mindbending Rock and Roll Hall of Fame and Museum. Pei originally declined the commission, until Rolling Stone founder Jann Wenner and Atlantic Records CEO Ahmet Ertegun convinced him to relent.

In a more recent project, the Miho Museum in Japan, which he built to house the vast art holdings of a wealthy religious sect, Pei buried most of the building underground, an allusion to a Chinese fable about a fisherman who enters a cave and finds paradise. A natty dresser, accessorized by his round-rimmed glasses, Pei is known to be quite voluble, especially when expounding on such passions as wine, Chinese cuisine and gardening.

QUINN   The high priestess of so-called "permanent" Washington society, Sally Quinn reigns as supreme hostess from the Georgetown mansion she shares with her husband, former editor of *The Washington Post*, Ben Bradlee. The former journalist and novelist, known for hosting dazzling parties for the political and media elite in the nation's capital, published a book in 1997 about the art of socializing, *The Party: A Guide to Adventurous Entertaining*. The book described a number of potential social disasters which were somehow averted, like the party at which the death of Vince Foster, White House counsel and friend of President Clinton, was whispered from ear to ear, or the event at which Nora Ephron, having just learned of husband Carl Bernstein's infidelities, poured a bottle of red wine over the Watergate journalist's head. The daughter of a general, Quinn earned recognition for her byline in the sixties by reporting on parties for the Post. A regular guest on national talk shows, the self-styled Washington establishment spokesperson has broadcast her anti-Clinton stance widely.

RILEY

Intense, debonair, passionate, Pat Riley is the world's most celebrated basketball coach. Famous as much for his sartorial style and outlandish temper as he is for his virtuosity on the sidelines, "Riles" commands large fees as he travels the world inspiring fans with motivational lines like "There's no such thing as coulda, shoulda, or woulda. If you shoulda and coulda, you woulda done it."

During the nine seasons in which Riley coached the Los Angeles Lakers, the team went to the NBA Finals seven times, winning four championships. The occasional sportscaster then joined the New York Knicks and proceeded to lead them through a series of their best seasons in decades. Now he is part-owner and coach of the Miami Heat.

The 6'4" former basketball star has famously justified what he calls his fits of "T.I."—temporary insanity. In his book *The Winner Within: A Life-Plan for Team Players*, Riley writes of "being angry at the right time to the right degree, at the right people. It requires a focused plan, and it demands a rapid follow-up of compassion to prevent lasting damage." As for his love of Armani suits? They add more "authority."

Photo: Patrick McMullan

RODHAM CLINTON

A consummate politician, Hillary Rodham Clinton has weathered many storms: rumors of her husband's infidelities while helping him campaign for the presidency; her failure to reform the nation's health-care system; her status as the only First Lady to testify before a federal grand jury; and, of course, standing by her man as he faced impeachment for his sexual indiscretions with Monica Lewinsky. Clinton was derided by those who thought her too tough when she announced early on that she had chosen a career over staying home to "bake cookies," but she has gained the respect of the American people for her competence, intelligence and ambition, tempered with compassion and steadfast loyalty. Her approval ratings rose from an unprecedented 43 percent to a staggering 70 percent at about the time the House Judiciary Committee began to consider impeaching the President.

Always a high achiever, the young Yale law school graduate was appointed staff counsel to the House Judiciary Committee during its Watergate investigations (where, ironically, she wrote the procedural rules for impeaching President Nixon). The first President's wife to form a working partnership with her husband while in office, she fulfilled the promise of her husband's campaign in which he declared that the nation would receive "two for the price of one!" as he and his wife continued to "do things together like we always have." Though she has yet to make her mark on public policy, the savvy stateswoman has managed to keep out of her husband's shadow while moving forward according to her own agenda. At the time of writing, the First Lady was considering a run for a New York Senate seat.

ROSE There are talk-show hosts. And then there is Charlie Rose. The 6'4" television journalist engages his interview subjects in conversation so personal that to view it is to feel as if you've eavesdropped on an intimate dinner. Millions of Americans tune in to absorb the in-depth discussions the acclaimed broadcaster has with world leaders, writers, athletes, entertainers, and other newsmakers. Among his many notable guests have been Nelson Mandela, Yitzhak Rabin, Mary Robinson, and Martin Scorcese—people of substance with "a great story to tell." Of course, they aren't always allowed to tell their stories with quite as much fluidity as some would like. Last year *Brill's Content* began tracking how often Rose interrupted his guests; on average, the magazine claimed, Rose cut his guests off 55 times per show.

Though many interviews are one-on-one, others are round table discussions in which Rose, celebrated for his intelligent, probing style, joins together such unlikely duos as Martin Amis and Elmore Leonard to compare intellectual notes. In the 1980s he anchored CBS's *Nightwatch* and found a way to communicate sensibly with convicted murderer Charles Manson. The interview won him an Emmy Award.

Raised in North Carolina over his father's general store, where the young Charlie helped out, the 57-year old lives between an apartment in midtown Manhattan and a new home in Bellport, on Long Island. Rising daily at 5 am, the avid reader takes a 45-minute nap in the afternoons. Rose's girlfriend of the last six years is Amanda Burden, a member of New York City's planning commission (and the daughter of Babe Paley).

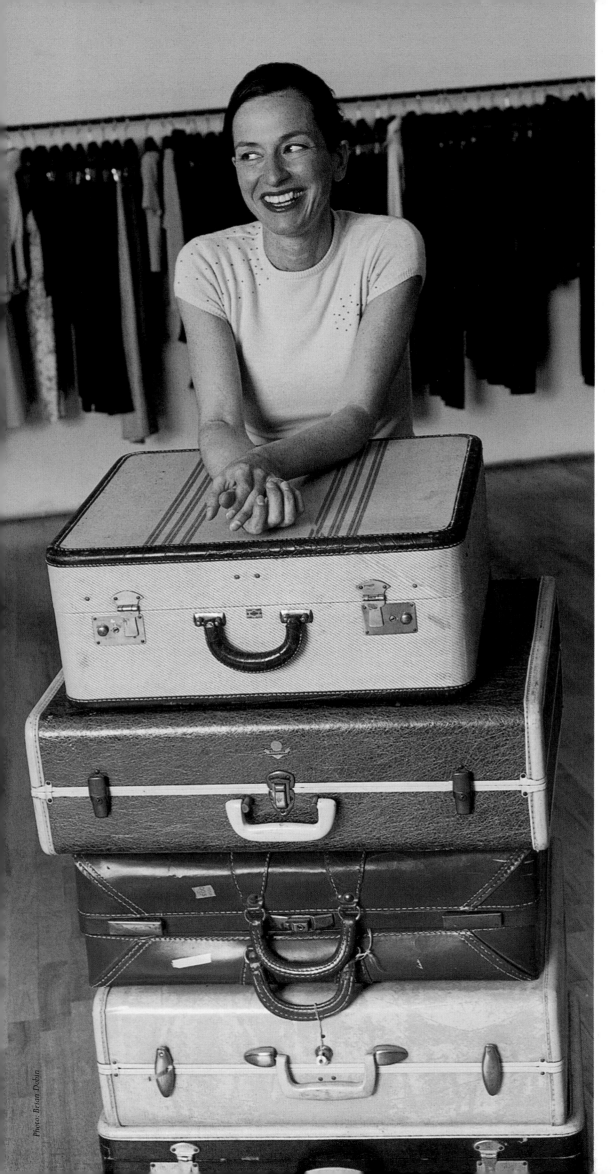

Photo: Brian Dobin

ROWLEY

This affable and delightfully eccentric designer created her first dress when she was seven years old. Nowadays she is celebrated as one of the hottest "downtown" designers around. Her life story will probably be used as the basis for a Hollywood biopic one day, but until then, here are the details: fumbling for direction at the Art Institute of Chicago, Cynthia Rowley's roommate suggested that with her talents for drawing and sewing she ought to go into fashion. She was soon spotted wearing a home made frock by a buyer from department store Marshall Fields. A few days later she received an order for five pieces. By the time she was a senior, Rowley had sold an eight-piece collection to Henri Bendel.

The Illinois native arrived in New York on New Year's Day, 1983, equipped with $4000, a couple of sewing machines and oodles of ambition. After many months of working alone in her apartment, drawing patterns on newspapers and cutting fabric, she waxed ecstatic to learn that she could subcontract her labor out to a factory. Before long she managed to get Bloomingdale's to give her an in-store boutique and Saks Fifth Avenue to hang her clothes in its Young Couture department. Fast forward to 1995, when Rowley received the prestigious New Fashion Talent award from the Council of Fashion Designers of America. At the time of going to press she was a nominee for 1999 Menswear Designer of the Year, with her own shops in New York, Chicago, Los Angeles and Tokyo. The appropriately titled *Swell: A Girl's Guide to the Good Life,* which Rowley wrote with Ilene Rosenzweig, has recently been published.

Rowley and husband Bill Keenan, sculptor and architect, live in New York and let off steam on their trampoline, in their "love shack" in Montauk, or one of their farms in Illinois. When we photographed Rowley she was due to have a baby within forty-eight hours. That she still manages to look this stunning is proof, as if it were needed, that some people have all the luck.

RUST Marina Rust's mother, scion of Marshall Field's department store fortune, sought to shield the youngster from 'materialism.' After leaving Rust's father when Marina was three, the post-hippie mother took her daughter to live on a commune in rural Oregon. But Rust yearned for the "correct" and "ordered" life provided by her father, David, then curator of French paintings at the National Gallery of Art in Washington, D.C.

Always impeccably dressed (although she winningly describes herself as "dishevelled") Rust is an affable, modest young woman whose singular style is an inspiration to many. She lives the life of a writer–hanging out with a literary crowd and working as contributing editor at *Vogue*.

At the age of 27, Rust published a novel called *Gatherings*. Among the critics who offered praise, Frances Fitzgerald applauded her deft, cool touch, describing it as "a daring and graceful first novel." She cites Evelyn Waugh as an influence and, among living American writers, Susan Minot.

Like her novel's protagonist, the 33-year old Rust knows intimately the world of shooting parties, coming out balls and plantations. But she is no prima donna: as a boardmember of the Henry Street Settlement, Rust has consciously addressed the grim disparities in American society. And her PBP Foundation has dispensed grants to such groups as the Harlem Literacy program. In time she may well "inherit" the city, as an article in *New York* magazine predicted last year. But it seems improbable that Marina Rust will let pre-eminence in the social pantheon go to her head. She is too smart and too sane to let that happen.

RYAN Who would have thought that Margaret Mary Hyra, a homecoming queen from Fairfield, Connecticut (voted "cutest girl" in high school), would one day command a colossal $10.5 million to star opposite Tom Hanks in *You've got Mail?* When America's future sweetheart was 15, her mother abandoned the family in search of her own fame as an actress, leaving her four children to be raised by their father, a high school math teacher and coach. Meg's mother later helped her to secure a coveted Screen Actors Guild card under her maiden name: Ryan. The bubbly blonde got her thespian legs playing in a popular soap opera. A few small film roles followed, including *Top Gun*, but it wasn't until *When Harry Met Sally* (and that memorable "faking" scene) that she rose to prominence as a true star.

Meg Ryan is married to Dennis Quaid, whom she met while they filmed together on *Inner Space*. Together with their seven-year old son, Jack, they divide their time between a home in Santa Monica and a hundred-acre ranch in Montana that once belonged to actor Warren Oates.

RYDER

Born Winona Horowitz to parents whom her godfather Timothy Leary (coincidentally, also Uma Thurman's godfather) called "hippie intellectuals and psychedelic scholars," this angelic young woman looks set to become one of Hollywood's more enduring stars.

Named after the town in Minnesota in which she was born, she moved with her parents to a commune at age seven. Bit by the acting bug, the young Winona enrolled in acting classes, where she was spotted by talent scouts. Redubbing herself Winona Ryder, the surname inspired by a Mitch Ryder album of her father's, she made waves as an eccentric teen in Tim Burton's 1988 hit *Beetlejuice*. In the following year she again portrayed the darker side of adolescence in the successful black comedy *Heathers*. Under Burton's wing again, she strayed from her typecast to play a perky cheerleader attracted to then fiancé Johnny Depp's eponymous hero, *Edward Scissorhands*. Excited by a screenplay based on Bram Stoker's novel *Dracula*, she coaxed Francis Ford Coppola to direct her in the project, which catapulted her into the stratosphere of leading ladies. Soon came an Oscar nomination for her role as the long-suffering wife in period piece *The Age of Innocence*.

Ryder's latest star vehicle also marks her producing debut in indie director James Mangold's *Girl, Interrupted*, an adaptation of Susanna Kaysen's 1993 memoir about the author's incarceration in a mental ward.

SAWYER

America's newscasting sweetheart has a voice that exudes authority, a face that glows with intelligence and a beauty just short of intimidating. She's tough, but polite; sweet, but probing; intellectual, but down to earth. Best of all, with a gift for raising the Nielsen ratings, she's a network darling.

Diane Sawyer wasn't always this brilliant. In the late 1980s, when she and co-anchor Dan Rather debuted the much ballyhooed news magazine program *PrimeTime Live,* reviews were so devastating that Sawyer considered leaving the business. She had forsaken a post at the prestigious *60 Minutes* only to find herself interviewing celebrities and losing her following. In her subsequent self-reinvention, the savvy former Junior Miss America recast herself as a high-minded investigative reporter. Snipping her famously blond locks (to avoid the glamour stigma), she went on to create what became the signature of *PTL:* hidden camera pieces. In one notorious episode, she entered a supermarket undercover to expose its practice of selling contaminated food. That week the chain store's market value plunged. When she signed a $7 million contract in 1994 to stay on the show, staffers scattered rose petals at her feet.

Sawyer's television career began inauspiciously with weather forecasts on local TV in her native South. She went on to become a press aide in the Nixon White House before helping the exiled president pen his memoirs. Upon her return to Washington she became a general assignment reporter for CBS. Hired early last year as a temporary parachute to slow the ratings free fall of *Good Morning America,* Sawyer worked such magic that she was kept on. Having dated the likes of screen legend Warren Beatty, she is now married to director Mike Nichols.

SCHRAGER

To stay at "an Ian Schrager hotel" is to know you are getting, if not the most opulent accommodation available, certainly the coolest. Schrager, who was born and bred in Brooklyn, has come full circle since he and Steve Rubell founded Studio 54, the Mecca for media, fashion and art trendies. Before it was raided by the IRS (based on a tip from a disgruntled ex-employee) and the partners thrown in jail for tax evasion, the former TV studio was the nightclub of choice for the likes of Andy Warhol, Mick Jagger and Calvin Klein.

Making a remarkable comeback from his 13-month prison term, Schrager is opening hostelries far and wide (and across an ocean to London and Paris) giving today's beautiful people new venues in which to flex their pecs, eat lavishly and party into the wee hours. French sultan of style Philippe Starck's radical, high-style designs set the cutting edge tone at both the Delano in the Art Deco District of Miami Beach, and the Mondrian in Los Angeles, a tribute to what Schrager calls "uncomplicated sophistication."

Schrager's other hotels include the Royalton, the Paramount and Morgans in New York. The new jewel in his crown is the fabled but down-at-heel St. Moritz Hotel on Central Park South. He intends to implement his high glitz/low cost formula at the 684-room, 35-story edifice for which he paid about $70 million. Last year Schrager's company pocketed $80 million in return for selling a controlling interest to NorthStar Capital Partners.

SCHWARZ

When Gerard Schwarz became musical director of the Seattle Symphony in 1985—at 96 years of age the oldest major cultural institution in the Pacific Northwest—the amiable conductor joined a list of renowned predecessors such as Sir Thomas Beecham, who headed the orchestra from 1941 to 1944. Continuing the symphony's long standing tradition of daring programming, the maestro has sustained a commitment to both 20th century music and American composers. Named Conductor of the Year for "bringing the Seattle Symphony to the upper echelon of American orchestras," Schwarz has been called "one of the great hopes for the future of American symphonic music." During his tenure the Seattle Symphony has recorded more than 70 compact discs, giving it the distinction of being one of the most recorded orchestras in the world. In total, Schwarz and his orchestra, which has grown along with Seattle's commercial and cultural boom, have received 10 Grammy nominations.

This year marks the Juilliard graduate's twenty-third season as music director of the New York Chamber Symphony. Music director of New York's Mostly Mozart Festival at Lincoln Center, he has also led the festival in Ravinia and Tokyo. Schwarz has received the Ditson Conductor's Award from Columbia University, an honorary Doctorate of Music from The Juilliard School, as well as honorary doctorates from Fairleigh Dickinson University, the University of Puget Sound, and Seattle University.

SHERMAN

As a kid, Cindy Sherman spent a lot of time creating homemade costumes and parading around the neighborhood to "fool the neighbors." In art school, the future art photographer was known to masquerade as the late Lucille Ball. Nowadays the postmodern lenswoman still dresses up—only now it's as a subject for her own photographs. Wearing masks and other props, she creates various personae in order to make "people recognize something of themselves rather than me."

Her "Untitled Film Still" series—of which all 69 black-and-white photos (executed in the 8 x 10 glossy format of standard publicity shots) were bought by the Museum of Modern Art for $1 million—parodied the fanzine images of blonde bombshell screen idols. Naturally, these portraits starred a be-wigged Sherman, impersonating the fictional icons in their supposed off-camera moments. As Andy Warhol said of her, "She's good enough to be a real actress." A MOMA retrospective of the series exhibited in 1997 was sponsored by Madonna.

In 1995 Sherman received a MacArthur "genius grant." More recently, while staying in Rome, the photographer/conceptual artist created huge Cibachrome prints in which she restaged bawdy renditions of various old-master paintings by the likes of Caravaggio and Raphael. Exploring female images and body language through themes from pornography to fairy-tales, her work has been questioned by some feminists who have accused her of perpetuating female stereotypes. Cindy Sherman recently joined the ranks of fellow artists such as Julian Schnabel to direct a film, *Office Killer*.

SMITH

"I'll never retire" says Liz Smith. "I'm just like an old quarter horse. When the bell rings, I rush out and start running for the story." The native-born Texan, who uses her clout to raise vast sums for causes like the Literacy Partners, has been running after stories for the last three decades. In the 1960s she worked as a ghost writer for the Hearst society column Cholly Knickerbocker, and as the entertainment editor of *Cosmopolitan*. But she made her name with a by-lined column in *The Daily News*. The most popular gossip column of its time ran for twenty years.

In 1991 Smith joined the *L.A. Times Mirror* syndicate, appearing daily in *New York Newsday* until, as she puts it herself, "the publishers pulled the edition out from under its devoted readers." Nowadays she is syndicated in more than 70 newspapers and her column can also be found on the internet.

Although she is described as a gossip columnist, Smith's great strength lies in the fact that she redefined the traditional role of the rumor-spreader, and usually scoops her competitors into the bargain. The woman who, in Gloria Steinem's words, "transcended a whole art form," brings wit and intelligence to bear on a vast array of subjects, including society, sports, theater, film, opera, dance, business and politics. "Gossip," says Liz Smith, "is news running ahead of itself in a red satin dress." She is currently writing her memoirs.

SPIELBERG

Legend has it that Steven Spielberg got his start by commandeering a janitor's closet at Universal Studios, converting it into an office, and donning a suit and tie to get past the guards each morning. Is the story true? It hardly matters. From the forty-minute *Escape from Nowhere,* which he made at the age of thirteen, to the multiple Oscar winning *Saving Private Ryan,* Steven Spielberg has always enjoyed telling tales. And with box office hits like *Jurassic Park, E.T.* and *Schindler's List* under his belt, he is the most celebrated director in the world today. When not behind a camera, Spielberg can be found working at the entrepreneurial endeavors which have raised his fortunes to an estimated $1 billion in 1998.

Unlike other wives of famous men, Kate Capshaw doesn't demonstrate a desperate need to distinguish herself from America's premier director. Not that she doesn't have a significant career in her own right: Capshaw, who abandoned a teaching career to become an actress, met her future husband on the set of *Indiana Jones and The Temple Of Doom,* in which she starred opposite Harrison Ford. And the stunning blonde has had numerous film leads since her betrothal to Spielberg. But at other times she has seemed content to put acting on the back burner while flaunting the domestic bliss she shares with her family. And her husband has publicly thanked her for providing him with a full home life.

Dividing their time between New York, Los Angeles and East Hampton, the couple are generous in their hospitality, hosting friends like Mr. and Mrs. Tom Hanks and the William Jefferson Clintons.

Photo: Patrick McMullan

Photo: Steve Sands

STEWART

When Americans want to preserve their own plums, trim a Christmas tree, or throw a memorable dinner party, they turn to the supreme voice of ambitiously tasteful living, Martha Stewart. American women may work 60 hour weeks and drive their kids to soccer practice, but they still make time to read the domestic diva's sumptuous magazine, lavishly photographed home decorating, gardening and cookbooks, and watch her Emmy-award winning television series, instructional videos, and television specials. Quite how much of the premier lifestyle authority's elaborate and labor-intensive advice is actually applied is another question altogether.

Born Martha Kostyra and raised by Polish parents of modest means in New Jersey, the doyenne of the hearth has helped to make homemaking chic, where once it was merely a series of chores. Meanwhile, as a consultant to K-Mart, a retail chain of low priced home goods, the former model, stockbroker and one-time caterer for Paloma Picasso has provided the middle classes with affordable and tasteful home furnishings. Stewart lives between East Hampton, Connecticut and Maine. Her daughter, Alexis, owns the East Hampton Gym.

Photo: Steve Sands

STREEP

Meryl Streep has played some of the era's most challenging stage and film roles with uncanny virtuosity. Her genius for probing the psychology of her characters has endowed her with a huge following. Noted for impeccable technique combined with raw emotional power, the 50-year old actress, who began her career on the stage, has impressively mastered a range of foreign accents, including Polish, English, Danish, Australian, Italian and Irish. As Sydney Pollack, who directed her in *Out of Africa,* said, "She can actually vanish into another person; in every role she becomes a totally new human being."

Before acting, the New Jersey native studied opera. Two years after appearing on the cinematic radar in *Julia,* the Vassar and Yale drama school graduate's role in *The Deer Hunter* catapulted her to stardom and earned her an Academy Award nomination, the first of 11 (making her the most nominated actress ever). When later that year she won an Emmy for her role in *Holocaust,* the provocative miniseries, she was dubbed "The Actress for the Eighties." Director Mike Nichols later said, "Meryl's got to be one of those phenomena, like Garbo, that happens only once in a generation."

Her performances in films like *Kramer Vs. Kramer, Sophie's Choice* and *The French Lieutenant's Woman* have made her one of the most respected actresses in the world today. Upcoming projects include *50 Violins* (for which she learned to play the fiddle); *Success,* about two duelling TV network executives; and *Still Life,* a family drama which co-stars Michael Douglas. Meryl Streep lives in Connecticut with her husband, sculptor Donald Gummer, and their four children.

TALLEY

André Leon Talley wants to be remembered as someone "who tried to embrace the world of style with joy and passion." As Editor-at-Large at *Vogue,* this tall, flamboyant figure has certainly had more influence than most on what we wear today.

As a student at Brown University in the 1970s, the man who famously hates the "grunge" look wore bell-bottoms that were four inches too short and put vaseline on his eyes. Upon moving to New York he became a volunteer at the Metropolitan Museum, where Diana Vreeland helped to foster his talent. Later Talley became part of Andy Warhol's Factory. In comparison to that period, when Warhol, "the world's greatest catalyst," brought directors, designers, writers, painters and musicians together, nowadays New York "is a dull grind, a city that is all about money."

"Hollywood used to dictate fashion," he says, "as designers were influenced by artists and icons like Hepburn, Kelly and Garbo." Today, he says, there are "few well-dressed people in Hollywood. The stylists promote what they feel is style, so the stars aren't given a chance to bring their own style to the fore."

André Leon Talley lives in Paris and has a home in New York. Beyond Paris, his favorite cities are St. Petersburg and San Francisco.

SULZBERGER

Publisher of *The New York Times,* Arthur Ochs Sulzberger Jr. has the words "It's the content, stupid" carved above his desk. What he means is that when you read the newspaper run by his father Arthur Ochs "Punch" Sulzberger Sr. until 1992, you get "judgement, talent, credibility." You also get "a little something special left over with which to wrap the fish." That hasn't stopped the trailblazer from investigating the possibility of switching from newsprint to electronic distribution systems. "Hell, if someone would be kind enough to invent a technology, I'll be pleased to beam it directly into your cortex," he has said. "We'll have the city edition, the late city edition, and the mind-meld edition."

Appointed chairman of *The New York Times* at age 46, "Young Arthur" presides over a media conglomerate that includes book-publishing companies, magazines, broadcasting stations, and a cable-TV system. But the august "Gray Lady" is the jewel in the empire's crown. Third in circulation (after *USA Today* and *The Wall Street Journal*) the paper with "All the News That's Fit to Print" is widely considered to be one of the finest in the world. This is despite the fact that under Sulzberger Jr.'s stewardship the paper added—*Gasp!*—color to its pages. He has also introduced more "soft sections" so that readers now get six sections of the daily editions to read with their coffee. Playing a key role in the development of the Times Square Business Improvement District, he served as its first chairman. Arthur Sulzberger lives in New York with his wife, artist Gail Gregg.

THURMAN

The thinking man's pin-up. Hailing from an intellectual and spiritual background—her father, who teaches Indo-Tibetan studies at Columbia University, was the first American to be ordained as a Buddhist monk; her mother, a former Swedish model, is a psychiatrist; her godfather was LSD guru Timothy Leary— even her name, Uma, means "The Bright One." Best known for her sultry role in the 1994 hit *Pulp Fiction*, the husky-voiced, 5'11" movie star with smoldering eyes and a body to rival Jayne Mansfield's garnered a Best Supporting Actress Oscar nomination. Although her last two films, *The Avengers* and *Les Miserables*, bombed both critically and commercially, she is still well regarded for memorable roles like the Venus de Milo in *Baron Munchausen*, the luscious babe in *The Truth About Cats & Dogs*, and the unrepressed June Miller in *Henry & June*, based on the life of Henry Miller. Uma Thurman recently appeared off-Broadway as Celimene, considered one of the theater's most difficult leading lady roles, in an adaptation of Moliere's *Misanthrope*. Wed for a year to actor Gary Oldman, she is now married to her *Gattaca* co-star Ethan Hawke. They have a daughter, Maya Ray.

VIDAL

A sort of latterday Oscar Wilde, wit, raconteur, author, playwright, social critic, screenwriter and sometime actor Gore Vidal stormed into the American consciousness in 1948 with his controversial third novel, a homosexual love story called *The City and the Pillar*, which divided the then conservative world of letters.

Raised in Washington, D.C. by his grandfather Thomas Pryor Gore, the blind Senator from Oklahoma (through whom the author is related to Vice President Al Gore) he attended the smart St. Albans school. Entering the world of Hollywood, he penned a number of screenplays including 1959's *Suddenly Last Summer*. The *soi disant* "gentleman bitch" of literature counts many best-sellers in his oeuvre including *Myra Breckinridge, Burr* and *Lincoln*—the latter two part of a series that elucidate his disenchantment with his country of birth. Spending much of his time at his villa in Ravello on Italy's Amalfi coast, Vidal plans to publish a new novel about America in the 1940s early next year.

This acerbic political theorist has been called one of America's finest essayists by *Time* magazine, while in another vein, the socially prominent memoirist has recounted his affiliations with the many celebrities whose lives have touched his, including Truman Capote, Tennessee Williams, John Kennedy ("the President-erect") and Jacqueline Kennedy Onassis, whom he characterizes as money hungry. Gore Vidal has co-habitated with Howard Austin for more than thirty years.

VINCENT

As a youth Billy Vincent divided his time between Muckross House, an extravagant Gothic pile in Ireland, and Filoli, a tycoon's mansion in California. In those prewar days it took two weeks to make the 6,000 mile journey to the Vincents' Irish mansion, which employed a staff of 95, including footmen, ghillies and two governesses (French and English) retained for the edification of their young master Billy.

After a spell at Cambridge, this swashbuckling scion of a California gold mining family enlisted in the Enniskillen Fusiliers and served with distinction in India, Persia, Iraq and Italy. He was badly injured at Monte Casino, but was still one of the first officers to lead his troups to liberate the Italian city. In 1947 Vincent and his sisters inherited a $5 million fortune. Embarking on a business career, his first job was selling a newfangled invention called the helicopter. A foray into oil exploration turned his investment to liquid gold when his company struck oil off Java. Nowadays this dapper dresser is Vice chairman of the American Ireland Fund and a director of Independent News and Media. He holds an honorary doctorate from Trinity College and a fellowship from Cambridge, where he helped to establish the Charles Stewart Parnell Chair of History.

Though Muckross House was given to the Irish government many years ago, the ardent Hibernophile bought a house nearby and regularly visits it with his French wife, Elizabeth, a painter of great distinction. They also have an apartment in Monte Carlo.

WINFREY Talk about a winning formula. Once upon a time Oprah Winfrey was a Mississippi farm girl. Now she combines authenticity, warmth, and a solid moral center to woo a huge audience of television fans year after year. One of the wealthiest women in America, the talk show hostess defies the country's inexhaustible appetite for external beauty by providing a much-admired inner strength.

Sexually abused as a child, Winfrey was a runaway teenager before beginning a radio career at age 18. The veteran broadcaster made her mark in 1986 when, with her uncanny ability to draw out guests, she turned a faltering Chicago television show into the number one nationally syndicated talk show in less than a year. The multiple Emmy Award winning *Oprah Winfrey Show* became the first TV talk show in history to be owned and produced by a woman. Abandoning the sleazy, confrontational formulas of her competitors, she manages to probe her subjects with a sense of compassion.

Winfrey's vulnerability, including perennial climbs up and down the weight ladder, combined with her honesty and spiritual quest, reflect her audience's own struggles and aspirations and have won her a special place in Americans' hearts. Her televised book club and TV and film production company have helped give life to under-appreciated literary works. As an actress she has had many roles, including an Oscar nominated performance in Steven Spielberg's *The Color Purple.* Oprah Winfrey lives with her partner, Stedman Graham, in Chicago.

WOLFE

The ultimate chronicler of pre-millennium American society, Tom Wolfe is celebrated for both his pioneering journalism and epoch-defining fiction. Blurring the lines between the two, Wolfe brings the textures and rhythms of fiction to his nonfiction and the prodigious reporting of society's complexities to his fiction. Although his first nine books were nonfiction (*The Electric Kool-Aid Acid Test, The Pump House Gang, The Painted Word*), he brashly invaded the hermetic literary community in 1987 with his first work of fiction, the Dickensian *The Bonfire of the Vanities*–which became one of the top ten bestselling books of the decade. The sweeping terrain of that masterpiece covered New York's race relations, class, power, and, of course, money (both new and old).

In his latest literary triumph, *A Man in Full,* Wolfe dissects the city of Atlanta. *The New York Times* gushed that the writing was as "powerful and as beautiful as anything…by any American novelist." Two weeks before *A Man in Full* was scheduled to arrive in bookstores, it was named a finalist for the National Book Award in fiction–a major triumph for a writer who had discarded 800 pages of manuscript (and nine years of writing) two years before and started again.

Wolfe grew up in Richmond, Virginia, and graduated from Washington and Lee University. After receiving his doctorate in American Studies from Yale, he worked as a reporter for publications from *The Washington Post* to *New York*. His first international success came with *The Right Stuff,* a 1979 bestseller, which won the American Book Award for general nonfiction. Tom Wolfe lives in New York City.

WOODS The name of this young sports hero is so ubiquitous that when author (and golf enthusiast) John Updike reviewed a new novel, he called it a "Tiger Woodsian debut." When the 21-year-old sensation won the Masters in 1997 his shining example inspired millions of golf neophytes to pick up clubs.

His father, Vietnam veteran Earl Woods, has said that Tiger knew how to swing a club before he could walk. At age five, he beat 10-year-olds. By 16 he was the youngest golfer ever to play in a Professional Golf Association tournament. It was soon time to quit his amateur status, so he dropped out of Stanford University and hit the professional circuit where, with his diverse ethnic roots—he boasts black, American Indian, Chinese, white and Thai blood—he became a dramatic emblem of multiculturalism.

In the same league as super athlete Michael Jordan, Woods commands similarly lucrative product endorsements, even if his performances are occasionally less than stellar. A Buddhist who attributes his calm focus to his religious practice, the young superstar conducts golf clinics for inner-city kids.

WYNN In Las Vegas, a desert town where art has traditionally meant paintings on velvet and where a museum is dedicated to Liberace, Stephen A. Wynn is exchanging tackiness for culture with a capital C. The chairman of Mirage Resorts, a billion dollar a year company that owns and operates casino-hotels, last year opened his 3,000-room, $1.6 billion flagship, Bellagio, a hotel-cum-museum in which $300 million worth of major artworks are displayed.

This would-be Frick started by acquiring Impressionists like Monet and Renoir, worked his way up to Post-Impressionists (Van Gogh's *Peasant Woman Against a Background of Wheat*, painted weeks before the artist's suicide, cost Wynn $47.5 million), became fascinated with Picasso, and later delved into abstract expressionists like De Kooning and Pollock. The most successful tycoon of the gambling-and-hotel business, Wynn spent about $140 million of his own money, under the guidance of New York dealer William Acquavella and former Kimbell Art Museum director William Pillsbury.

Wynn, who is gradually losing his sight to retinitis pigmentosa, an irreversible eye disease, teamed up with junk-bond king Michael Milken in the late 1970s to pioneer the casino as a family vacation destination. Before that he had studied medicine, English literature and business at the University of Pennsylvania. Nowadays, Wynn and his wife of 36 years, Elaine, live between New York, Idaho and a lavish mansion beside Shadow Creek, his golf course and country club on the outskirts of Las Vegas. Their friends include Ron Perelman, Rupert Murdoch and singer Paul Anka. Ⓐ

Summit's completely storable Sun Deck Collection by the ASID award-winning designer John Munford

Antibes • Atlanta • Chicago • Dallas • Dubai • Fort Lauderdale • Houston • Los Angeles
New York • Paris • Philadelphia • Phoenix • San Francisco • Seattle • Toronto • Vancouver

Summit Furniture, Inc.
5 Harris Court, Monterey, CA 93940
Telephone: 831.375.7811   *Facsimile:* 831.375.0940

Summit Furniture (Europe) Ltd.
198 Ebury Street, Orange Sq., London SW1W 8UN
Telephone: 207.259.9244   *Facsimile:* 207.259.9246

THE MODERN ACROPOLIS

Situated on a hilltop with breathtaking views of Los Angeles,
the Santa Monica Mountains and the Pacific Ocean,
the J. Paul Getty Center is truly a museum for the new century.
Here, Trevor White describes its genesis.

When Oscar Wilde returned from his tour of America in the last decade of the nineteenth century, he faithfully related the story of a miner who had struck it rich in the gold mines of California. Emboldened by his new success, the miner ordered a replica of the Venus de Milo. When the statue arrived with its arms broken off the miner was furious, and promptly sued the railroad. To Wilde's delight, the miner won the case, literally winning damages for his trouble.

California has changed a great deal in the last hundred years, although its reputation as a land unburdened by restraint or good taste has stuck to this day. It is hardly surprising, then, that when J. Paul Getty's Roman villa opened in Malibu in 1974, many critics dismissed it as the crowning achievement of a man whose life defined the term *nouveau riche*. Indeed, as John Walsh, the Director of the Getty museum, relates in his excellent history of the institution, it was even suggested that Getty had created "a kitsch new tourist attraction for Southern California; see Gettyland, then drive 60 miles to Disneyland."

Is it fair to dismiss Getty's endeavors in such a harsh manner? Of course not. Although the great oil man never actually visited this grand folly (preferring to live out his last years in an English Tudor mansion), Getty was acutely conscious of his role as a cultural benefactor. As he wrote in a book called *How to get rich:* "I am the last person in the world to question anyone's right to financial success. On the other hand I firmly believe that an individual who seeks financial success should be motivated by much more than merely a desire to amass a personal fortune." At the end of his life he repeated the sentiment with a little less sobriety: "I don't think there's any glory in being remembered as old moneybags."

Getty has often been characterized as an eccentric, and in some respects the expression seems tailor made for "the homeless billionaire" who was married and divorced six times; the tycoon who said that great success requires thirty five different qualities, while 99 percent of people only have thirty four (he neglected to tell the world what those qualities were). Who but the richest man on earth would install a payphone in his home?

However, there was nothing questionable about Getty's passion for art. Inspired by a visit to San Simeon, William Randolph Hearst's legendary estate, he began collecting in the 1930s. Initially he concentrated on acquiring antiquities and decorative arts, because he felt that most great paintings were overpriced. There was one simple dictum which informed Getty's purchases: buy what you like and like what you buy. It served him well. Over a fifty year period he acquired, among many other treasures, some of the best pieces of eighteenth century French furniture, like the massive double desk by Bernard van Risenburgh, and the Cabinet on Stand by André Charles Boulle.

Like many art enthusiasts, Getty tried periodically to stop collecting, but there was always some obscure delight which captivated his imagination and, in time, his wallet. In 1946 he decided to donate some of the works from his huge collection to museums in America and Europe. Four years later he left America for good and in May of 1954, the new J. Paul Getty Museum received its first visitors. Although he was busy making money on the oil fields of Kuwait, Getty sent a letter expressing his hope that "this modest and unpretentious" museum would give pleasure to the residents of Los Angeles. For fourteen years the ranch attracted a steady trickle of art lovers and curious locals. Then, at the age of 76, Getty decided to construct his Roman villa/museum. His advisers were aghast but Getty was not for turning: "Why not show Californians," he asked, "what an especially attractive Roman building would have looked like, with its gardens, fountains–even details such as the appropriate flowers?"

Above:
J. Paul Getty, 1892-1976

Page 274-275: The Museum's entrance facade,
seen from the tram arrival plaza at the
Getty Center. The Museum's collection of
paintings, sculpture, decorative arts, drawings,
illustrated manuscripts, and photographs
is exhibited in five gallery pavillions
around a central courtyard.

Page 276:
Top left: Photograph from the series Changing
Landscapes (1984-1997), part of the exhibition
Making Architecture: The Getty Center from
Concept through Construction.
Top right: Approaching the entrance to
the auditorium, facing west.
Bottom left: Exterior of the restaurant with
indoor and outdoor terrace seating, facing
north toward the Santa Monica Mountains.
Bottom right: Museum entrance hall.

Right:
View of the Peristyle Garden of the J. Paul Getty
Museum in Malibu. The Getty Villa, based on
the Villa dei Papiri in Herculaneum, is currently
closed for renovation and will reopen in 2001
as a center devoted to the display, conservation
and interpretation of ancient art.

Two years later the richest man on earth died. To the genuine astonishment of his staff in Malibu, who had often been warned that he would leave an endowment for operating expenses and no more, Getty left the museum four million shares of Getty oil stock worth $700 million. His instructions were simple: the money was to be spent on a library and "a museum that shall bear my name." It was the largest gift to the arts in modern history.

In December of 1997, fourteen years after the initial plan was hatched, the Getty Center finally opened to the public. Over two thousand people worked on the project, which cost over a billion dollars. Encompassing a museum, arts education, conservation and research complex, it was designed by Richard Meier, one of the most celebrated architects working in America today. Five pavilions, set around an open courtyard, house the permanent collections. Among the highlights are many master-pieces–including Van Gogh's *Irises* (which was bought for a world record $35m); four paintings by Rembrandt, the *Adoration of the Magi* by Andrea Mantegna and works by Monet, Renoir and Cezanne. Fourteen galleries of French furniture and decorative arts include four Eighteenth century paneled rooms. The museum also boasts enviable collections of rare books, illuminated manuscripts and the most distinguished photographic archive in the world today.

Is the Getty Center a great success? The answer to the question depends whether one is referring to the artworks on display, the design of the complex or the overall experience.

Most of the art is of the European tradition, and the youngest painting was finished in 1896; the collection can hardly be described as comprehensive. How can the decision to promote dead, white artists be justified in a city where people with African, Asian and Latin roots predominate? It does seem unusual (to say the least) but John Walsh defends the Getty's policy by saying that "there will always be a place for such a museum in the archipelago of specialized museums in Los Angeles, not for the sake of a white audience but for everyone."

This egalitarian spirit is confirmed by the fact that admission to the museum is free. And, since September 1998, the Getty Center has been open from 9 to 11am on weekdays exclusively for school groups. The museum's education department expects that over 100,000 school children will have visited by the turn of the new millennium.

Left Page: Nude Woman with a Snake, by Rembrandt van Rijn, 1606-1669. Red chalk heightened with white body color. Purchased in 1981, this superb drawing was the beginning of what eventually became a drawings collection of international importance.

Right Page:
Top: Man with a Hoe, by Jean-Francois Millet, French, 1814-1875. Oil on canvas.

Bottom: Adoration of the Magi, by Andrea Mantegna, Italian. circa 1431-1506. Distemper on linen.

Left:
Decorative arts gallery in the South Pavilion.
18th Century Paneled Room, from the library
of a house on the Place Vendome, Paris.

Page 284:
Top: Christ's Entry into Brussels in 1889,
by James Ensor, Belgian, 1860-1949.
Oil on canvas.
Bottom: Irises, by Vincent van Gogh,
Dutch, 1853-1890. Oil on canvas.

Page 285:
Top: Mythological Scene, by Dosso Dossi
(Giovanni di Niccoló de Lutero)
Italian, circa 1490-1542. Oil on canvas.

Bottom: Il Prospetto del Castel's St. Angiolo
con lo Sparo della Girandola,
by Francesco Panini, circa 1780-1785.
Hand colored (watercolor and gouache) etching.

J. Paul Getty loathed modernist architecture, frequently deriding it as an emblem of "this glib and brittle age." It is difficult to imagine that he would like the work of Richard Meier, an architect who believes that "whiteness is not the absence of color–it is the abundance of color." However, Meier has undoubtedly created one of the most spectacular public buildings of the late twentieth century. From the moment one steps into the driverless trams that shuttle visitors up from the car park to the entrance of the travertine-clad museum, one cannot but admire the singular vision of a man who battled for fourteen years to execute a design which even his fans thought wildly ambitious.

On an irregular site with magnificent views and arcane restrictions (during construction not a single bucket of soil could leave the site) Meier worked for six different branches of the Getty Trust. But it was his collaborators, rather than his clients, who often posed the greatest challenges. Meier's skirmishes with Robert Irwin are the stuff of legend. A renowned artist from Southern California, Irwin was hired to design the Center's landscaped garden (which completely changes with the seasons) mid-way through the project. The French decorator, Thierry Despont, who designed the gallery interiors, also clashed with Meier. Depending on your sympathies, creative tension resulted in a more measured and thoughtful space, or the introduction of collaborators compromised Meier's singular aesthetic.

The Getty Center has divided people like this since day one. And it seems inevitable that this sprawling receptacle for the vision of two very different men will continue to attract praise and vitriol in equal measure. Ultimately, however, it is difficult to argue with John Walsh, the Director of the museum, who doesn't seem to mind if people come to criticize the venture. "I don't care what their motive is. It could even be to get a better view of the city." "To get it," he says, "they'll have to come through the galleries. Something's going to rub off." Such pragmatic enthusiasm is shared by Walsh's staff. Their infectious sense of privilege lingers in the mind long after leaving this powerful monument to the timeless appeal of art. One can only conclude that Wilde would approve of the modern Acropolis. Ⓐ

James Kieran Pine
& Associates
Interior Design and Decoration

NEW YORK ◆ CHADDS FORD

(610) 637-3836   (610) 388-8491

THE PRIVATE PLAYGROUND

AN INSIDER'S GUIDE TO THE HAMPTONS

The Hamptons is America's answer to the Côte D'Azur—
an idyllic playground for the rich and famous.
Here, Norah Lawlor provides an insider's guide to this fabled enclave.

Some people say that the Hamptons wasn't built—rather, that it was born in 1929, the same year as Jacqueline Bouvier. Today it is the ultimate playground for America's moguls, movie stars, supermodels, millionaires, musicians and hordes of giggling socialites.

The phenomenon known as "summer in the Hamptons" starts on Memorial Day (usually the last weekend in May) and doesn't officially end until Labor Day. This is the time to see and be seen, unless, of course, you're a year round resident, in which case you'll stay in hibernation until October. That does seem unusual— but then, the Hamptons is a rather unusual place.

Southampton is where you will find the archetypal WASPs in all their curious finery. Most are members of at least one of the private beach clubs. Naturally, it is very difficult to become a member unless you are socially connected; almost as hard, in fact, as becoming connected if you are not a member. To avoid disappointment stay home and read Groucho Marx, who would never join a club that would have him as a member.

Page 288-289: Long Island Sound, photographed by Daniel Aubry.

Above: "The Caesars" in the East Garden of The Parrish Art Museum in Southampton.

The Southampton Bath and Tennis Corporation has a limit of 200 members; some of the lucky few include Revlon's Howard Gittes, fashion designer Vera Wang and tycoon Wilbur Ross. There is an initiation fee of $30,000 and yearly dues range from $4,000 to $7,000. Over at the Meadow Club there is a five-year waiting list; members include Gulfstream's Nick Forstmann, television news anchor Chuck Scarborough, billionaire George Soros, cosmetic surgeon Dan Baker and his socialite wife, Nina Griscom. The Southampton Bathing Corporation asks that you produce letters of recommendation from four current members. Members are up for readmission annually: if you bring the wrong people too many times, you're out, and your initiation fee won't be refunded. Members include philanthropist Carroll Petrie, Harry Hurt III, Henry Buhl and the Kempners. At the Maidstone Club, which has terrific facilities (swimming pool, beach, restaurant and golf course) you also need a member to sponsor your application: try actor Chevy Chase or singer Robert Goulet.

Being in the right tennis club is all well and good, but without the proper golf club, you're not quite swinging. Shinnecock Hills, former home of the US Open, has one of the longest waiting lists. Those who have made the cut include Charlotte Ford and Mai Hallingby. The Bridgehampton Club says it's not about money (the annual dues are quite reasonable) but getting in is an issue. You must know a member socially for at least three years and then he or she must invite you to become a member. If you don't cut the mustard, you might try the National Golf Links of America, where (at least) the golf course is said to be more challenging. Meanwhile, the Atlantic Golf Club has been unfairly described as the club that people come to if they were not "welcome" elsewhere. It opened seven years ago and membership is already closed. The lucky ones include Jonathan Tisch, David Koch, and real estate giant, Edward S. Gordon. Other Beach Clubs include: Sag Harbor Yacht Club, Southampton Yacht Club, Westhampton Country Club, Devon Yacht Club, Southampton Club and the Shinnecock Yacht Club.

Being a member of one of the private clubs is useful, but owning an estate home on one of Southampton's most exclusive streets is where it all begins. On Meadow Lane, the first castle you pass is the home of Francesco & Marina Galesi. They made a splash a few years ago, when they were the first to build a home resembling a French chateau. Galesi took over construction on the half-built home when the previous owners failed to make payments. His is one of the more unusual properties on the lane, with wall to wall aquariums and lavish formal gardens.

The Galesi's neighbors include David and Julia Koch, Linda Wachner, and Henry and Marie-Josée Kravis, who are building a new home right on the ocean. Then there is Gin Lane, where you can find the homes of Carroll Petrie, Herb Allen, Keith Barish and Marty Richards. First Neck Lane has the Bakers and South Main Street has the man in white, Tom Wolfe. Murray Lane has George Soros and Terry Allen Kramer (when she is away from her home in Palm Beach) and Ox Pasture Road has Howard Gittes and German industrialist Werner Otto.

Unlike the sedate Flying Point Beach, Cooper's Beach attracts a young, more social crowd: at the canteen you can get a snack or a phone number. If you don't want to be part of a scene, and you're officially designated as a resident (however temporary) you can use Dune Beach, Cryder Beach, Little Plains Beach or South Main Beach. Wherever you choose to tan your hide, the bottom line is that the Hamptons boast some of America's more enchanting beaches.

After a day at the beach, afternoon shopping is often on the agenda. Palm Beach designer Steven Stolman has the uniform for the WASP set, or you can try the Lilly Pulitzer department at Sak's Fifth Avenue on Main Street. The Men's Store is a few steps away. Hildreth's Department store is one of the oldest in the US, and it is still family owned. They have a second location in Bridgehampton. The Hildreth family has owned property here since the 17th century, along with the Gardiners, the Halseys, the Toppings and the Osbornes.

Book Hampton is where you can pick up one of several literary gems written about the Hamptons: *Philistines at the Hedgerow* by Steven Gaines (who now has his own web site called ihamptons.com), *Hamptons Babylon: Life Among The Super Rich On America's Riviera* by Peter Fearon and *The House That Ate The Hamptons* by James Brady, whose prolific writing has also included *Gin Lane* and *Further Lane*. A new Hamptons guidebook titled *Jodi's Shortcuts* by Jodi Della Femina provides an interesting and amusing potted guide to the area.

The most social restaurant in Southampton is Savanna's, which feels like a lifesize ad for Ralph Lauren; all crisp whites and talk of tennis. No wonder it is popular with clean cut men in fetching blazers. Daniel Ponton's Club Colette (which also has a Palm Beach branch) is an exclusive dinner club; members include Carroll Petrie, Dan Wassong and designer Arnold Scaasi. At the time of writing the club is organizing a junior committee where the membership fee will be $300 a year. Not a bad investment to dine and dance with the best of Palm Beach in the Hamptons.

David Lowenberg and Kirk Basnight, who own The Beacon in Sag Harbor, also own Red Bar Brasserie, which attracts more of a year round resident. You'll also find locals at the Coast Grill and 75 Main, which has a disco on Fridays and Saturdays in the summer. Incidentally, the best place for breakfast in any of the Hamptons is the Golden Pear, where you will see everyone you know before 1pm. Don't expect them to look their best.

The nightlife scene in Southampton is enjoying something of a renaissance. It all started a few summers ago when Jet East owner Andrew Sasson hired a host named Hugo, formerly of Les Caves du Roi in St. Tropez, who introduced "bottle service." To sit in the VIP area of the club with the likes of Sarah Jessica Parker and Sandra Bullock you must order at least a *bottle* of your favorite liquor. But first you have to get past the wretched velvet ropes, guarded by the doorman *du jour*. The best tables are those around the dance floor, which cheerful revellers are inclined to mount.

After you've finished your frolics at Jet (*never* call it Jet East), stop by Life at Tavern, the sister club to the New York hot spot. Brothers Gordon and Erik von Broock partnered up with Life owner Roy Stillman to create this giddy nightspot. In the VIP room you might find regulars like Jennifer Lopez, Oliver Stone or Ivana Trump. But the outdoor patio is much more comfortable: frontmen Mark Baker, Jeffrey Jah and Rocco Ancarola have no trouble filling it with a few hundred of their closest friends. Meanwhile, the twenty something crowd is at Conscience Point, where fashion designer Cynthia Rowley designed the VIP Shag Room. Incidentally, there are some quaint hotels in Southampton, like the Village Latch, the Southampton Inn and a newcomer, The Atlantic.

Bridgehampton is home to the Hampton Classic, which takes place during the last week of August. The most prestigious outdoor horse show in the nation usually features several Olympic veterans and World Champions. The closing day is particularly glamorous, with the Crown Royal Grand Prix, the Calvin Klein Show Jumping Derby and the Revlon Bonus Challenge.

The place to be is the Grand Prix Tent on closing day, where ringside tables can run $2,000. Some of the hottest tables include those of Calvin Klein (who sits with his celebrity chums), Revlon (where you'll see Ron Perelman and his

Below:
The American Hotel, Sag Harbor.

fiancée, actress Ellen Barkin), Louis Roederer Champagne (for obvious reasons!), David Yurman (who has the best view) and Jonathan Farkas (who gets all the socialites). The people to know are Hampton Classic President Dennis Suskind and Chair, Agneta Currey. Why? Because you have to be invited to sit at one of the VIP tables.

Polo players Neil Hirsch and Peter Brant started the Bridgehampton Polo Club, now better known as the Mercedes-Benz Polo Challenge. These matches are among the most exciting events of the summer, beginning in mid-July and running until mid-August. The Challenge attracts a very social crowd. Some of the best polo players from Palm Beach, Argentina and around the world come to Long Island to play.

Horseback riding is a big sport in the area; you can ride high at one of the status stables like Topping Riding Club, where Calvin Klein took his tumble, or Two Trees Stable, where there is plenty of room for polo ponies. Meanwhile, Sag Pond Farm is where you can ride with Rose and Tatiana Schlossberg, grand-daughters of the late Jackie Kennedy Onassis.

The Hamptons has a number of reasonable vineyards. Channing Daughters Winery, owned by Walter Channing, ex-husband of actress Stockard Channing, produces some of the finest New York Chardonnays, while Duck Walk Vineyards in Water Mill and Sag Pond Vineyard, owned by Christian Wolffer, are well worth checking out.

With more of a singles scene than any of the other Hamptons, the restaurants in Bridgehampton get more crowded and stay open much later. Open year round, 95 School Street is the place to be on the weekend. The Independent, which has a sister restaurant in New York, has a late night menu and newcomer Henry's is the spot for Sunday Brunch. The most romantic restaurant is Alison By The Beach in Sagaponack; its owners recently opened the equally seductive Alison In The Inn at the Inn at Quogue. Beaches like Peter's Pond and Sagg Beach also attract a singles scene and the place to stay is The Enclave.

East Hampton is where Def Jam President Russell Simmons and former Motown Records President André Harrell, who now works for Sean "Puffy" Combs, first threw parties for the society crowd who wanted to be with celebrities–and the celebrity crowd who wanted to be in society. There's nothing strange about that; at least, not anymore. This, after all, is the ultimate refuge for Hollywood stars, merchant princes, Wall Street heroes, shameless gold-diggers and society queens.

HOSTS, HONCHOS AND HOTSHOTS

In every enclave around the world there is a discernible pecking order, and the Hamptons is no different. European visitors are often informed that so-and-so is the ultimate dinner party guest, moving with ease in the smartest circles. Beware! That very same person is usually at the bottom of the smart set's list of last resorts. His intimate soirées mean dinner alone and the only star he really knows is Robert Redford playing Jay Gatsby. As Oscar Wilde said of one such cad, "He has dined in every house in London…once."

To save our European readers the tedium of enduring an evening in poor company, we have compiled the following wish list. There are two ground rules. Firstly, we have decided to exclude our *Amazing Americans,* on the premise that they are obviously good company. Secondly, siblings and spouses are chosen as representatives of their families. Here, then, are one hundred characters whose charm and style have made them the envy of everyone who plays the Hamptons game:

Brian Bantry	Tom Freston	Patricia Kennedy Lawford	Ann Rapp
Alec Baldwin	Larry Gagosian	David Koch	Marty Richards
Anne Barish	Francesco Galesi	Coco Kopelman	Felix Rohatyn
Peter Beard	David Geffen	John Kluge	Maer Roshan
Allen Beeber	Michael Gelman	Lulu de Kwiatkowski	Elizabeth Saltzman
Nicholas Berggruen	Nathalie Gerschel Kaplan	Amalia Lacroze de Fortabat	John Scanlon
Jason Binn	Dana Giacchetto	Aerin Lauder Zinterhofer	Peggy Siegal
Vanessa von Bismarck	Howard Gittes	Matt Lauer	Sally Singer
Samantha Boardman	Sarah Gore Reeves	Adam Lindemann	Barry Sonnenfeld
James Brady	Spalding Gray	Fern Mallis	George Soros
Christie Brinkley	Nina Griscom	Aileen Mehle	Regine Taulsen
Alison Brown	Allen Grubman	Nicole Miller	Judy Taubman
Jimmy Buffett	Joanne de Guardiola	Patrick McMullan	Michael Thomas
Henry Buhl	Marjorie Gubelmann	Chappy Morris	Andrew Tilberis
Patricia Burnham	Mai Hallingby	Tommy Mottola	Tinka Topping
David Patrick Columbia	Joseph Heller	Jimmy Nederlander	James Truman
Clive Cooke	Henry Hildreth	Billy Norwich	Adrienne Vittadini
Jennifer Creel	Neil Hirsch	Sheila O'Malley	Bruce Wasserstein
Agneta Currey	Jane Holtzer	Judy Peabody	Jann Wenner
Jerry Della Femina	Rachel Hovnanian	Ronald Perelman	Kevin West
Barry Diller	Harry Hurt III	Carroll Petrie	Christian Wolffer
Jonathan Farkas	Eric Javits	Bob Pittman	Monique Yazigi
Whitney Fairchild	Peter Jennings	George Plimpton	Toby Young
Ted Field	Billy Joel	Faith Popcorn	David Yurman
Teddy Forstmann	Betsey Johnson	Lee Radziwill	Mort Zuckerman

On Lily Pond Lane, Martha Stewart, Mort Zuckerman, Starbucks owner Howard Schultz and entertainment lawyer Allen Grubman all have homes. On Further Lane (in East Hampton and Amagansett) you will find *Saturday Night Live* creator, Lorne Michaels, musician Billy Joel with girlfriend Carolyn Beegan, art dealer Larry Gagosian and Bruce Wasserstein, who held a private dinner party for the Clintons when they visited the Hamptons in the summer of 1998. The President's visit was at the invitation of Allen and Susan Patricof, who live on Huntington Lane.

Publicist Peggy Siegal created quite a stir here when she started doing movie premieres for HBO and private screenings at the home of Bryan Bantry. Ted Field of Interscope Records held his annual party in East Hampton and rap impresario Sean "Puffy" Combs throws the closest thing to a night at Studio 54.

East Hampton has the Hamptons' largest selection of stores to shop in, with some of the biggest names in fashion. For the latest diamond settings you can try London Jewelers, or McCarver & Moser, which hosts cocktail parties to launch their collections throughout the season. Scoop Beach, owned by Stefani Greenfield, also has a lounge and carries designers like Shoshanna Lonstein and Jimmy Choo. Calypso is where you can find the latest swim wear, Cynthia Rowley has the coolest summer dresses and Biba is the place for that sexy little number. If all this shopping wears you out, check out the Naturopathica holistic health spa, which is run by Barbara Close, a cousin of actress Glenn Close.

East Hampton also boasts an impressive selection of restaurants. Husband and wife team Jeff Salaway and Toni Ross own Nick & Toni's, probably the most celebrated eatery in town. One usually ends up on a waiting list, but if you speak to Maitre d' Bonnie Murshin you may have better luck. Steven Spielberg, Kate Capshaw and Penny Marshall are all regulars and no matter what night you choose to go, you will always be surprised. A real Hamptons mainstay, Della Femina also attracts celebrities like Alan Alda, Ross Bleckner

Page 295-297:
Photographed by Daniel Aubry.

and Katie Couric. Owner Jerry Della Femina, who is a real Hamptons character, also owns Jerry's Red Horse Market and East Hampton Point, which is a beautiful place to have cocktails on the deck while watching the sunset. His home is right on the beach in East Hampton and his annual July 4th fete comes complete with a fireworks display. Both Della Femina and Nick & Toni's now have Manhattan branches.

NV Tsunami is a new supper club that is both a restaurant and a nightclub. The Palm Restaurant at the Hunting Inn is where you should go to have a quiet dinner on Sundays: speak to long time Maitre d' Tomas Romano for a reservation. Maya's, the celebrity packed restaurant from St. Barth's, has opened in Wainscott in the old Sapore di Mare space. Along with husband Randy Gurley, Maya will give Nick & Toni's stiff competition with their seafood specialties, but if they don't like how its working out in the Hamptons the Gurleys will probably give back the space to landlord, Pino Luongo. Chez & Chez (which is part-owned by Billy Joel) and The Laundry are alternatives if your first choice doesn't work out. Incidentally, Babette's is the place for breakfast, with its fresh juice bar and all-natural dishes.

In Amagansett, Pacific East is the place to go for dinner; for breakfast you can watch the likes of Alec Baldwin, Kim Basinger and Kathleen Turner at Estia. They also have another location, Estia's Little Kitchen in Sag Harbor. The Maidstone Arms is one of the best places to stay and the dining room is a great place to have dinner. East Hampton has some cozy Bed & Breakfast's such as the J. Harper Poor Cottage, The Pink House and The Hunting Inn.

Finally, Sag Harbor has a large year round community, including a host of literary residents like author and performer Spalding Gray. The best place to stay is the very grand American Hotel. Just around the corner, there is a quiet area called North Haven where celebrities like Christie Brinkley, Peter Cook and Nicole Miller call home. If you're really looking for peace and quiet, head to Shelter Island or Montauk, where the madding crowd are conspicuously absent.

A word of warning: wherever you end up during your sojourn, it is wise to remember that most of what you've heard is true. The Hamptons can be maddening or utterly enchanting, depending on how much credence you give to the social whirligig. My advice? Sit back, relax, try to be nice and enjoy the amazing views. As you'll discover, they certainly don't come cheap. In fact, the only thing cheap in the Hamptons is the train back to New York. And *no one* takes the train. Ⓐ

This earth has a

continent that has a

nation that has a

city that has a

street that has a

store that has

precisely what you want.

Did we mention we deliver?

WWW. BESTSELECTIONS.COM

BestSelections.com

INDEX I

LISTING BY ALPHABET

INDEX I

A

Aaron Basha 58
Abacus Security 58
ABC Carpet & Home 58
Abraham Moheban & Son 59
The Academy Awards 59
Acquavella Galleries 59
Addison on Madison 59
Admiral Limousine Service 60
Hotel Adolphus 58
Aida Thibiant European Day Spa 59
Akin, Gump, Strauss, Hauer & Feld 60
Alan Flusser 60
The Albuquerque Museum of Art & History 60
Alden Shoe Company 60
Alexandra Lind 60
Alexis Hotel 60
Alfred Bullard 60
Algabar 60
Allure Day Spa & Store 60
Along Came Mary! 60
Tina Alster, M.D 61
Amangani 61
Amaryllis, A Flower Shop 61
Ambria 61
American Antiques 61
The American Hotel 61
American Museum of Natural History 61
American Orient Express 62
American Safari Cruises 62
Andover Shop 62
Andrea Rosen Gallery 62
Andrew Dornenburg Private Dining 62
Andrew & Potter 62
Anthony A.P. Stuempfig 62
Antine Associates 63
L'Antiquaire & The Connoisseur 63
Antonio's Antiques 63
Architectural Accents 63
Architectural Digest 63
Armfield, Miller & Ripley 63
Art Luna Salon 63
Art of Eating 63
Art of Fitness 63
Artesia 64
Asanti Fine Jewelers 64
The Asia Society 64
The Aspen Club & Spa 64
Aspen Music Festival 64
Assets Protection Systems 64
Sherrell Aston, M.D. 64
At Home 65
Atlanta Rocks 65
Atlas Floral Decorators 65
Au Bon Climat Wineries 65
Auberge du Soleil 64
Auberge Le Grillon 65
Aubry 65

Augusta National Golf Club 65
Aujourd'hui 65
Auldridge Mead 66
Aureole 65
Aveda Institute 66
Aventura Limousines 66
Avenue 66
The Avon Centre 66
Axis Twenty 66
Azzura Point 66

B

B & B International 67
Babor Institut 67
Bacchanalia 67
Badgley-Mischka 67
Daniel Baker, M.D. 67
Baker & McKenzie 67
Baldwin Gallery 67
Balthazar 67
Bank of Boston 67
Barbara Gladstone Gallery 67
Barbara Israel Garden Antiques 68
Barbara Lockhart 68
Barbera Brooks Fine Flowers 68
Barclay Rex Pipe Shop 68
Barefoot Elegance 68
Barnard College 68
Barneys New York 68
Barrons 69
Barry Friedman 69
Barry Peterson Jewelers 69
Bartrum & Brakenhoff Yachts 69
Bath & Tennis Club 69
Bay Club 69
Bay Hill Club & Lodge 69
Beach Bistro 69
Beacon Hill Nannies 69
Beautique Day Spa and Salon 69
Beauvais Carpets 69
Le Bec-Fin 69
Bel-Air Country Club 70
Hotel Bel-Air 70
Belghiti Tailors 70
Bell'Occhio 70
Bellagio 70
Bergdorf Goodman 70
Beringer Wine Estates 70
Bernard & S. Dean Levy 70
Le Bernardin 70
Berry-Hill Galleries 70
Bessemer Trust 71
Best Domestic Services 71
BestSelections 71
The Beverly Hills Hotel 71
Biba 71
Bigsby & Kruthers 71
Bijan 72

Billy Blanks' World Training Center 72
Binion's Horseshoe 72
Lawrence Birnbaum, M.D. 72
Black Diamond Ranch 72
Black Pearl Antiques & Fine Arts 73
Blackberry Farm 72
Blackbird 72
Bliss 72
Blockheadia Ringnosii 72
Bloom 73
Boca Raton Resort and Club 73
Bonita Bay Club 73
The Boulders 73
Brandeis University 73
The Breakers 74
Breeder's Cup 74
Bridgehampton Polo Club 74
Brill's Content 74
Brinsmaid 74
The Broadmoor 74
The Brook 74
Brooklyn Museum of Art 74
Brown Brothers Harriman & Co. 74
Brown University 75
Brown-Davis Interiors 75
Brownes' & Co. Apothecary 75
Browns 75
Browns Restaurant 76
Bryan Cave 76
Bryn Mawr College 76
Bumble & Bumble 76
Bunny Williams 76
Burger Boat Company 76
The Burgundy Wine Co. 76

C

C & M Arts 77
Cacharel 77
Caesars Palace 77
Café Allegro 77
Café des Amis 77
Café L'Europe 78
Cakebread Cellars 77
Calabria 77
California Culinary Academy 78
Callahan Catering 78
Calligraphy Studios 78
Calvert Woodley 78
Calvin Klein 79
Camberley Brown 79
The Cambridge School of Culinary Arts 79
Campagne 79
Campanile 79
Campbell, Dettman & Panton Realty 79
Cannon/Bullock Interior Design 79
Canyon Ranch 79
Carapan Urban Spa & Store 79
Carey International 79
Caribou Club 80
Carleton Varney Design Group 80
The Carlyle 81
Carlyle Wines 80
Carol Dopkin Real Estate 80
Carolina Herrera 80
Carroll & Co. 80
Carswell Rush Berlin 80
Carter Landscaping 80
The Castle at Tarrytown 81
Century House Antiques 81

Cessna 81
Chaiken and Capone 81
Chalone Vineyard 82
Charles Nob Hill 82
Charles Perry-Chinese Export Porcelain 82
Charleston Grill 82
Charlie Trotter's 82
Charlotte Moss Interior Design 83
Chase International 82
Chase Manhattan Private Bank 82
Chateau du Sureau 84
Château Marmont 83
Chateau Montelena Winery 83
Chef Allen's 83
Chef Reto's Restaurant 83
Chez Francois 83
Chez Panisse 84
Chinese Porcelain Company 84
Chinois on Main 84
Chisholm Gallery 84
The Chopra Center for Well Being 84
Christie's 85
Christie's Great Estates 86
Chubb Group of Insurance Companies 86
Cigar Aficionado 86
The Cigar Box 86
Cindy Griem Fine Jewels 85
Cipriani 86
Dennis Cirillo, M.D. 86
Le Cirque 2000 86
Citibank Private Bank 87
Claremont Rug Company 87
Cleveland Museum of Art 87
Cline Fine Art Gallery 87
Clodagh Design 88
CLS Transportation 88
Club Colette 88
Club Macanudo Chicago 88
Coates, Reid & Waldron 88
Coeur d'Alene 88
Colin Cowie Lifestyles 89
The Colony Club 89
Colony Surf Hotel 89
Commander's Palace 89
Les Concierges 89
Congressional Country Club 89
Conover Real Estate 89
Continental Limousine 89
The Cooper-Hewitt National Design Museum 90
Michelle Copeland, M.D. 89
Le Coq au Vin 90
Corcoran Gallery of Art 90
The Corcoran Group 90
Cosentino 90
La Costa 90
Cove Landing 91
Covington & Burling 90
Craig F. Starr Associates 91
Crain's New York Business 91
Cravath, Swaine & Moore 91
Crème de la Mer 148
Crouch & Fitzgerald 91
The Culinary Institute of America 91
Cullman & Kravis 91
Cypress Point Club 91

PREVIOUS PAGE: *Portrait of Miss Helen Durham, by John Singer Sargent.*

D

D & M Champagne *92*
D'Amico Cucina *92*
Da Silvano *92*
Dallas Museum of Art *92*
Dallas Polo Club *92*
Dalva Brothers *92*
Dana Buchman *92*
Daniel *92*
Daniels, Daniels & Daniels Antiques *92*
Darrell Schmitt Design Associates *93*
Dartmouth College *93*
Dav El *93*
David Anthony Easton *93*
David Jones *93*
David LaVoy *93*
David Stern Designer Jewelers *94*
David Webb *93*
Davis, Polk & Wardwell *94*
De Pasquale, The Spa *94*
De Vera *94*
Deborah Koepper *94*
Deer Valley Resort *94*
Deerfield Academy *94*
Degustibus Cooking School *94*
Delano Hotel *95*
Delaware River Trading Company *95*
Della Femina *95*
Delmonico *95*
Dempsey & Carroll *95*
Departures *95*
Design Associates *95*
Despos *95*
Devon Yacht Club *95*
DHS Designs *96*
Dia Center for The Arts *95*
Diamond Creek Winery *96*
Didier Aaron *96*
Dillingham & Company *96*
Dimson Homma *96*
Distinctive Bookbinding & Stationery *97*
Diva Limousines *97*
Dixon and Dixon of Royal *97*
Dominus Estates *97*
Donald Young Gallery *97*
Donna Karan *97*
Doral Golf Resort & Spa *97*
Dormeuil Personal Tailoring *97*
Doubles *97*
Jeffrey Dover, M.D. *97*
Downtown *97*
Duckhorn Vineyards *98*
Duke University *98*
Dunemere Associates Real Estate *98*
Dunton Hot Springs *98*

E

East Bank Club *99*
East Hampton Gym *99*
East & Orient Company *99*
Edenhurst Gallery *99*
Edward Carter Gallery *99*
Edward Lee Cave *99*
Eleven Madison Park *99*
Eli Wilner & Company *100*
Elinor Gordon *99*
Elizabeth Arden Red Door Salon
   & Spa *100*
Eric Javits *100*

L'Ermitage Beverly Hills *100*
L'Espalier *100*
Estate Antiques *101*
Euphemia Haye Restaurant *101*
Evelyn Poole *101*
EventQuest *101*
Everest *101*
Everglades Club *101*

F

FAO Schwarz *101*
Far Niente Vineyards *101*
Lewis Feder, M.D. *102*
Felidia Ristorante *102*
Felissimo *103*
Fenton & Lang *102*
Ferrari Carano Wineries *102*
Ferrée Florsheim Catering *102*
Field Museum of Natural History *103*
15 degrees *102*
Fine Arts Museum of San Francisco *104*
Fioridella *103*
Firestone and Parson *104*
First Union National Bank *104*
Fish & Neave *104*
Fisher Travel *104*
Fisher Island Spa *104*
Fishers Island Country Club *104*
Fleet Bank *104*
Fleur de Lys *105*
FlexJet *105*
Flight Options *105*
Floral Events Unlimited *105*
Flowers *105*
Peter B. Fodor, M.D. *105*
The Ford Montreux Detroit Jazz
   Festival *105*
Fortune *105*
Fortunoff *106*
Fountain Pen Hospital *106*
Four Seasons Boston *106*
Four Seasons Las Vegas *106*
Four Seasons New York *106*
Four Seasons Palm Beach *106*
Four Seasons Restaurant *106*
Fox Residential Group *107*
Fraenkel Gallery *107*
Framed on Madison *107*
Franciscan Estates *107*
Frank & Barbara Pollack *107*
Fraser Yachts *107*
Frédéric Fekkai Beauté *107*
Freedman Jewelers *107*
Freer Gallery of Art *107*
The French Culinary Institute *108*
The French Laundry *108*
The French Room *108*
Frenchway Travel *108*
Frick Collection *108*

G

G. Ray Hawkins *109*
ga ga gifts of whimsy *109*
Gagosian Gallery *109*
Galerie Michael *109*
Galileo *109*
Gallery Paule Anglim *109*
Galper/Baldon Associates *109*
Game Creek Club *109*

Gardella's Elite Limousine Service *110*
Garden Gate *110*
The Gardener *110*
Gardner Colby Gallery *110*
Gary E. Young *110*
Gavert Atelier *110*
Gazelle Beauty Center and Day Spa *110*
Gearys of Beverly Hills *110*
Gene & Georgetti *111*
Gene Juarez Salon & Spa *111*
Genmar Holdings *111*
Genoa *111*
Geoffrey Bradfield *111*
Hotel George *111*
George L. Jewell Catering *111*
Gibson, Dunn & Crutcher *111*
Gilmartin Studios *111*
Mary Gingrass, M.D. *111*
Gioia *111*
Giovanni's *111*
Givenchy Hotel & Spa *113*
Gladstone Antiques Show *113*
Glen Gate *113*
Glorious Foods *113*
Golden Bear *113*
Golden Door *113*
Golden Nugget *113*
Golden West International *113*
Goldman, Sachs & Co. *113*
Gordon *114*
La Goulue *114*
Gramercy Tavern *114*
Grand Havana Room *114*
Green Classic Limousines *114*
Greenbaum Interiors *115*
Greenberg Van Doren Gallery *114*
The Greenbrier Hotel *114*
Greenhouse Gallery of Fine Art *114*
The Greenhouse Group *114*
Greenleaf & Crosby *114*
La Grenouille *115*
Grgich Hills Cellars *115*
The Grill on the Alley *115*
Groton School *116*
The Grove Park Inn Resort *116*
Guarisco Gallery *116*
Gulfstream Aerospace Corporation *116*
Gump's *116*
Gwathmey Siegel & Associates *116*

H

H. M. Luther Antiques *117*
H. S. Trask & Co. *117*
Hall and Hall Ranch Brokers *117*
Hamilton Cigar Bar *117*
Hamilton Jewelers *117*
Hammer Galleries *117*
Hampton Country Real Estate *117*
Hapa *117*
Harbour Town Golf Links *117*
Hargrave Yachts *118*
Harlan Estate *118*
Harrison K-9 Security *118*
Harry Winston Jewelers *118*
Hartmann Luggage & Leather Goods *118*
Harvard University *118*
Havana Studios *118*
Haverford College *119*
The Hay-Adams Hotel *118*
Kim Heirston *119*

Heitz Wine Cellars *119*
Helena Lehane *119*
Helmut Lang *119*
The Hess Collection Winery *119*
Hickox Salon and Spa *119*
High Museum of Art *119*
Hirschl & Adler Galleries *119*
Hirshhorn Museum and Sculpture
   Garden *120*
Hokanson *120*
The Hotchkiss School *120*
The Hotel *120*
The House on Bayou Road *120*
Houston Polo Club *120*
Howard Kaplan Antiques *120*
HR Beauty Gallery *120*
Hugh Newell Jacobsen *121*
The Huntington Hotel *121*
Huntington Private Financial Group *121*
Hyde Park Antiques *121*

I

Gerald Imber, M.D. *122*
Incredible Adventures *122*
The Inn at Little Washington *122*
The Inn at Spanish Bay *122*
Inn at the Market *123*
Interieurs *122*
Intermarine Yachting *122*
The International Fine Art and Antique
   Dealers Show *122*
International Fine Art Fair *123*
International House *123*
Iron Horse Vineyards *123*
Isabelle Greene & Associates *124*
Island Weiss Gallery *124*
Israel Sack *124*
The Ivy *124*

J

J. C. De Niro *125*
The J. Paul Getty Museum *125*
The Jack S. Blanton Museum of Art *125*
James Danziger Gallery *125*
James Kieran Pine *125*
James Robinson *126*
Janis Alridge *126*
Janos *126*
Japonesque *126*
Jardinière *126*
Jacqueline Jasper Portraits *125*
Jean Georges *126*
Jeffrey Bilhuber *126*
Jensen-Smith *126*
Hotel Jerome *126*
Jerry Dilts and Associates *126*
JetSource *127*
JFA Designs *127*
The Jockey Club *127*
Joel Soroka Gallery *127*
John Barrett Salon *127*
John Bartlett *127*
John Berggruen Gallery *127*
John Daugherty, Realtors *127*
John H. Surovek Gallery *127*
John & Paul Herring & Co. *127*
The John Sahag Workshop *127*
John's Island Club *128*
Jones, Day, Reavis & Pogue *128*

INDEX I

Jordan Vineyard & Winery *128*
Joseph A. Bank Clothiers *128*
Joseph Phelps *128*
Josephine Sasso *128*
Joshua & Company *128*
Josie Natori *128*
JP King Auction Company *129*
JP Morgan *129*
Juan Juan Salon *129*
Judith Leiber *129*
Judith Ripka *129*
Jupiter Hills *129*
Just Ask Peter *129*

K

Frank Kamer, M.D. *130*
Karl Kemp & Associates *131*
Kay Ledbetter & Associates *130*
Kemble Interiors *130*
Kennedy Galleries *130*
Kennedy & Violich *130*
Kensington Country Club *130*
Kent School *130*
Kentshire Galleries *130*
Kentucky Derby *130*
Kerry Joyce *130*
Key Lime Pie Salon and Wellness Spa *130*
The Keyes Company *131*
Kiawah Island Golf & Tennis Resort *131*
Kieselstein-Cord *133*
Kimbell Art Museum *133*
Kindel Furniture *134*
King & Spalding *133*
Kingsmill Resort *133*
Kinsey Marable Booksellers *133*
Kittansett Club *133*
The Knickerbocker Club *134*
Knight Security Systems *134*
Kroll Associates *134*
Kronish, Lieb, Weiner & Hellman, L.L.P. *134*
Kurt E. Schon *134*

L

L.A. Louver Gallery *135*
The L.A. Sports Club *135*
Lagos *135*
Lake Placid Lodge *135*
Lakeside Golf Club *135*
Lakeview Inn *135*
Lambertson Truex *135*
The Lark *136*
Latham & Watkins *136*
Laurels *136*
The Lawrenceville School *136*
Lazzara Yachts *136*
Leading Estates of the World *136*
Lee Epting *136*
Lehman Brothers Private Client Services *136*
Leo Castelli Gallery *136*
Leonard N. Stern School of Business *137*
Cap B. Lesesne, M.D. *138*
Leslie & Co. *137*
Lespinasse *137*
Lespinasse *137*
The Levison & Cullen Gallery *137*
Lexington Bar and Books *138*

Lighthouse Point Yacht & Racquet Club *138*
Lilly Pulitzer *138*
Ling Salon *138*
Ling Skin Care *138*
The Links Club *138*
Lisa Lindblad Travel Design *138*
The Little Nell *139*
The Lodge on Little St. Simons Island *140*
London Jewelers *139*
Los Angeles Times *139*
Lou Marotta, Inc. *141*
Louis, Boston *139*
Lowrance Interiors *140*
Lucques *139*
Lutsko Associates *140*
Luxuryfinder.com *140*
Lyman Perry *140*
Lynn Jachney Charters *140*

M

M. Finkel & Daughter *141*
M. Penner *141*
M. S. Rau Antiques *141*
Madison Avenue Bookshop *142*
Magnum Marine *142*
La Maisonette *142*
Malcolm Franklin *142*
Manhattan Anti-Aging Clinic *142*
Mansion on Turtle Creek *142*
Mansour *142*
Marc Friedland *142*
Marc Jacobs *143*
Marc Magnus *142*
Marguerite Riordan *143*
Marian Goodman Gallery *143*
Mario Buatta *143*
Mark Hampton *143*
The Mark *143*
Mark's Garden *143*
Mark's Las Olas *143*
Marlborough *144*
Martel Productions *144*
Martha Angus *145*
Martin Katz *144*
Marvin Alexander *144*
Mary Boone Gallery *144*
Mary Elaine's *144*
Mary McFadden *144*
Alice F. Mason *145*
Mason & Morse *145*
Masters Tournament *145*
Alan Matarasso, M.D. *145*
Matsuhisa *145*
Matthew Marks Gallery *145*
The Mauna Lani Bay *146*
Maurice Badler Fine Jewelry *145*
Maurice Bonamigo *146*
Maurice Jennings and David McKee *146*
Maxfield *146*
Maxwell Galleries *146*
The Mayflower Inn *146*
Mayle *147*
McCarty Pottery *147*
McMillen *147*
Meadowood Napa Valley *147*
Mecox Gardens *147*
MedFitness *147*
Mellon Bank *147*

La Mer *148*
Mercer Hotel *148*
The Mercury *148*
Merion Golf Club *148*
Merrill Lynch Financial Services *148*
Metropolitan Limousine *148*
Metropolitan Museum of Art *148*
The Metropolitan Opera *149*
Meurice Garment Care *149*
MGM Grand *149*
Michael Graves & Associates *149*
Michael Taylor Designs *149*
Michael Werner Gallery *149*
Michael's *149*
Mille Fleurs *150*
Milwaukee Art Museum *150*
Minardi Salon *150*
Mindy Weiss Party Consultants *150*
The Mirage *150*
Miraval *150*
Mitchell-Innes and Nash *150*
MLS Limousines *150*
Juan Pablo Molyneux *151*
Montrachet *151*
Montreux Golf & Country Club *151*
Moore Brothers Wine Company *151*
The Morgan Library *151*
Morgan Stanley Dean Witter *151*
Morgenthal Frederics Opticians *152*
Morrison & Foerster *152*
Murad Spa *152*
Museum of Contemporary Art San Diego *152*
Museum of Fine Arts, Boston *152*
Museum of Modern Art *152*
Myott Studio Workshop *152*

N

Nancy Goslee Power & Associates *153*
Naomi Leff & Associates *153*
Natalie Gerschel Kaplan *153*
Nathan Liverant and Son Antiques *153*
National Air and Space Museum *153*
National Gallery of Art *153*
National Golf Links of America *153*
Neal Auction Company *153*
Neiman Marcus *153*
Nelson & Nelson Antiques *155*
Nemati Collection *155*
NetJets *155*
Nevada Wine Cellar & Spirits *155*
New Life Clinic & Therapy Spa *155*
New Orleans Auction Galleries *155*
New Orleans Jazz & Heritage Festival *155*
New Orleans Museum of Art *155*
New York Aviation *155*
New York Botanical Garden *155*
The New York Observer *157*
New York Palace Hotel *157*
The New York Times *157*
New York Yacht Club *157*
Frederick A. Newman, M.D. *157*
Newport Art Museum *157*
Newport Music Festival *157*
Newseum *157*
Newton Vineyards *158*
Niall Smith Antiques *158*
Nick and Toni's *158*
Niebaum Coppola *158*

Nina Hovnanian Couture *158*
No. 9 Park *158*
Nobu *158*
Northern Trust *158*
Nova Limousine Service *158*
Nursery Lines *158*

O

Oakland Hills Country Club *159*
Oakmont Country Club *159*
Ober, Onet & Associates *159*
Ojai Valley Inn and Spa *159*
Old Chatham Sheepherding Company Inn *159*
Old Louisville Inn *159*
L'Olivier Floral Atelier *159*
One Pico *160*
Opus One Winery *160*
L'Orangerie *160*
Oregon Bach Festival *160*
Osteria del Circo *160*
Outside *160*

P

Pace Wildenstein *161*
Pacific Tall Ship Company *161*
Pacific Western Traders *161*
The Pacific-Union Club *161*
Pahlmeyer *161*
Le Palais *161*
Palm Beach International Art & Antique Fair *161*
Palm Beach Polo and Country Club *161*
Palmer Johnson Yachts *162*
Pamela Dennis *162*
Pascal *162*
Patina *162*
Paul, Hastings, Janofsky & Walker *162*
Paul Kasmin Gallery *162*
Paul Stuart *162*
Pauline Pocock Antiques *162*
Pavillion Agency *162*
Peabody Museum of Natural History *163*
The Peaks Resort and Golden Door Spa *163*
Pebble Beach Resorts *163*
The Peninsula Beverly Hills *163*
The Peninsula New York *164*
Performance Ski *163*
Jon Perlman, M.D. *163*
The Perlman Music Program *163*
Perna Luxury Real Estate *164*
Pete Dye Golf Club *164*
Peter Coppola Salon *164*
Peter Cummin & Associates *164*
Peter Marino & Associates *164*
Peter Michael *164*
Petersen Aviation *165*
Philadelphia Museum of Art *165*
Philip Baloun *164*
Philip H. Bradley *165*
Philip Johnson/Alan Ritchie Architects *165*
Philip Press *165*
Philips Exeter Academy *165*
Pine Valley Golf Club *165*
Pinehurst Polo Club *166*
Pinehurst Resort & Country Club *166*

Plantation 166
PNC Advisors 166
The Point 167
Post Ranch Inn 166
Prince Dimitri 167
Princeton University 166
Private Chefs, Inc. 166
Privé 167
Professional Nannies Institute 167
Pucci 167

Q

Quest 167
La Quinta 167

R

R.H. Love Galleries 168
Rabbit Ridge Vineyards 168
Racquet & Tennis Club 168
Radu Physical Culture 169
Ralph Lauren 169
Rancho Valencia Resort 169
Randolph Duke 169
Raytheon 169
Rebecca Moss 169
The Redfern Gallery 169
Reebok Sports Club 169
Regen-Leigh Antiques 169
The Regent Beverly Wilshire 170
John Reilly 169
Renaissance 170
Renny 170
Rialto 170
Richard Anderson Fine Arts 170
Richard Gould Antiques 170
Richard Gray Gallery 171
Richard Haynes & Associates 170
Richard J. Fisher Tinwork 170
Richard Keith Langham 171
Richard L. Feigen & Company 171
Richard York Gallery 171
Ridge Vineyards 171
The Rienzi House Museum 171
Rio 171
The Rittenhouse Hotel 172
Ritz-Carlton Hotel 171
Ritz-Carlton, Buckhead 171
Ritz-Carlton, Laguna Niguel 171
The River Café 173
Riviera Country Club 172
RL 172
Robert A.M. Stern Architects 172
Robert Isabell 172
Robert Long 173
Robert Mann Gallery 173
Robert Mondavi Winery 173
Robert Talbott Shirts 173
The Rockwell Group 173
Ron Herman L.A. 173
Ron Herman Landscape Architect 173
Rose Tarlow-Melrose House 174
Rosenberg & Stiebel 174
Roy's 174
Royal Fiesta Caterers 174
Royal Garden at Waikiki 174
Rudolf Steiner School 174
Ruggles Grill 174
The Ryland Inn 174

S

S. Bernstein & Co. 175
S.J. Shrubsole 175
Safra Bank 175
Saks Fifth Avenue 175
Salander-O'Reilly Galleries 175
Sallea Antiques 175
Salon AKS 175
Salon Cristophe 175
Salon d'Artiste 175
Salts 175
San Diego Museum of Art 176
San Diego Polo Club 176
San Francisco Golf Club 176
San Ysidro Ranch 176
Santa Barbara Polo and Racquet
    Club 176
Santa Fe Horse Park and Polo Club 177
Santa Fe Opera 177
Julian Schnabel 177
Schramsberg Vineyards 177
The Schwebel Company 177
Scott Snyder 177
Scottsdale Museum of Contemporary
    Art 177
Screaming Eagle Vineyards 177
Scully and Scully 177
Sea Island 178
Seaman Schepps 178
Sean Kelly Gallery 178
Seattle Art Museum 177
Seminole Golf Club 179
77 Maiden Lane 179
Shadow Creek 179
Shafer 179
Shapur Mozaffarian 178
Sharon Sacks Productions 179
Shearman & Sterling 179
Shelly Zegart Quilts 179
Sherry Lehmann 179
Shinnecock Hills Golf Club 180
Shipman House 180
Shreve & Co. 180
Shreve, Crump & Low 180
Shutters on the Beach 180
Sidley & Austin 180
Silver Oak Cellars 180
Silver Screen Security 180
Silverado Vineyards 180
Skadden, Arps, Slate, Meagher
    & Flom 181
Victor Skrebneski 181
Sokolin Wines 181
SOLE by Soledad Twombly 182
Soniat House 181
Soolip Paperie & Press 182
Sotheby's 182
Sotheby's International Realty 182
Souchi 182
Spago Hollywood 182
Spyglass Hill Golf Club 182
St. George's School 182
St. John Knits 183
St. Mark's School 183
St. Paul's School 183
St. Regis Hotel 183
Stag's Leap Wine Cellars 183
Stanford University 183
Starkey International 183
Steinway & Sons 184
Stella Salons 184

Stems 185
Steve Martino & Associates 184
Steven Holl Architects 184
Strategic Controls 184
Stribling & Associates 184
Studio Sofield 184
Styline Furniture 185
Sue Fisher King 185
Sullivan & Cromwell 185
Summit Aviation 186
Sumpter Priddy III 185
Sundance Hotel 185
Sunset Beach 186
Sunset Cottage 186
Susan Ciminelli Day Spa 186

T

The Taft School 187
Talbott 187
Tanglewood Music Festival 187
Thad Hayes Design 187
Thea Westreich Art Advisory
    Services 187
Therien & Company 187
Thierry Despont 187
Throckmorton Fine Art 188
Thunderbird Products 187
The Tides 187
Tiffany & Co. 187
Timberhill Ranch 188
Time Will Tell 188
Timothy Eaton Fine Art 188
Tocca 188
Todd Oldham 189
Tom Mathieu & Company 189
Tony Shafrazi Gallery 189
Adelaide Althin Toombs Sundin 189
Total Travel & Tickets 189
Town & Country 189
Town & Country Nannies & Mothers
    In Deed 189
Tracey Ross 190
Tracy Feith 190
Trinity School 190
Triple Creek Ranch 190
Troon Golf & Country Club 190
Troquet 190
Trump International Golf Club 190
Trump International Hotel 191
Tuleh 191
Turley Wine Cellars 191
20/20 Wines 191
Twin Farms 191
Two Design Group 191

U

U.S. Open Polo Tournament 192
U.S. Open Tennis 192
U.S. Security 192
Ultimo 192
Ultramarine 192
The Union Club 192
University of Pennsylvania 192
Urban Epicuria 192
US Trust 192

V

Valentino 193
Valerie Wilson Travel 193
Valley Club of Montecito 193
Vance Jordan Fine Art 194
Vanity Fair 193
Variety 193
Vassar College 193
Vera Wang 193
Veritas 194
Victoria Hagan 194
A La Vieille Russie 194
The Virginian Golf Club 194
Vision Aire 194
Vose Galleries of Boston 194

W

W 195
Wagwear 195
The Wall Street Journal 195
Walters Art Gallery 195
Warren-Tricomi Salon 195
The Washington Post 195
Wayne Pratt Antiques 195
Weisbrod Chinese Art 195
Wellesley College 196
Wendy Krispin 196
Patricia Wexler M.D. 196
Whistling Straits 198
Whitinsville Golf Club 196
Wildenstein & Co. 196
Wilkes Bashford 197
Will Rogers Polo Club 196
William A. Karges Fine Art 196
William B. May 197
William Calvert 197
William Doyle Galleries 197
William Pitt Real Estate 197
Wilmington Trust-FSB 197
Wilson Sonsini Goodrich & Rosati 197
Windows on the World Wine School 198
Windsor Court Hotel 198
Windsor Village 198
The Wine Cask 198
Winged Foot Golf Club 198
Winterthur Museum, Garden
    and Library 198
The Women's Center for Plastic and
    Reconstructive Surgery 198
The Woods 198

Y

Yachtscape 199
Yale School of Management 199
Yale University Golf Course 199
Yeamans Hall Club 199
York Furrier 199

Z

Zachy's 199

The Seductive Splendor Of Diamonds Platinum & Gold

PIRANESI

721 Madison Avenue;   New York, New York 10021   Tel: (212) 750-2799
521 East Cooper Avenue;   Aspen, Colorado 81611   Tel: (970) 920-7777

Visit us at: w w w . p i r a n e s i . c o m

INDEX II

LISTING BY STATE

INDEX II

ALABAMA

JP King Auction Company *129* AUCTION HOUSES *Gadsden*

ALASKA

Maurice Jennings and David McKee *146* ARCHITECTS AND INTERIOR DESIGNERS *Fayetteville*

ARIZONA

The Boulders *73* HOTELS *Carefree*
Canyon Ranch *79* SPAS AND CLINICS *Tucson*
Elizabeth Arden Red Door Salon & Spa *100* SPAS AND CLINICS *Phoenix*
Hapa *117* RESTAURANTS (RS) *Scottsdale*
Janos *126* RESTAURANTS *Tucson*
Mary Elaine's *144* RESTAURANTS *Scottsdale*
Miraval *150* SPAS AND CLINICS *Catalina*
Perna Luxury Real Estate *164* PROPERTY CONSULTANTS *Scottsdale*
Scottsdale Museum of Contemporary Art *177* MUSEUMS (RS) *Scottsdale*
Steve Martino & Associates *184* LANDSCAPE ARCHITECTS *Phoenix*
Troon Golf & Country Club *190* GOLF CLUBS *Scottsdale*

CALIFORNIA

Andrew & Potter *62* EMPLOYMENT AGENCIES (BKS) *Santa Barbara*
Art Luna Salon *63* HAIR AND BEAUTY *West Hollywood*
Asanti Fine Jewelers *64* JEWELRY AND WATCHES *San Marino*
Au Bon Climat Wineries *65* WINEMAKERS *Los Olivos*
Auberge du Soleil *64* HOTELS *Rutherford*
Azzura Point *66* RESTAURANTS *Corronado*
Barefoot Elegance *68* ARCHITECTS AND INTERIOR DESIGNERS *Newbury Park*
Beringer Wine Estates *70* WINEMAKERS *Napa*
Billy Blanks' World Training Center *72* FITNESS (BKS) *Sherman Oaks*
Blockheadia Ringnosii *72* WINEMAKERS (BKS) *St. Helena*
Browns *75* SPECIALTY SHOPS *Santa Monica*
Cakebread Cellars *77* WINEMAKERS *Rutherford*
Chalone Vineyard *82* WINEMAKERS *Soledad*
Chateau du Sureau *84* HOTELS *Oakhurst*
Château Marmont *83* HOTELS *Hollywood*
Chateau Montelena Winery *83* WINEMAKERS *Calistoga*
Chez Panisse *84* RESTAURANTS *Berkeley*
Chinois on Main *84* RESTAURANTS *Santa Monica*
The Chopra Center for Well Being *84* SPAS AND CLINICS *La Jolla*
Claremont Rug Company *87* SPECIALTY SHOPS *Oakland*
Cosentino *90* WINEMAKERS (BKS) *Yountville*
La Costa *90* SPAS AND CLINICS *Carlsbad*
Cypress Point Club *91* GOLF CLUBS *Pebble Beach*
De Vera *94* SPECIALTY SHOPS (RS) *San Francisco*
Diamond Creek Winery *96* WINEMAKERS *Calistoga*
Dominus Estates *97* WINEMAKERS *Yountville*
Duckhorn Vineyards *98* WINEMAKERS *St. Helena*
Far Niente Vineyards *101* WINEMAKERS *Oakville*
Ferrari Carano Wineries *102* WINEMAKERS *Healdsburg*
Flowers *105* WINEMAKERS (RS) *Cazadero*
Franciscan Estates *107* WINEMAKERS *St. Helena*
The French Laundry *108* RESTAURANTS *Yountville*
G. Ray Hawkins *109* ART DEALERS *Santa Monica*
Galper/Baldon Associates *109* LANDSCAPE ARCHITECTS *Venice*
The Gardener *110* SPECIALTY SHOPS *Berkeley*
Givenchy Hotel & Spa *113* SPAS AND CLINICS *Palm Springs*
Golden Door *113* SPAS AND CLINICS *San Marcos*
Grgich Hills Cellars *115* WINEMAKERS *Rutherford*

Harlan Estate *118* WINEMAKERS *Oakville*
Havana Studios *118* CIGAR BARS *Burbank*
Heitz Wine Cellars *119* WINEMAKERS *St. Helena*
The Hess Collection Winery *119* WINEMAKERS *Napa*
The Inn at Spanish Bay *122* HOTELS (BKS) *Pebble Beach*
Iron Horse Vineyards *123* WINEMAKERS *Sebastopol*
Isabelle Greene & Associates *124* LANDSCAPE ARCHITECTS *Santa Barbara*
JetSource *127* AIRPLANES *Carlsbad*
JFA Designs *127* JEWELRY AND WATCHES *Irvine*
Jordan Vineyard & Winery *128* WINEMAKERS *Healdsburg*
Joseph Phelps *128* WINEMAKERS *St. Helena*
L.A. Louver Gallery *135* ART DEALERS *Venice*
Lakeside Golf Club *135* GOLF CLUBS *Burbank*
Mansour *142* SPECIALTY SHOPS *West Hollywood*
Mark's Garden *143* FLORISTS *Sherman Oaks*
Meadowood Napa Valley *147* HOTELS *St. Helena*
Michael's *149* RESTAURANTS *Santa Monica*
Mille Fleurs *150* RESTAURANTS *Rancho Santa Fe*
Murad Spa *152* SPAS AND CLINICS *El Segundo*
Museum of Contemporary Art San Diego *152* MUSEUMS *San Diego*
Nancy Goslee Power & Associates *153* LANDSCAPE ARCHITECTS *Santa Monica*
Newton Vineyards *158* WINEMAKERS *St. Helena*
Niebaum Coppola *158* WINEMAKERS *Rutherford*
Ojai Valley Inn and Spa *159* SPAS AND CLINICS *Ojai*
One Pico *160* RESTAURANTS *Santa Monica*
Opus One Winery *160* WINEMAKERS *Oakville*
Pacific Western Traders *161* SPECIALTY SHOPS *Folsom*
Pahlmeyer *161* WINEMAKERS *Napa*
Pascal *162* RESTAURANTS *Newport Beach*
Pebble Beach Resorts *163* GOLF CLUBS *Pebble Beach*
Peter Michael *164* WINEMAKERS *Calistoga*
Petersen Aviation *165* AIRPLANES *Van Nuys*
Post Ranch Inn *166* HOTELS (BKS) *Big Sur*
La Quinta *167* GOLF CLUBS *La Quinta*
Rabbit Ridge Vineyards *168* WINEMAKERS *Healdsburg*
Rancho Valencia Resort *169* HOTELS *Rancho Santa Fe*
The Redfern Gallery *169* ART DEALERS *Laguna Beach*
Ridge Vineyards *171* WINEMAKERS *Cupertino*
Ritz-Carlton, Laguna Niguel *171* HOTELS *Dana Point*
Riviera Country Club *172* GOLF CLUBS *Pacific Palisades*
Robert Mondavi Winery *173* WINEMAKERS *Oakville*
Robert Talbott Shirts *173* FASHION *Carmel Valley*
Ron Herman Landscape Architect *173* LANDSCAPE ARCHITECTS *San Leandro*
San Diego Museum of Art *176* MUSEUMS *San Diego*
San Diego Polo Club *176* POLO CLUBS *Rancho Santa Fe*
San Ysidro Ranch *176* HOTELS *Santa Barbara*
Santa Barbara Polo and Racquet Club *176* POLO CLUBS *Carpinteria*
Schramsberg Vineyards *177* WINEMAKERS *Calistoga*
Screaming Eagle Vineyards *177* WINEMAKERS *Oakville*
Shafer *179* WINEMAKERS *Napa*
Sharon Sacks Productions *179* PARTY ORGANIZERS AND CATERERS *Reseda*
Shutters on the Beach *180* HOTELS *Santa Monica*
Silver Oak Cellars *180* WINEMAKERS *Geyserville*
Silverado Vineyards *180* WINEMAKERS *Napa*
Soolip Paperie & Press *182* SPECIALTY SHOPS (BKS) *West Hollywood*
Spago Hollywood *182* RESTAURANTS *West Hollywood*
Spyglass Hill Golf Club *182* GOLF CLUBS *Pebble Beach*
St. John Knits *183* FASHION *Irvine*
Stag's Leap Wine Cellars *183* WINEMAKERS *Napa*
Stanford University *183* COLLEGES *Stanford*
Talbott *187* WINEMAKERS *Gonzalez*
Timberhill Ranch *188* HOTELS *Cazadero*

Town & Country Nannies & Mothers In Deed *189* EMPLOYMENT AGENCIES *Palo Alto*
Troquet *190* RESTAURANTS (RS) *Costa Mesa*
Turley Wine Cellars *191* WINEMAKERS *St. Helena*
Urban Epicuria *192* SPECIALTY SHOPS (RS) *West Hollywood*
Valentino *193* RESTAURANTS *Santa Monica*
Valley Club of Montecito *193* GOLF CLUBS (BKS) *Santa Barbara*
William A. Karges Fine Art *196* ART DEALERS *Carmel*
Wilson Sonsini Goodrich & Rosati *197* LAW FIRMS *Palo Alto*
The Wine Cask *198* WINE MERCHANTS *Santa Barbara*

CALIFORNIA - BEVERLY HILLS/LOS ANGELES

The Academy Awards *59* EVENTS *Beverly Hills*
Aida Thibiant European Day Spa *59* SPAS AND CLINICS *Beverly Hills*
Algabar *60* SPECIALTY SHOPS (RS) *Los Angeles*
Along Came Mary! *60* PARTY ORGANIZERS AND CATERERS *Los Angeles*
Barbara Lockhart *68* ARCHITECTS AND INTERIOR DESIGNERS *Beverly Hills*
Bel-Air Country Club *70* PRIVATE CLUBS *Los Angeles*
Hotel Bel-Air *70* HOTELS *Los Angeles*
Best Domestic Services *71* EMPLOYMENT AGENCIES *Beverly Hills*
The Beverly Hills Hotel *71* HOTELS *Beverly Hills*
Bijan *72* FASHION *Beverly Hills*
Lawrence Birnbaum, M.D. *72* COSMETIC SURGEONS *Beverly Hills*
Campanile *79* RESTAURANTS *Los Angeles*
Cannon/Bullock Interior Design *79* SPECIALTY SHOPS (RS) *Los Angeles*
Carroll & Co. *80* FASHION *Beverly Hills*
CLS Transportation *88* CHAUFFEUR SERVICES *Los Angeles*
Colin Cowie Lifestyles *89* PARTY ORGANIZERS AND CATERERS *Los Angeles*
Darrell Schmitt Design Associates *93* ARCHITECTS AND INTERIOR DESIGNERS *Los Angeles*
David Jones *93* FLORISTS *Los Angeles*
Diva Limousines *97* CHAUFFEUR SERVICES *Los Angeles*
Downtown *97* SPECIALTY SHOPS *Los Angeles*
Edenhurst Gallery *99* ART DEALERS *Los Angeles*
L'Ermitage Beverly Hills *100* HOTELS *Beverly Hills*
Peter B. Fodor, M.D. *105* COSMETIC SURGEONS *Los Angeles*
ga ga gifts of whimsy *109* SPECIALTY SHOPS (RS) *Los Angeles*
Galerie Michael *109* ART DEALERS *Beverly Hills*
Gavert Atelier *110* HAIR AND BEAUTY (RS) *Beverly Hills*
Gearys of Beverly Hills *110* SPECIALTY SHOPS *Beverly Hills*
Gibson, Dunn & Crutcher *111* LAW FIRMS *Los Angeles*
Grand Havana Room *114* CIGAR BARS *Los Angeles*
The Grill on the Alley *115* RESTAURANTS *Beverly Hills*
The Ivy *124* RESTAURANTS *Los Angeles*
The J. Paul Getty Museum *125* MUSEUMS *Los Angeles*
The Jockey Club *127* PRIVATE CLUBS *Beverly Hills*
Juan Juan Salon *129* HAIR AND BEAUTY *Beverly Hills*
Frank Kamer, M.D. *130* COSMETIC SURGEONS *Beverly Hills*
Kerry Joyce *130* ARCHITECTS AND INTERIOR DESIGNERS *Los Angeles*
The L.A. Sports Club *135* FITNESS *Los Angeles*
Latham & Watkins *136* LAW FIRMS *Los Angeles*
Laurels *136* FLORISTS *Los Angeles*
Leading Estates of the World *136* PROPERTY CONSULTANTS *Los Angeles*
Los Angeles Times *139* MEDIA *Los Angeles*
Lowrance Interiors *140* ARCHITECTS AND INTERIOR DESIGNERS *Los Angeles*
Lucques *139* RESTAURANTS (RS) *Los Angeles*
Marc Friedland *142* SPECIALTY SHOPS *Los Angeles*
Martin Katz *144* JEWELRY AND WATCHES *Beverly Hills*
Matsuhisa *145* RESTAURANTS *Beverly Hills*
Maxfield *146* FASHION *Los Angeles*

PREVIOUS PAGE: *Room view from The Huntington Hotel, San Francisco, CA.*

Mindy Weiss Party Consultants *150* PARTY ORGANIZERS AND
CATERERS *Beverly Hills*
MLS Limousines *150* CHAUFFEUR SERVICES *Beverly Hills*
L'Orangerie *160* RESTAURANTS *Los Angeles*
Outside *160* SPECIALTY SHOPS (RS) *Los Angeles*
Patina *162* RESTAURANTS *Los Angeles*
Paul, Hastings, Janofsky & Walker *162* LAW FIRMS *Los Angeles*
The Peninsula Beverly Hills *163* HOTELS *Beverly Hills*
Jon Perlman, M.D. *163* COSMETIC SURGEONS *Beverly Hills*
Philip Press *165* JEWELRY AND WATCHES *Los Angeles*
Plantation *166* SPECIALTY SHOPS (RS) *Los Angeles*
Private Chefs, Inc. *166* EMPLOYMENT AGENCIES (BKS)
Beverly Hills
Privé *167* HAIR AND BEAUTY *Los Angeles*
The Regent Beverly Wilshire *170* HOTELS *Beverly Hills*
Richard Gould Antiques *170* ANTIQUES *Los Angeles*
Ron Herman L.A. *173* FASHION *Los Angeles*
Rose Tarlow–Melrose House *174* ARCHITECTS AND
INTERIOR DESIGNERS *Los Angeles*
Salon Cristophe *175* HAIR AND BEAUTY *Beverly Hills*
Sunset Cottage *186* ARCHITECTS AND INTERIOR
DESIGNERS *Los Angeles*
Therien & Company *187* ANTIQUES *Los Angeles*
Tracey Ross *190* FASHION (RS) *Los Angeles*
20/20 Wines *191* WINE MERCHANTS *Los Angeles*
Variety *193* MEDIA *Los Angeles*
Will Rogers Polo Club *196* POLO CLUBS *Los Angeles*
The Woods *198* FLORISTS *Los Angeles*

CALIFORNIA - SAN FRANCISCO

Antonio's Antiques *63* ANTIQUES *San Francisco*
Barbera Brooks Fine Flowers *68* FLORISTS (BKS) *San Francisco*
Bay Club *69* FITNESS *San Francisco*
Bell'Occhio *70* SPECIALTY SHOPS (BKS) *San Francisco*
California Culinary Academy *78* CULINARY SCHOOLS
San Francisco
Charles Nob Hill *82* RESTAURANTS *San Francisco*
Les Concierges *89* SPECIALTY SHOPS *San Francisco*
D & M Champagne *92* WINE MERCHANTS *San Francisco*
Dillingham & Company *96* ANTIQUES *San Francisco*
Fine Arts Museum of San Francisco *104* MUSEUMS *San Francisco*
Fioridella *103* FLORISTS *San Francisco*
Fleur de Lys *105* RESTAURANTS *San Francisco*
Fraenkel Gallery *107* ART DEALERS *San Francisco*
Gallery Paule Anglim *109* ART DEALERS *San Francisco*
Golden West International *113* WINE MERCHANTS
San Francisco
Gump's *116* SPECIALTY SHOPS *San Francisco*
The Huntington Hotel *121* HOTELS *San Francisco*
Japonesque *126* SPECIALTY SHOPS *San Francisco*
Jardinière *126* RESTAURANTS (RS) *San Francisco*
John Berggruen Gallery *127* ART DEALERS *San Francisco*
Lutsko Associates *140* LANDSCAPE ARCHITECTS *San Francisco*
Martha Angus *145* ARCHITECTS AND INTERIOR DESIGNERS
San Francisco
Maxwell Galleries *146* ART DEALERS *San Francisco*
Michael Taylor Designs *149* SPECIALTY SHOPS *San Francisco*
Morrison & Foerster *152* LAW FIRMS *San Francisco*
The Pacific-Union Club *161* PRIVATE CLUBS *San Francisco*
Ritz-Carlton Hotel *171* HOTELS *San Francisco*
S. Bernstein & Co. *175* ANTIQUES *San Francisco*
San Francisco Golf Club *176* GOLF CLUBS *San Francisco*
77 Maiden Lane *179* SPAS AND CLINICS *San Francisco*
Shapur Mozaffarian *178* JEWELRY AND WATCHES *San Francisco*
Shreve & Co. *180* JEWELRY AND WATCHES *San Francisco*
Souchi *182* FASHION (RS) *San Francisco*
Sue Fisher King *185* SPECIALTY SHOPS *San Francisco*
Wilkes Bashford *197* FASHION *San Francisco*

COLORADO

The Broadmoor *74* HOTELS *Colorado Springs*
Dunton Hot Springs *98* HOTELS (BKS) *Dolores*

15 degrees *102* RESTAURANTS (RS) *Boulder*
Game Creek Club *109* PRIVATE CLUBS (RS) *Vail*
Golden Bear *113* JEWELRY AND WATCHES *Vail*
The Peaks Resort and Golden Door Spa *163* SPAS AND CLINICS
Telluride
Starkey International *183* EMPLOYMENT AGENCIES *Denver*

COLORADO - ASPEN

The Aspen Club & Spa *64* FITNESS *Aspen*
Aspen Music Festival *64* EVENTS *Aspen*
Baldwin Gallery *67* ART DEALERS *Aspen*
Caribou Club *80* PRIVATE CLUBS *Aspen*
Carol Dopkin Real Estate *80* PROPERTY CONSULTANTS *Aspen*
Carol Dopkin Real Estate *80* PROPERTY CONSULTANTS *Aspen*
Cindy Griem Fine Jewels *85* JEWELRY AND WATCHES *Aspen*
Dennis Cirillo, M.D. *86* COSMETIC SURGEONS *Aspen*
Coates, Reid & Waldron *88* PROPERTY CONSULTANTS *Aspen*
Hotel Jerome *126* HOTELS *Aspen*
Joel Soroka Gallery *127* ART DEALERS *Aspen*
Joshua & Company *128* PROPERTY CONSULTANTS *Aspen*
Just Ask Peter *129* PARTY ORGANIZERS AND CATERERS
(BKS) *Aspen*
The Little Nell *139* HOTELS *Aspen*
Mason & Morse *145* PROPERTY CONSULTANTS *Aspen*
Nina Hovnanian Couture *158* FASHION (BKS) *Aspen*
Performance Ski *163* SPECIALTY SHOPS *Aspen*
Renaissance *170* RESTAURANTS (RS) *Aspen*

CONNECTICUT

Black Pearl Antiques & Fine Arts *73* ANTIQUES *Glastonbury*
Brinsmaid *74* JEWELRY AND WATCHES *New Canaan*
Cove Landing *91* ANTIQUES (RS) *Hadlyme*
Gardella's Elite Limousine Service *110* CHAUFFEUR SERVICES
Norwalk
Glen Gate *113* LANDSCAPE ARCHITECTS *Wilton*
The Hotchkiss School *120* SCHOOLS *Lakeville*
Jensen-Smith *126* PROPERTY CONSULTANTS *Southport*
Kent School *130* SCHOOLS *Kent*
Lakeview Inn *135* RESTAURANTS *New Preston*
Manhattan Anti-Aging Clinic *142* COSMETIC SURGEONS
New Haven
Marguerite Riordan *143* ANTIQUES *Stonington*
The Mayflower Inn *146* HOTELS *Washington*
Nathan Liverant and Son Antiques *153* ANTIQUES *Colchester*
Peabody Museum of Natural History *163* MUSEUMS *New Haven*
Peter Cummin & Associates *164* LANDSCAPE ARCHITECTS
Stonington
Sallea Antiques *175* ANTIQUES *New Canaan*
The Taft School *187* SCHOOLS *Watertown*
Wayne Pratt Antiques *195* ANTIQUES *Woodbury*
William Pitt Real Estate *197* PROPERTY CONSULTANTS
Stamford
Yale School of Management *199* COLLEGES *New Haven*
Yale University Golf Course *199* GOLF CLUBS *New Haven*

DELAWARE

Adelaide Althin Toombs Sundin *189* PORTRAIT PAINTERS
AND PHOTOGRAPHERS *Greenville*
Wilmington Trust–FSB *197* WEALTH MANAGEMENT
Wilmington
Winterthur Museum, Garden and Library *198* MUSEUMS (BKS)
Winterthur

WASHINGTON, D.C.

Admiral Limousine Service *60* CHAUFFEUR SERVICES
Washington, DC
Akin, Gump, Strauss, Hauer & Feld *60* LAW FIRMS
Washington, DC
Tina Alster, M.D *61* COSMETIC SURGEONS *Washington, DC*
Amaryllis, A Flower Shop *61* FLORISTS *Washington, DC*

Brown-Davis Interiors *75* ARCHITECTS AND INTERIOR
DESIGNERS *Washington, DC*
Calvert Woodley *78* WINE MERCHANTS *Washington, DC*
Carey International *79* CHAUFFEUR SERVICES *Washington, DC*
Corcoran Gallery of Art *90* MUSEUMS *Washington, DC*
Covington & Burling *90* LAW FIRMS *Washington, DC*
Freer Gallery of Art *107* MUSEUMS *Washington, DC*
Galileo *109* RESTAURANTS *Washington, DC*
Hotel George *111* HOTELS (RS) *Washington, DC*
Guarisco Gallery *116* ART DEALERS *Washington, DC*
The Hay-Adams Hotel *118* HOTELS *Washington, DC*
Hirshhorn Museum and Sculpture Garden *120* MUSEUMS
Washington, DC
Hugh Newell Jacobsen *121* ARCHITECTS AND INTERIOR
DESIGNERS *Washington, DC*
Janis Alridge *126* ANTIQUES *Washington, DC*
Lespinasse *137* RESTAURANTS *Washington, DC*
National Air and Space Museum *153* MUSEUMS *Washington, DC*
National Gallery of Art *153* MUSEUMS *Washington, DC*
The Washington Post *195* MEDIA *Washington, DC*

FLORIDA

Assets Protection Systems *64* SECURITY CONSULTANTS *Largo*
Atlas Floral Decorators *65* FLORISTS *Boca Raton*
Auberge Le Grillon *65* RESTAURANTS (BKS) *Boca Raton*
Aventura Limousines *66* CHAUFFEUR SERVICES *Aventura*
Bank of Boston *67* WEALTH MANAGEMENT *Boca Raton*
Bay Hill Club & Lodge *69* GOLF CLUBS *Orlando*
Beach Bistro *69* RESTAURANTS *Holmes Beach*
Black Diamond Ranch *72* GOLF CLUBS *Lecanto*
Boca Raton Resort and Club *73* HOTELS *Boca Raton*
Bonita Bay Club *73* GOLF CLUBS (RS) *Bonita Springs*
Brownes' & Co. Apothecary *75* HAIR AND BEAUTY *Miami Beach*
Campbell, Dettman & Panton Realty *79* PROPERTY
CONSULTANTS *Fort Lauderdale*
Chef Reto's Restaurant *83* RESTAURANTS *Boca Raton*
Chef Allen's *83* RESTAURANTS *Aventura*
Chisholm Gallery *84* ART DEALERS *Wellington*
Le Coq au Vin *90* RESTAURANTS *Orlando*
Daniels, Daniels & Daniels Antiques *92* ANTIQUES *Hallandale*
David Stern Designer Jewelers *94* JEWELRY AND WATCHES
Boca Raton
Delano Hotel *95* HOTELS *Miami Beach*
Doral Golf Resort & Spa *97* GOLF CLUBS *Miami*
Euphemia Haye Restaurant *101* RESTAURANTS *Longboat Key*
Evelyn Poole *101* ANTIQUES *Miami*
Fenton & Lang *102* PROPERTY CONSULTANTS (BKS)
Hobe Sound
Fisher Island Spa *104* SPAS AND CLINICS *Fisher Island*
Fraser Yachts *107* YACHTING *Fort Lauderdale*
Hargrave Yachts *118* YACHTING *Fort Lauderdale*
The Hotel *120* HOTELS (RS) *Miami Beach*
Huntington Private Financial Group *121* WEALTH
MANAGEMENT *Naples*
Incredible Adventures *122* TRAVEL CONSULTANTS *Sarasota*
J. C. DeNiro *125* PROPERTY CONSULTANTS *Miami Beach*
John's Island Club *128* GOLF CLUBS *Vero Beach*
Jupiter Hills *129* GOLF CLUBS *Tequesta*
Kensington Country Club *130* PRIVATE CLUBS *Naples*
The Keyes Company *131* PROPERTY CONSULTANTS
Miami Beach
Lazzara Yachts *136* YACHTING *Tampa*
Lighthouse Point Yacht & Racquet Club *138* FITNESS
Lighthouse Point
Ling Salon *138* HAIR AND BEAUTY *Miami*
Magnum Marine *142* YACHTING *Aventura*
Mark's Las Olas *143* RESTAURANTS *Fort Lauderdale*
New Life Clinic & Therapy Spa *155* SPAS AND CLINICS
Miami Beach
Palm Beach International Art & Antique Fair *161* EVENTS
Sewalls Point

Palm Beach Polo and Country Club *161* POLO CLUBS
Wellington
Pauline Pocock Antiques *162* ANTIQUES *Fort Lauderdale*
PNC Advisors *166* WEALTH MANAGEMENT *Vero Beach*
Royal Fiesta Caterers *174* PARTY ORGANIZERS AND
CATERERS *Deerfield Beach*
Stella Salons *184* HAIR AND BEAUTY *Miami Beach*
Styline Furniture *185* SPECIALTY SHOPS *Fort Lauderdale*
The Tides *187* HOTELS *Miami Beach*
Total Travel & Tickets *189* TRAVEL CONSULTANTS
Fort Lauderdale
U.S. Open Polo Tournament *192* EVENTS *Wellington*
Windsor Village *198* PROPERTY CONSULTANTS *Vero Beach*

FLORIDA - PALM BEACH

Babor Institut *67* SPAS AND CLINICS *Palm Beach*
Bath & Tennis Club *69* PRIVATE CLUBS *Palm Beach*
The Breakers *74* HOTELS *Palm Beach*
Café L'Europe *78* RESTAURANTS *Palm Beach*
Chase Manhattan Private Bank *82* WEALTH MANAGEMENT
Palm Beach
Club Colette *88* RESTAURANTS *Palm Beach*
Deborah Koepper *94* HAIR AND BEAUTY *Palm Beach*
Everglades Club *101* PRIVATE CLUBS *Palm Beach*
Four Seasons Palm Beach *106* HOTELS *Palm Beach*
Greenleaf & Crosby *114* JEWELRY AND WATCHES *Palm Beach*
John H. Surovek Gallery *127* ART DEALERS *Palm Beach*
Kemble Interiors *130* SPECIALTY SHOPS *Palm Beach*
Scott Snyder *177* ARCHITECTS AND INTERIOR DESIGNERS
Palm Beach
Seminole Golf Club *179* GOLF CLUBS *North Palm Beach*
Timothy Eaton Fine Art *188* ART DEALERS *West Palm Beach*
Tom Mathieu & Company *189* FLORISTS *Palm Beach*
Trump International Golf Club *190* GOLF CLUBS (RS)
West Palm Beach

GEORGIA

Architectural Accents *63* SPECIALTY SHOPS *Atlanta*
Atlanta Rocks *65* FITNESS *Doraville*
Augusta National Golf Club *65* GOLF CLUBS *Augusta*
Axis Twenty *66* SPECIALTY SHOPS *Atlanta*
Bacchanalia *67* RESTAURANTS *Atlanta*
Charles Perry-Chinese Export Porcelain *82* ANTIQUES *Atlanta*
David LaVoy *93* FLORISTS *Atlanta*
Gilmartin Studios *111* SPECIALTY SHOPS *Atlanta*
Green Classic Limousines *114* CHAUFFEUR SERVICES *Atlanta*
Gulfstream Aerospace Corporation *116* AIRPLANES *Savannah*
High Museum of Art *119* MUSEUMS *Atlanta*
Intermarine Yachting *122* YACHTING *Savannah*
Jerry Dilts and Associates *126* PARTY ORGANIZERS AND
CATERERS *Atlanta*
Key Lime Pie Salon and Wellness Spa *130* HAIR AND BEAUTY
Atlanta
King & Spalding *133* LAW FIRMS *Atlanta*
Lee Epting *136* PARTY ORGANIZERS AND CATERERS *Athens*
The Levison & Cullen Gallery *137* ANTIQUES *Atlanta*
The Lodge on Little St. Simons Island *140* HOTELS (BKS)
St. Simons Island
Masters Tournament *145* EVENTS *Augusta*
Myott Studio Workshop *152* SPECIALTY SHOPS *Atlanta*
Regen-Leigh Antiques *169* ANTIQUES *Atlanta*
Ritz-Carlton, Buckhead *171* RESTAURANTS *Atlanta*
Robert Long *173* FLORISTS *Atlanta*
Sea Island *178* GOLF CLUBS *Sea Island*

HAWAII

Colony Surf Hotel *89* HOTELS *Honolulu*
The Mauna Lani Bay *146* HOTELS *Kohala Coast*
Roy's *174* RESTAURANTS *Honolulu*
Royal Garden at Waikiki *174* HOTELS *Honolulu*
Shipman House *180* HOTELS (BKS) *Hilo*

IDAHO

Barry Peterson Jewelers *69* JEWELRY AND WATCHES *Ketchum*
Coeur d'Alene *88* SPAS AND CLINICS *Coeur d'Alene*

ILLINOIS

American Orient Express *62* TRAVEL CONSULTANTS
Downers Grove
Frank & Barbara Pollack *107* ANTIQUES *Highland Park*
Pacific Tall Ship Company *161* SPECIALTY SHOPS *Lemont*
York Furrier *199* FASHION *Elmhurst*

ILLINOIS - CHICAGO

Ambria *61* RESTAURANTS *Chicago*
Baker & McKenzie *67* LAW FIRMS *Chicago*
Bigsby & Kruthers *71* FASHION *Chicago*
Blackbird *72* RESTAURANTS (RS) *Chicago*
Charlie Trotter's *82* RESTAURANTS *Chicago*
Club Macanudo Chicago *88* CIGAR BARS *Chicago*
Despos *95* FASHION (BKS) *Chicago*
Distinctive Bookbinding & Stationery *97* SPECIALTY SHOPS
(BKS) *Chicago*
Donald Young Gallery *97* ART DEALERS *Chicago*
East Bank Club *99* FITNESS *Chicago*
Everest *101* RESTAURANTS *Chicago*
Ferrée Florsheim Catering *102* PARTY ORGANIZERS AND
CATERERS *Chicago*
Field Museum of Natural History *103* MUSEUMS *Chicago*
Gene & Georgetti *111* RESTAURANTS *Chicago*
George L. Jewell Catering *111* PARTY ORGANIZERS AND
CATERERS *Chicago*
Gordon *114* RESTAURANTS *Chicago*
Malcolm Franklin *142* ANTIQUES *Chicago*
Maurice Bonamigo *146* HAIR AND BEAUTY (BKS) *Chicago*
Metropolitan Limousine *148* CHAUFFEUR SERVICES *Chicago*
Northern Trust *158* WEALTH MANAGEMENT *Chicago*
Pucci *167* FASHION *Chicago*
R.H. Love Galleries *168* ART DEALERS *Chicago*
John Reilly *169* PORTRAIT PAINTERS AND
PHOTOGRAPHERS *Chicago*
Richard Gray Gallery *171* ART DEALERS *Chicago*
RL *172* RESTAURANTS (RS) *Chicago*
The Schwebel Company *177* ANTIQUES *Chicago*
Sidley & Austin *180* LAW FIRMS *Chicago*
Victor Skrebneski *181* PORTRAIT PAINTERS AND
PHOTOGRAPHERS *Chicago*
Ultimo *192* FASHION *Chicago*

INDIANA

Thunderbird Products *187* YACHTING *Decatur*

KANSAS

Cessna *81* AIRPLANES *Wichita*
Raytheon *169* AIRPLANES *Wichita*

KENTUCKY

Breeder's Cup *74* EVENTS *Lexington*
Camberley Brown *79* HOTELS *Louisville*
Kay Ledbetter & Associates *130* PROPERTY CONSULTANTS
Lexington
Kentucky Derby *130* EVENTS *Louisville*
Old Louisville Inn *159* HOTELS (BKS) *Louisville*
Shelly Zegart Quilts *179* SPECIALTY SHOPS *Louisville*

LOUISIANA

Artesia *64* RESTAURANTS (RS) *Abita Springs*
Commander's Palace *89* RESTAURANTS *New Orleans*
Delmonico *95* RESTAURANTS *New Orleans*
Dixon and Dixon of Royal *97* ANTIQUES (RS) *New Orleans*
The House on Bayou Road *120* HOTELS (BKS) *New Orleans*

International House *123* HOTELS (RS) *New Orleans*
Kurt E. Schon *134* ART DEALERS *New Orleans*
M. S. Rau Antiques *141* ANTIQUES *New Orleans*
Neal Auction Company *153* AUCTION HOUSES *New Orleans*
New Orleans Auction Galleries *155* AUCTION HOUSES
New Orleans
New Orleans Jazz & Heritage Festival *155* EVENTS *New Orleans*
New Orleans Museum of Art *155* MUSEUMS *New Orleans*
Soniat House *181* HOTELS (BKS) *New Orleans*
Windsor Court Hotel *198* HOTELS *New Orleans*

MASSACHUSETTS

Alden Shoe Company *60* FASHION *Middleborough*
Andover Shop *62* FASHION *Cambridge*
Aujourd'hui *65* RESTAURANTS *Boston*
Beacon Hill Nannies *69* EMPLOYMENT AGENCIES *Newton*
Biba *71* RESTAURANTS *Boston*
Brandeis University *73* COLLEGES *Waltham*
Brown Brothers Harriman & Co. *74* WEALTH MANAGEMENT
Boston
The Cambridge School of Culinary Arts *79* CULINARY
SCHOOLS *Cambridge*
Conover Real Estate *89* PROPERTY CONSULTANTS *Edgartown*
Dav El *93* CHAUFFEUR SERVICES *Chelsea*
Deerfield Academy *94* SCHOOLS *Deerfield*
Design Associates *95* ARCHITECTS AND INTERIOR
DESIGNERS *Cambridge*
Jeffrey Dover, M.D. *97* COSMETIC SURGEONS *Chestnut Hill*
L'Espalier *100* RESTAURANTS *Boston*
Firestone and Parson *104* ANTIQUES *Boston*
Fleet Bank *104* WEALTH MANAGEMENT *Boston*
Four Seasons Boston *106* HOTELS *Boston*
Gardner Colby Gallery *110* ART DEALERS *Edgartown*
Groton School *116* SCHOOLS *Groton*
Harvard University *118* COLLEGES *Cambridge*
Kennedy & Violich *130* ARCHITECTS AND INTERIOR
DESIGNERS *Boston*
Kittansett Club *133* GOLF CLUBS *Marion*
Louis, Boston *139* FASHION *Boston*
Lynn Jachney Charters *140* YACHTING *Marblehead*
Museum of Fine Arts, Boston *152* MUSEUMS *Boston*
No. 9 Park *158* RESTAURANTS (RS) *Boston*
Rialto *170* RESTAURANTS *Cambridge*
Salts *175* RESTAURANTS (RS) *Cambridge*
Shreve, Crump & Low *180* ANTIQUES *Boston*
St. Mark's School *183* SCHOOLS *Southborough*
Tanglewood Music Festival *187* EVENTS *Lenox*
Vose Galleries of Boston *194* ART DEALERS *Boston*
Wellesley College *196* COLLEGES *Wellesley*
Whitinsville Golf Club *196* GOLF CLUBS *Whitinsville*

MARYLAND

Congressional Country Club *89* GOLF CLUBS *Bethesda*
DHS Designs *96* SPECIALTY SHOPS *Annapolis*
Floral Events Unlimited *105* FLORISTS *Silver Spring*
Gary E. Young *110* ANTIQUES *Centreville*
Joseph A. Bank Clothiers *128* FASHION *Hampstead*
U.S. Security *192* SECURITY CONSULTANTS *Columbia*
Walters Art Gallery *195* MUSEUMS *Baltimore*

MICHIGAN

Continental Limousine *89* CHAUFFEUR SERVICES *Livonia*
The Ford Montreux Detroit Jazz Festival *105* EVENTS *Detroit*
Kindel Furniture *134* SPECIALTY SHOPS *Grand Rapids*
The Lark *136* RESTAURANTS *West Bloomfield*
Oakland Hills Country Club *159* GOLF CLUBS *Bloomfield Hills*

MINNESOTA

D'Amico Cucina *92* RESTAURANTS *Minneapolis*
Genmar Holdings *111* YACHTING *Minneapolis*

INDEX II

MISSISSIPPI
McCarty Pottery 147 SPECIALTY SHOPS (BKS) Merigold

MISSOURI
Bryan Cave 76 LAW FIRMS St. Louis
Café Allegro 77 RESTAURANTS Kansas City
Giovanni's 111 RESTAURANTS St. Louis
Greenberg Van Doren Gallery 114 ART DEALERS St. Louis
Vision Aire 194 AIRPLANES Chesterfield

MONTANA
H. S. Trask & Co. 117 FASHION Bozeman
Hall and Hall Ranch Brokers 117 PROPERTY CONSULTANTS
    Billings
Triple Creek Ranch 190 HOTELS (BKS) Darby

NEVADA
Aureole 65 RESTAURANTS Las Vegas
Bellagio 70 HOTELS (RS) Las Vegas
Binion's Horseshoe 72 CASINOS Las Vegas
Caesars Palace 77 CASINOS Las Vegas
Chase International 82 PROPERTY CONSULTANTS Lake Tahoe
Four Seasons Las Vegas 106 HOTELS (RS) Las Vegas
Golden Nugget 113 CASINOS (B) Las Vegas
Hamilton Cigar Bar 117 CIGAR BARS Las Vegas
MGM Grand 149 CASINOS Las Vegas
The Mirage 150 CASINOS Las Vegas
Montreux Golf & Country Club 151 GOLF CLUBS Reno
Nevada Wine Cellar & Spirits 155 WINE MERCHANTS (RS)
    Las Vegas
Rio 171 CASINOS Las Vegas
Shadow Creek 179 GOLF CLUBS (RS) Las Vegas

NEW HAMPSHIRE
Dartmouth College 93 COLLEGES Hanover
Philips Exeter Academy 165 SCHOOLS Exeter
St. Paul's School 183 SCHOOLS Concord

NEW JERSEY
Chubb Group of Insurance Companies 86 ART CONSULTANTS
    Warren
De Pasquale, The Spa 94 SPAS AND CLINICS Fairlawn
Delaware River Trading Company 95 SPECIALTY SHOPS (RS)
    Frenchtown
Gladstone Antiques Show 113 EVENTS (BKS) Gladstone
Greenbaum Interiors 115 SPECIALTY SHOPS Paterson
Hamilton Jewelers 117 JEWELRY AND WATCHES Princeton
The Lawrenceville School 136 SCHOOLS Lawrenceville
Michael Graves & Associates 149 ARCHITECTS AND
    INTERIOR DESIGNERS Princeton
Moore Brothers Wine Company 151 WINE MERCHANTS
    Pennsauken
Le Palais 161 RESTAURANTS Atlantic City
Pine Valley Golf Club 165 GOLF CLUBS Pine Valley
Princeton University 166 COLLEGES Princeton
The Ryland Inn 174 RESTAURANTS Whitehouse

NEW MEXICO
The Albuquerque Museum of Art & History 60 MUSEUMS
    Albuquerque
Christie's Great Estates 86 PROPERTY CONSULTANTS Santa Fe
Cline Fine Art Gallery 87 ART DEALERS Sante Fe
Richard J. Fisher Tinwork 170 SPECIALTY SHOPS (BKS) Tesuque
Santa Fe Horse Park and Polo Club 177 POLO CLUBS Santa Fe
Santa Fe Opera 177 EVENTS Santa Fe

NEW YORK
The American Hotel 61 HOTELS (BKS) Sag Harbor

Art of Eating 63 PARTY ORGANIZERS AND CATERERS
    East Hampton
Barbara Israel Garden Antiques 68 ANTIQUES Katonah
Brooklyn Museum of Art 74 MUSEUMS Brooklyn
Carter Landscaping 80 LANDSCAPE ARCHITECTS East Quogue
The Castle at Tarrytown 81 HOTELS Tarrytown
The Cigar Box 86 CIGAR BARS East Hampton
The Culinary Institute of America 91 CULINARY SCHOOLS
    Hyde Park
Della Femina 95 RESTAURANTS East Hampton
Devon Yacht Club 95 PRIVATE CLUBS Amagansett
Dunemere Associates Real Estate 98 PROPERTY
    CONSULTANTS East Hampton
East Hampton Gym 99 FITNESS East Hampton
Fishers Island Country Club 104 GOLF CLUBS (BKS)
    Fishers Island
Freedman Jewelers 107 JEWELRY AND WATCHES Huntington
Hampton Country Real Estate 117 PROPERTY
    CONSULTANTS Bridgehampton
Lake Placid Lodge 135 HOTELS (BKS) Lake Placid
London Jewelers 139 JEWELRY AND WATCHES Manhasset
Mecox Gardens 147 SPECIALTY SHOPS Southampton
Meurice Garment Care 149 SPECIALTY SHOPS (BKS) Manhasset
National Golf Links of America 153 GOLF CLUBS Southampton
New York Aviation 155 AIRPLANES Flushing
New York Botanical Garden 155 MUSEUMS Bronx
Frederick A. Newman, M.D. 157 COSMETIC SURGEONS
    Scarsdale
Nick and Toni's 158 RESTAURANTS East Hampton
Old Chatham Sheepherding Company Inn 159 HOTELS
    Old Chatham
The Perlman Music Program 163 EVENTS East Hampton
The Point 167 HOTELS Saranac Lake
The River Café 173 RESTAURANTS Brooklyn
Shinnecock Hills Golf Club 180 GOLF CLUBS Southampton
Silver Screen Security 180 SECURITY CONSULTANTS
    Staten Island
Sokolin Wines 181 WINE MERCHANTS Southampton
Steinway & Sons 184 SPECIALTY SHOPS Long Island City
Stems 185 FLORISTS Redhook
Summit Aviation 186 AIRPLANES East Farmingdale
Sunset Beach 186 HOTELS Shelter Island
U.S. Open Tennis 192 EVENTS Flushing
Vassar College 193 COLLEGES Poughkeepsie
Winged Foot Golf Club 198 GOLF CLUBS Mamaroneck
Zachy's 199 WINE MERCHANTS Scarsdale

NEW YORK - NEW YORK CITY
Aaron Basha 58 JEWELRY AND WATCHES New York
Abacus Security 58 SECURITY CONSULTANTS New York
ABC Carpet & Home 58 SPECIALTY SHOPS New York
Abraham Moheban & Son 59 ANTIQUES New York
Acquavella Galleries 59 ART DEALERS New York
Addison on Madison 59 FASHION (BKS) New York
Alan Flusser 60 FASHION New York
Alexandra Lind 60 FASHION (RS) New York
Allure Day Spa & Store 60 SPAS AND CLINICS New York
American Museum of Natural History 61 MUSEUMS New York
Andrea Rosen Gallery 62 ART DEALERS New York
Andrew Dornenburg Private Dining 62 PARTY ORGANIZERS
    AND CATERERS (BKS) New York
Antine Associates 63 ARCHITECTS AND INTERIOR
    DESIGNERS New York
L'Antiquaire & The Connoisseur 63 ANTIQUES New York
Architectural Digest 63 MEDIA New York
Art of Fitness 63 FITNESS New York
The Asia Society 64 MUSEUMS New York
Sherrell Aston, M.D. 64 COSMETIC SURGEONS New York
Aubry 65 PORTRAIT PAINTERS AND PHOTOGRAPHERS
    New York
Aveda Institute 66 HAIR AND BEAUTY New York

Avenue 66 MEDIA New York
The Avon Centre 66 SPAS AND CLINICS (RS) New York
B & B International 67 ART DEALERS New York
Badgley-Mischka 67 FASHION New York
Daniel Baker, M.D. 67 COSMETIC SURGEONS New York
Balthazar 67 RESTAURANTS New York
Barbara Gladstone Gallery 67 ART DEALERS New York
Barclay Rex Pipe Shop 68 SPECIALTY SHOPS New York
Barnard College 68 COLLEGES New York
Barneys New York 68 FASHION New York
Barrons 69 MEDIA New York
Barry Friedman 69 ART DEALERS New York
Beauvais Carpets 69 SPECIALTY SHOPS New York
Belghiti Tailors 70 FASHION (BKS) New York
Bergdorf Goodman 70 FASHION New York
Bernard & S. Dean Levy 70 ANTIQUES New York
Le Bernardin 70 RESTAURANTS New York
Berry-Hill Galleries 70 ART DEALERS New York
Bessemer Trust 71 WEALTH MANAGEMENT New York
BestSelections 71 SPECIALTY SHOPS New York
Bliss 72 SPAS AND CLINICS (RS) New York
Bloom 73 FLORISTS New York
Bridgehampton Polo Club 74 POLO CLUBS New York
Brill's Content 74 MEDIA (RS) New York
The Brook 74 PRIVATE CLUBS New York
Browns Restaurant 76 RESTAURANTS (RS) New York
Bumble & Bumble 76 HAIR AND BEAUTY New York
Bunny Williams 76 ARCHITECTS AND INTERIOR
    DESIGNERS New York
The Burgundy Wine Co. 76 WINE MERCHANTS (BKS) New York
C & M Arts 77 ART DEALERS New York
Calabria 77 FLORISTS New York
Callahan Catering 78 PARTY ORGANIZERS AND CATERERS
    New York
Calligraphy Studios 78 SPECIALTY SHOPS New York
Calvin Klein 79 FASHION New York
Carapan Urban Spa & Store 79 SPAS AND CLINICS New York
Carleton Varney Design Group 80 ARCHITECTS AND
    INTERIOR DESIGNERS New York
Carlyle Wines 80 WINE MERCHANTS New York
The Carlyle 81 HOTELS New York
Carolina Herrera 80 FASHION New York
Carswell Rush Berlin 80 ANTIQUES (BKS) New York
Chaiken and Capone 81 FASHION New York
Charlotte Moss Interior Design 83 ARCHITECTS AND
    INTERIOR DESIGNERS New York
Chinese Porcelain Company 84 ANTIQUES New York
Christie's 85 AUCTION HOUSES New York
Cigar Aficionado 86 MEDIA New York
Cipriani 86 RESTAURANTS New York
Le Cirque 2000 86 RESTAURANTS New York
Citibank Private Bank 87 WEALTH MANAGEMENT New York
Clodagh Design 88 ARCHITECTS AND INTERIOR
    DESIGNERS New York
The Colony Club 89 PRIVATE CLUBS New York
The Cooper-Hewitt National Design Museum 90 MUSEUMS
    New York
Michelle Copeland, M.D. 89 COSMETIC SURGEONS New York
The Corcoran Group 90 PROPERTY CONSULTANTS New York
Craig F. Starr Associates 91 ART DEALERS New York
Crain's New York Business 91 MEDIA New York
Cravath, Swaine & Moore 91 LAW FIRMS New York
Crème de la Mer 148 HAIR AND BEAUTY New York
Crouch & Fitzgerald 91 FASHION New York
Cullman & Kravis 91 ARCHITECTS AND INTERIOR
    DESIGNERS New York
Da Silvano 92 RESTAURANTS New York
Dalva Brothers 92 ANTIQUES New York
Dana Buchman 92 FASHION New York
Daniel 92 RESTAURANTS New York

David Anthony Easton *93* ARCHITECTS AND INTERIOR DESIGNERS *New York*
David Webb *93* JEWELRY AND WATCHES *New York*
Davis, Polk & Wardwell *94* LAW FIRMS *New York*
Degustibus Cooking School *94* CULINARY SCHOOLS *New York*
Dempsey & Carroll *95* SPECIALTY SHOPS *New York*
Departures *95* MEDIA *New York*
Dia Center for The Arts *95* MUSEUMS *New York*
Didier Aaron *96* ANTIQUES *New York*
Dimson Homma *96* SPECIALTY SHOPS *New York*
Donna Karan *97* FASHION *New York*
Dormeuil Personal Tailoring *97* FASHION *New York*
Doubles *97* PRIVATE CLUBS *New York*
Edward Carter Gallery *99* ART DEALERS *New York*
Edward Lee Cave *99* PROPERTY CONSULTANTS *New York*
Eleven Madison Park *99* RESTAURANTS *(RS) New York*
Eli Wilner & Company *100* SPECIALTY SHOPS *New York*
Eric Javits *100* FASHION *New York*
EventQuest *101* PARTY ORGANIZERS AND CATERERS *New York*
FAO Schwarz *101* SPECIALTY SHOPS *New York*
Lewis Feder, M.D. *102* COSMETIC SURGEONS *New York*
Felidia Ristorante *102* RESTAURANTS *New York*
Felissimo *103* SPECIALTY SHOPS *New York*
Fish & Neave *104* LAW FIRMS *New York*
Fisher Travel *104* TRAVEL CONSULTANTS *(BKS) New York*
Fortune *105* MEDIA *New York*
Fortunoff *106* JEWELRY AND WATCHES *New York*
Fountain Pen Hospital *106* SPECIALTY SHOPS *New York*
Four Seasons New York *106* HOTELS *New York*
Four Seasons Restaurant *106* RESTAURANTS *New York*
Fox Residential Group *107* PROPERTY CONSULTANTS *New York*
Framed on Madison *107* SPECIALTY SHOPS *New York*
Frédéric Fekkai Beauté *107* HAIR AND BEAUTY *New York*
The French Culinary Institute *108* CULINARY SCHOOLS *New York*
Frenchway Travel *108* TRAVEL CONSULTANTS *New York*
Frick Collection *108* MUSEUMS *New York*
Gagosian Gallery *109* ART DEALERS *New York*
Gazelle Beauty Center and Day Spa *110* HAIR AND BEAUTY *(RS) New York*
Geoffrey Bradfield *111* ARCHITECTS AND INTERIOR DESIGNERS *New York*
Gioia *111* JEWELRY AND WATCHES *New York*
Glorious Foods *113* PARTY ORGANIZERS AND CATERERS *New York*
Goldman, Sachs & Co. *113* WEALTH MANAGEMENT *New York*
La Goulue *114* RESTAURANTS *New York*
Gramercy Tavern *114* RESTAURANTS *New York*
La Grenouille *115* RESTAURANTS *New York*
Gwathmey Siegel & Associates *116* ARCHITECTS AND INTERIOR DESIGNERS *New York*
H. M. Luther Antiques *117* ANTIQUES *New York*
Hammer Galleries *117* ART DEALERS *New York*
Harry Winston Jewelers *118* JEWELRY AND WATCHES *New York*
Kim Heirston *119* ART CONSULTANTS *(RS) New York*
Helena Lehane *119* FLORISTS *New York*
Helmut Lang *119* FASHION *New York*
Hirschl & Adler Galleries *119* ART DEALERS *New York*
Howard Kaplan Antiques *120* ANTIQUES *New York*
HR Beauty Gallery *120* SPAS AND CLINICS *(RS) New York*
Hyde Park Antiques *121* ANTIQUES *New York*
Gerald Imber, M.D. *122* COSMETIC SURGEONS *New York*
Interieurs *122* SPECIALTY SHOPS *New York*
The International Fine Art and Antique Dealers Show *122* EVENTS *New York*
International Fine Art Fair *123* EVENTS *New York*
Island Weiss Gallery *124* ART DEALERS *New York*
Israel Sack *124* ANTIQUES *New York*
James Danziger Gallery *125* ART DEALERS *New York*

James Robinson *126* ANTIQUES *New York*
Jean Georges *126* RESTAURANTS *(RS) New York*
Jeffrey Bilhuber *126* ARCHITECTS AND INTERIOR DESIGNERS *New York*
John & Paul Herring & Co. *127* ART CONSULTANTS *(BKS) New York*
John Barrett Salon *127* HAIR AND BEAUTY *New York*
John Bartlett *127* FASHION *(RS) New York*
The John Sahag Workshop *127* HAIR AND BEAUTY *New York*
Josie Natori *128* FASHION *New York*
JP Morgan *129* WEALTH MANAGEMENT *New York*
Judith Leiber *129* FASHION *New York*
Judith Ripka *129* JEWELRY AND WATCHES *New York*
Karl Kemp & Associates *131* ANTIQUES *New York*
Kennedy Galleries *130* ART DEALERS *New York*
Kentshire Galleries *130* ANTIQUES *New York*
Kieselstein-Cord *133* FASHION *New York*
Kinsey Marable Booksellers *133* SPECIALTY SHOPS *New York*
The Knickerbocker Club *134* PRIVATE CLUBS *New York*
Kroll Associates *134* SECURITY CONSULTANTS *New York*
Kronish, Lieb, Weiner & Hellman, L.L.P. *134* LAW FIRMS *(BKS) New York*
Lambertson Truex *135* FASHION *(RS) New York*
Lehman Brothers Private Client Services *136* WEALTH MANAGEMENT *New York*
Leo Castelli Gallery *136* ART DEALERS *New York*
Leonard N. Stern School of Business *137* COLLEGES *New York*
Cap B. Lesesne, M.D. *138* COSMETIC SURGEONS *New York*
Lespinasse *137* RESTAURANTS *New York*
Lexington Bar and Books *138* CIGAR BARS *New York*
Ling Skin Care *138* HAIR AND BEAUTY *New York*
The Links Club *138* PRIVATE CLUBS *New York*
Lisa Lindblad Travel Design *138* TRAVEL CONSULTANTS *New York*
Lou Marotta, Inc. *141* ANTIQUES *New York*
Luxuryfinder.com *140* SPECIALTY SHOPS *(RS) New York*
Madison Avenue Bookshop *142* SPECIALTY SHOPS *(BKS) New York*
Marc Jacobs *143* FASHION *New York*
Marc Magnus *142* JEWELRY AND WATCHES *New York*
Marian Goodman Gallery *143* ART DEALERS *New York*
Mario Buatta *143* ARCHITECTS AND INTERIOR DESIGNERS *New York*
Mark Hampton *143* ARCHITECTS AND INTERIOR DESIGNERS *New York*
The Mark *143* HOTELS *New York*
Marlborough *144* ART DEALERS *New York*
Martel Productions *144* PARTY ORGANIZERS AND CATERERS *New York*
Marvin Alexander *144* ANTIQUES *New York*
Mary Boone Gallery *144* ART DEALERS *New York*
Mary McFadden *144* FASHION *New York*
Alice F. Mason *145* PROPERTY CONSULTANTS *New York*
Alan Matarasso, M.D. *145* COSMETIC SURGEONS *New York*
Matthew Marks Gallery *145* ART DEALERS *New York*
Maurice Badler Fine Jewelry *145* JEWELRY AND WATCHES *New York*
Mayle *147* FASHION *(RS) New York*
McMillen *147* ARCHITECTS AND INTERIOR DESIGNERS *New York*
MedFitness *147* FITNESS *New York*
La Mer *148* HAIR AND BEAUTY *New York*
Mercer Hotel *148* HOTELS *(RS) New York*
Merrill Lynch Financial Services *148* WEALTH MANAGEMENT *New York*
Metropolitan Museum of Art *148* MUSEUMS *New York*
The Metropolitan Opera *149* EVENTS *New York*
Michael Werner Gallery *149* ART DEALERS *New York*
Minardi Salon *150* HAIR AND BEAUTY *New York*
Mitchell-Innes and Nash *150* ART CONSULTANTS *New York*

Juan Pablo Molyneux *151* ARCHITECTS AND INTERIOR DESIGNERS *New York*
Montrachet *151* RESTAURANTS *New York*
The Morgan Library *151* MUSEUMS *(BKS) New York*
Morgan Stanley Dean Witter *151* WEALTH MANAGEMENT *New York*
Morgenthal Frederics Opticians *152* SPECIALTY SHOPS *New York*
Museum of Modern Art *152* MUSEUMS *New York*
Naomi Leff & Associates *153* ARCHITECTS AND INTERIOR DESIGNERS *New York*
Natalie Gerschel Kaplan *153* PARTY ORGANIZERS AND CATERERS *(RS) New York*
Nelson & Nelson Antiques *155* ANTIQUES *New York*
Nemati Collection *155* ANTIQUES *New York*
The New York Observer *157* MEDIA *New York*
New York Palace Hotel *157* HOTELS *New York*
The New York Times *157* MEDIA *New York*
New York Yacht Club *157* PRIVATE CLUBS *New York*
Niall Smith Antiques *158* ANTIQUES *(BKS) New York*
Nobu *158* RESTAURANTS *New York*
Nursery Lines *158* SPECIALTY SHOPS *New York*
Ober, Onet & Associates *159* PARTY ORGANIZERS AND CATERERS *New York*
L'Olivier Floral Atelier *159* FLORISTS *New York*
Osteria del Circo *160* RESTAURANTS *New York*
Pace Wildenstein *161* ART DEALERS *New York*
Pamela Dennis *162* FASHION *New York*
Paul Kasmin Gallery *162* ART DEALERS *New York*
Paul Stuart *162* FASHION *New York*
Pavillion Agency *162* EMPLOYMENT AGENCIES *(BKS) New York*
The Peninsula New York *164* HOTELS *New York*
Peter Coppola Salon *164* HAIR AND BEAUTY *New York*
Peter Marino & Associates *164* ARCHITECTS AND INTERIOR DESIGNERS *New York*
Philip Baloun *164* FLORISTS *New York*
Philip Johnson/Alan Ritchie Architects *165* ARCHITECTS AND INTERIOR DESIGNERS *New York*
Prince Dimitri *167* FASHION *New York*
Professional Nannies Institute *167* EMPLOYMENT AGENCIES *New York*
Quest *167* MEDIA *New York*
Racquet & Tennis Club *168* PRIVATE CLUBS *New York*
Radu Physical Culture *169* FITNESS *New York*
Ralph Lauren *169* FASHION *New York*
Randolph Duke *169* FASHION *(RS) New York*
Rebecca Moss *169* SPECIALTY SHOPS *New York*
Reebok Sports Club *169* FITNESS *New York*
Renny *170* FLORISTS *New York*
Richard Anderson Fine Arts *170* ART DEALERS *New York*
Richard Keith Langham *171* ARCHITECTS AND INTERIOR DESIGNERS *New York*
Richard L. Feigen & Company *171* ART DEALERS *New York*
Richard York Gallery *171* ART DEALERS *New York*
Robert A.M. Stern Architects *172* ARCHITECTS AND INTERIOR DESIGNERS *New York*
Robert Isabell *172* FLORISTS *New York*
Robert Mann Gallery *173* ART DEALERS *(RS) New York*
The Rockwell Group *173* ARCHITECTS AND INTERIOR DESIGNERS *New York*
Rosenberg & Stiebel *174* ART DEALERS *New York*
Rudolf Steiner School *174* SCHOOLS *New York*
S.J. Shrubsole *175* ANTIQUES *New York*
Safra Bank *175* WEALTH MANAGEMENT *New York*
Saks Fifth Avenue *175* FASHION *New York*
Salander-O'Reilly Galleries *175* ART DEALERS *New York*
Salon AKS *175* HAIR AND BEAUTY *New York*
Julian Schnabel *177* PORTRAIT PAINTERS AND PHOTOGRAPHERS *New York*
Scully and Scully *177* SPECIALTY SHOPS *New York*
Seaman Schepps *178* JEWELRY AND WATCHES *New York*
Sean Kelly Gallery *178* ART DEALERS *(RS) New York*

Shearman & Sterling *179* LAW FIRMS *New York*
Sherry Lehmann *179* WINE MERCHANTS *New York*
Skadden, Arps, Slate, Meagher & Flom *181* LAW FIRMS *New York*
SOLE by Soledad Twombly *182* FASHION *(RS) New York*
Sotheby's *182* AUCTION HOUSES *New York*
Sotheby's International Realty *182* PROPERTY CONSULTANTS *New York*
St. Regis Hotel *183* HOTELS *New York*
Steven Holl Architects *184* ARCHITECTS AND INTERIOR DESIGNERS *New York*
Strategic Controls *184* SECURITY CONSULTANTS *New York*
Stribling & Associates *184* PROPERTY CONSULTANTS *New York*
Studio Sofield *184* ARCHITECTS AND INTERIOR DESIGNERS *New York*
Sullivan & Cromwell *185* LAW FIRMS *New York*
Susan Ciminelli Day Spa *186* SPAS AND CLINICS *New York*
Thad Hayes Design *187* ARCHITECTS AND INTERIOR DESIGNERS *New York*
Thea Westreich Art Advisory Services *187* ART CONSULTANTS *New York*
Thierry Despont *187* ARCHITECTS AND INTERIOR DESIGNERS *New York*
Throckmorton Fine Art *188* ART DEALERS *New York*
Tiffany & Co. *187* JEWELRY AND WATCHES *New York*
Time Will Tell *188* JEWELRY AND WATCHES *New York*
Tocca *188* FASHION *(RS) New York*
Todd Oldham *189* FASHION *New York*
Tony Shafrazi Gallery *189* ART DEALERS *New York*
Town & Country *189* MEDIA *New York*
Tracy Feith *190* FASHION *(RS) New York*
Trinity School *190* SCHOOLS *New York*
Trump International Hotel *191* HOTELS *(RS) New York*
Tuleh *191* FASHION *(RS) New York*
Ultramarine *192* YACHTING *New York*
The Union Club *192* PRIVATE CLUBS *New York*
US Trust *192* WEALTH MANAGEMENT *New York*
Valerie Wilson Travel *193* TRAVEL CONSULTANTS *New York*
Vance Jordan Fine Art *194* ART DEALERS *New York*
Vanity Fair *193* MEDIA *New York*
Vera Wang *193* FASHION *New York*
Veritas *194* RESTAURANTS *(RS) New York*
Victoria Hagan *194* ARCHITECTS AND INTERIOR DESIGNERS *New York*
A La Vieille Russie *194* ANTIQUES *New York*
W *195* MEDIA *New York*
Wagwear *195* SPECIALTY SHOPS *New York*
The Wall Street Journal *195* MEDIA *New York*
Warren-Tricomi Salon *195* HAIR AND BEAUTY *(BKS) New York*
Weisbrod Chinese Art *195* ANTIQUES *New York*
Patricia Wexler M.D. *196* COSMETIC SURGEONS *New York*
Wildenstein & Co. *196* ART DEALERS *New York*
William B. May *197* PROPERTY CONSULTANTS *New York*
William Calvert *197* FASHION *(RS) New York*
William Doyle Galleries *197* AUCTION HOUSES *New York*
Windows on the World Wine School *198* CULINARY SCHOOLS *New York*

NORTH CAROLINA

Duke University *98* COLLEGES *Durham*
First Union National Bank *104* WEALTH MANAGEMENT *Charlotte*
The Grove Park Inn Resort *116* HOTELS *Asheville*
Pinehurst Polo Club *166* POLO CLUBS *(BKS) Whispering Pines*
Pinehurst Resort & Country Club *166* GOLF CLUBS *Pinehurst*
Yachtscape *199* YACHTING *Newbern*

OHIO

American Antiques *61* ANTIQUES *Columbus*
Chez Francois *83* RESTAURANTS *Vermilion*
Cleveland Museum of Art *87* MUSEUMS *Cleveland*
Flight Options *105* AIRPLANES *Richmond Heights*

Jones, Day, Reavis & Pogue *128* LAW FIRMS *Cleveland*
La Maisonette *142* RESTAURANTS *Cincinnati*
NetJets *155* AIRPLANES *Columbus*

OREGON

Café des Amis *77* RESTAURANTS *Portland*
Genoa *111* RESTAURANTS *Portland*
Hickox Salon and Spa *119* SPAS AND CLINICS *Portland*
Oregon Bach Festival *160* EVENTS *(BKS) Eugene*

PENNSYLVANIA

Alfred Bullard *60* ANTIQUES *Philadelphia*
Anthony A.P. Stuempfig *62* ANTIQUES *Philadelphia*
Auldridge Mead *66* HOTELS *(BKS) Ottsville*
Le Bec-Fin *69* RESTAURANTS *Philadelphia*
Bryn Mawr College *76* COLLEGES *Bryn Mawr*
Elinor Gordon *99* ANTIQUES *Villanova*
The Greenhouse Group *114* SPAS AND CLINICS *Ambler*
Haverford College *119* COLLEGES *Haverford*
James Kieran Pine *125* ARCHITECTS AND INTERIOR DESIGNERS *Chadds Ford*
Jacqueline Jasper Portraits *125* PORTRAIT PAINTERS AND PHOTOGRAPHERS *East Stroudsburg*
Josephine Sasso *128* FASHION *(RS) Paoli*
Lagos *135* JEWELRY AND WATCHES *Philadelphia*
Lilly Pulitzer *138* FASHION *King of Prussia*
Lyman Perry *140* ARCHITECTS AND INTERIOR DESIGNERS *Berwyn*
M. Finkel & Daughter *141* ANTIQUES *Philadelphia*
Mellon Bank *147* WEALTH MANAGEMENT *Pittsburgh*
Merion Golf Club *148* GOLF CLUBS *Ardmore*
Oakmont Country Club *159* GOLF CLUBS *Oakmont*
Philadelphia Museum of Art *165* MUSEUMS *Philadelphia*
Philip H. Bradley *165* ANTIQUES *Downingtown*
The Rittenhouse Hotel *172* HOTELS *Philadelphia*
Salon d'Artiste *175* SPAS AND CLINICS *Strafford*
University of Pennsylvania *192* COLLEGES *Philadelphia*

RHODE ISLAND

Bartrum & Brakenhoff Yachts *69* YACHTING *Newport*
Brown University *75* COLLEGES *Providence*
Newport Art Museum *157* MUSEUMS *Newport*
Newport Music Festival *157* EVENTS *Newport*
St. George's School *182* SCHOOLS *Newport*

SOUTH CAROLINA

Century House Antiques *81* SPECIALTY SHOPS *Charleston*
Charleston Grill *82* RESTAURANTS *Charleston*
Estate Antiques *101* ANTIQUES *Charleston*
Harbour Town Golf Links *117* GOLF CLUBS *Hilton Head Island*
Harrison K-9 Security *118* SECURITY CONSULTANTS *Aiken*
Kiawah Island Golf & Tennis Resort *131* HOTELS *Kiawah Island*
Yeamans Hall Club *199* GOLF CLUBS *(BKS) Charleston*

TENNESSEE

Blackberry Farm *72* HOTELS *Walland*
Mary Gingrass, M.D. *111* COSMETIC SURGEONS *Nashville*
Hartmann Luggage & Leather Goods *118* SPECIALTY SHOPS *Lebanon*

TEXAS

Beautique Day Spa and Salon *69* HAIR AND BEAUTY *Houston*
Cacharel *77* RESTAURANTS *Arlington*
Greenhouse Gallery of Fine Art *114* ART DEALERS *San Antonio*
Hokanson *120* SPECIALTY SHOPS *Houston*
Houston Polo Club *120* POLO CLUBS *Houston*
The Jack S. Blanton Museum of Art *125* MUSEUMS *Austin*
John Daugherty, Realtors *127* PROPERTY CONSULTANTS *Houston*

Kimbell Art Museum *133* MUSEUMS *Fort Worth*
Leslie & Co. *137* FASHION *Houston*
M. Penner *141* FASHION *Houston*
The Rienzi House Museum *171* MUSEUMS *(RS) Houston*
Ruggles Grill *174* RESTAURANTS *Houston*

TEXAS - DALLAS

Hotel Adolphus *58* HOTELS *Dallas*
At Home *65* SPECIALTY SHOPS *Dallas*
Dallas Museum of Art *92* MUSEUMS *Dallas*
Dallas Polo Club *92* POLO CLUBS *Dallas*
East & Orient Company *99* SPECIALTY SHOPS *Dallas*
FlexJet *105* AIRPLANES *Dallas*
The French Room *108* RESTAURANTS *Dallas*
Garden Gate *110* FLORISTS *Dallas*
Knight Security Systems *134* SECURITY CONSULTANTS *Dallas*
Mansion on Turtle Creek *142* HOTELS *Dallas*
The Mercury *148* RESTAURANTS *(RS) Dallas*
Neiman Marcus *153* FASHION *Dallas*
Nova Limousine Service *158* CHAUFFEUR SERVICES *Dallas*
Two Design Group *191* FLORISTS *Dallas*
Wendy Krispin *196* PARTY ORGANIZERS AND CATERERS *Dallas*
The Women's Center for Plastic and Reconstructive Surgery *198* COSMETIC SURGEONS *Dallas*

UTAH

Deer Valley Resort *94* HOTELS *Park City*
Sundance Hotel *185* HOTELS *Sundance*

VERMONT

Twin Farms *191* HOTELS *(BKS) Barnard*

VIRGINIA

Armfield, Miller & Ripley *63* PROPERTY CONSULTANTS *Middleburg*
The Inn at Little Washington *122* HOTELS *Washington*
Kingsmill Resort *133* SPAS AND CLINICS *Williamsburg*
Newseum *157* MUSEUMS *(BKS) Arlington*
Sumpter Priddy III *185* ANTIQUES *Alexandria*
The Virginian Golf Club *194* GOLF CLUBS *Bristol*

WASHINGTON

Alexis Hotel *60* HOTELS *(BKS) Seattle*
American Safari Cruises *62* HOTELS *Lynnwood*
Campagne *79* RESTAURANTS *Seattle*
Gene Juarez Salon & Spa *111* SPAS AND CLINICS *Seattle*
Inn at the Market *123* HOTELS *(BKS) Seattle*
Seattle Art Museum *177* MUSEUMS *(RS) Seattle*

WEST VIRGINIA

The Greenbrier Hotel *114* HOTELS *White Sulfur Springs*
Pete Dye Golf Club *164* GOLF CLUBS *Bridgeport*
Richard Haynes & Associates *170* SECURITY CONSULTANTS *Charleston*

WISCONSIN

Burger Boat Company *76* YACHTING *Manitowoc*
Milwaukee Art Museum *150* MUSEUMS *Milwaukee*
Palmer Johnson Yachts *162* YACHTING *Sturgeon Bay*
Whistling Straits *198* GOLF CLUBS *Kohler*

WYOMING

Amangani *61* HOTELS *Jackson*

INDEX II

DAVID WEBB

PRECIOUS JEWELS

INDEX III

LISTING BY
PRODUCT CATEGORY

AIRPLANES

Cessna 81
FlexJet 105
Flight Options 105
Gulfstream Aerospace Corporation 116
JetSource 127
NetJets 155
New York Aviation 155
Petersen Aviation 165
Raytheon 169
Summit Aviation 186
Vision Aire 194

ANTIQUES

Abraham Moheban & Son 59
Alfred Bullard 60
American Antiques 61
Anthony A.P. Stuempfig 62
L'Antiquaire & The Connoisseur 63
Antonio's Antiques 63
Barbara Israel Garden Antiques 68
Bernard & S. Dean Levy 70
Black Pearl Antiques & Fine Arts 73
Carswell Rush Berlin 80
Charles Perry-Chinese Export
    Porcelain 82
Chinese Porcelain Company 84
Cove Landing 91
Dalva Brothers 92
Daniels, Daniels & Daniels Antiques 92
Didier Aaron 96
Dillingham & Company 96
Dixon and Dixon of Royal 97
Elinor Gordon 99
Estate Antiques 101
Evelyn Poole 101
Firestone and Parson 104
Frank & Barbara Pollack 107
Gary E. Young 110
H. M. Luther Antiques 117
Howard Kaplan Antiques 120
Hyde Park Antiques 121
Israel Sack 124
James Robinson 126
Janis Alridge 126
Karl Kemp & Associates 131
Kentshire Galleries 130
The Levison & Cullen Gallery 137
Lou Marotta, Inc. 141
M. Finkel & Daughter 141
M. S. Rau Antiques 141
Malcolm Franklin 142
Marguerite Riordan 143
Marvin Alexander 144
Nathan Liverant and Son Antiques 153
Nelson & Nelson Antiques 155

Nemati Collection 155
Niall Smith Antiques 158
Pauline Pocock Antiques 162
Philip H. Bradley 165
Regen-Leigh Antiques 169
Richard Gould Antiques 170
S. Bernstein & Co. 175
S. J. Shrubsole 175
Sallea Antiques 175
The Schwebel Company 177
Shreve, Crump & Low 180
Sumpter Priddy III 185
Therien & Company 187
A La Vieille Russie 194
Wayne Pratt Antiques 195
Weisbrod Chinese Art 195

ARCHITECTS AND INTERIOR DESIGNERS

Antine Associates 63
Barbara Lockhart 68
Barefoot Elegance 68
Brown-Davis Interiors 75
Bunny Williams 76
Carleton Varney Design Group 80
Charlotte Moss Interior Design 83
Clodagh Design 88
Cullman & Kravis 91
Darrell Schmitt Design Associates 93
David Anthony Easton 93
Design Associates 95
Geoffrey Bradfield 111
Gwathmey Siegel & Associates 116
Hugh Newell Jacobsen 121
James Kieran Pine 125
Jeffrey Bilhuber 126
Kennedy & Violich 130
Kerry Joyce 130
Lowrance Interiors 140
Lyman Perry 140
Mario Buatta 143
Mark Hampton 143
Martha Angus 145
Maurice Jennings and David McKee 146
McMillen 147
Michael Graves & Associates 149
Juan Pablo Molyneux 151
Naomi Leff & Associates 153
Peter Marino & Associates 164
Philip Johnson/Alan Ritchie
    Architects 165
Richard Keith Langham 171
Robert A.M. Stern Architects 172
The Rockwell Group 173
Rose Tarlow-Melrose House 174

Scott Snyder 177
Steven Holl Architects 184
Studio Sofield 184
Sunset Cottage 186
Thad Hayes Design 187
Thierry Despont 187
Victoria Hagan 194

ART CONSULTANTS

Chubb Group of Insurance Companies 86
Kim Heirston 119
John & Paul Herring & Co. 127
Mitchell-Innes and Nash 150
Thea Westreich Art Advisory
    Services 187

ART DEALERS

Acquavella Galleries 59
Andrea Rosen Gallery 62
B & B International 67
Baldwin Gallery 67
Barbara Gladstone Gallery 67
Barry Friedman 69
Berry-Hill Galleries 70
C & M Arts 77
Chisholm Gallery 84
Cline Fine Art Gallery 87
Craig F. Starr Associates 91
Donald Young Gallery 97
Edenhurst Gallery 99
Edward Carter Gallery 99
Fraenkel Gallery 107
G. Ray Hawkins 109
Gagosian Gallery 109
Galerie Michael 109
Gallery Paule Anglim 109
Gardner Colby Gallery 110
Greenberg Van Doren Gallery 114
Greenhouse Gallery of Fine Art 114
Guarisco Gallery 116
Hammer Galleries 117
Hirschl & Adler Galleries 119
Island Weiss Gallery 124
James Danziger Gallery 125
Joel Soroka Gallery 127
John Berggruen Gallery 127
John H. Surovek Gallery 127
Kennedy Galleries 130
Kurt E. Schon 134
L.A. Louver Gallery 135
Leo Castelli Gallery 136
Marian Goodman Gallery 143
Marlborough 144
Mary Boone Gallery 144
Matthew Marks Gallery 145
Maxwell Galleries 146
Michael Werner Gallery 149
Pace Wildenstein 161

Paul Kasmin Gallery 162
R.H. Love Galleries 168
The Redfern Gallery 169
Richard Anderson Fine Arts 170
Richard Gray Gallery 171
Richard L. Feigen & Company 171
Richard York Gallery 171
Robert Mann Gallery 173
Rosenberg & Stiebel 174
Salander-O'Reilly Galleries 175
Sean Kelly Gallery 178
Throckmorton Fine Art 188
Timothy Eaton Fine Art 188
Tony Shafrazi Gallery 189
Vance Jordan Fine Art 194
Vose Galleries of Boston 194
Wildenstein & Co. 196
William A. Karges Fine Art 196

AUCTION HOUSES

Christie's 85
JP King Auction Company 129
Neal Auction Company 153
New Orleans Auction Galleries 155
Sotheby's 182
William Doyle Galleries 197

CASINOS

Binion's Horseshoe 72
Caesars Palace 77
Golden Nugget 113
MGM Grand 149
The Mirage 150
Rio 171

CHAUFFEUR SERVICES

Admiral Limousine Service 60
Aventura Limousines 66
Carey International 79
CLS Transportation 88
Continental Limousine 89
Dav El 93
Diva Limousines 97
Gardella's Elite Limousine Service 110
Green Classic Limousines 114
Metropolitan Limousine 148
MLS Limousines 150
Nova Limousine Service 158

CIGAR BARS

The Cigar Box 86
Club Macanudo Chicago 88
Grand Havana Room 114
Hamilton Cigar Bar 117
Havana Studios 118

INDEX III

Lexington Bar and Books *138*

COLLEGES

Barnard College *68*
Brandeis University *73*
Brown University *75*
Bryn Mawr College *76*
Dartmouth College *93*
Duke University *98*
Harvard University *118*
Haverford College *119*
Leonard N. Stern School of Business *137*
Princeton University *166*
Stanford University *183*
University of Pennsylvania *192*
Vassar College *193*
Wellesley College *196*
Yale School of Management *199*

COSMETIC SURGEONS

Tina Alster, M.D *61*
Sherrell Aston, M.D. *64*
Daniel Baker, M.D. *67*
Lawrence Birnbaum, M.D. *72*
Dennis Cirillo, M.D *86*
Michelle Copeland, M.D. *89*
Jeffrey Dover, M.D. *97*
Lewis Feder, M.D. *102*
Peter B. Fodor, M.D. *105*
Mary Gingrass, M.D. *111*
Gerald Imber, M.D. *122*
Frank Kamer, M.D. *130*
Cap B. Lesesne, M.D. *138*
Manhattan Anti-Aging Clinic *142*
Alan Matarasso, M.D. *145*
Frederick A. Newman, M.D. *157*
Jon Perlman, M.D. *163*
Patricia Wexler M.D. *196*
The Women's Center for Plastic and
    Reconstructive Surgery *198*

CULINARY SCHOOLS

California Culinary Academy *78*
The Cambridge School of Culinary
    Arts *79*
The Culinary Institute of America *91*
Degustibus Cooking School *94*
The French Culinary Institute *108*
Windows on the World Wine School *198*

EMPLOYMENT AGENCIES

Andrew & Potter *62*
Beacon Hill Nannies *69*
Best Domestic Services *71*

Pavillion Agency *162*
Private Chefs, Inc. *166*
Professional Nannies Institute *167*
Starkey International *183*
Town & Country Nannies & Mothers
    In Deed *189*

EVENTS

The Academy Awards *59*
Aspen Music Festival *64*
Breeder's Cup *74*
The Ford Montreux Detroit Jazz
    Festival *105*
Gladstone Antiques Show *113*
The International Fine Art and Antique
    Dealers Show *122*
International Fine Art Fair *123*
Kentucky Derby *130*
Masters Tournament *145*
The Metropolitan Opera *149*
New Orleans Jazz & Heritage
    Festival *155*
Newport Music Festival *157*
Oregon Bach Festival *160*
Palm Beach International Art &
    Antique Fair *161*
The Perlman Music Program *163*
Santa Fe Opera *177*
Tanglewood Music Festival *187*
U.S. Open Polo Tournament *192*
U.S. Open Tennis *192*

FASHION

Addison on Madison *59*
Alan Flusser *60*
Alden Shoe Company *60*
Alexandra Lind *60*
Andover Shop *62*
Badgley-Mischka *67*
Barneys New York *68*
Belghiti Tailors *70*
Bergdorf Goodman *70*
Bigsby & Kruthers *71*
Bijan *72*
Calvin Klein *79*
Carolina Herrera *80*
Carroll & Co. *80*
Chaiken and Capone *81*
Crouch & Fitzgerald *91*
Dana Buchman *92*
Despos *95*
Donna Karan *97*
Dormeuil Personal Tailoring *97*
Eric Javits *100*
H. S. Trask & Co. *117*
Helmut Lang *119*
John Bartlett *127*
Joseph A. Bank Clothiers *128*

Josephine Sasso *128*
Josie Natori *128*
Judith Leiber *129*
Kieselstein-Cord *133*
Lambertson Truex *135*
Leslie & Co. *137*
Lilly Pulitzer *138*
Louis, Boston *139*
M. Penner *141*
Marc Jacobs *143*
Mary McFadden *144*
Maxfield *146*
Mayle *147*
Neiman Marcus *153*
Nina Hovnanian Couture *158*
Pamela Dennis *162*
Paul Stuart *162*
Prince Dimitri *167*
Pucci *167*
Ralph Lauren *169*
Randolph Duke *169*
Robert Talbott Shirts *173*
Ron Herman L.A. *173*
Saks Fifth Avenue *175*
SOLE by Soledad Twombly *182*
Souchi *182*
St. John Knits *183*
Tocca *188*
Todd Oldham *189*
Tracey Ross *190*
Tracy Feith *190*
Tuleh *191*
Ultimo *192*
Vera Wang *193*
Wilkes Bashford *197*
William Calvert *197*
York Furrier *199*

FITNESS

Art of Fitness *63*
The Aspen Club & Spa *64*
Atlanta Rocks *65*
Bay Club *69*
Billy Blanks' World Training Center *72*
East Bank Club *99*
East Hampton Gym *99*
The L.A. Sports Club *135*
Lighthouse Point Yacht & Racquet
    Club *138*
MedFitness *147*
Radu Physical Culture *169*
Reebok Sports Club *169*

FLORISTS

Amaryllis, A Flower Shop *61*
Atlas Floral Decorators *65*
Barbera Brooks Fine Flowers *68*
Bloom *73*

Calabria *77*
David Jones *93*
David LaVoy *93*
Fioridella *103*
Floral Events Unlimited *105*
Garden Gate *110*
Helena Lehane *119*
Laurels *136*
Mark's Garden *143*
L'Olivier Floral Atelier *159*
Philip Baloun *164*
Renny *170*
Robert Isabell *172*
Robert Long *173*
Stems *185*
Tom Mathieu & Company *189*
Two Design Group *191*
The Woods *198*

GOLF CLUBS

Augusta National Golf Club *65*
Bay Hill Club & Lodge *69*
Black Diamond Ranch *72*
Bonita Bay Club *73*
Congressional Country Club *89*
Cypress Point Club *91*
Doral Golf Resort & Spa *97*
Fishers Island Country Club *104*
Harbour Town Golf Links *117*
John's Island Club *128*
Jupiter Hills *129*
Kittansett Club *133*
Lakeside Golf Club *135*
Merion Golf Club *148*
Montreux Golf & Country Club *151*
National Golf Links of America *153*
Oakland Hills Country Club *159*
Oakmont Country Club *159*
Pebble Beach Resorts *163*
Pete Dye Golf Club *164*
Pine Valley Golf Club *165*
Pinehurst Resort & Country Club *166*
La Quinta *167*
Riviera Country Club *172*
San Francisco Golf Club *176*
Sea Island *178*
Seminole Golf Club *179*
Shadow Creek *179*
Shinnecock Hills Golf Club *180*
Spyglass Hill Golf Club *182*
Troon Golf & Country Club *190*
Trump International Golf Club *190*
Valley Club of Montecito *193*
The Virginian Golf Club *194*
Whistling Straits *198*
Whitinsville Golf Club *196*
Winged Foot Golf Club *198*
Yale University Golf Course *199*
Yeamans Hall Club *199*

INDEX III

CHANEL

HAIR AND BEAUTY

Art Luna Salon 63
Aveda Institute 66
Beautique Day Spa and Salon 69
Brownes' & Co. Apothecary 75
Bumble & Bumble 76
Crème de la Mer 148
Deborah Koepper 94
Frédéric Fekkai Beauté 107
Gavert Atelier 110
Gazelle Beauty Center and Day Spa 110
John Barrett Salon 127
The John Sahag Workshop 127
Juan Juan Salon 129
Key Lime Pie Salon and Wellness Spa 130
Ling Salon 138
Ling Skin Care 138
Maurice Bonamigo 146
La Mer 148
Minardi Salon 150
Peter Coppola Salon 164
Privé 167
Salon AKS 175
Salon Cristophe 175
Stella Salons 184
Warren-Tricomi Salon 195

HOTELS

Hotel Adolphus 58
Alexis Hotel 60
Amangani 61
The American Hotel 61
American Safari Cruises 62
Auberge du Soleil 64
Auldridge Mead 66
Hotel Bel-Air 70
Bellagio 70
The Beverly Hills Hotel 71
Blackberry Farm 72
Boca Raton Resort and Club 73
The Boulders 73
The Breakers 74
The Broadmoor 74
Camberley Brown 79
The Carlyle 81
The Castle at Tarrytown 81
Chateau du Sureau 84
Château Marmont 83
Colony Surf Hotel 89
Deer Valley Resort 94
Delano Hotel 95
Dunton Hot Springs 98
L'Ermitage Beverly Hills 100
Four Seasons Boston 106
Four Seasons Las Vegas 106
Four Seasons New York 106
Four Seasons Palm Beach 106
Hotel George 111

The Greenbrier Hotel 114
The Grove Park Inn Resort 116
The Hay-Adams Hotel 118
The Hotel 120
The House on Bayou Road 120
The Huntington Hotel 121
The Inn at Little Washington 122
The Inn at Spanish Bay 122
Inn at the Market 123
International House 123
Hotel Jerome 126
Kiawah Island Golf & Tennis Resort 131
Lake Placid Lodge 135
The Little Nell 139
The Lodge on Little St. Simons
   Island 140
Mansion on Turtle Creek 142
The Mark 143
The Mauna Lani Bay 146
The Mayflower Inn 146
Meadowood Napa Valley 147
Mercer Hotel 148
New York Palace Hotel 157
Old Chatham Sheepherding Company
   Inn 159
Old Louisville Inn 159
The Peninsula Beverly Hills 163
The Peninsula New York 164
The Point 167
Post Ranch Inn 166
Rancho Valencia Resort 169
The Regent Beverly Wilshire 170
The Rittenhouse Hotel 172
Ritz-Carlton Hotel 171
Ritz-Carlton, Laguna Niguel 171
Royal Garden at Waikiki 174
San Ysidro Ranch 176
Shipman House 180
Shutters on the Beach 180
Soniat House 181
St. Regis Hotel 183
Sundance Hotel 185
Sunset Beach 186
The Tides 187
Timberhill Ranch 188
Triple Creek Ranch 190
Trump International Hotel 191
Twin Farms 191
Windsor Court Hotel 198

JEWELRY AND WATCHES

Aaron Basha 58
Asanti Fine Jewelers 64
Barry Peterson Jewelers 69
Brinsmaid 74
Cindy Griem Fine Jewels 85
David Stern Designer Jewelers 94
David Webb 93

Fortunoff 106
Freedman Jewelers 107
Gioia 111
Golden Bear 113
Greenleaf & Crosby 114
Hamilton Jewelers 117
Harry Winston Jewelers 118
JFA Designs 127
Judith Ripka 129
Lagos 135
London Jewelers 139
Marc Magnus 142
Martin Katz 144
Maurice Badler Fine Jewelry 145
Philip Press 165
Seaman Schepps 178
Shapur Mozaffarian 178
Shreve & Co. 180
Tiffany & Co. 187
Time Will Tell 188

LANDSCAPE ARCHITECTS

Carter Landscaping 80
Galper/Baldon Associates 109
Glen Gate 113
Isabelle Greene & Associates 124
Lutsko Associates 140
Nancy Goslee Power & Associates 153
Peter Cummin & Associates 164
Ron Herman Landscape Architect 173
Steve Martino & Associates 184

LAW FIRMS

Akin, Gump, Strauss, Hauer & Feld 60
Baker & McKenzie 67
Bryan Cave 76
Covington & Burling 90
Cravath, Swaine & Moore 91
Davis, Polk & Wardwell 94
Fish & Neave 104
Gibson, Dunn & Crutcher 111
Jones, Day, Reavis & Pogue 128
King & Spalding 133
Kronish, Lieb, Weiner & Hellman,
   L.L.P. 134
Latham & Watkins 136
Morrison & Foerster 152
Paul, Hastings, Janofsky & Walker 162
Shearman & Sterling 179
Sidley & Austin 180
Skadden, Arps, Slate, Meagher
   & Flom 181
Sullivan & Cromwell 185
Wilson Sonsini Goodrich & Rosati 197

MUSEUMS

The Albuquerque Museum of Art
   & History 60
American Museum of Natural History 61
The Asia Society 64
Brooklyn Museum of Art 74
Cleveland Museum of Art 87
The Cooper-Hewitt National Design
   Museum 90
Corcoran Gallery of Art 90
Dallas Museum of Art 92
Dia Center for The Arts 95
Field Museum of Natural History 103
Fine Arts Museum of San Francisco 104
Freer Gallery of Art 107
Frick Collection 108
High Museum of Art 119
Hirshhorn Museum and Sculpture
   Garden 120
The J. Paul Getty Museum 125
The Jack S. Blanton Museum of Art 125
Kimbell Art Museum 133
Metropolitan Museum of Art 148
Milwaukee Art Museum 150
The Morgan Library 151
Museum of Contemporary Art
   San Diego 152
Museum of Fine Arts, Boston 152
Museum of Modern Art 152
National Air and Space Museum 153
National Gallery of Art 153
New Orleans Museum of Art 155
New York Botanical Garden 155
Newport Art Museum 157
Newseum 157
Peabody Museum of Natural History 163
Philadelphia Museum of Art 165
The Rienzi House Museum 171
San Diego Museum of Art 176
Scottsdale Museum of Contemporary
   Art 177
Seattle Art Museum 177
Walters Art Gallery 195
Winterthur Museum, Garden and
   Library 198

PARTY ORGANIZERS & CATERERS

Along Came Mary! 60
Andrew Dornenburg Private Dining 62
Art of Eating 63
Callahan Catering 78
Colin Cowie Lifestyles 89
EventQuest 101
Ferrée Florsheim Catering 102
George L. Jewell Catering 111
Glorious Foods 113
Jerry Dilts and Associates 126

INDEX III

Just Ask Peter *129*
Lee Epting *136*
Martel Productions *144*
Mindy Weiss Party Consultants *150*
Natalie Gerschel Kaplan *153*
Ober, Onet & Associates *159*
Royal Fiesta Caterers *174*
Sharon Sacks Productions *179*
Wendy Krispin *196*

POLO CLUBS

Bridgehampton Polo Club *74*
Dallas Polo Club *92*
Houston Polo Club *120*
Palm Beach Polo and Country Club *161*
Pinehurst Polo Club *166*
San Diego Polo Club *176*
Santa Barbara Polo and Racquet
    Club *176*
Santa Fe Horse Park and Polo Club *177*
Will Rogers Polo Club *196*

PORTRAIT PAINTERS & PHOTOGRAPHERS

Aubry *65*
Jacqueline Jasper Portraits *125*
John Reilly *169*
Julian Schnabel *177*
Victor Skrebneski *181*
Adelaide Althin Toombs Sundin *189*

PROPERTY CONSULTANTS

Armfield, Miller & Ripley *63*
Campbell, Dettman & Panton Realty *79*
Carol Dopkin Real Estate *80*
Chase International *82*
Christie's Great Estates *86*
Coates, Reid & Waldron *88*
Conover Real Estate *89*
The Corcoran Group *90*
Dunemere Associates Real Estate *98*
Edward Lee Cave *99*
Fenton & Lang *102*
Fox Residential Group *107*
Hall and Hall Ranch Brokers *117*
Hampton Country Real Estate *117*
J. C. De Niro *125*
Jensen-Smith *126*
John Daugherty, Realtors *127*
Joshua & Company *128*
Kay Ledbetter & Associates *130*
The Keyes Company *131*
Leading Estates of the World *136*
Mason & Morse *145*
Alice F. Mason *145*
Perna Luxury Real Estate *164*

Sotheby's International Realty *182*
Stribling & Associates *184*
William B. May *197*
William Pitt Real Estate *197*
Windsor Village *198*

RESTAURANTS

Ambria *61*
Artesia *64*
Auberge Le Grillon *65*
Aujourd'hui *65*
Aureole *65*
Azzura Point *66*
Bacchanalia *67*
Balthazar *67*
Beach Bistro *69*
Le Bec-Fin *69*
Le Bernardin *70*
Biba *71*
Blackbird *72*
Browns Restaurant *76*
Cacharel *77*
Café Allegro *77*
Café des Amis *77*
Café L'Europe *78*
Campagne *79*
Campanile *79*
Charles Nob Hill *82*
Charleston Grill *82*
Charlie Trotter's *82*
Chef Reto's Restaurant *83*
Chef Allen's *83*
Chez Francois *83*
Chez Panisse *84*
Chinois on Main *84*
Cipriani *86*
Le Cirque 2000 *86*
Club Colette *88*
Commander's Palace *89*
Le Coq au Vin *90*
D'Amico Cucina *92*
Da Silvano *92*
Daniel *92*
Della Femina *95*
Delmonico *95*
Eleven Madison Park *99*
L'Espalier *100*
Euphemia Haye Restaurant *101*
Everest *101*
Felidia Ristorante *102*
15 degrees *102*
Fleur de Lys *105*
Four Seasons Restaurant *106*
The French Laundry *108*
The French Room *108*
Galileo *109*
Gene & Georgetti *111*
Genoa *111*
Giovanni's *111*

Gordon *114*
La Goulue *114*
Gramercy Tavern *114*
La Grenouille *115*
The Grill on the Alley *115*
Hapa *117*
The Ivy *124*
Janos *126*
Jardinière *126*
Jean Georges *126*
Lakeview Inn *135*
The Lark *136*
Lespinasse *137*
Lespinasse *137*
Lucques *139*
La Maisonette *142*
Mark's Las Olas *143*
Mary Elaine's *144*
Matsuhisa *145*
The Mercury *148*
Michael's *149*
Mille Fleurs *150*
Montrachet *151*
Nick and Toni's *158*
No. 9 Park *158*
Nobu *158*
One Pico *160*
L'Orangerie *160*
Osteria del Circo *160*
Le Palais *161*
Pascal *162*
Patina *162*
Renaissance *170*
Rialto *170*
Ritz-Carlton, Buckhead *171*
The River Café *173*
RL *172*
Roy's *174*
Ruggles Grill *174*
The Ryland Inn *174*
Salts *175*
Spago Hollywood *182*
Troquet *190*
Valentino *193*
Veritas *194*

SCHOOLS

Deerfield Academy *94*
Groton School *116*
The Hotchkiss School *120*
Kent School *130*
The Lawrenceville School *136*
Philips Exeter Academy *165*
Rudolf Steiner School *174*
St. George's School *182*
St. Mark's School *183*
St. Paul's School *183*
The Taft School *187*
Trinity School *190*

SECURITY CONSULTANTS

Abacus Security *58*
Assets Protection Systems *64*
Harrison K-9 Security *118*
Knight Security Systems *134*
Kroll Associates *134*
Richard Haynes & Associates *170*
Silver Screen Security *180*
Strategic Controls *184*
U.S. Security *192*

SPAS AND CLINICS

Aida Thibiant European Day Spa *59*
Allure Day Spa & Store *60*
The Avon Centre *66*
Babor Institut *67*
Bliss *72*
Canyon Ranch *79*
Carapan Urban Spa & Store *79*
The Chopra Center for Well Being *84*
Coeur d'Alene *88*
La Costa *90*
De Pasquale, The Spa *94*
Elizabeth Arden Red Door Salon
    & Spa *100*
Fisher Island Spa *104*
Gene Juarez Salon & Spa *111*
Givenchy Hotel & Spa *113*
Golden Door *113*
The Greenhouse Group *114*
Hickox Salon and Spa *119*
HR Beauty Gallery *120*
Kingsmill Resort *133*
Miraval *150*
Murad Spa *152*
New Life Clinic & Therapy Spa *155*
Ojai Valley Inn and Spa *159*
The Peaks Resort and Golden Door
    Spa *163*
Salon d'Artiste *175*
77 Maiden Lane *179*
Susan Ciminelli Day Spa *186*

SPECIALTY SHOPS

ABC Carpet & Home *58*
Algabar *60*
Architectural Accents *63*
At Home *65*
Axis Twenty *66*
Barclay Rex Pipe Shop *68*
Beauvais Carpets *69*
Bell'Occhio *70*
BestSelections *71*
Browns *75*
Calligraphy Studios *78*
Cannon/Bullock Interior Design *79*

INDEX III

Century House Antiques *81*

Claremont Rug Company *87*

Les Concierges *89*

De Vera *94*

Delaware River Trading Company *95*

Dempsey & Carroll *95*

DHS Designs *96*

Dimson Homma *96*

Distinctive Bookbinding & Stationery *97*

Downtown *97*

East & Orient Company *99*

Eli Wilner & Company *100*

FAO Schwarz *101*

Felissimo *103*

Fountain Pen Hospital *106*

Framed on Madison *107*

ga ga gifts of whimsy *109*

The Gardener *110*

Gearys of Beverly Hills *110*

Gilmartin Studios *111*

Greenbaum Interiors *115*

Gump's *116*

Hartmann Luggage & Leather Goods *118*

Hokanson *120*

Interieurs *122*

Japonesque *126*

Kemble Interiors *130*

Kindel Furniture *134*

Kinsey Marable Bookellers *133*

Luxuryfinder.com *140*

Madison Avenue Bookshop *142*

Mansour *142*

Marc Friedland *142*

McCarty Pottery *147*

Mecox Gardens *147*

Meurice Garment Care *149*

Michael Taylor Designs *149*

Morgenthal Frederics Opticians *152*

Myott Studio Workshop *152*

Nursery Lines *158*

Outside *160*

Pacific Tall Ship Company *161*

Pacific Western Traders *161*

Performance Ski *163*

Plantation *166*

Rebecca Moss *169*

Richard J. Fisher Tinwork *170*

Scully and Scully *177*

Shelly Zegart Quilts *179*

Soolip Paperie & Press *182*

Steinway & Sons *184*

Styline Furniture *185*

Sue Fisher King *185*

Urban Epicuria *192*

Wagwear *195*

TRAVEL CONSULTANTS

American Orient Express *62*

Fisher Travel *104*

Frenchway Travel *108*

Incredible Adventures *122*

Lisa Lindblad Travel Design *138*

Total Travel & Tickets *189*

Valerie Wilson Travel *193*

WEALTH MANAGEMENT

Bank of Boston *67*

Bessemer Trust *71*

Brown Brothers Harriman & Co. *74*

Chase Manhattan Private Bank *82*

Citibank Private Bank *87*

First Union National Bank *104*

Fleet Bank *104*

Goldman, Sachs & Co. *113*

Huntington Private Financial Group *121*

JP Morgan *129*

Lehman Brothers Private Client Services *136*

Mellon Bank *147*

Merrill Lynch Financial Services *148*

Morgan Stanley Dean Witter *151*

Northern Trust *158*

PNC Advisors *166*

Safra Bank *175*

US Trust *192*

Wilmington Trust-FSB *197*

WINE MERCHANTS

The Burgundy Wine Co. *76*

Calvert Woodley *78*

Carlyle Wines *80*

D & M Champagne *92*

Golden West International *113*

Moore Brothers Wine Company *151*

Nevada Wine Cellar & Spirits *155*

Sherry Lehmann *179*

Sokolin Wines *181*

20/20 Wines *191*

The Wine Cask *198*

Zachy's *199*

WINEMAKERS

Au Bon Climat Wineries *65*

Beringer Wine Estates *70*

Blockheadia Ringnosii *72*

Cakebread Cellars *77*

Chalone Vineyard *82*

Chateau Montelena Winery *83*

Cosentino *90*

Diamond Creek Winery *96*

Dominus Estates *97*

Duckhorn Vineyards *98*

Far Niente Vineyards *101*

Ferrari Carano Wineries *102*

Flowers *105*

Franciscan Estates *107*

Grgich Hills Cellars *115*

Harlan Estate *118*

Heitz Wine Cellars *119*

The Hess Collection Winery *119*

Iron Horse Vineyards *123*

Jordan Vineyard & Winery *128*

Joseph Phelps *128*

Newton Vineyards *158*

Niebaum Coppola *158*

Opus One Winery *160*

Pahlmeyer *161*

Peter Michael *164*

Rabbit Ridge Vineyards *168*

Ridge Vineyards *171*

Robert Mondavi Winery *173*

Schramsberg Vineyards *177*

Screaming Eagle Vineyards *177*

Shafer *179*

Silver Oak Cellars *180*

Silverado Vineyards *180*

Stag's Leap Wine Cellars *183*

Talbott *187*

Turley Wine Cellars *191*

YACHTING

Bartrum & Brakenhoff Yachts *69*

Burger Boat Company *76*

Fraser Yachts *107*

Genmar Holdings *111*

Hargrave Yachts *118*

Intermarine Yachting *122*

Lazzara Yachts *136*

Lynn Jachney Charters *140*

Magnum Marine *142*

Palmer Johnson Yachts *162*

Thunderbird Products *187*

Ultramarine *192*

Yachtscape *199*

INDEX III

EDITORIAL CONTRIBUTORS & RESEARCHERS

Karen Bressler, Kate Downing, Cedric Devitt, Richardson Dilworth, Sunshine Flint, Justin Haythe, Fiona Keane, Mary Kline, Nancy Millar, Seamus Moran, Monica Polanco, Arthur Prager, Jasbreet Rai, Nick Raskind, Susan Redstone, Elise Rosen, William Sokolin.

FEATURE WRITERS

Robinson Clark is a freelance business writer, principally for *Bloomberg News* and *SmartMoney*.

Tom Doak is President of Renaissance Golf Design, Traverse City, Michigan and the author of *The Confidential Guide to Golf Courses*.

Norah Lawlor is a New York City based society writer and publicist.

Lord McAlpine is the author of several books and an inveterate collector and traveler. His latest book is *Collecting and Display*.

Tom O'Gorman is a Contributing Editor at *The World of Hibernia,* the award-winning magazine for the Irish diaspora.

Debra Scott is the Editor of *Trump Style* magazine and has written for *The New York Post* and *The Times* of London.

ACKNOWLEDGEMENTS

Many people selflessly devoted time and energy to this project. The editors particularly wish to express their gratitude to the following individuals, who provided unstinting support and wise counsel: Harley Baldwin, John Brancati, Barbera Brooks, Tom Farley, Ralph Hersom, Patricia Higgins, Kate Kelly, Lisa Lindblad, Greg Midland, Patrick O'Connell, Christopher Peditto, John Reger, Joan Salwen-Fields, James Sherwin, Marianne Strong, Alicia White.

PHOTOGRAPHIC CREDITS

Ansel Adams: *Page 99*; Jerome Adamstein: *Page 105*; Ralph Alswang: *Page 51*; R. Valentine Atkinson: *Page 82*; Daniel Aubry: *Pages 65, 88*; Franklin Avery: *Page 84*; Balfour Walker Studios: *Page 126*; Paul Barton: *Page 104*; Gordon Beall: *Page 75*; Tom Bonner: *Pages 274-5, 282-3*; Antoine Bootz: *Page 103*; Rob Brown/Miller Brown: *Page 42*; Simon Bruty/Allsport: *Pages 34-5*; Alex Cao: *Page 262*; Dwight Carter: *Page 209*; Pierre Chanteau: *Page 122*; Geoffrey Clifford: *Page 167*; Dann Coffey: *Page 109*; Collins/Monkmeyer: *Page 11*; Susan Consentino: *Pages 287, 290-3*; Billy Cunningham: *Page 151*; Joe Deal: *Page 276*; Greg Delves: *Page 211*; Blaise-Alexandre Desgoffe: *Page 96*; Susan Dirk: *Page 177*; Brian Dobin: *Pages 208, 227, 233, 236, 238, 243, 256*; Miki Duisterhof: *Page 138*; Dunn/Monkmeyer: *Pages 14, 15*; John Earle: *Page 71*; Sigrid Estrada: *Page 252*; Jon Ferrey/Allsport: *Page 270*; Scott Frances/Esto: *Pages 273, 276*; Lois Ellen Frank: *Page 174*; George Gardner: *Page 140*; Andrew Garn: *Page 90*; Mark Gibson/SFCVB: *Page 9*; Ellen Graham: *Page 242*; Timothy Greenfield-Sanders: *Page 246*; Otto Gruele/Allsport: *Pages 33, 43*; George Holz/ABC: *Page 260*; Munawar Hosain/Rex USA: *Page 237*; Chris John: *Pages 33, 41*; Tom Johnson: *Page 229*; Jones: *Page 98*; Nils Jorgensen/Rex USA: *Page 239*; Catherine Karnow: *Page 62*; Elliot Kaufman: *Page 102*; Taka Kawachi: *Page 103*; Alan Kennedy: *Page 215*; Robert Kern: *Page 115*; Kinsella: *Page 45*; Paul Kolnik: *Page 245*; Kate Kunz: *Page 255*; Brigitte Lacombe: *Page 230*; Dan Lamont: *Page 261*; Dan Lecca: *Page 143*; Dave Lewis/Rex USA: *Page 248*; Andy Lyons/Allsport: *Page 253;* David O. Marlow: *Page 85*; Michael P. McLaughlin: *Page 218*; Patrick McMullan: *Page 138*; Patrick McNamara: *Pages 224, 244*; Barry Michlin: *Page 79*; Bill Munke: *Page 162*; National Park Service: *Page 9*; Gary Newkirk/Allsport: *Page 39*; The New York Times: *Pages 222, 265*; New York Convention & Visitors Bureau: *Pages 9, 10*; Victor Zbigniew Orlewicz: *Page 251;* Matthew Pace: *Page 78*; Erik Pendzich/Rex USA: *Page 210*; Matt Pfingsten: *Page 135*; Todd Phitt: *Page 92*; Gene Pollux: *Page 101*; Carl Purcell: *Page 157*; John Reck: *Page 86*; Allan Rosenberg: *Page 185*; Rex USA: *Pages 45, 54, 233, 251, 258*; William K. Sacco: *Page 163*; Jon Sall: *Page 47*; Francesco Scavullo: *Page 267*; David Seidner: *Page 249*; Carol Simowitz/SFCVB: *Pages 12-13*; Ron Solomon: *Page 118*; John Stephens: *Page 273*; Tim Street-Porter: *Page 83*; William Struhs: *Page 82*; John Sutton: *Page 197*; Charles Sykes/Rex USA: *Pages 268, 269*; Alex Vertikoff: *Pages 273, 278-9*; Peter Vitale: *Page 80;* Vogue: *Page 265*; Fritz von Schulenberg: *Page 76*; J. Weinstein: *Page 103*; Graydon Wood: *Page 165*; Bard Wrisley: *Page 119*; David Zaitz: *Page 88*.

AIRCRAFT · ANTIQUES · ARCHITECTS AND I
OUSES · CASINOS · CHAUFFEUR SERVICES ·
C SURGEONS · CULINARY SCHOOLS · EMPLO
FLORISTS · GOLF CLUBS · HAIR AND BEAU
CAPE ARCHITECTS · LAW FIRMS · MEDIA · M
OLO CLUBS · PORTRAIT PAINTERS AND PH
GENTS · RESTAURANTS · SCHOOLS · SECU
IALTY SHOPS · TRAVEL CONSULTANTS · WEA
AKERS · YACHTING · AIRCRAFT · ANTIQUES
EALERS · AUCTION HOUSES · CASINOS · CH
OLLEGES · COSMETIC SURGEONS · CULINAR
FASHION · FITNESS · FLORISTS · GOLF CLUB
ATCHES · LANDSCAPE ARCHITECTS · LAW F
ND CATERERS · POLO CLUBS · PORTRAIT PA
REAL ESTATE AGENTS · RESTAURANTS · SC
LINICS · SPECIALTY SHOPS · TRAVEL CONSU
HANTS · WINEMAKERS · YACHTING · AIRC
ESIGNERS · ART DEALERS · AUCTION HOU
ARS AND CLUBS · COLLEGES · COSMETIC SU
GENCIES · EVENTS · FASHION · FITNESS ·
OTELS · JEWELRY AND WATCHES · LANDSC
MS · PARTY ORGANIZERS AND CATERERS ·
OGRAPHERS · PRIVATE CLUBS · REAL ESTATE
ONSULTANTS · SPAS AND CLINICS · SPECI
ANAGEMENT · WINE MERCHANTS · WINE
RCHITECTS AND INTERIOR DESIGNERS ·
HAUFFEUR SERVICES · CIGAR BARS AND CL
ARY SCHOOLS · EMPLOYMENT AGENCIES ·
LUBS · HAIR AND BEAUTY · HOTELS · JEWE
AW FIRMS · MEDIA · MUSEUMS · PARTY OR
RAIT PAINTERS AND PHOTOGRAPHERS · PI
ANTS · SCHOOLS · SECURITY CONSULTANTS
CONSULTANTS · WEALTH MANAGEMENT